P9-EEO-361

Killing Hope

U.S. Military and CIA Interventions Since World War II

William Blum

Common Courage Press   Monroe, Maine

Copyright © William Blum 1995
All rights reserved.
Cover photo by Impact Visuals
Cover design by Matt Wuerker

Library of Congress Cataloging-in-Publication Data:
Blum, William.
Killing hope: U.S. military and CIA interventions since World War II/ William Blum
p. cm.
Rev. ed. of: The CIA. 1986
Includes bibliographical references and index.
ISBN 1-56751-053-1 (cloth).--ISBN 1-56751-052-3 (pbk.)
1. United States. Central Intelligence Agency. 2. United States-Foreign relations--1945-
1994. 3. United States--Foreign relations--1989- 4. United States--Military relations--
Foreign countries. 5. Intervention (International law) I. Blum, William. CIA. II. Title.
JK468.I6B59 1995
327.1273--dc20   95-11786
CIP

Revised and expanded version of The CIA, A Forgotten History,
published in 1986 by Zed Books, London.

Common Courage Press
P.O. Box 702
Monroe, ME 04951
207-525-0900 fax: 207-525-3068

First Printing

Contents

Author's Note

The Introduction to the original edition of this book is reprinted here, with some modifications, as it appeared in 1986. At that time the Soviet Union still existed and the cold war was very much alive, particularly with Ronald Reagan in the White House, and the Introduction reflects this. It is presented here because it offers a concise history of the cold war and a background to understanding the impetus behind, and the nature of, the many American interventions throughout the world. The actual case histories of the interventions presented in the book add to this analysis.

Many chapters have been significantly revised—by newly-disclosed information, such as in declassified documents, or by newly-discovered old information—and/or updated to the present time where applicable. Six new chapters have been added: Libya, Panama, Bulgaria, Iraq, Afghanistan, and Haiti. Unfortunately, the American government keeps people like me very busy.

> Who controls the past controls the future.
> Who controls the present controls the past.
>
> —George Orwell, *1984*

> Our fear that communism might someday take
> over most of the world blinds us to the fact
> that anti-communism already has.
>
> —Michael Parenti, *The Anti-Communist Impulse*

Introduction to the New Edition

In 1993, I came across a review of a book about people who deny that the Nazi Holocaust actually occurred. I wrote to the author, a university professor, telling her that her book made we wonder whether she knew that an American holocaust had taken place, and that the denial of it put the denial of the Nazi one to shame. So great and deep is the denial of the American holocaust, I said, that the denyers are not even aware that the claimers or their claim exist. Yet, a few million people have died in the American holocaust and many more millions have been condemned to lives of misery and torture as a result of US interventions extending from China and Greece in the 1940s to Afghanistan and Iraq in the 1990s. I enclosed a listing of these interventions, which is of course the subject of the present book.

In my letter I also offered to exchange a copy of the earlier edition of my book for a copy of hers, but she wrote back informing me that she was not in a position to do so. And that was all she said. She didn't ask to see my book. She made no comment whatsoever about the remainder of my letter—the part dealing with denying the American holocaust—not even to acknowledge that I had raised the matter. The irony of a scholar on the subject of denying the Nazi Holocaust engaging in such denial about the American holocaust was classic indeed. I was puzzled why the good professor had bothered to respond at all.

Clearly, if my thesis could receive such a non-response from such a person, I and my thesis faced an extremely steep uphill struggle. In the 1930s, and again after the war in the 1940s and '50s, anti-communists of various stripes in the United States tried their best to expose the crimes of the Soviet Union, such as the purge trials and the mass murders. But a strange thing happened. The truth did not seem to matter. American Communists and fellow travelers continued to support the Kremlin. Even allowing for the exaggeration and disinformation regularly disbursed by the anti-communists which damaged their credibility, the continued ignorance and/or denial by the American leftists is remarkable.

At the close of the Second World War, when the victorious Allies discovered the German concentration camps, in some cases German citizens from nearby towns were brought to the camp to come face-to-face with the institution, the piles of corpses, and the still-living skeletal people; some of the respectable burghers were even forced to bury the dead. What might be the effect upon the American psyche if the true-believers and deny-ers were compelled to witness the consequences of the past half-century of US foreign policy close up? What if all the nice, clean-cut, wholesome American boys who dropped an infinite tonnage of bombs, on a dozen different countries, on people they knew nothing about—characters in a video game—had to come down to earth and look upon and smell the burning flesh?

Our leaders understand how this works. They make it a point to keep our American eyes away from our foreign victims as much as possible, even on television. Before our boys were sent to Somalia, they were given psychological briefings from military psychiatrists to prepare them for the sights of starvation and misery. Our leaders are men not entirely insensitive. And it is because the American people see and hear their leaders expressing the right concern at the right time, with just the right catch in their throats to convey "I care!", they see them laughing and telling jokes, see them with their families, hear them speak of God and love, of peace and law, of democracy and freedom—it is because of such things that the idea that our government has done to the world's huddled masses what it did to the Seminoles has so difficult a time penetrating the American consciousness. It's like America has an evil twin.

1

George Bernard Shaw used three concepts to describe the positions of individuals in Nazi Germany: intelligence, decency, and Naziism. He argued that if a person was intelligent, and a Nazi, he was not decent. If he was decent and a Nazi, he was not intelligent. And if he was decent and intelligent, he was not a Nazi.

If, as we're told, the cold war is over and the United States won, it's proper to ask: What do we have to show for this victory? In human terms, that is. In terms of people's lives.

The trillions of dollars spent on the American military machine instead of on the cities, the infrastructure, housing, schools, health care, etc., etc., did little to improve the quality of life for the average person in the United States, though it did wonders for the folks of the military-industrial-intelligence complex. The M-I-I-C and their supporters in Congress successfully fought off the menace of a "peace dividend", and they show little sign of releasing their death grip on the society. Many years ago they insisted upon, and they got, a permanent war economy. There are, after all, always new enemies out there who threaten us—America, the perpetually aggrieved innocent in a treacherous world. In 1994, defense contractors began pitching the need for new advanced aircraft because so many countries of the world were now equipped with advanced fighters—sold to them by the United States—and "what if one of those ... countries turns against us?" asked the man from Lockheed.[1] When Lockheed announced a proposed $10 billion mega-merger with fellow defense giant Martin Marietta, it put to rest any lingering doubts about whether "defense conversion" had a future, collapsing decisively the bull market in high-tech plowshares.

In the same year, we learned for the first time of the almost-completed construction of new headquarters for the super secret National Reconnaissance Office. This espionage-mentality throwback to the 1950s dug into taxpayers' pockets for more than $300 million, but there's a whole planet out there to fly over and spy on, and ten thousand file cabinets, million-megabyte hard disks, and billion-megabyte CD-ROMs waiting to be filled with photos and maps and other vital information that hardly anyone will ever look at, and which will do nothing for people's lives. A little earlier, the Defense Department was not at all embarrassed to announce that it needed funding sufficient to enable it to fight two regional wars at the same time. In 1978 they were trying to be prepared to fight only "1 1/2 wars at once".[2] Is this just inflation, or is Dr. Strangelove alive and well at the Pentagon? After the "two-wars" declaration came the completely manufactured scare about North Korean nuclear weapons. And so it goes. Our rulers do their best to make sure that we shall never be at peace.

> Our first objective is to prevent the re-emergence of a new rival, either on the territory of the former Soviet Union or elsewhere, that poses a threat on the order of that posed formerly by the Soviet Union. ... we must account sufficiently for the interests of the advanced industrial nations to discourage them from challenging our leadership or seeking to overturn the established political and economic order. ... we must maintain the mechanisms for deterring potential competitors from even aspiring to a larger regional or global role.

So reads the Pentagon's Planning Guidance for the Fiscal Years 1994-1999.[3] Since the United States dispatched its breathtaking killing machine to the Persian Gulf in 1990, the American people have been treated to this world view on a number of occasions, along with chest-beating bragging by high-ranking military and civilian officials about the US being the world's only superpower, and assertions like that of former Assistant Secretary of Defense Richard Armitage that "the United States alone possesses sufficient moral, economic, political and military horsepower to jump-start and drive international efforts to curb international lawlessness"[4]—a manifesto, politically and poetically, on a par with "The defense of proletarian internationalism is a sacred duty of each communist and workers' party and of every Marxist-Leninist."

Why do Washington policy-makers trumpet their strategies, their victories, and their power so? Is it because the demise of the communist enemy has left the M-I-I-C thrashing about for a new mission, a new *raison d'être*? At those moments when their defense mechanisms are stilled, the more honest among them know that they've been çut off at the knees. And for this do they trumpet and cry: "Look! We *do* have a purpose! With a grand design!" Why else does the Pentagon make it all so public? Such policy planning used to be classified top-secret for 30 years.

The people of Utah and Nevada who lived downwind from the nuclear test sites don't have too much to show from the cold war except clusters of cancer; after 87 open-air tests more fallout had settled on St. George in Utah than on Hiroshima and Nagasaki ... and the hapless islanders of Micronesia who were terribly deceived about the H-test fallout; the Interior Department told the people of Bikini that they could return to their homes—provided they ate no home-grown food until the late 21st century ... and the soldiers who were forced to watch the tests from too close; and the uranium miners whose lungs inhaled radon gas; and the people who lived too close to the wrong nuclear reactors, Chernobyl in slow motion; and the unknowing guinea pigs of all the radiation experiments, injected with plutonium, uranium, radium, and other nice things ... and the folks whose brains were washed with LSD, "truth serums", and other nice things; and the people of Florida and New York and San Francisco who were secretly dusted and sprayed and chemicalized and biologicalized by the CIA and the Army, just to see what the (bad) effects would be ... and always, in each case, there were men in Washington who knew very well about the dangers of the fallout and the radiation and the germs, but said nothing; they knew about the accidents and the leaks, but said nothing; they knew about it early on, at least as early as 1947: "It is desired that no document be released which refers to experiments with humans and might have adverse effect on public opinion or result in legal suits. Documents covering such work field should be classified secret." ... and kindly old Ike who told the Atomic Energy Commission to keep the public "confused" with its explanations about fallout that had caused cancer concern in Utah ... and those that said anything were ignored, or fired.[5]

It was all called national security. The American republic had been replaced after World War II by a national security state, answerable to no one, an extra-constitutional government, secret from the American people, exempt from congressional oversight, above the law.

As to what the rest of world, primarily the Third World, derived from the cold war, the reader is referred to the pages that follow. It is not a pretty picture.

The end of communism in the Soviet Union and Eastern Europe has meant great tribulation for the large majority of the citizens, who had better and more secure lives before the great blind leap into the raging cold waters of capitalism. Perhaps the reason Americans have been so eager to help them—sending in a small army of industrial, financial and technical experts, and assorted cheerleaders, along with all the material goodies—is their almost childlike desire to be like us: they rush to copy our political system, our economic system, to wear our jeans, drink our Pepsi, drive our cars, listen to our music, read our novels, publish our novels, become "entrepreneurs"; they condemn communism, sing paeans to the market, and believe sincerely that there's no option other than the one or the other unadulterated; they confess their sins, abolish the Warsaw Pact, and plead to join NATO and the European Union. And our media eat it all up; we squeal with delight at each new sign of "democracy"; even the Russians making their first "horror" film is a newsworthy occasion in the West, like our baby is taking his first steps; our precocious babies we call "pro-democracy", the ugly little infants who still don't get it we call "hard-line"; we pooh-pooh our babies' setbacks, they're only growing pains, they have to learn how to live with freedom ... and it all makes us feel like we actually won something in the cold war; a validation of sorts. It ain't much, but it may be all there is.

At least that's how it was the first couple of years or so of reform. Now, the thought may be slowly penetrating that our baby is not growing normally, he's developing our worst habits, including huge gaps in wealth and all kinds of criminal rackets he never even knew existed; at times he even yearns for the good ol' days ...

A series of graffiti scrawled on a Warsaw building:

"Bring back communism!"

"We never had communism!"

"Then bring back what we had!"[6]

Is this malaise in the genes, or in the system? But there's no turning back, we insist— they haven't privatized enough yet, the shock therapy wasn't shocking enough. The quality of individual lives matters little, so long as the overall numbers and the graphs drawn up by the boys from the World Bank, the International Monetary Fund, and the Harvard and Washington think-tanks look good. It doesn't bother a ruling elite very much, noted Eduardo Galeano, "that politics be democratic so long as the economy is not."

The Stalinists in the Soviet Union used to denounce international financial organizations like the World Bank and the IMF as agencies by which the rich imperialist nations kept the poor countries in servitude. Now that Russia and its former fellow republics have thrown themselves on the mercy of these institutions, the born-again capitalists may decide that the Stalinists were right after all.

We've also been told that it was the relentlessly tough anti-communist policies of the Reagan Administration with its heated-up arms race that led to the collapse and reformation of the Soviet Union and its satellites. American history books may have already begun to chisel this thesis into marble. The Tories in Great Britain say that Margaret Thatcher and her unflinching policies contributed to the miracle as well. The East Germans were believers too. When Ronald Reagan visited East Berlin, the people there cheered him and thanked him "for his role in liberating the East". Even some leftist analysts, particularly those of a conspiracy bent, are believers.

But this view is not universally held.

Long the leading Soviet expert on the United States, Georgi Arbatov, head of the Moscow-based Institute for the Study of the U.S.A. and Canada, wrote his memoirs in 1992. A *Los Angeles Times* book review by Robert Scheer summed up a portion of it:

Arbatov understood all too well the failings of Soviet totalitarianism in comparison to the economy and politics of the West. It is clear from this candid and nuanced memoir that the movement for change had been developing steadily inside the highest corridors of power ever since the death of Stalin. Arbatov not only provides considerable evidence for the controversial notion that this change would have come about without foreign pressure, he insists that the U.S. military buildup during the Reagan years actually impeded this development.[7]

George F. Kennan agrees. The former US ambassador to the Soviet Union, and father of the theory of "containment" of the same country, asserts that "the suggestion that any United States administration had the power to influence decisively the course of a tremendous domestic political upheaval in another great country on another side of the globe is simply childish." He contends that the extreme militarization of American policy strengthened hard-liners in the Soviet Union. "Thus the general effect of Cold War extremism was to delay rather than hasten the great change that overtook the Soviet Union."[8]

Though the arms-race spending undoubtedly damaged the fabric of the Soviet civilian economy and society even more than it did in the United States, this had been going on for 40 years by the time Mikhail Gorbachev came to power without the slightest hint of impending doom. Gorbachev's close adviser, Aleksandr Yakovlev, when asked whether the Reagan administration's higher military spending, combined with its "Evil Empire" rhetoric, forced the Soviet Union into a more conciliatory position, responded:

> It played no role. None. I can tell you that with the fullest responsibility. Gorbachev and I were ready for changes in our policy regardless of whether the American president was Reagan, or Kennedy, or someone even more liberal. It was clear that our military spending was enormous and we had to reduce it.[9]

Understandably, some Russians might be reluctant to admit that they were forced to make revolutionary changes by their arch enemy, to admit that they lost the cold war. However, on this question we don't have to rely on the opinion of any individual, Russian or American. We merely have to look at the historical facts.

From the late 1940s to around the mid-1960s, it was an American policy objective to instigate the downfall of the Soviet government as well as several Eastern European regimes. Many hundreds of Russian exiles were organized, trained and equipped by the CIA, then sneaked back into their homeland to set up espionage rings, to stir up armed political struggle, and to carry out acts of assassination and sabotage, such as derailing trains, wrecking bridges, damaging arms factories and power plants, and so on. The Soviet government, which captured many of these men, was of course fully aware of who was behind all this.

Compared to this policy, that of the Reagan administration could be categorized as one of virtual capitulation. Yet what were the fruits of this ultra-tough anti-communist policy? Repeated serious confrontations between the United States and the Soviet Union in Berlin, Cuba and elsewhere, the Soviet interventions into Hungary and Czechoslovakia, creation of the Warsaw Pact (in direct reaction to NATO), no *glasnost*, no *perestroika*, only pervasive suspicion, cynicism and hostility on both sides. It turned out that the Russians were human after all—they responded to toughness with toughness. And the corollary: there was for many years a close correlation between the amicability of US-Soviet relations and the number of Jews allowed to emigrate from the Soviet Union.[10] Softness produced softness.

If there's anyone to attribute the changes in the Soviet Union and Eastern Europe to, both the beneficial ones and those questionable, it is of course Mikhail Gorbachev and the activists he inspired. It should be remembered that Reagan was in office for over four years before Gorbachev came to power (and Thatcher for six years), but in that period of time nothing of any significance in the way of Soviet reform took place despite Reagan's unremitting malice toward the communist state.

The argument is frequently advanced that it's easy in hindsight to disparage the American cold-war mania for a national security state, with all its advanced paranoia and absurdities, its NATO-supra-state-military juggernaut, its early-warning systems and air-raid drills, its nuclear silos and U-2s, but that after the War in Europe the Soviets did indeed appear to be a ten-foot-tall world-wide monster threat.

This argument breaks up on the rocks of a single question, which was all one had to ask back then: Why would the Soviets want to invade Western Europe or bomb the United States? They clearly had nothing to gain by such actions except the almost certain destruction of their country, which they were painstakingly rebuilding once again after the devastation of the war.

By the 1980s, the question that still dared not be asked had given birth to a $300 billion budget and Star Wars.

There are available, in fact, numerous internal documents from the State Department, the Defense Department, and the CIA from the postwar period, wherein one political analyst after another makes clear his serious skepticism of "The Soviet Threat"—revealing the Russians' critical military weaknesses and/or questioning their alleged aggressive intentions—while high officials, including the president, were publicly presenting a message explicitly the opposite.[11]

Historian Roger Morris, former member of the National Security Council under Presidents Johnson and Nixon, described this phenomenon:

> Architects of U.S. policy would have to make their case "clearer than the truth," and "bludgeon the mass mind of top government," as Secretary of State Dean Acheson ... puts it. They do. The new Central Intelligence Agency begins a systematic overstatement of Soviet military expenditures. Magically, the sclerotic Soviet economy is made to hum and climb on U.S. government charts. To Stalin's horse-drawn army—complete with shoddy equipment, war-torn roads and spurious morale—the Pentagon adds phantom divisions, then attributes invasion scenarios to the new forces for good measure.
>
> U.S. officials "exaggerated Soviet capabilities and intentions to such an extent," says a subsequent study of the archives, "that it is surprising anyone took them seriously." Fed by somber government claims and reverberating public fear, the U.S. press and people have no trouble.[12]

Nonetheless, the argument insists, the fact remains that there were many officials in high positions who simply and sincerely misunderstood the Soviet signals. The Soviet Union was, after all, a highly oppressive and secretive society, particularly before Stalin died in 1953. Apropos of this, former conservative member of the British Parliament Enoch Powell observed in 1983:

> International misunderstanding is almost wholly voluntary: it is that contradiction in terms, intentional misunderstanding—a contradiction, because in order to misunderstand deliberately, you must at least suspect if not actually understand what you intend to misunderstand. ... [The US misunderstanding of the USSR has] the function of sustaining a myth—the myth of the United States as "the last, best hope of mankind." St. George and the Dragon is a poor show without a real dragon, the bigger and scalier the better, ideally with flames coming out of its mouth. The misunderstanding of Soviet Russia has become indispensable to the self-esteem of the American nation: he will not be regarded with benevolence who seeks, however ineffectually, to deprive them of it.[13]

It can be argued as well that the belief of the Nazis in the great danger posed by the "International Jewish Conspiracy" must be considered before condemning the perpetrators of the Holocaust.

Both the Americans and the Germans believed their own propaganda, or pretended to. If one reads *Mein Kampf*, one is struck by the fact that a significant part of what Hitler wrote about Jews reads very much like an American anti-communist writing about communists: He starts with the premise that the Jews (communists) are evil and want to dominate the world; then, any behavior which appears to contradict this is regarded as simply a ploy to fool people and further their evil ends; this behavior is always part of a conspiracy and many people are taken in. He ascribes to the Jews great, almost mystical, power to manipulate societies and economies. He blames Jews for the ills arising from the industrial revolution, e.g., class divisions and hatred. He decries the Jews' internationalism and lack of national patriotism.

There were of course those cold warriors whose take on the Kremlin was that its master plan for world domination was nothing so gross as an invasion of Western Europe or dropping bombs on the United States. The ever more subtle—one could say fiendishly clever—plan was for subversion ... from the inside ... country by country ... throughout the Third World ... eventually surrounding and strangling the First World ... verily an International Communist Conspiracy, "a conspiracy," said Senator McCarthy, "on a scale so immense as to dwarf any previous such venture in the history of man."

This is the primary focus of this book: how the United States intervened all over the world to combat this subversion by the ICC, wherever and whenever it reared its ugly head.

Did this International Communist Conspiracy actually exist?

If it actually existed, why did the cold warriors of the CIA and other government agencies have to go to such extraordinary lengths of exaggeration? If they really and truly believed in the existence of a diabolic, monolithic International Communist Conspiracy, why did they have to invent so much about it to convince the American people, the Congress, and the rest of the world of its evil existence? Why did they have to stage manage, entrap, plant evidence, plant stories? The following pages are packed with double-density double-sided anti-commiespeak examples of US-government and media inventions about "the Soviet threat", "the Chinese threat", and "the Cuban threat". And all the while, at the same time, we were being flailed with scare stories: in the 1950s, there was "the Bomber Gap" between the US and the Soviet Union. Then came "the Missile Gap". Followed by "the Anti-ballistic missile (ABM) Gap". In the 1980s, it was "the Spending Gap". Finally, "the Laser Gap". And they were all lies.[14]

We now know that the CIA of Ronald Reagan and William Casey regularly "politicized intelligence assessments" to support the anti-Soviet bias of the administration, and suppressed reports, even those from its own analysts, which contradicted the bias. We now know that the CIA and the Pentagon, partly from the pressure of the conservative establishment, regularly overestimated the economic and military strength of the Soviet Union, and exaggerated the scale of Soviet nuclear tests and the number of "violations" of existing testban treaties, which Washington then accused the Russians of.[15] All to create a larger and meaner enemy, a bigger M-I-I-C budget, and give security and meaning to the cold warriors' own jobs.

Post-cold war, New-World-Order time, it looks good for the M-I-I-C and their global partners in crime, the World Bank and the IMF. They've got their NAFTA, and soon their GATT World Trade Organization. They're dictating economic, political and social development all over the Third World and Eastern Europe. Moscow's reaction to events anywhere is no longer a restraining consideration. The UN's Code of Conduct on Transnational Corporations, 15 years in the making, is dead. Everything in sight is being deregulated and privatized. Capital prowls the globe with a ravenous freedom it hasn't enjoyed since before World War I, operating free of friction, free of gravity. The world has been made safe for the transnational corporation.[16]

Will this mean any better life for the multitudes than the cold war brought? Any more regard for the common folk than there's been since they fell off the cosmic agenda centuries ago? "By all means," says Capital, offering another warmed-up version of the "trickle down" theory, the principle that the poor, who must subsist on table scraps dropped by the rich, can best be served by giving the rich bigger meals.

The boys of Capital, they also chortle in their martinis about the death of socialism. The word has been banned from polite conversation. And they hope that no one will notice that every socialist experiment of any significance in the twentieth century—without exception—has either been crushed, overthrown, or invaded, or corrupted, perverted, subverted, or destabilized, or otherwise had life made impossible for it, by the United States. Not one socialist government or movement—from the Russian Revolution to the Sandinistas in Nicaragua, from Communist China to the FMLN in Salvador—not one was permitted to rise or fall solely on its own merits; not one was left secure enough to drop its guard against the all-powerful enemy abroad and freely and fully relax control at home.

It's as if the Wright brothers' first experiments with flying machines all failed because the automobile interests sabotaged each test flight. And then the good and god-fearing folk of the world looked upon this, took notice of the consequences, nodded their collective heads wisely, and intoned solemnly: Man shall never fly.

Winning the cold war means never having to say you're sorry. The Germans have apologized to the Jews and the Poles. The Russians have apologized to the Poles as well, and to the Japanese for abuse of prisoners; the Soviet Communist Party has even apologized for foreign policy errors that "heightened tension with the West."[17] An East German TV newscaster apologized to viewers for years of dishonest reporting.[18] The Japanese have apologized to the Chinese and the Koreans; they've also apologized for failing to break off diplomatic relations with the US before attacking Pearl Harbor. When will the United States apologize to Japan for the atomizing of Hiroshima and Nagasaki, carried out after the Japanese were ready to surrender?[19] When will we apologize to the Russians, and the Vietnamese, the Laotians, and the Cambodians, the Chileans, the Guatemalans, and the Salvadoreans ... see the Table of Contents herein. And when will the FBI and CIA be brought to public account, as the Soviet KGB and the East German Stasi have, for their domestic crimes?

Los Angeles, October 1994

Introduction to the Original Edition

'It was in the early days of the fighting in Vietnam that a Vietcong officer said to his American prisoner: "You were our heroes after the War. We read American books and saw American films, and a common phrase in those days was 'to be as rich and as wise as an American'. What happened?"[1]

An American might have been asked something similar by a Guatemalan, an Indonesian or a Cuban during the ten years previous, or by a Uruguayan, a Chilean or a Greek in the decade subsequent. The remarkable international goodwill and credibility enjoyed by the United States at the close of the Second World War was dissipated country by country, intervention by intervention. The opportunity to build the war-ravaged world anew, to lay the foundations for peace, prosperity and justice, collapsed under the awful weight of anti-communism.

The weight had been accumulating for some time; indeed, since Day One of the Russian Revolution. By the summer of 1918 some 13,000 American troops could be found in the newly-born Union of Soviet Socialist Republics. Two years and thousands of casualties later, the American troops left, having failed in their mission to "strangle at its birth" the Bolshevik state, as Winston Churchill put it.[2]

The young Churchill was Great Britain's Minister for War and Air during this period. Increasingly, it was he who directed the invasion of the Soviet Union by the Allies (Great Britain, the US, France, Japan and several other nations) on the side of the counter-revolutionary "White Army". Years later, Churchill the historian was to record his views of this singular affair for posterity:

> Were they [the Allies] at war with Soviet Russia? Certainly not; but they shot Soviet Russians at sight. They stood as invaders on Russian soil. They armed the enemies of the Soviet Government. They blockaded its ports, and sunk its battleships. They earnestly desired and schemed its downfall. But war—shocking! Interference—shame! It was, they repeated, a matter of indifference to them how Russians settled their own internal affairs. They were impartial—Bang![3]

What was there about this Bolshevik Revolution that so alarmed the most powerful nations in the world? What drove them to invade a land whose soldiers had recently fought alongside them for over three years and suffered more casualties than any other country on either side of the World War?

The Bolsheviks had had the audacity to make a separate peace with Germany in order to take leave of a war they regarded as imperialist and not in any way *their* war, and to try and rebuild a terribly weary and devastated Russia. But the Bolsheviks had displayed the far greater audacity of overthrowing a capitalist-feudal system and proclaiming the first socialist state in the history of the world. This was uppitiness writ incredibly large. This was the crime the Allies had to punish, the virus which had to be eradicated lest it spread to their own people.

The invasion did not achieve its immediate purpose, but its consequences were nonetheless profound and persist to the present day. Professor D.F. Fleming, the Vanderbilt University historian of the cold war, has noted:

> For the American people the cosmic tragedy of the interventions in Russia does not exist, or it was an unimportant incident long forgotten. But for the Soviet peoples and their leaders the period was a time of endless killing, of looting and rapine, of plague and famine, of measureless suffering for scores of millions—an experience burned into the very soul of a nation, not to be forgotten for many generations, if ever. Also for many years the harsh Soviet regimentations could

9

all be justified by fear that the capitalist powers would be back to finish the job. It is not strange that in his address in New York, September 17, 1959, Premier Khrushchev should remind us of the interventions, "the time you sent your troops to quell the revolution", as he put it.[4]

In what could be taken as a portent of superpower insensitivity, a 1920 Pentagon report reads: "This expedition affords one of the finest examples in history of honorable, unselfish dealings ... under very difficult circumstances to be helpful to a people struggling to achieve a new liberty."[5]

History does not tell us what a Soviet Union, allowed to develop in a "normal" way of its own choosing, would look like today. We do know, however, the nature of a Soviet Union attacked in its cradle, raised alone in an extremely hostile world, and, when it managed to survive to adulthood, overrun by the Nazi war machine with the blessings of the Western powers. The resulting insecurities and fears have inevitably led to deformities of character not unlike that found in an individual raised in a similar life-threatening manner.

We in the West are never allowed to forget the political shortcomings (real and alleged) of the Soviet Union; at the same time we are never reminded of the history which lies behind it. The anti-communist propaganda campaign began even earlier than the military intervention. Before the year 1918 was over, expressions in the vein of "Red Peril", "the Bolshevik assault on civilization", and "menace to world by Reds is seen" had become commonplace in the pages of the *New York Times*.

During February and March 1919, a US Senate Judiciary Subcommittee held hearings before which many "Bolshevik horror stories" were presented. The character of some of the testimony can be gauged by the headline in the usually sedate *Times* of 12 February 1919.

DESCRIBE HORRORS UNDER RED RULE. R.E. SIMONS AND W.W. WELSH TELL SENATORS OF BRUTALITIES OF BOLSHEVIKI—STRIP WOMEN IN STREETS—PEOPLE OF EVERY CLASS EXCEPT THE SCUM SUBJECTED TO VIOLENCE BY MOBS.

Historian Frederick Lewis Schuman has written: "The net result of these hearings ... was to picture Soviet Russia as a kind of bedlam inhabited by abject slaves completely at the mercy of an organization of homicidal maniacs whose purpose was to destroy all traces of civilization and carry the nation back to barbarism."[6]

Literally no story about the Bolsheviks was too contrived, too bizarre, too grotesque, or too perverted to be printed and widely believed—from women being nationalized to babies being eaten (as the early pagans believed the Christians guilty of devouring their children; the same was believed of the Jews in the Middle Ages). The story about women with all the lurid connotations of state property, compulsory marriage, "free love", etc. "was broadcasted over the country through a thousand channels," wrote Schuman, "and perhaps did more than anything else to stamp the Russian Communists in the minds of most American citizens as criminal perverts".[7] This tale continued to receive great currency even after the State Department was obliged to announce that it was a fraud. (That the Soviets eat their babies was still being taught by the John Birch Society to its large audience at least as late as 1978.)[8]

By the end of 1919, when the defeat of the Allies and the White Army appeared likely, the *New York Times* treated its readers to headlines and stories such as the following:

30 Dec. 1919: "Reds Seek War With America"

9 Jan. 1920: "'Official quarters' describe the Bolshevist menace in the Middle East as ominous"

11 Jan. 1920: "Allied officials and diplomats [envisage] a possible invasion of Europe"

13 Jan. 1920: "Allied diplomatic circles" fear an invasion of Persia

16 Jan. 1920: A page-one headline, eight columns wide: "Britain Facing War With Reds, Calls Council In Paris."

"Well-informed diplomats" expect both a military invasion of Europe and a Soviet advance into Eastern and Southern Asia.

The following morning, however, we could read: "No War With Russia, Allies To Trade With Her"

7 Feb. 1920: "Reds Raising Army To Attack India"

11 Feb. 1920: "Fear That Bolsheviki Will Now Invade Japanese Territory"

Readers of the *New York Times* were asked to believe that all these invasions were to come from a nation that was shattered as few nations in history have been; a nation still recovering from a horrendous world war; in extreme chaos from a fundamental social revolution that was barely off the ground; engaged in a brutal civil war against forces backed by the major powers of the world; its industries, never advanced to begin with, in a shambles; and the country in the throes of a famine that was to leave many millions dead before it subsided.

In 1920, *The New Republic* magazine presented a lengthy analysis of the news coverage by the *New York Times* of the Russian Revolution and the intervention. Amongst much else, it observed that in the two years following the November 1917 revolution, the *Times* had stated no less than 91 times that "the Soviets were nearing their rope's end or actually had reached it."[9]

If this was reality as presented by the United States' "newspaper of record", one can imagine only with dismay the witch's brew the rest of the nation's newspapers were feeding to their readers.

This, then, was the American people's first experience of a new social phenomenon that had come upon the world, their introductory education about the Soviet Union and this thing called "communism". The students have never recovered from the lesson. Neither has the Soviet Union.

The military intervention came to an end but, with the sole and partial exception of the Second World War period, the propaganda offensive has never let up. In 1943 *Life* magazine devoted an entire issue in honor of the Soviet Union's accomplishments, going far beyond what was demanded by the need for wartime solidarity, going so far as to call Lenin "perhaps the greatest man of modern times".[10] Two years later, however, with Harry Truman sitting in the White House, such fraternity had no chance of surviving. Truman, after all, was the man who, the day after the Nazis invaded the Soviet Union, said: "If we see that Germany is winning, we ought to help Russia, and if Russia is winning, we ought to help Germany, and that way let them kill as many as possible, although I don't want to see Hitler victorious in any circumstances."[11] Much propaganda mileage has been squeezed out of the Soviet-German treaty of 1939, made possible only by entirely ignoring the fact that the Russians were forced into the pact by the repeated refusal of the Western powers, particularly the United States and Great Britain, to unite with Moscow in a stand against Hitler;[12] as they likewise refused to come to the aid of the socialist-oriented Spanish government under siege by the German, Italian and Spanish fascists.

From the Red Scare of the 1920s to the McCarthyism of the 1950s to the Reagan Crusade against the Evil Empire of the 1980s, the American people have been subjected to a relentless anti-communist indoctrination. It is imbibed with their mother's milk, pictured in their comic books, spelled out in their school books; their daily paper offers them headlines that tell them all they need to know; ministers find sermons in it, politicians are elected with it, and *Reader's Digest* becomes rich on it.

The fiercely-held conviction inevitably produced by this insidious assault upon the intellect is that a great damnation has been unleashed upon the world, possibly by the devil himself, but in the form of people; people not motivated by the same needs, fears, emotions, and personal morality that govern others of the species, but people engaged in an extremely clever, monolithic, international conspiracy dedicated to taking over the world and enslaving it; for reasons not always clear perhaps, but evil needs no motivation save evil itself. Moreover, any appearance or claim by these people to be rational human beings seeking a better kind of world or society is a sham, a cover-up, to delude others, and proof only of their cleverness; the repression and cruelties which have taken place in the Soviet Union are forever proof of the bankruptcy of virtue and the evil intentions of these people in whichever country they may be found, under whatever name they may call themselves: and, most important of all, the only choice open to anyone in the United States is between the American Way of Life and the Soviet Way of Life, that nothing lies between or beyond these two ways of making the world.

This is how it looks to the simple folk of America. One finds that the sophisticated, when probed slightly beneath the surface of their academic language, see it exactly the same way.

And lest we think that such beliefs belong to an earlier, less enlightened period, it should be noted that in the fall of 1987, two years after Gorbachev, when a Gallup poll asked Americans whether they agreed that "There is an international Communist conspiracy to rule the world", 60 percent replied in the affirmative; only 28 percent disagreed.[13]

To the mind carefully brought to adulthood in the United States, the truths of anti-communism are self-evident, as self-evident as the flatness of the world once was to an earlier mind; as the Russian people believed that the victims of Stalin's purges were truly guilty of treason.

The foregoing slice of American history must be taken into account if one is to make sense of the vagaries of American foreign policy since the end of World War II, specifically the record, as presented in this book, of what the CIA and other branches of the US government have done to the peoples of the world.

In 1918, the barons of American capital needed no reason for their war against communism other than the threat to their wealth and privilege, although their opposition was expressed in terms of moral indignation.

During the period between the two world wars, US gunboat diplomacy operated in the Caribbean to make "The American Lake" safe for the fortunes of United Fruit and W.R. Grace & Co., at the same time warning of the Bolshevik threat to righteousness from the likes of Augusto Sandino.

By the end of the Second World War, every American past the age of 40 had been subjected to some 25 years of anti-communist radiation, the average incubation period needed to produce a malignancy. Anti-communism had developed a life of its own, independent of its capitalist father. Increasingly, in the post-war period, middle-aged Washington policy makers and diplomats saw the world out there as one composed of "communists" and "anti-communists", whether of nations, movements or individuals. This comic-strip vision of the world, with American supermen fighting communist evil everywhere, had graduated from a cynical propaganda exercise to a moral imperative of US foreign policy.

Even the concept of "non-communist", implying some measure of neutrality, has generally been accorded scant legitimacy in this paradigm. John Foster Dulles, one of the major architects of post-war US foreign policy, expressed this succinctly in his typically simple, moralistic way: "For us there are two sorts of people in the world: there are those who are Christians and support free enterprise and there are the others."[14] As several of the case studies in the present book confirm, Dulles put that creed into rigid practice.

It is as true now as ever that American multinationals derive significant economic advantages from Third World countries due to their being under-industrialized, under-diversified, capitalist-oriented, and relatively powerless.

It is equally true that the consequence of American interventions has frequently been to keep Third World countries in just such an underdeveloped, impotent state.

There is thus at least a prima-facie case to be made for the contention that the engine of US foreign policy is still fueled predominantly by "economic imperialism".

But that the consequence illuminates the intent does not necessarily follow. The argument that economic factors have continued to exert an important and direct influence upon United States interventionist policy in modern times does not stand up to close or "micro" examination. When all the known elements of the interventions are considered, scarcely any cases emerge which actually conform to the economic model, and even in these the stage is shared with other factors. The upshot in the great majority of cases is that tangible economic gain, existing or potential, did not, and could not, play a determining role in the American decision to intervene. The economic model proves woefully inadequate not only as a means of explanation, but even more so as a tool of prediction. In each of the most recent cases, for example—Grenada, El Salvador, and Nicaragua—American intervention was foreseen and warned of well in advance simply, and only, because of the "communist" nature of the targets. But no one seriously suggested that some treasure lay in these impoverished lands luring the American pirates. Indeed, after the conquest and occupation of Grenada, the US business community displayed a marked indifference to setting up shop on the island, despite being implored to do so by Washington for political reasons. In other cases, where the American side failed to win a civil war, such as in China, Vietnam and Angola, Washington put up barriers to American corporations having any commercial dealings with the new regimes which were actually eager to do business with the United States.

But this, as mentioned, is the "micro" way of looking at the question. One can just as legitimately approach it from a "macro" point of view. Seen from this perspective, one must examine the role of the military-industrial-intelligence complex. The members of this network need enemies—the military and the CIA because enemies are their *raison d'être*, industry, specifically the defense contractors, because enemies are to be fought, with increasingly sophisticated weaponry and aircraft systems; enemies of our enemies are to be armed, to the teeth. It's made these corporations wealthier than many countries of the world; in one year the US spends on the military more than $17,000 per hour, for every hour since Jesus Christ was born. The executives of these corporations have long moved effortlessly through a revolving door between industry and government service, members in good standing of the good ol' boys club who continue to use their positions, their wealth, and their influence, along with a compliant and indispensable media, as we shall see, to nourish and perpetuate the fear of "communism, the enemy" now in its seventh decade and going strong. Given the nature and machinations of the military-industrial-intelligence complex, interventions against these enemies are inevitable, and, from the complex's point of view, highly desirable.

In cases such as the above-mentioned Grenada, El Salvador, and Nicaragua, even if the particular target of intervention does not present an immediate lucrative economic opportunity for American multinationals, the target's socialist-revolutionary program and rhetoric does present a threat and a challenge which the United States has repeatedly felt obliged to stamp out, to maintain the *principle*, and as a warning to others; for what the US has always feared from the Third World is the emergence of a good example: a flourishing socialist society independent of Washington.

Governments and movements with such programs and rhetoric are clearly not going to be cold-war allies, are clearly "communist", and thus are eminently credible candidates for the category of enemy.

Inextricably bound up with these motivations is a far older seducer of men and nations, the lust for power: the acquisition, maintenance, use and enjoyment of influence and prestige; the incomparable elation that derives from molding the world in your own beloved image.

In all these paradigms, "communist" is often no more than the name ascribed to those people who stand in the way of the realization of such ambitions (as "national security" is the name given for the *reason* for fighting "communists"). It is another twist of the old adage: if communists didn't exist, the United States would have to invent them. And so they have. The word "communist" (as well as "Marxist") has been so overused and so abused by American leaders and the media as to render it virtually meaningless. (The left has done the same to the word "fascist".) But merely having a name for something—witches or flying saucers—attaches a certain credence to it.

At the same time, the American public, as we have seen, has been soundly conditioned to react Pavlovianly to the term: it means, still, the worst excesses of Stalin, from wholesale purges to Siberian slave-labor camps; it means, as Michael Parenti has observed, that "Classic Marxist-Leninist *predictions* [concerning world revolution] are treated as statements of *intent* directing all present-day communist *actions*."[15] It means "us" against "them".

And "them" can mean a peasant in the Philippines, a mural-painter in Nicaragua, a legally-elected prime minister in British Guiana, or a European intellectual, a Cambodian neutralist, an African nationalist—all, somehow, part of the same monolithic conspiracy; each, in some way, a threat to the American Way of Life; no land too small, too poor, or too far away to pose such a threat, the "communist threat".

The cases presented in this book illustrate that it has been largely irrelevant whether the particular targets of intervention—be they individuals, political parties, movements or governments—called themselves "communist" or not. It has mattered little whether they were scholars of dialectical materialism or had never heard of Karl Marx; whether they were atheists or priests; whether a strong and influential Communist Party was in the picture or not; whether the government had come into being through violent revolution or peaceful elections ... all have been targets, all "communists".

It has mattered still less that the Soviet KGB was in the picture. The assertion has been frequently voiced that the CIA carries out its dirty tricks largely *in reaction to* operations of the KGB which have been "even dirtier". This is a lie made out of whole cloth. There may be an isolated incident of such in the course of the CIA's life, but it has kept itself well hidden. The relationship between the two sinister agencies is marked by fraternization and respect for fellow professionals more than by hand-to-hand combat. Former CIA officer John Stockwell has written:

> Actually, at least in more routine operations, case officers most fear the US ambassador and his staff, then restrictive headquarters cables, then curious, gossipy neighbors in the local communi-

ty, as potential threats to operations. Next would come the local police, then the press. Last of all is the KGB—in my twelve years of case officering I never saw or heard of a situation in which the KGB attacked or obstructed a CIA operation.[16]

Stockwell adds that the various intelligence services do not want their world to be "complicated" by murdering each other.

It isn't done. If a CIA case officer has a flat tire in the dark of night on a lonely road, he will not hesitate to accept a ride from a KGB officer—likely the two would detour to some bar for a drink together. In fact CIA and KGB officers entertain each other frequently in their homes. The CIA's files are full of mention of such relationships in almost every African station.[17]

Proponents of "fighting fire with fire" come perilously close at times to arguing that if the KGB, for example, had a hand in the overthrow of the Czechoslovak government in 1968, it is OK for the CIA to have a hand in the overthrow of the Chilean government in 1973. It's as if the destruction of democracy by the KGB deposits funds in a bank account from which the CIA is then justified in making withdrawals.

What then has been the thread common to the diverse targets of American intervention which has brought down upon them the wrath, and often the firepower, of the world's most powerful nation? In virtually every case involving the Third World described in this book, it has been, in one form or another, a policy of "self-determination": the desire, born of perceived need and principle, to pursue a path of development independent of US foreign policy objectives. Most commonly, this has been manifested in (a) the ambition to free themselves from economic and political subservience to the United States; (b) the refusal to minimize relations with the socialist bloc, or suppress the left at home, or welcome an American military installation on their soil; in short, a refusal to be a pawn in the cold war; or (c) the attempt to alter or replace a government which held to neither of these aspirations.

It cannot be emphasized too strongly that such a policy of independence has been viewed and expressed by numerous Third World leaders and revolutionaries as one not to be equated by definition to anti-Americanism or pro-communism, but as simply a determination to maintain a position of neutrality and non-alignment vis-à-vis the two superpowers. Time and time again, however, it will be seen that the United States was not prepared to live with this proposition. Arbenz of Guatemala, Mossadegh of Iran, Sukarno of Indonesia, Nkrumah of Ghana, Jagan of British Guiana, Sihanouk of Cambodia ... all, insisted Uncle Sam, must declare themselves unequivocally on the side of "The Free World" or suffer the consequences. Nkrumah put the case for non-alignment as follows:

The experiment which we tried in Ghana was essentially one of developing the country in co-operation with the world as a whole. Non-alignment meant exactly what it said. We were not hostile to the countries of the socialist world in the way in which the governments of the old colonial territories were. It should be remembered that while Britain pursued at home co-existence with the Soviet Union this was never allowed to extend to British colonial territories. Books on socialism, which were published and circulated freely in Britain, were banned in the British colonial empire, and after Ghana became independent it was assumed abroad that it would con-tinue to follow the same restrictive ideological approach. When we behaved as did the British in their relations with the socialist countries we were accused of being pro-Russian and introducing the most dangerous ideas into Africa.[18]

It is reminiscent of the 19th-century American South, where many Southerners were deeply offended that so many of their black slaves had deserted to the Northern side in the Civil War. They had genuinely thought that the blacks should have been grateful for all their white masters had done for them, and that they were happy and content with their lot. A Southern physician, Samuel Cartwright, argued that many of the slaves suffered from a form of mental illness, which he called "drapetomania", diagnosed as the uncontrollable urge to escape from slavery. In the second half of the 20th-century, this illness, in the Third World, has usually been called "communism".

When Washington officials equate nationalism or self-determination with "communism", there are times when they are "correct". At other times, they are "wrong". It doesn't particularly matter, for in either case they are referring to the same phenomenon. Although, in this book, the Soviet Union, China, various communist parties, etc., are sometimes referred to as "communist", this is primarily a shorthand convenience and a bow to custom, and is not meant to infer a political ideology or practice necessarily different in any way from those governments or parties *not* referred to as communist. Emphasis is placed upon what these bodies have actually done, not upon reference to what Marx or Lenin wrote.

Perhaps the most deeply ingrained reflex of knee-jerk anti-communism is the belief that the Soviet Union (or Cuba or Vietnam, etc., acting as Moscow's surrogate) is a clandestine force lurking behind the facade of self-determination, stirring up the hydra of revolution, or just plain trouble, here, there, and everywhere; yet another incarnation, although on a far grander scale, of the proverbial "outside agitator", he who has made his appearance regularly throughout history ... King George blamed the French for inciting the American colonies to revolt ... disillusioned American farmers and veterans protesting their onerous economic circumstances after the revolution (Shays' Rebellion) were branded as British agents out to wreck the new republic ... labor strikes in late-19th-century America were blamed on "anarchists" and "foreigners", during the First World War on "German agents", after the war on "Bolsheviks".

And in the 1960s, said the National Commission on the Causes and Prevention of Violence, J. Edgar Hoover "helped spread the view among the police ranks that any kind of mass protest is due to a conspiracy promulgated by agitators, often Communists, 'who misdirect otherwise contented people'."[19]

The last is the key phrase, one which encapsulates the conspiracy mentality of those in power—the idea that no people, except those living under the enemy, could be so miserable and discontent as to need recourse to revolution or even mass protest; that it is only the agitation of the outsider which misdirects them along this path.

Accordingly, if Ronald Reagan were to concede that the masses of El Salvador have every good reason to rise up against their god-awful existence, it would bring into question his accusation, and the rationale for US intervention, that it is principally (only?) the Soviet Union and its Cuban and Nicaraguan allies who instigate the Salvadoreans: that seemingly magical power of communists everywhere who, with a twist of their red wrist, can transform peaceful, happy people into furious guerrillas. The CIA knows how difficult a feat this is. The Agency, as we shall see, tried to spark mass revolt in China, Albania, Cuba, the Soviet Union, and elsewhere in Eastern Europe with a singular lack of success. The Agency's scribes have laid the blame for these failures on the "closed" nature of the societies involved. But in non-communist countries, the CIA has had to resort to military coups or extra-legal chicanery to get its people into power. It has never been able to light the fire of popular revolution.

For Washington to concede merit and virtue to a particular Third World insurgency would, moreover, raise the question: Why does not the United States, if it must intervene, take the side of the rebels? Not only might this better serve the cause of human rights and justice, but it would shut out the Russians from their alleged role. What better way to frustrate the International Communist Conspiracy? But this is a question that dares not speak its name in the Oval Office, a question that is relevant to many of the cases in this book.

Instead, the United States remains committed to its all-too-familiar policy of establishing and/or supporting the most vile tyrannies in the world, whose outrages against their own people confront us daily in the pages of our newspapers: brutal massacres; systematic, sophisticated torture; public whippings; soldiers and police firing into crowds; hunger, runaway unemployment, the homeless, the refugees, the tens of thousands of disappeared persons ... a way of life that is virtually a monopoly held by America's allies, from Guatemala, Chile and El Salvador to Turkey, Pakistan and Indonesia, all members in good standing of the Holy War Against Communism, all members of "The Free World", that little known region of which we hear so much and see so little.

The restrictions on civil liberties found in the communist bloc, as severe as they are, pale by comparison to the cottage-industry Auschwitzes of "The Free World", and, except in that curious mental landscape inhabited by The Compleat Anti-Communist, can have little or nothing to do with the sundry American interventions supposedly in the cause of a higher good.

It is interesting to note that as commonplace as it is for American leaders to speak of freedom and democracy while supporting dictatorships, so do Russian leaders speak of wars of liberation, anti-imperialism and anti-colonialism while doing extremely little to actually further these causes, American propaganda notwithstanding. The Soviets like to be thought of as champions of the Third World, but they have stood by doing little more than going "tsk, tsk" as progressive movements and governments, even Communist Parties, in Greece, Guatemala, British Guiana, Chile, Indonesia, the Philippines and elsewhere have gone to the wall with American complicity.

During the early 1950s, the Central Intelligence Agency instigated several military incursions into Communist China. In 1960, CIA planes, without any provocation, bombed the sovereign nation of Guatemala. In 1973, the Agency encouraged a bloody revolt against the government of Iraq. In the American mass media at the time, and therefore in the American mind, these events did not happen.

"We didn't know what was happening", became a cliché used to ridicule those Germans who claimed ignorance of the events which took place under the Nazis. Yet, was their stock answer as far-fetched as we'd like to think? It is sobering to reflect that in our era of instant world-wide communications, the United States has, on many occasions, been able to mount a large- or small-scale military operation or undertake another, equally blatant, form of intervention without the American public being aware of it until years later, if ever. Often the only report of the event or of US involvement was a passing reference to the fact that a communist government had made certain charges—just the kind of "news" the American public has been well conditioned to dismiss out of hand, and the press not to follow up; as the German people were taught that reports from abroad of Nazi wrong-doings were no more than communist propaganda.

With few exceptions, the interventions never made the headlines or the evening TV news.

With some, bits and pieces of the stories have popped up here and there, but rarely brought together to form a cohesive and enlightening whole; the fragments usually appear long after the fact, quietly buried within other stories, just as quietly forgotten, bursting into the foreground only when extraordinary circumstances have compelled it, such as the Iranian hostage crisis which produced a rash of articles on the role played by the United States in the overthrow of the Iranian government in 1953. It was as if editors had been spurred into thinking: "Hey, just what *did* we do in Iran to make all those people hate us so?"

There have been a lot of Irans in America's recent past, but in the absence of the *New York Daily News* or the *Los Angeles Times* conspicuously grabbing the reader by the collar and pressing against his face the full implication of the deed ... in the absence of NBC putting it all into real pictures of real people on the receiving end ... in such absence the incidents become non-events for the large majority of Americans, and they can honestly say "We didn't know what was happening."

Former Chinese Premier Chou En-lai once observed: "One of the delightful things about Americans is that they have absolutely no historical memory."

It's probably even worse than he realized. During the Three Mile Island nuclear power plant accident in Pennsylvania in 1979, a Japanese journalist, Atsuo Kaneko of the Japanese Kyoto News Service, spent several hours interviewing people temporarily housed at a hockey rink—mostly children, pregnant women and young mothers. He discovered that none of them had heard of Hiroshima. Mention of the name drew a blank.[20]

And in 1982, a judge in Oakland, California said he was appalled when some 50 prospective jurors for a death-penalty murder trial were questioned and "none of them knew who Hitler was".[21]

To the foreign policy oligarchy in Washington, it is more than delightful. It is *sine qua non.*

So obscured is the comprehensive record of American interventions that when, in 1975, the Congressional Research Service of the Library of Congress was asked to undertake a study of covert activities of the CIA to date, it was able to come up with but a very minor portion of the overseas incidents presented in this book for the same period.[22]

Yet, all the information is there for the reading. I have not had access to the secret archives of the CIA or other government agencies. The details of the interventions have been gathered from books, newspapers, periodicals, and US government publications freely available in one library or another. But for all that has made its way into popular consciousness, or into school texts, encyclopedias, or other standard reference works, there might as well exist strict censorship in the United States.

The reader is invited to look through the relevant sections of the three principal American encyclopedias, *Americana, Britannica,* and *Colliers,* after completing this book. The image of encyclopedias as the final repository of objective knowledge takes a beating. What is tantamount to a non-recognition of American interventions may very well be due to these esteemed works employing a criterion similar to that of Washington officials as reflected in the Pentagon Papers. The *New York Times* summarized this highly interesting phenomenon thusly:

> Clandestine warfare against North Vietnam, for example, is not seen ... as violating the Geneva Accords of 1954, which ended the French Indochina War, or as conflicting with the public policy pronouncements of the various administrations. Clandestine warfare, because it is covert, does not exist as far as treaties and public posture are concerned. Further, secret commitments to other nations are not sensed as infringing on the treaty-making powers of the Senate, because they are not publicly acknowledged.[23]

Introductions

The *de facto* censorship which leaves so many Americans functionally illiterate about the history of US foreign affairs may be all the more effective because it is not official, heavy-handed or conspiratorial, but woven artlessly into the fabric of education and media. No conspiracy is needed. The editors of *Reader's Digest* and *U.S. News and World Report* do not need to meet covertly with the man from NBC in an FBI safe-house to plan next month's stories and programs; for the simple truth is that these men would not have reached the positions they occupy if they themselves had not all been guided through the same tunnel of camouflaged history and emerged with the same selective memory and conventional wisdom.

As extensive as the historical record presented here is, it is by no means meant to be a complete catalogue of every instance and every kind of American intervention since the Second World War. We are, after all, dealing largely with events which were covert when they occurred and which, for the most part, remain officially classified. Moreover, with but a few exceptions, this study does not concern itself with espionage or counter-espionage other than in passing. These areas have been well documented in countless "spy" books. Generally speaking, the study is confined to the more significant or blatant cases of intervention: the use of armed aggression by American and/or native troops acting with the United States; an operation, successful or not, to overthrow a government; an attempt to suppress a popular rebellion or movement; an attempted assassination of a political leader; gross interference in an election, or other flagrant manipulation of a country's political or economic system.

To serve these ends, the CIA over the years has made use of an extraordinary arsenal of weapons. Because of space considerations and to avoid excess repetition, only selected examples are given here and there amongst the cases. In actuality, at least one, and usually more, of these tactics was brought to bear in virtually every instance. Principal among them are the following:

1) *CIA schools*: in the United States and Latin America, where many tens of thousands of Third World military and police personnel have been taught modern methods of controlling insurgency and "subversion"; instruction includes techniques of "interrogation" (often a euphemism for torture); members of the labor movement learn the how and why of organizing workers within a framework of free enterprise and anti-communism.

2) *Infiltration and manipulation of selected groups*: political parties, women's organizations, professional, youth and cultural associations, etc., for electoral and propaganda purposes; the creation of unions—local, regional, national and international—set up to counterpoise and weaken existing labor groups too closely oriented towards social change and the left.

3) *News manipulation*: the "hiring" of foreign editors, columnists and journalists ... "I guess I've bought as much newspaper space as the A & P," chortled a former CIA officer one day;[24] the creation and/or subsidizing of numerous periodicals, news services, radio stations, books, and book publishers. Considering all assets, the CIA, at least until the late 1970s, has run what probably amounts to the largest news organization in the world; its propaganda and disinformation effect is routinely multiplied by world-wide replay.

4) *Economic means*: in concert with other US government agencies, such as AID, private American corporations, and international lending institutions, the methods of manipulating and applying pressure to selected sectors of a country's economy, or the economy as a

whole, are without number.

5) *Dirty tricks department*: bugging, wire-tapping, forged documents, bogus personal letters, planting of evidence, spreading rumors, blackmail, etc., etc., to create incidents or obtain information to embarrass the left, locally and internationally, particularly to lend credence to charges of a Moscow or Havana conspiracy; to provoke the expulsion of communist-bloc diplomats or the breaking of relations with those countries; to foster distrust and dissension within the left.

Although the cases which follow are presented as more or less discrete stories, fixed in time and with beginnings and ends, this is done mainly to keep the information within manageable bounds and to highlight the more dramatic turns of events, and is not meant to indicate that there was no significant CIA activity in the particular country before or after the years specified. The reader should therefore keep in mind that the above types of operation as well as others are all ongoing programs, carried out routinely in numerous countries, including many not listed in this book. This is the Agency's "job", what its officers do for a living.

"The upheaval in China is a revolution which, if we analyze it, we will see is prompted by the same things that prompted the British, French and American revolutions."[25] A cosmopolitan and generous sentiment of Dean Rusk, then Assistant Secretary for Far Eastern Affairs, later Secretary of State. At precisely the same time as Mr. Rusk's talk in 1950, others in his government were actively plotting the downfall of the Chinese revolutionary government.

This has been a common phenomenon. For many of the cases described in the following pages, one can find statements of high or middle-level Washington officials which put into question the policy of intervention; which expressed misgivings based either on principle (sometimes the better side of American liberalism) or concern that the intervention would not serve any worthwhile end, might even result in disaster. I have attached little weight to such dissenting statements as, indeed, in the final analysis, did Washington decision-makers who, in controversial world situations, could be relied upon to play the anti-communist card. In presenting the interventions in this manner, I am declaring that American foreign policy is what American foreign policy does.

Though I am clearly opposed to the American interventions on both political and moral grounds, I have striven to not let this color my selection of facts; to not fall prey to that familiar failing: choosing one's facts to fit one's thesis. Which is to say, I have not knowingly omitted any facts which contradict in any significant way the information I have presented, or the implications of that information. Further, I have chosen not to take into account a number of intriguing disclosures concerning American interventions where I felt that the source could not be sufficiently trusted and/or the information was not presented or documented in a manner which made it credible to me. In any event, it is not demanded of the reader that he accept my biases, but that he reflect upon his own.[26]

London, March 1986

1. China 1945 to 1960s
Was Mao Tse-tung just paranoid?

For four years, numerous Americans, in high positions and obscure, sullenly harbored the conviction that World War II was "the wrong war against the wrong enemies". Communism, they knew, was the only genuine adversary on America's historical agenda. Was that not why Hitler had been ignored/tolerated/appeased? So that the Nazi war machine would turn East and wipe Bolshevism off the face of the earth once and for all? It was just unfortunate that Adolf turned out to be such a megalomaniac and turned West as well.

But that war was over. These Americans were now to have their day in every corner of the world. The ink on the Japanese surrender treaty was hardly dry when the United States began to use the Japanese soldiers still in China alongside American troops in a joint effort against the Chinese communists. (In the Philippines and in Greece, as we shall see, the US did not even wait for the war to end before subordinating the struggle against Japan and Germany to the anti-communist crusade.)

The communists in China had worked closely with the American military during the war, providing important intelligence about the Japanese occupiers, rescuing and caring for downed US airmen.[1] But no matter. Generalissimo Chiang Kai-shek would be Washington's man. He headed what passed for a central government in China. The Office of Strategic Services (OSS, forerunner of the CIA) estimated that the bulk of Chiang's military effort had been directed against the communists rather than the Japanese. He had also done his best to block the cooperation between the Reds and the Americans. Now his army contained Japanese units and his regime was full of officials who had collaborated with the Japanese and served in their puppet government.[2] But no matter. The Generalissimo was as anti-communist as they come. Moreover, he was a born American client. His forces would be properly trained and equipped to do battle with the men of Mao Tse-tung and Chou En-lai.

President Truman was up front about what he described as "using the Japanese to hold off the Communists":

> It was perfectly clear to us that if we told the Japanese to lay down their arms immediately and march to the seaboard, the entire country would be taken over by the Communists. We therefore had to take the unusual step of using the enemy as a garrison until we could airlift Chinese National [Chiang's] troops to South China and send Marines to guard the seaports.[3]

The deployment of American Marines had swift and dramatic results. Two weeks after the end of the war, Peking was surrounded by communist forces. Only the arrival of the Marines in the city prevented the Reds from taking it over.[4] And while Mao's forces were pushing into Shanghai's suburbs, US transport planes dropped Chiang's troops in to seize the city.[5]

In a scramble to get to key centers and ports before the communists, the US transported between 400,000 and 500,000 Nationalist troops by ship and plane all over the vastness of China and Manchuria, places they could never have reached otherwise.

As the civil war heated up, the 50,000 Marines sent by Truman were used to guard railway lines, coal mines, ports, bridges, and other strategic sites. Inevitably, they became involved in the fighting, sustaining dozens, if not hundreds of casualties. US troops, the communists charged, attacked areas controlled by the Reds, directly opened fire on them, arrested military officers, and disarmed soldiers.[6] The Americans found themselves blasting a small Chinese village "unmercifully", wrote a Marine to his congressman, not knowing "how many innocent people were slaughtered".[7]

United States planes regularly made reconnaissance flights over communist territory to scout the position of their forces. The communists claimed that American planes frequently strafed and bombed their troops and in one instance machine-gunned a communist-held town.[8] To what extent these attacks were carried out by US airmen is not known.

There were, however, American survivors in some of the many crashes of United States aircraft. Surprisingly, the Reds continued to rescue them, tend to their wounds, and return them to US bases. It may be difficult to appreciate now, but at this time the mystique and the myth of "America" still gripped the imagination of people all over the world, and Chinese peasants, whether labeled "communist" or not, were no exception. During the war the Reds had helped to rescue scores of American fliers and had transported them through Japanese lines to safety. "The Communists", wrote the *New York Times*, "did not lose one airman taken under their protection. They made a point of never accepting rewards for saving American airmen."[9]

When 1946 arrived, about 100,000 American military personnel were still in China, still supporting Chiang. The official United States explanation for the presence of its military was that they were there to disarm and repatriate the Japanese. Though this task was indeed carried out eventually, it was secondary to the military's political function, as Truman's statement cited above makes abundantly clear.

The American soldiers in China began to protest about not being sent home, a complaint echoed round the world by other GIs kept overseas for political (usually anti-communist) purposes. "They ask me, too, why they're here," said a Marine lieutenant in China at Christmas-time, 1945. "As an officer I am supposed to tell them, but you can't tell a man that he's here to disarm Japanese when he's guarding the same railway with [armed] Japanese."[10]

Strangely enough, the United States attempted to mediate in the civil war; this, while being an active, powerful participant on one side. In January 1946, President Truman, apparently recognizing that it was either compromise with the communists or see all of China fall under their sway, sent George Marshall to try and arrange a cease-fire and some kind of unspecified coalition government. While some temporary success was achieved in an on-and-off truce, the idea of a coalition government was doomed to failure, as unlikely as a marriage between the Czar and the Bolsheviks. As the historian D.F. Fleming has pointed out, "One cannot unite a dying oligarchy with a rising revolution."[11]

Not until early 1947 did the United States begin to withdraw some of its military forces, although aid and support to the Chiang government continued in one form or another long afterward. At about this same time, the Flying Tigers began to operate. The legendary American air squadron under the leadership of General Claire Chennault had fought for the Chinese against the Japanese before and during the world war. Now Chennault, Chiang's former air force adviser, had reactivated the squadron (under the name CAT) and its pilots-of-fortune soon found themselves in the thick of the fray, flying endless supply missions to Nationalist cities under siege, dodging communist shell bursts to airlift food, ammunition, and supplies of all kinds, or to rescue the wounded.[12] Technically, CAT was a private airline hired by the Chiang government, but before the civil war came to an end, the airline had formally interlocked with the CIA to become the first unit in the Agency's sprawling air-empire-to-be, best known for the Air America line.

By 1949, United States aid to the Nationalists since the war amounted to almost $2 billion in cash and $1 billion worth of military hardware; 39 Nationalist army divisions had been trained and equipped.[13] Yet the Chiang dynasty was collapsing all around in bits and pieces. It had not been only the onslaught of Chiang's communist foes, but the hostility of the Chinese people at large to his tyranny, his wanton cruelty, and the extraordinary corruption and decadence of his entire bureaucratic and social system. By contrast, the large areas under communist administration were models of honesty, progress and fairness; entire divisions of the Generalissimo's forces defected to the communists. American political and military leaders had no illusions about the nature and quality of Chiang's rule. The Nationalist forces, said General David Barr, head of the US Military Mission in China, were under "the world's worst leadership".[14]

The Generalissimo, his cohorts and soldiers fled to the offshore island of Taiwan (Formosa). They had prepared their entry two years earlier by terrorizing the islanders into submission—a massacre which took the lives of as many as 28,000 people.[15] Prior to the Nationalists' escape to the island, the US government entertained no doubts that Taiwan was a part of China. Afterward, uncertainty began to creep into the minds of Washington officials. The crisis was resolved in a remarkably simple manner: the US agreed with Chiang that the proper way to view the situation was not that Taiwan belonged to China, but that Taiwan *was* China. And so it was called.

In the wake of the communist success, China scholar Felix Greene observed, "Americans simply could not bring themselves to believe that the Chinese, however rotten their leadership, could have preferred a communist government."[16] It must have been the handiwork of a conspiracy, an international conspiracy, at the control panel of which sat, not unexpectedly, the Soviet Union. The evidence for this, however, was thin to the point of transparency. Indeed, ever since Stalin's credo of "socialism in one country" won out over Trotsky's internationalism in the 1920s, the Russians had sided with Chiang more than with Mao, advising the latter more than once to dissolve his army and join Chiang's government.[17] Particularly in the post-World War II years, when the Soviet Union was faced with its own staggering crisis of reconstruction, did it not relish the prospect of having to help lift the world's most populous nation into the modern age. In 1947, General Marshall stated publicly that he knew of no evidence that the Chinese communists were being supported by the USSR.[18]

But in the United States this did not prevent the rise of an entire mythology of how the US had "lost" China: Soviet intervention, State Department communists, White House cowards, military and diplomatic folly, communist dupes and fellow-travelers in the media ... treachery everywhere ...

The Truman administration, said Senator Joseph McCarthy with characteristic charm, was composed of "egg-sucking phony liberals" who protected the "Communists and queers" who had "sold China into atheistic slavery".[19]

Yet, short of an all-out invasion of the country by large numbers of American troops, it is difficult to see what more the US government could have done to prevent Chiang's downfall. Even after Chiang fled to Taiwan, the United States pursued a campaign of relentless assaults against the communist government, despite a request from Chou En-lai for aid and friendship. The Red leader saw no practical or ideological bar to this.[20] Instead, the United States evidently conspired to assassinate Chou on several occasions.[21]

Many Nationalist soldiers had taken refuge in northern Burma in the great exodus of 1949, much to the displeasure of the Burmese Government. There, the CIA began to regroup this stateless army into a fighting force, and during the early 1950s a number of large- and small-scale incursions into China were carried out. In one instance, in April 1951, a few thousand troops, accompanied by CIA advisers and supplied by air drops from American C46s and C47s, crossed the border into China's Yunnan province, but they were driven back by the communists in less than a week. The casualties were high and included several CIA advisers who lost their lives. Another raid that summer took the invaders 65 miles into China where they reportedly held a 100-mile-long strip of territory.

While the attacks continued intermittently, the CIA proceeded to build up the force's capabilities: American engineers arrived to help construct and expand airstrips in Burma, fresh troops were flown in from Taiwan, other troops were recruited from amongst Burmese hill tribes, CIA air squadrons were brought in for logistical services, and enormous quantities of American heavy arms were ferried in. Much of the supply of men and equipment came in via nearby Thailand.

The army soon stood at more than 10,000 men. By the end of 1952, Taiwan claimed that over 41,000 communists had been killed and more than 3,000 wounded. The figures were most likely exaggerated, but even if not, it was clear that the raids would not lead to Chiang's triumphant return to the mainland—although this was not their sole purpose. On the Chinese border two greater battles were raging: in Korea and Vietnam. It was the hope of the United States to force the Chinese to divert troops and military resources away from these areas. The infant People's Republic of China was undergoing a terrible test.

In between raids on China, the "Chinats" (as distinguished from the "Chicoms") found time to clash frequently with Burmese troops, indulge in banditry, and become the opium barons of The Golden Triangle, that slice of land encompassing parts of Burma, Laos and Thailand which was the world's largest source of opium and heroin. CIA pilots flew the stuff all over, to secure the cooperation of those in Thailand who were important to the military operation, as a favor to their Nationalist clients, perhaps even for the money, and, ironically, to serve as cover for their more illicit activities.

The Chinats in Burma kept up their harassment of the Chicoms until 1961 and the CIA continued to supply them militarily, but at some point the Agency began to phase itself out of a more direct involvement. When the CIA, in response to repeated protests by the Burmese Government to the United States and the United Nations, put pressure on the Chinats to leave Burma, Chiang responded by threatening to expose the Agency's covert support of his troops there. At an earlier stage, the CIA had entertained the hope that the Chinese would be provoked into attacking Burma, thereby forcing the strictly neutral Burmese to seek salvation in the Western camp.[22] In January 1961, the Chinese did just that, but as part of a combined force with the Burmese to overwhelm the Nationalists' main base and mark *finis* to their Burmese adventure. Burma subsequently renounced American aid and moved closer to Peking.[23] For many of the Chinats, unemployment was short-lived. They soon signed up with the CIA again; this time to fight with the Agency's grand army in Laos.

Burma was not the only jumping-off site for CIA-organized raids into China. Several islands within about five miles of the Chinese coast, particularly Quemoy and Matsu, were used as bases for hit-and-run attacks, often in battalion strength, for occasional bombing forays, and to blockade mainland ports. Chiang was "brutally pressured" by the US to build up his troops on the islands beginning around 1953 as a demonstration of Washington's new policy of "unleashing" him.[24]

The Chinese retaliated several times with heavy artillery attacks on Quemoy, on one occasion killing two American military officers. The prospect of an escalated war led the US later to have second thoughts and to ask Chiang to abandon the islands, but he then refused. The suggestion has often been put forward that Chiang's design was to embroil the United States in just such a war as his one means of returning to the mainland.[25]

Many incursions into China were made by smaller, commando-type teams air-dropped in for intelligence and sabotage purposes. In November 1952, two CIA officers, John Downey and Richard Fecteau, who had been engaged in flying these teams in and dropping supplies to them, were shot down and captured by the communists. Two years passed before Peking announced the capture and sentencing of the two men. The State Department broke its own two-year silence with indignation, claiming that the two men had been civilian employees of the US Department of the Army in Japan who were presumed lost on a flight from Korea to Japan. "How they came into the hands of the Chinese Communists is unknown to the United States ... the continued wrongful detention of these American citizens furnishes further proof of the Chinese Communist regime's disregard for accepted practices of international conduct."[26]

Fecteau was released in December 1971, shortly before President Nixon's trip to China; Downey was not freed until March 1973, soon after Nixon publicly acknowledged him to be a CIA officer.

The Peking announcement in 1954 also revealed that eleven American airmen had been shot down over China in January 1953 while on a mission which had as its purpose the "air-drop of special agents into China and the Soviet Union". These men were luckier, being freed after only 2 1/2 years. All told, said the Chinese, they had killed 106 American and Taiwanese agents who had parachuted into China between 1951 and 1954 and had captured 124 others. Although the CIA had little, if anything, to show for its commando actions, it reportedly maintained the program until at least 1960.[27]

There were many other CIA flights over China for purely espionage purposes, carried out by high-altitude U-2 planes, pilotless "drones", and other aircraft. These overflights began around the late 1950s and were not discontinued until 1971, to coincide with Henry Kissinger's first visit to Peking. The operation was not without incident. Several U-2 planes were shot down and even more of the drones, 19 of the latter by Chinese count between 1964 and 1969. China registered hundreds of "serious warnings" about violations of its air space, and on at least one occasion American aircraft crossed the Chinese border and shot down a Mig-l7.[28]

It would seem that no degree of failure or paucity of result was enough to deter the CIA from seeking new ways to torment the Chinese in the decade following their revolution. Tibet was another case in point. The Peking government claimed Tibet as part of China, as had previous Chinese governments for more than two centuries, although many Tibetans still regarded themselves as autonomous or independent. The United States made its position clear during the war:

> The Government of the United States has borne in mind the fact that the Chinese Government has long claimed suzerainty over Tibet and that the Chinese constitution lists Tibet among areas constituting the territory of the Republic of China. This Government has at no time raised a question regarding either of these claims.[29]

After the communist revolution, Washington officials tended to be more equivocal about the matter. But US actions against Tibet had nothing to do with the niceties of international law.

In the mid-1950s, the CIA began to recruit Tibetan refugees and exiles in neighboring countries such as India and Nepal. Amongst their number were members of the Dalai

Lama's guard, often referred to picturesquely as "the fearsome Khamba horsemen", and others who had already engaged in some guerrilla activity against Peking rule and/or the profound social changes being instituted by the revolution. (Serfdom and slavery were, literally, still prevalent in Tibet.) Those selected were flown to the United States, to an unused military base high in the Colorado mountains, an altitude approximating that of their mountainous homeland. There, hidden away as much as possible from the locals, they were trained in the fine points of paramilitary warfare.

After completing training, each group of Tibetans was flown to Taiwan or another friendly Asian country, thence to be infiltrated back into Tibet, or elsewhere in China, where they occupied themselves in activities such as sabotage, mining roads, cutting communication lines, and ambushing small communist forces. Their actions were supported by CIA aircraft and on occasion led by Agency contract mercenaries. Extensive support facilities were constructed in northeast India.

The operation in Colorado was maintained until some time in the 1960s. How many hundreds of Tibetans passed through the course of instruction will probably never be known. Even after the formal training program came to an end, the CIA continued to finance and supply their exotic clients and nurture their hopeless dream of reconquering their homeland.

In 1961, when the *New York Times* got wind of the Colorado operation, it acceded to a Pentagon request to probe no further. The matter was particularly sensitive because the CIA has traditionally been forbidden to conduct anything of this sort within the United States, although this question has never actually been adjudicated.[30]

Above and beyond the bedevilment of China on its own merits, there was the spillover from the Korean war into Chinese territory—numerous bombings and strafings by American planes which, the Chinese frequently reported, took civilian lives and destroyed homes. And there was the matter of germ warfare.

The Chinese devoted a great deal of effort to publicizing their claim that the United States, particularly during January to March 1952, had dropped quantities of bacteria and bacteria-laden insects over Korea and northeast China. It presented testimony of about 38 captured American airmen who had purportedly flown the planes with the deadly cargo. Many of the men went into voluminous detail about the entire operation: the kinds of bombs and other containers dropped, the types of insects, the diseases they carried, etc. At the same time, photographs of the alleged germ bombs and insects were published.   Then, in August, an "International Scientific Committee" was appointed, composed of scientists from Sweden, France, Great Britain, Italy, Brazil and the Soviet Union. After an investigation in China of more than two months, the committee produced a report of some 600 pages, many photos, and the conclusion that:

> The peoples of Korea and China have indeed been the objectives of bacteriological weapons. These have been employed by units of the U.S.A. armed forces, using a great variety of different methods for the purpose, some of which seem to be developments of those applied by the Japanese during the second world war.[31]

The last reference has to do with the bacteriological warfare experiments the Japanese had carried out against China between 1940 and 1942. The Japanese scientists responsible for this program were captured by the United States in 1945 and given immunity from prosecution in return for providing technical information about the experiments to American scientists from the Army biological research center at Fort Detrick, Maryland. The Chinese were aware of this at the time of the International Scientific Committee's investigation.[32]

It should be noted that some of the American airmen's statements contained so much technical biological information and were so full of communist rhetoric—"imperialist, capitalist Wall Street war monger" and the like—that their personal authorship of the statements must be seriously questioned. Moreover, it was later learned that most of the airmen had confessed only after being subjected to physical abuse.[33]

But in view of what we have since learned about American involvement with chemical and biological weapons, the Chinese claims cannot be dismissed out of hand. In 1970, for example, the *New York Times* reported that during the Korean War, when US forces were overwhelmed by "human waves" of Chinese, "the Army dug into captured Nazi chemical warfare documents describing Sarin, a nerve gas so lethal that a few pounds could kill thousands of people in minutes. ... By the mid-nineteen-fifties, the Army was manufacturing thousands of gallons of Sarin."[34]

And during the 1950s and 1960s, the Army and the CIA conducted numerous experiments with biological agents within the United States. To cite just two examples: In 1955, there is compelling evidence that the CIA released whooping-cough bacteria into the open air in Florida, followed by an extremely sharp increase in the incidence of the disease in the state that year.[35] The following year, another toxic substance was disseminated in the streets and tunnels of New York City.[36]

We will also see in the chapter on Cuba how the CIA conducted chemical and biological warfare against Fidel Castro's rule.

In March 1966, Secretary of State Dean Rusk spoke before a congressional committee about American policy toward China. Mr. Rusk, it seems, was perplexed that "At times the Communist Chinese leaders seem to be obsessed with the notion that they are being threatened and encircled." He spoke of China's "imaginary, almost pathological, notion that the United States and other countries around its borders are seeking an opportunity to invade mainland China and destroy the Peiping [Peking] regime". The Secretary then added:

> How much Peiping's "fear" of the United States is genuine and how much it is artificially induced for domestic political purposes only the Chinese Communist leaders themselves know. I am convinced, however, that their desire to expel our influence and activity from the western Pacific and Southeast Asia is not motivated by fears that we are threatening them.[37]

2. Italy 1947-1948

Free elections, Hollywood style

"Those who do not believe in the ideology of the United States, shall not be allowed to stay in the United States," declared the American Attorney General, Tom Clark, in January 1948.[1]

In March, the Justice Department, over which Clark presided, determined that Italians who did not believe in the ideology of the United States would not be allowed to emigrate to, or even enter, the United States.

This was but one tactic in a remarkable American campaign to ensure that Italians who did not believe in the ideology of the United States would not be allowed to form a government of a differing ideology in Italy in their election of 1948.

Two years earlier, the Italian Communist Party (PCI), one of the largest in the world, and the Socialist Party (PSI) had together garnered more votes and more seats in the Constituent Assembly election than the Christian Democrats. But the two parties of the left had run separate candidates and thus had to be content with some ministerial posts in a coalition cabinet under a Christian Democrat premier. The results, nonetheless, spoke plainly enough to put the fear of Marx into the Truman administration.

For the 1948 election, scheduled for 18 April, the PCI and PSI united to form the Popular Democratic Front (FDP) and in February won municipal elections in Pescara with a 10 percent increase in their vote over 1946. The Christian Democrats ran a poor second. The prospect of the left winning control of the Italian government loomed larger than ever before. It was at this point that the US began to train its big economic and political guns upon the Italian people. All the good ol' Yankee know-how, all the Madison Avenue savvy in the art of swaying public opinion, all the Hollywood razzmatazz would be brought to bear on the "target market".

Pressing domestic needs in Italy, such as agricultural and economic reform, the absence of which produced abysmal extremes of wealth and poverty, were not to be the issues of the day. The lines of battle would be drawn around the question of "democracy" vs. "communism" (the idea of "capitalism" remaining discreetly to one side). The fact that the Communists had been the single most active anti-fascist group in Italy during the war, undergoing ruthless persecution, while the Christian Democrat government of 1948 and other electoral opponents on the right were riddled through with collaborators, monarchists and plain unreconstructed fascists ... this too would be ignored; indeed, turned around. It was now a matter of Communist "dictatorship" vs. their adversaries' love of "freedom": this was presumed *a priori*. As one example, a group of American congressmen visited Italy in summer 1947 and casually and arbitrarily concluded that "The country is under great pressure from within and without to veer to the left and adopt a totalitarian-collective national organization."[2]

To make any of this at all credible, the whole picture had to be pushed and squeezed into the frame of The American Way of Life vs. The Soviet Way of Life, a specious proposition which must have come as somewhat of a shock to leftists who regarded themselves as Italian and neither Russian nor American.

In February 1948, after non-Communist ministers in Czechoslovakia had boycotted cabinet meetings over a dispute concerning police hiring practices, the Communist government dissolved the coalition cabinet and took sole power. The Voice of America pointed to this event repeatedly, as a warning to the Italian people of the fate awaiting them if Italy "went Communist" (and used as well by anti-communists for decades afterward as a prime example of communist duplicity). Yet, by all appearances, the Italian Christian Democrat government and the American government had conspired the previous year in an even more blatant usurpation of power.

In January 1947, when Italian Premier Alcide de Gasperi visited Washington at the United States' invitation, his overriding concern was to plead for crucial financial assistance for his war-torn, impoverished country. American officials may have had a different priority. Three days after returning to Italy, de Gasperi unexpectedly dissolved his cabinet, which included several Communists and Socialists. The press reported that many people in Italy believed that de Gasperi's action was related to his visit to the United States and was aimed at decreasing leftist, principally Communist, influence in the government. After two weeks of tortuous delay, the formation of a center or center-right government sought by de

Gasperi proved infeasible; the new cabinet still included Communists and Socialists although the left had lost key positions, notably the ministries of foreign affairs and finance.

From this point until May, when de Gasperi's deputy, Ivan Lombardo, led a mission to Washington to renew the request for aid, promised loans were "frozen" by the United States for reasons not very clear. On several occasions during this period the Italian left asserted their belief that the aid was being held up pending the ouster of leftists from the cabinet. The *New York Times* was moved to note that, "Some observers here feel that a further Leftward swing in Italy would retard aid." As matters turned out, the day Lombardo arrived in Washington, de Gasperi again dissolved his entire cabinet and suggested that the new cabinet would manage without the benefit of leftist members. This was indeed what occurred, and over the ensuing few months, exceedingly generous American financial aid flowed into Italy, in addition to the cancelation of the nation's $1 billion debt to the United States.[3]

At the very same time, France, which was also heavily dependent upon American financial aid, ousted all its Communist ministers as well. In this case there was an immediate rationale: the refusal of the Communist ministers to support Premier Ramadier in a vote of confidence over a wage freeze. Despite this, the ouster was regarded as a "surprise" and considered "bold" in France, and opinion was widespread that American loans were being used, or would be used, to force France to align with the US. Said Ramadier: "A little of our independence is departing from us with each loan we obtain."[4]

As the last month of the 1948 election campaign began, *Time* magazine pronounced the possible leftist victory to be "the brink of catastrophe".[5]

"It was primarily this fear," William Colby, former Director of the CIA, has written, "that had led to the formation of the Office of Policy Coordination, which gave the CIA the capability to undertake covert political, propaganda, and paramilitary operations in the first place."[6] But covert operations, as far as is known, played a relatively minor role in the American campaign to break the back of the Italian left. It was the very overtness of the endeavor, without any apparent embarrassment, that stamps the whole thing with such uniqueness and arrogance—one might say swagger. The fortunes of the FDP slid downhill with surprising acceleration during the final month in the face of an awesome mobilization of resources such as the following:[7]

• A massive letter writing campaign from Americans of Italian extraction to their relatives and friends in Italy—at first written by individuals in their own words or guided by "sample letters" in newspapers, soon expanded to mass-produced, pre-written, postage-paid form letters, cablegrams, "educational circulars", and posters, needing only an address and signature. And—from a group calling itself The Committee to Aid Democracy in Italy—half a million picture postcards illustrating the gruesome fate awaiting Italy if it voted for "dictatorship" or "foreign dictatorship". In all, an estimated 10 million pieces of mail were written and distributed by newspapers, radio stations, churches, the American Legion, wealthy individuals, etc.; and business advertisements now included offers to send letters airmail to Italy even if you didn't buy the product.
All this with the publicly expressed approval of the Acting Secretary of State and the Post Office which inaugurated special "Freedom Flights" to give greater publicity to the dispatch of the mail to Italy.

The form letters contained messages such as: "A communist victory would ruin Italy. The United States would withdraw aid and a world war would probably result." ... "We implore you not to throw our beautiful Italy into the arms of that cruel despot communism. America hasn't anything against communism in Russia [sic], but why impose it on other people, other lands, in that way putting out the torch of liberty?" ... "If the forces of true democracy should lose in the Italian election, the American Government will not send any more money to Italy and we won't send any more money to you, our relatives."

These were by no means the least sophisticated of the messages. Other themes emphasized were Russian domination of Italy, loss of religion and the church, loss of family life, loss of home and land.

Veteran newsman Howard K. Smith pointed out at the time that "For an Italian peasant a telegram from anywhere is a wondrous thing; and a cable from the terrestrial paradise of America is not lightly to be disregarded."

The letters threatening to cut off gifts may have been equally intimidating. "Such letters," wrote a Christian Democrat official in an Italian newspaper, "struck home in southern Italian and Sicilian villages with the force of lightning." A 1949 poll indicated that 16 percent of Italians claimed relatives in the United States with whom they were in touch; this, apparently, was in addition to friends there.

- The State Department backed up the warnings in the letters by announcing that "If the Communists should win ... there would be no further question of assistance from the United States." The Italian left felt compelled to regularly assure voters that this would not really happen; this, in turn, inspired American officials, including Secretary of State George Marshall, to repeat the threat. (Marshall was awarded the Nobel Peace Prize in 1953.)

- A daily series of direct short-wave broadcasts to Italy backed by the State Department and featuring prominent Americans. (The State Department estimated that there were 1.2 million short-wave receivers in Italy as of 1946.) The Attorney General went on the air and assured the Italian people that the election was a "choice between democracy and communism, between God and godlessness, between order and chaos." William Donovan, the wartime head of the OSS (fore-runner of the CIA) warned that "under a communist dictatorship in Italy," many of the "nation's industrial plants would be dismantled and shipped to Russia and millions of Italy's workers would be deported to Russia for forced labor." If this were not enough to impress the Italian listeners, a parade of unknown but passionate refugees from Eastern Europe went before the micro-phone to recount horror stories of life behind "The Iron Curtain".

- Several commercial radio stations broadcast to Italy special services held in American Catholic churches to pray for the Pope in "this, his most critical hour". On one station, during an entire week, hundreds of Italian-Americans from all walks of life delivered one-minute messages to Italy which were relayed through the short-wave station. Station WOV in New York invited Italian war brides to transcribe a personal message to their families back home. The station then mailed the recordings to Italy.

- Voice of America daily broadcasts into Italy were sharply increased, highlighting news of American assistance or gestures of friendship to Italy. A sky-full of show-biz stars, including Frank Sinatra and Gary Cooper, recorded a series of radio programs designed to win friends and influence the vote in Italy. Five broadcasts of Italian-American housewives were aired, and Italian-Americans with some leftist credentials were also enlisted for the cause. Labor leader Luigi Antonini called upon Italians to "smash the Muscovite fifth column" which "follows the orders of the ferocious Moscow tyranny," or else Italy would become an "enemy totalitarian country".

To counter Communist charges in Italy that negroes in the United States were denied opportunities, the VOA broadcast the story of a negro couple who had made a fortune in the junk business and built a hospital for their people in Oklahoma City. (It should be remembered that in 1948 American negroes had not yet reached the status of second-class citizens.)

- Italian radio stations carried a one-hour show from Hollywood put on to raise money for the orphans of Italian pilots who had died in the war. (It was not reported if the same was done for the orphans of German pilots.)

- American officials in Italy widely distributed leaflets extolling US economic aid and staged exhi-bitions among low-income groups. The US Information Service presented an exhibition on "The Worker in America" and made extensive use of documentary and feature films to sell the

American way of life. It was estimated that in the period immediately preceding the election more than five million Italians each week saw American documentaries. The 1939 Hollywood film "Ninotchka", which satirized life in Russia, was singled out as a particularly effective feature film. It was shown throughout working-class areas and the Communists made several determined efforts to prevent its presentation. After the election, a pro-Communist worker was reported as saying that "What licked us was 'Ninotchka'."

- The Justice Department served notice that Italians who joined the Communist Party would be denied that dream of so many Italians, emigration to America. The State Department then ruled that any Italians known to have *voted* for the Communists would not be allowed to even *enter* the terrestrial paradise. (A Department telegram to a New York politico read: "Voting Communist appears to constitute affiliation with Communist Party within meaning of Immigration Law and therefore would require exclusion from United States.") It was urged that this information be emphasized in letters to Italy.

- President Truman accused the Soviet Union of plotting the subjugation of Western Europe and called for universal military training in the United States and a resumption of military conscription to forestall "threatened communist control and police-state rule". During the campaign, American and British warships were frequently found anchored off Italian ports. *Time,* in an edition widely displayed and commented upon in Italy shortly before the election, gave its approval to the sentiment that "The U.S. should make it clear that it will use force, if necessary, to prevent Italy from going Communist."8

- The United States and Italy signed a ten-year treaty of "friendship, commerce and navigation". This was the first treaty of its kind entered into by the US since the war, a point emphasized for Italian consumption.

- A "Friendship Train" toured the United States gathering gifts and then traveled round Italy distributing them. The train was painted red, white and blue, and bore large signs expressing the friendship of American citizens toward the people of Italy.

- The United States government stated that it favored Italian trusteeship over some of its former African colonies, such as Ethiopia and Libya, a wholly unrealistic proposal that could never come to pass in the post-war world. (The Soviet Union made a similar proposal.)

- The US, Great Britain and France maneuvered the Soviet Union into vetoing, for the third time, a motion that Italy be admitted to the United Nations. (The first time, the Russians had expressed their opposition on the grounds that a peace treaty with Italy had not been signed. After the signing in 1947, they said they would accept the proposal if other World War II enemies, such as Bulgaria, Hungary and Rumania were also made members.)

- The same three allied nations proposed to the Soviet Union that negotiations take place with a view to returning Trieste to Italy. Formerly the principal Italian port on the Adriatic coast, bordering Yugoslavia, Trieste had been made a "free city" under the terms of the peace treaty. The approval of the Soviet Union was necessary to alter the treaty, and the Western proposal was designed to put the Russians on the spot. The Italian people had an intense sentimental attachment to Trieste, and if the Russians rejected the proposal it could seriously embarrass the Italian Communists. A Soviet acceptance, however, would antagonize their Yugoslav allies. The US prodded the Russians for a response, but none was forthcoming. From the Soviet point of view, the most obvious and safest path to follow would have been to delay their answer until after the election. Yet they chose to announce their rejection of the proposal only five days before the vote, thus hammering another nail into the FDP coffin.

- A "Manifesto of peace to freedom-loving Italians", calling upon them to reject Communism, was sent to Premier de Gasperi. Its signatories included two former US Secretaries of State, a former Assistant Secretary of State, a former Attorney General, a former Supreme Court Justice, a former Governor of New York, the former first lady Eleanor Roosevelt, and many other prominent personages. This message was, presumably, suitably publicized throughout Italy, a task easy in the extreme inasmuch as an estimated 82 percent of Italian newspapers were in the hands of those unsympathetic to the leftist bloc.

- More than 200 American labor leaders of Italian origin held a conference, out of which came a cable sent to 23 daily newspapers throughout Italy similarly urging thumbs down on the Reds. At the same time, the Italian-American Labor Council contributed $50,000 to anti-Communist labor organizations in Italy. The CIA was already secretly subsidizing such trade unions to counteract the influence of leftist unions,[9] but this was standard Agency practice independent of electoral considerations. (According to a former CIA officer, when, in 1945, the Communists came very near to gaining control of labor unions, first in Sicily, then in all Italy and southern France, co-operation between the OSS and the Mafia successfully stemmed the tide.)[10]

- The CIA, by its own later admission, gave $1 million to Italian "center parties", a king's ransom in Italy 1948,[11] although another report places the figure at $10 million. The Agency also forged documents and letters purported to come from the PCI which were designed to put the party in a bad light and discredit its leaders; anonymous books and magazine articles funded by the CIA told in vivid detail about supposed communist activities in Eastern Europe and the Soviet Union; pamphlets dealt with PCI candidates' sex and personal lives as well as smearing them with the fascist and/or anti-church brush.[12]

- An American group featuring noted Italian-American musicians traveled to Rome to present a series of concerts.

- President Truman chose a month before the election as the time to transfer 29 merchant ships to the Italian government as a "gesture of friendship and confidence in a democratic Italy". (These were Italian vessels seized during the war and others to replace those seized and lost.)

- Four days later, the House Appropriations Committee acted swiftly to approve $18.7 million in additional "interim aid" funds for Italy.

- Two weeks later, the United States gave Italy $4.3 million as the first payment on wages due to 60,000 former Italian war prisoners in the US who had worked "voluntarily" for the Allied cause. This was a revision of the peace treaty which stipulated that the Italian government was liable for such payments.

- Six days before election day, the State Department made it public that Italy would soon receive $31 million in gold in return for gold looted by the Nazis. (The fact that only a few years earlier Italy had been the "enemy" fighting alongside the Nazis was now but a dim memory.)

- Two days later, the US government authorized two further large shipments of food to Italy, one for $8 million worth of grains. A number of the aid ships, upon their arrival in Italy during the election campaign, had been unloaded amid ceremony and a speech by the American ambassador.

  A poster prominent in Italy read: "The bread that we eat—40 per cent Italian flour—60 per cent American flour sent free of charge." The poster neglected to mention whether the savings were passed on to the consumer or served to line the pockets of the baking companies.

- Four days before election day, the American Commission for the Restoration of Italian Monuments, Inc. announced an additional series of grants to the Italian Ministry of Fine Arts.

- April 15 was designated "Free Italy Day" by the American Sympathizers for a Free Italy with nation-wide observances to be held.

- The American ambassador, James Clement Dunn, traveled constantly throughout Italy pointing out to the population "on every possible occasion what American aid has meant to them and their country". At the last unloading of food, Dunn declared that the American people were saving Italy from starvation, chaos and possible domination from outside. His speeches usually received wide coverage in the non-left press. By contrast, the Italian government prohibited several of its own ambassadors abroad from returning home to campaign for the FDP.

In his historic speech of 12 March 1947, which came to be known as "The Truman Doctrine", the president had proclaimed:

I believe it must be the policy of the United States to support free peoples who are resisting attempted subjugation by armed minorities or by outside pressures. I believe that we must assist free peoples to work out their own destinies in their own way.[13]

It scarcely needs to be emphasized how hypocritical this promise proved to be, but the voices which spoke out in the United States against their government's crusade in Italy were few and barely audible above the roar. The Italian-American Committee for Free Elections in Italy held a rally to denounce the propaganda blitz, declaring that "Thousands of Americans of Italian origin feel deeply humiliated by the continuous flow of suggestions, advice and pressure put on the Italians, as though they were unable to decide for themselves whom to elect."[14]

The Progressive Party also went on record, stating: "As Americans we repudiate our Government's threat to cut off food from Italy unless the election results please us. Hungry children must not go unfed because their parents do not vote as ordered from abroad."[15] The party's candidate for president in 1948 was Henry Wallace, the former vice-president who was an outspoken advocate of genuine detente with the Soviet Union. History did not provide the opportunity to observe what the reaction would have been—amongst those who saw nothing wrong with what the United States was doing in Italy—if a similar campaign had been launched by the Soviet Union or the Italian left in the United States on behalf of Wallace.

Though some Italians must have been convinced at times that Stalin himself was the FDP's principal candidate, the actual Soviet intervention in the election hardly merited a single headline. The American press engaged in speculation that the Russians were pouring substantial sums of money into the Communist Party's coffers. However, a survey carried out by the Italian bureau of the United Press revealed that the anti-Communist parties spent 7 1/2 times as much as the FDP on all forms of propaganda, the Christian Democrats alone spending four times as much.[16] As for other Soviet actions, Howard K. Smith's observation is to the point:

> The Russians tried to respond with a few feeble gestures for a while—some Italian war prisoners were released; some newsprint was sent to Italy and offered to all parties for their campaign. But there was no way of resisting what amounted to a tidal wave.
>
> There is evidence that the Russians found the show getting too rough for them and actually became apprehensive of what the American and British reaction to a Communist victory at the polls might be. (Russia's concern about conflict with the West was also expressed within a month of the Italian elections in one of the celebrated Cominform letters to Tito, accusing the Yugoslavs of trying to involve the Soviets with the Western powers when "it should have been known ... that the U.S.S.R. after such a heavy war could not start a new one".)[17]

The evidence Smith was alluding to was the Soviet rejection of the Trieste proposal. By its timing, reported the *New York Times*, "the unexpected procedure caused some observers to conclude that the Russians had thrown the Italian Communist Party overboard."[18] The party's newspaper had a difficult time dealing with the story. Washington did as well, for it undermined the fundamental premise of the Italian campaign: that the Italian Communist Party and the Soviet Union were indistinguishable as to ends and means; that if you buy the one, you get the other as well. Thus the suggestion was put forth that perhaps the Soviet rejection was only a tactic to demonstrate that the US could not keep its promise on Trieste. But the Soviet announcement had not been accompanied by any such propaganda message, and it would not explain why the Russians had waited several weeks until near the crucial end to deliver its body blow to their Italian comrades. In any event, the United States could only come out smelling a lot sweeter than the Russians.

When the Broadway show had ended its engagement in Italy, the Christian Democrats stood as the clear winner with 48 percent of the vote. The leftist coalition had been humiliated with a totally unexpected polling of but 31 percent. It had been a crusade of the kind which Aneurin Bevan had ascribed to the Tories: "The whole art of Conservative politics in the 20th century," the British Labour leader wrote, "is being deployed to enable wealth to persuade poverty to use its political freedom to keep wealth in power."

3. Greece 1947 to early 1950s

From cradle of democracy to client state

Jorge Semprun is a Spaniard, a Frenchman, a novelist and film-writer, former Communist, former inmate of Buchenwald. He was at the infamous Nazi concentration camp in 1944 with other party members when they heard the news:

> For some days now, we had talked of nothing else. ... At first some of us had thought it was a lie. It had to be. An invention of Nazi propaganda, to raise the morale of the people. We listened to the news bulletins on the German radio, broadcast by all the loudspeakers, and we shook our heads. A trick to raise the morale of the German people, it had to be. But we soon had to face up to the evidence. Some of us listened in secret to the Allied broadcasts, which confirmed the news. There was no doubt about it: British troops really were crushing the Greek Resistance. In Athens, battle was raging, British troops were retaking the city from the ELAS forces, district by district. It was an unequal fight: ELAS had neither tanks nor planes.
>
> But Radio Moscow had said nothing, and this silence was variously interpreted.[1]

The British army had arrived in Greece during October and November 1944, shortly after the bulk of the Germans had fled, an evacuation due in no small part to ELAS, the People's Liberation Army. Founded during the course of 1941–42 on the initiative of the Greek Communist Party, ELAS and its political wing EAM cut across the entire left side of the political spectrum, numbering many priests and even a few bishops amongst its followers. The guerrillas had wrested large areas of the country from the Nazi invaders who had routed the British in 1941.

ELAS/EAM partisans could be ruthless and coercive toward those Greeks who did not cooperate with them or who were suspected of collaboration with the Germans. But they also provided another dramatic example of the liberating effects of a world war: the encrusted ways of the Greek old guard were cast aside; in their place arose communities which had at least the semblance of being run by the local residents, inchoate institutions and mechanisms which might have been the precursor of a regenerated Greek society after the war; education, perhaps geared toward propaganda, but for the illiterate education nonetheless; fighting battalions of women, housewives called upon for the first time to act independently of their husbands' control ... a phenomenon which spread irrepressibly until EAM came to number some one to two million Greeks out of a population of seven million.[2]

This was hardly the kind of social order designed to calm the ulcers of the British old guard (Winston Churchill for one) who had long regarded Greece as their private manor. The Great Man was determined that the Greek king should be restored to his rightful place, with all that that implied, and the British military in Greece lost no time in installing a government dedicated to that end. Monarchists, quislings, and conservatives of all stripes found themselves in positions of political power, predominant in the new Greek army and police; members of EAM/ELAS found themselves dead or in prison.[3]

In the early days of the world war, when defeating the Nazis was the Allies' overwhelming purpose, Churchill had referred to ELAS as "those gallant guerrillas", and ELAS's supporters had welcomed the British in early November 1944 with a sign reading, "We Greet the Brave English Army. ... EAM."[4]

But the following month, fighting broke out between ELAS and the British forces and their Greek comrades-in-arms, many of whom had fought against ELAS during the war and, in the process, collaborated with the Germans; others had simply served with the Germans. (The British Foreign Secretary, Ernest Bevin, acknowledged in August 1946 that there were 228 ex-members of the Nazi Security Battalions—whose main task had been to track down Greek resistance fighters and Jews—on active service in the new Greek army.)[5] Further support for the campaign against ELAS came from the US Air Force and Navy which transported more than two British divisions into Greece.[6] All this while the war against Germany still raged in Europe.

In mid-January 1945 ELAS agreed to an armistice, one that had much of the appearance and the effect of a surrender. There is disagreement amongst historians as to whether ELAS had been militarily defeated or whether the Communists in the ELAS and EAM hierarchy had received the word from Stalin to lay down the gun. If the latter were the case, it would have been consistent with the noted agreement between Stalin and Churchill in October 1944, whereby spheres of influence in Eastern Europe were allocated between the two powers. In this cynical (as Churchill acknowledged) Monopoly game Britain had landed on Greece. Churchill later wrote that Stalin had "adhered strictly and faithfully to our agreement of October, and during all the long weeks of fighting the Communists in the streets of Athens not one word of reproach came from *Pravda* or *Izvestia*".[7] Nor, as Jorge Semprun noted, from Radio Moscow.

"It is essential to remember," Professor D.F. Fleming has pointed out in his eminent history of the cold war, "that Greece was the first of the liberated states to be openly and forcibly compelled to accept the political system of the occupying Great Power. It was Churchill who acted first and Stalin who followed his example, in Bulgaria and then in Rumania, though with less bloodshed."[8]

A succession of Greek governments followed, serving by the grace of the British and the United States; thoroughly corrupt governments in the modern Greek tradition, which continued to terrorize the left, tortured them in notorious island prison camps, and did next to nothing to relieve the daily misery of the war-torn Greek people.[9] "There are few modern parallels for government as bad as this," CBS's chief European correspondent Howard K. Smith observed at the time.[10]

In the fall of 1946 the inevitable occurred: leftists took to the hills to launch phase two of the civil war. The Communists had wrenched Stalin's strangulating hand from their throats, for their very survival was at stake and everything that they believed in.

The British were weighed down by their own post-war reconstruction needs, and in February 1947 they informed the United States that they could no longer shoulder the burden of maintaining a large armed force in Greece nor provide sizeable military and economic aid to the country. Thus it was that the historic task of preserving all that is decent and good in Western Civilization passed into the hands of the United States.

Several days later, the State Department summoned the Greek chargé d'affaires in Washington and informed him that his government was to ask the US for aid. This was to be effected by means of a formal letter of request; a document, it turned out, to be written essentially by the State Department. The text of the letter, the chargé d'affaires later report-ed, "had been drafted with a view to the mentality of Congress ... It would also serve to protect the U.S. Government against internal and external charges that it was taking the ini-tiative of intervening in a foreign state or that it had been persuaded by the British to take over a bad legacy from them. The note would also serve as a basis for the cultivation of public opinion which was under study."[11]

In July, in a letter to Dwight Griswold, the head of the American Mission to Aid Greece (AMAG), Secretary of State George Marshall said:

> It is possible that during your stay in Greece you and the Ambassador will come to the conclu-sion that the effectiveness of your Mission would be enhanced if a reorganization of the Greek Government could be effected. If such a conclusion is reached, it is hoped that you and the Ambassador will be able to bring about such a reorganization indirectly through discreet sugges-tion and otherwise in such a manner that even the Greek political leaders will have a feeling that the reorganization has been effected largely by themselves and not by pressure from without.[12]

The Secretary spelled out a further guideline for Griswold, a man the *New York Times* shortly afterwards called the "most powerful man in Greece":[13]

> During the course of your work you and the members of your Mission will from time to time find that certain Greek officials are not, because of incompetence, disagreement with your poli-cies, or for some other reason, extending the type of cooperation which is necessary if the objec-tives of your Mission are to be achieved. You will find it necessary to effect the removal of these officials.[14]

These contrivances, however, were not the most cynical aspects of the American endeavor. Washington officials well knew that their new client government was so venal and so abusive of human rights that even confirmed American anti-communists were appalled. Stewart Alsop for one. On 23 February 1947 the noted journalist had cabled from Athens that most of the Greek politicians had "no higher ambition than to taste the prof-itable delights of a free economy at American expense".[15] The same year, an American investigating team found huge supplies of food aid rotting in warehouses at a time when an estimated 75 percent of Greek children were suffering from malnutrition.[16]

So difficult was it to gloss over this picture, that President Truman, in his address to Congress in March 1947 asking for aid to Greece based on the Greek "request" (the "Truman Doctrine" speech), attempted to pre-empt criticism by admitting that the Greek government was "not perfect" and that "it has made mistakes". Yet, somehow, by some ideological alchemy best known to the president, the regime in Athens was "democratic", its opponents the familiar "terrorists".[17]

There was no mention of the Soviet Union in this particular speech, but that was to be the relentless refrain of the American rationale over the next 2 1/2 years: the Russians were instigating the Greek leftists so as to kidnap yet another "free" country and drag it kicking and screaming behind the Iron Curtain.

The neighboring Communist states of Bulgaria, Albania, and particularly Yugoslavia, in part motivated by old territorial claims against Greece, did aid the insurgents by allowing them important sanctuary behind their borders and furnishing them with military supplies (whether substantial or merely token in amount is a debatable question). The USSR, howev-er, in the person of Joseph Stalin, was adamantly opposed to assisting the Greek "com-rades". At a meeting with Yugoslav leaders in early 1948 (a few months before Yugoslavia's break with the Soviet Union), described by Milovan Djilas, second-in-command to Tito, Stalin turned to the foreign minister Edvard Kardelj and asked: "Do you believe in the success of the uprising in Greece?"

> Kardelj replied, "If foreign intervention does not grow, and if serious political and military errors are not made."
> Stalin went on, without paying attention to Kardelj's opinion: "If, if! No, they have no prospect of success at all. What, do you think that Great Britain and the United States—the United States, the most powerful state in the world—will permit you to break their line of communication in the Mediterranean? Nonsense. And we have no navy. The uprising in Greece must be stopped, and as quickly as possible."[18]

The first major shiploads of military assistance under the new American operation arrived in the summer of 1947. (Significant quantities had also been shipped to the Greek government by the US while the British ran the show.) By the end of the year, the Greek military was being entirely supported by American aid, down to and including its clothing and food. The nation's war-making potential was transformed: continual increases in the size of the Greek armed forces ... fighter-bombers, transport squadrons, air fields, napalm bombs, recoilless rifles, naval patrol vessels, communication networks ... docks, railways, roads, bridges ... hundreds of millions of dollars of supplies and equipment, approaching a billion in total since the end of the world war ... and millions more to create a "Secret Army Reserve" fighting unit, composed principally of the ex-members of the Nazi Security Battalions referred to earlier.[19]

The US Military Mission took over the development of battle plans for the army from the ineffective Greek generals. The Mission, related British military writer Major Edgar O'Ballance, "took a tough line and insisted that all its recommendations be carried into effect, at once and in full".[20] Eventually, more than 250 American army officers were in the country, many assigned to Greek army divisions to ensure compliance with directives; others operated at the brigade level; another 200 or so US Air Force and Navy personnel were also on active duty in Greece.

All military training methods and programs were "revised, revitalized and tightened up" under American supervision[21]... infantry units made more mobile, with increased firepower; special commando units trained in anti-guerrilla tactics; training in mountain warfare, augmented by some 4,000 mules (sic) shipped to Greece by the United States ... at American insistence, whole sections of the population uprooted to eliminate the guerrillas' natural base of operation and source of recruits, just as would be done in Vietnam 20 years later.

"Both on the ground and in the air, American support was becoming increasingly active," observed C.M. Woodhouse, the British colonel and historian who served in Greece during the mid-1940s, "and the theoretical line between advice, intelligence and combat was a narrow one."[22]

The Greek leftists held out for three terrible years. Despite losses of many tens of thousands, they were always able to replenish their forces, even increase their number. But by October 1949, foreseeing nothing but more loss of lives to a vastly superior destruction-machine, the guerrillas announced over their radio a "cease fire". It was the end of the civil war.

The extent of American hegemony over Greece from 1947 onwards can scarcely be exaggerated. We have seen Marshall's directives to Griswold, and the American management of the military campaign. There were many other manifestations of the same phenomenon, of which the following are a sample:

In September 1947, Vice-Prime Minister Constantine Tsaldaris agreed to the dissolu-tion of the government and the creation of a new ruling coalition. In doing so, said the *New York Times*, Tsaldaris had "surrendered to the desires of Dwight P. Griswold ... of [US] Ambassador MacVeagh, and also of the King".[23] Before Tsaldaris addressed the Greek leg-islature on the matter, MacVeagh stepped in to make a change to the speech.[24]

Over the next several years, each of the frequent changes of prime minister came about only after considerable American input, if not outright demand.[25] One example of the latter occurred in 1950 when then American Ambassador Henry Grady sent a letter to Prime Minister Venizelos threatening to cut off US aid if he failed to carry out a government reor-ganization. Venizelos was compelled to step down.[26] The American influence was felt in regard to other high positions in Greek society as well. Andreas Papandreou, later to become prime minister himself, has written of this period that "Cabinet members and army generals, political party leaders and members of the Establishment, all made open references to American wishes or views in order to justify or to account for their own actions or posi-tions."[27]

Before undertaking a new crackdown on dissidents in July 1947, Greek authorities first approached Ambassador Macveagh. The ambassador informed them that the US govern-ment would have no objection to "preventive measures if they were considered necessary". Reassured, the Greeks went ahead and rounded up 4,000 people in one week.[28]

An example of what could land a Greek citizen in prison is the case of the EAM mem-ber who received an 18-month sentence for printing remarks deemed insulting to Dwight Griswold. He had referred to the American as "the official representative of a foreign coun-try".[29]

"In the economic sphere," Andreas Papandreou noted, the United States "exercised almost dictatorial control during the early fifties requiring that the signature of the chief of the U.S. Economic Mission appear alongside that of the Greek Minister of Co-ordination on any important documents."[30]

Earlier, American management of the economy may have been even tighter. A memo-randum from Athens dated 17 November 1947, from the American Mission to Aid Greece to the State Department in Washington, read in part: "we have established practical control ... over national budget, taxation, currency issuance, price and wage policies, and state eco-nomic planning, as well as over imports and exports, the issuance of foreign exchange and the direction of military reconstruction and relief expenditures."[31]

There was, moreover, the creation of a new internal security agency, named and mod-eled after the CIA (KYP in Greek). Before long, KYP was carrying out all the endearing practices of secret police everywhere, including systematic torture.

By the early 1950s, Greece had been molded into a supremely reliable ally-client of the United States. It was staunchly anti-communist and well integrated into the NATO system. It sent troops to Korea to support the United States' pretence that it was not simply an American war.

It is safe to say that had the left come to power, Greece would have been much more independent of the United States. Greece would likely have been independent as well of the Soviet Union, to whom the Greek left owed nothing. Like Yugoslavia, which is also free of a common border with the USSR, Greece would have been friendly towards the Russians, but independent.

When, in 1964, there came to power in Greece a government which entertained the novel idea that Greece was a sovereign nation, the United States and its Greek cohorts, as we shall see, quickly and effectively stamped out the heresy.

4. The Philippines 1940s and 1950s
America's oldest colony

I walked the floor of the White House night after night until midnight; and I am not ashamed to tell you, gentlemen, that I went down on my knees and prayed (to) Almighty God for light and guidance more than one night. And one night late it came to me this way—I don't know how it was, but it came: (1) That we could not give them [the Philippine Islands] back to Spain—that would be cowardly and dishonorable; (2) that we could not turn them over to France or Germany—our commercial rivals in the Orient—that would be bad business and discreditable; (3) that we could not leave them to themselves—they were unfit for self-government—and they would soon have anarchy and misrule over there worse than Spain's was; and (4) that there was nothing left for us to do but to take them all, and to educate the Filipinos, and uplift and civilize and Christianize them, and by God's grace do the very best we could by them, as our fellow-men for whom Christ also died.

—*William McKinley*, President of the United States, 1899[1]

William McKinley's idea of doing the very best by the Filipinos was to employ the United States Army to kill them in the tens of thousands, burn down their villages, subject them to torture, and lay the foundation for an economic exploitation which was proudly referred to at the time as "imperialism" by leading American statesmen and newspapers.

After the Spanish had been driven out of the Philippines in 1898 by a combined action of the United States and the Filipinos, Spain agreed to "cede" (that is, sell) the islands to the United States for $20 million. But the Filipinos, who had already proclaimed their own independent republic, did not take kindly to being treated like a plot of uninhabited real estate. Accordingly, an American force numbering at least 50,000 proceeded to instill in the population a proper appreciation of their status.

Thus did America's longest-lasting and most conspicuous colony ever come into being.

Nearly half a century later, the US Army again landed in the Philippines to find a nationalist movement fighting against a common enemy, this time the Japanese. While combatting the Japanese during 1945, the American military took many measures aimed at quashing this resistance army, the Huks (a shortening of Hukbalahap—"People's Army Against Japan" in Tagalog). American forces disarmed many Huk units, removed the local governments which the Huks had established, and arrested and imprisoned many of their high-ranking members as well as leaders of the Philippine Communist Party. Guerrilla forces, primarily organized and led by American officers and composed of US and Filipino soldiers of the so-called US Army Forces in the Far East, undertook police-type actions which resulted in a virtual reign of terror against the Huks and suspected sympathizers; disparaging rumors were spread about the Huks to erode their support amongst the peasants; and the Japanese were allowed to assault Huk forces unmolested.

This, while the Huks were engaged in a major effort against the Japanese invaders and Filipino collaborators and frequently came to the aid of American soldiers.[2]

In much of this anti-Huk campaign, the United States made use of Filipinos who were collaborating with the Japanese, such as landlords, large estate owners, many police constables, and other officials. In the post-war period, the US restored to power and position many of those tainted with collaboration, much to the distaste of other Filipinos.[3]

The Huk guerrilla forces had been organized in 1942, largely at the initiative of the Communist Party, in response to the Japanese occupation of the islands. Amongst American policy makers, there were those who came to the routine conclusion that the Huks were thus no more than a tool of the International Communist Conspiracy, to be opposed as all such groups were to be opposed. Others in Washington and Manila, whose reflexes were less knee-jerk, but more cynical, recognized that the Huk movement, if its growing influence was not checked, would lead to sweeping reforms of Philippine society.

The centerpiece of the Huk political program was land reform, a crying need in this largely agricultural society. (On occasion, US officials would pay lip-service to the concept, but during 50 years of American occupation, nothing of the sort had been carried out.) The other side of the Huk coin was industrialization, which the United States had long thwarted in order to provide American industries with a veritable playground in the Philippines. From the Huks' point of view, such changes were but prologue to raising the islanders from their state of backwardness, from illiteracy, grinding poverty, and the diseases of poverty like tuberculosis and beri-beri. "The Communist Hukbalahap rebellion," reported the *New York Times*, "is generally regarded as an outgrowth of the misery and discontent among the peasants of Central Luzon [the main island]."[4]

A study prepared years later for the US Army echoed this sentiment, stating that the Huks' "main impetus was peasant grievances, not Leninist designs".[5]

Nevertheless, the Huk movement was unmistakably a threat to the neo-colonial condition of the Philippines, the American sphere of influence, and those Philippine interests which benefited from the status quo.

By the end of 1945, four months after the close of World War II, the United States was training and equipping a force of 50,000 Filipino soldiers for the Cold War.[6] In testimony before a congressional committee, Major General William Arnold of the US Army candidly stated that this program was "essential for the maintenance of internal order, not for external difficulties at all".[7] None of the congressmen present publicly expressed any reservation about the international propriety of such a foreign policy.

At the same time, American soldiers were kept on in the Philippines, and in at least one infantry division combat training was re-established. This led to vociferous protests and demonstrations by the GIs who wanted only to go home. The inauguration of combat training, the *New York Times* disclosed, was "interpreted by soldiers and certain Filipino newspapers as the preparation for the repression of possible uprisings in the Philippines by disgruntled farm tenant groups." The story added that the soldiers had a lot to say "on the subject of American armed intervention in China and the Netherlands Indies [Indonesia]," which was occurring at the same time.[8]

To what extent American military personnel participated directly in the suppression of dissident groups in the Philippines after the war is not known.

The Huks, though not trusting Philippine and US authorities enough to voluntarily surrender their arms, did test the good faith of the government by taking part in the April 1946 national elections as part of a "Democratic Alliance" of liberal and socialist peasant political groups. (Philippine independence was scheduled for three months later—the Fourth of July to be exact.) As matters turned out, the commander-in-chief of the Huks, Luis Taruc, and several other Alliance members and reform-minded candidates who won election to

Congress (three to the Senate and seven to the House) were not allowed to take their seats under the transparent fiction that coercion had been used to influence voters. No investigation or review of the cases had even been carried out by the appropriate body, the Electoral Tribunal.[9] (Two years later, Taruc was temporarily allowed to take his seat when he came to Manila to discuss a ceasefire with the government.)

The purpose of denying these candidates their seats was equally transparent: the government was thus able to push through Congress the controversial Philippine-US Trade Act—passed by two votes more than required in the House, and by nothing to spare in the Senate—which yielded to the United States bountiful privileges and concessions in the Philippine economy, including "equal rights ... in the development of the nation's natural resources and the operation of its public utilities".[10] This "parity" provision was eventually extended to every sector of the Philippine economy.[11]

The debasement of the electoral process was followed by a wave of heavy brutality against the peasants carried out by the military, the police, and landlord goon squads. According to Luis Taruc, in the months following the election, peasant villages were destroyed, more than 500 peasants and their leaders killed, and about three times that number jailed, tortured, maimed or missing. The Huks and others felt they had little alternative but to take up arms once again.[12]

Independence was not likely to change much of significance. American historian George E.Taylor, of impeccable establishment credentials, in a book which bears the indication of CIA sponsorship, was yet moved to state that independence "was marked by lavish expressions of mutual good will, by partly fulfilled promises, and by a restoration of the old relationship in almost everything except in name. ... Many demands were made of the Filipinos for the commercial advantage of the United States, but none for the social and political advantage of the Philippines."[13]

The American military was meanwhile assuring a home for itself in the Philippines. A 1947 agreement provided sites for 23 US military bases in the country. The agreement was to last for 99 years. It stipulated that American servicemen who committed crimes outside the bases while on duty could be tried only by American military tribunals inside the bases.

By the terms of a companion military assistance pact, the Philippine government was prohibited from purchasing so much as a bullet from any arms source other than the US, except with American approval. Such a state of affairs, necessarily involving training, maintenance and spare parts, made the Philippine military extremely dependent upon their American counterparts. Further, no foreigners other than Americans were permitted to perform any function for or with the Philippine armed forces without the approval of the United States.[14]

By early 1950, the United States had provided the Philippines with over $200 million of military equipment and supplies, a remarkable sum for that time, and was in addition to the construction of various military facilities.[15] The Joint US Military Advisory Group (JUSMAG) reorganized the Philippine intelligence capability and defense department, put its chosen man, Ramon Magsaysay, at its head, and formed the Philippine army into battalion combat teams trained for counter-insurgency warfare.[16] The Philippines was to be a laboratory experiment for this unconventional type of combat. The methods and the terminology, such as "search-and-destroy" and "pacification", were later to become infamous in Vietnam.

By September, when Lt. Col. Edward G. Lansdale arrived in the Philippines, the civil war had all the markings of a long, drawn-out affair, with victory not in sight for either side. Ostensibly, Lansdale was just another American military adviser attached to JUSMAG, but in actuality he was the head of CIA clandestine and paramilitary operations in the country. His apparent success in the Philippines was to make him a recognized authority in counter-insurgency.

In his later reminiscences about this period in his life, Lansdale relates his surprise at hearing from informed Filipino civilian friends about how repressive the Quirino government was, that its atrocities matched those of (or attributed to) the Huks, that the government was "rotten with corruption" (down to the policeman in the street, Lansdale observed on his own), that Quirino himself had been elected the previous year through "extensive fraud", and that "the Huks were right", they were the "wave of the future", and violence was the only way for the people to get a government of their own. (The police, wrote a correspondent for the *Saturday Evening Post*, were "bands of uniformed thieves and rapists, more feared than bandits ... the army was little better.")[17]

Lansdale was undeterred. He had come to do a job. Accordingly, he told himself that if the Huks took over there would only be another form of injustice by another privileged few, backed by even crueller force. By the next chapter, he had convinced himself that he was working on the side of those committed to "defend human liberty in the Philippines".[18]

As a former advertising man, Lansdale was no stranger to the use of market research, motivation techniques, media, and deception. In CIA parlance, such arts fall under the heading of "psychological warfare". To this end, Lansdale fashioned a unit called the Civil Affairs Office. Its activities were based on the premise—one both new and suspect to most American military officers—that a popular guerrilla army cannot be defeated by force alone.

Lansdale's team conducted a careful study of the superstitions of the Filipino peasants living in Huk areas: their lore, taboos, and myths were examined for clues to the appropriate appeals that could wean them from supporting the insurgents. In one operation, Lansdale's men flew over these areas in a small plane hidden by a cloud cover and broadcast in Tagalog mysterious curses on any villagers who dared to give the Huks food or shelter. The tactic reportedly succeeded into starving some Huk units into surrender.[19]

Another Lansdale-initiated "psywar" operation played on the superstitious dread in the Philippine countryside of the *asuang*, a mythical vampire. A psywar squad entered a town and planted rumors that an *asuang* lived in the neighboring hill where the Huks were based, a location from which government forces were anxious to have them out. Two nights later, after giving the rumors time to circulate among Huk sympathizers in the town and make their way up the hill, the psywar squad laid an ambush for the rebels along a trail used by them. When a Huk patrol passed, the ambushers silently snatched the last man, punctured his neck vampire-fashion with two holes, held his body by the heels until the blood drained out, and put the corpse back on the trail. When the Huks, as superstitious as any other Filipinos, discovered the bloodless comrade, they fled from the region.[20]

Lansdale regularly held "coffee klatsches" with Filipino officials and military personnel in which new ideas were freely tossed back and forth, à la a Madison Avenue brain session. Out of this came the Economic Development Corps to lure Huks with a program of resettlement on their own patch of farm land, with tools, seeds, cash loans, etc. It was an undertaking wholly inadequate to the land problem, and the number that responded was very modest, but like other psywar techniques, a principal goal was to steal from the enemy his most persuasive arguments.[21] Among other tactics introduced or refined by Lansdale were: production of films and radio broadcasts to explain and justify government actions; infiltration of government agents into the ranks of the Huks to provide information and sow dissension; attempts to modify the behavior of government soldiers so as to curtail their abuse of people in rural areas (for the Huks had long followed an explicit code of proper conduct towards the peasants, with punishment meted out to violators), but on other occasions, government soldiers were allowed to run amok in villages—disguised as Huks.[22]

This last, revealed L. Fletcher Prouty, was a technique "developed to a high art in the Philippines" in which soldiers were "set upon the unwary village in the grand manner of a Cecil B. De Mille production".[23] Prouty, a retired US Air Force colonel, was for nine years the focal point officer for contacts between the Pentagon and the CIA. He has described another type of scenario by which the Huks were tarred with the terrorist brush, serving to obscure the political nature of their movement and mar their credibility:

> In the Philippines, lumbering interests and major sugar interests have forced tens of thousands of simple, backward villagers to leave areas where they have lived for centuries. When these poor people flee to other areas, it should be quite obvious that they in turn then infringe upon the territorial rights of other villagers or landowners. This creates violent rioting or at least sporadic outbreaks of banditry, that last lowly recourse of dying and terrorized people. Then when the distant government learns of the banditry and rioting, it must offer some safe explanation. The last thing that regional government would want to do would be to say that the huge lumbering or paper interests had driven the people out of their ancestral homeland. In the Philippines it is customary for the local/regional government to get a 10 percent rake-off on all such enterprise and for national politicians to get another 10 percent. So the safe explanation becomes "Communist-inspired subversive insurgency." The word for this in the Philippines is Huk.[24]

The most insidious part of the CIA operation in the Philippines was the fundamental manipulation of the nation's political life, featuring stage-managed elections and disinformation campaigns. The high-point of this effort was the election to the presidency, in 1953, of Ramon Magsaysay, the cooperative former defense department head.

Lansdale, it was said, "invented" Magsaysay.[25] His CIA front organizations ran the Filipino's campaign with all the license, impunity, and money that one would expect from the Democratic or Republican National Committees operating in the US, or perhaps more to the point, Mayor Daley operating in Chicago. One of these front organizations, the National Movement for Free Elections, was praised in a *New York Times* editorial for its contribution to making the Philippines "the showcase of democracy in Asia".[26]

The CIA, on one occasion, drugged the drinks of Magsaysay's opponent, incumbent president Elpido Quirino, before he gave a speech so that he would appear incoherent. On another occasion, when Magsaysay insisted on delivering a speech which had been written by a Filipino instead of one written by Lansdale's team, Lansdale reacted in a rage, finally hitting the presidential candidate so hard that he knocked him out.[27]

Magsaysay won the election, but not before the CIA had smuggled in guns for use in a coup in case their man lost.[28]

Once Magsaysay was in office, the CIA wrote his speeches, carefully guided his foreign policy, and used its press "assets" (paid editors and journalists) to provide him with a constant claque of support for his domestic programs and his involvement in the US-directed anti-communist crusade in southeast Asia, as well as to attack anti-US newspaper columnists. So beholden was Magsaysay to the United States, disclosed presidential assistant Sherman Adams, that he "sent word to Eisenhower that he would do anything the United States wanted him to do—even though his own foreign minister took the opposite view".[29]

One inventive practice of the CIA on behalf of Magsaysay was later picked up by Agency stations in a number of other Third World countries. This particular piece of chicanery consisted of selecting articles written by CIA writer-agents for the provincial press and republishing them in a monthly *Digest of the Provincial Press*. The *Digest* was then sent to congressmen and other opinion makers in Manila to enlighten them as to "what the provinces were thinking".[30]

Senator Claro M. Recto, Magsaysay's chief political opponent and a stern critic of American policy in the Philippines, came in for special treatment. The CIA planted stories that he was a Communist Chinese agent and it prepared packages of condoms labeled "Courtesy of Claro M. Recto—the People's Friend". The condoms all had holes in them at the most inappropriate place.[31]

The Agency also planned to assassinate Recto, going so far as to prepare a substance for poisoning him. The idea was abandoned "for pragmatic considerations rather than moral scruples."[32]

After Magsaysay died in a plane crash in 1957, various other Filipino politicians and parties were sought out by the CIA as clients, or offered themselves as such. One of the latter was Diosdado Macapagal, who was to become president in 1961. Macapagal provided the Agency with political information for several years and eventually asked for, and received, what he felt he deserved: heavy financial support for his campaign. (*Reader's Digest* called his election: "certainly a demonstration of democracy in action".)[33]

Ironically, Macapagal had been the bitterest objector to American intervention in the Magsaysay election in 1953, quoting time and again from the Philippine law that "No foreigner shall aid any candidate directly or indirectly or take part in or influence in any manner any election."[34]

Perhaps even more ironic, in 1957 the Philippine government adopted a law, clearly written by Americans, which outlawed both the Communist Party and the Huks, giving as one of the reasons for doing so that these organizations aimed at placing the government "under the control and domination of an alien power".[35]

By 1953 the Huks were scattered and demoralized, no longer a serious threat, although their death would be distributed over the next few years. It is difficult to ascertain to what extent their decline was due to the traditional military force employed against them, or to Lansdale's more unorthodox methods, or to the eventual debilitation of many of the Huks from malnutrition and disease, brought on by the impoverishment of the peasantry. Long before the end, many Huks were also lacking weapons and ammunition and proper military equipment, bringing into question the oft-repeated charge of Soviet and Chinese aid to them made by Filipino and American authorities.[36] Edward Lachica, a Filipino historian, has written that "The Kremlin did pay lip service to the Communist movement in the Philippines, praising the Huks for being part of the 'global struggle against the U.S.', but no material support was offered."[37]

"Since the destruction of Huk military power," noted George Taylor, "the social and political program that made the accomplishment possible has to a large extent fallen by the wayside."[38]

Fortress America, however, was securely in place in southeast Asia. From the Philippines would be launched American air and sea actions against Korea and China, Vietnam and Indonesia. The Philippine government would send combat forces to fight alongside the United States in Vietnam and Korea. On the islands' bases, the technology and art of counter-insurgency warfare would be imparted to the troops of America's other allies in the Pacific.

5. Korea 1945-1953
Was it all that it appeared to be?

To die for an idea; it is unquestionably
noble. But how much nobler it would be
if men died for ideas that were true.

—H.L. Mencken, 1919

How is it that the Korean War escaped the protests which surrounded the war in Vietnam? Everything we've come to love and cherish about Vietnam had its forerunner in Korea: the support of a corrupt tyranny, the atrocities, the napalm, the mass slaughter of civilians, the cities and villages laid to waste, the calculated management of the news, the sabotaging of peace talks. But the American people were convinced that the war in Korea was an unambiguous case of one country invading another without provocation. A case of the bad guys attacking the good guys who were being saved by the even better guys; none of the historical, political and moral uncertainty that was the dilemma of Vietnam. The Korean War was seen to have begun in a specific manner: North Korea attacked South Korea in the early morning of 25 June 1950; while Vietnam ... no one seemed to know how it all began, or when, or why.

And there was little in the way of accusations about American "imperialism" in Korea. The United States, after all, was fighting as part of a United Nations Army. What was there to protest about? And of course there was McCarthyism, so prevalent in the early 1950s, which further served to inhibit protest.

There were, in fact, rather different interpretations to be made of what the war was all about, how it was being conducted, even how it began, but these quickly succumbed to the heat of war fever.

Shortly after the close of the Second World War, the Soviet Union and the United States occupied Korea in order to expel the defeated Japanese. A demarcation line between the Russian and American forces was set up along the 38th Parallel. The creation of this line in no way had the explicit or implicit intention of establishing two separate countries, but the cold war was soon to intrude.

Both powers insisted that unification of North and South was the principal and desired goal. However, they also desired to see this carried out in their own ideological image, and settled thereby into a routine of proposal and counter-proposal, accusation and counter-accusation, generously intermixed with deviousness, and produced nothing in the way of an agreement during the ensuing years. Although both Moscow and Washington and their hand-picked Korean leaders were not always displeased about the division of the country (on the grounds that half a country was better than none), officials and citizens of both sides continued to genuinely call for unification on a regular basis.

That Korea was still one country, with unification still the goal, at the time the war began, was underscored by the chief US delegate to the UN, Warren Austin, in a statement he made shortly afterwards:

The artificial barrier which has divided North and South Korea has no basis for existence either

45

in law or in reason. Neither the United Nations, its Commission on Korea, nor the Republic of Korea [South Korea] recognize such a line. Now the North Koreans, by armed attack upon the Republic of Korea, have denied the reality of any such line.[1]

The two sides had been clashing across the Parallel for several years. What happened on that fateful day in June could thus be regarded as no more than the escalation of an ongoing civil war. The North Korean Government has claimed that in 1949 alone, the South Korean army or police perpetrated 2,617 armed incursions into the North to carry out murder, kidnapping, pillage and arson for the purpose of causing social disorder and unrest, as well as to increase the combat capabilities of the invaders. At times, stated the Pyongyang government, thousands of soldiers were involved in a single battle with many casualties resulting.[2]

A State Department official, Ambassador-at-large Philip C. Jessup, speaking in April 1950, put it this way:

> There is constant fighting between the South Korean Army and bands that infiltrate the country from the North. There are very real battles, involving perhaps one or two thousand men. When you go to this boundary, as I did ... you see troop movements, fortifications, and prisoners of war.[3]

Seen in this context, the question of who fired the first shot on 25 June 1950 takes on a much reduced air of significance. As it is, the North Korean version of events is that their invasion was provoked by two days of bombardment by the South Koreans, on the 23rd and 24th, followed by a surprise South Korean attack across the border on the 25th against the western town of Haeju and other places. Announcement of the Southern attack was broadcast over the North's radio later in the morning of the 25th.

Contrary to general belief at the time, no United Nations group—neither the UN Military Observer Group in the field nor the UN Commission on Korea in Seoul—witnessed, or claimed to have witnessed, the outbreak of hostilities. The Observer Group's field trip along the Parallel ended on 23 June. Its statements about what took place afterward are either speculation or based on information received from the South Korean government or the US military.

Moreover, early in the morning of the 26th, the South Korean Office of Public Information announced that Southern forces had indeed captured the North Korean town of Haeju. The announcement stated that the attack had occurred that same morning, but an American military status report as of nightfall on the 25th notes that all Southern territory west of the Imjin River had been lost to a depth of at least three miles inside the border except in the area of the Haeju "counter attack".

In either case, such a military victory on the part of the Southern forces is extremely difficult to reconcile with the official Western account, maintained to this day, that has the North Korean army sweeping south in a devastating surprise attack, taking control of everything that lay before it, and forcing South Korean troops to evacuate further south.

Subsequently, the South Korean government denied that its capture of Haeju had actually taken place, blaming the original announcement, apparently, on an exaggerating military officer. One historian has ascribed the allegedly incorrect announcement to "an error due to poor communications, plus an attempt to stiffen South Korean resistance by claiming a victory". Whatever actually lay behind the announcement, it is evident that very little reliance, if any, can be placed upon statements made by the South Korean government concerning the start of the war.[4]

There were, in fact, reports in the Western press of the attack on Haeju which made no mention of the South Korean government's announcement, and which appear to be independent confirmations of the event. The London *Daily Herald*, in its issue of 26 June, stated that "American military observers said the Southern forces had made a successful relieving counter-attack near the west coast, penetrated five miles into Northern territory and seized the town of Haeju." This was echoed in *The Guardian* of London the same day: "American officials confirmed that the Southern troops had captured Haeju."

Similarly, the *New York Herald Tribune* reported, also on the 26th, that "South Korean troops drove across the 38th Parallel, which forms the frontier, to capture the manufacturing town of Haeju, just north of the line. The Republican troops captured quantities of equipment." None of the accounts specified just when the attack took place.

On the 25th, American writer John Gunther was in Japan preparing his biography of General Douglas MacArthur. As he recounts in the book, he was playing tourist in the town of Nikko with "two important members" of the American occupation, when "one of these was called unexpectedly to the telephone. He came back and whispered, 'A big story has just broken. The South Koreans have attacked North Korea!'" That evening, Gunther and his party returned to Tokyo where "Several officers met us at the station to tell us correctly and with much amplification what had happened ... there was no doubt whatever that North Korea was the aggressor."

And the telephone call? Gunther explains: "The message may have been garbled in transmission. Nobody knew anything much at headquarters the first few hours, and probably people were taken in by the blatant, corrosive lies of the North Korean radio."[5]

There is something a little incongruous about the picture of American military and diplomatic personnel, practicing anti-communists each one, being taken in on so important a matter by communist lies—blatant ones no less.

The head of South Korea, Syngman Rhee, had often expressed his desire and readiness to compel the unification of Korea by force. On 26 June the *New York Times* reminded its readers that "on a number of occasions, Dr. Rhee has indicated that his army would have taken the offensive if Washington had given the consent." The newspaper noted also that before the war began: "The warlike talk strangely [had] almost all come from South Korean leaders."

Rhee may have had good reason for provoking a full-scale war apart from the issue of unification. On 30 May, elections for the National Assembly were held in the South in which Rhee's party suffered a heavy setback and lost control of the assembly. Like countless statesmen before and after him, Rhee may have decided to play the war card to rally support for his shaky rule. A labor adviser attached to the American aid mission in South Korea, Stanley Earl, resigned in July, expressing the opinion that the South Korean government was "an oppressive regime" which "did very little to help the people" and that "an internal South Korean rebellion against the Rhee Government would have occurred if the forces of North Korea had not invaded".[6]

Soviet leader Nikita Khrushchev, in his reminiscences, makes it plain that the North Koreans had contemplated an invasion of the South for some time and he reports their actual invasion without any mention of provocation on that day. This would seem to put that particular question to rest. However, Khrushchev's chapter on Korea is a wholly superficial account. It is not a serious work of history, nor was it intended to be. As he himself states:

"My memories of the Korean War are unavoidably sketchy." (He did not become Soviet leader until after the war was over.) His chapter contains no discussion of *any* of the previous fighting across the border, nothing of Rhee's belligerent statements, nothing at all even of the Soviet Union's crucial absence from the UN which, as we shall see, allowed the so-called United Nations Army to be formed and intervene in the conflict. Moreover, his reminiscences, as published, are an edited and condensed version of the tapes he made. A study based on a comparison between the Russian-language transcription of the tapes and the published English-language book reveals that some of Khrushchev's memories about Korea were indeed sketchy, but that the book fails to bring this out. For example, North Korean leader Kim Il-sung met with Stalin to discuss Kim's desire "to prod South Korea with the point of a bayonet". The book then states unambiguously: "Kim went home and then returned to Moscow when he had worked everything out." In the transcript, however, Khrushchev says: "In my opinion, either the date of his return was set, or he was to inform us as soon as he finished preparing all of his ideas. Then, I don't remember in which month or *year*, Kim Il-sung came and related his plan to Stalin" (emphasis added).[7]

On 26 June, the United States presented a resolution before the UN Security Council condemning North Korea for its "unprovoked aggression". The resolution was approved, although there were arguments that "this was a fight between Koreans" and should be treated as a civil war, and a suggestion from the Egyptian delegate that the word "unprovoked" should be dropped in view of the longstanding hostilities between the two Koreas.[8] Yugoslavia insisted as well that "there seemed to be lack of precise information that could enable the Council to pin responsibility", and proposed that North Korea be invited to present its side of the story.[9] This was not done. (Three months later, the Soviet foreign minister put forward a motion that the UN hear representatives from both sides. This, too, was voted down, by a margin of 46 to 6, because of North Korea's "aggression", and it was decided to extend an invitation to South Korea alone.)[10]

On the 27th, the Security Council recommended that members of the United Nations furnish assistance to South Korea "as may be necessary to repel the armed attack". President Truman had already ordered the US Navy and Air Force into combat by this time, thus presenting the Council with a *fait accompli*,[11] a tactic the US was to repeat several times before the war came to an end. The Council made its historic decision with the barest of information available to it, and all of it derived from and selected by only one side of the conflict. This was, as journalist I.F. Stone put it, "neither honorable nor wise".

It should be kept in mind that in 1950 the United Nations was in no way a neutral or balanced organization. The great majority of members were nations very dependent upon the United States for economic recovery or development. There was no Third World bloc which years later pursued a UN policy much more independent of the United States. And only four countries of the Soviet bloc were members at the time, none on the Security Council.[12]

Neither could UN Secretary-General Trygve Lie, of Norway, be regarded as neutral in the midst of cold war controversy. In his memoirs, he makes it remarkably clear that he was no objective outsider. His chapters on the Korean War are pure knee-reflex anti-communism and reveal his maneuvering on the issue.[13] In 1949, it was later disclosed, Lie had entered into a secret agreement with the US State Department to dismiss from UN employment individuals whom Washington regarded as having questionable political leanings.[14]

The adoption of these resolutions by the Security Council was possible only because the Soviet Union was absent from the proceedings due to its boycott of the United Nations over the refusal to seat Communist China in place of Taiwan. If the Russians had been present, they undoubtedly would have vetoed the resolutions. Their absence has always posed an awkward problem for those who insist that the Russians were behind the North Korean invasion. One of the most common explanations offered is that the Russians, as a CIA memorandum stated, wanted "to challenge the US specifically and test the firmness of US resistance to Communist expansion."[15] Inasmuch as, during the existence of the Soviet Union, the same analysis was put forth by American political pundits for virtually every encounter between the United States and leftists anywhere in the world, before and after Korea, it would appear that the test was going on for an inordinately long period and one can only wonder why the Soviets never came to a conclusion.

"The finishing touch," wrote I.F. Stone, "was to make the 'United Nations' forces subject to MacArthur without making MacArthur subject to the United Nations. This came on July 7 in a resolution introduced jointly by Britain and France. This is commonly supposed to have established a United Nations Command. Actually it did nothing of the sort."[16] The resolution recommended "that all members providing military forces and other assistance ... make such forces and other assistance available to a *unified command under the United States*" (emphasis added). It further requested "the United States to designate the commander of such forces."[17] This would be the redoubtable MacArthur.

It was to be an American show. Military personnel of some 16 other countries took part in one way or another but, with the exception of the South Koreans, there could be little doubt as to their true status or function. Eisenhower later wrote in his memoirs that when he was considering US military intervention in Vietnam in 1954, also as part of a "coalition", he recognized that the burden of the operation would fall on the United States, but "the token forces supplied by these other nations, *as in Korea*, would lend real moral standing to a venture that otherwise could be made to appear as a brutal example of imperialism" (emphasis added).[18]

The war, and a brutal one it was indeed, was fought ostensibly in defense of the Syngman Rhee regime. Outside of books published by various South Korean governments, it is rather difficult to find a kind word for the man the United States brought back to Korea in 1945 after decades of exile in America during the Japanese occupation of his country. Flown into Korea in one of MacArthur's airplanes, Rhee was soon maneuvered into a position of prominence and authority by the US Army Military Government in Korea (USAMGIK). In the process, American officials had to suppress a provisional government, the Korean People's Republic, that was the outgrowth of a number of regional governing committees set up by prominent Koreans and which had already begun to carry out administrative tasks, such as food distribution and keeping order. The KPR's offer of its services to the arriving Americans was dismissed out of hand.

Despite its communist-sounding name, the KPR included a number of conservatives; indeed, Rhee himself had been given the leading position of chairman. Rhee and the other conservatives, most of whom were still abroad when chosen, perhaps did not welcome the honor because the KPR, on balance, was probably too leftist for their tastes, as it was for the higher echelons of the USAMGIK. But after 35 years under the Japanese, any group or government set up to undo the effects of colonialism had to have a revolutionary tinge to it. It was the conservatives in Korea who had collaborated with the Japanese; leftists and other nationalists who had struggled against them; the make-up of the KPR necessarily reflected this, and it was reportedly more popular than any other political grouping.[19]

Whatever the political leanings or intentions of the KPR, by denying it any "authority, status or form",[20] the USAMGIK was regulating Korean political life as if the country were a defeated enemy and not a friendly state liberated from a common foe and with a right to independence and self-determination.

The significance of shunting aside the KPR went beyond this. John Gunther, hardly a radical, summed up the situation this way: "So the first—and best—chance for building a united Korea was tossed away."[21] And Alfred Crofts, a member of the American military government at the time, has written that "A potential unifying agency became thus one of the fifty-four splinter groups in South Korean political life."[22]

Syngman Rhee would be Washington's man: eminently pro-American, strongly anti-Communist, sufficiently controllable. His regime was one in which landlords, collaborators, the wealthy, and other conservative elements readily found a home. Crofts has pointed out that "Before the American landings, a political Right, associated in popular thought with colonial rule, could not exist; but shortly afterward we were to foster at least three conservative factions."[23]

Committed to establishing free enterprise, the USAMGIK sold off vast amounts of confiscated Japanese property, homes, businesses, industrial raw materials and other valuables. Those who could most afford to purchase these assets were collaborators who had grown rich under the Japanese, and other profiteers. "With half the wealth of the nation 'up for grabs', demoralization was rapid."[24]

While the Russians did a thorough house-cleaning of Koreans in the North who had collaborated with the Japanese, the American military government in the South allowed many collaborators, and at first even the Japanese themselves, to retain positions of administration and authority, much to the consternation of those Koreans who had fought against the Japanese occupation of their country. To some extent, these people may have been retained in office because they were the most experienced at keeping the country running. Another reason has been suggested: to prevent the Korean People's Republic from assuming a measure of power.[25]

And while the North soon implemented widespread and effective land reform and at least formal equality for women, the Rhee regime remained hostile to these ideals. Two years later, it enacted a land reform measure, but this applied only to former Japanese property. A 1949 law to cover other holdings was not enforced at all, and the abuse of land tenants continued in both old and new forms.[26]

Public resentment against the US/Rhee administration was aroused because of these policies as well as because of the suppression of the KPR and some very questionable elections. So reluctant was Rhee to allow an honest election, that by early 1950 he had become enough of an embarrassment to the United States for Washington officials to threaten to cut off aid if he failed to do so and also improve the state of civil liberties. Apparently because of this pressure, the elections held on May 30 were fair enough to allow "moderate" elements to participate, and, as mentioned earlier, the Rhee government was decisively repudiated.[27]

The resentment was manifested in the form of frequent rebellions, including some guerrilla warfare in the hills, from 1946 to the beginning of the war, and even during the war. The rebellions were dismissed by the government as "communist-inspired" and repressed accordingly, but, as John Gunther observed, "It can be safely said that in the eyes of Hodge [the commander of US forces in Korea] and Rhee, particularly at the beginning, almost any Korean not an extreme rightist was a communist and potential traitor."[28]

General Hodge evidently permitted US troops to take part in the repression. Mark

Gayn, a correspondent in Korea for the *Chicago Sun*, wrote that American soldiers "fired on crowds, conducted mass arrests, combed the hills for suspects, and organized posses of Korean rightists, constabulary and police for mass raids."[29] Gayn related that one of Hodge's political advisers assured him (Gayn) that Rhee was not a fascist: "He is two centuries before fascism—a pure Bourbon."[30]

Describing the government's anti-guerrilla campaign in 1948, pro-Western political scientist John Kie-Chiang Oh of Marquette University has written: "In these campaigns, the civil liberties of countless persons were often ignored. Frequently, hapless villagers, suspected of aiding the guerrillas, were summarily executed."[31]

A year later, when a committee of the National Assembly launched an investigation of collaborators, Rhee had his police raid the Assembly: 22 people were arrested, of whom 16 were later found to have suffered either broken ribs, skull injuries or broken eardrums.[32]

At the time of the outbreak of war in June 1950, there were an estimated 14,000 political prisoners in South Korean jails.[33]

Even during the height of the war, in February 1951, reported Professor Oh, there was the "Koch'ang Incident", again involving suspicion of aiding guerrillas, "in which about six hundred men and women, young and old, were herded into a narrow valley and mowed down with machine guns by a South Korean army unit."[34]

Throughout the war, a continuous barrage of accusations was leveled by each side at the other, charging the enemy with engaging in all manner of barbarity and atrocity, against troops, prisoners of war, and civilians alike, in every part of the country (each side occupied the other's territory at times), trying to outdo each other in a verbal war of superlatives almost as heated as the combat. In the United States this produced a body of popular myths, not unlike those emerging from other wars which are widely supported at home. (By contrast, during the Vietnam War the inclination of myths to flourish was regularly countered by numerous educated protestors who carefully researched the origins of the war, monitored its conduct, and publicized studies sharply at variance with the official version(s), eventually influencing the mass media to do the same.)

There was, for example, the consensus that the brutality of the war in Korea must be laid overwhelmingly on the doorstep of the North Koreans. The Koch'ang Incident mentioned above may be relevant to providing some counterbalance to this belief. Referring to the incident, the British Korea scholar Jon Halliday observed:

> This account not only serves to indicate the level of political violence employed by the UN side, but also confers inherent plausibility on DPRK [North Korea] and Southern opposition accusations of atrocities and mass executions by the UN forces and Rhee officials during the occupation of the DPRK in late 1950. After all, if civilians could be mowed down in the South on *suspicion* of aiding (not even *being*) guerrillas—what about the North, where millions could reasonably be assumed to be Communists, or political militants?[35](Emphasis in original.)

Oh's account is but one of a number of reports of slaughter carried out by the South Koreans against their own people during the war. The *New York Times* reported a "wave of [South Korean] Government executions in Seoul" in December 1950.[36] René Cutforth, a correspondent for the BBC in Korea, later wrote of "the shooting without trial of civilians, designated by the police as 'communist'. These executions were done, usually at dawn, on any patch of waste ground where you could dig a trench and line up a row of prisoners in front of it."[37] And Gregory Henderson, a US diplomat who served seven years in Korea in the 1940s and '50s, has stated that "probably over 100,000 were killed without any trial whatsoever" by Rhee's forces in the South during the war.[38] Following some of the massacres of civilians in the South, the Rhee government turned around and attributed them to Northern troops.

One way in which the United States contributed directly to the war's brutality was by introducing a weapon which, although used in the last stage of World War II, and in Greece, was new to almost all observers and participants in Korea. It was called napalm. Here is one description of its effect from the *New York Times*.

> A napalm raid hit the village three or four days ago when the Chinese were holding up the advance, and nowhere in the village have they buried the dead because there is nobody left to do so. ... The inhabitants throughout the village and in the fields were caught and killed and kept the exact postures they had held when the napalm struck—a man about to get on his bicycle, fifty boys and girls playing in an orphanage, a housewife strangely unmarked, holding in her hand a page torn from a Sears-Roebuck catalogue crayoned at Mail Order No. 3,811,294 for a $2.98 "bewitching bed jacket—coral". There must be almost two hundred dead in the tiny hamlet.[39]

The United States may also have waged germ warfare against North Korea and China, as was discussed earlier in the chapter on China.

At the same time, the CIA reportedly was targeting a single individual for termination—North Korean leader Kim Il Sung. Washington sent a Cherokee Indian, code-named Buffalo, to Hans V. Tofte, a CIA officer stationed in Japan, after Buffalo had agreed to serve as Kim Il Sung's assassin. Buffalo was to receive a considerable amount of money if his mission succeeded. It obviously did not, and nothing further has been revealed about the incident.[40]

Another widely-held belief in the United States during the war was that American prisoners in North Korean camps were dying off like flies because of Communist neglect and cruelty. The flames of this very emotional issue were fanned by the tendency of US officials to exaggerate the numbers involved. During November 1951, for example—long before the end of the war—American military announcements put the count of POW deaths at between 5,000 and 8,000.[41] However, an extensive study completed by the US Army two years after the war revealed that the POW death toll for the entire war was 2,730 (out of 7,190 held in camps; an unknown number of other prisoners never made it to the camps, being shot in the field because of the inconvenience of dealing with them in the midst of combat, a practice engaged in by both sides).

The study concluded that "there was evidence that the high death rate was not due primarily to Communist maltreatment ... it could be accounted for largely by the ignorance or the callousness of the prisoners themselves."[42] "Callousness" refers here to the soldiers' lack of morale and collective spirit. Although not mentioned in the study, the North Koreans, on several occasions, claimed that many American POWs also died in the camps as a result of the heavy US bombing.

The study of course could never begin to catch up with all the scare headlines to which the Western world had been treated for three years. Obscured as well was the fact that several times as many Communist prisoners had died in US/South Korean camps—halfway through the war the official figure stood at 6,600[43]—though these camps did hold many more prisoners than those in the North.

The American public was also convinced, and probably still is, that the North Koreans and Chinese had "brainwashed" US soldiers. This story arose to explain the fact that as many as 30 percent of American POWs had collaborated with the enemy in one way or another, and "one man in every seven, or more than thirteen per cent, was guilty of serious collaboration—writing disloyal tracts ... or agreeing to spy or organize for the Communists after the war."[44] Another reason the brainwashing theme was promoted by Washington was to increase the likelihood that statements made by returning prisoners which questioned the official version of the war would be discounted.

In the words of Yale psychiatrist Robert J. Lifton, brainwashing was popularly held to be an "all-powerful, irresistible, unfathomable, and magical method of achieving total control over the human mind."[45] Although the CIA experimented, beginning in the 1950s, to develop just such a magic, neither they nor the North Koreans or Chinese ever possessed it. The Agency began its "behavior-control" or "mind-control" experiments on human subjects (probably suspected double agents), using drugs and hypnosis, in Japan in July 1950, shortly after the beginning of the Korean War. In October, they apparently used North Korean prisoners of war as subjects.[46] In 1975, a US Navy psychologist, Lt. Com. Thomas Narut, revealed that his naval work included establishing how to induce servicemen who may not be naturally inclined to kill, to do so under certain conditions. He referred to these men using the words "hitmen" and "assassin". Narut added that convicted murderers as well had been released from military prisons to become assassins.[47]

Brainwashing, said the Army study, "has become a catch phrase, used for so many things that it no longer has any precise meaning" and "a precise meaning is necessary in this case".[48]

> The prisoners, as far as Army psychiatrists have been able to discover, were not subjected to anything that could properly be called brainwashing. Indeed, the Communist treatment of prisoners, while it came nowhere near fulfilling the requirements of the Geneva Convention, rarely involved outright cruelty, being instead a highly novel blend of leniency and pressure ... The Communists rarely used physical torture ... and the Army has not found a single verifiable case in which they used it for the specific purpose of forcing a man to collaborate or to accept their convictions.[49]

According to the study, however, some American airmen, of the 90 or so who were captured, were subjected to physical abuse in an attempt to extract confessions about germ warfare. This could reflect either a greater Communist resentment about the use of such a weapon, or a need to produce some kind of corroboration of a false or questionable claim.

American soldiers were instead subjected to political indoctrination by their jailers. Here is how the US Army saw it:

> In the indoctrination lectures, the Communists frequently displayed global charts dotted with our military bases, the names of which were of course known to many of the captives. "See those bases?" the instructor would say, tapping them on the chart with his pointer. "They are American—full of war materiel. You *know* they are American. And you can see they are ringing Russia and China. Russia and China do not have *one* base outside their own territory. From this it's clear which side is the warmonger. Would America have these bases and spend millions to maintain them were it not preparing to war on Russia and China?" This argument seemed plausible to many of the prisoners. In general they had no idea that these bases showed not the United States' wish for war, but its wish for peace, that they had been established as part of a series of treaties aimed not at conquest, but at curbing Red aggression.[50]

The Chinese Communists, of course, did not invent this practice. During the American Civil War, prisoners of both the South and the North received indoctrination about the respective merits of the two sides. And in the Second World War, "democratization courses" were held in US and British POW camps for Germans, and reformed Germans were granted privileges. Moreover, the US Army was proud to state that Communist prisoners in

American camps during the Korean War were taught "what democracy stands for".[51]

The predicted Chinese aggression manifested itself about four months after the war in Korea began. The Chinese entered the war after American planes had violated their air space on a number of occasions, had bombed and strafed Chinese territory several times (always "in error"), when hydro-electric plants on the Korean side of the border, vital to Chinese industry, stood in great danger, and US or South Korean forces had reached the Chinese border, the Yalu River, or come within a few miles of it in several places.

The question must be asked: How long would the United States refrain from entering a war being waged in Mexico by a Communist power from across the sea, which strafed and bombed Texas border towns, was mobilized along the Rio Grande, and was led by a general who threatened war against the United States itself?

American airpower in Korea was fearsome to behold. As would be the case in Vietnam, its use was celebrated in the wholesale dropping of napalm, the destruction of villages "suspected of aiding the enemy", bombing cities so as to leave no useful facilities standing, demolishing dams and dikes to cripple the irrigation system, wiping out rice crops ... and in those moving expressions like "scorched-earth policy", "saturation bombing", and "operation killer".[52]

"You can kiss that group of villages good-bye," exclaimed Captain Everett L. Hundley of Kansas City, Kansas after a bombing raid.[53]

"I would say that the entire, almost the entire Korean Peninsula is just a terrible mess," testified Major General Emmett O'Donnell before the Senate when the war was one year old. "Everything is destroyed. There is nothing standing worthy of the name."[54]

And here, the words of the venerable British military guide, *Brassey's Annual*, in its 1951 yearbook:

> It is no exaggeration to state that South Korea no longer exists as a country. Its towns have been destroyed, much of its means of livelihood eradicated, and its people reduced to a sullen mass dependent upon charity and exposed to subversive influences. When the war ends no gratitude can be expected from the South Koreans, but it is to be hoped that the lesson will have been learned that it is worse than useless to destroy to liberate. Certainly, western Europe would never accept such a "liberation".[55]

The worst of the bombing was yet to come. That began in the summer of 1952 and was Washington's way of putting itself in a better bargaining position in the truce discussions with the Communists, which had been going on for a full year while the battles raged. The extended and bitter negotiations gave rise to another pervasive Western belief—that it was predominantly Communist intransigence, duplicity, and lack of peaceful intentions which frustrated the talks and prolonged the war.

This is a lengthy and entangled chapter of the Korean War story, but one does not have to probe too deeply to discover the unremarkable fact that the barriers were erected by the anti-Communist side as well. Syngman Rhee, for example, was so opposed to any outcome short of total victory that both the Truman and Eisenhower administrations drew up plans for overthrowing him;[56] which is not to suggest that the American negotiators were negotiating in the best of faith. The last thing they wanted to be accused of was having allowed the commies to make suckers of them. Thus it was that in November of 1951 we could read in the *New York Times*:

The unadorned way that an apparently increasing number of them [American soldiers in Korea] see the situation right now is that the Communists have made important concessions, while the United Nations Command, as they view it, continues to make more and more demands. ... The United Nations truce team has created the impression that it switches its stand whenever the Communists indicate that they might go along with it.[57]

At one point during this same period, when the Communists proposed that a ceasefire and a withdrawal of troops from the combat line should take place while negotiations were going on, the United Nations Command reacted almost as if this were a belligerent and devious act. "Today's stand by the Communists," said the UNC announcement, "was virtually a renunciation of their previously stated position that hostilities should continue during armistice talks."[58]

Once upon a time, the United States fought a great civil war in which the North attempted to reunite the divided country through military force. Did Korea or China or any other foreign power send in an army to slaughter Americans, charging Lincoln with aggression?

Why did the United States choose to wage full-scale war in Korea? Only a year earlier, in 1949, in the Arab-Israeli fighting in Palestine and in the India-Pakistani war over Kashmir, the United Nations, with American support, had intervened to mediate an armistice, not to send in an army to take sides and expand the fighting. And both these conflicts were less in the nature of a civil war than was the case in Korea. If the US/UN response had been the same in these earlier cases, Palestine and Kashmir might have wound up as the scorched-earth desert that was Korea's fate. What saved them, what kept the US armed forces out, was no more than the absence of a communist side to the conflict.

6. Albania 1949-1953
The proper English spy

"To simultaneously plan and sabotage this ill-fated venture must have been a severe test of his energy and ingenuity," wrote one of Kim Philby's biographers.[1] The venture was the clandestine attempt, begun in 1949, by the United States and Great Britain to overthrow the pro-Soviet regime of Enver Hoxha through guerrilla-fomented uprisings.

It ended in disaster, in part because the Russians had apparently been alerted by Philby, the proper Englishman who had gone to all the right schools and penetrated the highest ranks of British and American intelligence, though he had been a Soviet spy since the age of 21.

Philby had moved to Washington the year before to act as the British Secret Intelligence Service (SIS) liaison to the CIA. In that capacity he served as a co-director of the CIA-SIS task force engaged in planning the Albanian operation. The choice had fallen upon Albania because it was regarded as the most vulnerable of the socialist states, the smallest and the weakest, not sharing a border with the Soviet Union, isolated between a US-controlled Greece and a Yugoslavia that was a renegade from the Soviet bloc. Moreover, a recent agreement between the Soviet Union and Albania involved aid for Albania in return for a Soviet right to build a submarine base with direct access to the Mediterranean. By the rules and logic of the cold-war board game, this was a move the United States was obliged to thwart.[2]

The task force began by recruiting scattered Albanian émigrés who were living in Italy, Greece and elsewhere. They were exposed to basic military training, with a touch of guerrilla warfare thrown in, at sites established on the British island of Malta in the Mediterranean, in the American occupation zone of West Germany, and, to a lesser extent, in England itself.[4] "Whenever we want to subvert any place," confided Frank Wisner, the CIA's head of covert operations, to Philby, "we find that the British own an island within easy reach."[5]

Intermittently, for some three-and-a-half years, the émigrés were sent back into their homeland: slipping up into the mountains of Greece and over the border, parachuting in from planes which had taken off from bases in Western Europe, entering by sea from Italy. American planes and balloons dropped propaganda leaflets and goods as well, such items in scarce supply in Albania as flour, halvah, needles, and razor blades, along with a note announcing that they were a gift from the "Albanian National Liberation Front"[6]—another instance of the subtle "marketing" touch that the CIA, born and raised in America, was to bring to so many of its operations.

In outline, the plan, or the hope, was for the guerrillas to make for their old home regions and try to stir up anti-Soviet and anti-Communist sentiments, eventually leading to uprisings. They were to distribute propaganda, obtain political, economic and military information, engage in sabotage, recruit individuals into cells, and supply them with equipment. Later infusions of men and material would expand these cells into "centers of resistance".[6]

Cold-war conventional wisdom dictated that the masses of Eastern Europe were waiting to be sparked into open rebellion for their freedom. Even if this were the case, the choice of ignition was highly dubious, for the guerrillas included amongst their numbers many who supported a reinstitution of the Albanian monarchy in the person of the reactionary King Zog, then in exile, and others who had collaborated with the Italian fascists or Nazis during their wartime occupations of Albania.

To be sure, there were those of republican and democratic leanings in the various émigré committees as well, but State Department papers, later declassified, reveal that prominent Albanian collaborators played leading roles in the formation of these committees. These were individuals the State Department characterized as having "somewhat checkered" political backgrounds, who "might sooner or later occasion embarrassment to this government". They were admitted to the United States over the Department's objections because of "intelligence considerations". One of the checkered gentlemen was Xhafer Deva, minister of interior during the Italian occupation, who had been responsible for deportations of "Jews, Communists, partisans and suspicious persons" (as a captured Nazi report put it) to extermination camps in Poland.[7]

In the name of the CIA-funded National Committee for a Free Albania, a powerful underground radio station began broadcasting inside the country, calling for the nation's liberation from the Soviet Union. In early 1951, several reports came out of Albania of open organized resistance and uprisings.[8] To what extent these happenings were a consequence of the Western infiltration and agitation is impossible to determine. Overall, the campaign had little to show for its efforts. It was hounded throughout by logistical foul-ups, and the grim reality that the masses of Albanians greeted the émigrés as something less than liberators, either from fear of the harsh Hoxha regime, or because they supported the social changes taking place more than they trusted what the émigrés had to offer.

Worst of all, the Albanian authorities usually seemed to know in which area the guerrillas would be arriving, and when. Kim Philby was not the only potential source of disclosure. The Albanian groups were almost certainly infiltrated, and careless talk indulged in by the motley émigrés could have contributed to the fiasco. Philby, referring to the CIA-SIS task force members' habit of poking fun at Albanians, wrote: "Even in our more serious moments, we Anglo-Saxons never forgot that our agents were just down from the trees."[9]

So lax was security that *New York Times* correspondent Cyrus L. Sulzberger filed several dispatches from the Mediterranean area touching upon the intervention which required virtually no reading between the lines.[10] (The articles carried no attention-grabbing headlines, there was no public comment about them from Washington, no reporters asked government officials any embarrassing questions ... ergo: a "non-event" for Americans.)

Despite one failure after another, and without good reason to expect anything different in the future, the operation continued until the spring of 1953, resulting in the death or imprisonment of hundreds of men. It was not simply the obsession with chopping off one of Stalin's fingers. Professional prestige and careers had been invested, a visible success was needed to "recoup past losses" and "justify earlier decisions".[11] And the men who were being lost were, after all, only Albanians, who spoke not a word of the Queen's English, and did not yet walk upright properly.

There was, however, the danger of the action escalating into conflict with the Soviet Union. The Soviets did in fact send some new fighter planes to Albania, presumably in the hope that they could shoot down the foreign aircraft making drops.[12] The operation could not fail to remind Stalin, Hoxha, and the entire socialist bloc of another Western intervention 30 years earlier in the Soviet Union. It could only serve to make them yet more "paranoid" about Western intentions and convince them to turn the screw of internal security yet tighter. Indeed, every now and again over the ensuing years, Hoxha mentioned the American and British "invasion" and used it to justify his policy of isolation.[13]

In the early 1960s, Hoxha himself did what the CIA and SIS had failed to do: He pulled Albania out of the Soviet orbit. The Albanian leader purged pro-Soviet officials in his government and aligned his country with China. There was no military retaliation on the part of the USSR. In the mid-1970s, Hoxha forsook China as well.

7. Eastern Europe 1948-1956
Operation Splinter Factor

Jozef Swiatlo surfaced at a press conference in Washington on 28 September 1954. Swiatlo was a Pole; he had been a very important one, high up in the Ministry of Public Security, the secret police. The story went that he had defected in West Berlin the previous December while on a shopping trip, and now the State Department was presenting him to the world to clear up the mystery of the Fields, the American citizens who had disappeared in 1949. Swiatlo revealed that Noel Field and his wife Herta had been arrested in Hungary, and that brother Hermann Field had suffered the same fate in Poland at the hands of Swiatlo himself, all in connection with the trial of a leading Hungarian Communist. The State Department had already dispatched strong letters to the governments of Hungary and Poland.[1]

There is a more expanded and more sinister version of the Jozef Swiatlo story. This story has Swiatlo seeking to defect to the British in Warsaw back in 1948 at a time when he was already in his high security position. The British, for various reasons, turned his case over to the United States and, at the request of Allen Dulles, Swiatlo was told to remain at his post until further notice.

At this time Dulles was not yet Director of the CIA, but was a close consultant to the Agency, had his own men in key positions, and was waiting only until November for Thomas Dewey to win the presidential election and appoint him to the top position. (Harry Truman's surprising re-election postponed this for four years, but Dulles did become Deputy Director in 1951.)

Noel Field, formerly a State Department Foreign Service Officer, was a long-time Communist fellow-traveler, if not a party member in the United States or Europe. During the Second World War, his path converged with Dulles's in intrigue-filled Switzerland. Dulles was an OSS man, Field the representative of the Unitarian Church in Boston helping refugees from Nazi occupation. Field made it a point particularly to help Communist refugees, of which there were many inasmuch as Communists were second only to Jews on the German persecution list. The OSS aided the operation financially; the Communists in turn were an excellent source of information about happenings in Europe of interest to Washington and its allies.

Toward the end of the war, Field induced Dulles to provide American support for a project which placed agents in various European countries to prepare the way for the advancing Allied troops. The men chosen by Field, unsurprisingly, were all Communists and their placement in certain Eastern European countries helped them to get their hands on the reins of power long before non-Communist forces were able to regroup and organize themselves.

It could be concluded from this that Allen Dulles had been duped. Moreover, the OSS, under Dulles's direction and again with Field involved, had financed the publication of a clandestine newspaper inside Germany; anti-fascist and left-wing, the paper was called *Neues Deutschland*, and immediately upon liberation became the official newspaper of the East German Communist Party.

After the war these incidents served as jokes which intelligence services of both East and West could and did appreciate. Before long, the joke fell heavily upon Noel Field.

In 1949 when Field visited Poland he was regarded with grave suspicion by Polish authorities. He was seen to have worked during the war in a position which could easily have been a front for Western espionage, a position which brought him into regular contact with senior Communist Party members; and he had, after all, worked closely with Allen Dulles, famous already as a spymaster, and the brother of John Foster Dulles, prominent in Washington official circles and already making his calls for the "liberation" of the Soviet bloc nations.

At the time of Field's arrival in Poland, Jozef Swiatlo was looking to implicate Jakub Berman, a high party and state official whom Swiatlo was suspicious of and detested. It was his failure to convince the Polish president to act against Berman that reportedly drove Swiatlo to try to defect the year before. When Noel Field wrote to Berman asking his help in obtaining a job in Eastern Europe, Swiatlo learned of the letter and saw his chance to nail Berman.

But first Noel Field had to be established as an American spy. Given the circumstantial evidence pointing in that direction, that would not be too difficult for a man of Swiatlo's high position and low character. Of course, if Field really *was* working with US intelligence, Swiatlo couldn't very well be exposing him since the Polish security officer was now himself an American agent. Accordingly, he sent his first message to the CIA, describing his plan about Berman and Field and the harm it could do to the Communist Party in Poland. He concluded with: "Any objections?"

Allen Dulles had none. His reaction to Swiatlo's message was one of pleasure and amusement. The time had come to settle accounts with Noel Field. More importantly, Dulles saw that Swiatlo, using Noel Field, "the American spy", as a bludgeon could knock off countless leading Communist officials in the Soviet bloc. It could put the whole of the bloc into a state of acute paranoia and set off a wave of repression and Stalinist tyranny that could eventually lead to uprisings. Dulles called his plan: Operation Splinter Factor.

Thus it was that Jozef Swiatlo was directed to find spies everywhere in Eastern Europe. He would uncover American plots and British plots, "Trotskyist" conspiracies and "Titoist" conspiracies. He would report to Soviet secret-police chief Lavrenti Beria himself that at the center of the vast network was a man named Noel Haviland Field.

Field was arrested and wound up in a prison in Hungary, as did his wife Herta when she came looking for him. And when his brother Hermann Field sought to track down the two of them, he met the same fate in Poland.

Swiatlo was in a unique position to carry out Operation Splinter Factor. Not only did he have the authority and command, he had the files on countless Communist Party members in the bloc countries. Any connection they had had with Noel Field, anything that Field had done, could be interpreted to show the hand of American intelligence or an act of real or potential subversion of the socialist states. The Soviets, and Stalin himself, were extremely interested in the "Fieldists". Noel Field had known almost everyone who was anyone in the Soviet bloc.

Just in case the level of paranoia in the infant, insecure governments of Eastern Europe was not high enough, a CIA double agent would "corroborate" a vital piece of information, or introduce the right rumor at the right time; or the Agency's Radio Free Europe would broadcast certain tantalizing, seemingly-coded messages; or the CIA would direct the writing of letters from "East European expatriates" in the United States to leading Communists in their homelands, containing just the bit of information, or the phrase, carefully designed to lift the eyebrows of a security officer.

Many of the victims of Swiatlo's purges were people who had spent the war years in the West rather than in the Soviet Union and thus had crossed Field's path. These were people who tended to be more nationalist Communists, who wanted to put greater distance between their countries and the Soviet Union, as Tito had done in Yugoslavia, and who favored a more liberal regime at home. Dulles brushed aside the argument that these were people to be supported, not eliminated. He felt that they were potentially the more dangerous to the West because if their form of Communism were allowed to gain a foothold in Eastern Europe then Communism might become respectable and accepted; particularly with Italy and France threatening to vote Communists into power, Communism had to be shown at its worst.

There were hundreds of trials all over Eastern Europe—"show trials" and lesser spectacles—in which the name of Noel Field played an important part. What Operation Splinter Factor began soon took on a life of its own: following the arrest of a highly-placed person, others fell under suspicion because they knew him or had been appointed by him; or any other connection to an arrested person might serve to implicate some unlucky soul.

Jozef Swiatlo had his counterpart in Czechoslovakia, a man firmly entrenched in the upper rungs of the Czech security apparatus. The man, whose name is not known, had been recruited by General Reinhard Gehlen, the former Nazi intelligence chief who went to work for the CIA after the war.

Czechoslovakia was the worst case. By 1951 an unbelievable 169,000 card-carrying members of the Czech Communist Party had been arrested—ten percent of the entire membership. There were tens of thousands more in Poland, Hungary, East Germany, and Bulgaria. Hundreds were put to death, others died in prison or went insane.[2]

After Swiatlo defected in December 1953, East European intelligence services came to realize that he had been working for the other side all along. Four weeks after Swiatlo held his Washington press conference, the Polish government announced that it was releasing Hermann Field because investigation had revealed that the charges which had been brought against him by "an American agent and provocateur", Jozef Swiatlo, were "baseless".[3] Field was later paid $50,000 for his imprisonment as well as having his convalescence at a sanitorium paid for.[4]

Three weeks after Hermann Field's release, Noel and Herta Field were freed in Hungary. The government in Budapest stated that it could not justify the charges against them.[5] They were also compensated and chose to remain in Hungary.

Once Noel Field had been officially declared innocent, the cases of countless others in East Europe had to be reviewed. First in trickles, then in rushes, the prisoners were released. By 1956 the vast majority stood outside prison walls.

Throughout the decade following the war, the CIA was fanning the flames of discontent in Eastern Europe in many ways other than Operation Splinter Factor. Radio Free Europe (RFE, cf. Soviet Union chapter), broadcasting from West Germany, never missed a (dirty) trick. In January 1952, for example, after RFE learned that Czechoslovakia was planning to devalue its currency, it warned the population, thus stimulating a nation-wide buying panic.[6] RFE's commentaries about various European Communists were described by Blanche Wiesen Cook in her study of the period, *The Declassified Eisenhower*. She wrote that the broadcasts:

> involved a wide range of personal criticism, tawdry and slanderous attacks ranging from rumors of brutality and torture, to corruption, and to madness, perversion, and vice. Everything was used that could be imagined in order to make communists, whether in England or in Poland, look silly, undignified, and insignificant.[7]

One of the voices heard frequently over RFE on the subject of Communist obnoxiousness was none other than Jozef Swiatlo, who had earned the nickname of "Butcher" for his proclivity to torture. Needless to say, the born-again humanitarian made no mention of Splinter Factor or his double role, although some of his broadcasts reportedly shook up the Polish security system for the better.[8]

Any way the US could stir up trouble and nuisance ... supporting opposition groups in Rumania[9] ... setting up an underground radio station in Bulgaria[10] ... dropping propaganda from balloons over Hungary, Czechoslovakia, and Poland (on one day in August 1951 alone, 11,000 balloons carrying 13 million leaflets)[11] ... dropping people as well: four American airmen, presumably intelligence operatives, landing in Hungary[12] ...

In 1955, Eastern Europeans could be found at Fort Bragg, North Carolina training with the Green Berets, learning guerrilla warfare tactics, hopefully to be used in their native lands.[13]

By the following year, hundreds of Hungarians, Rumanians, Poles and others were being trained by CIA paramilitary specialists at a secret installation in West Germany.

When, in October 1956, the uprising in Hungary occurred, these men, according to the CIA, were not used because they were not yet ready.[14] But the Agency did send its agents in Budapest into action to join the rebels and help organize them.[15] In the meantime, RFE was exhorting the Hungarian people to continue their resistance, offering tactical advice, and implying that American military assistance was on the way. It never came.

There is no evidence that Operation Splinter Factor contributed to the Hungarian uprising or to the earlier ones in Poland and East Germany. Nonetheless, the CIA could point to all the cold-war, anti-Communist propaganda points it had won because of the witch hunts in the East, the human cost notwithstanding.

8. Germany 1950s
Everything from juvenile delinquency to terrorism

Within a period of 30 years and two world wars with Germany, the Soviet Union suffered more than 40 million dead and wounded, enormous devastation to its land, and to its cities razed to the ground. At the close of the Second World War, the Russians were not kindly disposed toward the German people. With their own country to rebuild, they placed the reconstruction of Germany far down on their list of priorities.

The United States emerged from the war with relatively minor casualties and its territory completely unscathed. It was ready, willing and able to devote itself to its main priority in Europe: the building of an anti-Communist bulwark in the West, particularly in the strategic location of Germany.

In 1945, former Secretary of State Dean Acheson has written, official American policy was explicitly "to bring home to the Germans that they could not escape the suffering they had brought upon themselves ... [and] to control [the] German economy to ... prevent any higher standard of living than in neighboring nations."[1]

"From the outset," Acheson added, US officials in Germany believed this plan "to be unworkable".[2]

Acheson did not explain what lay behind this prognosis, but its correctness soon became apparent for three distinct reasons: (1) influential American business and financial leaders, some of them occupying important government positions, had too great a stake in a highly-industrialized Germany (usually dating back to before the war) to allow the country to sink to the depths that some American policy-makers advocated as punishment; (2) a revitalized West Germany was seen as an indispensable means of combatting Soviet influence in the Eastern sector of the country, if not in all of Eastern Europe. West Germany was to become "the showcase of Western democracy"—dramatic, living proof of the superiority of capitalism over socialism; (3) in American conservative circles, and some liberal ones as well, wherein a Soviet invasion of Western Europe remained perpetually imminent, the idea of tying West Germany's industrial hands was one which came perilously close to being "soft on communism", if not worse.[3]

Dwight Eisenhower echoed this last sentiment when he later wrote:

> Had certain officials in the Roosevelt administration had their way, Germany would have been far worse off, for there were those who advocated the flooding of the Ruhr mines, the wrecking of German factories, and the reducing of Germany from an industrial to an agricultural nation. Among

others, Harry Dexter White, later named by Attorney General Brownell as one who had been heavily involved in a Soviet espionage ring operating within our government ... proposed exactly that.[4]

Thus it was that the de-industrialization of West Germany met the same fate as the demilitarization of the country would in the coming years, as the United States poured in massive economic assistance: $4 billion of Marshall Plan aid and an army of industrial and technical experts.

At the same time, the Soviet Union was pouring massive economic assistance *out* of East Germany. The Soviets dismantled and moved back home entire factories with large amounts of equipment and machinery, and thousands of miles of railroad track. When added to war reparations, the toll reached into the billions of dollars.

By the early 1950s, though social services, employment, and cultural life in East Germany were on a par or superior to that in West Germany, the Western sector had the edge in those areas of prosperity with the most sex appeal: salaries were higher, the eating was better, consumer goods more available, and the neon lights emblazoned the nights along the Kurfürstendamm.

American cold warriors, however, as if discontent with the game score or with leaving so much to chance, instituted a crude campaign of sabotage and subversion against East Germany designed to throw the economic and administrative machinery out of gear. The CIA and other US intelligence and military services in West Germany (with occasional help from the likes of British intelligence and the West German police) recruited, equipped, trained and financed German activist groups and individuals of West and East. Finding recruits for such a crusade was not difficult, for in post-war Germany, anti-communism lived on as the only respectable vestige of Naziism.

The most active of these groups, which went by the name of Fighting Group Against Inhumanity, admitted that it had received financial support from the Ford Foundation and the West Berlin government.[5] Subsequently, an East Berlin news magazine published a copy of a letter from the Ford Foundation confirming a grant of $150,000 to the National Committee for a Free Europe "so that it, in turn, could support the humanitarian activities of 'The Fighting Group Against Inhumanity'."[6] The National Committee for a Free Europe, in turn, was a CIA front organization which also ran Radio Free Europe.[7]

The Association of Political Refugees from the East, and the Investigating Committee of Freedom-minded Jurists of the Soviet Zone, were two of the other groups involved in the campaign against East Germany. The actions carried out by these operatives ran the spectrum from juvenile delinquency to terrorism; anything "to make the commies look bad". It added up to the following remarkable record:[8]

- through explosives, arson, short circuiting, and other methods they damaged power stations, shipyards, a dam, canals, docks, public buildings, gas stations, shops, a radio station, outdoor stands, public transportation;

- derailed freight trains, seriously injuring workers; burned 12 cars of a freight train and destroyed air pressure hoses of others;

- blew up road and railway bridges; placed explosives on a railway bridge of the Berlin-Moscow line but these were discovered in time—hundreds would have been killed;

- used special acids to damage vital factory machinery; put sand in the turbine of a factory, bringing it to a standstill; set fire to a tile-producing factory; promoted work slow-downs in factories; stole blueprints and samples of new technical developments;

- killed 7,000 cows of a co-operative dairy by poisoning the wax coating of the wire used to bale the cows' corn fodder;

- added soap to powdered milk destined for East German schools;
- raided and wrecked left-wing offices in East and West Berlin, stole membership lists; assaulted and kidnapped leftists and, on occasion, murdered them;
- set off stink bombs to disrupt political meetings;
- floated balloons which burst in the air, scattering thousands of propaganda pamphlets down upon East Germans;
- were in possession, when arrested, of a large quantity of the poison cantharidin with which it was planned to produce poisoned cigarettes to kill leading East Germans;
- attempted to disrupt the World Youth Festival in East Berlin by sending out forged invitations, false promises of free bed and board, false notices of cancellations; carried out attacks on participants with explosives, firebombs, and tire-puncturing equipment; set fire to a wooden bridge on a main motorway leading to the festival;
- forged and distributed large quantities of food ration cards—for example, for 60,000 pounds of meat—to cause confusion, shortages and resentment;
- sent out forged tax notices and other government directives and documents to foster disorganization and inefficiency within industry and unions;
- "gave considerable aid and comfort" to East Germans who staged an uprising on 17 June 1953; during and after the uprising, the US radio station in West Berlin, RIAS (Radio In the American Sector), issued inflammatory broadcasts into East Germany appealing to the populace to resist the government; RIAS also broadcast warnings to witnesses in at least one East German criminal case being monitored by the Investigating Committee of Freedom-minded Jurists of the Soviet Zone that they would be added to the committee's files of "accused persons" if they lied.

Although many hundreds of the American agents were caught and tried by East Germany, the ease with which they could pass back and forth between the two sectors and infiltrate different enterprises without any language barrier provided opportunities for the CIA unmatched anywhere else in Eastern Europe.

Throughout the 1950s, the East Germans and the Soviet Union repeatedly lodged complaints with the Soviets' erstwhile allies in the West and with the United Nations about specific sabotage and espionage activities and called for the closure of the offices in West Germany they claimed were responsible, and for which they provided names and addresses. Inevitably the East Germans began to tighten up entry into the country from the West.

The West also bedeviled the East with a vigorous campaign of recruiting East German professionals and skilled workers. Eventually, this led to a severe labor and production crisis in the East, and in August 1961, to the building of the infamous Berlin Wall.

While staging their commando attacks upon East Germany, American authorities and their German agents were apparently convinced that the Soviet Union had belligerent designs upon West Germany; perhaps a textbook case of projection. On 8 October 1952, the Minister-President of the West German state of Hesse, Georg August Zinn, disclosed that the United States had created a secret civilian army in his state for the purpose of resisting a Russian invasion.

This force of between 1,000 and 2,000 men belonged to the so-called "Technical Service" of the German Youth Federation, the latter characterized by the *New York Times* as "a Right-wing youth group frequently charged with extremist activities" (a reference to the terrorist tactics described above). The stalwarts of the Technical Service were hardly youths, however, for almost all appeared to be between 35 and 50 and most, said Zinn, were "former officers of the Luftwaffe, the Wehrmacht and the S.S. [Hitler's Black-shirts]".

For more than a year they had received American training in infantry weapons and explosives and "political instruction" in small groups at a secluded site in the countryside and at a US military installation.

The intelligence wing of the Technical Service, the state president revealed, had drawn up lists and card indexes of persons who were to be "put out of the way" when the Soviet tanks began to roll. These records, which contained detailed descriptions and intimate biographical information, were of some 200 leading Social Democrats (including Zinn himself), 15 Communists, and various others, all of whom were deemed "politically untrustworthy" and opponents of West German militarization. Apparently, support for peaceful co-existence and detente with the Soviet bloc was sufficient to qualify one for inclusion on the hit-list, for one man was killed at the training site, charged with being an "East-West bridge builder". It was this murder that led to the exposure of the entire operation.

The United States admitted its role in the creation and training of the guerrilla army, but denied any involvement in the "illegal, internal, and political activities" of the organization. But Zinn reported that the Americans had learned of the plotting in May and had not actually dissolved the group until September, the same month that German Security Police arrested a number of the group's leaders. At some point, the American who directed the training courses, Sterling Garwood, had been "supplied with carbon copies of the card-index entries". It appears that at no time did US authorities communicate anything of this matter to the West German Government.

As the affair turned out, those who had been arrested were quickly released and the United States thwarted any further investigation in this the American Zone of occupied Germany. Commented Herr Zinn: "The only legal explanation for these releases can be that the people in Karlsruhe [the Federal Court] declared that they acted upon American direction."[9]

To add to the furor, the national leader of the Social Democrats accused the United States of financing an opposition group to infiltrate and undermine his party. Erich Ollenhauer, whose name had also appeared on the Technical Service's list, implied that American "clandestine" agencies were behind the plot despite the disapproval of high-ranking US officials.[10]

The revelations about the secret army and its hit-list resulted in a storm of ridicule and denunciation falling upon the United States from many quarters in West Germany. In particular, the delicious irony of the Americans working hand-in-glove with "ex"-Nazis did not escape the much-castigated German people.

This operation in Germany, it was revealed many years later, was part of a much wider network—called "Operation Gladio"—created by the CIA and other European intelligence services, with similar secret armies all over Western Europe. (See Western Europe chapter.)

9. Iran 1953

Making it safe for the King of Kings

"So this is how we get rid of that madman Mossadegh," announced John Foster Dulles to a group of top Washington policy makers one day in June 1953.[1] The Secretary of State held in his hand a plan of operation to overthrow the prime minister of Iran prepared by Kermit (Kim) Roosevelt of the CIA. There was scarcely any discussion amongst the high-powered men in the room, no probing questions, no legal or ethical issues raised.

"This was a grave decision to have made," Roosevelt later wrote. "It involved tremendous risk. Surely it deserved thorough examination, the closest consideration, somewhere at the very highest level. It had not received such thought at this meeting. In fact, I was morally certain that almost half of those present, if they had felt free or had the courage to speak, would have opposed the undertaking."[2]

Roosevelt, the grandson of Theodore and distant cousin of Franklin, was expressing surprise more than disappointment at glimpsing American foreign-policy-making undressed.

The original initiative to oust Mossadegh had come from the British, for the elderly Iranian leader had spearheaded the parliamentary movement to nationalize the British-owned Anglo-Iranian Oil Company (AIOC), the sole oil company operating in Iran. In March 1951, the bill for nationalization was passed, and at the end of April Mossadegh was elected prime minister by a large majority of Parliament. On 1 May, nationalization went into effect. The Iranian people, Mossadegh declared, "were opening a hidden treasure upon which lies a dragon".[3]

As the prime minister had anticipated, the British did not take the nationalization gracefully, though it was supported unanimously by the Iranian parliament and by the overwhelming majority of the Iranian people for reasons of both economic justice and national pride. The Mossadegh government tried to do all the right things to placate the British: It offered to set aside 25 percent of the net profits of the oil operation as compensation; it guaranteed the safety and the jobs of the British employees; it was willing to sell its oil without disturbance to the tidy control system so dear to the hearts of the international oil giants. But the British would have none of it. What they wanted was their oil company back. And they wanted Mossadegh's head. A servant does not affront his lord with impunity.

A military show of force by the British navy was followed by a ruthless international economic blockade and boycott, and a freezing of Iranian assets which brought Iran's oil exports and foreign trade to a virtual standstill, plunged the already impoverished country into near destitution, and made payment of any compensation impossible. Nonetheless, and long after they had moved to oust Mossadegh, the British demanded compensation not only for the physical assets of the AIOC, but for the value of their enterprise in developing the oil fields; a request impossible to meet, and, in the eyes of Iranian nationalists, something which decades of huge British profits had paid for many times over.

The British attempt at economic strangulation of Iran could not have gotten off the ground without the active co-operation and support of the Truman and Eisenhower administrations and American oil companies. At the same time, the Truman administration argued with the British that Mossadegh's collapse could open the door to the proverbial communist takeover.[4] When the British were later expelled from Iran, however, they had no alternative but to turn to the United States for assistance in toppling Mossadegh. In November 1952, the Churchill government approached Roosevelt, the de facto head of the CIA's Middle East division, who told the British that he felt that there was "no chance to win approval from the outgoing administration of Truman and Acheson. The new Republicans, however, might be quite different."[5]

John Foster Dulles was certainly different. The apocalyptic anti-communist saw in Mossadegh the epitome of all that he detested in the Third World: unequivocal neutralism in the cold war, tolerance of Communists, and disrespect for free enterprise, as demonstrated by the oil nationalization. (Ironically, in recent years Great Britain had nationalized several of its own basic industries, and the government was the majority owner of the AIOC.) To the likes of John Foster Dulles, the eccentric Dr. Mohammed Mossadegh was indeed a madman. And when the Secretary of State considered further that Iran was a nation exceedingly rich in the liquid gold, and that it shared a border with the Soviet Union more than

1,000 miles long, he was not unduly plagued by indecision as to whether the Iranian prime minister should finally retire from public life.

As matters turned out, the overthrow of Mossadegh in August 1953 was much more an American operation than a British one. Twenty-six years later, Kermit Roosevelt took the unusual step of writing a book about how he and the CIA carried out the operation. He called his book *Countercoup* to press home the idea that the CIA coup was staged only to prevent a takeover of power by the Iranian Communist Party (The Tudeh) closely backed by the Soviet Union. Roosevelt was thus arguing that Mossadegh had to be removed to prevent a Communist takeover, whereas the Truman administration had felt that Mossadegh had to be kept in power to prevent one.

It would be incorrect to state that Roosevelt offers little evidence to support his thesis of the Communist danger. It would be more precise to say that he offers *no* evidence at all. Instead, the reader is subjected to mere assertions of the thesis which are stated over and over, apparently in the belief that enough repetition will convince even the most skeptical. Thus are we treated to variations on the theme such as the following:

"The Soviet threat [was] indeed genuine, dangerous and imminent" ... Mossadegh "had formed an alliance" with the Soviet Union to oust the Shah ... "the obvious threat of Russian takeover" ... "the alliance between [Mossadegh] and the Russian-dominated Tudeh was taking on a threatening shape" ... Mossadegh's "increasing dependence on the Soviet Union" ... "the hand of the Tudeh, and behind them the Russians, is showing more openly every day" ... "Russian backing of the Tudeh and Tudeh backing of [Mossadegh] became ever more obvious" ... the Soviet Union was "ever more active in Iran. Their control over Tudeh leadership was growing stronger all the time. It was exercised often and, to our eyes, with deliberate ostentation" ...[6]

But none of this subversive and threatening activity was, apparently, ever open, obvious, or ostentatious enough to provide Roosevelt with a single example he could impart to a curious reader.

In actuality, although the Tudeh Party more or less faithfully followed the fluctuating Moscow line on Iran, the relation of the party to Mossadegh was much more complex than Roosevelt and other cold-war chroniclers have made it out to be. The Tudeh felt very ambiguous about the wealthy, eccentric, land-owning prime minister who, nonetheless, was standing up to imperialism. Dean Acheson, Truman's Secretary of State, described Mossadegh as "essentially a rich, reactionary, feudal-minded Persian",[7] hardly your typical Communist Party fellow-traveler.

On occasion the Tudeh had supported Mossadegh's policies; more often it had attacked them bitterly, and in one instance, on 15 July 1951, a Tudeh-sponsored demonstration was brutally suppressed by Mossadegh, resulting in some 100 deaths and 500 injured. The Iranian leader, moreover, had campaigned successfully against lingering Soviet occupation of northern Iran after World War II, and in October 1947 had led Parliament in its rejection of a government proposal that a joint Irano-Soviet oil company be set up to exploit the oil of northern Iran.[8]

What, indeed, did Mossadegh have to gain by relinquishing any of his power to the Tudeh and/or the Soviet Union? The idea that the Russians even desired the Tudeh to take power is no more than speculation. There was just as much evidence, or as little, to conclude that the Russians, once again, were more concerned about their relationship with Western governments than with the fate of a local Communist Party in a country outside the socialist bloc of Eastern Europe.

A secret State Department intelligence report, dated 9 January 1953, in the closing days of the Truman administration, stated that Mossadegh had not sought any alliance with the Tudeh, and that "The major opposition to the National Front [Mossadegh's governing coalition] arises from the vested interests, on the one hand, and the Tudeh Party on the other."[9]

The Tudeh Party had been declared illegal in 1949 and Mossadegh had not lifted that ban although he allowed the party to operate openly, at least to some extent because of his democratic convictions, and had appointed some Tudeh sympathizers to government posts.

Many of the Tudeh's objectives paralleled those espoused by the National Front, the State Department report observed, but "An open Tudeh move for power ... would probably unite independents and non-Communists of all political leanings and would result ... in energetic efforts to destroy Tudeh by force."[10]

The National Front itself was a coalition of highly diverse political and religious elements including right-wing anti-communists, held together by respect for Mossadegh's personal character and honesty, and by nationalistic sentiments, particularly in regard to the nationalization of oil.

In 1979, when he was asked about this State Department report, Kermit Roosevelt replied: "I don't know what to make of that ... Loy Henderson [US ambassador to Iran in 1953] thought that there was a serious danger that Mossadegh was going to, in effect, place Iran under Soviet domination."[11] Though he was the principal moving force behind the coup, Roosevelt was now passing the buck, and to a man who, as we shall see in the Middle East chapter, was given to alarmist statements about "communist takeovers".

One can but wonder what Roosevelt, or anyone else, made of a statement by John Foster Dulles before a Senate committee in July 1953, when the operation to oust Mossadegh was already in process. The Secretary of State, the press reported, testified "that there was 'no substantial evidence' to indicate that Iran was cooperating with Russia. On the whole, he added, Moslem opposition to communism is predominant, although at times the Iranian Government appears to rely for support on the Tudeh party, which is communistic."[12]

The young Shah of Iran had been relegated to little more than a passive role by Mossadegh and the Iranian political process. His power had been whittled away to the point where he was "incapable of independent action", noted the State Department intelligence report. Mossadegh was pressing for control of the armed forces and more say over expenditures of the royal court, and the inexperienced and indecisive Shah—the "King of Kings"—was reluctant to openly oppose the prime minister because of the latter's popularity.

The actual sequence of events instigated by Roosevelt which culminated in the Shah's ascendancy appears rather simple in hindsight, even naive, and owed not a little to luck. The first step was to reassure the Shah that Eisenhower and Churchill were behind him in his struggle for power with Mossadegh and were willing to provide whatever military and political support he needed. Roosevelt did not actually know what Eisenhower felt, or even knew, about the operation and went so far as to fabricate a message from the president to the Shah expressing his encouragement.[13]

At the same time, the Shah was persuaded to issue royal decrees dismissing Mossadegh as prime minister and replacing him with one Fazlollah Zahedi, a general who had been imprisoned during the war by the British for collaboration with the Nazis.[14] Late in the night of 14/15 August, the Shah's emissary delivered the royal decree to Mossadegh's home, which was guarded by troops. Not surprisingly, he was received very coolly and did not get in to see the prime minister. Instead, he was obliged to leave the decree with a servant who signed a receipt for the piece of paper dismissing his master from power. Equally unsurprising, Mossadegh did not abdicate. The prime minister, who maintained that only Parliament could dismiss him, delivered a radio broadcast the following morning in which he stated that the Shah, encouraged by "foreign elements", had attempted a *coup d'état*. Mossadegh then declared that he was, therefore, compelled to take full power unto himself. He denounced Zahedi as a traitor and sought to have him arrested, but the general had been hidden by Roosevelt's team.

The Shah, fearing all was lost, fled with his queen to Rome via Baghdad without so much as packing a suitcase. Undeterred, Roosevelt went ahead and directed the mimeographing of copies of the royal decrees for distribution to the public, and sent two of his Iranian agents to important military commanders to seek their support. It appears that this crucial matter was left to the last minute, almost as an afterthought. Indeed, one of the two Iranians had been recruited for the cause only the same day, and it was only he who succeeded in winning a commitment of military support from an Iranian colonel who had tanks and armored cars under his command.[15]

Beginning on 16 August, a mass demonstration arranged by the National Front, supporting Mossadegh and attacking the Shah and the United States, took place in the capital city, Teheran. Roosevelt characterizes the demonstrators simply as "the Tudeh, with strong Russian encouragement", once again failing to offer any evidence to support his assertion. The *New York Times* referred to them as "Tudeh partisans and Nationalist extremists", the latter term being one which could have applied to individuals comprising a wide range of political leanings.[16]

Among the demonstrators there were as well a number of individuals working for the CIA. According to Richard Cottam, an American academic and author reportedly in the employ of the Agency in Teheran at this time, these agents were sent "into the streets to act as if they were Tudeh. They were more than just provocateurs, they were shock troops, who acted as if they were Tudeh people throwing rocks at mosques and priests", the purpose of which was to stamp the Tudeh and, by implication, Mossadegh as being anti-religion.[17]

During the demonstrations, the Tudeh raised their familiar demand for the creation of a democratic republic. They appealed to Mossadegh to form a united front and to provide them with arms to defend against the coup, but the prime minister refused.[18] Instead, on 18 August he ordered the police and army to put an end to the Tudeh demonstrations which they did with considerable force. According to the accounts of Roosevelt and Ambassador Henderson, Mossadegh took this step as a result of a meeting with Henderson in which the ambassador complained of the extreme harassment being suffered by US citizens at the hands of the Iranians. It is left unclear by both of the Americans how much of this harassment was real and how much manufactured by them for the occasion. In any event, Henderson told Mossadegh that unless it ceased, he would be obliged to order all Americans to leave Iran at once. Mossadegh, says Henderson, begged him not to do this for an American evacuation would make it appear that his government was unable to control the country, although at the same time the prime minister was accusing the CIA of being behind the issuance of the royal decrees.[19] (The Tudeh newspaper at this time was demanding the expulsion of "interventionist" American diplomats.)[20]

Whatever Mossadegh's motivation, his action was again in sharp contradiction to the idea that he was in alliance with the Tudeh or that the party was in a position to grab the reins of power. Indeed, the Tudeh did not take to the streets again.

The following day, 19 August, Roosevelt's Iranian agents staged a parade through Teheran. With a fund of some one million dollars having been established in a safe in the American embassy, the "extremely competent professional 'organizers'," as Roosevelt called them, had no difficulty in buying themselves a mob, probably using but a small fraction of the fund. (The various accounts of the CIA role in Iran have the Agency spending from $10,000 to $19 million to overthrow Mossadegh. The larger amounts are based on reports that the CIA engaged in heavy bribery of members of Parliament and other influential Iranians to enlist their support against the prime minister.)

Soon a line of people could be seen coming out of the ancient bazaar, led by circus and athletic performers to attract the public. The marchers were waving banners, shouting "Long live the Shah!" Along the edges of the procession, men were passing out Iranian currency adorned with a portrait of the Shah. The demonstrators gathered followers as they went, people joining and picking up the chants, undoubtedly for a myriad of political and personal reasons. The balance of psychology had swung against Mossadegh.

Along the way, some marchers broke ranks to attack the offices of pro-Mossadegh newspapers and political parties, Tudeh and government offices. Presently, a voice broke in over the radio in Teheran announcing that "The Shah's instruction that Mossadegh be dismissed has been carried out. The new Prime Minister, Fazlollah Zahedi, is now in office. And His Imperial Majesty is on his way home!"

This was a lie, or a "pre-truth" as Roosevelt suggested. Only then did he go to fetch Zahedi from his hiding place. On the way, he happened to run into the commander of the air force who was among the marching throng. Roosevelt told the officer to get hold of a tank in which to carry Zahedi to Mossadegh's house in proper fashion.[21]

Kermit Roosevelt would have the reader believe that at this point it was all over but the shouting and the champagne he was soon to uncork: Mossadegh had fled, Zahedi had assumed power, the Shah had been notified to return—a dramatic, joyful, and peaceful triumph of popular will. Inexplicably, he neglects to mention at all that in the streets of Teheran and in front of Mossadegh's house that day, a nine-hour battle raged, with soldiers loyal to Mossadegh on one side and those supporting Zahedi and the Shah on the other. Some 300 people were reported killed and hundreds more wounded before Mossadegh's defenders finally succumbed.[22]

Roosevelt also fails to mention any contribution of the British to the whole operation, which considerably irritated the men in MI6, the CIA's counterpart, who claim that they, as well as AIOC staff, local businessmen and other Iranians, had indeed played a role in the events. But they have been tight-lipped about what that role was precisely.[23]

The US Military Mission in Iran also claimed a role in the action, as Major General George C. Stewart later testified before Congress:

> Now, when this crisis came on and the thing was about to collapse, we violated our normal criteria and among the other things we did, we provided the army immediately on an emergency basis, blankets, boots, uniforms, electric generators, and medical supplies that permitted and created the atmosphere in which they could support the Shah ... The guns that they had in their hands, the trucks that they rode in, the armored cars that they drove through the streets, and the radio communications that permitted their control, were all furnished through the military defense assistance program.[24]

The latter part of the General's statement would, presumably, apply to the other side as well.

"It is conceivable that the Tudeh could have turned the fortunes of the day against the royalists," wrote Kennett Love, a *New York Times* reporter who was in Teheran during the crucial days of August. "But for some reason they remained completely aloof from the conflict. ... My own conjecture is that the Tudeh were restrained by the Soviet Embassy because the Kremlin, in the first post-Stalin year, was not willing to take on such consequences as might have resulted from the establishment of a communist-controlled regime in Teheran."

Love's views, contained in a paper he wrote in 1960, may well have been inspired by information received from the CIA. By his own admission, he was in close contact with the Agency in Teheran and even aided them in their operation.[25]

Earlier in the year, the *New York Times* had noted that "prevailing opinion among detached observers in Teheran" was that "Mossadegh is the most popular politician in the country". During a period of more than 40 years in public life, Mossadegh had "acquired a reputation as an honest patriot".[26]

In July, the State Department Director of Iranian Affairs had testified that "Mossadegh has such tremendous control over the masses of people that it would be very difficult to throw him out."[27]

A few days later, "at least 100,000" people filled the streets of Teheran to express strong anti-US and anti-Shah sentiments. Though sponsored by the Tudeh, the turnout far exceeded any estimate of party adherents.[28]

But popularity and masses, of the unarmed kind, counted for little, for in the final analysis what Teheran witnessed was a military showdown carried out on both sides by soldiers obediently following the orders of a handful of officers, some of whom were staking their careers and ambitions on choosing the winning side; some had a more ideological commitment. The *New York Times* characterized the sudden reversal of Mossadegh's fortunes as "nothing more than a mutiny ... against pro-Mossadegh officers" by "the lower ranks" who revered the Shah, had brutally quelled the demonstrations the day before, but refused to do the same on 19 August, and instead turned against their officers.[29]

What connection Roosevelt and his agents had with any of the pro-Shah officers beforehand is not clear. In an interview given at about the same time that he finished his book, Roosevelt stated that a number of pro-Shah officers were given refuge in the CIA compound adjoining the US Embassy at the time the Shah fled to Rome.[30] But inasmuch as Roosevelt mentions not a word of this rather important and interesting development in his book, it must be regarded as yet another of his assertions to be approached with caution.

In any event, it may be that the 19 August demonstration organized by Roosevelt's team was just the encouragement and spark these officers were waiting for. Yet, if so, it further illustrates how much Roosevelt had left to chance.

In light of all the questionable, contradictory, and devious statements which emanated at times from John Foster Dulles, Kermit Roosevelt, Loy Henderson and other American officials, what conclusions can be drawn about American motivation in the toppling of Mossadegh? The consequences of the coup may offer the best guide.

For the next 25 years, the Shah of Iran stood fast as the United States' closest ally in the Third World, to a degree that would have shocked the independent and neutral Mossadegh. The Shah literally placed his country at the disposal of US military and intelligence organizations to be used as a cold-war weapon, a window and a door to the Soviet Union—electronic listening and radar posts were set up near the Soviet border; American aircraft used Iran as a base to launch surveillance flights over the Soviet Union; espionage agents were infiltrated across the border; various American military installations dotted the Iranian landscape. Iran was viewed as a vital link in the chain being forged by the United States to "contain" the Soviet Union. In a telegram to the British Acting Foreign Secretary in September, Dulles said: "I think if we can in coordination move quickly and effectively in Iran we would close the most dangerous gap in the line from Europe to South Asia."[31] In February 1955, Iran became a member of the Baghdad Pact, set up by the United States, in Dulles's words, "to create a solid band of resistance against the Soviet Union".[32]

One year after the coup, the Iranian government completed a contract with an international consortium of oil companies. Amongst Iran's new foreign partners, the British lost the exclusive rights they had enjoyed previously, being reduced now to 40 percent. Another 40 percent now went to American oil firms, the remainder to other countries. The British, however, received an extremely generous compensation for their former property.[33]

In 1958, Kermit Roosevelt left the CIA and presently went to work for Gulf Oil Co., one of the American oil firms in the consortium. In this position, Roosevelt was director of Gulf's relations with the US government and foreign governments, and had occasion to deal with the Shah. In 1960, Gulf appointed him a vice president. Subsequently, Roosevelt formed a consulting firm, Downs and Roosevelt, which, between 1967 and 1970, reportedly received $116,000 a year above expenses for its efforts on behalf of the Iranian government. Another client, the Northrop Corporation, a Los Angeles-based aerospace company, paid Roosevelt $75,000 a year to aid in its sales to Iran, Saudi Arabia and other countries.[34] (See the Middle East chapter for Roosevelt's CIA connection with King Saud of Saudi Arabia.)

Another American member of the new consortium was Standard Oil Co. of New Jersey (now Exxon), a client of Sullivan and Cromwell, the New York law firm of which John Foster Dulles had long been the senior member. Brother Allen, Director of the CIA, had also been a member of the firm.[35] Syndicated columnist Jack Anderson reported some years later that the Rockefeller family, who controlled Standard Oil and Chase Manhattan Bank, had "helped arrange the CIA coup that brought down Mossadegh". Anderson listed a number of ways in which the Shah demonstrated his gratitude to the Rockefellers, including heavy deposits of his personal fortune in Chase Manhattan, and housing developments in Iran built by a Rockefeller family company.[36]

The standard "textbook" account of what took place in Iran in 1953 is that—whatever else one might say for or against the operation—the United States saved Iran from a Soviet/Communist takeover. Yet, during the two years of American and British subversion of a bordering country, the Soviet Union did nothing that would support such a premise. When the British Navy staged the largest concentration of its forces since World War II in Iranian waters, the Soviets took no belligerent steps; nor when Great Britain instituted draconian international sanctions which left Iran in a deep economic crisis and extremely vulnerable, did the oil fields "fall hostage" to the Bolshevik Menace; this, despite "the whole of the Tudeh Party at its disposal" as agents, as Roosevelt put it.[37] Not even in the face of the coup, with its imprint of foreign hands, did Moscow make a threatening move; neither did Mossadegh at any point ask for Russian help.

One year later, however, the *New York Times* could editorialize that "Moscow ... counted its chickens before they were hatched and thought that Iran would be the next 'People's Democracy'." At the same time, the newspaper warned, with surprising arrogance, that "underdeveloped countries with rich resources now have an object lesson in the heavy cost that must be paid by one of their number which goes berserk with fanatical nationalism."[38]

A decade later, Allen Dulles solemnly stated that communism had "achieved control of the governmental apparatus" in Iran.[39] And a decade after that, *Fortune* magazine, to cite one of many examples, kept the story alive by writing that Mossadegh "plotted with the Communist party of Iran, the Tudeh, to overthrow Shah Mohammed Reza Pahlevi and hook up with the Soviet Union."[40]

And what of the Iranian people? What did being saved from communism do for them? For the preponderance of the population, life under the Shah was a grim tableau of grinding poverty, police terror, and torture. Thousands were executed in the name of fighting communism. Dissent was crushed from the outset of the new regime with American assistance. Kennett Love wrote that he believed that CIA officer George Carroll, whom he knew personally, worked with General Farhat Dadsetan, the new military governor of Teheran, "on preparations for the very efficient smothering of a potentially dangerous dissident movement emanating from the bazaar area and the Tudeh in the first two weeks of November, 1953".[41]

The notorious Iranian secret police, SAVAK, created under the guidance of the CIA and Israel,[42] spread its tentacles all over the world to punish Iranian dissidents. According to a former CIA analyst on Iran, SAVAK was instructed in torture techniques by the Agency.[43] Amnesty International summed up the situation in 1976 by noting that Iran had the "highest rate of death penalties in the world, no valid system of civilian courts and a history of torture which is beyond belief. No country in the world has a worse record in human rights than Iran."[44]

When to this is added a level of corruption that "startled even the most hardened observers of Middle Eastern thievery",[45] it is understandable that the Shah needed his huge military and police force, maintained by unusually large US aid and training programs,[46] to keep the lid down for as long as he did. Said Senator Hubert Humphrey, apparently with some surprise:

> Do you know what the head of the Iranian Army told one of our people? He said the Army was in good shape, thanks to U.S. aid—it was now capable of coping with the civilian population. That Army isn't going to fight the Russians. It's planning to fight the Iranian people.[47]

Where force might fail, the CIA turned to its most trusted weapon—money. To insure support for the Shah, or at least the absence of dissent, the Agency began making payments to Iranian religious leaders, always a capricious bunch. The payments to the ayatollahs and mullahs began in 1953 and continued regularly until 1977 when President Carter abruptly halted them. One "informed intelligence source" estimated that the amount paid reached as much as $400 million a year; others thought that figure too high, which it certainly seems to be. The cut-off of funds to the holy men, it is believed, was one of the elements which precipitated the beginning of the end for the King of Kings.[48]

10. Guatemala 1953-1954

While the world watched

To whom do you turn for help when the police are assaulting you? The old question.

To whom does a poor banana republic turn when a CIA army is advancing upon its territory and CIA planes are overhead bombing the country?

The leaders of Guatemala tried everyone—the United Nations, the Organization of

American States, other countries individually, the world press, even the United States itself, in the desperate hope that it was all a big misunderstanding, that in the end, reason would prevail.

Nothing helped. Dwight Eisenhower, John Foster Dulles and Allen Dulles had decided that the legally-elected government of Jacobo Arbenz was "communist", therefore must go; and go it did, in June 1954.

In the midst of the American preparation to overthrow the government, the Guatemalan Foreign Minister, Guillermo Toriello, lamented that the United States was categorizing "as 'communism' every manifestation of nationalism or economic independence, any desire for social progress, any intellectual curiosity, and any interest in progressive liberal reforms."[1]

Toriello was close to the truth, but Washington officials retained enough contact with reality and world opinion to be aware of the inappropriateness of coming out against nationalism, independence or reform. Thus it was that Secretary of State Dulles asserted that Guatemalans were living under a "Communist type of terrorism"[2] ... President Eisenhower warned about "the Communist dictatorship" establishing "an outpost on this continent to the detriment of all the American nations"[3] ... the US Ambassador to Guatemala, John Peurifoy, declared that "We cannot permit a Soviet Republic to be established between Texas and the Panama Canal"[4] ... others warned that Guatemala could become a base from which the Soviet Union might actually seize the Canal ... Senator Margaret Chase Smith hinted, unmistakably, that the "unjustified increases in the price of coffee" imported from Guatemala were due to communist control of the country, and called for an investigation[5] ... and so it went.

The Soviet Union could be excused if it was somewhat bewildered by all the rhetoric, for the Russians had scant interest in Guatemala, did not provide the country with any kind of military assistance, did not even maintain diplomatic relations with it, thus did not have the normally indispensable embassy from which to conduct such nefarious schemes. (During this period, the height of McCarthyist "logic", there were undoubtedly those Americans who reasoned: "All the better to deceive us!")

With the exception of one occasion, the countries of Eastern Europe had as little to do with Guatemala as did the Soviet Union. A month before the coup, that is, long after Washington had begun preparation for it, Czechoslovakia made a single arms sale to Guatemala for cash, something the Czechs would no doubt have done for any other country willing to pay the price. The weapons, it turned out, were, in the words of the *New York Times*, "worthless military junk". *Time* magazine pooh-poohed the newspaper's report and cited US military men giving a better appraisal of the weapons. It may be that neither *Time* nor the military men could conceive that one member of the International Communist Conspiracy could do such a thing to another member.[6]

The American propaganda mill made much of this arms transaction. Less publicized was the fact that Guatemala had to seek arms from Czechoslovakia because the United States had refused to sell it any since 1948 due to its reformist governments, and had pressured other countries to do the same despite Arbenz's repeated pleas to lift the embargo.[7]

Like the Soviets, Arbenz had reason to wonder about the American charges. The Guatemalan president, who took office in March 1951 after being elected by a wide margin, had no special contact or spiritual/ideological ties with the Soviet Union or the rest of the Communist bloc. Although American policymakers and the American press, explicitly and implicitly, often labeled Arbenz a communist, there were those in Washington who knew better, at least during their more dispassionate moments. Under Arbenz's administration, Guatemala had voted at the United Nations so closely with the United States on issues of "Soviet imperialism" that a State Department group occupied with planning Arbenz's overthrow concluded that propaganda concerning Guatemala's UN record "would not be particularly helpful in our case".[8] And a State Department analysis paper reported that the Guatemalan president had support "not only from Communist-led labor and the radical fringe of professional and intellectual groups, but also among many anti-Communist nationalists in urban areas".[9]

Nonetheless, Washington repeatedly and adamantly expressed its displeasure about the presence of communists working in the Guatemalan government and their active participation in the nation's political life. Arbenz maintained that this was no more than proper in a democracy, while Washington continued to insist that Arbenz was too tolerant of such people—not because of anything they had done which was intrinsically threatening or offensive to the US or Western civilization, but simply because they were of the species communist, well known for its infinite capacity for treachery. Ambassador Peurifoy—a diplomat whose suit might have been pinstriped, but whose soul was a loud check—warned Arbenz that US-Guatemalan relations would remain strained so long as a single communist remained on the public payroll.[10]

The centerpiece of Arbenz's program was land reform. The need for it was clearly expressed in the all-too-familiar underdeveloped-country statistics: In a nation overwhelmingly rural, 2.2 percent of the landowners owned 70 percent of the arable land; the annual per capita income of agricultural workers was $87. Before the revolution of 1944, which overthrew the Ubico dictatorship, "farm laborers had been roped together by the Army for delivery to the low-land farms where they were kept in debt slavery by the landowners."[11]

The expropriation of large tracts of uncultivated acreage which was distributed to approximately 100,000 landless peasants, the improvement in union rights for the workers, and other social reforms, were the reasons Arbenz had won the support of Communists and other leftists, which was no more than to be expected. When Arbenz was criticized for accepting Communist support, he challenged his critics to prove their good faith by backing his reforms themselves. They failed to do so, thus revealing where the basis of their criticism lay.[12]

The party formed by the Communists, the Guatemalan Labor Party, held four seats in Congress, the smallest component of Arbenz's ruling coalition which commanded a total of 51 seats in the 1953-54 legislature.[13] Communists held several important sub-cabinet posts but none was ever appointed to the cabinet. In addition, there were Communists employed in the bureaucracy, particularly in the administration of land reform.[14]

Lacking anything of substance they could accuse the Guatemalan left of, Washington officials were reduced to condemnation by semantics. Thus, communists, unlike normal human beings, did not take jobs in the government—they "infiltrated" the government. Communists did not support a particular program—they "exploited" it. Communists did not back Arbenz—they "used" him. Moreover, communists "controlled" the labor movement and land reform—but what type of person is it who devotes himself in an under-developed country to furthering the welfare of workers and peasants? None other than the type that Washington calls "communist".

The basic idea behind the employment of such language—which was standard Western fare throughout the cold war—was to deny the idea that communists could be people sincerely concerned about social change. American officials denied it to each other as well as to the world. Here, for example, is an excerpt from a CIA report about Guatemala, prepared in 1952 for the edification of the White House and the intelligence community:

Communist political success derives in general from the ability of individual Communists and fellow travelers to identify themselves with the nationalist and social aspirations of the Revolution of 1944. In this manner, they have been successful in infiltrating the Administration and pro-Administration political parties and have gained control of organized labor ... [Arbenz] is essentially an opportunist whose politics are largely a matter of historical accident ... The extension of [communist] influence has been facilitated by the applicability of Marxist 'cliches' to the anti-colonial and social aims of the Guatemalan Revolution.[15]

The first plan to topple Arbenz was a CIA operation approved by President Truman in 1952, but at the eleventh hour, Secretary of State Dean Acheson persuaded Truman to abort it.[16] However, soon after Eisenhower became president in January 1953, the plan was resurrected.

Both administrations were pressured by executives of United Fruit Company, much of whose vast and uncultivated land in Guatemala had been expropriated by the Arbenz government as part of the land reform program. The company wanted nearly $16 million for the land, the government was offering $525,000, United Fruit's own declared valuation for tax purposes.[17]

United Fruit functioned in Guatemala as a state within a state. It owned the country's telephone and telegraph facilities, administered its only important Atlantic harbor, and monopolized its banana exports. A subsidiary of the company owned nearly every mile of railroad track in the country. The fruit company's influence amongst Washington's power elite was equally impressive. On a business and/or personal level, it had close ties to the Dulles brothers, various State Department officials, congressmen, the American Ambassador to the United Nations, and others. Anne Whitman, the wife of the company's public relations director, was President Eisenhower's personal secretary. Under-secretary of State (and formerly Director of the CIA) Walter Bedell Smith was seeking an executive position with United Fruit at the same time he was helping to plan the coup. He was later named to the company's board of directors.[18]

Under Arbenz, Guatemala constructed an Atlantic port and a highway to compete with United Fruit's holdings, and built a hydro-electric plant to offer cheaper energy than the US-controlled electricity monopoly. Arbenz's strategy was to limit the power of foreign companies through direct competition rather than through nationalization, a policy not feasible of course when it came to a fixed quantity like land. In his inaugural address, Arbenz stated that:

> Foreign capital will always be welcome as long as it adjusts to local conditions, remains always subordinate to Guatemalan laws, cooperates with the economic development of the country, and strictly abstains from intervening in the nation's social and political life.[19]

This hardly described United Fruit's role in Guatemala. Amongst much else, the company had persistently endeavored to frustrate Arbenz's reform programs, discredit him and his government, and induce his downfall.

Arbenz was, accordingly, wary of multinationals and could not be said to welcome them into his country with open arms. This attitude, his expropriation of United Fruit's land, and his "tolerance of communists" were more than enough to make him a marked man in Washington. The United States saw these policies as being inter-related: that is, it was communist influence—not any economic or social exigency of Guatemalan life—which was responsible for the government's treatment of American firms.

In March 1953, the CIA approached disgruntled right-wing officers in the Guatemalan army and arranged to send them arms. United Fruit donated $64,000 in cash. The following month, uprisings broke out in several towns but were quickly put down by loyal troops. The rebels were put on trial and revealed the fruit company's role in the plot, but not the CIA's.[20]

The Eisenhower administration resolved to do the job right the next time around. With cynical glee, almost an entire year was spent in painstaking, step-by-step preparation for the overthrow of Jacobo Arbenz Guzman. Of the major CIA undertakings, few have been as well documented as has the coup in Guatemala. With the release of many formerly classified government papers, the following story has emerged.[21]

Headquarters for the operation were established in Opa Locka, Florida, on the outskirts of Miami. The Nicaraguan dictator Anastasio Somoza lent/leased his country out as a site for an airstrip and for hundreds of men—Guatemalan exiles and US and Central American mercenaries—to receive training in the use of weapons and radio broadcasting, as well as in the fine arts of sabotage and demolition. Thirty airplanes were assigned for use in the "Liberation", stationed in Nicaragua, Honduras and the Canal Zone, to be flown by American pilots. The Canal Zone was set aside as a weapons depot from which arms were gradually distributed to the rebels who were to assemble in Honduras under the command of Colonel Carlos Castillo Armas before crossing into Guatemala. Soviet-marked weapons were also gathered for the purpose of planting them inside Guatemala before the invasion to reinforce US charges of Russian intervention. And, as important as arms, it turned out, hidden radio transmitters were placed in and around the perimeter of Guatemala, including one in the US Embassy.

An attempt was made to blow up the trains carrying the Czech weapons from portside to Guatemala City; however, a torrential downpour rendered the detonators useless, whereupon the CIA paramilitary squad opened fire on one train, killing a Guatemalan soldier and wounding three others; but the convoy of trains made it safely to its destination.

After the Czech ship had arrived in Guatemala, Eisenhower ordered the stopping of "suspicious foreign-flag vessels on the high seas off Guatemala to examine cargo".[22] The State Department's legal adviser wrote a brief which concluded in no uncertain terms that "Such action would constitute a violation of international law." No matter. At least two foreign vessels were stopped and searched, one French and one Dutch. It was because of such actions by the British that the United States had fought the War of 1812.

The Guatemalan military came in for special attention. The US ostentatiously signed mutual security treaties with Honduras and Nicaragua, both countries hostile to Arbenz, and dispatched large shipments of arms to them in the hope that this would signal a clear enough threat to the Guatemalan military to persuade it to withdraw its support of Arbenz. Additionally, the US Navy dispatched two submarines from Key West, saying only that they were going "south". Several days later, the Air Force, amid considerable fanfare, sent three B-36 bombers on a "courtesy call" to Nicaragua.

The CIA also made a close study of the records of members of the Guatemalan officer corps and offered bribes to some of them. One of the Agency's clandestine radio stations broadcast appeals aimed at military men, as well as others, to join the liberation movement. The station reported that Arbenz was secretly planning to disband or disarm the armed forces and replace it with a people's militia. CIA planes dropped leaflets over Guatemala carrying the same message.

Eventually, at Ambassador Peurifoy's urging, a group of high-ranking officers called on Arbenz to ask that he dismiss all communists who held posts in his administration. The president assured them that the communists did not represent a danger, that they did not run the government, and that it would be undemocratic to dismiss them. At a second meeting, the officers also demanded that Arbenz reject the creation of the "people's militia".

Arbenz himself was offered a bribe by the CIA, whether to abdicate his office or something less is not clear. A large sum of money was deposited in a Swiss bank for him, but he, or a subordinate, rejected the offer.

On the economic front, contingency plans were made for such things as cutting off Guatemalan credit abroad, disrupting its oil supplies, and causing a run on its foreign reserves.[23] But it was on the propaganda front that American ingenuity shone at its brightest. Inasmuch as the Guatemalan government was being overthrown because it was communist, the fact of its communism would have to be impressed upon the rest of Latin America. Accordingly, the US Information Agency (USIA) began to place unattributed articles in foreign newspapers labeling particular Guatemalan officials as communist and referring to various actions by the Guatemalan government as "communist-inspired". In the few weeks prior to Arbenz's fall alone, more than 200 articles about Guatemala were written and placed in scores of Latin American newspapers.

Employing a method which was to become a standard CIA/USIA feature all over Latin America and elsewhere, as we shall see, articles placed in one country were picked up by newspapers in other countries, either as a result of CIA payment or unwittingly because the story was of interest. Besides the obvious advantage of multiplying the potential audience, the tactic gave the appearance that independent world opinion was taking a certain stand and further obscured the American connection.

The USIA also distributed more than 100,000 copies of a pamphlet entitled "Chronology of Communism in Guatemala" throughout the hemisphere, as well as 27,000 copies of anti-communist cartoons and posters. The American propaganda agency, moreover, produced three films on Guatemala, with predictable content, and newsreels favorable to the United States for showing free in cinemas.

Francis Cardinal Spellman of New York, a prelate possessed of anti-communism, a man who feared social change more than he feared God, was visited by the CIA. Would his Reverence arrange CIA contact with Archbishop Mariano Rossell Arellano of Guatemala? The Cardinal would be delighted. Thus it came to pass that on 9 April 1954, a pastoral letter was read in Guatemalan Catholic churches calling to the attention of the congregations the presence in the country of a devil called communism and demanding that the people "rise as a single man against this enemy of God and country", or at least not rally in Arbenz's defense. To appreciate the value of this, one must remember that Guatemala's peasant class was not only highly religious, but that very few of them were able to read, and so could receive the Lord's Word only in this manner. For those who could read, many thousands of pamphlets carrying the Archbishop's message were air-dropped around the country.

In May, the CIA covertly sponsored a "Congress Against Soviet Intervention in Latin America" in Mexico City. The same month, Somoza called in the diplomatic corps in Nicaragua and told them, his voice shaking with anger, that his police had discovered a secret Soviet shipment of arms (which had been planted by the CIA) near the Pacific Coast, and suggested that the communists wanted to convert Nicaragua into "a new Korean situation". A few weeks later, an unmarked plane parachuted arms with Soviet markings onto Guatemala's coast.

On such fare did the people of Latin America dine for decades. By such tactics were they educated about "communism".

In late January 1954 the operation appeared to have suffered a serious setback when photostat copies of Liberation documents found their way into Arbenz's hands. A few days later, Guatemala's newspapers published copies of correspondence signed by Castillo Armas, Somoza and others under banner headlines. The documents revealed the existence of some of the staging, training and invasion plans, involving, amongst others, the "Government of the North".[24]

The State Department labeled the accusations of a US role "ridiculous and untrue" and said it would not comment further because it did not wish to give them a dignity they did not deserve. Said a Department spokesperson: "It is the policy of the United States not to interfere in the internal affairs of other nations. This policy has repeatedly been reaffirmed under the present administration."

Time magazine gave no credence whatsoever to the possibility of American involvement in such a plot, concluding that the whole exposé had been "masterminded in Moscow".[25]

The *New York Times* was not so openly cynical, but its story gave no indication that there might be any truth to the matter. "Latin American observers in New York," reported the newspaper, "said the 'plot' charges savored of communist influence." This article was followed immediately on the page by one headed "Red Labor Chiefs Meet. Guatemalan Confederation Opens Its Congress".[26]

And the CIA continued with its preparations as if nothing had happened.

The offensive began in earnest on 18 June with planes dropping leaflets over Guatemala demanding that Arbenz resign immediately or else various sites would be bombed. CIA radio stations broadcast similar messages. That afternoon, the planes returned to machine-gun houses near military barracks, drop fragmentation bombs and strafe the National Palace.

Over the following week, the air attacks continued daily—strafing or bombing ports, fuel tanks, ammunition dumps, military barracks, the international airport, a school, and several cities; nine persons, including a three-year-old girl, were reported wounded; an unknown number of houses were set afire by incendiary explosives. During one night-time raid, a tape recording of a bomb attack was played over loudspeakers set up on the roof of the US Embassy to heighten the anxiety of the capital's residents. When Arbenz went on the air to try and calm the public's fear, the CIA radio team jammed the broadcast.

Meanwhile, the Agency's army had crossed into Guatemala from Honduras and captured a few towns, but its progress in the face of resistance by the Guatemalan army was unspectacular. On the broadcasts of the CIA's "Voice of Liberation" the picture was different: The rebels were everywhere and advancing; they were of large numbers and picking up volunteers as they marched; war and upheaval in all corners; fearsome battles and major defeats for the Guatemalan army. Some of these broadcasts were transmitted over regular public and even military channels, serving to convince some of Arbenz's officers that the reports were genuine. In the same way, the CIA was able to answer real military messages with fake responses. All manner of disinformation was spread and rumors fomented; dummy parachute drops were made in scattered areas to heighten the belief that a major invasion was taking place.

United Fruit Company's publicity office circulated photographs to journalists of mutilated bodies about to be buried in a mass grave as an example of the atrocities committed by the Arbenz regime. The photos received extensive coverage. Thomas McCann of the company's publicity office later revealed that he had no idea what the photos represented: "They could just as easily have been the victims of either side—or of an earthquake. The point is, they were widely accepted for what they were purported to be—victims of communism."[27]

In a similar vein, Washington officials reported on political arrests and censorship in Guatemala without reference to the fact that the government was under siege (let alone who was behind the siege), that suspected plotters and saboteurs were the bulk of those being arrested, or that, overall, the Arbenz administration had a fine record on civil liberties. The performance of the American press in this regard was little better.

The primary purpose of the bombing and the many forms of disinformation was to make it appear that military defenses were crumbling, that resistance was futile, thus provoking confusion and division in the Guatemalan armed forces and causing some elements to turn against Arbenz. The psychological warfare conducted over the radio was directed by E. Howard Hunt, later of Watergate fame, and David Atlee Phillips, a newcomer to the CIA. When Phillips was first approached about the assignment, he asked his superior, Tracy Barnes, in all innocence, "But Arbenz became President in a free election. What right do we have to help someone topple his government and throw him out of office?"

"For a moment," wrote Phillips later, "I detected in his face a flicker of concern, a doubt, the reactions of a sensitive man." But Barnes quickly recovered and repeated the party line about the Soviets establishing "an easily expandable beachhead" in Central America.[28]

Phillips never looked back. When he retired from the CIA in the mid-1970s, he founded the Association of Retired Intelligence Officers, an organization formed to counteract the flood of unfavorable publicity sweeping over the Agency at the time.

American journalists reporting on the events in Guatemala continued to exhibit neither an investigative inclination nor a healthy conspiracy mentality. But what was obscure to the US press was patently obvious to large numbers of Latin Americans. Heated protests against the United States broke out during this week in June in at least eleven countries and was echoed by the governments of Ecuador, Argentina, Uruguay, and Chile which condemned American "intervention" and "aggression".

Life magazine noted these protests by observing that "world communism was efficiently using the Guatemalan show to strike a blow at the U.S." It scoffed at the idea that Washington was behind the revolt.[29] *Newsweek* reported that Washington "officials interpreted" the outcry "as an indication of the depth of Red penetration into the Americas".[30] A State Department memo at the time, however, privately acknowledged that much of the protest emanated from non-communist and even pro-American moderates.[31]

On 21 and 22 June, Guatemalan Foreign Minister Toriello made impassioned appeals to the United Nations for help in resolving the crisis. American UN Ambassador Henry Cabot Lodge tried to block the Security Council from discussing a resolution to send an investigating team to Guatemala, characterizing Toriello's appeals as communist maneuvers. But under heavy pressure from UN Secretary-General Dag Hammarskjöld, the Council was convened. Before the vote, while Lodge worked on the smaller nations represented on the Council, Eisenhower and Dulles came down hard on France and Great Britain, both of whom favored the resolution. Said the President of the United States to his Secretary of State: "The British expect us to give them a free ride and side with them on Cyprus. And yet they won't even support us on Guatemala! Let's give them a lesson."[32]

As matters turned out, the resolution was defeated by five votes to four, with Britain and France abstaining, although their abstentions were not crucial inasmuch as seven votes were required for passage. Hammarskjöld was so upset with the American machinations, which he believed undercut the strength of the United Nations, that he confided that he might be forced "to reconsider my present position in the United Nations".[33]

During this same period, the CIA put into practice a plan to create an "incident". Agency planes were dispatched to drop several harmless bombs on Honduran territory. The Honduran government then complained to the UN and the Organization of American States, claiming that the country had been attacked by Guatemalan planes.[34]

Arbenz finally received an ultimatum from certain army officers: Resign or they would come to an agreement with the invaders. The CIA and Ambassador Peurifoy had been offering payments to officers to defect, and one army commander reportedly accepted $60,000 to surrender his troops. With his back to the wall, Arbenz made an attempt to arm civilian supporters to fight for the government, but army officers blocked the disbursement of weapons. The Guatemalan president knew that the end was near.

The Voice of Liberation meanwhile was proclaiming that two large and heavily armed columns of invaders were moving towards Guatemala City. As the hours passed, the further advance of the mythical forces was announced, while Castillo Armas and his small band had actually not progressed very far from the Honduran border. The American disinformation and rumor offensive continued in other ways as well, and Arbenz, with no one he could trust to give him accurate information, could no longer be certain that there wasn't at least some truth to the radio bulletins.

Nothing would be allowed to threaten the victory so near at hand: A British freighter docked in Guatemala and suspected of having arrived with fuel for Arbenz's military vehicles, was bombed and sunk by a CIA plane after the crew had been warned to flee. It turned out that the ship had come to Guatemala to pick up a cargo of coffee and cotton.

A desperate Toriello pleaded repeatedly with Ambassador Peurifoy to call off the bombings, offering even to reopen negotiations about United Fruit's compensation. In a long cable to John Foster Dulles, the foreign minister described the aerial attacks on the civilian population, expressed his country's defenselessness against the bombings, and appealed to the United States to use its good offices to put an end to them. In what must have been a deeply humiliating task, Toriello stated all of this without a hint that the United States was, or could be, a party to any of it. The pleas were not simply too late. They had *always* been too late.

The Castillo Armas forces could not have defeated the much larger Guatemalan army, but the air attacks, combined with the belief in the invincibility of the enemy, persuaded Guatemalan military officers to force Arbenz to resign. No Communists, domestic or foreign, came to his aid. He asked the head of the officers, Army Chief of Staff Col. Carlos Díaz, only that he give his word not to negotiate with Castillo Armas, and Díaz, who despised the rebel commander as much as Arbenz did, readily agreed. What Díaz did not realize was that the United States would not be satisfied merely to oust Arbenz. Castillo Armas had been groomed as the new head of government, and that was not negotiable.

A CIA official, Enno Hobbing, who had just arrived in Guatemala to help draft a new constitution (sic) for the incoming regime, told Díaz that he had "made a big mistake" in taking over the government. "Colonel," said Hobbing, "you're just not convenient for the requirements of American foreign policy."

Presently, Peurifoy confronted Díaz with the demand that he deal directly with Castillo Armas. At the same time, the Ambassador showed the Guatemalan general a long list of names of some leaders, requiring that Díaz shoot them all within 24 hours.

"But why?" Díaz asked.

"Because they're communists," replied Peurifoy.[35]

Although Díaz was not a communist sympathizer, he refused both requests, and indicated that the struggle against the invaders would continue.[36] Peurifoy left, livid with anger. He then sent a simple cable to CIA headquarters in Florida: "We have been doubled-crossed. BOMB!" Within hours, a CIA plane took off from Honduras, bombed a military base and destroyed the government radio station. Col. Castillo Armas, whose anti-communism the United States could trust, was soon the new leader of Guatemala.

The propaganda show was not yet over. At the behest of the CIA, Guatemalan military officers of the new regime took foreign correspondents on a tour of Arbenz's former residence where they could see for themselves rooms filled with school textbooks published in ... yes, the Soviet Union. The *New York Times* correspondent, Paul Kennedy, considered to be strongly anti-Arbenz, concluded that the "books had been planted" and did not bother to report the story.[37] *Time* made no mention of the books either, but somehow came upon the story that mobs had plundered Arbenz's home and found "stacks of communist propaganda and four bags of earth, one each from Russia, China, Siberia and Mongolia."[38] *Time*'s article made it clear enough that it now knew of the American role in Arbenz's downfall (although certainly not the full story), but the magazine had nothing to say about the propriety of overthrowing a democratically elected government by force.

Castillo Armas celebrated the liberation of Guatemala in various ways. In July alone, thousands were arrested on suspicion of communist activity. Many were tortured or killed. In August a law was passed and a committee set up which could declare anyone a communist, with no right of appeal. Those so declared could be arbitrarily arrested for up to six months, could not own a radio or hold public office. Within four months the committee had registered 72,000 names. A committee official said it was aiming for 200,000.[39] Further implementation of the agrarian reform law was stopped and all expropriations of land already carried out were declared invalid.[40] United Fruit Company not only received all its land back, but the government banned the banana workers' unions as well. Moreover, seven employees of the company who had been active labor organizers were found mysteriously murdered in Guatemala City.[41]

The new regime also disenfranchised three-quarters of Guatemala's voters by barring illiterates from the electoral rolls and outlawed all political parties, labor confederations and peasant organizations. To this was added the closing down of opposition newspapers (which Arbenz had not done) and the burning of "subversive" books, including Victor Hugo's *Les Miserables*, Dostoyevsky novels, and the works of Guatemala's Nobel Prize-winning author Miguel Angel Asturias, a biting critic of United Fruit.[42]

Meanwhile, John Foster Dulles, who was accused by Toriello of seeking to establish a "banana curtain" in Central America,[43] was concerned that some "communists" might escape retribution. In cables he exchanged with Ambassador Peurifoy, Dulles insisted that the government arrest those Guatemalans who had taken refuge in foreign embassies and that "criminal charges" be brought against them to prevent them leaving the country, charges such as "having been covert Moscow agents". The Secretary of State argued that communists should be automatically denied the right of asylum because they were connected with an international conspiracy. The only way they should be allowed to leave, he asserted, was if they agreed to be sent to the Soviet Union. But Castillo Armas refused to accede to Dulles's wishes on this particular issue, influenced perhaps by the fact that he, as well as some of his colleagues, had been granted political asylum in an embassy at one time or another.[44]

One of those who sought asylum in the Argentine Embassy was a 25-year-old

Argentine doctor named Ernesto "Che" Guevara. Guevara, who had been living in Guatemala since sometime in 1953, had tried to spark armed resistance to the invading forces, but without any success. Guevara's experience in Guatemala had a profound effect upon his political consciousness. His first wife, Hilda Gadea, whom he met there, later wrote:

> Up to that point, he used to say, he was merely a sniper, criticizing from a theoretical point of view the political panorama of our America. From here on he was convinced that the struggle against the oligarchic system and the main enemy, Yankee imperialism, must be an armed one, supported by the people.[45]

In the wake of the coup, the United States confiscated a huge amount of documents from the Guatemalan government, undoubtedly in the hope of finally uncovering the hand of The International Communist Conspiracy behind Arbenz. If this is what was indeed discovered, it has not been made public.

On 30 June, while the dust was still settling, Dulles summed up the situation in Guatemala in a speech which was a monument to coldwarspeak:

> [The events in Guatemala] expose the evil purpose of the Kremlin to destroy the inter-American system ... having gained control of what they call the mass organizations, [the communists] moved on to take over the official press and radio of the Guatemalan Government. They dominated the social security organization and ran the agrarian reform program ... dictated to the Congress and to the President ... Arbenz ... was openly manipulated by the leaders of communism ... The Guatemalan regime enjoyed the full support of Soviet Russia ... [the] situation is being cured by the Guatemalans themselves.[46]

When it came to rewriting history, however, Dulles's speech had nothing on these lines from a CIA memo written in August 1954 and only for internal consumption no less: "When the communists were forced by outside pressure to attempt to take over Guatemala completely, they forced Arbenz to resign (deleted). They then proceeded to establish a Communist Junta under Col. Carlos Díaz."[47]

And in October, John Peurifoy sat before a congressional committee and told them:.

> My role in Guatemala prior to the revolution was strictly that of a diplomatic observer ... The revolution that overthrew the Arbenz government was engineered and instigated by those people in Guatemala who rebelled against the policies and ruthless oppression of the Communist-controlled government.[48]

Later, Dwight Eisenhower was to write about Guatemala in his memoirs. The former president chose not to offer the slightest hint that the United States had anything to do with the planning or instigation of the coup, and indicated that his administration had only the most tangential of connections to its execution.[49] (When Soviet leader Nikita Khrushchev's memoirs were published in the West, the publisher saw fit to employ a noted Kremlinologist to annotate the work, pointing out errors of omission and commission.)

Thus it was that the educated, urbane men of the State Department, the CIA and the United Fruit Company, the pipe-smoking, comfortable men of Princeton, Harvard and Wall Street, decided that the illiterate peasants of Guatemala did not deserve the land which had been given to them, that the workers did not need their unions, that hunger and torture were a small price to pay for being rid of the scourge of communism.

The terror carried out by Castillo Armas was only the beginning. It was, as we shall see, to get much worse in time. It has continued with hardly a pause for 40 years.

In 1955, the *New York Times* reported from the United Nations that "The United States has begun a drive to scuttle a section of the proposed Covenant of Human Rights that poses a threat to its business interests abroad." The offending section dealt with the right of peoples to self-determination and to permanent sovereignty over their natural wealth and resources. Said the newspaper: "It declares in effect that any country has the right to nationalize its resources ..."[50]

11. Costa Rica mid-1950s
Trying to topple an ally, part I

If ever the CIA maintained a love-hate relationship, it was with José Figueres, three times the head of state of Costa Rica.

On the one hand, Figueres, by his own admission in 1975, worked for the CIA "in 20,000 ways ... all over Latin America" for 30 years.[1] "I collaborated with the CIA when we were trying to topple Trujillo," he divulged, speaking of the Dominican Republic dictator.[2]

On the other hand, Figueres revealed that the Agency had twice tried to kill him.[3] He did not elaborate, although he stated at the same time that he had tried for two years to get the Bay of Pigs invasion called off. This may have precipitated one or both of the assassination attempts.

The CIA also tried to overthrow the Figueres government. In 1964, the first significant exposé of the Agency, *The Invisible Government*, disclosed that:

in the mid-1950s CIA agents intruded deeply into the political affairs of Costa Rica, the most stable and democratic republic in Latin America. Knowledgeable Costa Ricans were aware of the CIA's role. The CIA's purpose was to promote the ouster of José (Pepe) Figueres, the moderate socialist who became President in a fair and open election in 1953.[4]

Figueres remained in office until 1958, in this his first term as president; he had headed a liberal junta in the late 1940s.

The Agency's "major grievance was that Figueres had scrupulously recognized the right of asylum in Costa Rica—for non-Communists and Communists alike. The large influx of questionable characters complicated the agency's job of surveillance and forced it to increase its staff."[5]

The CIA's problems with Figueres actually went somewhat deeper. Costa Rica was a haven for hundreds of exiles fleeing from various Latin American right-wing dictatorships, such as in the Dominican Republic, Nicaragua, and Venezuela, and Figueres was providing groups of them with material and moral support in their plans to overthrow these regimes.[6] To Figueres, this was entirely in keeping with his anti-totalitarian beliefs, directed against the left as well as the right. The problem was that the dictators targeted for overthrow were all members in good standing of the United States' anti-Communist, "Free-World" club.

(The American attitude toward Trujillo was later modified.) Moreover, Figueres had on occasion expressed criticism of the American policy of supporting such dictatorships while neglecting the economic and social problems of the hemisphere.

These considerations could easily outweigh the fact that Figueres had established his anti-Communist credentials, albeit not of the "ultra" variety, and was no more a "socialist" than US Senator Hubert Humphrey. Although Figueres spoke out strongly at times against foreign investment, as president he was eminently accommodating to Central America's *bêtes noires*, the multinational fruit companies.[7]

In addition to providing support to Figueres's political opponents,[8] the CIA, reported *The Invisible Government*, tried:

> to stir up embarrassing trouble within the Communist Party in Costa Rica, and to attempt to link Figueres with the Communists. An effort to produce evidence that Figueres had been in contact with leading Communists during a trip to Mexico was unsuccessful. But CIA agents had better luck with the first part of their strategy—stirring up trouble for the Communists. They succeeded in planting a letter in a Communist newspaper. The letter, purportedly from a leading Costa Rican Communist, put him on record in opposition to the Party line on the [1956] Hungarian revolution. Unaware that the letter was a CIA plant, the leading officials in the American Embassy held an urgent meeting to ponder its meaning. The political officer then dispatched a long classified report to Washington, alerting top policy makers to the possibility of a startling turn in Latin American Communist politics.[9]

In 1955 the Agency carried out an action against Figueres that was more immediately threatening. A deep personal and political animosity between Figueres and Nicaraguan dictator Anastasio Somoza had escalated into violence: an attempt against Somoza's life, launched from Costa Rica with Figueres's support, was countered by an invasion from Nicaragua by land and air. Figueres's biographer, Charles Ameringer, has related that:

> Figueres accused the U.S. Central Intelligence Agency of aiding the Somoza movement against him. He claimed that the CIA felt indebted to Somoza for the help he had given in overthrowing the Arbenz regime. He asserted that the same pilots and planes (the F-47) that had participated in the attack upon Guatemala, "afterwards came from Nicaragua and machine-gunned eleven defenseless towns in our territory." According to Figueres, at the same time that the U.S. Department of State arranged the sale of fighter planes for Costa Rica's defense, CIA planes and pilots were flying sorties for the rebels.[10]

It is interesting to note that during this period, when virtually nothing had yet been revealed about such blatant CIA covert activities, the fact that the Agency had been caught red-handed tapping Figueres's telephone was worthy of condemnatory editorial comment by the *Washington Post* and a like statement by Senator Mike Mansfield on the floor of the Senate.[11]

José Figueres did not regain the presidency of Costa Rica until 1970, at which time a renewed CIA effort to overthrow him was undertaken, for not very different reasons.

12. Syria 1956-1957

Purchasing a new government

"Neutrality," proclaimed John Foster Dulles in 1956, "has increasingly become an obsolete conception, and, except under very exceptional circumstances, it is an immoral and shortsighted conception."[1]

The short-sightedness of the neutralist government lay perhaps in its inability to perceive that its neutralism would lead to John Foster Dulles attempting to overthrow it.

Syria was not behaving like Washington thought a Third World government should. For one thing, it was the only state in the area to refuse all US economic or military assistance. Damascus did not much care for the strings which came attached—the acceptance of military aid usually meant the presence of American military advisers and technicians; furthermore, the US Mutual Security Act of 1955 specified that the recipient country agree to make a contribution to "the defensive strength of the free world", and declared it US policy "to encourage the efforts of other free nations ... to foster private initiative and competition [i.e., capitalism]."[2]

Another difficulty posed by Syria was that, although its governments of recent years had been more or less conservative and had refrained from unpleasant leftist habits like nationalizing American-owned companies, US officials—suffering from what might be called anti-communist paranoia or being victims of their own propaganda—consistently saw the most ominous handwritings on the walls. To appreciate this, one has to read some of the formerly-secret-now-declassified documents of the National Security Council (NSC), based in part on reports received from the American embassy in Damascus during 1955 and 1956 ...

"If the popular leftward trend in Syria continues over any considerable period, there is a real danger that Syria will fall completely under left-wing control either by coup or usurpation of authority" ... "the fundamental anti-US and anti-West orientation of the Syrians is stimulated by inevitable political histrionics about the Palestine problem" ... "Four successive short-lived governments in Syria have permitted continuous and increasing Communist activities" ... "the Communists support the leftist cliques [in] the army" ... "apathy towards Communism on the part of politicians and army officers" is a threat to security ... "the Arab Socialist Resurrectionist Party (ASRP)" and "the Communist Party of Syria are capable of bringing about further deterioration of Syrian internal security" ... danger of ASRP "coup d'etat" and "increased Communist penetration of government and army" ... "Of all the Arab states Syria is at the present time the most wholeheartedly devoted to a neutralist policy with strong anti-Western overtones" ... "If the present trend continues there is a strong possibility that a Communist-dominated Syria will result, threatening the peace and stability of the area and endangering the achievement of our objectives in the Near East" ... we "should give priority consideration to developing courses of action in the Near East designed to affect the situation in Syria and to recommending specific steps to combat communist subversion" ...[3]

It would appear that the idea of military men who were leftist and/or apathetic to communists must truly have been an incongruous phenomenon to the American official mind. But nowhere in any of the documents is there mention of the leftists/Communists/ASRP having in fact done anything illegal or wicked, although the language employed is similar to what we saw in the Guatemala chapter: These people don't join anything, they "infiltrate", they "penetrate"; they "control", they're "opportunistic". In actuality, the behavior described is like that of other political animals: trying to influence key sectors of the society and win allies. But to the men holding positions of responsibility in the National Security Council and the State Department, the evil intent and danger of such people was so self-evident as not to require articulation.

There is one exception, perhaps expressed to explain away an uncomfortable observation:

In fact, the Communist Party does not appear to have as its immediate objective seizure of power. Rather it seeks to destroy national unity, to strengthen support for Soviet policies and opposition to Western policies and to exacerbate tensions in the Arab world. It has made significant progress toward these objectives.[4]

There is no indication of what the author had in mind by "national unity".

A leftist-oriented or communist-dominated Syrian government, reasoned the US ambassador to Syria, James Moose, Jr., would clearly threaten American interests in neighboring Turkey, which, in turn, could outflank all the states of the NATO alliance, and so forth and so on.[5] It was clear that since the Syrian government could not be relied upon to do anything about this major impending disaster, something would have to be done about the Syrian government.

To this we add the usual Middle-Eastern intrigue: in this case, Iraq plotting with the British to topple the governments in both Syria and Nasser's Egypt; the British pressuring the Americans to join the conspiracy;[6] and the CIA compromising—leave Nasser alone, at least for the time being, and we'll do something about Syria.[7]

An implausible scenario, scandalous, but in the time-honored tradition of the Middle East. The British were old hands at it. Dulles and the Americans, still exulting in their king-making in Iran, were looking to further remake the oil region in their own image.

Wilbur Crane Eveland was a staff member of the National Security Council, the high-level inter-agency group in Washington which, in theory, monitors and controls CIA clandestine activities. Because of Eveland's background and experience in the Middle East, the CIA had asked that he be lent to the Agency for a series of assignments there.

Archibald Roosevelt was, like his cousin Kermit Roosevelt, a highly-placed official of the CIA; both were grandsons of Teddy. Kermit had masterminded the overthrow of the Iranian government in 1953. Archie had fond hopes of doing the same in Syria.

Michail Bey Ilyan had once served as Syria's foreign minister. In 1956 he was the leader of the conservative Populist Party.

At a meeting of these three men in Damascus, Syria on 1 July 1956, as described by Eveland in his memoirs, Roosevelt asked Ilyan "what would be needed to give the Syrian conservatives enough control to purge the communists and their leftist sympathizers. Ilyan responded by ticking off names and places: the radio stations in Damascus and Aleppo; a few key senior officers; and enough money to buy newspapers now in Egyptian and Saudi hands."

"Roosevelt probed further. Could these things, he asked Ilyan, be done with U.S. money and assets alone, with no other Western or Near Eastern country involved?"

"Without question, Ilyan replied, nodding gravely."

On 26 July, Egyptian President Gamal Abdul Nasser announced that his government was taking over the operation of the Suez Canal. The reaction of the British and French was swift and inflamed. The United States was less openly hostile, though it was critical and Egyptian government funds in the US were frozen. This unexpected incident put a crimp in the CIA's plans, for—as Ilyan explained to Eveland in despair—Nasser was now the hero of the Arab world, and collaboration with any Western power to overthrow an Arab government was politically indefensible.

Eventually the coup was scheduled for 25 October. The logistics, as outlined by Ilyan, called for senior colonels in the Syrian army to:

take control of Damascus, Aleppo, Homs, and Hamah. The frontier posts with Jordan, Iraq, and

Lebanon would also be captured in order to seal Syria's borders until the radio stations announced that a new government had taken over under Colonel Kabbani, who would place armored units at key positions throughout Damascus. Once control had been established, Ilyan would inform the civilians he'd selected that they were to form a new government, but in order to avoid leaks none of them would be told until just a week before the coup.

For this operation, money would have to change hands. Ilyan asked for and received half a million Syrian pounds (approximately $167,000). The Syrian further stipulated that to guarantee their participation the Syrian plotters would require assurance from the highest level of the American government that the US would both back the coup and immediately grant recognition to the new government. This, Ilyan explained, could be communicated as follows: in April, President Eisenhower had said that the United States would oppose aggression in the Middle East, but not without congressional approval. Could the president repeat this statement, in light of the Suez crisis, he asked, on a specified date when Ilyan's colleagues would be told to expect it? Eisenhower's words would provide the guarantees they were seeking.

An affirmative reply to Ilyan's plan arrived in Damascus from Washington the next day. A proper occasion for the requested statement would have to be found and Secretary Dulles would be the one to use it. The scheme was for Dulles to make public reference to Eisenhower's statement between 16 and 18 October, thus giving Ilyan the week he needed to assemble his civilian team.

Before long, John Foster Dulles held a press conference. In light of recent Israeli attacks on Jordan, one of the reporters present asked whether the United States might come to Jordan's aid per "our declaration of April 9".

Yes, replied the Secretary of State, repeating the reference to the April statement. The date was 16 October.

But following close on the heels of this was a message from Ilyan in Damascus to Eveland in Beirut postponing the date of the coup for five days to 30 October because Colonel Kabbani had told Ilyan that his people weren't quite ready.

The postponement was crucial. Early in the morning of the 30th, a very distraught Michail Ilyan appeared at Eveland's door. "Last night," he cried, "the Israelis invaded Egypt and are right now heading for the Suez Canal! How could you have asked us to over-throw our government at the exact moment when Israel started a war with an Arab state?"[8]

The leftist-trend-in-Syria bell continued to ring in Washington. In January 1957, wrote President Eisenhower later, CIA Director Allen Dulles "submitted reports indicating that the new Syrian Cabinet was oriented to the left".[9] Two months later, Dulles prepared a "Situation Report on Syria" in which he wrote of an "increasing trend toward a decidedly leftist, pro-Soviet government". Dulles was concerned with "organized leftist officers belonging to the Arab Socialist Resurrection Party".[10] That same month, a State Department internal document stated:

> The British are believed to favor active stimulation of a change in the present regime in Syria, in an effort to assure a pro-Western orientation on the part of future Syrian governments. ... The United States shares the concern of the British Government over the situation in Syria.[11]

Then, in June, an internal Department of Defense memorandum spoke of a possible "leftist coup". This was to be carried out, according to the memo, against "the leftist Syrian Government".[12]

Thus it was that in Beirut and Damascus, CIA officers were trying their hands again at stage-managing a Syrian coup. On this occasion, Kermit Roosevelt, rather than cousin Archibald, was pulling the strings. He arranged for one Howard ("Rocky") Stone to be transferred to Damascus from the Sudan to be sure that the "engineering" was done by a "pro". Stone was, at thirty-two, already a legend in the CIA's clandestine service as the man who had helped Kim Roosevelt overthrow the Iranian government four years earlier, though what Stone's precise contribution was has remained obscure.

The proposed beneficiary of this particular plot was to be Adib Shishakly, former right-wing dictator of Syria, living covertly in Lebanon. Shishakly's former chief of security, Colonel Ibrahim Husseini, now Syrian military attaché in Rome, was secretly slipped into Lebanon under cover of a CIA-fabricated passport. Husseini was then to be smuggled across the Syrian border in the trunk of a US diplomatic car in order to meet with key Syrian CIA agents and provide assurances that Shishakly would come back to rule once Syria's government had been overthrown.

But the coup was exposed before it ever got off the ground. Syrian army officers who had been assigned major roles in the operation walked into the office of Syria's head of intelligence, Colonel Sarraj, turned in their bribe money and named the CIA officers who had paid them. Lieut. Col. Robert Molloy, the American army attaché, Francis Jeton, a career CIA officer, officially Vice Consul at the US Embassy, and the legendary Howard Stone, with the title of Second Secretary for Political Affairs, were all declared *personae non gratae* and expelled from the country in August.

Col. Molloy was determined to leave Syria in style. As his car approached the Lebanese border, he ran his Syrian motorcycle escort off the road and shouted to the fallen rider that "Colonel Sarraj and his commie friends" should be told that Molloy would "beat the shit out of them with one hand tied behind his back if they ever crossed his path again."

The Syrian government announcement which accompanied the expulsion order stated that Stone had first made contact with the outlawed Social Nationalist Party and then with the army officers. When the officers reported the plot, they were told to continue their contacts with the Americans and later met Shishakly and Husseini at the homes of US Embassy staff members. Husseini reportedly told the officers that the United States was prepared to give a new Syrian government between 300 and 400 million dollars in aid if the government would make peace with Israel.

An amusing aside to the affair occurred when the Syrian Defense Minister and the Syrian Ambassador to Italy disputed the claim that Husseini had anything to do with the plot. The Ambassador pointed out that Husseini had not been in Syria since 20 July and his passport showed no indication that he had been out of Italy since that time.

The State Department categorized the Syrian charge as "complete fabrications" and retaliated by expelling the Syrian ambassador and a Second Secretary and recalling the American ambassador from Syria. It marked the first time since 1915 that the United States had expelled a chief of mission of a foreign country.[13]

In the wake of the controversy, the *New York Times* reported that:

There are numerous theories about why the Syrians struck at the United States. One is that they acted at the instigation of the Soviet Union. Another is that the Government manufactured an anti-U.S. spy story to distract public attention from the significance of Syria's negotiations with Moscow.[14]

In the same issue, a *Times* editorial speculated upon other plausible-sounding explanations.[15] Neither in its news report nor in its editorial did the *New York Times* seem to consider even the possibility that the Syrian accusation might be true.

President Eisenhower, recalling the incident in his memoirs, offered no denial to the accusation. His sole comment on the expulsions was: "The entire action was shrouded in mystery but the suspicion was strong that the Communists had taken control of the government. Moreover, we had fresh reports that arms were being sent into Syria from the Soviet bloc."[16]

Syria's neutralism/"leftism" continued to obsess the United States. Five years later, when John F. Kennedy was in the White House, he met with British Prime Minister Macmillan and the two leaders agreed, according to a CIA report, on "Penetration and cultivation of disruptive elements in the Syrian armed forces, particularly in the Syrian army, so that Syria can be guided by the West."[17]

Decades later, Washington was still worried, though Syria had still not "gone communist".

13. The Middle East 1957-1958

The Eisenhower Doctrine claims another backyard for America

On 9 March 1957, the United States Congress approved a presidential resolution which came to be known as the Eisenhower Doctrine. This was a piece of paper, like the Truman Doctrine and the Monroe Doctrine before it, whereby the US government conferred upon the US government the remarkable and enviable right to intervene militarily in other countries. With the stroke of a pen, the Middle East was added to Europe and the Western hemisphere as America's field of play.

The resolution stated that "the United States regards as vital to the national interest and world peace the preservation of the independence and integrity of the nations of the Middle East." Yet, during this very period, as we have seen, the CIA initiated its operation to overthrow the government of Syria.

The business part of the resolution was contained in the succinct declaration that the United States "is prepared to use armed forces to assist" any Middle East country "requesting assistance against armed aggression from any country controlled by international communism". Nothing was set forth about non-communist or anti-communist aggression which might endanger world peace.

Wilbur Crane Eveland, the Middle East specialist working for the CIA at the time, had been present at a meeting in the State Department two months earlier called to discuss the resolution. Eveland read the draft, which stated that "many, if not all" of the Middle East states "are aware of the danger that stems from international communism". Later he wrote:

> I was shocked. Who, I wondered, had reached this determination of what the Arabs considered a danger? Israel's army had just invaded Egypt and still occupied all of the Sinai Peninsula and the Gaza Strip. And, had it not been for Russia's threat to intervene on behalf of the Egyptians, the British, French, and Israeli forces might now be sitting in Cairo, celebrating Nasser's ignominious fall from power.[1]

The simplistic and polarized view of the world implicit in the Eisenhower Doctrine ignored not only anti-Israeli sentiments but currents of nationalism, pan-Arabism, neutralism and socialism prevalent in many influential quarters of the Middle East. The framers of the resolution saw only a cold-war battlefield and, in doing so, succeeded in creating one.

In April, King Hussein of Jordan dismissed his prime minister, Suleiman Nabulsi, amidst rumors, apparently well-founded, of a coup against the King encouraged by Egypt and Syria and Palestinians living in Jordan. It was the turning point in an ongoing conflict between the pro-West policy of Hussein and the neutralist leanings of the Nabulsi regime. Nabulsi had announced that in line with his policy of neutralism, Jordan would develop closer relations with the Soviet Union and accept Soviet aid if offered. At the same time, he rejected American aid because, he said, the United States had informed him that economic aid would be withheld unless Jordan "severs its ties with Egypt" and "consents to settlement of Palestinian refugees in Jordan", a charge denied by the State Department. Nabulsi added the commentary that "communism is not dangerous to the Arabs".

Hussein, conversely, accused "international communism and its followers" of direct responsibility for "efforts to destroy my country". When pressed for the specifics of his accusation, he declined to provide any.

When rioting broke out in several Jordanian cities, and civil war could not be ruled out, Hussein showed himself equal to the threat to his continued rule. He declared martial law, purged the government and military of pro-Nasser and leftist tendencies, and abolished all political opposition. Jordan soon returned to a state of relative calm.

The United States, however, seized upon Hussein's use of the expression "international communism" to justify rushing units of the Sixth Fleet to the eastern Mediterranean—a super aircraft carrier, two cruisers, and 15 destroyers, followed shortly by a variety of other naval vessels and a battalion of marines which put ashore in Lebanon—to "prepare for possible future intervention in Jordan".[2]

Despite the fact that nothing resembling "armed aggression from any country controlled by international communism" had taken place, the State Department openly invited the King to invoke the Eisenhower Doctrine.[3] But Hussein, who had not even requested the show of force, refused, knowing that such a move would only add fuel to the fires already raging in Jordanian political life. He survived without it.

Sometime during this year the CIA began making secret annual payments to King Hussein, initially in the millions of dollars per year. The practice was to last for 20 years, with the Agency providing Hussein female companions as well. As justification for the payment, the CIA later claimed that Hussein allowed American intelligence agencies to operate freely in Jordan. Hussein himself provided intelligence to the CIA and distributed part of his payments to other government officials who also furnished information or cooperated with the Agency.[4]

A few months later, it was Syria which occupied the front stage in Washington's melodrama of "International Communism". The Syrians had established relations with the Soviet Union via trade, economic aid, and military purchases and training. The United States chose to see something ominous in this although it was a state of affairs engendered in no small measure by John Foster Dulles, as we saw in the previous chapter. American antipathy toward Syria was heightened in August following the Syrian government's exposure of the CIA-directed plot to overthrow it.

Washington officials and the American media settled easily into the practice of referring to Syria as a "Soviet satellite" or "quasi-satellite". This was not altogether objective or spontaneous reporting. Kennett Love, a *New York Times* correspondent in close contact to the CIA (see Iran chapter), later disclosed some of the background:

> The US Embassy in Syria connived at false reports issued in Washington and London through diplomatic and press channels to the effect that Russian arms were pouring into the Syrian port of Latakia, that "not more than 123 Migs" had arrived in Syria, and that Lieutenant Colonel Abdel Hameed Serraj, head of Syrian intelligence, had taken over control in a Communist-inspired coup. I travelled all over Syria without hindrance in November and December [1956] and found there were indeed "not more than 123 Migs". There were none. And no Russian arms had arrived for months. And there had been no coup, although some correspondents in Beirut, just a two-hour drive from Damascus, were dispatching without attribution false reports fed to them by embassy visitors from Damascus and a roving CIA man who worked in the guise of a US Treasury agent. Serraj, who was anti-Communist, had just broken the clumsy British-US-Iraqi-supported plot [to overthrow the Syrian government]. Syria was quiet but worried lest the propaganda presage a new *coup d'état* or a Western-backed invasion.[5]

As if to further convince any remaining skeptics, Eisenhower dispatched a personal emissary, Loy Henderson, on a tour of the Middle East. Henderson, not surprisingly, returned with the conclusion that "there was a fear in all Middle East countries that the Soviets might be able to topple the regimes in each of their countries through exploiting the crisis in Syria".[6] He gave no indication as to whether the Syrians themselves thought they were going through a crisis.

As an indication of how artificial were the crises announced by the White House, how arbitrary were the doomsday pronouncements about the Soviet Union, let us consider the following from a Department of Defense internal memorandum of June 1957, about two months before Henderson went to the Middle East:

> The USSR has shown no intention of direct intervention in any of the previous Mid-Eastern crises, and we believe it is unlikely that they would intervene, directly, to assure the success of a leftist coup in Syria.[7]

In early September, the day after Henderson returned, the United States announced that the Sixth Fleet was once again being sent to the Mediterranean and that arms and other military equipment were being rushed to Jordan, Lebanon, Iraq and Turkey. A few days later, Saudi Arabia was added to the list. The Soviet Union replied with arms shipments to Syria, Egypt and Yemen.

The Syrian government accused the US of sending warships close to her coast in an "open challenge" and said that unidentified planes had been flying constantly over the Latakia area day and night for four days, Latakia being the seaport where Soviet ships arrived.

Syria further claimed that the US had "incited" Turkey to concentrate an estimated 50,000 soldiers on Syria's border. The Syrians ridiculed the explanation that the Turkish troops were only on maneuvers. Eisenhower later wrote that the troops were at the border with "a readiness to act" and that the United States had already assured the leaders of Turkey, Iraq and Jordan that if they "felt it necessary to take actions against aggression by the Syrian government, the United States would undertake to expedite shipments of arms already committed to the Middle Eastern countries and, further, would replace losses as quickly as possible." The president had no quarrel with the idea that such action might be taken to repel, in his words, the "*anticipated* aggression" of Syria, for it would thus be "basically defensive in nature" (emphasis added).[8]

The American role here may have been more active than Eisenhower suggests. One of his advisers, Emmet John Hughes, has written of how Under-Secretary of State Christian Herter, later to replace an ailing John Foster Dulles as Secretary, "reviewed in rueful detail

... some recent clumsy clandestine American attempts to spur Turkish forces to do some vague kind of battle with Syria".[9]

Dulles gave the impression in public remarks that the United States was anxious to somehow invoke the Eisenhower Doctrine, presumably as a "justification" for taking further action against Syria. But he could not offer any explanation of how this was possible. Certainly Syria was not going to make the necessary request.

The only solution lay in Syria attacking another Arab country which would then request American assistance. This appears to be one rationale behind the flurry of military and diplomatic activity directed at Syria by the US. A study carried out for the Pentagon some years later concluded that in "the 1957 Syrian crisis ... Washington seem[ed] to seek the *initial* use of force by target"[10] (emphasis added; "target" refers to Syria).

Throughout this period, Washington officials alternated between striving to enlist testimonials from other Arab nations that Syria was indeed a variety of Soviet satellite and a threat to the region, and assuring the world that the United States had received a profusion of just such testimony. But Jordan, Iraq and Saudi Arabia all denied that they felt threatened by Syria. Egypt, Syria's closest ally, of course concurred. At the height of the "crisis", King Hussein of Jordan left for a vacation in Europe. The Iraqi premier declared that his country and Syria had arrived at a "complete understanding". And King Saud of Saudi Arabia, in a message to Eisenhower, said that US concern over Syria was "exaggerated" and asked the president for "renewed assurances that the United States would refrain from any interference in the internal affairs of Arab states". Saud added that "efforts to overturn the Syrian regime would merely make the Syrians more amenable to Soviet influence", a view shared by several observers on all sides.

At the same time, the *New York Times* reported:

> From the beginning of the crisis over Syria's drift to the left, there has been less excitement among her Arab neighbors than in the United States. Foreign diplomats in the area, including many Americans, felt that the stir caused in Washington was out of proportion to the cause.

Eventually, Dulles may have been influenced by this lack of support for the American thesis, for when asked specifically to "characterize what the relation is between Soviet aims in the area and the part that Syria adds to them", he could only reply that "The situation internally in Syria is not entirely clear and fluctuates somewhat." Syria, he implied, was not yet in the grip of international Communism.

The next day, Syria, which had no desire to isolate itself from the West, similarly moderated its tone by declaring that the American warships had been 15 miles offshore and had continued "quietly on their way".[11]

It appears that during this same restless year of 1957, the United States was also engaged in a plot to overthrow Nasser and his troublesome nationalism, although the details are rather sketchy. In January, when King Saud and Iraqi Crown Prince Abdul Illah were in New York at the United Nations, they were approached by CIA Director Allen Dulles and one of his top aides, Kermit Roosevelt, with offers of CIA covert planning and funding to topple the Egyptian leader whose radical rhetoric, inchoate though it was, was seen by the royal visitors as a threat to the very idea of monarchy. Nasser and other army officers had overthrown King Farouk of Egypt in 1952. Ironically, Kermit Roosevelt and the CIA have traditionally been given credit for somehow engineering this coup. However, it is by no means certain that they actually carried this out.[12]

"Abdul Illah," wrote Eveland, "insisted on British participation in anything covert, but the Saudis had severed relations with Britain and refused. As a result, the CIA dealt separately with each: agreeing to fund King Saud's part in a new area scheme to oppose Nasser and eliminate his influence in Syria; and to the same objective, coordinating in Beirut a covert working group composed of representatives of the British, Iraqi, Jordanian, and Lebanese intelligence services."[13]

The conspiracy is next picked up in mid-spring at the home of Ghosn Zogby in Beirut. Zogby, of Lebanese ancestry, was the chief of the CIA Beirut station. He and Kermit Roosevelt, who was staying with him, hosted several conferences of the clandestine planners. "So obvious," Eveland continued, "were their 'covert' gyrations, with British, Iraqi, Jordanian and Lebanese liaison personnel coming and going nightly, that the Egyptian ambassador in Lebanon was reportedly taking bets on when and where the next U.S. coup would take place." At one of these meetings, the man from the British Secret Intelligence Service (SIS) informed the gathering that teams had been fielded to assassinate Nasser.

Shortly afterwards, Eveland learned from a CIA official that John Foster Dulles, as well as his brother Allen, had directed Roosevelt to work with the British to bring down Nasser. Roosevelt now spoke in terms of a "palace revolution" in Egypt.[14]

From this point on we're fishing in murky waters, for the events which followed produced more questions than answers. With the six countries named above, plus Turkey and Israel apparently getting in on the act, and less than complete trust and love existing amongst the various governments, a host of plots, sub-plots and side plots inevitably sprang to life; at times it bordered on low comedy, though some would call it no more than normal Middle East "diplomacy".

Between July 1957 and October 1958, the Egyptian and Syrian governments and media announced the uncovering of what appear to be at least eight separate conspiracies to overthrow one or the other government, to assassinate Nasser, and/or prevent the expected merger of the two countries. Saudi Arabia, Iraq and the United States were most often named as conspirators, but from the entanglement of intrigue which surfaced it is virtually impossible to unravel the particular threads of the US role.[15]

Typical of the farcical goings-on, it seems that at least one of the plots to assassinate Nasser arose from the Dulles brothers taking Eisenhower's remark that he hoped "the Nasser problem could be eliminated" to be an order for assassination, when the president, so the story goes, was merely referring to improved US-Egyptian relations. Upon realizing the error, Secretary Dulles ordered the operation to cease.[16] (Three years later, Allen Dulles was again to "misinterpret" a remark by Eisenhower as an order to assassinate Patrice Lumumba of the Congo.)

Official American pronouncements during this entire period would have had the world believe that the Soviet Union was the *eminence grise* behind the strife in Jordan, the "crisis" in Syria, and unrest generally in the Middle East; that the Soviet aim was to dominate the area, while the sole purpose of US policy was to repel this Soviet thrust and maintain the "independence" of the Arab nations. Yet, on three separate occasions during 1957—in February, April and September—the Soviet Union called for a four-power (US, USSR, Great Britain and France) declaration renouncing the use of force and interference in the internal affairs of the Middle Eastern countries. The February appeal had additionally called for a four-power embargo on arms shipments to the region, withdrawal of all foreign troops, liquidation of all foreign bases, and a conference to reach a general Middle East settlement.

The Soviet strategy was clearly to neutralize the Middle East, to remove the threat it had long felt from the potentially hostile control of the oil region by, traditionally, France and Great Britain, and now the United States, which sought to fill the "power vacuum" left by the decline of the two European nations as Middle East powers.

History does not relate what a Middle East free from big-power manipulation would have been like, for neither France, Great Britain, nor the United States was amenable to even calling the Soviet "bluff", if that was what it was. The *New York Times* summarized the attitude of the three Western nations to the first two overtures as one that "deprecated the Soviet proposals as efforts to gain recognition of a Soviet right to a direct voice in the affairs of the Middle East. They have told the Russians to take up their complaints through the United Nations."

Following the September proposal, John Foster Dulles, replying to a question at a press conference, said that "the United States is skeptical of these arrangements with the Soviet Union for 'hands-off'. What they are apt to mean is our hands off and their hands under the table." This appears to be the only public comment the US government saw fit to make on the matter.[17]

It may be instructive to speculate upon the reaction of the Western nations if the Soviet Union had announced a "Khrushchev Doctrine", ceding to itself the same scope of action in the Middle East as that stipulated in the Eisenhower Doctrine.

In January 1958, Syria and Egypt announced their plans to unite, forming the new nation of the United Arab Republic (UAR). The initiative for the merger had come from Syria who was motivated in no small part by her fear of further American power plays against her. Ironically, under the merger arrangement, the Communist Party, already outlawed in Egypt, was dissolved in Syria, an objective which a year and a half of CIA covert activity had failed to achieve.

Two weeks after the birth of the UAR, and in direct response to it, Iraq and Jordan formed the Arab Union, with the United States acting as midwife. This union was short lived, for in July a bloody coup in Iraq overthrew the monarchy, the new regime establishing a republic and promptly renouncing the pact. The trumpets of Armageddon could once more be heard distinctly in the Oval Office. "This somber turn of events," wrote Eisenhower in his memoirs, "could, without vigorous response on our part, result in a complete elimination of Western influence in the Middle East."[18] Although the president would not be so crass as to mention a concern about oil, his anxiety attack was likely brought on by the fact that one of the greatest oil reserves in the world was now under rule of a government led by pro-Nasserites, which might well prove to be not as pliable an ally as the previous regime, and too independent of Washington.

The time for a mere show of force was over. The very next day, the marines, along with the American navy and air force, were sent in—not to Iraq, but to Lebanon.

Of all the Arab states, Lebanon was easily the United States' closest ally. She alone had supported the Eisenhower Doctrine with any enthusiasm or unequivocally echoed Washington's panic about Syria. To be more precise, it was the president of Lebanon, Camille Chamoun, and the foreign minister, Charles Malik, a Harvard Ph.D. in philosophy, who had put all their cold-war eggs into the American basket. Chamoun had ample reason to be beholden to the United States. The CIA apparently played a role in his 1952 election,[19] and in 1957 the Agency furnished generous sums of money to Chamoun to use in support of candidates in the Chamber of Deputies (Parliament) June elections who would back him and, presumably, US policies. Funds were also provided to specifically oppose, as punishment, those candidates who had resigned in protest over Chamoun's adherence to the Eisenhower Doctrine.

As is customary in such operations, the CIA sent an "election specialist" along with the money to Beirut to assist in the planning. American officials in Washington and Lebanon proceeded on the assumption, they told each other, that Egypt, Syria and Saudi Arabia would also intervene financially in the elections. The American ambassador to Lebanon, Donald Heath, argued as well, apparently without ironic intention, that "With both the president and the new chamber of deputies supporting American principles, we'd also have a demonstration that representative democracy could work" in the Middle East.

To what extent the American funding helped, or even how the money was spent, is not known, but the result was a landslide for pro-government deputies; so much so, that it caused considerable protest within Lebanon, including the charge that Chamoun had stacked the parliament in order to amend the constitution to permit him to seek an other-wise prohibited second six-year term of office the following year.[20]

By late April 1958, tensions in Lebanon had reached bursting point. The inordinate pro-American orientation of Chamoun's government and his refusal to dispel rumors that he would seek a second term incensed both Lebanese nationalists and advocates of the Arab nationalism which Nasser was promoting throughout the Middle East. Demands were made that the government return to the strict neutrality provided for in the National Pact of 1943 at the time of Lebanon's declaration of independence from France.

A rash of militant demonstrations, bombings and clashes with police took place, and when, in early May, the editor of an anti-government newspaper was murdered, armed rebellion broke out in several parts of the country, and US Information Agency libraries in Tripoli and Beirut were sacked. Lebanon contained all the makings of a civil war.

"Behind everything," wrote Eisenhower, "was our deep-seated conviction that the Communists were principally responsible for the trouble and that President Chamoun was motivated only by a strong feeling of patriotism."

The president did not clarify who or what he meant by "Communists". However, in the next paragraph he refers, without explanation, to the Soviet Union as "stirring up trouble" in the Middle East. And on the following page, the old soldier writes that "there was no doubt in our minds" about Chamoun's charge that "Egypt and Syria had been instigating the revolt and arming the rebels".[21]

In the midst of the fighting, John Foster Dulles announced that he perceived "international communism" as the source of the conflict and for the third time in a year the Sixth Fleet was dispatched to the eastern Mediterranean; police supplies to help quell rioters, as well as tanks and other heavy equipment, were airlifted to Lebanon.

At a subsequent news conference, Dulles declared that even if international communism were not involved, the Eisenhower Doctrine was still applicable because one of its provisions stated that "the independence of these countries is vital to peace and the national interest of the United States." "That is certainly a mandate," he said, "to do something if we think that our peace and vital interests are endangered from any quarter."[22] Thus did one of the authors of the doctrine bestow upon himself a mandate.

Egypt and Syria, from all accounts, supported the rebels' cause with arms, men and money, in addition to inflammatory radio broadcasts from Cairo, although the extent of the material support is difficult to establish. A UN Observation Group went to Lebanon in June at the request of Foreign Minister Malik and reported that they found no evidence of UAR intervention of any significance. A second UN report in July confirmed this finding. It is open to question, however, what degree of reliance can be placed upon these reports, dealing as they do with so thorny an evaluation and issued by a body in the business of promoting compromise.

In any event, the issue was whether the conflict in Lebanon represented a legitimate, home-grown civil war, or whether it was the doing of the proverbial "outside agitators". On this point, historian Richard Barnet has observed:

> No doubt the Observation Group did minimize the extent of UAR participation. But essentially they were correct. Nasser was trying to exploit the political turmoil in Lebanon, but he did not create it. Lebanon, which had always abounded in clandestine arsenals and arms markets, did not need foreign weapons for its domestic violence. Egyptian intervention was neither the stimulus nor the mainstay of the civil strife. Once again a government that had lost the power to rule effectively was blaming its failure on foreign agents.[23]

President Eisenhower—continuing his flip-flop thinking on the issue—wrote that it now seemed that Nasser "would be just as happy to see a temporary end to the struggle ... and contacted our government and offered to attempt to use his influence to end the trouble."[24]

Camille Chamoun had sacrificed Lebanon's independence and neutrality on the altar of personal ambition and the extensive American aid that derived from subscribing to the Eisenhower Doctrine. Lebanese Muslims, who comprised most of Chamoun's opposition, were also galled that the Christian president had once again placed the country outside the mainstream of the Arab world, as he had done in 1956 when he refused to break relations with France and Great Britain following their invasion of Egypt.

Chamoun himself had admitted the significance of his pro-American alignment in a revealing comment to Wilbur Crane Eveland. Eveland writes that in late April,

> I'd suggested that he might ease tensions by making a statement renouncing a move for reelection. Chamoun had snorted and suggested that I look at the calendar: March 23 was a month behind us, and no amendment to permit another term could legally be passed after that date. Obviously, as he pointed out, the issue of the presidency was not the real issue; renunciation of the Eisenhower Doctrine was what his opponents wanted.[25]

Instead of renouncing the doctrine, Chamoun invoked it. Although scattered fighting, at times heavy, was continuing in Lebanon, it was the coup in Iraq on 14 July that tipped the scales in favor of Chamoun making the formal request for military assistance and the United States immediately granting it. A CIA report of a plot against King Hussein of Jordan at about the same time heightened even further Washington's seemingly unceasing sense of urgency about the Middle East.

Chamoun had, by this time, already announced his intention to step down from office when his term expired in September. He was now concerned about American forces helping him to stay alive until that date, as well as their taking action against the rebels. For the previous two months, fear of assassination had kept him constantly inside the presidential palace, never so much as approaching a window. The murder of the Iraqi king and prime minister during the coup was not designed to make him feel more secure.

The Eisenhower Doctrine was put into motion not only in the face of widespread opposition to it within Lebanon, but in disregard of the fact that, even by the doctrine's own dubious provisions, the situation in Lebanon did not qualify: It could hardly be claimed that Lebanon had suffered "armed aggression from any country controlled by international communism". If further evidence of this were needed, it was provided by veteran diplomat Robert Murphy who was sent to Lebanon by Eisenhower a few days after the US troops had landed. Murphy concluded, he later wrote, that "communism was playing no direct or substantial part in the insurrection".[26]

Yet, Eisenhower could write that the American Government "was moving in accord with the provisions of the Middle East Resolution [Eisenhower Doctrine], but if the conflict expanded into something that the Resolution did not cover, I would, given time, go to the Congress for additional authorization".[27] Apparently the president did not place too much weight on John Foster Dulles having already determined that the Resolution's mandate was open-ended.

Thus it was that American military forces were dispatched to Lebanon. Some 70 naval vessels and hundreds of aircraft took part in the operation, many remaining as part of the visible American presence. By 25 July, the US forces on shore totaled at least 10,600. By August 13, their number came to 14,000, more than the entire Lebanese Army and gendarmerie combined.[28]

"In my [radio-TV] address," wrote Eisenhower, "I had been careful to use the term 'stationed in' Lebanon rather than 'invading'."[29] This was likely a distinction lost upon many Lebanese, both high and low, supporters of the rebels and supporters of the government, including government tank forces who were prepared to block the entrance into Beirut of US troops; only the last-minute intercession on the spot by the American ambassador may have averted an armed clash.[30]

At a meeting between Robert Murphy and Lebanese Commander-in-Chief General Faud Chehab—related by Eveland who was briefed by Murphy afterwards—the American diplomat was warned that the Lebanese people were "restless, resentful, and determined that Chamoun should resign and U.S. troops leave at once. Otherwise the general could not be responsible for the consequences. For fifteen years his officers had acted behind his back; now, he feared, they might revolt and attack the American forces."

Murphy had listened patiently, Eveland relates, and then ...

> escorted the general to a window overlooking the sea. Pointing to the supercarrier *Saratoga*, swinging at anchor on the horizon, the President's envoy had quietly explained that just one of its aircraft, armed with nuclear weapons, could obliterate Beirut and its environs from the face of the earth. To this, Murphy quickly added that he'd been sent to be sure that it wouldn't be necessary for American troops to fire a shot. Shehab [Chehab], he was certain, would ensure that there were no provocations on the Lebanese side. That, Murphy told me, ended the conversation. It now seemed that the general had "regained control" of his troops.[31]

None of the parties seem to have considered what would have been the fate of the thousands of American military personnel in a Beirut obliterated from the face of the earth.

Civil warfare in Lebanon increased in intensity in the two weeks following the American intervention. During this period, CIA transmitters in the Middle East were occupied in sending out propaganda broadcasts of disguised origin, a tactic frequently employed by the Agency. In the case of one broadcast which has been reported, the apparent aim was to deflect anti-US feelings onto the Soviet Union and other targets. But the residents of the Middle East were not the only ones who may have been taken in by the spurious broadcast, for it was picked up by the American press and passed on to an unwitting American public; the following appeared in US newspapers:

BEIRUT, July 23 (UPI)—A second mysterious Arab radio station went on the air yesterday calling itself the "Voice of Justice" and claiming to be broadcasting from Syria. Its program heard here consisted of bitter criticism against Soviet Russia and Soviet Premier Khrushchev. Earlier the "Voice of Iraq" went on the air with attacks against the Iraqi revolutionary government. The "Voice of Justice" called Khrushchev the "hangman of Hungary"and warned the people of the Middle East they would suffer the same fate as the Hungarians if the Russians got a foothold in the Middle East.[32]

On 31 July, the Chamber of Deputies easily chose General Chehab to succeed Chamoun as president in September, an event that soon put a damper on the fighting in Lebanon and marked the beginning of the end of the conflict which, in the final analysis, appears to have been more a violent protest than a civil war. Tension was further eased by the US announcement shortly afterwards of its intention to withdraw a Marine battalion as a prelude to a general withdrawal.

The last American troops left Lebanon in late October without having fired a shot in anger. What had their presence accomplished?

The authors of the Pentagon study referred to earlier concluded that "A balanced assessment of U.S. behavior in the Lebanon crisis is made difficult by the suspicion that the outcome might have been much the same if the United States had done nothing. Even Eisenhower expressed some doubt on this score."[33]

American intervention against the new Iraqi government was more covert. A secret plan for a joint US-Turkish invasion of the country, code-named Operation CANNON-BONE, was drafted by the US Joint Chiefs of Staff shortly after the coup in 1958. Reportedly, only Soviet threats to intercede on Iraq's side forced Washington to hold back. But in 1960, the United States began to fund the Kurdish guerrillas in Iraq who were fighting for a measure of autonomy.[34]

At the same time, the Iraqis, under Brig. General Abdul Karim Kassem, started to work towards the creation of an international organization to counter the power of the Western oil monopolies. This was to become OPEC, and was not received with joy in certain Western quarters. In February 1960, the Near East Division of the CIA's clandestine services requested that the Agency find a way to "incapacitate" Kassem for "promoting Soviet bloc political interests in Iraq". "We do not consciously seek subject's permanent removal from the scene," said the Near East Division. "We also do not object should this complication develop."

As matters turned out, the CIA mailed a monogrammed handkerchief containing an "incapacitating agent" to Kassem from an Asian country. If the Iraqi leader did in fact receive it, it certainly didn't kill him. That was left to his own countrymen who executed him three years later.[35]

The significance of the Lebanese intervention, as well as the shows of force employed in regard to Jordan and Syria, extended beyond the immediate outcomes. In the period before and after the intervention, Eisenhower, Dulles and other Washington officials offered numerous different justifications for the American military action in Lebanon: protecting American lives; protecting American property; the Eisenhower Doctrine, with various interpretations; Lebanese sovereignty, integrity, independence, etc.; US national interest; world peace; collective self-defense; justice; international law; law and order; fighting "Nasserism" ... the need to "do something" ...[36]

In summing up the affair in his memoirs, president Eisenhower seemed to settle upon one rationale in particular, and this is probably the closest to the truth of the matter. This was to put the world—and specifically the Soviet Union and Nasser—on notice that the United States had virtually unlimited power, that this power could be transported to any corner of the world with great speed, that it could and would be used to deal decisively with any situation with which the United States was dissatisfied, for whatever reason.[37]

At the same time, it was a message to the British and the French that there was only one Western superpower in the post-war world, and that their days as great powers in the Lands of Oil were over.

14. Indonesia 1957-1958
War and pornography

"I think it's time we held Sukarno's feet to the fire," said Frank Wisner, the CIA's Deputy Director of Plans (covert operations), one day in autumn 1956.[1] Wisner was speaking of the man who had led Indonesia since its struggle for independence from the Dutch following the war. A few months earlier, in May, Sukarno had made an impassioned speech before the US Congress asking for more understanding of the problems and needs of developing nations like his own.[2]

The ensuing American campaign to unseat the flamboyant leader of the fifth most populous nation in the world was to run the gamut from large-scale military maneuvers to seedy sexual intrigue.

The previous year, Sukarno had organized the Bandung Conference as an answer to the Southeast Asia Treaty Organization (SEATO), the US-created political-military alliance of area states to "contain communism". In the Indonesian city of Bandung, the doctrine of neutralism had been proclaimed as the faith of the underdeveloped world. To the men of the CIA station in Indonesia the conference was heresy, so much so that their thoughts turned toward assassination as a means of sabotaging it.

In 1975, the Senate committee which was investigating the CIA heard testimony that Agency officers stationed in an East Asian country had suggested that an East Asian leader be assassinated "to disrupt an impending Communist [sic] Conference in 1955".[3] (In all likelihood, the leader referred to was either Sukarno or Chou En-lai of China.) But, said the committee, cooler heads prevailed at CIA headquarters in Washington and the suggestion was firmly rejected.

Nevertheless, a plane carrying eight members of the Chinese delegation, a Vietnamese, and two European journalists to the Bandung Conference crashed under mysterious circumstances. The Chinese government claimed that it was an act of sabotage carried out by the US and Taiwan, a misfired effort to murder Chou En-lai. The chartered Air India plane had taken off from Hong Kong on 11 April 1955 and crashed in the South China Sea. Chou En-lai was scheduled to be on another chartered Air India flight a day or two later. The Chinese government, citing what it said were press reports from the *Times of India*, stated that the crash was caused by two time bombs apparently placed aboard the plane in Hong Kong. A clockwork mechanism was later recovered from the wrecked airliner and the Hong Kong police called it a case of "carefully planned mass murder". Months later, British police in Hong Kong announced that they were seeking a Chinese Nationalist for conspiracy to cause the crash, but that he had fled to Taiwan.[4]

99

In 1967 a curious little book appeared in India, entitled *I Was a CIA Agent in India*, by John Discoe Smith, an American. Published by the Communist Party of India, it was based on articles written by Smith for *Literaturnaya Gazeta* in Moscow after he had defected to the Soviet Union around 1960. Smith, born in Quincy, Mass. in 1926, wrote that he had been a communications technician and code clerk at the US Embassy in New Delhi in 1955, performing tasks for the CIA as well. One of these tasks was to deliver a package to a Chinese Nationalist which Smith later learned, he claimed, contained the two time bombs used to blow up the Air India plane. The veracity of Smith's account cannot be determined, although his employment at the US Embassy in New Delhi from 1954 to 1959 is confirmed by the *State Department Biographic Register*.[5]

Elsewhere the Senate committee reported that it had "received some evidence of CIA involvement in plans to assassinate President Sukarno of Indonesia", and that the planning had proceeded to the point of identifying an agent whom it was believed might be recruited for the job.[6] (The committee noted that at one time, those at the CIA who were concerned with possible assassinations and appropriate methods were known internally as the "Health Alteration Committee".)

To add to the concern of American leaders, Sukarno had made trips to the Soviet Union and China (though to the White House as well), he had purchased arms from Eastern European countries (but only after being turned down by the United States),[7] he had nationalized many private holdings of the Dutch, and, perhaps most disturbing of all, the Indonesian Communist Party (PKI) had made impressive gains electorally and in union-organizing, thus earning an important role in the coalition government.

It was a familiar Third World scenario, and the reaction of Washington policy-makers was equally familiar. Once again, they were unable, or unwilling, to distinguish nationalism from pro-communism, neutralism from wickedness. By any definition of the word, Sukarno was no communist. He was an Indonesian nationalist and a "Sukarnoist" who had crushed the PKI forces in 1948 after the independence struggle had been won.[8] He ran what was largely his own show by granting concessions to both the PKI and the Army, balancing one against the other. As to excluding the PKI, with its more than one million members, from the government, Sukarno declared: "I can't and won't ride a three-legged horse."[9]

To the United States, however, Sukarno's balancing act was too precarious to be left to the vagaries of the Indonesian political process. It mattered not to Washington that the Communist Party was walking the legal, peaceful road, or that there was no particular "crisis" or "chaos" in Indonesia, so favored as an excuse for intervention. Intervention there would be.

It would not be the first. In 1955, during the national election campaign in Indonesia, the CIA had given a million dollars to the Masjumi party, a centrist coalition of Muslim organizations, in a losing bid to thwart Sukarno's Nationalist Party as well as the PKI. According to former CIA officer Joseph Burkholder Smith, the project "provided for complete write-off of the funds, that is, no demand for a detailed accounting of how the funds were spent was required. I could find no clue as to what the Masjumi did with the million dollars."[10]

In 1957, the CIA decided that the situation called for more direct action. It was not difficult to find Indonesian colleagues-in-arms for there already existed a clique of army officers and others who, for personal ambitions and because they disliked the influential position of the PKI, wanted Sukarno out, or at least out of their particular islands. (Indonesia is the world's largest archipelago, consisting of some 3,000 islands.)

The military operation the CIA was opting for was of a scale that necessitated significant assistance from the Pentagon, which could be secured for a political action mission only if approved by the National Security Council's "Special Group" (the small group of top NSC officials who acted in the president's name, to protect him and the country by evaluating proposed covert actions and making certain that the CIA did not go off the deep end; known at other times as the 5412 Committee, the 303 Committee, the 40 Committee, or the Operations Advisory Group).

The manner in which the Agency went about obtaining this approval is a textbook example of how the CIA sometimes determines American foreign policy. Joseph Burkholder Smith, who was in charge of the Agency's Indonesian desk in Washington from mid-1956 to early 1958, has described the process in his memoirs: Instead of first proposing the plan to Washington for approval, where "premature mention ... might get it shot down"...

> we began to feed the State and Defense departments intelligence that no one could deny was a useful contribution to understanding Indonesia. When they had read enough alarming reports, we planned to spring the suggestion we should support the colonels' plans to reduce Sukarno's power. This was a method of operation which became the basis of many of the political action adventures of the 1960s and 1970s. In other words, the statement is false that CIA undertook to intervene in the affairs of countries like Chile *only after* being ordered to do so by ... the Special Group. ... In many instances, we made the action programs up ourselves after we had collected enough intelligence to make them appear required by the circumstances. Our activity in Indonesia in 1957-1958 was one such instance.[11] (Emphasis in original.)

When the Communist Party did well again in local elections held in July, the CIA viewed it as "a great help to us in convincing Washington authorities how serious the Indonesian situation was. The only person who did not seem terribly alarmed at the PKI victories was Ambassador Allison. This was all we needed to convince John Foster Dulles finally that he had the wrong man in Indonesia. The wheels began to turn to remove this last stumbling block in the way of our operation."[12] John Allison, wrote Smith, was not a great admirer of the CIA to begin with. And in early 1958, after less than a year in the post, he was replaced as ambassador by Howard Jones, whose selection "pleased" the CIA Indonesia staff.[13]

On 30 November 1957, several hand grenades were tossed at Sukarno as he was leaving a school. He escaped injury, but 10 people were killed and 48 children injured. The CIA in Indonesia had no idea who was responsible, but it quickly put out the story that the PKI was behind it "at the suggestion of their Soviet contacts in order to make it appear that Sukarno's opponents were wild and desperate men". As it turned out, the culprits were a Muslim group not associated with the PKI or with the Agency's military plotters.[14]

The issue of Sukarno's supposed hand-in-glove relationship with Communists was pushed at every opportunity. The CIA decided to make capital of reports that a good-looking blonde stewardess had been aboard Sukarno's aircraft everywhere he went during his trip in the Soviet Union and that the same woman had come to Indonesia with Soviet President Kliment Voroshilov and had been seen several times in the company of Sukarno. The idea was that Sukarno's well-known womanizing had trapped him in the spell of a Soviet female agent. He had succumbed to Soviet control, CIA reports implied, as a result of her influence or blackmail, or both.

"This formed the foundation of our flights of fancy," wrote Smith. "We had as a matter of fact, considerable success with this theme. It appeared in the press around the world, and when *Round Table*, the serious British quarterly of international affairs, came to analyze the Indonesian revolt in its March 1958 issue, it listed Sukarno's being blackmailed by a Soviet female spy as one of the reasons that caused the uprising."

Seemingly, the success of this operation inspired CIA officers in Washington to carry the theme one step further. A substantial effort was made to come up with a pornographic film or at least some still photographs that could pass for Sukarno and his Russian girl friend engaged in "his favorite activity". When scrutiny of available porno films (supplied by the Chief of Police of Los Angeles) failed to turn up a couple who could pass for Sukarno (dark and bald) and a beautiful blonde Russian woman, the CIA undertook to produce its own films, "the very films with which the Soviets were blackmailing Sukarno". The Agency developed a full-face mask of the Indonesian leader which was to be sent to Los Angeles where the police were to pay some porno-film actor to wear it during his big scene. This project resulted in at least some photographs, although they apparently were never used.[15]

Another outcome of the blackmail effort was a film produced for the CIA by Robert Maheu, former FBI agent and intimate of Howard Hughes. Maheu's film starred an actor who resembled Sukarno. The ultimate fate of the film, which was entitled "Happy Days", has not been reported.[16]

In other parts of the world, at other times, the CIA has done better in this line of work, having produced sex films of target subjects caught in *flagrante delicto* who had been lured to Agency safe-houses by female agents.

In 1960, Col. Truman Smith, US Army Ret., writing in *Reader's Digest* about the KGB, declared: "It is difficult for most of us to appreciate its menace, as its methods are so debased as to be all but beyond the comprehension of any normal person with a sense of right and wrong." One of the KGB methods the good colonel found so debased was the making of sex films to be used as blackmail. "People depraved enough to employ such methods," he wrote, "find nothing distasteful in more violent methods."[17]

Sex could be used at home as well to further the goals of American foreign policy. Under the cover of the US foreign aid program, at that time called the Economic Cooperation Administration, Indonesian policemen were trained and then recruited to provide information on Soviet, Chinese and PKI activities in their country. Some of the men singled out as good prospects for this work were sent to Washington for special training and to be softened up for recruitment. Like Sukarno, reportedly, these police officers invariably had an obsessive desire to sleep with a white woman. Accordingly, during their stay they were taken to Baltimore's shabby sex district to indulge themselves.[18]

The Special Group's approval of the political action mission was forthcoming in November 1957,[19] and the CIA's paramilitary machine was put into gear. In this undertaking, as in others, the Agency enjoyed the advantage of the United States' far-flung military empire. Headquarters for the operation were established in neighboring Singapore, courtesy of the British; training bases set up in the Philippines; airstrips laid out in various parts of the Pacific to prepare for bomber and transport missions; Indonesians, along with Filipinos, Taiwanese, Americans, and other "soldiers of fortune" were assembled in Okinawa and the Philippines along with vast quantities of arms and equipment.

For this, the CIA's most ambitious military operation to date, tens of thousands of rebels were armed, equipped and trained by the US Army. US Navy submarines, patrolling off the coast of Sumatra, the main island, put over-the-beach parties ashore along with supplies and communications equipment. The US Air Force set up a considerable Air Transport force which air-dropped many thousands of weapons deep into Indonesian territory. And a fleet of 15 B-26 bombers was made available for the conflict after being "sanitized" to ensure that they were "non-attributable" and that all airborne equipment was "deniable".

In the early months of 1958, rebellion began to break out in one part of the Indonesian island chain, then another. CIA pilots took to the air to carry out bombing and strafing missions in support of the rebels. In Washington, Col. Alex Kawilarung, the Indonesian military attaché, was persuaded by the Agency to "defect". He soon showed up in Indonesia to take charge of the rebel forces. Yet, as the fighting dragged on into spring, the insurgents proved unable to win decisive victories or take the offensive, although the CIA bombing raids were taking their toll. Sukarno later claimed that on a Sunday morning in April, a plane bombed a ship in the harbor of the island of Ambon—all those aboard losing their lives—as well as hitting a church, which demolished the building and killed everyone inside. He stated that 700 casualties had resulted from this single run.

On 15 May, a CIA plane bombed the Ambon marketplace, killing a large number of civilians on their way to church on Ascension Thursday. The Indonesian government had to act to suppress public demonstrations.

Three days later, during another bombing run over Ambon, a CIA pilot, Allen Lawrence Pope, was shot down and captured. Thirty years old, from Perrine, Florida, Pope had flown 55 night missions over Communist lines in Korea for the Air Force. Later he spent two months flying through Communist flak for the CIA to drop supplies to the French at Dien Bien Phu. Now his luck had run out. He was to spend four years as a prisoner in Indonesia before Sukarno acceded to a request from Robert Kennedy for his release.

Pope was captured carrying a set of incriminating documents, including those which established him as a pilot for the US Air Force and the CIA airline CAT. Like all men flying clandestine missions, Pope had gone through an elaborate procedure before taking off to "sanitize" him, as well as his aircraft. But he had apparently smuggled the papers aboard the plane, for he knew that to be captured as an "anonymous, stateless civilian" meant having virtually no legal rights and running the risk of being shot as a spy in accordance with custom. A captured US military man, however, becomes a commodity of value for his captors while he remains alive.

The Indonesian government derived immediate material concessions from the United States as a result of the incident. Whether the Indonesians thereby agreed to keep silent about Pope is not known, but on 27 May the pilot and his documents were presented to the world at a news conference, thus contradicting several recent statements by high American officials.[20] Notable amongst these was President Eisenhower's declaration on 30 April concerning Indonesia: "Our policy is one of careful neutrality and proper deportment all the way through so as not to be taking sides where it is none of our business."[21]

And on 9 May, an editorial in the *New York Times* had stated:

> It is unfortunate that high officials of the Indonesian Government have given further circulation to the false report that the United States Government was sanctioning aid to Indonesia's rebels. The position of the United States Government has been made plain, again and again. Our Secretary of State was emphatic in his declaration that this country would not deviate from a correct neutrality ... the United States is not ready ... to step in to help overthrow a constituted government. Those are the hard facts. Jakarta does not help its case, here, by ignoring them.

With the exposure of Pope and the lack of rebel success in the field, the CIA decided that the light was no longer worth the candle, and began to curtail its support. By the end of June, Indonesian army troops loyal to Sukarno had effectively crushed the dissident military revolt.

The Indonesian leader continued his adroit balancing act between the Communists and the army until 1965, when the latter, likely with the help of the CIA, finally overthrew his regime.

15. Western Europe 1950s and 1960s
Fronts within fronts within fronts

At the British Labour Party conference in 1960, Michael Foot, the party's future leader and a member of its left wing, was accused of being a "fellow traveller" by then-leader Hugh Gaitskell. Foot responded with a reference to Gaitskell and others of the party's right wing: "But who," he asked, "are *they* travelling with?"[1]

They, it turned out, had been travelling with the CIA for some years. Fellow passengers were Frenchmen, Germans, Dutch, Italians, and a host of other West Europeans; all taking part in a CIA operation to win the hearts and minds of liberals, social democrats, and assorted socialists, to keep them from the clutches of the Russian bear.

It was an undertaking of major proportions. For some 20 years, the Agency used dozens of American foundations, charitable trusts and the like, including a few of its own creation, as conduits for payments to all manner of organizations in the United States and abroad, many of which, in turn, funded other groups. So numerous were the institutions involved, so many were the interconnections and overlaps, that it is unlikely that anyone at the CIA had a grasp of the full picture, let alone exercised broad control over it or proper accounting. (See Appendix I for a partial organizational chart.)

The ultimate beneficiaries of this flow of cash were political parties, magazines, news agencies, journalists' unions, other unions and labor organizations, student and youth groups, lawyers' associations, and other enterprises already committed to "The Free World" which could be counted upon to spread the gospel further if provided with sufficient funding.

The principal front organization set up by the CIA in this period was the grandly named Congress for Cultural Freedom (CCF). In June 1950, prominent literati and scientists of the United States and Europe assembled in the Titiana Palace Theatre, in the American Zone of Berlin, before a large audience to launch the organization whose purpose was to "defend freedom and democracy against the new tyranny sweeping the world". The CCF was soon reaching out in all directions with seminars, conferences, and a wide program of political and cultural activities in Western Europe as well as India, Australia, Japan, Africa and elsewhere. It had, moreover, more than 30 periodicals under its financial wing, including, in Europe:

> *Socialist Commentary, Censorship, Science and Freedom, Minerva, Soviet Survey* (or *Survey*), *China Quarterly*, and *Encounter* in Great Britain;
>
> *Preuves, Censure Contre les Artes et la Pensée, Mundo Nuevo*, and *Cuadernos* in France (the last two in Spanish, aimed at Latin America);
>
> *Perspektiv* in Denmark, *Argumenten* in Sweden, *Irodalmi Ujsag* in Hungary, *Der Monat* in Germany, *Forum* in Austria, *Tempo Presente* in Italy, and *Vision* in Switzerland.

There were as well CCF links to *The New Leader, Africa Report, East Europe* and *Atlas* in New York.[2]

Generally, the CCF periodicals were well-written political and cultural magazines which, in the words of former CIA executive Ray Cline, "would not have been able to survive financially without CIA funds".[3]

Amongst the other media-related organizations subsidized by the CIA in Europe at this time were the West German news agency DENA (later known as DPA),[4] the international association of writers PEN, located in Paris, certain French newspapers,[5] the International

Federation of Journalists, and Forum World Features, a news feature service in London whose stories were bought by some 140 newspapers around the world, including about 30 in the United States, amongst which were the *Washington Post* and four other major dailies. The Church committee of the US Senate reported that "major U.S. dailies" which took the service were informed that Forum World Features was "CIA-controlled". *The Guardian* and *The Sunday Times* of Great Britain also used the service, which earlier had been called Forum Service. By 1967, according to one of Forum's leading writers, the news service had become perhaps "the principal CIA media effort in the world", no small accomplishment when one considers that the CIA, in its heyday, was devoting a reported 29 percent of its budget to media and propaganda.[6]

Another important recipient of CIA beneficence was Axel Springer, the West German press baron who was secretly funneled about $7 million in the early 1950s to help him build up his vast media empire. Springer, until he died in 1985, was the head of the largest publishing conglomerate in Western Europe, standing as a tower of pro-Western and anti-communist sentiment. The publisher of the influential West German weekly *Der Spiegel*, Rudolph Augstein, has observed: "No single man in Germany, before or after Hitler, with the possible exception of Bismarck or the two emperors, has had so much power as Springer." His relationship with the CIA reportedly continued until at least the early 1970s.[7]

The originator of the American program, the head of the CIA's International Organizations Division, Tom Braden, later wrote that the Agency placed one operative in the CCF and that another became an editor of the CCF's most important magazine, *Encounter*.[8] Presumably there was at least one CIA agent or officer in each of the funded groups. Braden stated that "The agents could ... propose anti-Communist programs to the official leaders of the organizations." He added, however, that it was a policy to "protect the integrity of the organization by not requiring it to support every aspect of official American policy."[9]

The Cultural Freedom journals appealed to the non-Marxist left (Forum, by contrast, was conservative), generally eschewing the class struggle and excessive nationalization of industry. They subscribed to Daniel Bell's "the end of ideology" thesis, the *raison d'être* of which was that since no one could call for dying for capitalism with a straight face, the idea of dying for socialism or any other ideology had to be discredited. At the same time, the journals advocated a reformed capitalism, a capitalism with a human face.

To the cold warriors in Washington who were paying the bills, however, the idea of reforming capitalism was of minimal interest. What was of consequence was the commitment of the magazines to a strong, well-armed, and united Western Europe, allied to the United States, which would stand as a bulwark against the Soviet bloc; support for the Common Market and NATO; critical analysis of what was seen as the intellectual component of international communist subversion; skepticism of the disarmament, pacifism, and neutralism espoused by the likes of the prominent Campaign for Nuclear Disarmament (CND) in Great Britain. Criticism of US foreign policy took place within the framework of cold-war assumptions; for example, that a particular American intervention was not the most effective way of combatting communism, not that there was anything wrong with intervention *per se* or that the United States was supporting the wrong side.

"Private" publications such as these could champion views which official US government organs like the Voice of America could not, and still be credible. The same was true of the many other private organizations on the CIA payroll at this time.

In 1960, CND and other elements of the Labour Party's left wing succeeded in winning over the party's conference to a policy of complete, unilateral nuclear disarmament and neutrality in the cold war. In addition, two resolutions supporting NATO were voted down. Although the Labour Party was not in power at the time, the actions carried considerable propaganda and psychological value. Washington viewed the turn of events with not a little anxiety, for such sentiments could easily spread to the major parties of other NATO countries.

The right wing of the Labour Party, which had close, not to say intimate, connections to the Congress for Cultural Freedom, *Encounter, New Leader,* and other CIA "assets" and fronts, undertook a campaign to reverse the disarmament resolution. The committee set up for the purpose issued an appeal for funds, and soon could report that many small donations had been received, together with a large sum from a source that wished to remain anonymous. Over the next year, there was sufficient funding for a permanent office, a full-time, paid chairman and paid staff, field workers, traveling expenses, tons of literature sent to a large mailing list within the movement, a regular bulletin sent free, etc.

Their opponents could not come close to matching this propaganda blitz. At the 1961 conference, the unilateralist and neutralist decisions were decisively overturned and the Labour Party returned to the NATO fold.[10]

Supporters of the CIA have invariably defended the Agency's sundry activities in Western Europe on the grounds that the Russians were the first to be so engaged there and had to be countered. Whatever truth there may be in this assertion, the fact remains, as Tom Braden has noted, that the American effort spread to some fields "where they [the Russians] had not even begun to operate".[11] Braden doesn't specify which fields, but it seems that political parties was one: The CIA had working/financial relationships with leading members of the West German Social Democratic Party, two parties in Austria, the Christian Democrats of Italy, and the Liberal Party, in addition to the Labour Party, in Britain,[12] and probably at least one party in every other Western European country, all of which purported to be independent of either superpower, something the various Communist parties, whether supported by the Soviet Union or not, could never get away with.

The media provides another case in point. Neither Braden, nor anyone else apparently, has cited examples of publications or news agencies in Western Europe—pro-Communist or anti-Nato, etc.—which, ostensibly independent in the cold war, were covertly funded by the Soviet Union.

More importantly, it should be borne in mind that all the different types of enterprises and institutions supported by the CIA in Western Europe were supported by the Agency all over the Third World for decades on a routine basis without a Russian counterpart in sight. The growing strength of the left in post-war Europe was motivation enough for the CIA to develop its covert programs, and this was a circumstance deriving from World War II and the economic facts of life, not from Soviet propaganda and manipulation.

Operation Gladio

The rationale behind it was your standard cold-war paranoia: There's a good chance the Russians will launch an unprovoked invasion of Western Europe. And if they defeated the Western armies and forced them to flee, certain people had to remain behind to harass the Russians with guerrilla warfare and sabotage, and act as liaisons with those abroad. The "stay-behinds" would be provided with funds, weapons, communication equipment and training exercises. The planning for this covert paramilitary network, code-named

"Operation Gladio" (Italian for "sword"), began in 1949, involving initially the British, the Americans and the Belgians. It eventually established units in every non-communist country in Europe—including Greece and Turkey and neutral Sweden and Switzerland—with the apparent exceptions of Ireland and Finland. The question of whether the units were more under the control of national governments or NATO remains purposely unclear, although from an operational point of view, it appears that the CIA and various other intelligence services were calling the shots.

As matters turned out, in the complete absence of any Russian invasions, the operation was used almost exclusively to inflict political damage upon domestic leftist movements.

The Gladio story broke in Italy in the fall of 1990, stemming from a judicial investigation into a 1972 car-bombing which discovered that the explosives had come from one of the 139 secret weapons depots kept for Gladio's forces in Italy. Subsequently, the head of the Italian parliamentary inquiry into the matter revealed that "When Gladio was started, the Americans would often insist ... that the organization also had to be used to counter any insurgencies." Retired Greek Gen. Nikos Kouris told a similar story, declaring that a Greek force was formed with CIA help in 1955 to intervene in case of Communist threat, whether external or internal. "There were ex-military men, specially trained soldiers and also civilians. What held them together was one ideological common denominator: extreme rightism."

As in Germany (see Germany chapter), the Italian operation was closely tied to terrorists. A former Gladio agent, Roberto Cavallero, went public to charge that there was a direct link between Gladio and Italy's wave of terrorist bombings in the 1970s and early 1980s which left at least 300 dead. He said that Gladio had trained him and many others "to prepare groups which, in the event of an advance by left wing forces in our country, would fill the streets, creating a situation of such tension as to require military intervention." Cavallero was of course referring to electoral advances of the Italian Communist Party, not an invasion by the Soviet Union.

The single worst terrorist action was the bombing at the Bologna railway station in August 1980 which claimed 86 lives. The *Observer* of London later reported:

> The Italian railway bombings were blamed on the extreme Left as part of a strategy to convince voters that the country was in a state of tension and that they had no alternative to voting the safe Christian Democrat ticket. All clues point to the fact that they were masterminded from within Gladio.

One of the men sought for questioning in Italy about the Bologna bombing, Roberto Fiore, has lived in London ever since and the British government has refused to extradite him. He is apparently under the protective wing of MI6 (Britain's CIA) for whom he has provided valuable intelligence.

The kidnapping and murder in 1978 of Aldo Moro, the leader of the Christian Democrats, which was attributed to the Red Brigades, appears now to have also been the work of Gladio agents provocateurs who infiltrated the organization. Just prior to his abduction, Moro had announced his intention to enter into a governmental coalition with the Communist Party. Colonel Oswald Le Winter of the CIA, who served as a US liaison officer with Gladio, has stated that the planning staff of the Red Brigades was made up of intelligence agents.

In Belgium, in 1983, to convince the public that a security crisis existed, Gladio operatives as well as police officers staged a series of seemingly random shootings in supermarkets which, whether intended or not, led to several deaths. A year later, a party of US Marines parachuted into Belgium with the intention of attacking a police station. One

Belgian citizen was killed and one of the Marines lost an eye in the operation, that was intended to jolt the local Belgian police into a higher state of alert, and to give the impression to the comfortable population at large that the country was on the brink of Red revolution. Guns used in the operation were later planted in a Brussels house used by a Communist splinter group.

As late as 1990, large stockpiles of weapons and explosives for Operation Gladio could still be found in some member countries, and Italian Prime Minister Giulio Andreotti disclosed that more than 600 people still remained on the Gladio payroll in Italy.[13]

16. British Guiana 1953-1964
The CIA's international labor mafia

For a period of 11 years, two of the oldest democracies in the world, Great Britain and the United States, went to great lengths to prevent a democratically elected leader from occupying his office.

The man was Dr. Cheddi Jagan. The grandson of indentured immigrants from India, Jagan had become a dentist in the United States, then returned to his native Guiana. In 1953, at the age of 35, he and the People's Progressive Party (PPP) were elected by a large majority to head the government of the British colony. Jagan's victory was due in part to the fact that Indians comprised about 46 percent of the population; those of African origin made up about 36 percent.

The PPP's program in office was hardly revolutionary. It encouraged foreign investment in the mining sectors while attempting to institute liberal reforms such as strengthening the rights of unionists and tenant farmers, creating a public school system that would lessen church control of education, and removing a ban on the import of "undesirable" publications, films and records. But the British Conservative government was not disposed to live with such policies advocated by a man who talked suspiciously like a socialist. The government and the British media, as well as the American media, subjected the Jagan administration to a campaign of red-scare accusations and plain lies in the fashion of Senator McCarthy whose -ism was then all the rage in the United States.

Four and a half months after Jagan took office, the government of Winston Churchill flung him out. The British sent naval and army forces, suspended the constitution and removed the entire Guianese government. At the same time, the barristers drew up some papers which the Queen signed, so it was all nice and legal.[1]

"Her Majesty's Government," said the British Colonial Secretary during a debate in Parliament, "are not prepared to tolerate the setting up of Communist states in the British Commonwealth."[2]

The American attitude toward this slap in the face of democracy can be surmised by the refusal of the US government to allow Jagan to pass in transit through the United States when he tried to book a flight to London to attend the parliamentary debate. According to Jagan, Pan Am would not even sell him a ticket. (Pan Am has a long history of collaboration with the CIA, a practice initiated by the airline's president, Juan Trippe, the son-in-law of Roosevelt's Secretary of State, Edward R. Stettinius.)[3]

By this time the CIA had already gotten its foot in the door of the British Guiana labor movement, by means of the marriage of the Agency to the American Federation of Labor in the United States. One of the early offsprings of this union was the Inter-American Regional Labor Organization (ORIT from the Spanish). In the early 1950s, ORIT was instrumental in the conversion of the leading confederation of unions in Guiana, the Trades Union Council, from a militant labor organization to a vehicle of anti-communism. Wrote Serafino Romualdi, at one time the head of AIFLD (see below) and a long-time CIA collaborator: "Since my first visit to British Guiana in 1951, I did everything in my power to strengthen the democratic [i.e., anti-communist] trade union forces opposed to him [Jagan]."[4]

This was to have serious repercussions for Jagan in later years.

In 1957, running on a program similar to that of four years earlier, Jagan won the election again. This time the British deemed it wiser to employ more subtle methods for his removal and the CIA was brought into the picture, one of the rare instances in which the Agency has been officially allowed to operate in a British bailiwick. The CIA has done so, unofficially, on numerous occasions, to the displeasure of British authorities.

The CIA set to work to fortify those unions which already tended somewhat toward support of Jagan's leading political opponent, Forbes Burnham of the African Party. One of the most important of these was the civil servants' union, dominated by blacks.

Consequently, the CIA turned to Public Services International (PSI) in London, an international trade union secretariat for government employees, one of the international networks which exist to export the union know-how of advanced industrial countries to less-developed countries.

According to a study undertaken by *The Sunday Times* of London, by 1958 the PSI's "finances were low, and its stocks were low with its own parent body, the International Confederation of Free Trade Unions [set up by the CIA in 1949 to rival the Soviet-influenced World Federation of Trade Unions]. It needed a success of some kind. The financial crisis was resolved, quite suddenly, by the PSI's main American affiliate union, the American Federation of State, County and Municipal Employees (AFSCME)." AFSCME's boss, Dr Arnold Zander, told the PSI executive that he had "been shopping" and had found a donor.

"The spoils were modest at first—only a couple of thousand pounds in 1958. It was, the kind donor had said, for Latin America. The money went towards a PSI 'recruiting drive' in the northern countries of Latin America by one William Doherty, Jr., a man with some previous acquaintance of the CIA." (Doherty was later to become the Executive Director of the American Institute for Free Labor Development, the CIA's principal labor organization in Latin America.)

"The donor was presumably pleased, because next year, 1959, Zander was able to tell the PSI that his union was opening a full-time Latin American section in the PSI's behalf. The PSI was charmed."

The PSI's representative, said Zander, would be William Howard McCabe (a CIA labor apprentice). The *Times* continued:

> McCabe, a stocky, bullet-headed American, appeared to have no previous union history, but the PSI liked him. When he came to its meetings, he distributed cigarette lighters and photographs of himself doling out food parcels to the peasants. The lighters and the parcels were both inscribed "with the compliments of the PSI".[5]

In 1967, in the wake of numerous revelations about CIA covert financing, the new head of AFSCME admitted that the union had been heavily funded by the Agency until 1964 through a foundation conduit (see Appendix I). It was revealed that AFSCME's

International Affairs Department, which had been responsible for the British Guiana operation, had actually been run by two CIA "aides".[6]

CIA work within Third World unions typically involves a considerable educational effort, the basic premise of which is that all solutions will come to working people under a system of free enterprise, class co-operation and collective bargaining, and by opposing communism in collaboration with management and government, unless, of course, the government, as in this case, is itself "communist". The most promising students, those perhaps marked as future leaders, are singled out to be sent to CIA schools in the United States for further education.

The CIA, said *The Sunday Times*, also "appears to have had a good deal of success in encouraging politicians to break away from Jagan's party and government. Their technique of financing sympathetic figures was to take out heavy insurance policies for them."[7]

During the 1961 election campaign, the CIA's ongoing program was augmented by ad hoc operations from other American quarters. The US Information Service took the most unusual step of showing its films, depicting the evils of Castroism and communism, on street corners of British Guiana. And the Christian Anti-Communist Crusade brought its traveling road show down and spent a reported $76,000 on electoral propaganda which lived up to the organization's name.[8] One historian has described this as "a questionable activity for a private organization, which the State Department did nothing to discourage".[9] On the other hand, the activities of US government agencies in British Guiana were no less questionable.

Despite the orchestrated campaign directed against him, Jagan was re-elected by a comfortable majority of legislative seats, though with only a plurality of the popular vote.

In October, at his request, Jagan was received at the White House in Washington. He had come to talk about assistance for his development program. President Kennedy and his advisers, however, were interested in determining where Jagan stood on the political spectrum before granting any aid. Oddly, the meeting, as described by Kennedy aide Arthur Schlesinger, Jr. who was present, seemed to be conducted as if the Kennedy men were totally unaware of American destabilization activities in British Guiana.

To Jagan's expressed esteem for the politics of British Labour leader Aneurin Bevan, those in the room "all responded agreeably".

To Jagan's professed socialism, Kennedy asserted that "We are not engaged in a crusade to force private enterprise on parts of the world where it is not relevant."

But when Jagan, perhaps naively, mentioned his admiration for the scholarly, leftist journal, *Monthly Review*, it appears that he crossed an ideological line, which silently and effectively sealed his country's fate. "Jagan," wrote Schlesinger later, "was unquestionably some sort of Marxist."[10]

No economic aid was given to British Guiana while Jagan remained in power, and the Kennedy administration pressured the British to delay granting the country its independence, which had been scheduled to occur within the next year or two.[11] Not until 1966, when Jagan no longer held office, did British Guiana become the independent nation of Guyana.

In February 1962, the CIA helped to organize and finance anti-Jagan protests which used the newly announced budget as a pretext. The resulting strikes, riots and arson were wholly out of proportion to the alleged instigation. A Commonwealth Commission of Enquiry later concluded (perhaps to the discomfort of the British Colonial Office which had appointed it) that:

There is very little doubt that, despite the loud protestations of the trades union leaders to the contrary, political affinities and aspirations played a large part in shaping their policy and formulating their programme of offering resistance to the budget and making a determined effort to change the government in office.[12]

The CIA arranged, as it has on similar occasions, for North American and Latin American labor organizations, with which it had close ties, to support the strikers with messages of solidarity and food, thus enhancing the appearance of a genuine labor struggle. The agency also contrived for previously unheard-of radio stations to go on the air and for newspapers to print false stories about approaching Cuban warships.[13]

The centerpiece of the CIA's program in British Guiana was the general strike (so called, although its support was considerably less than total) which began in April 1963. It lasted for 80 days, the longest general strike in history, it is said.[14]

This strike, as in 1962, was called by the Trades Union Council (TUC) which, as we have seen, was a member in good standing of the CIA's international labor mafia. The head of the TUC was one Richard Ishmael who had been trained in the US at the CIA's American Institute for Free Labor Development along with other Guianese labor officials.

The strike period was marked by repeated acts of violence and provocation, including attacks on Jagan's wife and some of his ministers. Ishmael himself was later cited in a secret British police report as having been part of a terrorist group which had carried out bombings and arson attacks against government buildings during the strike.[15]

No action was taken against Ishmael and others in this group by British authorities who missed no opportunity to exacerbate the explosive situation, hoping that it would culminate in Jagan's downfall.

Meanwhile, CIA agents were giving "advice to local union leaders on how to organize and sustain" the strike, the *New York Times* subsequently reported. "They also provided funds and food supplies to keep the strikers going and medical supplies for pro-Burnham workers injured in the turmoil. At one point, one of the agents even served as a member of a bargaining committee from a Guiana dike workers' union that was negotiating with Dr. Jagan." This agent was later denounced by Jagan and forbidden to enter the country.[16] This is probably a reference to Gene Meakins, one of the CIA's main labor operatives, who had been serving as public relations advisor and education officer to the TUC. Meakins edited a weekly paper and broadcast a daily radio program by means of which he was able to generate a great deal of anti-Jagan propaganda.[17]

The *Sunday Times* study concluded that:

Jagan seems to have thought that the unions could hold out a month. But McCabe was providing the bulk of the strike pay, plus money for distress funds, for the strikers' daily 15 minutes on the radio and their propaganda, and considerable travelling expenses. All over the world, it seemed brother unions were clubbing together.

The mediator sent from London, Robert Willis, the general secretary of the London Typographical Society and a man not noted for his mercy in bargaining with newspaper managements was shocked. "It was rapidly clear to me that the strike was wholly political", he said. "Jagan was giving in to everything the strikers wanted, but as soon as he did they erected more demands".[18]

Financial support for the strike alone, channeled through the PSI and other labour organizations by the CIA, reached the sum of at least one million dollars.

American oil companies provided a further example of the multitude of resources the US can bring to bear upon a given target. The companies co-operated with the strikers by refusing to provide petroleum, forcing Jagan to appeal to Cuba for oil. During Jagan's remaining year in office, in the face of a general US economic embargo, he turned increasingly to the Soviet bloc. This practice of course provided ammunition to those critics of Jagan in British Guiana, the United States and Great Britain who insisted that he was a communist and thus fraught with all the dangers that communists are fraught with.

The strike was maintained primarily by black supporters of Forbes Burnham and by employers who locked out many of Jagan's Indian supporters. This inevitably exacerbated the already existing racial tensions, although *The Sunday Times* asserted that the "racial split was fairly amicable until the 1963 strike divided the country". Eventually, the tension broke out into bloodshed leaving hundreds dead and wounded and "a legacy of racial bitterness".[19]

Jagan was certainly aware, to some extent at least, of what was transpiring around him during the general strike. After it was over he charged that:

> The United States, in spite of protestations to the contrary by some of its leaders, is not prepared to permit a Socialist government or a government committed to drastic and basic reforms to exist in this hemisphere, even when this government has been freely elected ... It is all too clear that the United States will only support a democratic government if it favors a classic private enterprise system.[20]

In an attempt to surmount the hurdle of US obsession with the Soviet Union and "another Cuba in the Western hemisphere", Jagan proposed that British Guiana be "neutralized" by an agreement between the United States and the Soviet Union, as the two powers had done in the case of Austria. Officials in Washington had no comment on the suggestion.[21]

Cheddi Jagan's government managed to survive all the provocations and humiliations. With elections on the agenda for 1964, the British and their American cousins turned once again to the gentlemanly way of the pen.

The British Colonial Secretary, Duncan Sandys, who had been a leading party to the British-CIA agreement concerning Jagan, cited the strike and general unrest as proof that Jagan could not run the country or offer the stability that the British government required for British Guiana to be granted its independence. (Sandys was the founder, in 1948, of The European Movement, a CIA-funded cold-war organization.)[22]

This was, of course, a contrived position. Syndicated American columnist Drew Pearson, writing about the meeting between President Kennedy and British Prime Minister Macmillan in the summer of 1963, stated that "the main thing they agreed on was that the British would refuse to grant independence to Guiana because of a general strike against pro-Communist Prime Minister, Cheddi Jagan. That strike was secretly inspired by a combination of U.S. Central Intelligence money and British intelligence. It gave London the excuse it wanted."[23]

The excuse was used further to justify an amendment to the British Guiana constitution providing for a system of proportional representation in the election, a system that appeared certain to convert Jagan's majority of legislative seats into a plurality. Subsequently, the British-appointed Governor of British Guiana announced that he would not be bound to call on the leader of the largest party to form a government if it did not have a majority of seats, a procedure in striking contrast to that followed in Great Britain.

When, in October 1964, the Labour Party succeeded the Conservative Party to power in Great Britain, Jagan had hopes that the conspiracy directed against him would be squashed, for several high-ranking Labour leaders had stated publicly, and to Jagan personally, their opposition to the underhanded and anti-democratic policy of their Conservative Party foes. Within days of taking office, however, the Labour Party dashed these hopes.[24]

"Bowing to United States wishes," the *New York Times* disclosed, the Labour Party "ruled out early independence for British Guiana" and was going ahead with the proportional representation elections. Secretary of State Dean Rusk, it was reported, had left the new British Foreign Secretary, Patrick Gordon-Walker, "in no doubt that the United States would resist a rise of British Guiana as an independent Castro-type state".[25] On a previous occasion, Rusk had urged Gordon-Walker's Conservative predecessor, Lord Home, to suspend the British Guiana constitution again and "revert to direct colonial government".[26]

The intensive American lobbying effort against British Guiana (the actual campaign of subversion aside), led Conservative MP and former Colonial Secretary, Iain Macleod, to observe in the House of Commons: "There is an irony which we all recognize in the fact of America urging us all over the world towards colonial freedom except when it approaches her own doorstep."[27]

The day before the election of 7 December, a letter appeared in a British Guiana newspaper—a bogus pro-Communist letter, a tactic the CIA has used successfully the world over. The letter was purportedly written by Jagan's wife Janet to Communist Party members, in which she stated: "We can take comfort in the thought that the PNC [Burnham's party] will not be able to stay in power long ... our communist comrades abroad will continue to help us win eventual total victory."

Ms. Jagan quickly retorted that she would not be so stupid as to write a letter like that, but, as in all such cases, the disclaimer trailed weakly and too late behind the accusation.[28]

As expected, Jagan won only a plurality of the legislative seats, 24 of 53. The governor then called upon Forbes Burnham, who had come in second, to form a new government. Burnham had also been named as a terrorist in the British police report referred to earlier, as had several of his new government ministers.

Jagan refused to resign. British Army troops were put on full alert in the capital city of Georgetown. A week later, Her Majesty's Government waved its hand over a piece of paper, thereby enacting another amendment to the British Guiana constitution and closing a loophole which was allowing Jagan to stall for time. He finally surrendered to the inevitable.[29]

In 1990, at a conference in New York City, Arthur Schlesinger publicly apologized to Cheddi Jagan, who was also present. Schlesinger said that it was his recommendation to the British that led to the proportional representation tactic. "I felt badly about my role thirty years ago," the former Kennedy aide admitted. "I think a great injustice was done to Cheddi Jagan."[30]

Four years later, with Jagan again president—having won, in 1992, the country's first free election since he had been ousted—the Clinton administration prepared to nominate a new ambassador to Guyana: William Doherty, Jr. Jagan was flabbergasted and made his feelings known, such that Doherty was dropped from consideration.[31]

When it was time, in 1994, for the US government to declassify its British Guiana documents under the 30-year rule, the State Department and CIA refused to do so, reported the *New York Times*, because "it is not worth the embarrassment". The newspaper added:

Still-classified documents depict in unusual detail a direct order from the President to unseat Dr. Jagan, say Government officials familiar with the secret papers. Though many Presidents have ordered the CIA to undermine foreign leaders, they say the Jagan papers are a smoking gun: a clear written record, without veiled words or plausible denials, of a President's command to depose a Prime Minister.[32]

"They made a mistake putting Burnham in," said Janet Jagan looking back at it all. "The regrettable part is that the country went backwards." And so it had. One of the better-off countries in the region 30 years ago, Guyana in 1994 was among the poorest. Its principal export was people.[33]

17. Soviet Union late 1940s to 1960s
From spy planes to book publishing

Information ... hundreds of young Americans and émigré Russians gave their lives so that the United States could amass as much information as possible about the Soviet Union ... almost any information at all about the land Churchill had described as "a riddle wrapped in a mystery inside an enigma".

There is no evidence, however, that any of the information collected ever saved any lives, or served any other useful purpose for the world. Today, tons of files stuffed with reports, volumes of computer printouts, tapes, photographs, etc., lie in filing cabinets, gathering dust in warehouses in the United States and West Germany. Probably a good part of the material has already been shredded. Much of it has never been looked at, and never will be.

Beginning in the late 1940s, the US military, the CIA and the National Security Agency regularly sent aircraft along the borders of the Soviet Union to collect visual, photographic and electronic data of a military or industrial nature, particularly to do with Soviet missile and nuclear capability. The increasingly sophisticated planes and equipment, as well as satellites, submarines, and electronic listening posts in Turkey and Iran, produced vast amounts of computer input. At times, the planes would unintentionally drift over Soviet territory. At other times, they would do so intentionally in order to photograph a particular target, or to activate radar installations so as to capture their signals, or to evaluate the reaction of Soviet ground defenses against an attack. It was a dangerous game of aerial "chicken" and on many occasions the planes were met by anti-aircraft fire or Soviet fighter planes.

In both 1950 and 1951, an espionage airplane with a crew of ten was shot down, with no survivors. In 1969, a crew of 31 was lost, this time to North Korean fighters over the Sea of Japan. During the intervening years, there were dozens of air incidents involving American aircraft and Communist firepower, arising from hundreds, if not thousands, of espionage flights. Some of the spy planes made it safely back to base (which might be Turkey, Iran, Greece, Pakistan, Japan or Norway) after being attacked, and even hit; others were downed with loss of life or with crew members captured by the Soviets.[1]

There has been considerable confusion concerning the number and the fate of US airmen captured by the Soviets after their planes made forced landings or were shot down during the 1950s and '60s. Russian president Boris Yeltsin stated in 1992 that nine US planes had been shot down in the early 1950s and twelve American survivors had been held prisoner, their ultimate fate not yet discovered. Five months later, Dmitri Volkogonov, former Soviet general and co-chairman of a Russian-US commission investigating the whole question of missing Americans, told a US Senate committee that 730 airmen had been captured on cold war spy flights, their fate likewise unclear.[2]

The most notable of these incidents was of course the downing of the U-2 piloted by Francis Gary Powers on 1 May 1960. The ultra high-flying U-2 had been developed because of the vulnerability to being shot down of planes flying at normal altitudes. The disappearance of Powers and his U-2 somewhere in the Soviet Union ensnared the United States government publicly in an entanglement of a false cover story, denials, and amendments to denials. Finally, when the Russians presented Powers and his plane to the world, President Eisenhower had no alternative but to admit the truth. He pointedly added, however, that flights such as the U-2's were "distasteful but vital", given the Russian "fetish of secrecy and concealment".[3] One of Eisenhower's advisers, Emmet John Hughes, was later to observe that it thus took the administration only six days "to transform an unthinkable falsehood into a sovereign right."[4]

On several occasions, the United States protested to the Soviet Union about Soviet attacks on American planes which were not actually over Soviet territory, but over the Sea of Japan, for example. Though engaged in espionage, such flights, strictly speaking, appear to be acceptable under international law.

The most serious repercussion of the whole U-2 affair was that it doomed to failure the Eisenhower-Khrushchev summit meeting which took place two weeks later in Paris, and upon which so much hope for peace and detente had been placed by people all over the world.

Was the U-2 affair the unfortunate accident of timing that history has made it out to be? Col. L. Fletcher Prouty, US Air Force, Ret. has suggested otherwise. From 1955 to 1963, Prouty served as the liaison between the CIA and the Pentagon on matters concerning military support of "special operations". In his book, *The Secret Team*, Prouty suggests that the CIA and certain of the Agency's colleagues in the Pentagon sabotaged this particular U-2 flight, the last one scheduled before the summit. They did this, presumably, because they did not relish a lessening of cold-war tensions, their *raison d'être*.

The method employed, Prouty surmises, was remarkably simple. The U-2's engine needed infusions of liquid hydrogen to maintain the plane's incredible altitude, which placed it outside the range of Soviet firepower and interceptor aircraft. If the hydrogen container were only partly filled upon takeoff from Turkey, it would be simply a matter of time—calculable to coincide with the plane being over Soviet territory—before the U-2 was forced to descend to a lower altitude. At this point, whether the plane was shot down or Powers bailed out, allowing it to crash, is not certain. The Soviet Union claimed that it had shot down the U-2 at its normal high altitude with a rocket, but this was probably a falsehood born of four years of frustrating failure to shoot a single U-2 from the sky. In any event, the Russians were able to present to the world a partially intact spy plane along with a fully intact spy pilot, complete with all manner of incriminating papers on him, and an unused suicide needle. The presence of identification papers was no oversight, says Prouty: deliberately, "neither pilot nor plane were sanitized on this flight as was required on other flights".[5]

Powers, in his book, doesn't discuss the liquid hydrogen at all. He believed his plane was disabled and forced to descend by the shock waves of a Soviet near-miss. But he recounts technical problems with the plane even before the presumed near-miss.[6]

In light of the furor raised by the shooting down of a South Korean commercial airliner by the Soviet Union in 1983, which the Russians claimed was spying, it is interesting to note that Prouty also makes mention of the United States at one time using "a seemingly clean national commercial airline" of an unspecified foreign country "to do some camera spying or other clandestine project".[7]

To the Russians, the spy planes were more than simply a violation of their air space, and they rejected the notion put forth by the US that the flights were just another form of espionage—"intelligence collection activities are practiced by all countries", said Washington.[8] (At the time there had been no indication of Soviet flights over the United

States.)[9] The Russians viewed the flights as particularly provocative because airplanes are a means of conducting warfare, they can be considered as the beginning of hostilities, and may even be carrying bombs. The Russians could not forget that the Nazis had preceded their invasion of the Soviet Union with frequent reconnaissance overflights. Neither could they forget that in April 1958, US planes carrying nuclear bombs had flown over the Arctic in the direction of the USSR due to a false warning signal on American radar. The planes were called back when only two hours flying time separated them from the Soviet Union.[10]

No American plane dropped bombs on the Soviet Union but many of them dropped men assigned to carry out hostile missions. The men who fell from the sky were Russians who had emigrated to the West where they were recruited by the CIA and other Western intelligence organizations.

The leading émigré organization was known as National Alliance of Russian Solidarists, or the National Union of Labor (NTS). It was composed largely of two distinct groups: the sons of the Russians who had gone to the West following the revolution, and those Russians who, through circumstance or choice, had wound up in Western Europe at the close of the Second World War. Members of both groups had collaborated with the Nazis during the war. Although NTS was generally classified in the right wing of the various émigré organizations, their collaboration had been motivated more by anti-Stalinism than by pro-Nazi sentiments.

NTS was based primarily in West Germany where, throughout the 1950s, the CIA was the organization's chief benefactor, often its sole support. At a CIA school set up in Germany, under the imposing name of the Institute for the Study of the USSR, as well as at schools in Great Britain and the United States, the Agency provided NTS members with extensive training before airdropping them into Soviet territory. The men landed on their native soil elaborately equipped, with everything from weapons to collapsible bicycles, frog-men suits, and rubber mats for crossing electrically-charged barbed-wire fences.

The Russians were returned to their homeland for a variety of reasons: to gather intelligence about military and technological installations; commit assassinations; obtain current samples of identification documents; assist Western agents to escape; engage in sabotage, for which they were well trained (methods of derailing trains and wrecking bridges, actions against arms factories and power plants, etc.); or instigate armed political struggle against Communist rule by linking up with resistance movements—a wholly unrealistic goal given the feeble state of such movements, but one which some NTS fanatics swore by.

It will never be known just how many men the CIA infiltrated into the Soviet Union, not only by air but by border crossings and by boat as well; many hundreds at least. As to their fate ... the Soviet Union published a book in 1961 called *Caught In the Act* (= CIA), in which were listed the names and other details of about two dozen infiltrators the Russians claimed to have captured, often almost immediately upon arrival. Some were executed, others received prison sentences, one allegedly was an individual who had taken part in a mass execution of Jews in German-occupied Soviet territory. The book asserts that there were many more caught who were not listed. This may have been a self-serving statement, but it was a relatively simple matter for the Russians to infiltrate the émigrés' ranks in Western Europe and learn the entire operation.

The CIA, to be sure, was not naive about this practice. The Agency went so far as to torture suspected defectors in Munich—using such esoteric methods as applying turpentine to a man's testicles or sealing someone in a room and playing Indonesian music at deafening levels until he cracked.[11]

The Russians further claimed that some of those smuggled in were furnished with special radio beacons to guide planes where to land other agents, and which could also be used to direct US bombers in the event of war.

Some of the émigrés made it back to Western Europe with their bits and pieces of information, or after attempting to carry out some other assignment. Others, provided with a complete set of necessary documents, were instructed to integrate themselves back into Soviet society and become "agents in place". Still others, caught up in the emotions of being "home", turned themselves in—once again, "the human factor", which no amount of training or indoctrination can necessarily circumvent.[12]

No American operation against the Soviet Union would be complete without its propaganda side: bringing the gospel to the heathen, in a myriad of ways that displayed the creativity of the CIA and its team of émigrés.

Novel mechanisms were developed to enable airplanes and balloons to drop anti-Communist literature over the Soviet Union. When the wind was right, countless leaflets and pamphlets were scattered across the land; or quantities of literature were floated downstream in waterproof packages.

Soviet citizens coming to the West were met at every turn by NTS people handing out their newspapers and magazines in Russian and Ukrainian. To facilitate contact, NTS at times engaged in black market operations and opened small shops which catered to Russians at cheap prices. From North Africa to Scandinavia, the CIA network confronted Soviet seamen, tourists, officials, athletes, even Soviet soldiers in East Germany, to present them with the Truth as seen by the "Free World", as well as to pry information from them, to induce them to defect, or to recruit them as spies. Hotel rooms were searched, phones tapped, bribes offered, or blackmail threatened in attempts to reach these ends. Actions were also undertaken to entrap or provoke Soviet diplomatic personnel so as to cause their expulsion and/or embarrass the Soviet Union.[13]

The propaganda offensive led the US government into the book publishing business. Under a variety of arrangements with American and foreign publishers, distributors, literary agents and authors, the CIA and the United States Information Agency (USIA) produced, subsidized or sponsored "well over a thousand books" by 1967 which were deemed to serve a propaganda need.[14] Many of the books were sold in the United States as well as abroad. None bore any indication of US government involvement. Of some, said the USIA, "We control the things from the very idea down to the final edited manuscript."[15]

Some books were published, and at times written, only after the USIA or the CIA agreed to purchase a large number of copies. There is no way of determining what effect this financial incentive had upon a publisher or author concerning a book's tone and direction. In some cases, Washington released classified information to an author to assist him or her in writing the book. In 1967, following revelations about CIA domestic activities, this practice purportedly came to an end in the US although it continued abroad. A Senate committee in 1976 stated that during the preceding few years, the CIA had been connected with the publication of some 250 books, mostly in foreign languages.[16] Some of these were most likely later reprinted in the United States.

The actual identity of most of the books, however, is still classified. Among those which have been revealed are: *The Dynamics of Soviet Society* by Walt Rostow, *The New Class* by Milovan Djilas, *Concise History of the Communist Party* by Robert A. Burton, *The Foreign Aid Programs of the Soviet Bloc and Communist China* by Kurt Muller, *In Pursuit of World Order* by Richard N. Gardner, *Peking and People's Wars* by Major

General Sam Griffith, *The Yenan Way* by Eudocio Ravines, *Life and Death in Soviet Russia* by Valentin Gonzalez, *The Anthill* by Suzanne Labin, *The Politics of Struggle: The Communist Front and Political Warfare* by James D. Atkinson, *From Colonialism to Communism* by Hoang Van Chi, *Why Vietnam?* by Frank Trager, and *Terror in Vietnam* by Jay Mallin. In addition, the CIA financed and distributed throughout the world the animated cartoon film of George Orwell's *Animal Farm*.[17.]

The most pervasive propaganda penetration of the socialist bloc was by means of the airwaves: Numerous transmitters, tremendous wattage, and often round-the-clock programming brought Radio Liberty and Radio Free Russia to the Soviet Union, Radio Free Europe and Radio in the American Sector to Eastern Europe, and the Voice of America to all parts of the world. With the exception of the last, the stations were ostensibly private organizations financed by "gifts" from American corporations, nickel-and-dime donations from the American public, and other private sources. In actuality, the CIA covertly funded almost all of the costs until 1971; exposure of the Agency's role in 1967 (although it had been widely assumed long before then) led to Congress eventually instituting open governmental financing of the stations.

The stations served the purpose of filling in some of the gaps and correcting the falsehoods of the Communist media, but could not escape presenting a picture of the world, both East and West, shot through with their own omissions and distortions. Their mission in life was to emphasize whatever could make the Communist regimes look bad. "To many in the CIA," wrote Victor Marchetti, former senior official of the Agency, "the primary value of the radios was to sow discontent in Eastern Europe and, in the process, to weaken the communist governments".[18]

Many of the Russians who worked for the various stations, which broadcast at length about freedom, democracy and other humanitarian concerns, were later identified by the US Justice Department as members of Hitler's notorious *Einsatzgruppen*, which rounded up and killed numerous Jews in the Soviet Union. One of these worthies was Stanislaw Stankievich, under whose command a mass murder of Jews in Byelorussia was carried out in which babies were buried alive with the dead, presumably to save ammunition. Stankievich wound up working for Radio Liberty. German war criminals as well were employed by the CIA in a variety of anti-Soviet operations.[19]

By every account, the sundry programs to collect strategic information about the Soviet Union, particularly via infiltration into the country and encountering Soviet nationals in the West, were a singular flop. The information reported was usually trivial, spotty, garbled, or out-of-date. Worse, it was often embellished, if not out-and-out fabricated. Many post-war émigrés in Western Europe made their living in the information business. It was their most saleable commodity. From a real or fictitious meeting with a Soviet citizen they would prepare a report which was often just ordinary facts with a bit of political color added on. At times, as many as four versions of the report would be produced, differing in style and quantity of "facts"; written by four different people, the reports would then be sold separately to US, British, French and West German intelligence agencies. The CIA's version contained everything in the other three versions, which were eventually transmitted to the Agency by the other countries without their source being revealed. Analysis of all the reports tended to bring the CIA to the conclusion that the NTS was giving them the fullest picture of all, and that the information all tallied. NTS looked good, and the files grew thick.[20]

The CIA's Russian files in Washington, meanwhile, approached mountainous proportions with the data acquired from opening mail between the Soviet Union and the United

States, a practice begun in the early 1950s and continued at least into the 1970s.[21] (Said a Post Office counsel in 1979: "If there was no national security mail cover program, the FBI might be inhibited in finding out if a nation was planning war against us.")[22]

Former CIA officer Harry Rositzke, who was closely involved with anti-Soviet operations after the war, later wrote that the primary task of the émigrés infiltrated into the Soviet Union during the early years—and the same could probably be said of the spyplanes—was to provide "early warning" of a Soviet military offensive against the West, an invasion which, in the minds of cold-warriors in the American government, appeared perpetually "imminent". This apprehension was reminiscent of the alarms sounded following the Russian Revolution (see Introduction to the Original Edition) and similarly flourished despite the fact of a Russia recently devastated by a major war and hardly in a position to undertake a military operation of any such magnitude. Nevertheless, wrote Rositzke, "It was officially estimated that Soviet forces were capable of reaching the English Channel in a matter of weeks. ... It was an axiom in Washington that Stalin was plotting war. When would it come?" He pointed out, however, that "The mere existence of radio-equipped agents on Soviet terrain with no early warnings to report had some cautionary value in tempering the war scare among the military estimators at the height of the Cold War."[23]

A secret report of the National Security Resources Board of January 1951 warned: "As things are now going, by 1953 if not 1952, the Soviet aggressors will assume complete control of the world situation."[24]

Rositzke, although a committed anti-Communist, recognized the unreality of such thinking. But, as he explained, his was a minority opinion in official Washington:

> The facts available even at the time suggested the far greater likelihood that Moscow's postwar strategy, including the conversion of Eastern Europe into a western buffer, was basically defensive. I argued this thesis with some of the CIA analysts working on Soviet estimates and with some Pentagon audiences, but it was not a popular view at the time. It is nonetheless a simple fact that no scenario was written then, nor has it been written since, to explain *why* the Russians would want to conquer Western Europe by force or to bomb the United States. Neither action would have contributed in any tangible way to the Soviet national interest and would have hazarded the destruction of the Soviet state. This basic question was never raised, for the Cold War prism created in the minds of the diplomatic and military strategists a clear-cut world of black and white; there were no grays.[25]

Several years were to pass, Rositzke pointed out, before it became clear to Washington that there were no warnings, early or otherwise, to report. This, however, had no noticeable effect upon the United States' military build-up or cold-war propaganda.

18. Italy 1950s to 1970s
Supporting the Cardinal's orphans and techno-fascism

After the multifarious extravaganza staged by the United States in 1948 to exorcise the spectre of Communism that was haunting Italy, the CIA settled in place for the long haul with a less flamboyant but more insidious operation.

A White House memorandum, prepared after the 1953 election, reported that "Neither the Moscow war stick nor the American economic carrot was being visibly brandished over the voters in this election."[1] Covert funding was the name of the game. Victor Marchetti, former executive assistant to the Deputy Director of the CIA, has revealed that in the 1950s the Agency "spent some $20 to $30 million a year, or maybe more, to finance its programs in Italy." Expenditures in the 1960s, he added, came to about $10 million annually.[2]

The CIA itself has admitted that between 1948 and 1968, it paid a total of $65,150,000 to the Christian Democrats and other parties, to labor groups, and to a wide variety of other organizations in Italy.[3] It also spent an undisclosed amount in support of magazines and book publishers and other means of news and opinion manipulation, such as planting news items in non-American media around the world which cast unfavorable light upon communism, then arranging for these stories to be reprinted in friendly Italian publications.[4]

It is not known when, if ever, the CIA ended its practice of funding anti-Communist groups in Italy. Internal Agency documents of 1972 reveal contributions of some $10 million to political parties, affiliated organizations, and 21 individual candidates in the parliamentary elections of that year.[5] At least $6 million was passed to political leaders for the June 1976 elections.[6] And in the 1980s, CIA Director William Casey arranged for Saudi Arabia to pay $2 million to prevent the Communists from achieving electoral gains in Italy.[7]

Moreover, the largest oil company in the United States, Exxon Corp., admitted that between 1963 and 1972 it had made political contributions to the Christian Democrats and several other Italian political parties totaling $46 million to $49 million. Mobil Oil Corp. also contributed to the Italian electoral process to the tune of an average $500,000 a year from 1970 through 1973. There is no report that these corporate payments derived from persuasion by the CIA or the State Department, but it seems rather unlikely that the firms would engage so extravagantly in this unusual sideline with complete spontaneity.[8]

Much of the money given by the CIA to Italian political parties since World War II, said a former high-level US official, ended up "in villas, in vacation homes and in Swiss bank accounts for the politicians themselves."[9]

A more direct American intervention into the 1976 elections was in the form of propaganda. Inasmuch as political advertising is not allowed on Italian television, the US Ambassador to Switzerland, Nathaniel Davis, arranged for the purchase of large blocks of time on Monte Carlo TV to present a daily "news" commentary by the editorial staff of the Milan newspaper *Il Giornale Nuovo,* which was closely associated to the CIA. It was this newspaper that, in May 1981, set in motion that particular piece of international disinformation known as "The KGB Plot to Kill the Pope".

Another Italian newspaper, the *Daily American* of Rome, for decades the country's leading English-language paper, was for a long period in the 1950s to the '70s partly owned and/or managed by the CIA. "We 'had' at least one newspaper in every foreign capital at any given time," the CIA admitted in 1977, referring to papers owned outright or heavily subsidized, or infiltrated sufficiently to have stories printed which were useful to the Agency or suppress those it found detrimental.[10]

Ambassador Davis also arranged for news items which had been placed in various newspapers by the Agency to be read on Monte Carlo TV and Swiss TV, both of which were received in Italy. The programs were produced in Milan by Franklin J. Tonnini of the US Diplomatic Corps, and Michael Ledeen, a reporter with *Il Giornale Nuovo.*[11] (Ledeen, an American, was later a consultant to the Reagan administration and a senior fellow at the conservative think-tank of Georgetown University in Washington, the Center for Strategic and International Studies.)

The relentless fight against the Italian Communist Party took some novel twists. One, in the 1950s, was the brainchild of American Ambassador Clare Booth Luce. The celebrated Ms. Luce (playwright and wife of *Time* magazine publisher Henry Luce) decided to make it known that no US Department of Defense procurement contracts would be awarded to Italian firms whose employees had voted to be represented by the Communist-controlled labor union. In the case of Fiat, this had dramatic results: The Communist union's share of the vote promptly fell from 60 to 38 percent.[12]

Then there was the case of Cardinal Giovanni Battista Montini, another beneficiary of CIA largesse. The payments made to him reveal something of the Agency's mechanistic thinking about why people become radicals. It seems that the good Cardinal was promoting orphanages in Italy during the 1950s and 1960s and, says Victor Marchetti, "The thinking was that if such institutions were adequately supported, many young people would be able to live well there and so would not one day fall into Communist hands."[13] The Cardinal, as a Monsignor, had been involved with the Vatican's operation to smuggle Nazis to freedom after World War II. He had a long history of association with Western governments and their intelligence agencies. In 1963, he became Pope Paul VI.[14]

In a 1974 interview, Marchetti also spoke of the training provided by the Agency to the Italian security services:

> They are trained, for example, to confront disorders and student demonstrations, to prepare dossiers, to make the best possible use of bank data and tax returns of individual citizens, etc. In other words, to watch over the population of their country with the means offered by technology. This is what I call techno-fascism.[15]

William Colby, later Director of the CIA, arrived in Italy in 1953 and devoted the next five years of his life to financing and advising center/right organizations for the express purpose of inducing the Italian people to turn away from the leftist bloc, particularly the Communist Party, and keep it from taking power in the 1958 elections. In his account of that period he justifies this program on the grounds of supporting "democracy" or "center democracy" and preventing Italy from becoming a Soviet satellite. Colby perceived all virtue and truth to be bunched closely around the center of the political spectrum, and the Italian Communist Party to be an extremist organization committed to abolishing democracy and creating a society modeled after the (worst?) excesses of Stalinist Russia. He offers no evidence to support his conclusion about the Communists, presumably because he regards it as self-evident, as much to the reader as to himself. Neither, for that matter, does he explain what was this thing called "democracy" which he so cherishes and which the Communists were so eager to do away with.[16]

Colby comes across as a technocrat who carried out the orders of his "side" and mouthed the party line without serious examination. When Oriana Fallaci, the Italian journalist, interviewed him in 1976, she remarked at the close of a frustrating conversation, "Had you been born on the other side of the barricade, you would have been a perfect Stalinist." To which, Colby replied: "I reject that statement. But ... well ... it might be. No, no. It might not."[17]

American policy makers dealing with Italy in the decades subsequent to Colby's time there did not suffer any less than he from hardening of the categories. Colby, after all, took pains to point out his *liberal* leanings. These were men unable to view the Italian Communist Party in its indigenous political context, but only as a "national security" threat to the United States and NATO. Yet, all those years, the party was proceeding along a path revisionist enough to make Lenin turn in his grave if he were in one. The path was marked by billboards proclaiming the "democratic advance to socialism" and the "national road to socialism", the abandonment of "the dictatorship of the proletariat" and the denunciation of the Soviet invasion of Czechoslovakia. The party pushed its "national" role as responsible opposition, participated in "the drive for productivity", affirmed its support for a multiparty system and for Italy remaining in the Common Market and in NATO, and was second to none in its condemnation of any form of terrorism. On many occasions, it was the principal political force in city governments including Rome, Florence and Venice, without any noticeable return to barbarism, and was a *de facto* participant in the running of the Italian state. (The Socialist Party, a prime target of the United States in the 1948 elections, was a formal member of the government for much of the 1960s to the 1990s.)

In the files of the State Department and the CIA lie any number of internal reports prepared by anonymous analysts testifying to the reality of the Communist Party's "historic compromise" and the evolution of its estrangement from the Soviet Union known as "Eurocommunism."

In the face of this, however—in the face of everything—American policy remained rooted in place, fixed in a time that was no longer, and probably never was; a policy that had nothing to do with democracy (by whatever definition) and everything to do with the conviction that a Communist government in Italy would not have been the supremely pliant cold-war partner that successive Christian Democrat regimes were for decades. It would not have been enough for such a government to be independent of Moscow. The problem with a Communist government was that it would probably have tried to adopt the same position towards Washington.

19. Vietnam 1950-1973

The hearts and minds circus

Contrary to repeated statements by Washington officials during the 1960s that the United States did not intervene in Vietnam until, and only because, "North Vietnam invaded South Vietnam", the US was deeply and continually involved in that woeful land from the year 1950 onwards.

The initial, fateful step was the decision to make large-scale shipments of military equipment (tanks, transport planes, etc.) to the French in Vietnam in the spring and summer of 1950. In April, Secretary of State Dean Acheson had told French officials that the United States government was set against France negotiating with their Northern-based Vietnamese foes, the Vietminh[1] (also spelled Viet Minh or Viet-Minh: the name was short for League for the Independence of Vietnam, a broadly-based nationalist movement led by Communists). Washington was not particularly sympathetic to France's endeavor to regain control of its colony of 100 years and had vacillated on the issue, but the rise to power of the Communists in China the previous autumn had tipped the scale in favor of supporting the French. To the Truman administration, the prospect of another Communist government in Asia was intolerable. There was a secondary consideration as well at the time: the need to persuade a reluctant France to support American plans to include Germany in West European defense organizations.

During World War II, the Japanese had displaced the French. Upon the defeat of Japan, the Vietminh took power in the North, while the British occupied the South, but soon turned it back to the French. Said French General Jean Leclerc in September 1945: "I didn't come back to Indochina to give Indochina back to the Indochinese."[2] Subsequently, the French emphasized that they were fighting for the "free world" against communism, a claim made in no small part to persuade the United States to increase its aid to them.

American bombers, military advisers and technicians by the hundreds were to follow the first aid shipments, and over the next few years direct American military aid to the French war effort ran to about a billion dollars a year. By 1954, the authorized aid had reached the sum of $1.4 billion and constituted 78 percent of the French budget for the war.[3]

The extensive written history of the American role in Indochina produced by the Defense Department, later to be known as "The Pentagon Papers", concluded that the decision to provide aid to France "directly involved" the United States in Vietnam and "set" the course for future American policy.[4]

There had been another path open. In 1945 and 1946, Vietminh leader Ho Chi Minh had written at least eight letters to President Truman and the State Department asking for America's help in winning Vietnamese independence from the French. He wrote that world peace was being endangered by French efforts to reconquer Indochina and he requested that the "four powers" (US, USSR, China, and Great Britain) intervene in order to mediate a fair settlement and bring the Indochinese issue before the United Nations.[5] (This was a remarkable repeat of history. In 1919, following the First World War, Ho Chi Minh had appealed to US Secretary of State Robert Lansing for America's help in achieving basic civil liberties and an improvement in the living conditions for the colonial subjects of French Indochina. This plea, too, was ignored.)[6]

Despite the fact that Ho Chi Minh and his followers had worked closely with the American OSS (the forerunner of the CIA) during the recently ended world war, while the French authorities in Indochina had collaborated with the Japanese, the United States failed to answer any of the letters, did not reveal that it had received them, and eventually sided with the French. In 1950, part of the publicly stated rationale for the American position was that Ho Chi Minh was not really a "genuine nationalist" but rather a tool of "international communism", a conclusion that could be reached only by deliberately ignoring the totality of his life's work. He and the Vietminh had, in fact, been long-time admirers of the United States. Ho trusted the US more than he did the Soviet Union and reportedly had a picture of George Washington and a copy of the American Declaration of Independence on his desk. According to a former OSS officer, Ho sought his advice on framing the Vietminh's own declaration of independence. The actual declaration of 1945 begins with the familiar "All men are created equal. They are endowed by their Creator with certain inalienable rights, among these are Life, Liberty and the pursuit of Happiness."[7]

But it was the French who were to receive America's blessing. Ho Chi Minh was, after all, some kind of communist.

The United States viewed the French struggle in Vietnam and their own concurrent intervention in Korea as two links in the chain aimed at "containing" China. Washington was adamantly opposed to the French negotiating an end to the war which would leave the Vietminh in power, in the northern part of the country, and, at the same time, free the Chinese to concentrate exclusively on their Korean border. In 1952, the US exerted strong pressure upon France not to pursue peace feelers extended by the Vietminh, and a French delegation, scheduled to meet with Vietminh negotiators in Burma, was hastily recalled to Paris.

Bernard Fall, the renowned French scholar on Indochina, believed that the canceled negotiations "could perhaps have brought about a cease-fire on a far more acceptable basis" for the French "than the one obtained two years later in the shadow of crushing military defeat".[8]

Subsequently, to keep the French from negotiating with the Vietminh, the United States used the threat of a cessation of their substantial economic and military aid.[9] (This prompted a French newspaper to comment that "the Indochina War has become France's number one dollar-earning export".)[10]

In November 1953, the omnipresent CIA airline, CAT, helped the French air force airlift 16,000 men into a fortified base the French had established in a valley in the North called Dien Bien Phu. When the garrison was later surrounded and cut off by the Vietminh, CAT pilots, flying US Air Force C-119s, often through anti-aircraft fire, delivered supplies to the beleaguered French forces, in this their Waterloo.[11]

By 1954, the *New York Times* could report that "The French Air Force is now almost entirely equipped with American planes."[12] The United States had also constructed a number of airfields, ports and highways in Indochina to facilitate the war effort, some of which American forces were to make use of in their later wars in that area.

In April 1954, when a French military defeat was apparent and negotiations at Geneva were scheduled, the National Security Council urged President Eisenhower "to inform Paris that French acquiescence in a Communist take-over of Indochina would bear on its status as one of the Big Three" and that "U.S. aid to France would automatically cease".[13]

A Council paper recommended that "It be U.S. policy to accept nothing short of a military victory in Indo-China" and that the "U.S. actively oppose any negotiated settlements in Indo-China at Geneva". The Council stated further that, if necessary, the US should consider continuing the war without French participation.[14]

The Eisenhower administration had for some time very seriously considered committing American combat troops to Vietnam. Apparently this move was not made only because of uncertainty about congressional approval and the refusal of other countries to send even a token force, as they had done in Korea, to remove the appearance of a purely American operation.[15] "We are confronted by an unfortunate fact," lamented Secretary of State John Foster Dulles at a 1954 Cabinet meeting. "Most of the countries of the world do not share our view that Communist control of any government anywhere is in itself a danger and a threat."[16]

In May, the Chairman of the Joint Chiefs of Staff, Admiral Arthur Radford, sent a memorandum to Defense Secretary Charles Wilson on "Studies With Respect to Possible U.S. Actions Regarding Indochina" which stated that "The employment of atomic weapons is contemplated in the event that such course appears militarily advantageous."[17] (General Charles Willoughby, MacArthur's director of intelligence, put it a bit more poetically when he advocated the use of atomic bombs "to create a belt of scorched earth across the avenues of communism to block the Asiatic hordes".)[18]

By this time, two American aircraft carriers equipped with atomic weapons had been ordered into the Gulf of Tonkin, in the North of Vietnam,[19] and Dulles is, in fact, reported to have offered his French counterpart, Georges Bidault, atomic bombs to save Dien Bien Phu. Bidault was obliged to point out to Dulles that the use of atomic bombs in a war of such close armed conflict would destroy the French troops as well as the Vietminh.[20]

Dulles regularly denounced China, in the ultra-sanctimonious manner he was known for, for assisting the Vietminh, as if the Chinese had no cause or right to be alarmed about an anti-communist military crusade taking place scant miles from their border. As the Geneva conference approached, a CIA propaganda team in Singapore began to disseminate fabricated news items to advance the idea that "the Chinese were giving full armed support to the Viet-Minh" and to "identify" the Viet-Minh "with the world Communist movement". The CIA believed that such stories would strengthen the non-Communist side at the Geneva talks.[21]

Joseph Burkholder Smith was a CIA officer in Singapore. His "press asset" was one Li Huan Li, an experienced local journalist. It is instructive to note the method employed in the creation and dissemination of one such news report about the Chinese. After Smith and Li had made up their story, Li attended the regular press conference held by the British High Commissioner in Singapore, Malcolm MacDonald. At the conference, Li mentioned the report and asked the Commissioner if he had any comment. As expected, MacDonald had nothing to say about it one way or the other. The result was the following news item:

> MORE CHINESE SUPPLIES AND TROOPS SPOTTED EN ROUTE TO HAIPHONG. At the press conference of the British High Commissioner for Southeast Asia today, reports of the sightings of Chinese naval vessels and supply ships in the Tonkin Gulf en route from Hainan to Haiphong were again mentioned.
> According to these reports, the most recent of many similar sightings occurred one week ago when a convoy of ten ships were spotted. Among them were two armed Chinese naval vessels indicating that the convoy consisted of troops as well as arms and supplies.
> High Commissioner Malcolm MacDonald would not elaborate further about these reports.[22]

The story was put onto a wire service in the morning, and by the evening had gone around the world, coming back to Singapore on the European relay to Asia.

The Geneva conference, on 20 July 1954, put a formal end to the war in Vietnam. The United States was alone in refusing to sign the Final Declaration, purely because it was peeved at the negotiated settlement, which precluded any further military effort to defeat the Vietminh. There had been ample indication of American displeasure with the whole process well before the end of the conference. Two weeks earlier, for example, President Eisenhower had declared at a news conference: "I will not be a party to any treaty that makes anybody a slave; now that is all there is to it."[23] But the US did issue a "unilateral declaration" in which it agreed to "refrain from the threat or the use of force to disturb" the accords.[24]

The letter and the spirit of the ceasefire agreement and the Final Declaration looked forward to a Vietnam free from any military presence other than Vietnamese or French, and free from any aggressive operations. However, while the conference was still in session in June, the United States began assembling a paramilitary team inside Vietnam. By August, only days after the close of the conference, the team was in place. Under the direction of CIA leading-light Edward Lansdale, fresh from his success in the Philippines, a campaign of military and psychological warfare was carried out against the Vietminh. (Lansdale's activities in Vietnam were later enshrined in two semi-fictional works, *The Ugly American* and *The Quiet American*.) Over the next six months, Lansdale's clandestine team executed such operations as the following:

- Encouraged the migration of Vietnamese from the North to the South through "an extremely intensive, well-coordinated, and, in terms of its objective, very successful ... psychological warfare operation. Propaganda slogans and leaflets appealed to the devout Catholics with such themes as 'Christ has gone to the South' and the 'Virgin Mary has departed from the North'."[25]

- Distributed other bogus leaflets, supposedly put out by the Vietminh, to instill trepidation in the minds of people in the North about how life would be under Communist rule. The following day, refugee registration to move South tripled. (The exodus of Vietnamese to the South during the "regrouping" period that followed the Geneva Accords was often cited by American officials in the 1960s, as well as earlier, as proof of the fact that the people did not want to live under communism—"They voted with their feet" was the catchphrase.) Still other "Vietminh" leaflets were aimed at discouraging people in the South from returning to the North.

- Infiltrated paramilitary forces into the North under the guise of individuals choosing to live there.
- Contaminated the oil supply of the bus company in Hanoi so as to lead to a gradual wreckage of the bus engines.
- Took "the first actions for delayed sabotage of the railroad (which required teamwork with a CIA special technical team in Japan who performed their part brilliantly)."
- Instigated a rumor campaign to stir up hatred of the Chinese, with the usual stories of rapes.
- Created and distributed an almanac of astrological predictions carefully designed to play on Vietnamese fears and superstitions and undermine life in the North while making the future of the South appear more attractive.
- Published and circulated anti-Communist articles and "news" reports in newspapers and leaflets.
- Attempted, unsuccessfully, to destroy the largest printing establishment in the North because it intended to remain in Hanoi and do business with the Vietminh.
- Laid some of the foundation for the future American war in Vietnam by: sending selected Vietnamese to US Pacific bases for guerrilla training; training the armed forces of the South who had fought with the French; creating various military support facilities in the Philippines; smuggling into Vietnam large quantities of arms and military equipment to be stored in hidden locations; developing plans for the "pacification of Vietminh and dissident areas".[26]

At the same time, the United States began an economic boycott against the North Vietnamese and threatened to blacklist French firms which were doing business with them.[27]

Another development during this period that had very profound consequences for the coming tragedy was the cancelation of the elections that would have united North and South Vietnam as one nation.

The Geneva Accords specified that elections under international supervision were to be held in July 1956, with "consultations" to prepare for them to be held "from 20 July 1955 onwards". The United States, in its unilateral declaration, had reiterated this pledge: "In the case of nations now divided against their will, we shall continue to seek to achieve unity through free elections supervised by the United Nations to insure that they are conducted fairly."

The elections were never held. On 16 July 1955, four days before the consultations were scheduled to begin, President Ngo Dinh Diem of South Vietnam issued a statement that made it clear that he had no intention of engaging in the consultations, much less the elections.[28] Three days later, North Vietnam sent Diem a formal note calling for the talks, but Diem remained firm in his position. Efforts by France and Great Britain to persuade Diem to begin the talks were to no avail.

The reason for Diem's intransigence is well known. He, like President Eisenhower and John Foster Dulles, knew that Ho Chi Minh would be a certain winner of any national elections. A CIA National Intelligence Estimate in the autumn concluded that the Diem regime (which Lansdale himself called "fascistic")[29] "almost certainly would not be able to defeat the communists in country-wide elections."[30] Later, Eisenhower was to write in his memoirs: "I have never talked or corresponded with a person knowledgeable in Indochinese affairs who did not agree that had elections been held as of the time of the fighting, possibly 80 percent of the population would have voted for the Communist Ho Chi Minh as their leader rather than Chief of State Bao Dai."[31] (The latter was Diem's predecessor.)

The study of the Pentagon papers cited "State Department cables and National Security Council memorandums indicating that the Eisenhower Administration wished to postpone the elections as long as possible and communicated its feelings to Mr. Diem."[32]

This was support that Diem could not have done without, for, as the Pentagon historians point out: "Without the threat of U.S. intervention, South Vietnam could not have refused to even discuss the elections called for in 1956 under the Geneva settlement without being immediately overrun by the Vietminh armies."[33]

The public statements of Diem and Dulles spoke only of their concern that the elections would not be "free", which served to obscure the fact that Ho Chi Minh did not need to resort to fraud in order to win, as well as ignoring the announcements of both the United Nations and the International Control Commission (set up in Vietnam by the Geneva Accords) that they were ready to supervise the elections.

In any event, Diem's commitment to free elections may be surmised from a referendum he held in October 1955 in South Vietnam to invest his regime with a semblance of legality, in which he received 98.2 percent of the vote. *Life* magazine later reported that Diem's American advisers had told him that a 60 percent margin would be quite sufficient and would look better, "but Diem insisted on 98 percent".[34]

With the elections canceled, the nation still divided, and Diem with his "mandate" free to continue his heavy, tyrannical rule, the turn to violence in South Vietnam became inevitable.

As if in knowledge of and preparation for this, the United States sent 350 additional military men to Saigon in May 1956, an "example of the U.S. ignoring" the Geneva Accords, stated the Pentagon study.[35] Shortly afterwards, Dulles confided to a colleague: "We have a clean base there now, without a taint of colonialism. Dienbienphu was a blessing in disguise."[36]

The Later Phase

"If you grab 'em by the balls, the hearts and minds will follow" ... "Give us your hearts and minds or we'll burn down your goddamn village" ... the end result of America's anticommunist policy in Vietnam; also its beginning and its middle.

There was little serious effort to win the hearts and minds of the Vietnamese people, even less chance of success, for the price of success was social change, of the kind that Diem was unwilling to accept in Vietnam, the kind the United States was not willing to accept anywhere in the Third World. If Washington had been willing to accept such change— which they have always routinely and disparagingly dismissed as "socialist"—there would have been no need to cancel the elections or to support Diem, no need for intervention in the first place. There was, consequently, no way the United States could avoid being seen by the people of Vietnam as other than the newest imperialist occupiers, following in the footsteps of first the Chinese, then the French, then the Japanese, then the French again.

We will not go into a detailed recounting of all the horrors, all the deceptions, the destruction of a society, the panorama of absurdities and ironies; only a selection, a montage, lest we forget.

To the men who walked the corridors of power in Washington, to the military men in the field, Indochina—nay, southeast Asia—was a single, large battlefield.

Troops of South Vietnam were used in Laos and Cambodia.

Troops of Thailand were used in Laos, Cambodia and South Vietnam.

Thailand and the Philippines were used as bases from which to bomb the three countries of Indochina.

Military officers in South Vietnam, Thailand, and Taiwan were trained at American schools in the Philippines.

CIA-supported forces carried out incursions and invasions into China from Laos, Burma and Taiwan.

When there was a (much-publicized) pause in the bombing of North Vietnam, more American planes were thus available to increase the bombing of Laos.

And so it went.

From 1955 to 1959, Michigan State University, under a US government contract, conducted a covert police training program for the South Vietnamese. With the full knowledge of certain MSU officials, five CIA operatives were concealed in the staff of the program and carried on the university's payroll as its employees. By the terms of a 1957 law, drawn up by the MSU group, every Vietnamese 15 years and older was required to register with the government and carry ID cards. Anyone caught without the proper identification was considered as a National Liberation Front (Vietcong) suspect and subject to imprisonment or worse. At the time of registration, a full set of fingerprints was obtained and information about the person's political beliefs was recorded.[37]

When popular resistance to Ngo Dinh Diem reached the level where he was more of a liability than an asset he was sacrificed. On 1 November 1963, some of Diem's generals overthrew him and then murdered both him and his brother after they had surrendered. The coup, wrote *Time* magazine, "was planned with the knowledge of Dean Rusk and Averill Harriman at the State Department, Robert S. McNamara and Roswell Gilpatrick at the Defense Department and the late Edward R. Murrow at the U.S Information Agency."[38]

Evidently Washington had not planned on assassinations accompanying the coup, but as General Maxwell Taylor, President Kennedy's principal military adviser, has observed: "The execution of a coup is not like organizing a tea party; it's a very dangerous business. So I didn't think we had any right to be surprised ... when Diem and his brother were murdered."[39]

Donald Duncan was a member of the Green Berets in Vietnam. He has written about his training, part of which was called "countermeasures to hostile interrogation", ostensibly how Americans captured by Communists could deal with being tortured. Translations of an alleged Soviet interrogation manual were handed out to the class. The manual described in detail such methods as the "Airplane Ride" (hanging by the thumbs), the Cold-Hot Water Treatment, and the lowering of a man's testicles into a jeweler's vise, while the instructor, a Sergeant Lacey, explained some variations of these methods. Then a student had a question:

"Sergeant Lacey, the name of this class is 'Countermeasures to Hostile Interrogation,' but you have spent most of the period telling us there are no countermeasures. If this is true, then the only reason for teaching them [the torture methods], it seems to me, is so that we'll know how to use them. Are you suggesting we use these methods?"

The class laughs, and Lacey looks down at the floor creating a dramatic pause. When he raises his head, his face is solemn but his deep set eyes are dancing. "We can't tell you that, Sergeant Harrison. The Mothers of America wouldn't approve." The class bursts into laughter at the sarcastic cynicism. "Furthermore," a conspiratorial wink, "we will deny that any such thing is taught or intended."[40]

At the US Navy's schools in San Diego and Maine during the 1960s and 1970s, the course had a different name. There, the students were supposedly learning about methods of "survival, evasion, resistance and escape" which they could use as prisoners of war. There was in the course something of survival in a desert, where students were forced to eat lizards, but the naval officers and cadets were also subjected to beatings, jarring judo flips, "tiger cages"—hooded and placed in a 16-cubic-foot box for 22 hours with a coffee can for their excrement—and a torture device called the "water board": the subject strapped to an inclined board, head downward, a towel placed over his face, and cold water poured over the towel; he would choke, gag, retch and gurgle as he experienced the sensation of drowning, just as was done to Vietcong prisoners in Vietnam, along with the tiger cages.

A former student, Navy pilot Lt. Wendell Richard Young, claimed that his back was broken during the course and that students were tortured into spitting, urinating and defecating on the American flag, masturbating before guards, and, on one occasion, engaging in sex with an instructor.[41]

Fabrications were required to support the varied State Department claims about the nature of the war and the reasons for the American military actions. A former CIA officer, Philip Liechty, stated in 1982 that in the early 1960s he saw written plans to take large amounts of Communist-bloc arms, load them on a Vietnamese boat, fake a battle in which the boat would be sunk in shallow water, then call in Western reporters to see the captured weapons as proof of outside aid to the Vietcong. This is precisely what occurred in 1965. The State Department's white paper, "Aggression From the North", which came out at the end of February 1965, relates that a "suspicious vessel" was "sunk in shallow water" off the coast of South Vietnam on 16 February 1965 after an attack by South Vietnamese forces. The boat was reported to contain at least 100 tons of military supplies "almost all of communist origin, largely from Communist China and Czechoslovakia as well as North Vietnam". The white paper noted that "Representatives of the free press visited the sunken North Vietnamese ship and viewed its cargo."

Liechty said that he had also seen documents involving an elaborate operation to print large numbers of postage stamps showing a Vietnamese shooting down a US Army helicopter. The former CIA officer stated that this was a highly professional job and that the very professionalism required to produce the multicolor stamps was meant to indicate that they were produced by the North Vietnamese because the Vietcong would not have had the capabilities. Liechty claimed that letters in Vietnamese were then written and mailed all over the world with the stamp on them "and the CIA made sure journalists would get hold of them". *Life* magazine, in its issue of 26 February 1965, did in fact feature a full color blow-up of the stamp on its cover, referring to it as a "North Vietnam stamp". This was just two days before the State Department's white paper appeared.

In reporting Liechty's statements, the *Washington Post* noted:

> Publication of the white paper turned out to be a key event in documenting the support of North Vietnam and other communist countries in the fighting in the South and in preparing American public opinion for what was to follow very soon: the large-scale commitment of U.S. forces to the fighting.[42]

Perhaps the most significant fabrication was that of the alleged attack in August 1964 on two US destroyers in the Tonkin Gulf off the coast of North Vietnam. President Johnson used the incident to induce a resolution from Congress to take "all necessary steps, including the use of armed forces" to prevent further North Vietnamese aggression. It was a blanket endorsement for escalation heaped upon escalation. Serious enough doubts were raised at the time about the reality of the attack, but over the years other information has come to light which has left the official story in tatters.[43]

And probably the silliest fabrication: the 1966 US Army training film, "County Fair", in which the sinister Vietcong are shown in a jungle clearing heating gasoline and soap bars, concocting a vicious communist invention called napalm.[44]

The Johnson administration's method of minimizing public concern about escalation of the war, as seen by a psychiatrist:

First step: Highly alarming rumors about escalation are "leaked".

Second step: The President officially and dramatically sets the anxieties to rest by announcing a much more moderate rate of escalation, and accompanies this announcement with assurances of the Government's peaceful intentions.

Third step: After the general sigh of relief, the originally rumored escalation is gradually put into effect.

The succession of "leaks", denials of leaks, and denials of denials thoroughly confuses the individual. He is left bewildered, helpless, apathetic.

The end result is that the people find themselves deeply committed to large-scale war, without being able to tell how it came about, when and how it all began.[45]

Senator Stephen Young of Ohio was reported to have said that while he was in Vietnam he was told by the CIA that the Agency disguised people as Vietcong to commit atrocities, including murder and rape, so as to discredit the Communists. After the report caused a flurry in Washington, Young said that he had been misquoted, that the CIA was not the source of the story. Congressman Cornelius Gallagher, who had accompanied Young on the trip, suggested that it "may well be that he [Young] spoke to a Vietcong disguised as a CIA man".[46]

From a speech by Carl Oglesby, President of Students for a Democratic Society (SDS), during the March on Washington, 27 November 1965:

The original commitment in Vietnam was made by President Truman, a mainstream liberal. It was seconded by President Eisenhower, a moderate liberal. It was intensified by the late President Kennedy, a flaming liberal. Think of the men who now engineer that war—those who study the maps, give the commands, push the buttons, and tally the dead: Bundy, McNamara, Rusk, Lodge, Goldberg, the President [Johnson] himself. They are not moral monsters. They are all honorable men. They are all liberals.[47]

The International Communist Conspiracy in action:

During the heat of the fighting in 1966-67, the Soviet Union sold to the United States over $2 million worth of magnesium—a metal vital in military aircraft production—when there was a shortage of it in the United States. This occurred at a time when Washington maintained an embargo on supplying Communist nations with certain alloys of the same metal.[48] At about the same time, China sold several thousand tons of steel to the United States in South Vietnam for use in the construction of new Air and Army bases when no one else could meet the American military's urgent need: this, while Washington maintained a boycott on all Chinese products; even wigs imported into the US from Hong Kong had to be accompanied by a certificate of origin stating that they contained no Chinese hair. The sale of steel may have been only the tip of the iceberg of Chinese sales to the United States during the war.[49]

In a visit to China in January 1972, White House envoy Alexander Haig met with Premier Chou En-lai. Years later, Haig wrote: "Though he never stated the case in so many words, I reported to President Nixon that the import of what Zhou [Chou] said to me was: don't lose in Vietnam; don't withdraw from Southeast Asia."[50]

In 1975, a Senate investigating committee began looking into allegations that the CIA had counterfeited American money during the Vietnam war to finance secret operations.[51]

"Two Vietcong prisoners were interrogated on an airplane flying toward Saigon. The first refused to answer questions and was thrown out of the airplane at 3,000 feet. The second immediately answered all the questions. But he, too, was thrown out." Variations of the water torture were also used to loosen tongues or simply to torment. "Other techniques, usually designed to force onlooking prisoners to talk, involve cutting off the fingers, ears, fingernails or sexual organs of another prisoner."[52]

It is not clear whether these particular Vietnamese were actual prisoners of war, i.e., captured in combat, or whether they were amongst the many thousands of civilians arrested as part of the infamous Phoenix Program. Phoenix was the inevitable consequence of fighting a native population: You never knew who was friend, who was enemy. Anyone was a potential informer, bomb-thrower, or assassin. Safety demanded that, unless proved otherwise, everyone was to be regarded as the enemy, part of what the CIA called the Vietcong infrastructure (VCI).

In 1971, CIA officer William Colby, the director of Phoenix, was asked by a congressman: "Are you certain that we know a member of the VCI from a loyal member of the South Vietnam citizenry?"

"No, Mr. Congressman," replied Colby, "I am not."[53]

Phoenix was a coordinated effort of the United States and South Vietnam to wipe out this infrastructure. Under the program, Vietnamese citizens were rounded up and jailed, often in tiger cages, often tortured, often killed, either in the process of being arrested or subsequently. By Colby's records, during the period between early 1968 and May 1971, 20,587 alleged Vietcong cadres met their death as a result of the Phoenix Program.[54] A similar program, under different names, had existed since 1965 and been run by the United States alone.[55]

Colby claims that more than 85 percent of the 20,587 figure were actually killed in military combat and only identified afterward as members of the VCI.[56] It strains credulity, however, to think that the tens of thousands of Vietcong killed in combat during this period were picked over, body by body, on the battlefield, for identification and that their connection to the VCI was established.

The South Vietnam government credited Phoenix with 40,994 VCI deaths.[57] The true figure will probably never be known.

A former US military-intelligence officer in Vietnam, K. Barton Osborn, testified before a House Committee that suspects caught by Phoenix were interrogated in helicopters and sometimes pushed out. He also spoke of the use of electric shock torture and the insertion into the ear of a six-inch dowel which was tapped through the brain until the victim died.[58]

Osborn's colleague, Michael J. Uhl, testified that most suspects were captured during sweeping tactical raids and that all persons detained were classified as Vietcong. None of those held for questioning, said Osborn, had ever lived through the process.[59]

Arthur Sylvester, Assistant Secretary of Defense for Public Affairs, was the man most responsible for "giving, controlling and managing the war news from Vietnam". One day in July 1965, Sylvester told American journalists that they had a patriotic duty to disseminate only information that made the United States look good. When one of the newsmen exclaimed: "Surely, Arthur, you don't expect the American press to be handmaidens of government," Sylvester replied, "That's exactly what I expect," adding: "Look, if you think any American official is going to tell you the truth, then you're stupid. Did you hear that?— stupid." And when a correspondent for a New York paper began a question, he was interrupted by Sylvester who said: "Aw, come on. What does someone in New York care about the war in Vietnam?"[60]

Meanwhile, hundreds of US servicemen in Asia and Europe were being swindled by phoney American auto dealers who turned up to take down-payments on cars which they never delivered. Commented an Illinois congressman: "We cannot expect our servicemen to fight to protect the free enterprise system if the very system which they fight to protect takes advantage of them."[61]

On 27 January 1973, in Paris, the United States signed the "Agreement on Ending the War and Restoring Peace in Vietnam". Among the principles to which the United States agreed was the one stated in Article 21: "In pursuance of its traditional policy, the United States will contribute to healing the wounds of war and to postwar reconstruction of the Democratic Republic of Vietnam [North Vietnam] and throughout Indochina."

Five days later, 1 February, President Nixon sent a message to the Prime Minister of North Vietnam reiterating and expanding upon this pledge. The first two principles put forth in the President's message were:

(1) The Government of the United States of America will contribute to postwar reconstruction in North Vietnam without any political conditions. (2) Preliminary United States studies indicate that the appropriate programs for the United States contribution to postwar reconstruction will fall in the range of $3.25 billion of grant aid over 5 years. Other forms of aid will be agreed upon between the two parties. This estimate is subject to revision and to detailed discussion between the Government of the United States and the Government of the Democratic Republic of Vietnam.[62]

For the next two decades, the only aid given to any Vietnamese people by the United States was to those who left Vietnam and those who were infiltrated back in to stir up trouble. At the same time, the US imposed a complete embargo on trade and assistance to the country, which lasted until 1994.

Are the victims of the Vietnam War also to be found in generations yet unborn? Tens of millions of gallons of herbicides were unleashed over the country; included in this were quantities of dioxin, which has been called the most toxic man-made substance known; three ounces of dioxin, it is claimed, in the New York City water supply could wipe out the entire populace. Studies in Vietnam since the war have pointed to abnormally high rates of cancers, particularly of the liver, chromosomal damage, birth defects, long-lasting neurological disorders, etc. in the heavily-sprayed areas. Other victims were Americans. Thousands of Vietnam veterans fought for years to receive disability compensation, claiming irreparable damage from simply handling the toxic herbicides.

After the Second World War, the International Military Tribunal convened at Nuremberg, Germany. Created by the victorious Allies, the Tribunal sentenced to prison or execution numerous Nazis who pleaded that they had been "only following orders". In an opinion handed down by the Tribunal, it declared that "the very essence of the [Tribunal's] Charter is that individuals have international duties which transcend the national obligations of obedience imposed by the individual state."

During the Vietnam war, a number of young Americans refused military service on the grounds that the United States was committing war crimes in Vietnam and that if they took part in the war they too, under the principles laid down at Nuremberg, would be guilty of war crimes.

One of the most prominent of these cases was that of David Mitchell of Connecticut. At Mitchell's trial in September 1965, Judge William Timbers dismissed his defense as "tommyrot" and "degenerate subversion", and found the Nuremberg principles to be "irrelevant" to the case. Mitchell was sentenced to prison. Conservative columnist William F. Buckley, Jr., not celebrated as a champion of draft resistance, noted shortly afterward:

> I am glad I didn't have Judge Timbers' job. Oh, I could have scolded Mr. Mitchell along with the best of them. But I'd have to cough and wheeze and clear my throat during that passage in my catechism at which I explained to Mr. Mitchell wherein the Nuremberg Doctrine was obviously not at his disposal.[63]

In 1971, Telford Taylor, the chief United States prosecutor at Nuremberg, suggested rather strongly that General William Westmoreland and high officials of the Johnson administration such as Robert McNamara and Dean Rusk could be found guilty of war crimes under criteria established at Nuremberg.[64] Yet every American court and judge, when confronted by the Nuremberg defense, dismissed it without according it any serious consideration whatsoever.

The West has never been allowed to forget the Nazi holocaust. For 40 years there has been a continuous outpouring of histories, memoirs, novels, feature films, documentaries, television series ... played and replayed in every Western language; there have been museums, memorial sculptures, photo exhibitions, remembrance ceremonies ... Never Again! But who hears the voice of the Vietnamese peasant? Who has access to the writings of the Vietnamese intellectual? What was the fate of the Vietnamese Anne Frank? Where, asks the young American, is Vietnam?

20. Cambodia 1955-1973
Prince Sihanouk walks the high-wire of neutralism

> John Foster Dulles had called on me in his capacity as Secretary of State, and he had exhausted every argument to persuade me to place Cambodia under the protection of the South-East Asia Treaty Organization. I refused ... I considered SEATO an aggressive military alliance directed against neighbors whose ideology I did not share but with whom Cambodia had no

quarrel. I had made all this quite clear to John Foster, an acidy, arrogant man, but his brother [CIA Director Allen Dulles] soon turned up with a briefcase full of documents "proving" that Cambodia was about to fall victim to "communist aggression" and that the only way to save the country, the monarchy and myself was to accept the protection of SEATO. The "proofs" did not coincide with my own information, and I replied to Allen Dulles as I had replied to John Foster: Cambodia want- ed no part of SEATO. We would look after ourselves as neutrals and Buddhists. There was nothing for the secret service chief to do but pack up his dubious documents and leave.

Prince Norodom Sihanouk, in his memoirs[1]

The visits of the Brothers Dulles in 1955 appear to have been the opening salvos in a campaign of extraordinary measures aimed at pressuring the charismatic Cambodian leader into aligning his nation with the West and joining The Holy War Against Communism. The coercion continued intermittently until 1970 when Sihanouk was finally overthrown in an American-backed coup and the United States invaded Cambodia.

In March 1956, after Sihanouk had visited Peking and criticized SEATO, the two coun- tries which sandwich Cambodia—Thailand and South Vietnam, both heavily dependent upon and allied with the United States—suddenly closed their borders. It was a serious move, for the bulk of Cambodia's traffic with the outside world at that time passed either along the Mekong River through South Vietnam or by railway through Thailand.

The danger to the tiny kingdom was heightened by repeated military provocations. Thai troops invaded Cambodian territory and CIA-financed irregulars began to make com- mando raids from South Vietnam. Deep intrusions were made into Cambodian air space by planes based in the two countries.

To Sihanouk, these actions "looked more and more like preliminary softening-up probes" for his overthrow. He chose to thrust matters out into the open. At a press confer- ence he scolded the US, defended Cambodia's policy of neutrality, and announced that the whole question would be on the agenda of his party's upcoming national congress. There was the implication that Cambodia would turn to the socialist bloc for aid.

The United States appeared to retreat in the face of this unorthodox public diplomacy. The State Department sent a couple of rather conciliatory messages which nullified a threat- ened cut-off of certain economic aid and included this remarkable piece of altruism: "The only aim of American policy to Cambodia is to help her strengthen and defend her indepen- dence." Two days before the national congress convened, Thailand and South Vietnam opened their frontiers. The local disputes which the two countries had cited as the reasons for the blockade had not been resolved at all.[2]

The measures taken against Cambodia were counter-productive. Not only did Sihanouk continue to attack SEATO, but he established relations with the Soviet Union and Poland and accepted aid from China. He praised the latter lavishly for treating Cambodia as an equal and for providing aid without all the strings which, he felt, came attached to American aid.[3]

Such behavior should not obscure the fact that Sihanouk was as genuine a neutralist as one could be in such a highly polarized region of the world in the midst of the cold war. He did not shy away from denouncing China, North Vietnam or communism on a number of occasions when he felt that Cambodia's security or neutrality was being threatened. "I fore- see perfectly well," he said at one time, "the collapse of an independent and neutral Cambodia after the complete triumph of Communism in Laos and South Vietnam."[4]

In May 1957, a National Security Council (NSC) paper acknowledged that "the United States has been unable to influence Cambodia in the direction of a stable [i.e., pro-Western] government and non-involvement in the communist bloc."[5]

The following year, five battalions of Saigon troops, supported by aircraft, crossed the Cambodian border again, penetrated to a depth of almost 10 miles and began putting up new boundary markers. Sihanouk's impulse was to try and repel the invaders but, to his amazement, he was informed by the American Ambassador to Cambodia, Carl Strom, that US military aid was provided exclusively for the purpose of opposing "communist aggression" and in no case could be used against an American ally. The ambassador cautioned that if a single bullet were fired at the South Vietnamese or a single US-supplied truck used to transport Cambodian troops to a military confrontation with them, this would constitute grounds for canceling aid.[6]

Ambassador Strom was called back to Washington, told that Sihanouk would now have to go and that US aid would be cut off to precipitate his fall. Strom, however, did not think that this was the wisest move to make at that point and was able to convince the State Department to hold off for the time being.[7]

William Shawcross, in his elaborately-researched book, *Sideshow: Kissinger, Nixon and the Destruction of Cambodia*, notes that "NSC papers of the period cited in the Pentagon papers confirm that Washington saw Thai and Vietnamese pressure across the borders as one of the principal weapons to be used in an effort to move Sihanouk toward a more pro-American position."[8]

In addition to Thai and South Vietnamese troops, the CIA had at its disposal two other forces, the Khmer Serei and the Khmer Krom, composed largely of ethnic Cambodians opposed to Sihanouk's rule, who operated out of the two neighboring countries. The Khmer Serei ("Free Cambodians") were described by Shawcross as the "Cambodian organization with which American officials had had the closest contact".[9] Sihanouk once equated them to the "free" Cubans the United States maintained in Florida.[10]

These forces—recruited, financed, armed and trained by the CIA and the US Special Forces (Green Berets)[11]—began to infiltrate into Cambodia in the latter part of 1958 as part of a complex conspiracy which included, amongst others, a disloyal Cambodian general named Dap Chhuon who was plotting an armed uprising inside the country. At its most optimistic, the conspiracy aimed at overthrowing Sihanouk.

Sihanouk discovered the plan, partly through reports from Chinese and French intelligence. The French were not happy about the American intrusion into what had been their domain for close to a century.

By February 1959 the conspirators had been apprehended or had fled, including Victor Masao Matsui, a member of the CIA station in Cambodia's capital city Phnom Penh, who hurriedly left the country after Sihanouk accused him of being a party to the plot. Matsui, an American of Japanese descent, had been operating under State Department cover as an attaché at the embassy.

The intrigue, according to Sihanouk, began in September 1958 at a SEATO meeting in Thailand and was carried a step further later that month in New York when he visited the United Nations. While Sihanouk was away in Washington for a few days, a member of his delegation, Slat Peou, held several conferences with Americans in his New York hotel room which he did not mention to any of his fellow delegates. Slat Peou, it happened, was a close friend of Victor Matsui and was the brother of General Dap Chhuon. In the aftermath of the aborted conspiracy, Slat Peou was executed for treason.[12] Sihanouk was struck by the bitter irony of the CIA plotting against him in New York while he was in Washington being honored by President Eisenhower with a 21-gun salute.[13]

In a similar vein, several years later President Kennedy assured Sihanouk "on his honour" that the United States had played no role in the affairs of the Khmer Serei. "I considered President Kennedy to be an honourable man," wrote Sihanouk, "but, in that case, who really represented the American government?"[14]

CIA officer (later Director) William Colby, stationed in Vietnam at the time of the Dap Chhuon plot, has written that the Agency was well aware of the plot and had recruited someone on Dap Chhuon's staff and furnished him with a radio with which to keep the CIA informed. The Agency wanted to be kept informed, Colby asserts, in order to "dissuade the Thai and Vietnamese" from overthrowing Sihanouk. Colby adds:

> Unfortunately, in putting down the coup, Sihanouk had captured our agent and his radio. And, not unnaturally, he drew the conclusion that CIA was one of the participants, and that the gold and arms furnished from Bangkok and Saigon to be used against him were only part of the overall plot of which the radio was a key element.[15]

The Cambodian leader has attested to several other plots he lays at the doorstep of the CIA. Amongst these was a 1959 effort to murder him which was foiled when the police picked a nervous young man, Rat Vat by name, out of a crowd surrounding Sihanouk. He was found to be carrying a hand grenade and a pistol. Investigation showed, writes Sihanouk, that the would-be assassin was instigated by the CIA and the Khmer Serei. Sihanouk also cites three incidents occurring in 1963: an attempt to blow up a car carrying him and the visiting president of China, Liu Shao Chi; an attempt to smuggle arms into Cambodia in a number of crates addressed to the US Embassy; and a partially successful venture aimed at sabotaging the Cambodian economy and subverting key government personnel through the setting up of a bank in Phnom Penh.[16]

On 20 November of the same year, two days before the assassination of John F. Kennedy, the Cambodian National Congress, at Sihanouk's initiative, vote to "end all aid granted by the United States in the military, economic, technical and cultural fields". It was perhaps without precedent that a country receiving American aid voluntarily repudiated it. But Sihanouk held strong feelings on the subject. Over the years he had frequently recited from his register of complaints about American aid to Cambodia: how it subverted and corrupted Cambodian officials and businessmen who wound up "constituting a clientele necessarily obedient to the demands of the lavish bestower of foreign funds"; and how the aid couldn't be used for state institutions, only private enterprise, nor, as mentioned earlier, used against attacks by US allies.[17]

After some American bombings of Cambodian villages near the South Vietnam border in pursuit of North Vietnamese and Vietcong, the Cambodian government, in October 1964, announced that "in case of any new violation of Cambodian territory by US ground, air, or naval forces, Cambodia will immediately sever diplomatic relations with the United States". The government did just that the following May when American planes bombarded several villages, killing or wounding dozens of peasants.[18]

The pattern over the next few years, as the war in Indochina intensified, was one of repeated forays into Cambodian territory by American, Saigon and Khmer Serei forces in search of Communist supply lines and sanctuaries along the Ho Chi Minh Trail; bombing and strafing, napalming, and placing land mines, with varying numbers of Cambodian civilian casualties; angry accusations by the Cambodian government, followed on occasion by an American apology, promise of an investigation, and the taking of "measures to prevent any recurrence of such incidents".[19]

Sihanouk did not at all relish the intrusions into Cambodia by the Vietnamese Communists, nor was he wholly or consistently antagonistic to American pursuit of them, particularly when there was no loss of Cambodian lives. On at least one occasion he disclosed the location of Communist bases which were promptly bombed by the US. However, Sihanouk then went on the radio and proceeded to denounce the bombings.[20] Opportunist that he often revealed himself to be, Sihanouk was nonetheless truly caught between the devil and the deep blue sea, and by the late 1960s his predicament had compelled him to resume American aid and re-establish diplomatic relations with the United States.

Despite all the impulsiveness of his personality and policies, Sihanouk's neutralist high-wire balancing act did successfully shield his country from the worst of the devastation that was sweeping through the land and people of Vietnam and Laos. Cambodia had its own Communist insurgents, the Khmer Rouge, who surely would have unleashed a full-scale civil war if faced with a Cambodian government nestled comfortably in the American camp. This is precisely what later came to pass following the overthrow of Sihanouk and his replacement by Lon Nol who was closely tied to the United States.

In March 1969, the situation began to change dramatically. Under the new American president, Richard Nixon, and National Security Affairs adviser Henry Kissinger, the isolated and limited attacks across the Cambodian border became sustained, large-scale B-52 bombings—"carpet bombings", in the euphemistic language so dear to the hearts of military men.

Over the next 14 months, no less than 3,630 B-52 bombing raids were flown over Cambodia.[21] To escape the onslaught, the Vietnamese Communists moved their bases further inside the country. The B-52s of course followed, with a concomitant increase in civilian casualties.

The Nixon administration artfully played down the nature and extent of these bombings, going so far as to falsify military records, and was largely successful in keeping it all a secret from the American public, the press and Congress.[22] Not until 1973, in the midst of the Watergate revelations, did a fuller story begin to emerge.

It was frequently argued that the United States had every right to attack Cambodia because of its use as a sanctuary by America's foes in Vietnam. Apropos of this claim, William Shawcross has pointed out that:

> During the Algerian war of independence the United States rejected France's claimed right to attack a Tunisian town inhabited by Algerian guerrillas, and in 1964 Adlai Stevenson, at the U.N., condemned Britain for assaulting a Yemeni town used as a base by insurgents attacking Aden. Even Israel had frequently been criticized by the United States for attacks on enemy bases outside its territory.[23]

On 18 March 1970, Sihanouk, while on a trip abroad, was deposed as Head of State by two of his leading ministers, Lon Nol and Sirik Matak. To what extent, if any, the United States played a direct role in the coup has not been established, but there are circumstances and testimony pointing to American complicity, among which are the following:

- According to Frank Snepp, the CIA's principal political analyst in Vietnam at this time, in early 1970 the Agency was cultivating both Lon Nol and Son Ngoc Thanh, leader of the Khmer Serei, as possible replacements for Sihanouk. The CIA believed, he says, that if Lon Nol came to power, "He would welcome the United States with open arms and we would accomplish everything."[24] (This, presumably, meant *carte blanche* to wipe out Vietnamese Communist forces and sanctuaries in Cambodia, as opposed to Sihanouk's extremely equivocal position on the matter.) Both men, as matters turned out, served as prime minister in the new government, for which diplomatic recognition was immediately forthcoming from Washington.

- The United States could seemingly also rely on Sirik Matak, a committed anti-Communist who had been profiled by the Pentagon's Defense Intelligence Agency as "a friend of the West and ... co-operative with U.S. officials during the 1950s."[25]

- Investigative journalist Seymour Hersh, in his biographic work on Kissinger, states that Sihanouk's "immediate overthrow had been for years a high priority of the Green Berets reconnaissance units operating inside Cambodia since the late 1960s. There is also incontrovertible evidence that Lon Nol was approached by agents of American military intelligence in 1969 and asked to overthrow the Sihanouk government. Sihanouk made similar charges in his 1973 memoir, *My War With The CIA*, but they were not taken seriously then."[26]

- An opponent of Sihanouk, Prom Thos, who became a minister in the new government, has said that whether Lon Nol had specific promises of American help before the coup is unimportant: "We all just knew that the United States would help us; there had been many stories of CIA approaches and offers before then."[27]

- The CIA's intimate links to the conspiratorial circle are exemplified by an Agency report prepared six days before the coup, entitled "Indications of Possible Coup in Phnom Penh". It disclosed that anti-Communist demonstrations against the Vietcong and North Vietnamese embassies in the capital the previous day had been planned by Sirik Matak and Lon Nol as part of a showdown policy against Sihanouk and his followers, and that the two men had put the army on alert "to prepare ... for a coup against Sihanouk if Sihanouk refused to support" them.[28]

- General William Rosson, deputy to General Creighton Abrams, the Commander of US Forces in Vietnam at the time, has declared that American commanders were informed several days beforehand that a coup was being planned and that United States support was solicited.[29]

- Roger Morris, who was serving under Henry Kissinger on the National Security Council staff when the coup took place, reported that "It was clear in the White House that the CIA station in Phnom Penh knew the plotters well, probably knew their plans, and did nothing to alert Sihanouk. They informed Washington well in advance of the coup."[30]

- William Shawcross asserts that had Sihanouk "returned quickly and calmly to Phnom Penh [following the anti-communist demonstrations] he would most likely have been able to avert disaster." That he did not do so may not have been by chance. Frank Snepp has revealed that the CIA persuaded Sihanouk's mother, the Queen, to send a message to her son abroad reassuring him that the situation was not serious enough to warrant his return.[31]

With Sihanouk and his irritating neutralism no longer an obstacle, American military wheels began to spin. Within hours of the coup, US and South Vietnam forces stationed in border districts were directed to establish communication with Cambodian commanders on the other side and take steps toward military co-operation. The next day, the Cambodian army called in an American spotter plane and South Vietnamese artillery during a sweep of a Vietcong sanctuary by a battalion of Cambodian troops inside Cambodia. The *New York Times* declared that "The battle appeared to be the most determined Cambodian effort yet to drive the Vietcong out of border areas."[32] The Great Cambodian War had begun. It was to persist for five terrible years.

The enemy confronting the United States and its Saigon and Phnom Penh allies was now not simply the North Vietnamese and the Vietcong. The Cambodian Communists—the Khmer Rouge—under the leadership of Pol Pot, had entered the conflict, as had sundry Cambodian supporters of Prince Sihanouk.

On 30 April 1970, the first full-scale American invasion of the new war was launched. It produced a vast outcry of protest in the United States, rocking university campuses from coast to coast. Perhaps the most extraordinary reaction was the angry resignations of four men from Henry Kissinger's National Security Council staff, including Roger Morris. (Kissinger labeled the resignations as "the cowardice of the Eastern establishment".)[33]

By the end of May, scores of villages had been reduced to rubble and ashes by US air power; the long train of Cambodian refugees had begun their march.

Three years and more than a hundred thousand tons of bombs later, 27 January 1973 to be precise, an agreement was signed in Paris putting an end to a decade of American warfare in Vietnam. The bombing of Cambodia, however, continued.

Prior to the Paris agreement, the official position of the Nixon administration, repeatedly asserted, was that the sole purpose of bombing Cambodia was to protect American lives in Vietnam. Yet now, the US not only did not cease the bombing, it increased it, in a last desperate attempt to keep the Khmer Rouge from coming to power. During March, April and May, the tonnage of bombs unloosed over Cambodia was more than double that of the entire previous year. The society's traditional economy had vanished. The old Cambodia was being destroyed forever.

Under increasing pressure from Congress, the Nixon administration finally ended the bombing in August. More than two million Cambodians had been made homeless.

It does appear rather ludicrous, in the light of this application of brute force, that the CIA was at the same time carrying out the most subtle of psychological tactics. To spread dissatisfaction about the exiled Sihanouk amongst the Cambodian peasantry who revered him, a CIA sound engineer, using sophisticated electronics, fashioned an excellent counterfeit of the Prince's distinctive voice and manner of speaking—breathless, high-pitched, and full of giggles. This voice was beamed from a clandestine radio station in Laos with messages artfully designed to offend any good Cambodian. In one of the broadcasts, "Sihanouk" exhorted young women to aid the cause by sleeping with the valiant Vietcong.[34]

In a farewell press conference in September 1973, the American Ambassador to Cambodia, Emory Swank, called what had taken place there "Indochina's most useless war".[35]

Later, California Congressman Pete McClosky, following a visit to Cambodia, had harsher words. He was moved to declare that what the United States had "done to the country is greater evil than we have done to any country in the world, and wholly without reason, except for our own benefit to fight against the Vietnamese."[36]

On 17 April 1975, the Khmer Rouge entered Phnom Penh in victory. Two weeks later, Saigon fell to the North Vietnamese and the Vietcong. Incredibly, the Khmer Rouge were to inflict even greater misery upon this unhappy land. And to add to the irony—or to multiply it—the United States supported the Khmer Rouge after their subsequent defeat by the Vietnamese, both by defending their right to the United Nations Cambodian seat, and in their military struggle against the Cambodian government and its Vietnamese allies. In November 1980, Ray Cline, former Deputy Director of the CIA, visited a Khmer Rouge enclave in Cambodia in his capacity as senior foreign policy adviser to President-elect Ronald Reagan. A Khmer Rouge press release spoke of the visit in warm terms.[37] This was in keeping with the Reagan administration's subsequent opposition to the Vietnamese-supported Phnom Penh government. A lingering bitter hatred of Vietnam by unreconstructed American cold warriors appears to be the only explanation for this policy.

21. Laos 1957-1973

L'Armée Clandestine

For the past two years the US has carried out one of the most sustained bombing campaigns in history against essentially civilian targets in northeastern Laos.... Operating from Thai bases and from aircraft carriers, American jets have destroyed the great majority of villages and towns in the northeast. Severe casualties have been inflicted upon the inhabitants ... Refugees from the Plain of Jars report they were bombed almost daily by American jets last year. They say they spent most of the past two years living in caves or holes.

Far Eastern Economic Review, Hong Kong, 1970[1]

[The Laos operation] is something of which we can be proud as Americans. It has involved virtually no American casualties. What we are getting for our money there ... is, I think, to use the old phrase, very cost effective.

U. Alexis Johnson, US Under Secretary of State, 1971[2]

The United States undertook the bombing campaign because its ground war against the Pathet Lao had failed.

The ground war had been carried out because the Pathet Lao were led by people whom the State Department categorized as "communist", no more, no less.

The Pathet Lao (re)turned to warfare because of their experiences in "working within the system".

In 1957 the Pathet Lao ("Lao nation") held two ministerial posts in the coalition "government of national union". This was during John Foster Dulles's era, and if there was anything the fanatic Secretary of State hated more than neutralism it was a coalition with communists. This government featured both. There could be little other reason for the development of the major American intervention into this impoverished and primitive land of peasants. The American ambassador to Laos at the time, J. Graham Parsons, was to admit later: "I struggled for sixteen months to prevent a coalition."[3]

In addition to its demand for inclusion in the coalition government, the Pathet Lao had called for diplomatic relations with the countries of the Soviet bloc and the acceptance of aid from them, as was already the case with Western nations. "Agreement to these conditions," said Washington, "would have given the Communists their most significant gains in Southeast Asia since the partition of Indochina."[4] Others would say that the Pathet Lao's conditions were simply what neutralism is all about.

In May 1958, the Pathet Lao and other leftists, running a campaign based on government corruption and indifference, won 13 of 21 contested seats for the National Assembly and wound up controlling more than one-third of the new legislature.[5] Two months later, however, Prime Minister Souvanna Phouma, a man universally categorized as a neutralist, "resigned" to form a new government which would exclude the Pathet Lao ministers.[6] (He subsequently claimed that he was forced to resign due to continued American opposition to Laotian neutrality; as it happened, one Phoui Sananikone, backed by the US, became premier in the reorganized government.)[7] Then, in January 1959, the non-left majority in the National Assembly voted, in effect, to dissolve the Assembly in order "to counteract communist influence and subversion". The left was now altogether excluded from the government, and the elections scheduled for December were canceled.[8]

If this wasn't enough to disenchant the Pathet Lao or anyone else with the Laotian political process, there was, in the late 1950s and early 1960s, the spectacle of a continuous parade of coups and counter-coups, of men overthrown winding up in the new government, and regimes headed by men who had sided with the French in their war against Indochinese independence, while the Pathet Lao had fought against the colonialists.[9] There were as well government-rigged elections, with the CIA stuffing ballot boxes;[10] different regimes-cum-warlords governing simultaneously from different "capitals", their armies fighting each other, switching allies and enemies when it suited them; hundreds of millions of US dollars pouring into a tiny kingdom which was 99 percent agricultural, with an economy based more on barter than money, the result being "unimaginable bribery, graft, currency manipulation and waste".[11]

The CIA and the State Department alone could take credit for engineering coups, through force, bribery or other pressures, at least once in each of the years 1958, 1959 and 1960, if not in others.[12] "By merely withholding the monthly payment to the troops," wrote Roger Hilsman (whose career encompassed both agencies, perhaps covertly simultaneously), "the United States could create the conditions for toppling any Lao government whose policies it opposed. As it turned out, in fact, the United States used this weapon twice—to bring down the government of one Lao leader and to break the will of another."[13]

The American wheeling and dealing centered around giving power to the CIA's hand-picked rightist strongman Phoumi Nosavan, ousting Souvanna Phouma and other neutralists, and jailing Pathet Lao leaders, including the movement's head, Souphanouvong (the half-brother of Souvanna Phouma, both being princes of the royal family). Souphanouvong insisted that neither he nor the Pathet Lao were communist, but were rather "ultra-nationalist".[14] Crucial to understanding his statements, of course, is the question of exactly what he meant by the term "communist". This is not clear, but neither is it clear what the State Department meant when it referred to him as such. The Pathet Lao were the only sizable group in the country serious about social change, a characteristic which of course tends to induce Washington officials to apply the communist label.

In August 1960, Kong Le, a military officer with his own troop following, staged a coup and set up a neutralist government under Souvanna Phouma, rejecting Pathet Lao help.[15] But when this government became a casualty of a CIA coup in December, Kong Le allied himself with the Pathet Lao; later he turned to the United States for aid and fought against the Pathet Lao. Such was the way of the Laotian circus.

No study of Laos of this period appears to have had notable success in untangling the muddle of who exactly replaced whom, and when, and how, and why. After returning from Laos, writer Norman Cousins stated in 1961 that "if you want to get a sense of the universe unraveling, come to Laos. Complexity such as this has to be respected."[16]

One thing that came through unambiguously, however, was the determination of the United States to save Laos from communism and neutralism. To this end, the CIA set about creating its now-famous *Armée Clandestine*, a process begun by the US Army in the mid-1950s when it organized Meo hill tribesmen (the same ethnic group organized in Vietnam). Over the years, other peoples of Laos were added, reaching at least 30,000 in the mid-1960s, half of them more or less full-time soldiers ... many thousands more from Thailand ... hundreds of other Asians came on board, South Vietnamese, Filipinos, Taiwanese, South Koreans, men who had received expert training from their American mentors in their home countries for other wars, now being recycled ... an army, said the *New York Times*, "armed, equipped, fed, paid, guided, strategically and tactically, and often transported into and out of action by the United States" ... trained and augmented by the CIA, and by men of every branch of the US military with their multiple specialties, the many pilots of the CIA's Air America, altogether some 2,000 Americans in and over Laos, and thousands more in Asia helping with the logistics. A Secret Army, secret, that is, from the American people and Congress—US military personnel were there under various covers, some as civilians in mufti, having "resigned" from the service for the occasion and been hired by a private company created by the CIA; others served as embassy attachés; CIA pilots were officially under contract to the Agency for International Development (AID); Americans who were killed in Laos were reported to have died in Vietnam[17] ... all this in addition to the "official" government forces, the Royal Laotian Army, greatly expanded and totally paid for by the United States ...[18]

Laos was an American plantation, a CIA playground. During the 1960s, the Agency roamed over much of the land at will, building an airstrip, a hangar, or a base here, a warehouse, barracks, or a radar site there;[19] relocating thousands of people, entire villages, whole tribes, to suit strategic military needs; recruiting warriors "through money and/or the threat or use of force and/or promises of independent kingdoms which it had no intention of fulfilling, and then keeping them fighting long beyond the point when they wished to stop;"[20] while the "legendary" pilots of Air America roamed far and wide as well, hard drinking, daredevil flying, death defying, great stories to tell the guys back home, if you survived.[21]

Some of the stories had to do with drugs. Flying opium and heroin all over Indochina to serve the personal and entrepreneurial needs of the CIA's various military and political allies, ultimately turning numerous GIs in Vietnam into addicts. The operation was not a paragon of discretion. Heroin was refined in a laboratory located on the site of CIA headquarters in northern Laos. After a decade of American military intervention, Southeast Asia had become the source of 70 percent of the world's illicit opium and the major supplier of raw materials for America's booming heroin market.[22]

At the same time, the hearts and minds of the Laotian people, at least of those who could read, were not overlooked. The US Information Agency was there to put out a magazine with a circulation of 43,000; this, in a country where the circulation of the largest newspaper was 3,300; there were as well USIA wall newspapers, films, leaflet drops, and radio programs.[23]

In the face of it all, the Pathet Lao more than held their own. The CIA was overextended, and, unlike the motley band of Asians assembled by the Agency, the soldiers of the Pathet Lao had some idea of what they were fighting for. The Soviet Union, aware of what the United States was doing in Laos, even if the American public was not, was alarmed by the establishment of a pro-American government in the country, and acceded to a cold-war knee-reflex by sending military supplies to the Pathet Lao, though nothing remotely on the order of the US commitment.[24]

Beginning in the early 1960s, the North Vietnamese were aiding them as well. Hanoi's overriding interest in Laos was not necessarily the creation of a Communist state, but the prevention of a belligerent government on its border. In January 1961, the *New York Times* reported that "Many Western diplomats in Vientiane [capital of Laos] ... feel the Communists would have been content to leave Laos alone provided she remained neutral and outside the United States sphere of influence."[25]

Hanoi was concerned not only by the American political and military operations in Laos, but by the actions of US Special Forces teams which were entering North Vietnam to engage in espionage, sabotage, and assassination,[26] and by the bombings of the country being carried out by the US Air Force[27] at a time when the war in South Vietnam was still but a shadow of what was to come. Later, as the wars in Vietnam and Laos became intertwined, Laos formed part of the Ho Chi Minh Trail, the principal route by which Hanoi supplied its comrades in South Vietnam, and the North Vietnamese fought to protect it as well as attacking American radar installations in Laos used to aid US bombing of North Vietnam.

The nature and extent of North Vietnam's aid to the Pathet Lao before this period is difficult to ascertain from Western sources, because such charges typically emanated from the Laotian government or the State Department. On a number of occasions, their report of a North Vietnamese military operation in Laos turned out to be a fabrication. William Lederer and Eugene Burdick, in *A Nation of Sheep*, summarized one of these non-events from the summer of 1959:

> The people of the United States were led to believe that Laos physically had been invaded by foreign Communist troops from across its northern border. Our Secretary of State called the situation grave; our ambassador to the U.N. called for world action; our press carried scare headlines; our senior naval officer implied armed intervention and was seconded by ranking Congressmen ... The entire affair was a fraud. No military invasion of Laos had taken place ... There seemed no doubt that a war embracing thousands of troops, tanks, planes, and mass battles, was raging.
>
> Regardless of how the accounts were worded, this was the picture given the nation.[28]

It had all been a ploy to induce Congress not to reduce aid for Laos, something seriously being considered because of the pervasive corruption which had been exposed concerning the aid program.[29] The Laotian government and the large American establishment in Laos, each for their own reasons, were not about to let the golden goose slip away that easily.

On the last day of 1960, the Laotian government announced to the world that seven battalions of North Vietnamese troops had invaded the country. By all accounts, and by the utter lack of evidence, this claim as well cannot be taken seriously.[30]

And in 1962, reported Bernard Fall, the renowned French scholar on Indochina: After a battle between government forces and the Pathet Lao, in spite of the fact that Col. Edwin Elder, the American commander in the area of the battle, immediately stated that there was

> "no evidence to show that Chinese or [North] Vietnamese had participated in the attack", the Laotians—and much of the U.S. press, and official Washington with them—immediately claimed that they were again faced with a large-scale "foreign invasion".[31]

Shortly after Kennedy became president in January 1961, he made a sustained diplomatic effort to establish a coalition government in Laos, precisely what the Eisenhower administration and the CIA had done their best to sabotage. Although he sometimes fell back on conventional cold-war rhetoric when speaking of Laos, one part of John F. Kennedy realized the absurdity of fighting for the backward country, a land he considered not "worthy of engaging the attention of great powers".[32] Soviet Premier Khrushchev, for his part, was reportedly "bored" with the question of Laos, and irritably asked Kennedy's emissary why Washington bothered so much about the country.[33]

Eventually, in July 1962, a multi-nation conference in Geneva signed an agreement for a coalition government in Laos. But in the mountains and the plains of the country, this was no longer a viable option. The CIA had too much time, effort, material and emotion invested in its Secret Army; it was the best war the Agency had going anywhere; it was great adventure. And the Pathet Lao were much stronger now than a few years earlier. They were not about to buy such shopworn, suspect goods again, although everyone went through the motions.

Both sides regularly accused each other of violating the agreement, and not without justification. The North Vietnamese, for example, did not withdraw all of their troops from Laos, while the US left behind all manner of military personnel, American and Asian, who remained under AID and other civilian cover, but this was nonetheless a violation of the agreement. Moreover, Christopher Robbins, in his study of Air America, has noted that US "Military advisers and CIA personnel moved across the border into Thailand, where they were flown in every day [to Laos] like commuters by Air America, whose entire helicopter operation was based in Udorn [Thailand]."[34] Air America, by the early 1970s, had no less than 4,000 employees in Thailand.[35]

Thus it was that the fighting dragged on, though only sporadically. In April 1964, the coalition government, such as it was, was overthrown by the right wing, with the CIA's man Phoumi Nosavan emerging as part of a rightist government headed by the perennial survivor Souvanna Phouma to give it a neutralist fig leaf.[36] The Pathet Lao were once again left out in the cold. For them it was the very last straw. The fighting greatly intensified, the skirmishes were now war, and the Pathet Lao offensive soon scored significant advances. Then the American bombing began.

Between 1965 and 1973, more than two million tons of bombs rained down upon the people of Laos,[37] considerably more than the US had dropped on both Germany and Japan during the Second World War, albeit for a shorter period. For the first few years, the bombing was directed primarily at the provinces controlled by the Pathet Lao. Of the bombing, Fred Branfman, a former American community worker in Laos, wrote: "village after village was leveled, countless people buried alive by high explosives, or burnt alive by napalm and white phosphorous, or riddled by anti-personnel bomb pellets"[38] ... "The United States has undertaken," said a Senate report, "... a large-scale air war over Laos to destroy the physical and social infrastructure of Pathet Lao held areas and to interdict North Vietnamese infiltration ... throughout all this there has been a policy of subterfuge and secrecy ... through such things as saturation bombing and the forced evacuation of population from enemy held or threatened areas—we have helped to create untold agony for hundreds of thousands of villagers."[39]

The American military, however, kept proper records. AID could report to Congress that wounds suffered by civilian war casualties were as follows:

1. Type: Soft tissue, 39 percent. Compound fracture, 30 percent. Amputation, 12 percent. Intra-abdominal, 10 percent. Intra-thoracic, 3 percent. Intra-cranial, 1 percent.
2. Location: Lower extremities, 60 percent. Upper extremities, 15 percent. Trunk, 18 percent. Head, 7 percent.[40]

There was no happy way out for the Laotian people. In October 1971, one could read in *The Guardian* of London ...

although US officials deny it vehemently, ample evidence exists to confirm charges that the Meo villages that do try to find their own way out of the war—even if it is simply by staying neutral and refusing to send their 13-year-olds to fight in the CIA army—are immediately denied American rice and transport, and ultimately bombed by the US Air Force.[41]

The fledgling society that the United States was trying to make extinct—the CIA dropped millions of dollars in forged Pathet Lao currency as well, in an attempt to wreck the economy[42]—was one which Fred Branfman described thus:

The Pathet Lao rule over the Plain of Jars begun in May 1964 brought its people into a post-colonial era. For the first time they were taught pride in their country and people, instead of admiration for a foreign culture; schooling and massive adult literacy campaigns were conducted in Laotian instead of French; and mild but thorough social revolution—ranging from land reform to greater equality for women—was instituted.[43]

Following on the heels of events in Vietnam, a ceasefire was arrived at in Laos in 1973, and yet another attempt at coalition government was undertaken. (This one lasted until 1975 when, after renewed fighting, the Pathet Lao took over full control of the country.) Laos had become a land of nomads, without villages, without farms; a generation of refugees; hundreds of thousands dead, many more maimed. When the US Air Force closed down its radio station, it signed off with the message: "Good-by and see you next war."[44]

Thus it was that the worst of Washington's fears had come to pass: All of Indochina—Vietnam, Cambodia and Laos—had fallen to the Communists. During the initial period of US involvement in Indochina in the 1950s, John Foster Dulles, Dwight Eisenhower and other American officials regularly issued doomsday pronouncements of the type known as the "Domino Theory", warning that if Indochina should fall, other nations in Asia would topple over as well. In one instance, President Eisenhower listed no less than Taiwan, Australia, New Zealand, the Philippines and Indonesia amongst the anticipated "falling dominos".[45]

Such warnings were repeated periodically over the next decade by succeeding administrations and other supporters of US policy in Indochina as a key argument in defense of such policy. The fact that these ominous predictions turned out to have no basis in reality did not deter Washington officialdom from promulgating the same dogma up until the 1990s about almost each new world "trouble-spot", testimony to their unshakable faith in the existence and inter-workings of the International Communist Conspiracy.

22. Haiti 1959-1963
The Marines land, again

"Duvalier has performed an economic miracle," remarked a Haitian of his country's dictator. "He has taught us to live without money ... to eat without food ... to live without life."[1]

And when Francois "Papa Doc" Duvalier's voodoo magic wore thin, he could always count on the US Marines to continue his people's education.

During the night of 12-13 August 1959, a boat landed on the northern coast of Haiti with a reported 30 men, Haitians and Cubans and perhaps others aboard. The men had set sail from Cuba some 50 miles away. Their purpose was to overthrow the tyrannical Haitian government, a regime whose secret police, it was said, outnumbered its army.

In short order, the raiding party, equipped with heavy weapons, captured a small army post and began to recruit and arm villagers for the cause.[2] The government reported that about 200 persons had joined them.[3] Haitian exiles in Venezuela, in an apparently coordinated effort, broadcast appeals to their countrymen to aid the invaders. They set at 120 the number of men who had landed in Haiti, although this appears to be an exaggeration.[4]

The initial reaction of the Duvalier government was one of panic, and the police began rounding up opposition sympathizers.[5] It was at this point that the US military mission, in Haiti to train Duvalier's forces, stepped in. The Americans instituted an air and sea reconnaissance to locate the rebels. Haitian soldiers, accompanied by US Marines, were airlifted to the area and went into the field to do battle with them.[6] Two other US Navy planes and

145

a helicopter arrived from Puerto Rico.[7]

According to their commander, Col. Robert Debs Heinl, Jr., the American Marines took part in the fighting, which lasted until 22 August.[8] The outcome was a complete rout of the rebel forces.

Information about the men who came from Cuba derives almost exclusively from the Haitian government and the American military mission. These sources claim that the raiding party was composed of about 30 men and that, with the exception of one or two Haitians who led them, they were all Cubans. Another report, referred to in the *New York Times*, stated that there were ten Haitians and two Venezuelans amongst the 30 invaders.[9] The latter ratio is probably closer to the truth, for there was a considerable number of Haitian exiles living in Cuba, many of whom had gained military experience during the recent Cuban revolution; for obvious reasons of international politics and fighting incentive, such men were the most likely candidates to be part of an invasion of their homeland.

The Castro government readily admitted that the raiding party had come from Cuba but denied that the government had known or approved of it. This claim would seem rather suspect were it not for the fact that the Cuban coast guard had thwarted a similar undertaking in April.[10]

The first members of the American military mission had arrived in Haiti in January, largely in response to another invasion attempt the previous July (originating probably in the Dominican Republic). Regardless of all the horror stories about the Haitian regime— such as the one Col. Heinl tells of his 12-year-old son being arrested when he was overheard expressing sympathy for a group of hungry peasants he saw—Duvalier was Washington's man. After all was said and done, he could be counted upon to keep his Black nation, which was usually accorded the honor of being Latin America's poorest, from turning Red. Heinl has recounted the instructions he received from a State Department Under Secretary in January:

> Colonel, the most important way you can support our objectives in Haiti is to help keep Duvalier in power so he can serve out his full term in office, and maybe a little longer than that if everything works out.[11]

The Kennedy administration, which came to power in January 1961, had little use for Papa Doc, and supported his overthrow as well as his possible assassination. According to the later testimony of CIA official Walter Elder before a Senate investigating committee, the Agency furnished arms to Haitian dissidents seeking to topple the dictator. Elder added that while the assassination of Duvalier was not contemplated, the arms were provided "to help [the dissidents] take what measures were deemed necessary to replace the government," and it was realized, he said, that Duvalier might be killed in the course of the overthrow.[12]

But as Cuba increasingly became the United States' *bête noire*, the CIA's great obsession, Washington's policy changed. Haiti's cooperation was needed for the success of US efforts to have Cuba expelled from the Organization of American States in 1963. From that point on, Duvalier enjoyed the full diplomatic and economic support of the US. When the Haitian leader died on 12 April 1971, the American Ambassador Clinton Knox was the only diplomat present at the midnight swearing-in of 19-year-old Jean-Claude "Baby Doc" Duvalier as the new President for Life, who was to receive the same economic, political and military support as had "Papa Doc", with only the occasional hiccup of a protest from Washington when the level of repression became difficult to ignore.[13]

23. Guatemala 1960
One good coup deserves another

In November 1960, as John F. Kennedy was preparing to succeed Dwight Eisenhower, the obsessive priority of American foreign policy—to invade Cuba—proceeded without pause. On the beaches and in the jungles of Guatemala, Nicaragua and Florida, the Bay of Pigs invasion was being rehearsed.

On the 13th of the month, five days after Kennedy's victory, Guatemalan military personnel broke out in armed rebellion against the government of General Miguel Ydigoras Fuentes, seizing two military bases and the port city of Puerto Barrios. Reports of the number of officers involved in the uprising vary from 45 to 120, the latter figure representing almost half the Guatemalan Army's officer corps. The officers commanded as many as 3,000 troops, a significant percentage of the armed forces. Their goals, it later developed, were more nationalistic than ideological. The officers were fed up with the corruption in the Ydigoras regime and in the army, and were particularly incensed about the use of their country by a foreign power as a springboard for an invasion of Cuba, some of them being admirers of Fidel Castro for his nationalist policies. One of the dissident officers later characterized the American training base in Guatemala as "a shameful violation of our national sovereignty. And why was it permitted? Because our government is a puppet."[1]

The rebellion was crushed within a matter of days, reportedly by the sole power of the Guatemalan Air Force. Some years later, a different picture was to emerge.

The rebels were a force to be reckoned with. The ease with which they had taken over the two garrisons and the real possibility of their mutiny spreading to other bases set alarms ringing at the CIA base, a large coffee plantation in a remote corner of southwestern Guatemala, where the Agency and the US Air Force were training the army of Cuban exiles who were to launch the attack upon their homeland. The CIA feared, and rightly so, that a new regime would send them, the Cubans, and the whole operation packing.

In Washington, President Eisenhower ordered US naval and air units to patrol the Caribbean coast and "shoot if necessary" to prevent any "communist-led" invasion of Guatemala or Nicaragua.[2] Eisenhower, like Ydigoras, saw the hand of international communism, particularly Cuba, behind the uprising, although no evidence of this was ever presented.[3] It was all most ironic in light of the fact that it was the conspiracy of the two leaders to overthrow Cuba that was one of the reasons for the uprising; and that the US naval fleet ordered into action was deployed from Guantánamo Naval Base in Cuba, an American military installation present in that country against the vociferous objections of the Cuban government.

In Guatemala, meanwhile, the CIA decided upon a solution to the dilemma that was both remarkably simple and close at hand: American and Cuban pilots took off from their training ground and bombed and strafed rebel headquarters outside Guatemala City, and bombed the town and airfield of Puerto Barrios. Caught completely by surprise, and defenseless against this superior force, the rebels' insurrection collapsed.[4]

Back at the coffee plantation, the CIA resumed the function which had been so rudely interrupted, the preparation for the overthrow of the Cuban government.

No announcement about the bombings was made in Washington, nor did a report appear in the American press.

The CIA actions were probably not widely known about in Guatemala either, but it became public knowledge that President Ydigoras had asked Washington for the naval and air support, and had even instructed the Guatemalan Ambassador in Washington to "Get in touch immediately with [Assistant Secretary of State for Inter-American Affairs] Thomas Mann to coordinate your action."[5] Thus it was that the Guatemalan president, needing afterward to distance himself a little from so much Yanqui protection, was moved to state that countries like Guatemala are at a disadvantage because "Cuba is a satellite of powerful Russia", but "we are not a satellite of the United States."[6]

The final irony was that some of the dissident officers who went into hiding became more radicalized by their experience. During their revolt they had spurned offers of support from some of the peasants—though this would necessarily have been very limited in any case—because fighting for social change was not at all what the officers had in mind at the time. But as fugitives, thrown into greater contact with the peasants, they eventually came to be moved by the peasants' pressing need for land and for a way out of their wretched existence.[7] In 1962, several of the officers were to emerge as leaders of a guerrilla movement which incorporated "November Thirteen" as part of its name. In their opening statement, the guerrillas declared:

> Democracy vanished from our country long ago. No people can live in a country where there is no democracy. That is why the demand for changes is mounting in our country. We can no longer carry on in this way. We must overthrow the Ydigoras government and set up a government which represents human rights, seeks ways and means to save our country from its hardships, and pursues a serious self-respecting foreign policy.[8]

A simple sentiment, stated even simpler, but, as we shall see, a movement fated to come up against the wishes of the United States. For if Washington could casually do away with an elected government in Guatemala, as it had in 1954, it could be moved by a guerrilla army only as rocks by waves or the moon by howling wolves.

24. France/Algeria 1960s
L'état, c'est la CIA

When John F. Kennedy assumed office in January 1961, he was confronted with a CIA at the zenith of its power and credibility. In the Agency's first 14 years, no formal congressional investigation of it had taken place, nor had any "watchdog" committee been established; four investigations of the CIA by independent task forces during this period had ensured that everything relating to things covert remained just that; with the exception of the U-2 incident the year before, no page-one embarrassments, scandals, or known failures; what had received a measure of publicity—the coups in Guatemala and Iran—were widely regarded as CIA success stories. White House denials and a compliant media had kept the Agency's misadventure in Indonesia in 1958 from the public scrutiny it deserved.

It is probable that the CIA had more staff officers overseas, under official and unofficial covers, than the State Department, and this in addition to its countless paid agents. Often the CIA Chief of Station had been in a particular country longer than the American ambassador, had more money at his disposal, and exerted more influence. When it suited their purposes, Agency officers would completely bypass the ambassador and normal protocol to deal directly with the country's head of state and other high officials.

The CIA had its own military capabilities, including its own air force; for all intents and purposes, its own foreign service with, indeed, its own foreign policy, though never at cross-purposes with fundamental US cold-war, anti-communist ideology and goals.

Seemingly without fear of exposure or condemnation, the Agency felt free to carry out sundry Dr. Strangelove experiments involving control of the human mind and all manner of biochemical weapons, including the release of huge amounts of bacteria into the air in the United States which resulted in much illness and a number of deaths.

It was all very heady stuff for the officers of the CIA, playing their men's games with their boys' toys. They recognized scarcely any limitation upon their freedom of action. British colonial governors they were, and all the world was India.

Then, in mid-April, came the disaster at the Bay of Pigs in Cuba. The international repercussions had barely begun to subside when the Agency was again catapulted into world headlines. On 22 April four French generals in Algeria seized power in an attempt to maintain the country's union with France. The *putsch*, which held out but four days, was a direct confrontation with French President Charles de Gaulle, who had dramatically proclaimed a policy leading "not to an Algeria governed from France, but to an Algerian Algeria".

The next day, the leftist Italian newspaper, *Il Paese,* stated that "It is not by chance that some people in Paris are accusing the American secret service headed by Allen Dulles of having participated in the plot of the four 'ultra' generals."[1]

Whether *Il Paese* was the original source of this charge remains a mystery. Dulles himself later wrote that the Italian daily was "*one* of the first to launch it" (emphasis added). He expressed the opinion that "This particular myth was a Communist plant, pure and simple."[2]

The *New York Times* reported that the rumors apparently began circulating by word of mouth on the day of the *putsch*,[3] a report echoed by the *Washington Star* which added that some of the rumors were launched "by minor officials at the Elysée Palace itself" who gave reporters "to understand that the generals' plot was backed by strongly anti-communist elements in the United States Government and military services."[4]

Whatever its origins, the story spread rapidly around the world, and the French Foreign Office refused to refute the allegation. *Le Monde* asserted in a front-page editorial on 28 April that "the behavior of the United States during the recent crisis was not particularly skillful. It seems established that American agents more or less encouraged Challe [the leader of the *putsch*] ... President Kennedy, of course, knew nothing of all this."[5]

Reports from all sources were in agreement that if the CIA had indeed been involved in the *putsch*, it had been so for two reasons: (1) the concern that if Algeria were granted its independence, "communists" would soon come to power, being those in the ranks of the National Liberation Front (NLF) which had been fighting the French Army in Algeria for several years—the legendary Battle of Algiers. It was with the NLF that de Gaulle was expected to negotiate a settlement; (2) the hope that it would precipitate the downfall of de Gaulle, an end desired because the French President was a major stumbling block to US aspirations concerning NATO: among other things, he refused to incorporate French troops into an integrated military command, and he opposed exclusive American control over the alliance's nuclear weapons.

By all accounts, it appears that the rebel officers had counted on support from important military and civilian quarters in France to extend the rebellion to the home country and overthrow de Gaulle. Fanciful as this may sound, the fact remains that the French government took the possibility seriously—French Premier Michel Debré went on television to warn the nation of an imminent paratroop invasion of the Paris area and to urge mass opposition.[6]

Reaction in the American press to the allegations had an unmistakably motley quality. *Washington Post* columnist Marquis Childs said that the French were so shocked by the generals' coup that they had to find a scapegoat. At the same time he quoted "one of the highest officials of the French government" as saying:

Of course, your government, neither your State Department nor your President, had anything to do with this. But when you have so many hundreds of agents in every part of the world, it is not to be wondered at that some of them should have got in touch with the generals in Algiers.[7]

Time magazine discounted the story, saying too that the United States was being made a scapegoat and that the CIA had become a "favorite target in recent weeks".[8]

James Reston wrote in the *New York Times* that the CIA:

was involved in an embarrassing liaison with the anti-Gaullist officers who staged last week's insurrection in Algiers ... [the Bay of Pigs and Algerian events have] increased the feeling in the White House that the CIA has gone beyond the bounds of an objective intelligence-gathering agency and has become the advocate of men and policies that have embarrassed the Administration.[9]

However, C.L. Sulzberger, who had been the man at the *New York Times* closest to the CIA since its founding, stated flatly that "No American in Algeria had to do with any insurrectional leader ... No consular employee saw any rebel." (A few days later, though, Secretary of State Dean Rusk disclosed that an emissary of the rebellious French generals had visited the US Consulate in Algiers to request aid but had been summarily rebuffed.)

The affair, wrote Sulzberger, was "a deliberate effort to poison Franco-American relationships" begun in Moscow but abetted by "anti-American French officials" and "naive persons in Washington ... When one checks, one finds all this began in a Moscow *Izvestia* article April 25."[10] This last, as we have seen, was incorrect.

Dean of American columnists, Walter Lippmann, who had seen de Gaulle in Paris shortly before the *putsch*, wrote:

the reason why the French Government has not really exculpated the CIA of encouraging the Algerian rebel generals is that it was already so angry with the CIA for meddling in French internal politics. The French grievance, justified or not, has to do with recent French legislation for the French nuclear weapon, and the alleged effort of CIA agents to interfere with that legislation.[11]

Newsweek repeated the claim that it was "French officials" who had been "the main sources" of the rumors in the first place. When challenged by the American administration the French denied their authorship and tended to soften the charges. Some French officials eventually declared the matter to be closed, though they still failed to explicitly rule out the allegations about American involvement.[12]

In early May 1961, *L'Express*, the widely-read French liberal weekly, published what was perhaps the first detailed account of the mysterious affair. Their Algerian correspondent, Claude Krief, reported:[13]

Both in Paris and Washington the facts are now known, though they will never be publicly admitted. In private, the highest French personalities make no secret of it. What they say is this: "The CIA played a direct part in the Algiers coup, and certainly weighed heavily on the decision taken by ex-general Challe to start his *putsch*."

Not long before, Challe had held the position of NATO Commander-in-Chief, Allied Forces, Central Europe, as a result of which he had been in daily contact with US military officers.[14] Krief wrote that certain American officials in NATO and the Pentagon had encouraged Challe, and that the general had several meetings with CIA officers who told him that "to get rid of de Gaulle would render the Free World a great service". Krief noted that Challe, despite an overweening ambition, was very cautious and serious-minded: "All the people who know him well, are deeply convinced that he had been encouraged by the CIA to go ahead."

At a luncheon in Washington the previous year, Jacques Soustelle, the former Governor-General of Algeria who had made public his disagreement with de Gaulle's Algeria policy, had met with CIA officials, including Richard Bissell, head of covert operations. Soustelle convinced the Agency officials, according to Krief, that Algeria would become, through de Gaulle's blundering, "a Soviet base". This luncheon became something of a *cause célèbre* in the speculation concerning the CIA's possible role. The *New York Times* and others reported that it had been given by the Agency for Soustelle.[15] US officials, however, insisted that the luncheon had been arranged by someone at the French Embassy at Soustelle's request. This French official, they said, had been present throughout the meeting and thus there could have been no dark conspiracy.[16] Why the French Embassy would host a luncheon for a prominent and bitter foe of de Gaulle, a man who only two months earlier had been kicked out of de Gaulle's cabinet for his "ultra" sympathies, was not explained. Nor, for that matter, why in protocol-minded Washington of all places, the CIA would attend. In any event, it seems somewhat fatuous to imply that this was the only chance Soustelle and the CIA had to talk during his stay in the United States, which lasted more than a week.

A clandestine meeting in Madrid also received wide currency within the controversy. Krief dates it 12 April 1961, and describes it as a meeting of "various foreign agents, including members of the CIA and the Algiers conspirators, who disclosed their plans to the CIA men". The Americans were reported to have angrily complained that de Gaulle's policy was "paralyzing NATO and rendering the defense of Europe impossible", and assured the generals that if they and their followers succeeded, Washington would recognize the new Algerian Government within 48 hours.

It may well be that the French Government did have evidence of the CIA's complicity. But in the unnatural world of international diplomacy, this would not necessarily lead to an unambiguous public announcement. Such a move could result in an open confrontation between France and the United States, a predicament both sides could be expected to take pains to avoid. Moreover, it might put the French in the position of having to *do* something about it. And what could they do? Breaking relations with the United States was not a realistic option; neither were the French in any position to retaliate economically or militarily. But French leaders were too angry to simply let the matter pass into obscurity. Thus, to complete the hypothetical scenario, they took the backdoor approach with all its shortcomings.

In a similar vein, the United States knew that the Russians, for at least one year, were intercepting telephone calls in the US of government and congressional officials, but said nothing publicly because it was unable to end the practice for technical reasons.[17] And this concerned an "enemy", not an ally.

Between 1958 and the middle of the 1960s, there occurred some 30 serious assassination attempts upon the life of Charles de Gaulle, in addition to any number of planned attempts which didn't advance much beyond the planning stage.[18] A world record for a head of state, it is said. In at least one of the attempts, the CIA may have been a co-conspirator against the French president. By the mid-1960s, differences between de Gaulle and Washington concerning NATO had almost reached the breaking point; in February 1966, he gave NATO and the United States a deadline to either place their military bases in France under French control or dismantle them.

In 1975, the *Chicago Tribune* featured a front-page story which read in part:

Congressional leaders have been told of Central Intelligence Agency involvement in a plot by French dissidents to assassinate the late French President Charles De Gaulle. Within the last two weeks, a CIA representative disclosed sketchy details of the scheme ... Sometime in the mid-1960s—probably in 1965 or 1966—dissidents in the De Gaulle government are said to have made contact with the CIA to seek help in a plot to murder the French leader. Which party instigated the contact was not clear ... According to the CIA briefing officer, discussions were held on how best to eliminate De Gaulle, who by then had become a thorn in the side of the Johnson administration because of his ouster of American military bases from French soil and his demands that United States forces be withdrawn from the Indochina War. Thus the following plan is said to have evolved after discussions between CIA personnel and the dissident French. There is, however, no evidence the plot got beyond the talking stage.

A hired assassin, armed with a poison ring, was to be slipped into a crowd of old soldiers of France when General De Gaulle was to be the host at a reception for them. The killer would make his appearance late in the day when it could be presumed De Gaulle's hand would be weary and perhaps even numb from shaking hundreds of hands. The assassin would clasp the general's hand in lethal friendship and De Gaulle would fail to detect the tiny pin prick of poison as it penetrated his flesh. The executioner would stroll off to become lost in the crowd as the poison began coursing through De Gaulle's veins either to his heart or brain, depending on the deadly poison used. How quickly death would come was not divulged, if that was even discussed at the time ...

In the outline presented to the congressional leaders, there is no hint of what the CIA's actual role might have been had the plot reached fruition.[19]

The dissidents involved in the alleged plot were embittered French army officers and former Algerian settlers who still bore deep resentment toward de Gaulle for having "sold out French honor" by his retreat from the North African colony.

There was no mention in the reported CIA testimony about any involvement of Lyndon Johnson, although it was well known that there was no love lost between Johnson and de Gaulle. The French leader was firmly convinced that the United States was behind the failure of his trip to South America in 1964. He believed that the CIA had used its network of agents in South America to prevent a big turnout of crowds.[20] There is some evidence to indicate that the General was not just paranoid. In 1970, Dr Alfred Stepan, a professor of political science at Yale, testified before Congress about his experience in South America in 1964 when he was a journalist for *The Economist*.

When De Gaulle was going to make his trip through Latin America, many of the Latin Americans interviewed [officers of various embassies] said that they were under very real pressure by various American groups not to be very warm towards De Gaulle, because we considered Latin America within the United States area of influence.[21]

After the appearance of the *Chicago Tribune* story, CIA Director William Colby confirmed that "foreigners" had approached the Agency with a plot to kill de Gaulle. The Agency rejected the idea, Colby said, but he did not know if the French government had been advised of the plot.[22] It is not clear whether the incident referred to by Colby was related to the one discussed in the *Tribune*.

In the early evening of Monday, 9 November 1970, Charles de Gaulle died peacefully at the age of 80, sitting in his armchair watching a sentimental television serial called "Nanou".

25. Ecuador 1960-1963
A textbook of dirty tricks

If the *Guinness Book of World Records* included a category for "cynicism", one could suggest the CIA's creation of "leftist" organizations which condemned poverty, disease, illiteracy, capitalism, and the United States in order to attract committed militants and their money away from legitimate leftist organizations.

The tiny nation of Ecuador in the early 1960s was, as it remains today, a classic of banana-republic underdevelopment; virtually at the bottom of the economic heap in South America; a society in which one percent of the population received an income comparable to United States upper-class standards, while two-thirds of the people had an average family income of about ten dollars per month—people simply outside the money economy, with little social integration or participation in the national life; a tale told many times in Latin America.

In September 1960, a new government headed by José María Velasco Ibarra came to power. Velasco had won a decisive electoral victory, running on a vaguely liberal, populist, something-for-everyone platform. He was no Fidel Castro, he was not even a socialist, but he earned the wrath of the US State Department and the CIA by his unyielding opposition to the two stated priorities of American policy in Ecuador: breaking relations with Cuba, and clamping down hard on activists of the Communist Party and those to their left.

Over the next three years, in pursuit of those goals, the CIA left as little as possible to chance. A veritable textbook on covert subversion techniques unfolded. In its pages could be found the following, based upon the experiences of Philip Agee, a CIA officer who spent this period in Ecuador.[1]

Almost all political organizations of significance, from the far left to the far right, were infiltrated, often at the highest levels. Amongst other reasons, the left was infiltrated to channel young radicals away from support to Cuba and from anti-Americanism; the right, to instigate and co-ordinate activities along the lines of CIA priorities. If, at a point in time, there was no organization that appeared well-suited to serve a particular need, then one would be created.

Or a new group of "concerned citizens" would appear, fronted with noted personalities, which might place a series of notices in leading newspapers denouncing the penetration of the government by the extreme left and demanding a break with Cuba. Or one of the noted personalities would deliver a speech prepared by the CIA, and then a newspaper editor, or a well-known columnist, would praise it, both gentlemen being on the CIA payroll.

Some of these fronts had an actual existence; for others, even their existence was phoney. On one occasion, the CIA Officer who had created the non-existent "Ecuadorean Anti-Communist Front" was surprised to read in his morning paper that a real organization with that name had been founded. He changed the name of his organization to "Ecuadorean Anti-Communist Action".

Wooing the working class came in for special emphasis. An alphabet-soup of labor organizations, sometimes hardly more than names on stationery, were created, altered, combined, liquidated, and new ones created again, in an almost frenzied attempt to find the right combination to compete with existing left-oriented unions and take national leadership away from them. Union leaders were invited to attend various classes conducted by the CIA in Ecuador or in the United States, all expenses paid, in order to impart to them the dangers of communism to the union movement and to select potential agents.

This effort was not without its irony either. CIA agents would sometimes jealously vie with each other for the best positions in these CIA-created labor organizations; and at times Ecuadorean organizations would meet in "international conferences" with CIA labor fronts from other countries, with almost all of the participants blissfully unaware of who was who or what was what.

In Ecuador, as throughout most of Latin America, the Agency planted phoney anti-communist news items in co-operating newspapers. These items would then be picked up by other CIA stations in Latin America and disseminated through a CIA-owned news agency, a CIA-owned radio station, or through countless journalists being paid on a piece-work basis, in addition to the item being picked up unwittingly by other media, including those in the United States. Anti-communist propaganda and news distortion (often of the most far-fetched variety) written in CIA offices would also appear in Latin American newspapers as unsigned editorials of the papers themselves.

In virtually every department of the Ecuadorean government could be found men occupying positions, high and low, who collaborated with the CIA for money and/or their own particular motivation. At one point, the Agency could count amongst this number the men who were second and third in power in the country.

These government agents would receive the benefits of information obtained by the CIA through electronic eavesdropping or other means, enabling them to gain prestige and promotion, or consolidate their current position in the rough-and-tumble of Ecuadorean politics. A high-ranking minister of leftist tendencies, on the other hand, would be the target of a steady stream of negative propaganda from any or all sources in the CIA arsenal; staged demonstrations against him would further increase the pressure on the president to replace him.

The Postmaster-General, along with other post office employees, all members in good standing of the CIA Payroll Club, regularly sent mail arriving from Cuba and the Soviet bloc to the Agency for its perusal, while customs officials and the Director of Immigration kept the Agency posted on who went to or came from Cuba. When a particularly suitable target returned from Cuba, he would be searched at the airport and documents prepared by the CIA would be "found" on him. These documents, publicized as much as possible, might include instructions on "how to intensify hatred between classes", or some provocative language designed to cause a split in Communist Party ranks. Generally, the documents "verified" the worst fears of the public about communist plans to take over Ecuador under the masterminding of Cuba or the Soviet Union; at the same time, perhaps, implicating an important Ecuadorean leftist whose head the Agency was after. Similar revelations, staged by CIA stations elsewhere in Latin America, would be publicized in Ecuador as a warning that Ecuador was next.

Agency financing of conservative groups in a quasi-religious campaign against Cuba and "atheistic communism" helped to seriously weaken President Velasco's power among the poor, primarily Indians, who had voted overwhelmingly for him, but who were even more deeply committed to their religion. If the CIA wished to know how the president was reacting to this campaign it need only turn to his physician, its agent, Dr. Felipe Ovalle, who would report that his patient was feeling considerable strain as a result.

CIA agents would bomb churches or right-wing organizations and make it appear to be the work of leftists. They would march in left-wing parades displaying signs and shouting slogans of a very provocative anti-military nature, designed to antagonize the armed forces and hasten a coup.

The Agency did not always get away clean with its dirty tricks. During the election campaign, on 19 March 1960, two senior colonels who were the CIA's main liaison agents within the National Police participated in a riot aimed at disrupting a Velasco demonstration. Agency officer Bob Weatherwax was in the forefront directing the police during the riot in which five Velasco supporters were killed and many wounded. When Velasco took office, he had the two colonels arrested and Weatherwax was asked to leave the country.

CIA-supported activities were carried out without the knowledge of the American ambassador. When the Cuban Embassy publicly charged the Agency with involvement in various anti-Cuban activities, the American ambassador issued a statement that "had everyone in the [CIA] station smiling". Stated the ambassador: "The only agents in Ecuador who are paid by the United States are the technicians invited by the Ecuadorean government to contribute to raising the living standards of the Ecuadorean people."

Finally, in November 1961, the military acted. Velasco was forced to resign and was replaced by Vice-President Carlos Julio Arosemana. There were at this time two prime candidates for the vice-presidency. One was the vice-president of the Senate, a CIA agent. The other was the rector of Central University, a political moderate. The day that Congress convened to make their choice, a notice appeared in a morning paper announcing support for the rector by the Communist Party and a militant leftist youth organization. The notice had been placed by a columnist for the newspaper who was the principal propaganda agent for the CIA's Quito station. The rector was compromised rather badly, the denials came too late, and the CIA man won. His Agency salary was increased from $700 to $1,000 a month.

Arosemana soon proved no more acceptable to the CIA than Velasco. All operations continued, particularly the campaign to break relations with Cuba, which Arosemana steadfastly refused to do. The deadlock was broken in March 1962 when a military garrison, led by Col. Aurelio Naranjo, gave Arosemana 72 hours to send the Cubans packing and fire the leftist Minister of Labor. (There is no need to point out here who Naranjo's financial benefactor was.) Arosemana complied with the ultimatum, booting out the Czech and Polish delegations as well at the behest of the new cabinet which had been forced upon him.

At the CIA station in Quito there was a champagne victory celebration. Elsewhere in Ecuador, people angry about the military's domination and desperate about their own lives, took to arms. But on this occasion, like others, it amounted to naught ... a small band of people, poorly armed and trained, infiltrated by agents, their every move known in advance—confronted by a battalion of paratroopers, superbly armed and trained by the United States. That was in the field. In press reports, the small band grew to hundreds; armed not only to the teeth, but with weapons from "outside the country" (read Cuba), and the whole operation very carefully planned at the Communist Party Congress the month before.

On 11 July 1963 the Presidential Palace in Quito was surrounded by tanks and troops. Arosemana was out, a junta was in. Their first act was to outlaw communism; "communists" and other "extreme" leftists were rounded up and jailed, the arrests campaign being facilitated by data from the CIA's Subversive Control Watch List. (Standard at many Agency stations, this list would include not only the subject's name, but the names and addresses of his relatives and friends and the places he frequented—anything to aid in tracking him down when the time came).

Civil liberties were suspended; the 1964 elections canceled; another tale told many times in Latin America.

And during these three years, what were the American people told about this witch's brew of covert actions carried out, supposedly, in their name? Very little, if anything, if the *New York Times* is any index. Not once during the entire period, up to and including the coup, was any indication given in any article or editorial on Ecuador that the CIA or any other arm of the US government had played any role whatever in any event which had occurred in that country. This is the way the writings read even if one looks back at them with the advantage of knowledge and hindsight and reads between the lines.

There is a solitary exception. Following the coup, we find a tiny announcement on the very bottom of page 20 that Havana radio had accused the United States of instigating the military takeover.[2] The Cuban government had been making public charges about American activities in Ecuador regularly, but this was the first one to make the *New York Times*. The question must be asked: Why were these charges deemed unworthy of reporting or comment, let alone investigation?

26. The Congo 1960-1964
The assassination of Patrice Lumumba

Within days of its independence from Belgium on 30 June 1960, the land long known as the Belgian Congo, and later as Zaire, was engulfed in strife and chaos as multiple individuals, tribes, and political groups struggled for dominance or independence. For the next several years the world press chronicled the train of Congolese governments, the endless confusion of personalities and conspiracies, exotic place names like Stanleyville and Leopoldville, shocking stories of European hostages and white mercenaries, the brutality and the violence from all quarters with its racist overtones.

Into this disorder the Western powers were "naturally" drawn, principally Belgium to protect its vast mineral investments, and the United States, mindful of the fabulous wealth as well, and obsessed, as usual, with fighting "communism".

Successive American administrations of Eisenhower, Kennedy and Johnson, looking through cold-war binoculars perceived an East-West battleground. The CIA station in the Congo cabled Washington in August that "Embassy and station believe Congo experiencing classic communist effort [to] takeover government." CIA Director Allen Dulles warned of a "communist takeover of the Congo with disastrous consequences ... for the interests of the free world". At the same time, Dulles authorized a crash-program fund of up to $100,000 to replace the existing government of Patrice Lumumba with a "pro-western group".[1]

It's not known what criteria the CIA applied to determine that Lumumba's government was going communist, but we do know how the *Washington Post* arrived at the same conclusion:

> Western diplomats see ... the part [of the Congo] controlled by volatile Premier Patrice Lumumba sliding slowly but surely into the Communist bloc. ... Apart from the fevered activity of Communist bloc nations here, the pattern of events is becoming apparent to students of Communist policy. Premier Lumumba's startling changes of position, his open challenge of the United Nations and Secretary General Dag Hammarskjold, his constant agitation of the largely illiterate Congolese can be explained in no other way, veteran observers say.[2]

Years later, Under Secretary of State C. Douglas Dillon told a Senate investigating committee (the Church committee) that the National Security Council and President Eisenhower had believed in 1960 that Lumumba was a "very difficult if not impossible person to deal with, and was dangerous to the peace and safety of the world."[3] This statement moved author Jonathan Kwitny to observe:

> How far beyond the dreams of a barefoot jungle postal clerk in 1956, that in a few short years he would be *dangerous to the peace and safety of the world!* The perception seems insane, particularly coming from the National Security Council, which really does have the power to end all human life within hours.[4]

Patrice Lumumba became the Congo's first prime minister after his party received a plurality of the votes in national elections. He called for the nation's economic as well as political liberation and did not shy away from contact with socialist countries. At the Independence Day ceremonies he probably managed to alienate all the attending foreign dignitaries with his speech, which read in part:

> Our lot was eighty years of colonial rule ... We have known tiring labor exacted in exchange for salary which did not allow us to satisfy our hunger ... We have known ironies, insults, blows which we had to endure morning, noon, and night because we were "Negroes" ... We have known that the law was never the same depending on whether it concerned a white or a Negro ... We have known the atrocious sufferings of those banished for political opinions or religious beliefs ... We have known that there were magnificent houses for the whites in the cities and tumble-down straw huts for the Negroes.[5]

In 1960, it must be borne in mind, this was indeed radical and inflammatory language in such a setting.

On 11 July, the province of Katanga—home to the bulk of the Congo's copper, cobalt, uranium, gold, and other mineral wealth—announced that it was seceding. Belgium, the principal owner of this fabulous wealth, never had any intention of giving up real control of the country, and it now supported the move for Katanga's independence, perceiving the advantage of having its investments housed in their own little country, not accountable to nor paying taxes to the central government in Leopoldville. Katanga, moreover, was led by Moise Tshombe, a man eminently accommodating to, and respectful of, whites and their investments.

The Eisenhower administration supported the Belgian military intervention on behalf of Katanga; indeed, the American embassy had previously requested such intervention. Influencing this policy, in addition to Washington's ideological aversion to Lumumba, was the fact that a number of prominent administration officials had financial ties to the Katanga wealth.[6]

The Belgian intervention, which was a very violent one, was denounced harshly by the Soviet Union, as well as many countries from the Afro-Asian bloc, leading the UN Security Council on the 14th to authorize the withdrawal of Belgian troops and their replacement by a United Nations military force. This was fine with the United States, for the UN under Dag Hammarskjöld was very closely allied to Washington. The UN officials who led the Congo operation were Americans, in secret collaboration with the State Department, and in exclusion of the Soviet bloc; the latter's citizens who worked at the UN Secretariat were kept from seeing the Congo cables. Hammarskjöld himself was quite hostile toward Lumumba.[7]

The UN force entered Katanga province and replaced the Belgian troops, but made no effort to end the secession. Unable to put down this uprising on his own, as well as one in another province, Lumumba had appealed to the United Nations as well as the United States to supply him with transport for his troops. When they both refused, he turned to the

Soviet Union for aid, and received it,[8] though military success still eluded him.

The Congo was in turmoil in many places. In the midst of it, on 5 September, President Joseph Kasavubu suddenly dismissed Lumumba as prime minister—a step of very debatable legality, taken with much American encouragement and assistance, as Kasavubu "sat at the feet of the CIA men".[9] The action was taken, said the Church committee later, "despite the strong support for Lumumba in the Congolese Parliament."[10]

During the early 1960s, according to a highly-placed CIA executive, the Agency "regularly bought and sold Congolese politicians".[11] US diplomatic sources subsequently confirmed that Kasavubu was amongst the recipients.[12]

Hammarskjöld publicly endorsed the dismissal before the Security Council, and when Lumumba tried to broadcast his case to the Congolese people, UN forces closed the radio station. Instead, he appeared before the legislature, and by dint of his formidable powers of speech, both houses of Parliament voted to reaffirm him as prime minister. But he could taste the fruits of his victory for only a few days, for on the 14th, army strongman Joseph Mobutu took power in a military coup.

Even during this period, with Lumumba not really in power, "CIA and high Administration officials continued to view him as a threat" ... his "talents and dynamism appear [to be the] overriding factor in reestablishing his position each time it seems half lost" ... "Lumumba was a spellbinding orator with the ability to stir masses of people to action" ... "if he ... started to talk to a battalion of the Congolese Army he probably would have had them in the palm of his hand in five minutes" ...[13]

In late September, the CIA sent one of its scientists, Dr. Sidney Gottlieb, to the Congo carrying "lethal biological material" (a virus) specifically intended for use in Lumumba's assassination. The virus, which was supposed to produce a fatal disease indigenous to the Congo area of Africa, was transported via diplomatic pouch.[14]

In 1975, the Church committee went on record with the conclusion that Allen Dulles had ordered Lumumba's assassination as "an urgent and prime objective" (Dulles's words).[15] After hearing the testimony of several officials who believed that the order to kill the African leader had emanated originally from President Eisenhower, the committee decided that there was a "reasonable inference" that this was indeed the case.[16]

As matters evolved in the Congo, the virus was never used, for the CIA's Congo station was unable to come up with "a secure enough agent with the right access" to Lumumba before the potency of the biological material was no longer reliable.[17]

The Church committee observed, however, that the CIA station in Leopoldville

continued to maintain close contact with Congolese who expressed a desire to assassinate Lumumba. CIA officers encouraged and offered to aid these Congolese in their efforts against Lumumba, although there is no evidence that aid was ever provided for the specific purpose of assassination.[18]

Fearing for his life, Lumumba was on the run. For a while he was protected from Mobutu by the United Nations, which, under considerable international pressure, had been forced to put some distance between itself and Washington.[19] But on 1 December, Lumumba was taken into custody by Mobutu's troops. A 28 November CIA cable indicates that the Agency was involved in tracking down the charismatic Congo leader. The cable spoke of the CIA station working with the Congolese government to get the roads blocked and troops alerted to close a possible escape route of Lumumba's.[20]

The United States had also been involved in the takeover of government by Mobutu—

whom author and CIA-confidant Andrew Tully described as having been "discovered" by the CIA.[21] Mobutu detained Lumumba until 17 January 1961 when he transferred his prisoner into the hands of Moise Tshombe of Katanga province, Lumumba's bitter enemy. Lumumba was assassinated the same day.

In 1978, former CIA Africa specialist John Stockwell related in his book how a ranking Agency officer had told him of driving around with Lumumba's body in the trunk of his car, "trying to decide what to do with it".[22] What he did do with it has not yet been made public.

During the period of Lumumba's imprisonment, US diplomats in the Congo were pursuing a policy of "deploring" his beatings and trying to secure "humane treatment" for him, albeit due to "considerations of international opinion and not from tender feelings toward him".[23] The immediate and the long-term effect of Lumumba's murder was to make him the martyr and symbol of anti-imperialism all over Africa and elsewhere in the Third World which such American officials had feared. Even Mobutu later felt compelled to build a memorial to his victim.

Without a clearcut "communist" enemy like Lumumba, the Kennedy administration, which came to power on 20 January 1961, was very divided on the Katanga question. Although the United States wound up supporting—in the name of Congolese stability—the UN military operation in the summer to suppress the secession, Tshombe had outspoken support in the US Congress, and sentiment amongst officials at the State Department and the White House mirrored this division. The sundry economic and diplomatic ties of these officials appear to have been more diverse and contradictory than under the Eisenhower administration, and this is reflected in the lack of a unified policy. However, according to Kennedy adviser and biographer, Arthur Schlesinger, opinions on both sides of the issue were expressed in terms of hindering supposed malevolent Soviet/communist designs in the Congo.[24]

In an even more marked policy division, US Air Force C-130s were flying Congolese troops and supplies against the Katangese rebels, while at the same time the CIA and its covert colleagues in the Pentagon were putting together an air armada of heavy transport aircraft, along with mercenary units, to aid the very same rebels.[25] (This marked at least the third instance of the CIA acting in direct military opposition to another arm of the US government.)[26]

Washington officials were more in unison when dealing with another prominent leftist—Antoine Gizenga, who had been Vice-Prime Minister under Lumumba. Following the latter's dismissal, according to the Church committee, the CIA station chief in the Congo, Lawrence Devlin, urged "a key Congolese leader" (presumably Mobutu) to "arrest" or undertake a "more permanent disposal of Lumumba, Gizenga, and Mulele." (Pierre Mulele was another Lumumba lieutenant.)[27] Gizenga was in fact arrested shortly after Mobutu took power, but a UN contingent from Ghana, whose leader, Kwame Nkrumah, was Lumumba's ally, intervened and freed him.[28]

In the continuous musical-chairs game of Congolese politics, the first of August 1961 found Gizenga as the Vice-Prime Minister under one Cyrille Adoula. By the end of the month, Gizenga was as well, and simultaneously, the leader of a rebel force that had set up a regime in the Stanleyville area which it proclaimed as the legitimate government of the entire Congo. He fancied himself the political and spiritual successor to Lumumba.

The Soviet Union may have believed Gizenga, for apparently they were sending him arms and money, using Sudan, which borders the Congo on the north, as a conduit. When the CIA learned that a Czech ship was bound for Sudan with a cargo of guns disguised as Red Cross packages for refugee relief in the Congo, the Agency turned to its most practiced art, bribery, to persuade a crane operator to let one of the crates drop upon arrival. On that day, the dockside was suddenly covered with new Soviet Kalashnikov rifles. Through an equally clever ploy at the Khartoum (Sudan) airport, the CIA managed to separate a Congolese courier from his suitcase of Soviet money destined for Gizenga.[29]

The State Department, meanwhile, was, in its own words,

urging Adoula to ... dismiss Gizenga and declare him in rebellion against the national government so that police action can now be taken against him. We are also urging the U.N. to take military action to break his rebellion ... We are making every effort to keep Gizenga isolated from potential domestic and foreign support ... We have taken care to insure that this [US] aid has been channelled through the central government in order to provide the economic incentive to encourage support for that government.[30]

The CIA was supplying arms and money to Adoula's supporters, as well as to Mobutu's.[31] Adoula, who had a background of close ties to both the American labor movement and the CIA international labor movement (via the International Confederation of Free Trade Unions—see British Guiana chapter), was chosen to be prime minister instead of Gizenga by a parliamentary conference during which the parliamentarians were bribed by the CIA and even by the United Nations. A subsequent CIA memorandum was apparently paying tribute to this when it stated: "The U.N. and the United States, in closely coordinated activities, played essential roles in this significant success over Gizenga."[32]

In January 1962, United Nations forces with strong American backing ousted Gizenga and his followers from Stanleyville, and a year later finally forced Tshombe to end his secession in Katanga. These actions were carried out in the name of "uniting the Congo", as if this were a matter to be decided by other than Congolese. Never before had the UN engaged in such offensive military operations, and the world organization was criticized in various quarters for having exceeded its charter. In any event, the operations served only to temporarily slow down the dreary procession of changing leaders, attempted coups, autonomous armies, shifting alliances, and rebellions.

Adding an ironic and absurd touch to the American Congo policy, three months after the successful action against Gizenga, Allen Dulles (thanks to the Bay of Pigs, now the *former* Director of the CIA) informed a television audience that the United States had "overrated the danger" of Soviet involvement ... "It looked as though they were going to make a serious attempt at takeover in the Belgian Congo, well it did not work out that way at all."[33]

Nonetheless, by the middle of 1964, when rebellion—by the heirs of Lumumba and Gizenga—was more widespread and furious than ever and the collapse of the central government appeared as a real possibility, the United States was pouring in a prodigious amount of military aid to the Leopoldville regime. In addition to providing arms and planes, Washington dispatched some 100 to 200 military and technical personnel to the Congo to aid government troops, and the CIA was conducting a paramilitary campaign against the insurgents in the eastern part of the country.[34]

The government was now headed by none other than Moise Tshombe, a man called "Africa's most unpopular African" for his widely-recognized role in the murder of the popular Lumumba and for his use of white mercenaries, many of them South Africans and Rhodesians, during his secession attempt in Katanga. Tshombe defended the latter action by explaining that his troops would not fight without white officers.[35]

Tshombe once again called upon his white mercenary army, numbering 400 to 500 men, and the CIA called upon its own mercenaries as well, a band which included Americans, Cuban-exile veterans of the Bay of Pigs, Rhodesians, and South Africans, the latter having been recruited with the help of the South African government. "Bringing in our own animals" was the way one CIA operative described the operation. The Agency's pilots carried out regular bombing and strafing missions against the insurgents, although some of the Cubans were reported to be troubled at being ordered to make indiscriminate attacks upon civilians.[36] Looking back at the affair in 1966, the *New York Times* credited the CIA with having created "an instant air force" in the Congo.[37]

When China protested to the United States about the use of American pilots in the Congo, the State Department issued an explicit denial, then publicly reversed itself, but insisted that the Americans were flying "under contract with the Congolese government". The next day, the Department said that the flights would stop, after having obtained assurances from "other arms of the [U.S] Government", although it still held to the position that the matter was one between the Congolese government and civilian individuals who were not violating American law.[38]

The Congolese against whom this array of military might was brought to bear were a coalition of forces. Some of the leading figures had spent time in Eastern Europe, the Soviet Union or China and were receiving token amounts of arms and instruction from those countries; but they were never necessarily in the communist camp any more than the countless Third Worlders who have gone to university in the United States and have been courted afterwards are necessarily in the Western/capitalist camp. (This does not hold for professional military officers who, unlike students, tend to be a particularly homogeneous group—conservative, authoritarian, and anti-communist.)

Africa scholar M. Crawford Young has observed that amongst the coalition leadership, "The destruction of the [Leopoldville] regime, a vigorous reassertion of Congolese control over its own destiny, and a vague socialist commitment were recurrent themes. But at bottom it appeared far more a frame of mind and a style of expression, than an interrelated set of ideas."[39] The rebels had no revolutionary program they could, or did, proclaim.

Co-existing with this element within the coalition were currents of various esoteric churches, messianic sects, witch-finding movements, and other occult inspirations as well as plain opportunists. Many believed that the magic of their witch doctors would protect them against bullets. One of their leaders, Pierre Mulele, was a quasi-Catholic who baptized his followers in his own urine to also make them immune to bullets. The insurgents were further divided along tribal lines and were rent by debilitating factionalism. No single group or belief could dominate.[40]

"Rebel success created the image of unified purpose and revolutionary promise," wrote Young. "Only in its subsequent phase of decay and disintegration" did the coalition's "dramatic lack of cohesion" and "disparity in purpose and perception" become fully evident.[41]

The *New York Times* addressed the question of the coalition's ideology as follows:

> There is evidence that most supporters of the Stanleyville regime have no ideological commitment but are mainly Congolese who are disillusioned with the corruption and irresponsibility that has characterized the Leopoldville regimes. The rebel leaders have received advice and money from Communists but few if any of the rebels consider themselves Communists. It is probable that few have heard of Karl Marx.[42]

In the coalition-controlled area of Stanleyville, between 2,000 and 3,000 white foreigners found themselves trapped by the war. One of the rebel leaders, Christopher Gbenye, conditioned their safe release upon various military concessions, principally a cessation of American bombing, but negotiations failed to produce an agreement.[43]

Instead, on 24 November 1964, the United States and Belgium staged a dramatic rescue mission in which over 500 Belgian paratroopers were dropped at dawn into Stanleyville from American transport planes. Much chaos followed, and the reports are conflicting, but it appears that more than 2,000 hostages were rescued, in the process of which the fleeing rebels massacred about 100 others and dragged several hundred more into the bush.

American and Belgian officials took great pains to emphasize the purely "humanitarian" purpose of the mission. However, the rescuers simultaneously executed a key military maneuver when they "seized the strategic points of the city and coordinated their operation with the advancing columns of Tshombe's mercenary army that was moving swiftly towards the city."[44] Moreover, in the process of the rescue, the rescuers killed dozens of rebels and did nothing to curtail Tshombe's troops when they reached Stanleyville and began an "orgy of looting and killing".[45]

Tshombe may have provided a reminder of the larger-than-humanitarian stake at hand in the Congo when, in the flush of the day's success, he talked openly with a correspondent of *The Times* of London who reported that Tshombe "was confident that the fall of Stanleyville would give a new impetus to the economy and encourage investors. It would reinforce a big development plan announced this morning in collaboration with the United States, Britain and West Germany."[46]

The collapse of the rebels' stronghold in Stanleyville marked the beginning of the end for their cause. By spring 1965 their fortune was in sharp decline, and the arrival of about 100 Cuban revolutionaries, amongst whom was Che Guevara himself, had no known effect upon the course of events. Several months later, Guevara returned to Cuba in disgust at the low level of revolutionary zeal exhibited by the Congolese guerrillas and the local populace.[47]

The concluding tune for the musical chairs was played in November, when Joseph Mobutu overthrew Tshombe and Kasavubu. Mobutu, later to adopt the name Mobutu Sese Seko, has ruled with a heavy dictatorial hand ever since.

In the final analysis, it mattered precious little to the interests of the US government whether the forces it had helped defeat were really "communist" or not, by whatever definition. The working premise was that there was now fixed in power, over a more-or-less unified Congo, a man who would be more co-operative with the CIA in its African adventures and with Western capital, and less accessible to the socialist bloc, than the likes of Lumumba, Gizenga, et al. would have been. The CIA has chalked this one up as a victory.

What the people of the Congo (now Zaire) won is not clear. Under Mobutu, terror and repression became facts of daily life, civil liberties and other human rights were markedly absent. The country remains one of the poorest to be found anywhere despite its vast natural riches. Mobutu, however, is reputed to be one of the richest heads of state in the world. (See Zaire chapter.)

William Atwood, US Ambassador to Kenya in 1964-65, who played a part in the hostage negotiations, also saw the US role in the Congo in a positive light. Bemoaning African suspicions toward American motives there, he wrote: "It was hard to convince people that we had provided the Congo with $420 million in aid since independence just to prevent chaos; they couldn't believe any country could be that altruistic."[48]

Atwood's comment is easier to understand when one realizes that the word "chaos" has long been used by American officials to refer to a situation over which the United States has insufficient control to assure that someone distinctly pro-Western will remain in, or come to, power. When President Eisenhower, for example, decided to send troops into Lebanon in 1958, he saw it as a move, he later wrote, "to stop the trend towards chaos".[49]

27. Brazil 1961-1964
Introducing the marvelous new world of Death Squads

When the leading members of the US diplomatic mission in Brazil held a meeting one day in March 1964, they arrived at the consensus that President João Goulart's support of social and economic reforms was a contrived and thinly veiled vehicle to seize dictatorial power.[1]

The American ambassador, Lincoln Gordon, informed the State Department that "a desperate lunge [by Goulart] for totalitarian power might be made at any time."[2]

The Brazilian army chief of staff, General Humberto de Alencar Castelo (or Castello) Branco, provided the American Embassy with a memorandum in which he stated his fear that Goulart was seeking to close down Congress and initiate a dictatorship.[3]

Within a week after the expression of these concerns, the Brazilian military, with Castelo Branco at its head, overthrew the constitutional government of President Goulart, the culmination of a conspiratorial process in which the American Embassy had been intimately involved. The military then proceeded to install and maintain for two decades one of the most brutal dictatorships in all of South America.

What are we to make of all this? The idea that men of rank and power lie to the public is commonplace, not worthy of debate. But do they as readily lie to each other? Is their need to rationalize their misdeeds so great that they provide each other a moral shoulder to lean on? "Men use thoughts only to justify their injustices," wrote Voltaire, "and speech only to conceal their thoughts."

The actual American motivation in supporting the coup was something rather less heroic than preserving democracy, even mundane as such matters go. American opposition to Goulart, who became president in 1961, rested upon a familiar catalogue of complaints:

US Defense Secretary Robert McNamara questioned Brazil's neutral stand in foreign policy. The Brazilian ambassador in Washington, Roberto Campos, responded that "neutralism" was an inadequate term and explained that "what was involved was really a deep urge of the Brazilian people to assert their personality in world affairs."[4]

American officials did not approve of some of the members of Goulart's cabinet, and said so. Ambassador Campos pointed out to them that it was "quite inappropriate" for the United States "to try to influence the composition of the cabinet."[5]

Attorney-General Robert Kennedy met with Goulart and expressed his uneasiness about the Brazilian president allowing "communists" to hold positions in government agencies. (Bobby was presumably acting on the old and very deep-seated American belief that once you welcome one or two communists into your parlor, they take over the whole house and sign the deed over to Moscow.) Goulart did not see this as a danger. He replied that he was in full control of the situation, later remarking to Campos that it was as if he had been told that he had no capacity for judging the men around him.[6]

The American Defense Attaché in Brazil, Col. Vernon Walters, reported that Goulart showed favoritism towards "ultra-nationalist" military officers over "pro-U.S." officers. Goulart saw it as promoting those officers who appeared to be most loyal to his government. He was, as it happens, very concerned about American-encouraged military coups and said so explicitly to President Kennedy.[7]

Goulart considered purchasing helicopters from Poland because Washington was delaying on his request to purchase them from the United States. Ambassador Gordon told him that he "could not expect the United States to like it".[8]

The Goulart administration, moreover, passed a law limiting the amount of profits multinationals could transmit out of the country, and a subsidiary of ITT was nationalized. Compensation for the takeover was slow in coming because of Brazil's precarious financial position, but these were the only significant actions taken against US corporate interests.

Inextricably woven into all these complaints, yet at the same time standing apart, was Washington's dismay with Brazil's "drift to the left" ... the communist/leftist influence in the labor movement ... leftist "infiltration" wherever one looked ..."anti-Americanism" among students and others (the American Consul General in São Paulo suggested to the State Department that the United States "found competing student organizations") ... the general erosion of "U.S. influence and the power of people and groups friendly to the United States"[9]... one might go so far as to suggest that Washington officials felt unloved, were it not for the fact that the coup, as they well knew from much past experience, could result only in intensified anti-Americanism all over Latin America.

Goulart's predecessor, Jânio da Silva Quadros, had also irritated Washington. "Why should the United States trade with Russia and her satellites but insist that Brazil trade only with the United States?" he asked, and proceeded to negotiate with the Soviet Union and other Communist countries to (re)establish diplomatic and commercial relations. He was, in a word, independent.[10]

Quadros was also more-or-less a conservative who clamped down hard on unions, sent federal troops to the northeast hunger dens to squash protest, and jailed disobedient students.[11] But the American ambassador at the time, John Moors Cabot, saw fit to question Brazil's taking part in a meeting of "uncommitted" (non-aligned) nations. "Brazil has signed various obligations with the United States and American nations," he said. "I am sure Brazil is not going to forget her obligations ... It is committed. It is a fact. Brazil can uncommit itself if it wants."[12]

In early 1961, shortly after Quadros took office, he was visited by Adolf Berle, Jr., President Kennedy's adviser on Latin American affairs and formerly ambassador to Brazil. Berle had come as Kennedy's special envoy to solicit Quadros's backing for the impending Bay of Pigs invasion. Ambassador Cabot was present and some years later described the meeting to author Peter Bell. Bell has written:

> Ambassador Cabot remembers a "stormy conversation" in which Berle stated the United States had $300 million in reserve for Brazil and in effect "offered it as a bribe" for Brazilian cooperation ... Quadros became "visibly irritated" after Berle refused to heed his third "no". No Brazilian official was at the airport the next day to see the envoy off.[13]

Quadros, who had been elected by a record margin, was, like Goulart, accused of seeking to set up a dictatorship because he sought to put teeth into measures unpopular with the oligarchy, the military, and/or the United States, as well as pursuing a "pro-communist" foreign policy. After but seven months in office he suddenly resigned, reportedly under military pressure, if not outright threat. In his letter of resignation, he blamed his predicament on "reactionaries" and "the ambitions of groups of individuals, some of whom are foreigners ... the terrible forces that arose against me."[14]

A few months later, Quadros reappeared, to deliver a speech in which he named Berle, Cabot, and US Treasury Secretary Douglas Dillon as being among those who had contributed to his downfall. Dillon, he said, sought to mix foreign policy with Brazil's needs for foreign credits.[15] (Both Berle and Cabot had been advocates of the 1954 overthrow of Guatemalan President Arbenz, whose sins, in Washington's eyes, were much the same as those Goulart was now guilty of.)[16] At the same time, Quadros announced his intention to lead a "people's crusade" against the "reactionaries, the corrupt and the Communists".[17]

As Quadros's vice president, Goulart succeeded to the presidency in August 1961 despite a virtual coup and civil war initiated by segments of the military to block him because he was seen as some sort of dangerous radical. Only the intervention of loyalist military units and other supporters of the constitutional process allowed Goulart to take office.[18] The military opposition to Goulart arose, it should be noted, before he had the opportunity to exhibit his alleged tendencies toward dictatorship. Indeed, as early as 1954, the military had demonstrated its antipathy toward him by forcing President Vargas to fire him from his position as Minister of Labor.[19] The American doubts about Goulart also predated his presidency. In 1960, when Goulart was elected vice president, "concern at the State Department and the Pentagon turned to panic" according to an American official who served in Brazil.[20]

Goulart tried to continue Quadros's independent foreign policy. His government went ahead with resumption of relations with socialist countries, and at a meeting of the Organization of American States in December 1961 Brazil abstained on a vote to hold a special session aimed at discussing "the Cuban problem", and stood strongly opposed to sanctions against the Castro government.[21] A few months later, speaking before the US Congress, Goulart affirmed Brazil's right to take its own stand on some of the cold-war issues. He declared that Brazil identified itself "with the democratic principles which unite the peoples of the West", but was "not part of any politico-military bloc".[22]

Time magazine, in common with most US media, had (has) a difficult time understanding the concept and practice of independence amongst America's allies. In November 1961, the magazine wrote that Brazil's domestic politics were "confused" and that the country was "also adrift in foreign affairs. Goulart is trying to play the old Quadros game of international 'independence', which means wooing the East while panhandling from the West." *Time* was critical of Goulart in that he had sought an invitation to visit Washington and on the same day he received it he "called in Communist Poland's visiting Foreign Minister, Adam Rapacki, [and] awarded him the Order of the Southern Cross—the same decoration that Quadros hung on Cuba's Marxist mastermind, Che Guevara".[23]

Former *Time* editor and Latin America correspondent, John Gerassi, commented that every visiting foreign dignitary received this medal, the *Cruzeiro do Sul*, as part of protocol. He added:

Apparently *Time* thinks that any President who wants to visit us must necessarily hate our enemies as a consequence, and is "confused" whenever this does not occur. But, of course, *Time* magazine is so unused to the word "independent" that an independent foreign policy must be very confusing indeed. In South America, where everyone would like to follow an independent foreign policy but where only Brazil has, at times, the courage, no one was confused.[24]

Goulart, a millionaire land-owner and a Catholic who wore a medal of the Virgin around his neck, was no more a communist than was Quadros, and he strongly supported the United States during the "Cuban Missile Crisis" of October 1962. He offered Ambassador Gordon a toast "To the Yankee Victory!",[25] perhaps unaware that only three weeks earlier, during federal and state elections in Brazil, CIA money had been liberally expended in support of anti-Goulart candidates. Former CIA officer Philip Agee has stated that the Agency spent between 12 and 20 million dollars on behalf of hundreds of candidates.[26] Lincoln Gordon says the funding came to no more than 5 million.[27]

In addition to the direct campaign contributions, the CIA dipped into its bag of dirty tricks to torment the campaigns of leftist candidates.[28] At the same time, the Agency for International Development (AID), at the express request of President Kennedy, was allocating monies to projects aimed at benefiting chosen gubernatorial candidates.[29] (While Goulart was president, no new US economic assistance was given to the central government, while regional assistance was provided on a markedly ideological basis. When the military took power, this pattern was sharply altered.)[30]

Agee adds that the CIA carried out a consistent propaganda campaign against Goulart which dated from at least the 1962 election operation and which included the financing of mass urban demonstrations, "proving the old themes of God, country, family and liberty to be as effective as ever" in undermining a government.[31]

CIA money also found its way to a chain of right-wing newspapers, Diarias Associades, to promote anti-communism; for the distribution of 50 thousand books of similar politics to high school and college students; and for the formation of women's groups with their special Latin mother's emphasis on the godlessness of the communist enemy. The women and other CIA operatives also went into the rumor-mongering business, spreading stories about outrages Goulart and his cronies were supposed to be planning, such as altering the constitution so as to extend his term, and gossip about Goulart being a cuckold and a wife-beater.[32]

All this to overthrow a man who, in April 1962, had received a ticker-tape parade in New York City, was warmly welcomed at the White House by President Kennedy, and had addressed a joint session of Congress.

The intraservice confrontation which had attended Goulart's accession to power apparently kept a rein on coup-minded officers until 1963. In March of that year the CIA informed Washington, but not Goulart, of a plot by conservative officers.[33] During the course of the following year, the plots thickened. Brazilian military officers could not abide by Goulart's attempts at populist social reforms, though his program was timid, his rhetoric generally mild, and his actions seldom matched either. (He himself pointed out that General Douglas MacArthur had carried out a more radical distribution of land in Japan after the Second World War than anything planned by the Brazilian Government.) The military men were particularly incensed at Goulart's support of a weakening of military discipline and his attempts to build up a following among non-commissioned officers.[34] This the president was genuinely serious about because of his "paranoia" about a coup.

Goulart's wooing of NCOs and his appeals to the population over the heads of a hostile Congress and state governors (something President Reagan later did on several occasions) were the kind of tactics his enemies labeled as dictatorial.

In early 1964, disclosed *Fortune* magazine after the coup, an emissary was sent by some of the military plotters "to ask U.S. Ambassador Lincoln Gordon what the U.S. position would be if civil war broke out". The emissary "reported back that Gordon was cautious and diplomatic, but he left the impression that if the [plotters] could hold out for forty-eight hours they would get U.S. recognition and help."[35]

The primary American contact with the conspirators was Defense Attaché Vernon Walters who arrived in Brazil after having been apprised that President Kennedy would not be averse to the overthrow of João Goulart.[36] Walters, who later became Deputy Director of the CIA, had an intimacy with leading Brazilian military officers, particularly General Castelo Branco, going back to World War II when Walters had served as interpreter for the Brazilian Expeditionary Force then fighting in Italy with the Allies. Brazil was the only Latin American country to send ground combat troops to the war, and it allowed the United States to build huge aircraft staging bases on its territory.[37] The relationship between US and Brazilian officers was continued and enhanced after the war by the creation of the Higher War College (*Escola Superior de Guerra*) in Rio de Janeiro in 1949. Latin America historian Thomas E. Skidmore has observed:

> Under the U.S.-Brazilian military agreements of the early 1950s, the U.S. Army received exclusive rights to render assistance in the organization and operation of the college, which had been modeled on the National War College in Washington. In view of the fact that the Brazilian War College became a rallying point for leading military opponents of civilian populist politicians, it would be worth examining the extent to which the strongly anti-Communist ideology—bordering on an anti-political attitude—[of certain officers] was reinforced (or moderated?) by their frequent contacts with United States officers.[38]

There was, moreover, the ongoing US Military Assistance Program, which Ambassador Gordon described as a "major vehicle for establishing close relationships with personnel of the armed forces" and "a highly important factor in influencing [the Brazilian] military to be pro-US."[39]

A week before the coup, Castelo Branco, who emerged as the leader of the conspirators, gave Walters a copy of a paper he had written which was in effect a justification for a military coup, another variation on the theme of upholding the constitution by preventing Goulart from instituting a dictatorship.[40]

To Lincoln Gordon and other American officials, civil war appeared a real possibility as the result of a coup attempt. As the scheduled day approached, contingency plans were set up.

A large quantity of petroleum would be sent to Brazil and made available to the insurgent officers, an especially vital commodity if Goulart supporters in the state oil union were to blow up or control the refineries.[41]

A US Navy task force would be dispatched to Brazilian coastal waters, the presence of which would deliver an obvious message to opponents of the coup.[42]

Arms and ammunition would be sent to Branco's forces to meet their fighting needs.[43]

Concerned that the coup attempt might be met by a general strike, Washington discussed with Gordon the possible need "for the U.S. to mount a large material program to assure the success of the takeover."[44] The conspirators had already requested economic aid from the United States, in the event of their success, to get the government and economy moving again, and had received a generally favorable response.[45]

At the same time, Gordon sent word to some anti-Goulart state governors emphasizing the necessity, from the American point of view, that the new regime have a claim to legitimacy. The ambassador also met with former president Juscelino Kubitschek to urge him to take a stronger position against Goulart and to use his considerable influence to "swing a large congressional group and thereby influence the legitimacy issue".[46]

Of the American contingency measures, indications are that it was the naval show of force—which, it turned out, included an aircraft carrier, destroyers, and guided missiles—which most encouraged the Brazilian military plotters or convinced those still wavering in their commitment.[47]

Another actor in the unfolding drama was the American Institute for Free Labor Development. The AIFLD came formally into being in 1961 and was technically under the direction of the American labor movement (AFL-CIO), but was soon being funded almost exclusively by the US government (AID) and serving consistently as a CIA instrument in most countries of Latin America. In May 1963, the AIFLD founded the *Instituto Cultural Trabalho* in Brazil which, over the next few years, gave courses to more than 7,000 union leaders and members.[48] Other Brazilians went to the United States for training. When they returned to Brazil, said AIFLD executive William Doherty, Jr., some of them:

> became intimately involved in some of the clandestine operations of the revolution before it took place on April 1. What happened in Brazil on April 1 did not just happen—it was planned—and planned months in advance. Many of the trade union leaders—some of whom were actually trained in our institute—were involved in the revolution, and in the overthrow of the Goulart regime.[49]

Doherty did not spell out any details of the AIFLD role in the coup (or revolution as he called it), although *Reader's Digest* later reported that one of the AIFLD-trained labor leaders set up courses for communication workers in combatting communism in the labor movement in Brazil, and "After every class he quietly warned key workers of coming trouble and urged them to keep communications going no matter what happened."[50] Additionally, Richard Martinez, an unwitting CIA contract employee who was sent to Brazil to work with the Agency's Post, Telegraph and Telephone Workers International (formerly Doherty's domain), has revealed that his field workers in Brazil burned down Communist Party headquarters at the time of the coup.[51]

The coup began on 31 March 1964 with the advance upon Rio of troops and tanks. Officers obtained the support of some units of enlisted men by telling them they were heading for the city to secure it against Goulart's enemies. But at the main air force base pro-Goulart enlisted men, hearing of the move toward Rio, seized the base and put their officers under arrest. Indecision and cold feet intervened, however, and what might have reversed the course of events instead came to nought. Other military units loyal to Goulart took actions elsewhere, but these too fizzled out.[52]

Here and there a scattering of workers went out on strike; several short-lived, impotent demonstrations took place, but there was little else. A number of labor leaders and radicals were rounded up on the orders of certain state governors; those who were opposed to what was happening were not prepared for violent resistance; in one incident a group of students staged a protest—some charged up the stairs of an Army organization, but the guard fired into their midst, killing two of them and forcing the others to fall back.[53]

Most people counted on loyal armed forces to do their duty, or waited for the word from Goulart. Goulart, however, was unwilling to give the call for a civil war; he did not want to be responsible, he said, for bloodshed amongst Brazilians, and fled to Uruguay.[54]

Lincoln Gordon cabled Washington the good news, suggesting the "avoidance of a jubilant posture". He described the coup as "a great victory for the free world", adding, in a remark that might have had difficulty getting past the lips of even John Foster Dulles, that without the coup there could have been a "total loss to the West of all South American Republics". Following a victory parade in Rio on 2 April by those pleased with the coup—a March of Family with God for Liberty—Gordon informed the State Department that the "only unfortunate note was the obviously limited participation in the march of the lower classes."[55]

His cable work done, the former Harvard professor turned his attention back to trying to persuade the Brazilian Congress to bestow a seal of "legitimacy" upon the new government.[56]

Two years later, Gordon was to be questioned by a senator during hearings to consider his nomination as Secretary of State for Inter-American Affairs. "I am particularly concerned," said the senator, "with the part you may have played, if any, in encouraging, promoting, or causing that overthrow."

Said Lincoln Gordon: "The answer to that, senator, is very simple. The movement which overthrew President Goulart was a purely, 100 percent—not 99.44—but 100 percent purely Brazilian movement. Neither the American Embassy nor I personally played any part in the process whatsoever."[57]

Gordon's boss, Dean Rusk, was not any more forthright. When asked about Cuban charges that the United States was behind the coup, the Secretary of State responded: "Well, there is just not one iota of truth in this. It's just not so in any way, shape, or form."[58] While Attorney General Robert Kennedy's view of the affair, stated to Gordon, was: "Well, Goulart got what was coming to him. Too bad he didn't follow the advice we gave him when I was there."[59]

Gordon artfully combined fast talk with omission of certain key facts about Brazilian politics—his summary of Goulart's rise and fall made no mention at all of the military's move to keep him from taking office in 1961—to convince the assembled senators that Goulart was indeed seeking to set up a personal dictatorship.[60]

Depending on the setting, either "saving Brazil from dictatorship" or "saving Brazil from communism" was advanced as the rationale for what took place in 1964. (General Andrew O'Meara, head of the US Southern [Latin America] Command, had it both ways. He told a House committee that "The coming to power of the Castelo Branco government in Brazil last April saved that country from an immediate dictatorship which could only have been followed by Communist domination.")[61]

The rescue-from-communism position was especially difficult to support, the problem being that the communists in Brazil did not, after all, *do* anything which the United States could point to. Moreover, the Soviet Union was scarcely in the picture. Early in 1964, reported a Brazilian newspaper, Russian leader Khrushchev told the Brazilian Communist Party that the Soviet government did not wish either to give financial aid to the Goulart regime or to tangle with the United States over the country.[62] In his reminiscences—albeit, as mentioned earlier, not meant to be a serious work of history—Khrushchev does not give an index reference to Brazil.

A year after the coup, trade between Brazil and the USSR was running at $120 million per year and a Brazilian mission was planning to go to Moscow to explore Soviet willingness to provide a major industrial plant.[63] The following year, the Russians invited the new Brazilian president-to-be, General Costa e Silva, to visit the Soviet Union.[64]

During the entire life of the military dictatorship, extending into the 1980s, Brazil and the Soviet bloc engaged in extensive trade and economic cooperation, reaching billions of dollars per year and including the building of several large hydroelectric plants in Brazil. A similar economic relationship existed between the Soviet bloc and the Argentine military dictatorship of 1976-83, so much so that in 1982, when Soviet leader Brezhnev died, the Argentine government declared a national day of mourning.[65]

It was only by ignoring facts like these during the cold war that the anti-communist propaganda machine of the United States could preach about the International Communist Conspiracy and claim that the coup in Brazil had saved the country from communism. For a typical example of this propaganda, one must read "The Country That Saved Itself," which appeared in *Reader's Digest* several months after the coup. The innumerable lies about what occurred in Brazil, fed by the magazine to its millions of readers, undoubtedly played a role in preparing the American public for the great anti-communist crusade in Vietnam just picking up steam at the time. The article began:

> Seldom has a major nation come closer to the brink of disaster and yet recovered than did Brazil in its recent triumph over Red subversion. The communist drive for domination—marked by propaganda, infiltration, terror—was moving in high gear. Total surrender seemed imminent— and then the people said *No!*[66]

The type of independence shown by the Brazilian military government in its economic relations with the Soviet Union was something Washington could accept from a conservative government, even the occasional nationalization of American property, when it knew that the government could be relied upon to keep the left suppressed at home and to help in the vital cold-war, anti-communist campaigns abroad. In 1965, Brazil sent 1,100 troops to the Dominican Republic in support of the US invasion, the only country in Latin America to send more than a token force. And in 1971 and 1973, the Brazilian military and intelligence apparatuses contributed to the American efforts in overthrowing the governments of Bolivia and Chile.

The United States did not rest on its laurels. CIA headquarters immediately began to generate hemisphere-wide propaganda, as only the Agency's far-flung press-asset network could, in support of the new Brazilian government and to discredit Goulart.[67] Dean Rusk, concerned that Goulart might be received in Uruguay as if he were still Brazil's president on the grounds that he had not resigned, cabled the American Embassy in Montevideo that "it would be useful if you could quietly bring to the attention of appropriate officials the fact that despite his allegations to the contrary Goulart has abandoned his office."[68]

At the same time, the CIA station in Uruguay undertook a program of surveillance of Brazilian exiles who had fled from the military takeover, to prevent them from instigating any kind of insurgency movement in their homeland. It was a simple matter for the Agency to ask their (paid) friend, the head of Uruguayan intelligence, to place his officers at the residences of Goulart and other key Brazilians. The officers kept logs of visitors while posing as personal security men for the exiles, although it is unlikely that the exiles swallowed the story.[69]

In the first few days following the coup, "several thousand" Brazilians were arrested, "communist and suspected communist" all.[70] AIFLD graduates were promptly appointed by the new government to purge the unions.[71] Though Ambassador Gordon had assured the State Department before the coup that the armed forces "would be quick to restore constitutional institutions and return power to civilian hands,"[72] this was not to be. Within days, General Castelo Branco assumed the presidency and over the next few years his regime instituted all the features of military dictatorship which Latin America has come to know and love: Congress was shut down, political opposition was reduced to virtual extinction, habeas corpus for "political crimes" was suspended, criticism of the president was forbidden by law, labor unions were taken over by government interveners, mounting protests were met by police and military firing into crowds, the use of systematic "disappearance" as a form of repression came upon the stage of Latin America, peasants' homes were burned down, priests were brutalized ... the government had a name for its program: the "moral rehabilitation" of Brazil ... then there was the torture and the death squads, both largely undertakings of the police and the military, both underwritten by the United States.[73]

In the chapters on Guatemala and Uruguay, we shall see how the US Office of Public Safety (OPS), the CIA and AID combined to provide the technical training, the equipment, and the indoctrination which supported the horrors in those countries. It was no less the case in Brazil. Dan Mitrione of the OPS, whom we shall encounter in his full beauty in Uruguay, began his career in Brazil in the 1960s. By 1969, OPS had established a national police force for Brazil and had trained over 100,000 policemen in the country, in addition to 523 receiving more advanced instruction in the United States.[74] About one-third of the students' time at the police academies was devoted to lectures on the "communist menace" and the need to battle against it.[75] The "bomb school" and techniques of riot control were other important aspects of their education.

> Tortures range from simple but brutal blows from a truncheon to electric shocks. Often the torture is more refined: the end of a reed is placed in the anus of a naked man hanging suspended downwards on the *pau de arara* [parrot's perch] and a piece of cotton soaked in petrol is lit at the other end of the reed. Pregnant women have been forced to watch their husbands being tortured. Other wives have been hung naked beside their husbands and given electric shocks on the sexual parts of their body, while subjected to the worst kind of obscenities. Children have been tortured before their parents and vice versa. At least one child, the three month old baby of Virgilio Gomes da Silva was reported to have died under police torture. The length of sessions depends upon the resistance capacity of the victims and have sometimes continued for days at a time.
>
> Amnesty International[76]

> Judge Agamemnon Duarte indicated that the CCC [Commandos to Hunt Communists, a death squad armed and aided by the police] and the CIA are implicated in the murder of Father Henrique Neto. He admitted that ... the American Secret Service (CIA) was behind the CCC.
>
> *Jornal do Brazil*[77]

Chief of Staff of the Brazilian Army, General Breno Borges Forte, at the Tenth Conference of American Armies in 1973:

> The enemy is undefined ... it adapts to any environment and uses every means, both licit and illicit, to achieve its aims. It disguises itself as a priest, a student or a campesino, as a defender of democracy or an advanced intellectual, as a pious soul or as an extremist protestor; it goes into the fields and the schools, the factories and the churches, the universities and the magistracy; if necessary, it will wear a uniform or civil garb; in sum, it will take on any role that it considers appropriate to deceive, to lie, and to take in the good faith of Western peoples."[78]

In 1970, a US Congress study group visited Brazil. It gave this summary of statements by American military advisers there:

> Rather than dwell on the authoritarian aspects of the regime, they emphasize assertions by the Brazilian armed forces that they believe in, and support, representative democracy as an ideal and would return government to civilian control if this could be done without sacrifice to security and development. This withdrawal from the political arena is not seen as occurring in the near future. For that reason they emphasize the continued importance of the military assistance training program as a means of exerting U.S. influence and retaining the current pro-U.S. attitude of the Brazilian armed forces. Possible disadvantages to U.S. interests in being so closely identified with an authoritarian regime are not seen as particularly important.[79]

The CIA never rests ... a footnote: the *New York Times* reported in 1966 ...

When the CIA learned last year that a Brazilian youth had been killed in 1963, allegedly in an auto accident, while studying on a scholarship at the Lumumba University in Moscow, it mounted a massive publicity campaign to discourage other South American families from sending their youngsters to the Soviet Union.[80]

28. Peru 1960-1965
Fort Bragg moves to the jungle

It was a CIA dream come true. A commando raid by anti-Castro Cubans upon the Cuban Embassy in Lima had uncovered documentary proof that Cuba had paid out "hundreds of thousands" of dollars in Peru for propaganda to foster favorable attitudes toward the Cuban revolution and to promote Communist activities within the country.

This was no standard broad-brush, cold-war accusation, for the documents disclosed all manner of details and names—the culprits who had been on the receiving end of the tainted money; men in unions and universities and in politics; men who had secretly visited Cuba, all expenses paid.[1] To top it all off, these were men the CIA looked upon as enemies.

The only problem—and it wasn't really a problem—was that some of the documents were counterfeit. The raid had certainly taken place, on 8 November 1960 to be exact. And documents had indeed been seized, at gunpoint. But the most incriminating of the documents, presented a month later with the authentic ones, had been produced by the experts of the CIA's Technical Services Division.[2]

It was a propaganda windfall. The story received wide media coverage in Latin America and the United States, accompanied by indignant anti-communist articles and editorials. The *Wall Street Journal* was moved to run an extremely long, slightly hysterical piece, obviously based on Washington handouts, strikingly unquestioned, which warned that "mountainous stacks of intelligence data from the 20 nations stretching from Mexico to Argentina tell of a widening Communist push into the hemisphere".[3]

To be sure, the Cubans insisted that the documents were not genuine, but that was only to be expected. The affair was to cast a shadow over Castro's foreign relations for some time to come.

The most propitious outcome, from the CIA's standpoint, was that within days after the disclosure the Peruvian government broke diplomatic relations with Cuba. This was a major priority of the Agency in Lima, as in most other CIA stations in Latin America, and led further to the Cuban news agency, *Prensa Latina*, being barred from operating in Peru. The news agency's dispatches, the Peruvian authorities now decided, were "controlled from Moscow".[4]

A week later, there was further welcome fallout from the incident. The government enacted legislation making it easier to arrest members of the Communist Party, although this was repealed a year later. During its deliberations the Peruvian legislature accepted a sworn statement from one Francisco Ramos Montejo, a recent defector from the Cuban Embassy who had been present during the raid, who "confirmed" that all the documents were genuine. Ramos, who was now living in Miami and working for the CIA, added fresh revelations that there had been detailed plans for the assassination of Peruvian officials and for the overthrow of the government, and that arms had been smuggled into Peru from Bolivia and Ecuador, presumably for these purposes.[5]

Of such stuff is the battle for the hearts and minds of Latin Americans made.

The political history of Peru has been of the classic South American mold—an oligarchy overthrown by a military coup replaced by another oligarchy ... periodically punctuated by an uprising, sporadic violence from the forgotten below to remind those above that they are still alive, albeit barely. Veteran Latin America newsman John Gerassi described the state of those below in the Peru of the early 1960s:

> In Lima, the capital, whose colonial mansions enveloped by ornate wooden balconies help make it one of the most beautiful cities in the world, half of the 1.3 million inhabitants live in rat-infested slums. One, called El Montón, is built around, over, and in the city dump. There, when I visited it, naked children, some too young to know how to walk, competed with pigs for a few bits of food scraps accidentally discarded by the garbage men ... [The peasants] chew cocaine-producing coca leaves to still hunger pains, and average 500 calories a day. Where there is grass, the Peruvian Andes Indian eats it—and also the sheep he kills when it gets so hungry that it begins tearing another sheep's wool off for its food. The peons who work the land of the whites average one sol (4 cents) a day, and ... labor from sunup to sundown.[6]

During this period, a movement led by Hugo Blanco organized peasants into unions, staged strikes and seized land. The movement engaged in little which could be termed guerrilla warfare, using its meagre arms to defend the squatters, and was easily and brutally put down by the police and army, apparently without significant American assistance other than the "routine" arming and training of such forces.

By 1965, however, several guerrilla groups had evolved in the eastern slopes of the Andes, cognizant of the bare truth that organizing peasants was, by itself, painfully inadequate; some would say suicidal. Inspired by the Cuban revolution, impressed with the social gains which had followed, and, in some cases, trained by the Cubans, these sons of the middle class met in May to plan a common strategy. Guerrilla warfare began in earnest the following month. By the end of the year, however, a joint Peruvian-American counter-insurgency operation had broken the back of three rebel groups, two of them in less than two months. Those guerrillas who remained alive and active were reduced to futile and impotent skirmishes over the next year or so.[7]

The role of the CIA in this definitive military mop-up has been concisely depicted by the former high official of the Agency, Victor Marchetti:

> Green Berets participated ... in what was the CIA's single large-scale Latin American intervention of the post-Bay of Pigs era. This occurred in the mid-1960s, when the agency secretly came to the aid of the Peruvian government, then plagued by guerrilla troubles in its remote eastern regions. Unable to cope adequately with the insurgent movement, Lima had turned to the U.S. government for aid, which was immediately and covertly forthcoming.
>
> The agency financed the construction of what one experienced observer described as "a miniature Fort Bragg" in the troubled Peruvian jungle region, complete with mess halls, classrooms, barracks, administrative buildings, parachute jump towers, amphibious landing facilities, and all the other accoutrements of paramilitary operations. Helicopters were furnished under cover of official military aid programs, and the CIA flew in arms and other combat equipment. Training was provided by the agency's Special Operations Division personnel and by Green Beret instructors on loan from the Army.[8]

In February 1966, Secretary of Defense Robert McNamara summed up this effort in a Senate hearing: "In Peru, the Government has already made good progress against guerrilla concentrations, and U.S. trained and supported Peruvian army and air force units have played prominent roles in this counter-guerrilla campaign."[9]

Typically, and ironically, such training would have included instilling in the Peruvian officers the motivation for doing battle with the insurgents in the first place. As US military affairs scholar Michael Klare has pointed out:

> Many Latin American military officers would rather command elite units like jet fighter squadrons, naval flotillas, or armored brigades than slug it out with the guerrillas in long, unspectacular jungle campaigns. U.S. training programs are designed, therefore, to emphasize the importance of counterguerrilla operations (and to suggest, thereby, that the United States will reward those officers who make a good showing at this kind of warfare).[10]

The extent to which American military personnel engaged directly in combat is not known. They did, however, set up their headquarters in the center of an area of heavy fighting, in the village of Mazanari, and in September 1965 the *New York Times* reported that when the Peruvian army opened a major drive against the guerrillas, "At least one United States Army counter-insurgency expert was said to have helped plan and direct the attack."[11]

In the urban areas a concurrent round-up of guerrilla supporters was carried out, based materially on CIA intelligence: the list of "subversives" regularly compiled by Agency stations throughout the world for just such occasions.[12] The CIA is usually in a much better position to collect this information than the host government, due to its superior experience in the field, funds available for hiring informants, technical equipment for eavesdropping, and greater motivation.

While this was taking place the war in Vietnam and the militant protest against it had already captured the front pages of American newspapers, and the isolated *New York Times* dispatch referred to above easily passed into oblivion. Yet, the American objective in Peru—to crush a movement aimed at genuine land reform and the social and political changes inevitably stemming from such—was identical to its objective in Vietnam. And the methods employed were similar: burning down peasants' huts and villages to punish support for the guerrillas, defoliating the countryside to eliminate guerrilla sanctuaries, saturation bombing with napalm and high explosives, even throwing prisoners out of helicopters.[13]

The essential difference, one which spelled disaster for the Peruvian insurgents, was that their ranks were not augmented in any appreciable number by the Indian peasants, a group with little revolutionary consciousness and even less daring; four centuries of dehumanization had robbed them of virtually all hope and the sense of a right to revolt; and when this sense stirred even faintly, such as under Hugo Blanco, it was met head-on by the brick wall of official violence.

As common in the Third World as it is ludicrous, the bulk of the armed forces employed to keep the peasants pacified were soldiers of peasant stock themselves. It is a measure of the ultimate cynicism of the Peruvian and American military authorities that soldiers were stationed outside their home areas to lessen their resistance when the order was given to shoot.[14]

But it all worked. It worked so well that more than a decade was to pass before desperate men took to arms again in Peru.

29. Dominican Republic 1960-1966

Saving democracy from communism by getting rid of democracy

On the night of 30 May 1961, Generalissimo Rafael Trujillo, mass murderer, torturer par excellence, absolute dictator, was shot to death on a highway in the outskirts of the capital city, Ciudad Trujillo.

The assassination set off a chain of events over the next five years which featured sustained and remarkably gross intervention into the internal affairs of the Dominican Republic by the United States, the likes of which had not been seen in Latin America since the heyday of American gunboat diplomacy.

The United States had been an accomplice in the assassination itself of the man it had helped to climb to power and to endure for some 30 years. It marked one of the rare occasions that the US government acted to overthrow a right-wing despot, albeit anti-communism was still the motivating force.

Whatever repugnance individual Washington policy makers may have felt toward Trujillo's incredible violations of human rights over the years, his fervent adherence to American policies, his repression of the left, and, as a consequence, the vigorous support he enjoyed in Congress (where Trujillo's money was no stranger) and in other influential American circles, were enough to keep successive United States administrations looking the other way.

When, in January 1959, Fulgencio Batista fell before the forces of Fidel Castro in nearby Cuba, a reconsideration of this policy was thrust upon Washington's agenda. This historic event seemed to suggest that support of right-wing governments might no longer be the best way of checking the rise of revolutionary movements in Latin America, but rather might be fostering them. Indeed, in June a force of Dominican exiles launched an invasion of their homeland from Cuba. Although the invasion was a complete failure, it could only serve to heighten Washington's concern about who was swimming around in "The American Lake".

"'Batista is to Castro as Trujillo is to _____' was the implicit assumption, and Washington wanted to ensure that it could help fill in the blank," is the way one analysis formulated the problem. "As a result, the United States began to cast about for a way to get rid of Trujillo and at the same time to ensure a responsible successor."[1] Ironically, it was to Trujillo's Dominican Republic that Batista had fled.

The decision to topple Trujillo was reinforced in early 1960 when the United States sought to organize hemispheric opposition to the Castro regime. This policy ran head-on into the familiar accusation that the United States opposed only leftist governments, never those of the right, no matter how tyrannical. The close association with Trujillo, widely regarded as Washington's "protegé", was proving increasingly to be an embarrassment. The circumstances were such that President Eisenhower was led to observe that "It's certain that American public opinion won't condemn Castro until we have moved against Trujillo."[2] (The president's apparent belief in the independence of the American mind may have been overly generous, for Washington was supporting right-wing dictatorships in Guatemala, Nicaragua, Haiti and elsewhere before and after Trujillo's assassination, yet the American public fell readily into line in condemning Castro.)

As early as 1958, the then-CIA chief of station in the Dominican Republic, Lear Reed, along with several Dominicans, had plotted an assassination of Trujillo, one which never got off the ground.[3] What the Agency's motivation was, and whether it was acting on its own or at the behest of higher echelons in Washington, is not known. However, in February 1960 the National Security Council's Special Group in Washington gave consideration to a program of covert aid to anti-Trujillo Dominicans.[4] Two months later, Eisenhower approved a contingency plan which provided, in part, that if the situation deteriorated still further: "the United States would immediately take political action to remove Trujillo from the Dominican Republic as soon as a suitable successor regime can be induced to take over with the assurance of U.S. political, economic, and—if necessary—military support."[5]

Seemingly unaware of the currents swirling about him, Trujillo continued to live up to his gangster reputation. In June, his henchmen blew up a car carrying Venezuelan President Romulo Betancourt, an outspoken critic of the Dominican dictator. As a result, Washington came under renewed pressure from several of the more democratic Caribbean countries for action against Trujillo. Betancourt, who had survived the blast, told US Secretary of State Christian Herter: "If you don't eliminate him, we will invade."[6]

For a full year, the dissidents and various American officials played cloak-and-dagger games: There were meetings in New York and Washington, in Ciudad Trujillo and Venezuela; Americans living in the Dominican Republic were enlisted for the cause by the CIA; schemes to overthrow Trujillo were drawn up at different times by the State Department, the CIA, and the dissidents, some approved by the Special Group. A training camp was set up in Venezuela for Dominican exiles flown there from the United States and Puerto Rico by the CIA; the dissidents made numerous requests for weapons, from sniper rifles to remote-control detonating devices, for the understood purpose of assassinating Trujillo and other key members of his regime. Several of the requests were approved by the State Department or the CIA; support for the dissidents was regularly reiterated at high levels of the US government ... yet, after all was said and done, none of the ambitious plans was even attempted (the actual assassination was essentially a spur-of-the-moment improvised affair), only three pistols and three carbines were ever passed to the anti-Trujillistas, and it is not certain that any of these guns were used in the assassination.[7]

In the final analysis, the most significant aid received by the dissidents from the United States was the assurance that the "Colossus to the North" would not intervene militarily to prevent the assassination and would support them afterwards if they set up a "suitable" government. In Latin America this is virtually a *sine qua non* for such undertakings, notably in the Dominican Republic where American marines have landed on four separate occasions in this century, the last intervention having created a centralized Dominican National Guard which the US placed under the control of a young officer it had trained named Rafael Trujillo.

The gap between the word and the deed of the American government concerning the assassination appears to have been the consequence of a growing uncertainty in Washington about what would actually take place in the wake of Trujillo's demise—would a pro-Castro regime emerge from the chaos? A secondary consideration, perhaps, was a reluctance to engage in political assassination, both as a matter of policy and as a desire to avoid, as one State Department official put it, "further tarnishing in the eyes of the world" of the "U.S. moral posture".[8] This was particularly the expressed feeling of President John Kennedy and others in his administration who had assumed office in January 1961, although they were later to undertake several assassination attempts against Castro.

The dismal failure of the Bay of Pigs invasion in April further dampened the enthusiasm of Washington officials for Caribbean adventures (except against Cuba in revenge) and induced them to request a postponement of the assassination. The plotters, however, were well past the point of no return.

The Dominicans who pulled the triggers and their fellow conspirators were in no way revolutionaries. They came from the ranks of the conservative, privileged sectors of Dominican society and were bound together primarily by an intense loathing of Trujillo, a personal vendetta—each of them, or someone close to them, had suffered a deep humiliation at the hands of the diabolical dictator, if not torture or murder.

Their plan as to what would follow the elimination of Trujillo was only half-baked, and even this fell apart completely. As matters turned out, the day after the assassination, Rafael ("Ramfis") Trujillo, Jr. rushed home from his playboy's life in Paris to take over the reins of government. Little had been resolved, either in the Dominican Republic or in Washington. The Kennedy administration was confronted with the same ideological questions which had caused them so much indecision before the assassination, as they had the Eisenhower administration. To wit: What is the best way of preventing the establishment of left-wing governments intent upon radical social change? The traditional iron fist of right-wing dictatorship, or a more democratic society capable of meeting many of the legitimate demands of the populace? How much democracy? Would too much open the door for even greater, and unacceptable, demands and provide the left with a legal platform from which to sway ("dupe", Washington would call it) the public? And if it is a dictatorship that is to be supported, how are liberal American leaders to explain this to the world and to their own citizens?

John F. Kennedy and his men from Harvard tended to treat such policy questions in a manner more contemplative than American political figures are usually inclined to do: on occasion, it might be said, they even agonized over such questions. But in the end, their Latin American policy was scarcely distinguishable from that of conservative Republican administrations. A leader who imposed "order" with at least the facade of democracy, who kept the left submerged without being notoriously brutal about it; in short, the anti-communist liberal, still appeared to be the safest ally for the United States.

"There are three possibilities," Kennedy said, "in descending order of preference: a decent democratic regime, a continuation of the Trujillo regime or a Castro regime. We ought to aim at the first but we really can't renounce the second until we are sure we can avoid the third."[9]

Rafael Trujillo, Jr. was clearly not ideal. Besides bearing the inescapable stigma of his name and family, he proceeded to carry out a bloodbath of revenge over the next six months.[10] But, unlike his father in his last years, Ramfis could be prodded by Washington into making a few token reforms, and both parties might have been content to continue in this fashion indefinitely had not many people of the Dominican Republic felt terribly cheated by the turn of events. Their elation over the assassination had soured in the face of business-as-usual.

Resentment spilled over into the streets. By October, the protests were occurring daily and were being put down by tanks; students were shot dead by government troops. The United States began to make moves, for the situation in the streets and high places of the government was anarchic enough, Washington feared, to provide an opening for the proverbial (and seemingly magical) "communist takeover", although, in fact, the left in the Dominican Republic was manifestly insignificant from years of repression.

American diplomats met in the capital city with the Trujillo clan and Dominican military leaders and bluntly told them that US military power would, if necessary, be used to compel the formation of a provisional government headed by Joachín Balaguer until elections could be held. Balaguer had been closely tied to the Trujillo family for decades, was serving as president under Trujillo at the time of the assassination, and had remained in the same capacity under Ramfis, but he was not regarded as a threat to continue the tyranny. As Kennedy put it: "Balaguer is our only tool. The anticommunist liberals aren't strong enough. We must use our influence to take Balaguer along the road to democracy."[11] Just how committed John F. Kennedy was to democracy in the Dominican Republic we shall presently see.

To make certain that the Dominicans got the message, a US naval task force of eight ships with 1,800 Marines aboard appeared off the Dominican coast on 19 November, just outside the three-mile limit but in plain sight of Ciudad Trujillo. Spanish-language broadcasts from the offshore ships warned that the Marines were prepared to come ashore; while overhead, American jet fighters streaked along the coastline. Brigadier General Pedro Rodriguez Echevarría, a key military figure, was persuaded by the United States to put aside any plans for a coup he may have been harboring and to support the American action. Rodriguez proceeded—whether of his own initiative is not clear—to order the bombing of the air base outside the capital where Trujillistas had been massing troops. Over the next two days, Ramfis returned to the pleasure temples of Europe while other prominent Trujillistas left for the good life in Florida.[12]

However, when Balaguer proved to be a major obstacle to beginning the process of democratization and indicated that he did not regard his regime as temporary, the United States added its own special pressure to that of Balaguer's domestic opposition to force him to resign after only two months in office. Washington then turned around and issued another stern warning to General Rodriguez, threatened Dominican leaders with a large loss of aid if they supported a coup, and mounted another naval show-of-force to help other military officers block the general's attempt to seize power.[13]

While a seven-man "Council of State" then administered the affairs of government, the US continued to treat the Dominican Republic as its private experiment in the prevention of communism. The American Ambassador, John Bartlow Martin, pressed the Council to curb left-wing activity. By his own admission, Martin urged the use of "methods once used by the police in Chicago": harassment of suspects by repeated arrests, midnight raids on their homes, beatings, etc.[14]

When street disturbances erupted, US Attorney General Robert Kennedy arranged for riot-control equipment to be sent to Santo Domingo (the original name of the capital, now restored). The equipment came complete with two Spanish-speaking Los Angeles detectives to impart to their Dominican counterparts the fine art of quelling such uprisings that they had acquired in the Mexican barrios of east Los Angeles. In a few weeks, Ambassador Martin could report that the Council had "rewon the streets, thanks almost entirely to those two detectives".[15]

This riot-control unit remained as a permanent part of the Santo Domingo police force. Known as the *Cascos Blancos* (white helmets), they came to be much hated by the populace. Shortly afterwards, the US military undertook a long-range program to transform the country's armed forces into what was hoped would be an efficient anti-guerrilla organization, though guerrillas were as rare on the Caribbean island as members of the Trujillo family.[16]

Finally, in December 1962, elections were held, under terms dictated in large part by Ambassador Martin to the two major candidates. His purpose was to introduce into the Dominican Republic some of the features that Americans regard as necessary to a viable and democratic electoral system, but Martin's fiat was inescapably a highly condescending intrusion into the affairs of a supposedly sovereign nation. His instructions extended down to the level of what the loser should say in his concession speech.

Further, under an "Emergency Law", the United States and the Council arranged for the deportation of some 125 Trujillistas and "Castro communists" to the United States, from where they were not allowed to leave until after the election in order "to help maintain stability so elections could be held".[17]

The winner, and first more-or-less-democratically elected president of the Dominican Republic since 1924, was Juan Bosch, a writer who had spent many years in exile while Trujillo reigned. Here at last was Kennedy's liberal anti-communist, non-military and legally elected by a comfortable majority as well. Bosch's government was to be the long-sought-after "showcase of democracy" that would put the lie to Fidel Castro. He was given the grand treatment in Washington shortly before he took office in February 1963.

Bosch was true to his beliefs. He called for land reform, including transferring some private land to the public sector as required; low-rent housing; modest nationalization of business; an ambitious project of public works, serving mass needs more than vested interests; a reduction in the import of luxury items; at the same time, he favored incentives to private enterprise and was open to foreign investment provided it was not excessively exploitative of the country—all in all, standard elements in the program of any liberal Third World leader serious about social change. He was likewise serious about the thing called civil liberties: Communists, or those labeled as such, or anyone else, were not to be persecuted unless they actually violated the law.

A number of American officials and congressmen expressed their discomfort with Bosch's plans, as well as his stance of independence from the United States. Land reform and nationalization are always touchy issues in Washington, the stuff that "creeping socialism" is made of. In several quarters of the US press Bosch was red-baited and compared with Castro, and the Dominican Republic with Cuba. (Castro, for his part, branded Bosch a "Yankee puppet".) Some of the press criticism was clearly orchestrated, in the manner of many CIA campaigns.[18]

In both the United States and the Dominican Republic, the accusations most frequently cast at Bosch were the ones typically used against Latin American leaders who do not vigorously suppress the left (cf. Arbenz and Goulart): Bosch was allowing "communists" to "infiltrate" into the country and into the government, and he was not countering "communist subversion", the latter referring to no more than instances of people standing up for their long-denied rights. Wrote a reporter for the *Miami News*: "Communist penetration of the Dominican Republic is progressing with incredible speed and efficiency." He did not, however, name a single communist in the Bosch government. As it happens, the reporter, Hal Hendrix, was a valuable press asset and a "secret operative" of the CIA in the 1960s.[19]

The CIA made a further contribution to the anti-Bosch atmosphere. Ambassador Martin has reported that the Agency "gave rumors [about communists in the Dominican Republic] a credibility far higher than I would have ... In reporting a Castro/Communist plot, however wildly implausible, it is obviously safer to evaluate it as 'could be true' than as nonsense."[20]

John F. Kennedy also soured on Bosch, particularly for his refusal to crack down on radicals. Said the president to Ambassador Martin one day:

> I'm wondering if the day might not come when he'd [Bosch] like to get rid of some of the left. Tell him we respect his judgment, we're all for him, but the time may come when he'll want to deport 30 or 50 people, when it'd be better to deport them than to let them go. I suppose he'd have to catch them in something.[21]

When the United States failed to commit any new economic assistance to the Dominican Republic and generally gave the indication that Juan Bosch was a doomed venture, right-wing Dominican military officers could only be encouraged in their craving to be rid of the president and his policies. Sam Halper, former Caribbean Bureau Chief of *Time* magazine, later reported that the military coup ousting Bosch went into action "as soon as they got a wink from the U.S. Pentagon".[22]

In July, a group of officers formally presented Bosch with a statement of principle-cum-ultimatum: Their loyalty to his regime was conditioned upon his adoption of a policy of rigorous anti-communism. Bosch reacted by going on television and delivering a lecture about the apolitical role required of the military in a democratic society, surely an occult subject to these products of 31 years of Trujilloism.

The beleaguered president could see that a premature demise lay ahead for his government. His speech on television had sounded very much like a farewell. The failure of Washington to intervene on his behalf could only enlarge the writing on the wall. Indeed, Bosch and some of his aides strongly suspected that the US military and the CIA were already conspiring with the Dominican officers. Several American military officers had disregarded diplomatic niceties by expressing their reservations about Bosch's politics loud enough to reach his ears.[23]

A week before the inevitable coup, the CIA/AIFLD-created union federation in the Dominican Republic, CONATRAL, which had been set up to counter and erode Bosch's support in the labor movement, placed an ad in a leading newspaper urging the people to put their faith in the army to defend them against communism.[24]

The end came in September, a scant seven months after Bosch had taken office. He had not had the time to accomplish much that was worthwhile in this hopelessly corrupt society before the military boots marched, as they have always marched in Latin America.

The United States, which can discourage a military coup in Latin America with a frown, did nothing to stand in the way of the Dominican officers. There would be no display of American military might this time—although Bosch asked for it—"unless a Communist takeover were threatened," said the State Department.[25]

"Democracy," said *Newsweek* magazine, "was being saved from Communism by getting rid of democracy."[26]

There were the customary expressions of regret in Washington about the death of democracy, and there was the *de rigueur* withholding of recognition of the new regime. But two months later, when opposition to the yet-again repressive dictatorship began to manifest itself noticeably, the junta yelled "communist" and was quickly embraced by the United States with recognition and the other perquisites which attach to being a member in good standing of the "Free World".[27]

Nineteen months later, a revolution broke out in the Dominican Republic which promised to put the exiled Bosch back in power at the hands of a military-civilian force that would be loyal to his program. But for the fifth time in the century, the American Marines landed and put an abrupt end to such hopes.

In the early morning of Saturday, 24 April 1965, a group of young army officers of middle rank, acting in concert with civilian Bosch partisans, declared themselves in revolt against the government. The "constitutionalists", as they called themselves, were soon joined by other officers and their units. Spurred by ecstatic radio proclamations, thousands of Dominicans poured into the streets shouting "Viva Bosch" and grabbed up the arms handed out by the rebel military forces.

The television station was taken over and for two days a "potpourri of politicians, soldiers, women, children, adventurers, hoodlums and anyone who wished to, shouted against the status quo."[28]

The participants in the uprising were a mixed bag, not all of them sympathetic to Bosch or to social reform; some were on the right, with their own varied motivations. But the impetus clearly lay with the constitutionalists, and the uprising was thus viewed with alarm by the rest of the military and the US Embassy as a movement to restore Bosch to power with all that that implied.

Philip Geyelin of the *Wall Street Journal* (and formerly with the CIA), who had access to the official embassy cables and the key actors in the drama, has written:

> What the record reveals, in fact, is that from the very outset of the upheaval, there was a concerted U.S. Government effort, if not actually a formal decision, to checkmate the rebel movement by whatever means and at whatever cost.
> By Sunday, April 25 ... the Santo Domingo embassy had clearly cast its lot with the "loyalist" military cabal and against the rebellion's original aim: the return of Juan Bosch ... Restoration of the Bosch regime would be "against U.S. interests", the embassy counseled. Blocking Bosch could mean further bloodshed, the embassy conceded. Nonetheless, Washington was advised, the embassy military attaches had given "loyalist" leaders a go-ahead to do "everything possible" to prevent what was described as the danger of a "Communist take-over".[29]

The attachés as well as the US Consul made emergency visits to several still-uncommitted Dominican military commanders to persuade them, apparently with notable success, to support the government.[30]

A bloody civil war had broken out in the streets of Santo Domingo. During the first few days, the momentum of battle swung to one side, then the other. By the night of 28 April, however, the military and police inside Santo Domingo had collapsed, and the constitutionalists were preparing to attack the military's last bastion, San Isidro, their main base about 10 miles away.[31]

"The Generals at San Isidro were dejected, several were weeping, and one was hysterically urging 'retreat'," read the cable sent by the American ambassador, W. Tapley Bennett, to Washington in the early evening of the 28th. (Bennett, as we shall see, was given to hyperbole of the worst sort, but the Dominican military certainly were isolated and demoralized.) Bennett added, whether in the same cable or another one is not clear, that if US troops did not immediately land, American lives would be lost and "Castro-type elements" would be victorious.[32]

Within hours, the first 500 US Marines were brought in by helicopter from ships stationed a few miles off the coast. Two days later, American forces ashore numbered over 4,000. At the peak, some 23,000 troops, Marine and Army, were to take up positions in the beleaguered country, with thousands more standing by on a 35-ship task force offshore.

The American action was in clear violation of several international agreements, including the Charter of the Organization of American States (OAS) which prohibited intervention "directly or indirectly, for any reason whatever, in the internal or external affairs of any other state".

During the entire course of the US military occupation, American pronouncements would have had the world believe that its forces were in the Dominican Republic in a "neutral" capacity: to protect the lives of Americans and other foreigners, establish a ceasefire, ensure free elections, etc. As we have seen, however, the United States had committed itself to one side from the start of hostilities. This continued to be the case. The morning after the landing of the first Marines, Ambassador Bennett was instructed by the State Department that US military officers should be used "to help San Isidro develop operational plans to take the rebel stronghold downtown".33

Within a few days, American troops were deployed in an armed corridor through the center of Santo Domingo so as to divide the constitutionalists' zone and cut off their main body from access to the rest of the country, bottling them up in a small downtown area with their backs to the sea. Other American forces were stationed throughout the countryside. The rebel offensive against San Isidro had been prevented. It was the end of their revolution.

The American forces came to the aid of the Dominican military in a number of ways, supplying them with equipment, food and even their salaries, but it was the direct military involvement that was most telling. On one striking occasion, the sea of American troops parted to allow the Dominican military to pass through and brutally attack and mop up the northern section of the rebel zone while the main rebel force in the south remained helplessly blocked behind the American line. This "smashing victory," the New York Times reported, was "visibly aided by United States troops". Other American journalists also reported that US troops took part in the fighting, although Washington officials angrily denied it.34

The rebels were reduced to little more than sniping attacks on American soldiers, for which they paid a heavy price. US forces blasted apart a building in downtown Santo Domingo from which sniper fire was coming; advancing into a constitutionalist zone, again after sniper fire, they killed some 67 rebels and bystanders; American paratroops were seen firing at rebels who were retreating, and the constitutionalists' Minister of Justice and Police was "reported to have been killed by United States machine-gun fire as he attempted to capture the empty Presidential Palace in midtown with a squad of his troops."35

When the Johnson administration was not denying such actions outright, it was claiming that they were either contrary to orders, "individual indiscretions", or "isolated incidents".

A covert team of Green Berets arrived at one point to help ensure the safety of American civilians. But when they discovered that some of the Americans were assisting rebel forces, "their main objective shifted from protecting their fellow countrymen to spying on them".36

The Green Berets also found the time to lay the groundwork for the assassination of one of the leading constitutionalist leaders, Col. Francisco Caamaño. The plot was canceled at the last moment due to the excessive risk involved.37

Another group of American visitors was that of some leaders of the National Student Association, ostensibly come to the Dominican Republic to talk with their counterparts about educational matters, but actually there at the behest of the CIA to gather information on local students. This was still two years before the exposé of the long-lasting relationship between the CIA and the prominent student organization.38

Throughout this period, the communication guns of the US government were aimed at the people of the United States, the Dominican Republic and the world to convince them that "communists" were a dominant element amongst the constitutionalists, that they represented a threat to take over the movement, or that they had already taken it over, with frightening consequences for all concerned.

At various times the Johnson administration released lists of "communists and Castroites" in the ranks of the rebels. These lists totaled 53 or 58 or 77 names and became a cause célèbre as well as an object of media ridicule. Besides the laughably small numbers involved (in a rebellion of tens of thousands with numerous leaders), several of those on the lists, it turned out, were in prison while others were out of the country.

The American Embassy in Santo Domingo assured reporters that if they went to rebel headquarters, they would see the named communist in the flesh. The newspeople went and looked but could find no identifiable communists (however one identifies a communist). Subsequently, administration officials explained that the reason that newspeople had seen such little evidence of communist activity was that the American landings had scared the Reds into hiding.

Eventually, American officials admitted their doubt that they could prove that communists had gained control of the constitutionalists, although President Johnson had pressed the CIA and FBI into an intensive search for evidence. (A CIA cable to Washington on 25 April reported that the Communist Party [Partido Socialista Dominicano] had been "unaware of the coup attempt".)[39]

Former CIA officer Philip Agee, stationed in Uruguay at the time, wrote later that the new password at his station became "Fifty-eight trained communists". The proper reply was "Ten thousand marines".[40]

The embassy, and Ambassador Bennett in particular, poured forth "a rising stream of hysterical rumors, atrocity stories, and alarmist reports"[41] about the rebels, reminiscent of the Bolshevik horror stories which had filled the pages of the American press following the Russian Revolution: embassies being ransacked ... "Castroite-style mass executions" ... rebels parading in the streets with the heads of their victims on poles ...

President Johnson made reference to the "atrocities" in public statements, but none of the stories were ever proven, for none were true; no one ever located any of the many headless Dominicans; and American officials, in a monument to *chutzpah*, later denounced the press for reporting such unverified rumors.[42]

Meanwhile, the CIA, the Defense Intelligence Agency and the US Information Agency were conducting their own intensive propaganda campaign in the Dominican Republic to give credence to the American position and discredit Dominican groups opposed to it. Experts on psychological warfare arrived to ply their trade, radio stations and newspapers were covertly set up, rebel radio stations jammed, leaflets airdropped in the countryside. The USIA also secretly subsidized the publication of pro-administration material aimed for distribution in the United States.[43]

From all the wild charges and the frequent contradictory statements made by American officials, the expression "credibility gap" entered the American popular language and soon came to haunt the Johnson presidency.[44]

Historian Richard Barnet has noted another interesting side to the American propaganda effort:

> To justify the intervention, which had aroused violent opposition from traditional friends of the United States because of its crudeness and the swathe of lies in which it was wrapped ... [Washington] began a direct assault on the concept of non-intervention, the rhetorical foundation stone of Latin-American policy enshrined in numerous treaties, declarations, and Pan-American Day speeches ... Under Secretary Thomas Mann told newspaper correspondents that the OAS and UN charters were drawn up in "19th-century terms" ... Averell Harriman remarked in Montevideo that the principle of non-intervention was becoming "obsolete". By a vote of 315 to 52 the House of Representatives passed a resolution ... justifying the unilateral use of force on foreign territory by any nation which considers itself threatened by "international communism, directly or indirectly." ... The President [declared in a speech]: "The first reality is that old concepts and old labels are largely obsolete. In today's world, with enemies of freedom talking about 'Wars of national liberation,' the old distinction between 'Civil War' and 'International War' has already lost much of its meaning ... The moment of decision must become the moment of action."

"This is the essence of the Johnson Doctrine," wrote Barnet, "a virtually unlimited claim of legitimacy for armed intervention in civil strife."[45]

The last American troops did not leave the Dominican Republic until September 1966. The interim period witnessed a succession of ceasefires, broken truces, and protracted negotiations under provisional governments.

In June 1966, elections were held in which Joaquín Balaguer defeated Juan Bosch by a surprisingly large margin. Yet, it was not all that surprising. For five long years the people of the Dominican Republic had lived under a cloud of chaos and violence. The experience had instilled in them a deep longing for a return to "normalcy", to order, without foreign intervention, without soldiers patrolling their streets, without curfews, tear gas and bloodshed. With the US Army still very much in evidence and the American distaste for Bosch well known ... with the ubiquitous American propaganda hammering home fear of The Red Menace and associating the constitutionalists, and thus Bosch, with communism ... with the Dominican military still largely Trujillista in personnel and ideology ... a victory for Bosch would be seen by many voters as a danger that all the horrors would rain down upon their heads once more. Bosch, who had returned several months prior to the election, was himself so fearful for his personal safety that he never left his home during the campaign.

Joachim Balaguer remained in office for the next 12 years, ruling his people in the grand Latin American style: The rich became richer and the poor had babies, hungry babies; democracy remained an alien concept; the police and military regularly kidnapped, tortured and murdered opponents of the government and terrorized union organizers.[46]

But the man was not, personally, the monster that Trujillo was. There was relative calm and peace. No "communist threat" hovered over the land. The pot was sweetened for foreign investors, and American corporations moved in with big bucks. There was stability and order. And the men who ran the United States looked and were satisfied. Perhaps some of them had come to the realization that the anti-communist liberal government was an impossible ideal; for any movement seeking genuine democracy and social reform would invariably attract individuals whom the United States would invariably categorize as "communist"; the United States would then feel driven to discredit, subvert and eventually overturn the movement. A Catch 22.

30. Cuba 1959 to 1980s
The unforgivable revolution

The existence of a revolutionary socialist government with growing ties to the Soviet Union only 90 miles away, insisted the United States Government, was a situation which no self-respecting superpower should tolerate, and in 1961 it undertook an invasion of Cuba.

But less than 50 miles from the Soviet Union sat Pakistan, a close ally of the United States, a member since 1955 of the South-East Asia Treaty Organization (SEATO), the US-created anti-communist alliance. On the very border of the Soviet Union was Iran, an even closer ally of the United States, with its relentless electronic listening posts, aerial surveillance, and infiltration into Russian territory by American agents. And alongside Iran, also bordering the Soviet Union, was Turkey, a member of the Russians' mortal enemy, NATO, since 1951.

In 1962 during the "Cuban Missile Crisis", Washington, seemingly in a state of near-panic, informed the world that the Russians were installing "offensive" missiles in Cuba. The US promptly instituted a "quarantine" of the island—a powerful show of naval and marine forces in the Caribbean would stop and search all vessels heading towards Cuba; any found to contain military cargo would be forced to turn back.

The United States, however, had missiles and bomber bases already in place in Turkey and other missiles in Western Europe pointed toward the Soviet Union. Russian leader Nikita Khrushchev later wrote:

> The Americans had surrounded our country with military bases and threatened us with nuclear weapons, and now they would learn just what it feels like to have enemy missiles pointing at you; we'd be doing nothing more than giving them a little of their own medicine. ... After all, the United States had no moral or legal quarrel with us. We hadn't given the Cubans anything more than the Americans were giving to their allies. We had the same rights and opportunities as the Americans. Our conduct in the international arena was governed by the same rules and limits as the Americans.[1]

Lest anyone misunderstand, as Khrushchev apparently did, the rules under which Washington was operating, *Time* magazine was quick to explain. "On the part of the Communists," the magazine declared, "this equating [referring to Khrushchev's offer to mutually remove missiles and bombers from Cuba and Turkey] had obvious tactical motives. On the part of neutralists and pacifists [who welcomed Khrushchev's offer] it betrayed intellectual and moral confusion." The confusion lay, it seems, in not seeing clearly who were the good guys and who were the bad guys, for "The purpose of the U.S. bases [in Turkey] was not to blackmail Russia but to strengthen the defense system of NATO, which had been created as a safeguard against Russian aggression. As a member of NATO, Turkey welcomed the bases as a contribution to her own defense." Cuba, which had been invaded only the year before, could have, it seems, no such concern. *Time* continued its sermon:

> Beyond these differences between the two cases, there is an enormous moral difference between U.S. and Russian objectives ... To equate U.S. and Russian bases is in effect to equate U.S. and Russian purposes ... The U.S. bases, such as those in Turkey, have helped keep the peace since World War II, while the Russian bases in Cuba threatened to upset the peace. The Russian bases were intended to further conquest and domination, while U.S. bases were erected to preserve freedom. The difference should have been obvious to all.[2]

Equally obvious was the right of the United States to maintain a military base on Cuban soil—Guantánamo Naval Base by name, a vestige of colonialism staring down the throats of the Cuban people, which the US, to this day, refuses to vacate despite the vehement protest of the Castro government.

In the American lexicon, in addition to good and bad bases and missiles, there are good and bad revolutions. The American and French Revolutions were good. The Cuban Revolution is bad. It must be bad because so many people have left Cuba as a result of it.

But at least 100,000 people left the British colonies in America during and after the American Revolution. These Tories could not abide by the political and social changes, both actual and feared, particularly that change which attends all revolutions worthy of the name: Those looked down upon as inferiors no longer know their place. (Or as the US Secretary of State put it after the Russian Revolution: the Bolsheviks sought "to make the ignorant and incapable mass of humanity dominant in the earth.")[3]

The Tories fled to Nova Scotia and Britain carrying tales of the godless, dissolute, barbaric American revolutionaries. Those who remained and refused to take an oath of allegiance to the new state governments were denied virtually all civil liberties. Many were jailed, murdered, or forced into exile. After the American Civil War, thousands more fled to South America and other points, again disturbed by the social upheaval. How much more is such an exodus to be expected following the Cuban Revolution?—a true social revolution, giving rise to changes much more profound than anything in the American experience. How many more would have left the United States if 90 miles away lay the world's wealthiest nation welcoming their residence and promising all manner of benefits and rewards?

After the Cuban Revolution in January 1959, we learned that there are also good and bad hijackings. On several occasions Cuban planes and boats were hijacked to the United States but they were not returned to Cuba, nor were the hijackers punished. Instead, some of the planes and boats were seized by US authorities for non-payment of debts claimed by American firms against the Cuban government.[4] But then there were the bad hijackings—planes forced to fly from the United States to Cuba. When there began to be more of these than flights in the opposite direction, Washington was obliged to reconsider its policy.

It appears that there are as well good and bad terrorists. When the Israelis bombed PLO headquarters in Tunis in 1985, Ronald Reagan expressed his approval. The president asserted that nations have the right to retaliate against terrorist attacks "as long as you pick out the people responsible".[5]

But if Cuba had dropped bombs on any of the headquarters of the anti-Castro exiles in Miami or New Jersey, Ronald Reagan would likely have gone to war, though for 25 years the Castro government had been on the receiving end of an extraordinary series of terrorist attacks carried out in Cuba, in the United States, and in other countries by the exiles and their CIA mentors. (We shall not discuss the consequences of Cuba bombing CIA headquarters.)

Bombing and strafing attacks of Cuba by planes based in the United States began in October 1959, if not before.[6] In early 1960, there were several fire-bomb air raids on Cuban cane fields and sugar mills, in which American pilots also took part—at least three of whom died in crashes, while two others were captured. The State Department acknowledged that one plane which crashed, killing two Americans, had taken off from Florida, but insisted that it was against the wishes of the US government.[7]

In March a French freighter unloading munitions from Belgium exploded in Havana taking 75 lives and injuring 200, some of whom subsequently died. The United States denied Cuba's accusation of sabotage but admitted that it had sought to prevent the shipment.[8]

And so it went ... reaching a high point in April of the following year in the infamous CIA-organized invasion of Cuba at the Bay of Pigs. Over 100 exiles died in the attack. Close to 1,200 others were taken prisoner by the Cubans. It was later revealed that four American pilots flying for the CIA had lost their lives as well.[9]

The Bay of Pigs assault had relied heavily on the Cuban people rising up to join the invaders,[10] but this was not to be the case. As it was, the leadership and ranks of the exile forces were riddled with former supporters and henchmen of Fulgencio Batista, the dictator overthrown by Castro, and would not have been welcomed back by the Cuban people under any circumstances.

Despite the fact that the Kennedy administration was acutely embarrassed by the unmitigated defeat—indeed, *because* of it—a campaign of smaller-scale attacks upon Cuba was initiated almost immediately. Throughout the 1960s, the Caribbean island was subjected to countless sea and air commando raids by exiles, at times accompanied by their CIA supervisors, inflicting damage upon oil refineries, chemical plants and railroad bridges, cane fields, sugar mills and sugar warehouses; infiltrating spies, saboteurs and assassins ... anything to damage the Cuban economy, promote disaffection, or make the revolution look bad ... taking the lives of Cuban militia members and others in the process ... pirate attacks on Cuban fishing boats and merchant ships, bombardments of Soviet vessels docked in Cuba, an assault upon a Soviet army camp with 12 Russian soldiers reported wounded ... a hotel and a theatre shelled from offshore because Russians and East Europeans were supposed to be present there ...[11]

These actions were not always carried out on the direct order of the CIA or with its foreknowledge, but the Agency could hardly plead "rogue elephant". It had created an operations headquarters in Miami that was truly a state within a city—over, above, and outside the laws of the United States, not to mention international law, with a staff of several hundred Americans directing many more Cuban agents in just such types of actions, with a budget in excess of $50 million a year, and an arrangement with the local press to keep operations in Florida secret except when the CIA wanted something publicized.[12]

Title 18 of the US Code declares it to be a crime to launch a "military or naval expedition or enterprise" from the United States against a country with which the United States is not (officially) at war. Although US authorities now and then aborted an exile plot or impounded a boat—sometimes because the Coast Guard or other officials had not been properly clued in—no Cubans were prosecuted under this act. This was no more than to be expected inasmuch as Attorney General Robert Kennedy had determined after the Bay of Pigs that the invasion did not constitute a military expedition.[13]

The commando raids were combined with a total US trade and credit embargo, which continues to this day, and which genuinely hurt the Cuban economy and chipped away at the society's standard of living. So unyielding has the embargo been that when Cuba was hard hit by a hurricane in October 1963, and Casa Cuba, a New York social club, raised a large quantity of clothing for relief, the United States refused to grant it an export license on the grounds that such shipment was "contrary to the national interest".[14]

Moreover, pressure was brought to bear upon other countries to conform to the embargo, and goods destined for Cuba were sabotaged: machinery damaged, chemicals added to lubricating fluids to cause rapid wear on diesel engines, a manufacturer in West Germany paid to produce ball-bearings off-center, another to do the same with balanced wheel gears—"You're talking about big money," said a CIA officer involved in the sabotage efforts, "when you ask a manufacturer to go along with you on that kind of project because he has to reset his whole mold. And he is probably going to worry about the effect on future business. You might have to pay him several hundred thousand dollars or more."[15]

One manufacturer who defied the embargo was the British Leyland Company, which sold a large number of buses to Cuba in 1964. Repeated expressions of criticism and protest by Washington officials and congressmen failed to stem deliveries of some of the buses. Then, in October, an East German cargo ship carrying another 42 buses to Cuba collided in thick fog with a Japanese vessel in the Thames. The Japanese ship was able to continue on, but the cargo ship was beached on its side; the buses would have to be "written off", said the Leyland company. In the leading British newspapers it was just an accident story.[16] In the *New York Times* it was not even reported. A decade was to pass before the American columnist Jack Anderson disclosed that his CIA and National Security Agency sources had confirmed that the collision had been arranged by the CIA with the cooperation of British intelligence.[17] Subsequently, another CIA officer stated that he was skeptical about the collision story, although admitting that "it is true that we were sabotaging the Leyland buses going to Cuba from England, and that was pretty sensitive business."[18]

What undoubtedly was an even more sensitive venture was the use of chemical and biological weapons against Cuba by the United States. It is a remarkable record.

In August 1962, a British freighter under Soviet lease, having damaged its propeller on a reef, crept into the harbor at San Juan, Puerto Rico for repairs. It was bound for a Soviet port with 80,000 bags of Cuban sugar. The ship was put into dry dock and 14,135 sacks of sugar were unloaded to a warehouse to facilitate the repairs. While in the warehouse, the sugar was contaminated by CIA agents with a substance that was allegedly harmless but unpalatable. When President Kennedy learned of the operation he was furious because it had taken place in US territory and if discovered could provide the Soviet Union with a pro-paganda field-day and could set a terrible precedent for chemical sabotage in the cold war. He directed that the sugar not be returned to the Russians, although what explanation was given to them is not publicly known.[19] Similar undertakings were apparently not canceled. The CIA official who helped direct worldwide sabotage efforts, referred to above, later revealed that "There was lots of sugar being sent out from Cuba, and we were putting a lot of contaminants in it."[20]

The same year, a Canadian agricultural technician working as an adviser to the Cuban government was paid $5,000 by "an American military intelligence agent" to infect Cuban turkeys with a virus which would produce the fatal Newcastle disease. Subsequently, 8,000 turkeys died. The technician later claimed that although he had been to the farm where the turkeys had died, he had not actually administered the virus, but had instead pocketed the money, and that the turkeys had died from neglect and other causes unrelated to the virus. This may have been a self-serving statement. The *Washington Post* reported that "According to U.S. intelligence reports, the Cubans—and some Americans—believe the turkeys died as the result of espionage."[21]

Authors Warren Hinckle and William Turner, citing a participant in the project, have reported in their book on Cuba that:

> During 1969 and 1970, the CIA deployed futuristic weather modification technology to ravage Cuba's sugar crop and undermine the economy. Planes from the China Lake Naval Weapons Center in the California desert, where hi tech was developed, overflew the island, seeding rain clouds with crystals that precipitated torrential rains over non-agricultural areas and left the cane fields arid (the downpours caused killer flash floods in some areas).[22]

In 1971, also according to participants, the CIA turned over to Cuban exiles a virus which causes African swine fever. Six weeks later, an outbreak of the disease in Cuba forced the slaughter of 500,000 pigs to prevent a nationwide animal epidemic. The outbreak, the first ever in the Western hemisphere, was called the "most alarming event" of the year by the United Nations Food and Agricultural Organization.[23]

Ten years later, the target may well have been human beings, as an epidemic of dengue fever swept the Cuban island. Transmitted by blood-eating insects, usually mosquitos, the disease produces severe flu symptoms and incapacitating bone pain. Between May and October 1981, over 300,000 cases were reported in Cuba with 158 fatalities, 101 of which were children under 15.[24] In 1956 and 1958, declassified documents have revealed, the US Army loosed swarms of specially bred mosquitos in Georgia and Florida to see whether dis-ease-carrying insects could be weapons in a biological war. The mosquitos bred for the tests were of the *Aedes Aegypti* type, the precise carrier of dengue fever as well as other diseases.[25] In 1967 it was reported by *Science* magazine that at the US government center in Fort Detrick, Maryland, dengue fever was amongst those "diseases that are at least the objects of considerable research and that appear to be among those regarded as potential BW [biological warfare] agents."[26] Then, in 1984, a Cuban exile on trial in New York testified that in the latter part of 1980 a ship travelled from Florida to Cuba with

a mission to carry some germs to introduce them in Cuba to be used against the Soviets and against the Cuban economy, to begin what was called chemical war, which later on produced results that were not what we had expected, because we thought that it was going to be used against the Soviet forces, and it was used against our own people, and with that we did not agree.[27]

It's not clear from the testimony whether the Cuban man thought that the germs would somehow be able to confine their actions to only Russians, or whether he had been misled by the people behind the operation.

The full extent of American chemical and biological warfare against Cuba will never be known. Over the years, the Castro government has in fact blamed the United States for a number of other plagues which afflicted various animals and crops.[28] And in 1977, newly-released CIA documents disclosed that the Agency "maintained a clandestine anti-crop warfare research program targeted during the 1960s at a number of countries throughout the world."[29]

It came to pass that the United States felt the need to put some of its chemical and biological warfare (CBW) expertise into the hands of other nations. As of 1969, some 550 students, from 36 countries, had completed courses at the US Army's Chemical School at Fort McClellan, Alabama. The CBW instruction was provided to the students under the guise of "defense" against such weapons—just as in Vietnam, as we have seen, torture was taught. As will be described in the chapter on Uruguay, the manufacture and use of bombs was taught under the cover of combating terrorist bombings.[30]

The ingenuity which went into the chemical and biological warfare against Cuba was apparent in some of the dozens of plans to assassinate or humiliate Fidel Castro. Devised by the CIA or Cuban exiles, with the cooperation of American mafiosi, the plans ranged from poisoning Castro's cigars and food to a chemical designed to make his hair and beard fall off and LSD to be administered just before a public speech. There were also of course the more traditional approaches of gun and bomb, one being an attempt to drop bombs on a baseball stadium while Castro was speaking; the B-26 bomber was driven away by anti-aircraft fire before it could reach the stadium.[31] It is a combination of such Cuban security measures, informers, incompetence, and luck which has served to keep the bearded one alive to the present day.

Attempts were also made on the lives of Castro's brother Raul and Che Guevara. The latter was the target of a bazooka fired at the United Nations building in New York in December 1964.[32] Various Cuban exile groups have engaged in violence on a regular basis in the United States with relative impunity for decades. One of them, going by the name of Omega 7 and headquartered in Union City, New Jersey, was characterized by the FBI in 1980 as "the most dangerous terrorist organization in the United States".[33] Attacks against Cuba itself began to lessen around the end of the 1960s, due probably to a lack of satisfying results combined with ageing warriors, and exile groups turned to targets in the United States and elsewhere in the world.

During the next decade, while the CIA continued to pour money into the exile community, more than 100 serious "incidents" took place in the United States for which Omega 7 and other groups claimed responsibility. (Within the community, the distinction between a terrorist and a non-terrorist group is not especially precise; there is much overlapping identity and frequent creation of new names.) There occurred repeated bombings of the Soviet UN Mission, its Washington Embassy, its automobiles, a Soviet ship docked in New Jersey, the offices of the Soviet airline Aeroflot, with a number of Russians injured from these attacks; several bombings of the Cuban UN Mission and its Interests Section in Washington, many attacks upon Cuban diplomats, including at least one murder; a bomb discovered at New York's Academy of Music in 1976 shortly before a celebration of the Cuban Revolution was to begin; a bombing two years later of the Lincoln Center after the Cuban ballet had performed ...[34]

The single most violent act of this period was the blowing up of a Cubana Airlines plane shortly after it took off from Barbados on 6 October 1976, which took the lives of 73 people including the entire Cuban championship fencing team. CIA documents later revealed that on 22 June, a CIA officer abroad had cabled a report to Agency headquarters that he had learned from a source that a Cuban exile group planned to bomb a Cubana airliner flying between Panama and Havana. The group's leader was a baby doctor named Orlando Bosch. After the plane crashed in the sea in October, it was Bosch's network of exiles that claimed responsibility. The cable showed that the CIA had the means to penetrate the Bosch organization, but there's no indication in any of the documents that the Agency undertook any special monitoring of Bosch and his group because of their plans, or that the CIA warned Havana.[35]

In 1983, while Orlando Bosch sat in a Venezuelan prison charged with masterminding the plane bombing, the City Commission of Miami proclaimed a "Dr. Orlando Bosch Day."[36] In 1968, Bosch had been convicted of a bazooka attack on a Polish ship in Miami.

Cuban exiles themselves have often come in for harsh treatment. Those who have visited Cuba for any reason whatever, or publicly suggested, however timidly, a rapprochement with the homeland, they too have been the victims of bombings and shootings in Florida and New Jersey. American groups advocating a resumption of diplomatic relations or an end to the embargo have been similarly attacked, as have travel agencies handling trips to Cuba and a pharmaceutical company in New Jersey which shipped medicines to the island. Dissent in Miami has been effectively silenced, while the police, city officials, and the media look the other way, when not actually demonstrating support for the exiles' campaign of intimidation.[37] In Miami and elsewhere, the CIA—ostensibly to uncover Castro agents—has employed exiles to spy on their countrymen, to keep files on them, as well as on Americans who associate with them.[38]

Although there has always been the extreme lunatic fringe in the Cuban exile community (as opposed to the normal lunatic fringe) insisting that Washington has sold out their cause, over the years there has been only the occasional arrest and conviction of an exile for a terrorist attack in the United States, so occasional that the exiles can only assume that Washington's heart is not wholly in it. The exile groups and their key members are well known to the authorities, for the anti-Castroites have not excessively shied away from publicity. At least as late as the early 1980s, they were training openly in southern Florida and southern California; pictures of them flaunting their weapons appeared in the press.[39] The CIA, with its countless contacts-cum-informers amongst the exiles, could fill in many of the missing pieces for the FBI and the police, if it wished to. In 1980, in a detailed report on Cuban-exile terrorism, *The Village Voice* of New York reported:

Two stories were squeezed out of New York police officials ... "You know, it's funny," said one cautiously, "there have been one or two things ... but let's put it this way. You get just so far on a case and suddenly the dust is blown away. Case closed. You ask the CIA to help, and they say they aren't really interested. You get the message." Another investigator said he was working on a narcotics case involving Cuban exiles a couple of years ago, and telephone records he obtained showed a frequently dialed number in Miami. He said he traced the number to a company called Zodiac, "which turned out to be a CIA front." He dropped his investigation.[40]

In 1961, amid much fanfare, the Kennedy administration unveiled its showpiece program, the Alliance for Progress. Conceived as a direct response to Castro's Cuba, it was meant to prove that genuine social change could take place in Latin America without resort to revolution or socialism. "If the only alternatives for the people of Latin America are the status quo and communism," said John F. Kennedy, "then they will inevitably choose communism."[41]

The multi-billion dollar Alliance program established for itself an ambitious set of goals which it hoped to achieve by the end of the decade. These had to do with economic growth, more equitable distribution of national income, reduced unemployment, agrarian reform, education, housing, health, etc. In 1970, the Twentieth Century Fund of New York—whose list of officers read like a Who's Who in the government/industry revolving-door world—undertook a study to evaluate how close the Alliance had come to realizing its objectives. One of the study's conclusions was that Cuba, which was not one of the recipient countries, had

> come closer to some of the Alliance objectives than most Alliance members. In education and public health, no country in Latin America has carried out such ambitious and nationally comprehensive programs. Cuba's centrally planned economy has done more to integrate the rural and urban sectors (through a national income distribution policy) than the market economies of the other Latin American countries.[42]

Cuba's agrarian reform program as well was recognized as having been more widesweeping than that of any other Latin American country, although the study took a wait-and-see attitude towards its results.[43]

These and other economic and social gains were achieved despite the US embargo and the inordinate amount of resources and labor Cuba was obliged to devote to defense and security because of the hovering giant to the north. Moreover, though not amongst the stated objectives of the Alliance, there was another area of universal importance in which Cuba stood apart from many of its Latin neighbors: there were no legions of *desaparecidos*, no death squads, no systematic torture.

Cuba had become what Washington had always feared from the Third World—a good example.

Parallel to the military and economic belligerence, the United States has long maintained a relentless propaganda offensive against Cuba. A number of examples of this occurring in other countries can be found in other chapters of this book. In addition to its vast overseas journalistic empire, the CIA has maintained anti-Castro news-article factories in the United States for decades. The Agency has reportedly subsidized at times such publications in Miami as *Avance*, *El Mundo*, *El Prensa Libre*, *Bohemia* and *El Diario de Las Americas*, as well as AIP, a radio news agency that produced programs sent free of charge to more than 100 small stations in Latin America. Two CIA fronts in New York, Foreign Publications, Inc, and Editors Press Service, also served as part of the propaganda network.[44]

Was it inevitable that the United States would attempt to topple the Cuban government? Could relations between the two neighboring countries have taken a different path? Based on the American record of invariable hostility towards even moderately leftist governments, the answer would appear to be that there's no reason to believe that Cuba's revolutionary government could have been an exception. Washington officials, however, were not immediately ill-disposed towards the Cuban Revolution. There were those who even expressed their tentative approval or optimism. This was evidently based on the belief that what had taken place in Cuba was little more than another Latin American change in government, the kind which had occurred with monotonous regularity for over a century, where the names and faces change but subservience to the United States remains fixed. (The fact that John Foster Dulles was dying of cancer at this time could only contribute to the atmosphere of tolerance. Dulles left the State Department in early February 1959, a month after the revolution. One of his last acts was to withdraw the US military mission from Cuba.)

Then Castro revealed himself to be cut from a wholly different cloth. It was not to be business as usual in the Caribbean. He soon became outspoken in his criticism of the United States. He referred acrimoniously to the 60 years of American control of Cuba; how, at the end of those 60 years, the masses of Cubans found themselves impoverished; how the United States used the sugar quota as a threat. He spoke of the unacceptable presence of the Guantánamo base; and he made it clear enough to Washington that Cuba would pursue a policy of independence and neutralism in the cold war. It was for just such reasons that Castro and Che Guevara had forsaken the prosperous bourgeois careers awaiting them in law and medicine to lead the revolution in the first place. Serious compromise was not on their agenda; nor on Washington's, which was not prepared to live with such men and such a government. Soon, Castro and his regime were consigned to the "communist" slot, a word known to instantly cut off the flow of blood to the brain cells of the user.

A National Security Council meeting of 10 March 1959 included on its agenda the feasibility of bringing "another government to power in Cuba".[45] This was before Castro had nationalized any US property. The following month, after meeting with Castro in Washington, Vice President Richard Nixon wrote a memo in which he stated that he was convinced that Castro was "either incredibly naive about Communism or under Communist discipline" and that the Cuban leader would have to be treated and dealt with accordingly. Nixon later wrote that his opinion at this time was a minority one within the Eisenhower administration.[46] But before the year was over, CIA Director Allen Dulles had decided that an invasion of Cuba was necessary. In March of 1960, it was approved by President Eisenhower.[47] Then came the embargo, leaving Castro no alternative but to turn more and more to the Soviet Union, thus confirming in the minds of Washington officials that Castro was indeed a communist. Some speculated that he had been a covert Red all along.

In this context, it's interesting to note that the Cuban Communist Party had long supported Batista, had served in his cabinet, and had been unsupportive of Castro and his followers until their accession to power appeared imminent.[48] To add to the irony, during 1957-58 the CIA was channeling funds to Castro's movement; this while the US continued to support Batista with weapons to counter the rebels; in all likelihood, another example of the Agency hedging its bets.[49]

If Castro had toned down his early rhetoric and observed the usual diplomatic niceties, but still pursued the policies of self-determination and socialism which he felt were best for Cuba (or inescapable if certain changes were to be realized), he could only have postponed the day of reckoning, and that not for long. Jacobo Arbenz of Guatemala, Mossadegh of Iran, Cheddi Jagan of British Guiana, and other Third World leaders have gone out of their way to avoid stepping on Washington's very sensitive toes unnecessarily, and were much less radical in their programs and in their stance toward the United States than Castro; nonetheless, all of them fell under the CIA axe.

In 1974, by way of marking 15 years of American hostility towards Cuba, Castro observed that "Cuba is the only country in the world where John Foster Dulles is still Secretary of State."[50]

31. Indonesia 1965
Liquidating President Sukarno ... and 500,000 others

Armed with wide-bladed knives called *parangs*, Moslem bands crept at night into the homes of communists, killing entire families. ... Travellers ... tell of small rivers and streams that have been literally clogged with bodies. River transportation has at places been seriously impeded.

Time magazine, December 1965 [1]

Nearly 100 Communists, or suspected Communists, were herded into the town's botanical garden and mowed down with a machine gun ... the head that had belonged to the school principal, a P.K.I. [Communist Party] member, was stuck on a pole and paraded among his former pupils, convened in special assembly.

New York Times, May 1966 [2]

Estimates of the total number of Indonesians murdered over a period of several years following an aborted coup range from 500,000 to one million.[3]

In the early morning hours of 1 October 1965, a small force of junior military officers abducted and killed six generals and seized several key points in the capital city of Jakarta. They then went on the air to announce that their action was being taken to forestall a *putsch* by a "Generals' Council" scheduled for Army Day, the fifth of October. The *putsch*, they said, had been sponsored by the CIA and was aimed at capturing power from President Sukarno. By the end of the day, however, the rebel officers in Jakarta had been crushed by the army under the direction of General Suharto, although some supportive army groups in other cities held out for a day or two longer.[4]

Suharto—a man who had served both the Dutch colonialists and the Japanese invaders[5]—and his colleagues charged that the large and influential PKI was behind the junior officers' "coup attempt", and that behind the party stood Communist China. The triumphant armed forces moved in to grab the reins of government, curb Sukarno's authority (before long he was reduced to little more than a figurehead), and carry out a bloodbath to eliminate once and for all the PKI with whom Sukarno had obliged them to share national power for many years. Here at last was the situation which could legitimate these long-desired actions.

Anti-Communist organizations and individuals, particularly Muslims, were encouraged to join in the slaying of anyone suspected of being a PKI sympathizer. Indonesians of Chinese descent as well fell victim to crazed zealots. The Indonesian people were stirred up in part by the display of photographs on television and in the press of the badly decomposed bodies of the slain generals. The men, the public was told, had been castrated and their eyes gouged out by Communist women. (The army later made the mistake of allowing official medical autopsies to be included as evidence in some of the trials; and the extremely detailed reports of the injuries suffered mentioned only bullet wounds and some bruises, no eye gougings or castration.)[6]

What ensued was called by the *New York Times* "one of the most savage mass slaughters of modern political history."[7] Violence, wrote *Life* magazine, "tinged not only with fanaticism but with blood-lust and something like witchcraft."[8]

Twenty-five years later, American diplomats disclosed that they had systematically compiled comprehensive lists of "Communist" operatives, from top echelons down to village cadres, and turned over as many as 5,000 names to the Indonesian army, which hunted those persons down and killed them. The Americans would then check off the names of those who had been killed or captured. Robert Martens, a former member of the US Embassy's political section in Jakarta, stated in 1990: "It really was a big help to the army. They probably killed a lot of people, and I probably have a lot of blood on my hands, but that's not all bad. There's a time when you have to strike hard at a decisive moment."

"I know we had a lot more information [about the PKI] than the Indonesians themselves," said Marshall Green, US Ambassador to Indonesia at the time of the coup. Martens "told me on a number of occasions that ... the government did not have very good information on the Communist setup, and he gave me the impression that this information was superior to anything they had."

"No one cared, as long as they were Communists, that they were being butchered," said Howard Federspiel, who in 1965 was the Indonesia expert at the State Department's Bureau of Intelligence and Research. "No one was getting very worked up about it."

Although the former deputy CIA station chief in Indonesia, Joseph Lazarsky, and former diplomat Edward Masters, who was Martens' boss, confirmed that CIA agents contributed in drawing up the death lists, the CIA in Langley categorically denied any involvement.[9]

The massacre put a horrific end to the well-organized PKI national organization. But it did not put to rest the basic questions underlying the events of 1965, to wit:

Was there in actual fact a Generals' Council aiming to take over the government within a matter of days? A semi-official account of the whole affair published in Indonesia in 1968 denied the existence of the Council.[10] However, a study written and published by the CIA the same year confirmed that there was indeed a Generals' Council but that its purpose was only to devise a way to protect itself from a purported plan of Sukarno to crush the army.[11]

What was the nature and extent, if any, of PKI involvement in the alleged coup attempt? Did some members of the party know of the junior officers' plans in advance and simply lend moral support, or did they take a more active role? The semi-official account stated that the PKI's aim was not to seize political power for itself but to "prevent the army from eliminating the Party after Sukarno's death."[12] (Sukarno had suffered a kidney attack in August, although he quickly recovered. His part in the affair also remains largely a mystery.) The CIA study comes to a similar conclusion: "It now seems clear that the Indonesian coup was not a move to overthrow Sukarno and/or the established government of Indonesia. Essentially, it was a purge of the Army leadership."[13]

What was the role, if any, of the CIA? Was the coup attempt instigated by an agent provocateur who spread the story of the Generals' Council and its imminent putsch? (The killing, or even the abduction, of the six generals probably could not have been foreseen—

three of them were actually slain resisting abduction.)[14] Was PKI participation induced to provide the excuse for its destruction? There are, in fact, indications of an agent provocateur in the unfolding drama, one Kamarusaman bin Ahmed Mubaidah, known as "Sjam". According to the later testimony of some of the arrested officers, it was Sjam who pushed the idea of the hostile Generals' Council and for the need to counteract it. At the trials and in the CIA Study, the attempt is made to establish that, in so doing, Sjam was acting on behalf of PKI leader Aidit. Presentation of this premise may explain why the CIA took the unique step of publishing such a book; i.e., to assign responsibility for the coup attempt to the PKI so as to "justify" the horror which followed.

But Sjam could just as easily have been acting for the CIA and/or the generals in the same manner. He apparently was a trusted aide of Aidit and could have induced the PKI leader into the plot instead of the other way around. Sjam had a politically checkered and mysterious background, and his testimony at one of the trials, in which he appeared as a defendant, was aimed at establishing Aidit as the sole director of the coup attempt.[15]

The CIA, in its intimate involvement in Indonesian political affairs since at least the mid-1950s (see Indonesia, 1957-58 chapter), had undoubtedly infiltrated the PKI at various levels, and the military even more so, and was thus in a good position to disseminate disinformation and plant the ideas for certain actions, whether through Sjam or others.

The desire of the US government to be rid of Sukarno—a leader of the non-aligned and anti-imperialist movements of the Third World, and a protector of the PKI—did not diminish with the failure of the Agency-backed military uprising in 1958. Amongst the various reports of the early 1960s indicating a continuing interest in this end, a CIA memorandum of June 1962 is strikingly to the point. The author of the memo, whose name is deleted, was reporting on the impressions he had received from conversations with "Western diplomats" concerning a recent meeting between President Kennedy and British Prime Minister Macmillan. The two leaders agreed, said the memo, to attempt to isolate Sukarno in Asia and Africa. Further, "They agreed to liquidate President Sukarno, depending upon the situation and available opportunities. (It is not clear to me [the CIA officer] whether murder or overthrow is intended by the word liquidate.)"[16]

Whatever was intended, Sukarno was now, for all practical purposes, eliminated as an international thorn in the flesh. Of even greater significance, the PKI, which had been the largest Communist Party in the world outside the Soviet bloc and China, had been decimated, its tattered remnants driven underground. It could not have worked out better for the United States and the new military junta if it had been planned.

If the generals had been planning their own coup as alleged, the evidence is compelling that the United States was intimately involved before, during and after the events of 30 September/1 October. One aspect of this evidence is the closeness of the relationship between the American and Indonesian military establishments which the United States had been cultivating for many years. President Kennedy, his former aide Arthur Schlesinger has written, was "anxious to strengthen the anti-communist forces, especially the army, in order to make sure that, if anything happened to Sukarno, the powerful Indonesian Communist Party would not inherit the country."[17]

Roger Hilsman, whose career spanned the CIA and the State Department, has noted that by 1963 ...

one-third of the Indonesian general staff had had some sort of training from Americans and almost half of the officer corps. As a result of both the civic action project and the training program, the American and Indonesian military had come to know each other rather well. Bonds of personal respect and even affection existed.[18]

This observation is reinforced by reports of the House Committee on Foreign Affairs:

At the time of the attempted Communist coup and military counter-coup [sic] of October 1965, more than 1,200 Indonesian officers including senior military figures, had been trained in the United States. As a result of this experience, numerous friendships and contacts existed between the Indonesian and American military establishments, particularly between members of the two armies. In the post-coup period, when the political situation was still unsettled, the United States, using these existing channels of communication, was able to provide the anti-Communist forces with moral and token material support.[19]

When the average MAP [Military Assistance Program] trainee returns home he may well have some American acquaintances and a fair appreciation of the United States. This impact may provide some valuable future opportunity for communication as occurred in Indonesia during and immediately after the attempted Communist-backed coup of October 1965.[20]

The CIA, wrote the *New York Times*, was said "to have been so successful at infiltrating the top of the Indonesian government and army that the United States was reluctant to disrupt CIA covering operations by withdrawing aid and information programs in 1964 and 1965. What was presented officially in Washington as toleration of President Sukarno's insults and provocations was in much larger measure a desire to keep the CIA fronts in business as long as possible."[21]

Finally, we have the testimony of Secretary of Defense Robert McNamara before a Senate Committee in 1966:

Senator Sparkman: At a time when Indonesia was kicking up pretty badly—when we were getting a lot of criticism for continuing military aid—at that time we could not say what that military aid was for. Is it secret any more?

McNamara: I think in retrospect, that the aid was well justified.

Sparkman: You think it paid dividends?

McNamara: I do, sir.[22]

There are other statements which may be pertinent to the question of American involvement. Former US Ambassador Marshall Green, speaking in Australia in 1973 where he was then ambassador, is reported as saying: "In 1965 I remember, Indonesia was poised at the razor's edge. I remember people arguing from here that Indonesia wouldn't go communist. But when Sukarno announced in his August 17 speech that Indonesia would have a communist government within a year [?] then I was almost certain. ... What we did we had to do, and you'd better be glad we did because if we hadn't Asia would be a different place today."[23]

James Reston, writing in the *New York Times* in 1966:

Washington is being careful not to claim any credit for this change [from Sukarno to Suharto] ... but this does not mean that Washington had nothing to do with it. There was a great deal more contact between the anti-Communist forces in that country and at least one very high official in Washington before and during the Indonesian massacre than is generally realized. General Suharto's forces, at times severely short of food and munitions, have been getting aid from here through various third countries, and it is doubtful if the [Suharto] coup would ever have been attempted without the American show of strength in Vietnam or been sustained without the clandestine aid it has received indirectly from here.[24]

Neville Maxwell, Senior Research Officer, Institute of Commonwealth Studies, Oxford University:

A few years ago I was researching in Pakistan into the diplomatic background of the 1965 Indo-Pakistan conflict, and in foreign ministry papers to which I had been given access came across a letter to the then foreign minister, Mr Bhutto, from one of his ambassadors in Europe (I believe Mr J.A. Rahim, in Paris) reporting a conversation with a Dutch intelligence officer with NATO. According to my note of that letter, the officer had remarked to the Pakistani diplomat that Indonesia was "ready to fall into the Western lap like a rotten apple". Western intelligence agencies, he said, would organize a "premature communist coup ... [which would be] foredoomed to fail, providing a legitimate and welcome opportunity to the army to crush the communists and make Soekarno a prisoner of the army's goodwill". The ambassador's report was dated December 1964.[25]

It should be remembered that Indonesia had been a colony of the Netherlands, and the Dutch still had some special links to the country.

The record of the "New Order" imposed by General Suharto upon the people of Indonesia for almost three decades has been remarkable. The government administers the nation on the level of Chicago gangsters of the 1930s running a protection racket. Political prisoners overflow the jails. Torture is routine.[26] ... Death squads roam at will, killing not only "subversives" but "suspected criminals" by the thousands.[27] ... "An army officer [in the province of Aceh] fires a single shot in the air, at which point all young males must run to a central square before the soldier fires a second shot. Then, anyone arriving late—or not leaving his home—is shot on the spot."[28]

And 200,000 more

In 1975 Indonesia invaded the former Portuguese colony of East Timor, which lies at the eastern end of the Indonesian archipelago and which had proclaimed its independence after Portugal relinquished control. It was the beginning of a massacre that continues into the 1990s. By 1989, Amnesty International estimated that Indonesian troops, with the aim of forcibly annexing East Timor, had killed 200,000 people out of a population of between 600,000 and 700,000.[29] The level of atrocity has often been on a par with that carried out against the PKI in Indonesia itself.

The invasion of 7 December 1975—of which, said the *New York Times*: "By any definition, Indonesia is guilty of naked aggression"[30]—was launched the day after US President Gerald Ford and Secretary of State Henry Kissinger left Indonesia following a meeting with President Suharto. Columnist Jack Anderson later reported:

By December 3, 1975, an intelligence dispatch to Washington reported that "Ranking Indonesian civilian government leaders have decided that the only solution in the Portuguese Timor situation is for Indonesia to launch an open offensive against Fretilin [the leading East Timorese resistance movement]."

But it was essential to neutralize the United States. For the Indonesian army relied heavily on U.S. arms which, under our laws, could not be used for aggression.

As it happened, President Gerald Ford was on his way to Indonesia for a state visit. An intelligence report forewarned that Suharto would bring up the Timor issue and would "try and elicit a sympathetic attitude."

That Suharto succeeded is confirmed by Ford himself. The United States had suffered a devastating setback in Vietnam, leaving Indonesia as the most important American ally in the area. The U.S. national interest, Ford concluded, "had to be on the side of Indonesia."

Ford gave his tacit approval on December 6, 1975 ... Five days after the invasion, the United Nations voted to condemn the attack as an arrant act of international aggression. The United

States abstained. Thereafter, the U.S. delegate maneuvered behind the scenes to resist U.N. moves aimed at forcing Indonesia to give up its conquest.[31]

Throughout the late 1970s and the 1980s, US State Department officials, in statements to the press and in testimony before Congress, consistently supported Indonesia's claim to East Timor (unlike the United Nations and the European Community), and downplayed the slaughter to a remarkable extent. Meanwhile, the omnipresent American military advisers, the training, the weapons, the helicopter gunships, and all the other instruments indispensable to efficient, modern, counter-insurgency warfare, were kept flowing into the hands of the Indonesian military. This may not be all, for Fretilin reported on a number of occasions that American advisers were directing and even participating in the combat.[32]

32. Ghana 1966
Kwame Nkrumah steps out of line

In October of the year 1965, Kwame Nkrumah, the President of Ghana, published his famous-to-be book, *Neo-Colonialism—The Last Stage of Imperialism*, dedicated to "the Freedom Fighters of Africa, living and dead". In the book, Nkrumah accused the CIA of being behind numerous setbacks and crises in the Third World and Eastern Europe. He later wrote that "the American Government sent me a note of protest, and promptly refused Ghana $35 million of 'aid'."[1] Four months later he was overthrown in a CIA-backed military coup.

To be sure, the coup-makers—members of the Ghanaian army and police—had their own motivations. They were fearful of having their powers stripped from them by a suspicious Nkrumah who was building up his own private army, and they were intent upon furthering their individual professional careers and status. Within days, even hours, of the successful coup in February 1966, majors had become colonels and colonels had become generals. There was more than a touch of the Keystone Kops to the whole episode.

Kwame Nkrumah was a man who, as a student in the United States during the Great Depression, had roamed Harlem, slept in the subway and lined up at Father Divine's soup kitchens. Later he was to be hailed as "Africa's brightest star", a leader in the call for an anti-imperialist, pan-African organization and an international movement of nations non-aligned in the cold war. But from all accounts, Nkrumah engaged in idiosyncratic, one-man rule and thought that socialism could be promoted by edict from above. And though he spoke out boldly against neo-colonialism, he was unable, ultimately, to keep Ghana from falling under the sway of the multinationals. When he attempted to lessen his country's dependence on the West by strengthening economic and military ties to the Soviet Union, China and East Germany, he effectively sealed his fate.

The United States wanted him out. Great Britain, the former colonial power in Ghana when it was known as the Gold Coast, wanted him out. France and West Germany wanted him out. Those Ghanaians who carried out the coup suffered from no doubts that a move against Nkrumah would be supported by the Western powers.

At the time of the coup, the Soviet press charged that the CIA had been involved, and in 1972 *The Daily Telegraph*, the conservative London newspaper, reported that "By 1965 the Accra [capital of Ghana] CIA Station had two-score active operators, distributing largesse among President Nkrumah's secret adversaries." By February, 1966, the report continued, the CIA had its plans ready to end Nkrumah's regime: "The patient and assiduous work of the Accra CIA station was fully rewarded."[2]

It wasn't until 1978, however, that the story "broke" in the United States. Former CIA officer John Stockwell, who had spent most of his career in Africa, published a book in which he revealed the Agency's complicity. Shortly afterwards, the *New York Times*, quoting "first-hand intelligence sources", corroborated that the CIA had advised and supported the dissident Ghanaian army officers.

Stockwell disclosed that the CIA station in Accra "was given a generous budget, and maintained intimate contact with the plotters as a coup was hatched. So close was the station's involvement that it was able to coordinate the recovery of some classified Soviet military equipment by the United States as the coup took place."[3]

The CIA station had also proposed to headquarters in Washington that a small squad of paramilitary experts, members of the agency's Special Operations Group, be on hand at the moment of the coup, with their faces blacked, storm the Chinese Embassy, kill everyone inside, steal their secret records, and blow up the building to cover the fact.[4]

"This proposal was squashed," Stockwell wrote, "but inside CIA headquarters the Accra station was given full, if unofficial credit for the eventual coup, in which eight Soviet advisers were killed."[5] (The Soviet Union categorically denied that any of its advisers had been killed.)

Other intelligence sources who were in Ghana at the time of the coup have taken issue with Stockwell's view that the CIA deserved full credit for Nkrumah's downfall. But they considered the Agency's role to have been pivotal, and at least some officials in Washington apparently agreed, for the CIA station chief in Accra, Howard T. Bane, was quickly promoted to a senior position in the agency.[6]

"When he was successful," one of the *New York Times* sources said of Bane, "everyone in the African division knew it. If it had failed, he would have been transferred and no CIA involvement revealed."

Bane, nevertheless, was enraged by the CIA's high-level decision not to permit the raid on the Chinese Embassy, at the time the Peking government's only embassy in Africa. "They didn't have the guts to do it," he subsequently told an associate.[7]

After the coup, the CIA made a payment of "at least $100,000" to the new Ghanaian regime for the confiscated Soviet material, one item of which was a cigarette lighter that also functioned as a camera.[8]

The Ghanaian leaders soon expelled large numbers of Russians as well as Chinese and East Germans. Virtually all state-owned industries were allowed to pass into private hands. In short order the channels of aid, previously clogged, opened wide, and credit, food and development projects flowed in from the United States, the European powers, and the International Monetary Fund. Washington, for example, three weeks after the coup, approved substantial emergency food assistance in response to an urgent request from Ghana. A food request from Nkrumah four months earlier had been turned down.[9] One month after his ouster, the international price of cocoa—Ghana's economic lifeblood—had risen 14 percent.[10]

The CIA's reluctance to approve the action at the Chinese Embassy may have stemmed from the fact that the National Security Council had specifically refused to authorize the Agency's involvement in the coup at all. This was, as we have seen, not the first instance of the CIA taking American foreign policy into its own hands. On such occasions, the *modus operandi* calls for putting as little into writing as feasible, or keeping records out of official CIA files, thus making them immune to Freedom of Information disclosures or congressional investigations; technically the records do not exist, legally they can be destroyed at any time. This was the case with the Ghanaian coup and may explain why more details of the CIA role have never been revealed.

The American right-wing view of what happened

According to John Barron, the *Reader's Digest's* resident KGB expert, Nkrumah was overthrown by only native insurgents, the only foreigners in the picture being 11 KGB officers who were found in Nkrumah's headquarters and summarily executed. The Soviet Union didn't say a word about this, he wrote, because they didn't want "the world to know that KGB officers were actually sitting in the Ghanian President's office running the country." Barron offers no evidence at all to support his claim of the KGB running the country, nor does he explain why the new government didn't publicize this very interesting fact.

He goes on to write of "the copious secret files of the Nkrumah regime" which were discovered and then studied and analyzed. The files revealed, he says, that "the KGB had converted Ghana into one vast base of subversion, which the Soviet Union fully intended to use to capture the continent of Africa". For reasons best known to himself perhaps, Barron fails to offer the reader a single quotation from any of the copious secret files to support his allegations.[11]

33. Uruguay 1964-1970
Torture—as American as apple pie

"The precise pain, in the precise place, in the precise amount, for the desired effect."[1]

The words of an instructor in the art of torture. The words of Dan Mitrione, the head of the Office of Public Safety (OPS) mission in Montevideo.

Officially, OPS was a division of the Agency for International Development, but the director of OPS in Washington, Byron Engle, was an old CIA hand. His organization maintained a close working relationship with the CIA, and Agency officers often operated abroad under OPS cover, although Mitrione was not one of them.[2]

OPS had been operating formally in Uruguay since 1965, supplying the police with the equipment, the arms, and the training it was created to do. Four years later, when Mitrione arrived, the Uruguayans had a special need for OPS services. The country was in the midst of a long-running economic decline, its once-heralded prosperity and democracy sinking fast toward the level of its South American neighbors. Labor strikes, student demonstrations, and militant street violence had become normal events during the past year; and, most worrisome to the Uruguayan authorities, there were the revolutionaries who called themselves Tupamaros. Perhaps the cleverest, most resourceful and most sophisticated urban guerrillas the world has ever seen, the Tupamaros had a deft touch for capturing the public's imagination with outrageous actions, and winning sympathizers with their Robin Hood philosophy. Their members and secret partisans held key positions in the government, banks, universities, and the professions, as well as in the military and police.

"Unlike other Latin-American guerrilla groups," the *New York Times* stated in 1970, "the Tupamaros normally avoid bloodshed when possible. They try instead to create embarrassment for the Government and general disorder."[3] A favorite tactic was to raid the files of a private corporation to expose corruption and deceit in high places, or kidnap a prominent figure and try him before a "People's Court". It was heady stuff to choose a public villain whose acts went uncensored by the legislature, the courts and the press, subject him to an informed and uncompromising interrogation, and then publicize the results of the intriguing dialogue. Once they ransacked an exclusive high-class nightclub and scrawled on the walls perhaps their most memorable slogan: *O Bailan Todos O No Baila Nadie* ... Either everyone dances or no one dances.

Dan Mitrione did not introduce the practice of torturing political prisoners to Uruguay. It had been perpetrated by the police at times from at least the early 1960s. However, in a surprising interview given to a leading Brazilian newspaper in 1970, the former Uruguayan Chief of Police Intelligence, Alejandro Otero, declared that US advisers, and in particular Mitrione, had instituted torture as a more routine measure; to the means of inflicting pain, they had added scientific refinement; and to that a psychology to create despair, such as playing a tape in the next room of women and children screaming and telling the prisoner that it was his family being tortured.[4]

"The violent methods which were beginning to be employed," said Otero, "caused an escalation in Tupamaro activity. Before then their attitude showed that they would use violence only as a last resort."[5]

The newspaper interview greatly upset American officials in South America and Washington. Byron Engle later tried to explain it all away by asserting: "The three Brazilian reporters in Montevideo all denied filing that story. We found out later that it was slipped into the paper by someone in the composing room at the *Jornal do Brasil*."[6]

Otero had been a willing agent of the CIA, a student at their International Police Services school in Washington, a recipient of their cash over the years, but he was not a torturer. What finally drove him to speak out was perhaps the torture of a woman who, while a Tupamaro sympathizer, was also a friend of his. When she told him that Mitrione had watched and assisted in her torture, Otero complained to him, about this particular incident as well as his general methods of extracting information. The only outcome of the encounter was Otero's demotion.[7]

William Cantrell was a CIA operations officer stationed in Montevideo, ostensibly as a member of the OPS team. In the mid-1960s he was instrumental in setting up a Department of Information and Intelligence (DII), and providing it with funds and equipment.[8] Some of the equipment, innovated by the CIA's Technical Services Division, was for the purpose of torture, for this was one of the functions carried out by the DII.[9]

"One of the pieces of equipment that was found useful," former *New York Times* correspondent A. J. Langguth learned, "was a wire so very thin that it could be fitted into the mouth between the teeth and by pressing against the gum increase the electrical charge. And it was through the diplomatic pouch that Mitrione got some of the equipment he needed for interrogations, including these fine wires."[10]

Things got so bad in Mitrione's time that the Uruguayan Senate was compelled to undertake an investigation. After a five-month study, the commission concluded unanimously that torture in Uruguay had become a "normal, frequent and habitual occurrence", inflicted upon Tupamaros as well as others. Among the types of torture the commission's report made reference to were electric shocks to the genitals, electric needles under the fingernails, burning with cigarettes, the slow compression of the testicles, daily use of psychological torture ... "pregnant women were subjected to various brutalities and inhuman treatment" ... "certain women were imprisoned with their very young infants and subjected to the same treatment" ...[11]

Eventually the DII came to serve as a cover for the *Escuadrón de la Muerte* (Death Squad), composed, as elsewhere in Latin America, primarily of police officers, who bombed and strafed the homes of suspected Tupamaro sympathizers and engaged in assassination and kidnapping. The Death Squad received some of its special explosive material from the Technical Services Division and, in all likelihood, some of the skills employed by its members were acquired from instruction in the United States.[12] Between 1969 and 1973, at least 16 Uruguayan police officers went through an eight-week course at CIA/OPS schools in Washington and Los Fresnos, Texas in the design, manufacture and employment of bombs and incendiary devices.[13] The official OPS explanation for these courses was that policemen needed such training in order to deal with bombs placed by terrorists. There was, however, no instruction in destroying bombs, only in making them; moreover, on at least one reported occasion, the students were not policemen, but members of a private right-wing organization in Chile (see chapter on Chile). Another part of the curriculum which might also have proven to be of value to the Death Squad was the class on Assassination Weapons— "A discussion of various weapons which may be used by the assassin" is how OPS put it.[14]

Equipment and training of this kind was in addition to that normally provided by OPS: riot helmets, transparent shields, tear gas, gas masks, communication gear, vehicles, police batons, and other devices for restraining crowds. The supply of these tools of the trade was increased in 1968 when public disturbances reached the spark-point, and by 1970 American training in riot-control techniques had been given to about a thousand Uruguayan policemen.[15]

Dan Mitrione had built a soundproofed room in the cellar of his house in Montevideo. In this room he assembled selected Uruguayan police officers to observe a demonstration of torture techniques. Another observer was Manuel Hevia Cosculluela, a Cuban who was with the CIA and worked with Mitrione. Hevia later wrote that the course began with a description of the human anatomy and nervous system ...

> Soon things turned unpleasant. As subjects for the first testing they took beggars, known in Uruguay as *bichicomes*, from the outskirts of Montevideo, as well as a woman apparently from the frontier area with Brazil. There was no interrogation, only a demonstration of the effects of different voltages on the different parts of the human body, as well as demonstrating the use of a drug which induces vomiting—I don't know why or what for—and another chemical substance. The four of them died.[16]

In his book Hevia does not say specifically what Mitrione's direct part in all this was, but he later publicly stated that the OPS chief "personally tortured four beggars to death with electric shocks".[17]

On another occasion, Hevia sat with Mitrione in the latter's house, and over a few drinks the American explained to the Cuban his philosophy of interrogation. Mitrione considered it to be an art. First there should be a softening-up period, with the usual beatings and insults. The object is to humiliate the prisoner, to make him realize his helplessness, to cut him off from reality. No questions, only blows and insults. Then, only blows in silence.

Only after this, said Mitrione, is the interrogation. Here no pain should be produced other than that caused by the instrument which is being used. "The precise pain, in the precise place, in the precise amount, for the desired effect," was his motto.

During the session you have to keep the subject from losing all hope of life, because this can lead to stubborn resistance. "You must always leave him some hope ... a distant light."

"When you get what you want, and I always get it," Mitrione continued, "it may be good to prolong the session a little to apply another softening-up. Not to extract information now, but only as a political measure, to create a healthy fear of meddling in subversive activities."

The American pointed out that upon receiving a subject the first thing is to determine his physical state, his degree of resistance, by means of a medical examination. "A premature death means a failure by the technician ... It's important to know in advance if we can permit ourselves the luxury of the subject's death."[18]

Not long after this conversation, Manual Hevia disappeared from Montevideo and turned up in Havana. He had been a Cuban agent—a double agent—all along.

About half a year later, 31 July 1970 to be exact, Dan Mitrione was kidnapped by the Tupamaros. They did not torture him. They demanded the release of some 150 prisoners in exchange for him. With the determined backing of the Nixon administration, the Uruguayan government refused. On 10 August, Mitrione's dead body was found on the back seat of a stolen car. He had turned 50 on his fifth day as a prisoner.

Back in Mitrione's home town of Richmond, Indiana, Secretary of State William Rogers and President Nixon's son-in-law David Eisenhower attended the funeral for Mitrione, the city's former police chief. Frank Sinatra and Jerry Lewis came to town to stage a benefit show for Mitrione's family.

And White House spokesman, Ron Ziegler, solemnly stated that "Mr. Mitrione's devoted service to the cause of peaceful progress in an orderly world will remain as an example for free men everywhere."[19]

"A perfect man," his widow said.

"A great humanitarian," said his daughter Linda.[20]

The military's entry into the escalating conflict signaled the beginning of the end for the Tupamaros. By the end of 1972, the curtain was descending on their guerrilla theatre. Six months later, the military was in charge, Congress was dissolved, and everything not prohibited was compulsory. For the next 11 years, Uruguay competed strongly for the honor of being South America's most repressive dictatorship. It had, at one point, the largest number of political prisoners per capita in the world. And, as every human rights organization and former prisoner could testify, each one of them was tortured. "Torture," said an activist priest, "was routine and automatic."[21]

No one was dancing in Uruguay.

In 1981, at the Fourteenth Conference of American Armies, the Uruguayan Army offered a paper in which it defined subversion as "actions, violent or not, with ultimate purposes of a political nature, in all fields of human activity within the internal sphere of a state and whose aims are perceived as not convenient for the overall political system."[22]

The dissident Uruguayan writer, Eduardo Galeano, summed up his country's era of dictatorship thusly: "People were in prison so that prices could be free."[23]

The film "State of Siege" appeared in 1972. It centered around Mitrione and the Tupamaros and depicted a Uruguayan police officer receiving training at a secret bomb school in the United States, though the film strove more to provide a composite picture of the role played by the US in repression throughout Latin America. A scheduled premier showing of the film at the federally-funded John F. Kennedy Arts Center in Washington was canceled. There was already growing public and congressional criticism of this dark side of American foreign policy without adding to it. During the mid-1970s, however, Congress enacted several pieces of legislation which abolished the entire Public Safety Program. In its time, OPS had provided training for more than one million policemen in the Third World. Ten thousand of them had received advance training in the United States. An estimated $150 million worth of equipment had been shipped to police forces abroad.[24] Now, the "export of repression" was to cease.

That was on paper. The reality appears to be somewhat different.

To a large extent, the Drug Enforcement Administration (DEA) simply picked up where OPS had left off. The drug agency was ideally suited for the task, for its agents were already deployed all over Latin America and elsewhere overseas in routine liaison with foreign police forces. The DEA acknowledged in 1975 that 53 "former" employees of the CIA were now on its staff and that there was a close working relationship between the two agencies. The following year, the General Accounting Office reported that DEA agents were engaging in many of the same activities the OPS had been carrying out.

In addition, some training of foreign policemen was transferred to FBI schools in Washington and Quantico, Virginia; the Defense Department continued to supply police-type equipment to military units engaged in internal security operations; and American arms manufacturers were doing a booming business furnishing arms and training to Third World governments. In some countries, contact between these companies and foreign law enforcement officials was facilitated by the US Embassy or military mission. The largest of the arms manufacturers, Smith and Wesson, ran its own Academy in Springfield, Massachusetts, which provided American and foreign "public and industrial security forces with expert training in riot control".[25]

Said Argentine Minister Jose Lopez Rega at the signing of a US-Argentina anti-drug treaty in 1974: "We hope to wipe out the drug traffic in Argentina. We have caught guerrillas after attacks who were high on drugs. The guerrillas are the main drug users in Argentina. Therefore, this anti-drug campaign will automatically be an anti-guerrilla campaign as well."[26]

And in 1981, a former Uruguayan intelligence officer declared that US manuals were being used to teach techniques of torture to his country's military. He said that most of the officers who trained him had attended classes run by the United States in Panama. Among other niceties, the manuals listed 35 nerve points where electrodes could be applied.[27]

※ ※

Philip Agee, after he left Ecuador, was stationed in Uruguay from March 1964 to August 1966. His account of CIA activities in Montevideo is further testimony to the amount of international mischief money can buy. Amongst the multifarious dirty tricks pulled off with impunity by Agee and his Agency cohorts, the following constitute an interesting sample:[28]

A Latin American students' conference with a leftist leaning, held in Montevideo, was undermined by promoting the falsehood that it was nothing more than a creature of the

Soviet Union—originated, financed and directed by Moscow. Editorials on this theme authored by the CIA appeared in leading newspapers to which the Agency had daily access. This was followed by publication of a forged letter of a student leader thanking the Soviet cultural attaché for his assistance. A banner headline in one paper proclaimed: "Documents for the Break with Russia", which was indeed the primary purpose of the operation.

An inordinate amount of time, energy and creativity was devoted, with moderate success, to schemes aimed at encouraging the expulsion of an assortment of Russians, East Germans, North Koreans, Czechs, and Cubans from Uruguayan soil, if not the breaking of relations with these countries. In addition to planting disparaging media propaganda, the CIA tried to obtain incriminating information by reading the mail and diplomatic cables to and from these countries, tapping embassy phones, and engaging in sundry bugging and surreptitious entry. The Agency would then prepare "Intelligence" reports, containing enough factual information to be plausible, which then made their way innocently into the hands of officials of influence, up to and including the president of the republic.

Anti-communist indoctrination of secondary-level students was promoted by financing particular school organizations and publications.

A Congress of the People, bringing together a host of community groups, labor organizations, students, government workers, etc., Communist and non-Communist, disturbed the CIA because of the potential for a united front being formed for electoral purposes. Accordingly, newspaper editorials and articles were generated attacking the Congress as a classic Communist takeover/duping tactic and calling upon non-Communists to refrain from participating; and a phoney handbill was circulated in which the Congress called upon the Uruguayan people to launch an insurrectional strike with immediate occupation of their places of work. Thousands of the handbills were handed out, provoking angry denials from the Congress organizers, but, as is usual in such cases, the damage was already done.

The Uruguayan Communist Party planned to host an international conference to express solidarity with Cuba. The CIA merely had to turn to their (paid) friend, the Minister of the Interior, and the conference was banned. When it was shifted to Chile, the CIA station in Santiago performed the same magic.

Uruguay at this time was a haven for political exiles from repressive regimes such as in Brazil, Argentina, Bolivia and Paraguay. The CIA, through surveillance and infiltration of the exile community, regularly collected information on exiles' activities, associates, etc., to be sent to CIA stations in the exiles' homelands with likely transmission to their governments, which wanted to know what these troublemakers were up to and which did not hesitate to harass them across frontiers.

"Other operations," wrote Agee, "were designed to take control of the streets away from communists and other leftists, and our squads, often with the participation of off-duty policemen, would break up their meetings and generally terrorize them. Torture of communists and other extreme leftists was used in interrogation by our liaison agents in the police."

The monitoring and harassment of Communist diplomatic missions by the CIA, as described above, was standard Agency practice throughout the Western world. This rarely stemmed from anything more than a juvenile cold-war reflex: making life hard for the commies. Looked at from any angle, it was politically and morally pointless. Richard Gott, the Latin America specialist of *The Guardian* of London, related an anecdote which is relevant:

In January 1967 a group of Brazilians and a Uruguayan asked for political asylum in the Czech embassy in Montevideo, stating that they wished to go to a Socialist country to pursue their revolutionary activities. They were, they said, under constant surveillance and harassment from the Uruguayan police. The Czech ambassador was horrified by their request and threw them out, saying that there was no police persecution in Uruguay. When the revolutionaries camped in his garden the ambassador called the police.[29]

34. Chile 1964-1973

A hammer and sickle stamped on your child's forehead

When Salvador Allende, a committed Marxist, came within three percent of winning the Chilean presidency in 1958, the United States decided that the next election, in 1964, could not be left in the hands of providence, or democracy.

Washington took it all very gravely. At the outset of the Kennedy administration in 1961, an electoral committee was established, composed of top-level officials from the State Department, the CIA and the White House. In Santiago, a parallel committee of embassy and CIA people was set up.[1]

"U.S. government intervention in Chile in 1964 was blatant and almost obscene," said one intelligence officer strategically placed at the time. "We were shipping people off right and left, mainly State Dept. but also CIA, with all sorts of covers." All in all, as many as 100 American operatives were dedicated to the operation.[2]

They began laying the groundwork for the election years ahead, a Senate investigating committee has disclosed, "by establishing operational relationships with key political parties and by creating propaganda and organizational mechanisms capable of influencing key sectors of the population." Projects were undertaken "to help train and organize 'anti-communists'" among peasants, slum dwellers, organized labor, students, the media, etc.[3]

After channeling funds to several non-leftist parties, the electoral team eventually settled on a man of the center, Eduardo Frei, the candidate of the Christian Democratic Party, as the one most likely to block Allende's rise to power. The CIA underwrote more than half the party's total campaign costs,[4] one of the reasons that the Agency's overall electoral operation reduced the U.S. Treasury by an estimated $20 million[5]—much more per voter than that spent by the Johnson and Goldwater campaigns combined in the same year in the United States. The bulk of the expenditures went toward propaganda. As the Senate committee described it:

> In addition to support for political parties, the CIA mounted a massive anti-communist propaganda campaign. Extensive use was made of the press, radio, films, pamphlets, posters, leaflets, direct mailings, paper streamers, and wall painting. It was a "scare campaign", which relied heavily on images of Soviet tanks and Cuban firing squads and was directed especially to women. Hundreds of thousands of copies of the anti-communist pastoral letter of Pope Pius XI were distributed by Christian Democratic organizations. They carried the designation, "printed privately by citizens without political affiliation, in order more broadly to disseminate its content." "Disinformation" and "black propaganda"—material which purported to originate from another source, such as the Chilean Communist Party—were used as well.[6]

The scare campaign played up to the fact that women in Chile, as elsewhere in Latin America, are traditionally more religious than men, more susceptible to being alarmed by the specter of "godless, atheist communism". One radio spot featured the sound of a machine gun, followed by a woman's cry: "They have killed my child—the communists." The announcer then added in impassioned tones: "Communism offers only blood and pain. For this not to happen in Chile, we must elect Eduardo Frei president."[7]

Other scare tactics centered around warnings of Russian control, and that the left would confiscate everything near, dear and holy.

The committee report continued:

> The propaganda campaign was enormous. During the first week of intensive propaganda activity (the third week of June 1964), a CIA-funded propaganda group produced twenty radio spots per day in Santiago and on 44 provincial stations; twelve-minute news broadcasts five times daily on three Santiago stations and 24 provincial outlets; thousands of cartoons, and much paid press advertising. By the end of June, the group produced 24 daily newscasts in Santiago and the provinces, 26 weekly "commentary" programs, and distributed 3,000 posters daily.[8]

One poster which appeared in the thousands showed children with a hammer and sickle stamped on their foreheads.[9]

Newspaper articles from elsewhere in Latin America which supported the political lines of the CIA campaign were collected and reprinted in Chile. Undoubtedly, many of these articles had been written in the first place by CIA stations in the particular countries. There were also endorsements of Frei solicited from famous personages abroad, advertisements such as a "message from the women of Venezuela",[10] and a vitriolic anti-communist radio broadcast by Juanita Castro, sister of Fidel, who was on a CIA-organized speaking tour of South America: "If the Reds win in Chile," she said, "no type of religious activity will be possible ... Chilean mother, I know you will not allow your children to be taken from you and sent to the Communist bloc, as in the case of Cuba."[11]

The Senate committee also revealed that:

> In addition to buying propaganda piecemeal, the [CIA] Station often purchased it wholesale by subsidizing Chilean media organizations friendly to the United States. Doing so was propaganda writ large. Instead of placing individual items, the CIA supported—or even founded—friendly media outlets which might not have existed in the absence of Agency support.
>
> From 1953 through 1970 in Chile, the Station subsidized wire services, magazines written for intellectual circles, and a right-wing weekly newspaper.[12]

Of one subsidized newspaper, a State Department veteran of the campaign recalls that "The layout was magnificent. The photographs were superb. It was a Madison Avenue product far above the standards of Chilean publications."[13]

The same could be said about the electioneering itself. Besides running political action projects on its own in a number of important voting blocks, the CIA directed the Christian Democrats' campaign along American-style lines, with voter registration, get-out-the-vote drives, and professional management firms to carry out public opinion surveys.[14] To top it all off, they sent for a ringer—an election specialist from the staff of that eminent connoisseur and guardian of free elections, Mayor Richard Daley of Chicago.[15] What the function of Daley's man in Chile was, can only be guessed at.

Several of the grassroots programs funded by the CIA were those run by Roger Vekemans, a Belgian Jesuit priest who arrived in Chile in 1957 and founded a network of social-action organizations, one of which grew to have 100 employees and a $30 million annual budget. By his own declaration in 1963, Vekemans received $5 million from the CIA as well as a like amount from AID to guide his organizations' resources in support of the

Christian Democrats and Eduardo Frei, with whom Vekemans had close relations.[16] The Jesuit's programs served the classic function of channeling revolutionary zeal along safe reformist paths. Church people working for the CIA in the Third World have typically been involved in gathering information about the activities and attitudes of individual peasants and workers, spotting the troublemakers, recruiting likely agents, preaching the gospel of anti-communism, acting as funding conduits, and serving as a religious "cover" for various Agency operations. An extreme anti-communist, Vekemans was a front-line soldier in the struggle of the Christian Democrats and the Catholic Church against the "liberation theology" then gaining momentum amongst the more liberal clergy in Latin America and which would lead to the historic dialogue between Christianity and Marxism.[17]

The operation worked. It worked beyond expectations. Frei received 56 percent of the vote to Allende's 39 percent. The CIA regarded "the anti-communist scare campaign as the most effective activity undertaken", noted the Senate committee.[18] This was the tactic directed toward Chilean women in particular. As things turned out, Allende won the men's vote by 67,000 over Frei (in Chile men and women vote separately), but amongst the women Frei came out ahead by 469,000 ... testimony, once again, to the remarkable ease with which the minds of the masses of people can be manipulated, in any and all societies.

What was there about Salvador Allende that warranted all this feverish activity? What threat did he represent, this man against whom the great technical and economic resources of the world's most powerful nation were brought to bear? Allende was a man whose political program, as described by the Senate committee report, was to "redistribute income [two percent of the population received 46 percent of the income] and reshape the Chilean economy, beginning with the nationalization of major industries, especially the copper companies; greatly expanded agrarian reform; and expanded relations with socialist and communist countries."[19]

A man committed to such a program could be expected by American policy makers to lead his country along a path independent of the priorities of US foreign policy and the multinationals. (As his later term as president confirmed, he was independent of any other country as well.)

The CIA is an ongoing organization. Its covert activities are ongoing, each day, in each country. Between the 1964 and 1970 presidential elections many of the programs designed to foster an anti-leftist mentality in different sections of the population continued; much of the propaganda and electioneering mechanisms remained in place to support candidates of the 1965 and 1969 congressional elections; in the latter election, financial support was given to a splinter socialist party in order to attract votes away from Allende's Socialist Party; this reportedly deprived the party of a minimum of seven congressional seats.[20]

The Senate committee described some of the other individual covert projects undertaken by the CIA during this period:

- Wresting control of Chilean university student organizations from the communists;
- Supporting a women's group active in Chilean political and intellectual life;
- Combatting the communist-dominated *Central Unica de Trabajadores Chilenos* (CUTCh) and supporting democratic [i.e., anti-communist] labor groups; and,
- Exploiting a civic action front group to combat communist influence within cultural and intellectual circles.[21]

In 1968, at the same time the CIA was occupied in subverting unions dominated by the Chilean Communist Party, a US Senate committee was concluding that the Latin American labor movement had largely abandoned its revolutionary outlook: "Even the Communist-dominated unions, especially those which follow the Moscow line, now generally accept the peaceful road as a viable alternative."[22]

"I don't see why we need to stand by and watch a country go communist because of the irresponsibility of its own people."[23]

Thus spoke Henry Kissinger, principal adviser to the President of the United States on matters of national security. The date was 27 June 1970, a meeting of the National Security Council's 40 Committee, and the people Kissinger suspected of imminent irresponsibility were the Chileans whom he feared might finally elect Salvador Allende as their president.

The United States did not stand by idly. At this meeting approval was given to a $300,000 increase in the anti-Allende "spoiling" operation which was already underway. The CIA trained its disinformation heavy artillery on the Chilean electorate, firing shells marked: "An Allende victory means violence and Stalinist repression."[24] Black propaganda was employed to undermine Allende's coalition and support by sowing dissent between the Communist Party and the Socialist Party, the main members of the coalition, and between the Communist Party and the CUTCh.[25]

Nonetheless, on 4 September Allende won a plurality of the votes. On 24 October, the Chilean Congress would meet to choose between him and the runnerup, Jorge Alessandri of the conservative National Party. By tradition, Allende was certain to become president.

The United States had seven weeks to prevent him from taking office. On 15 September, President Nixon met with Kissinger, CIA Director Richard Helms, and Attorney General John Mitchell. Helms' handwritten notes of the meeting have become famous: "One in 10 chance perhaps, but save Chile! ... not concerned with risks involved ...$10,000,000 available, more if necessary ... make the economy scream ..."[26]

Funds were authorized by the 40 Committee to bribe Chilean congressmen to vote for Alessandri,[27] but this was soon abandoned as infeasible, and under intense pressure from Richard Nixon, American efforts were concentrated on inducing the Chilean military to stage a coup and then cancel the congressional vote altogether.[28] At the same time, Nixon and Kissinger made it clear to the CIA that an assassination of Allende would not be unwelcome. One White House options-paper discussed various ways this could be carried out.[29]

A fresh propaganda campaign was initiated in Chile to impress upon the military, amongst others, the catastrophe which would befall the nation with Allende as president. In addition to the standard communist horror stories, it was made known that there would be a cutoff of American and other foreign assistance; this was accompanied by predictions/rumors of the nationalization of everything down to small shops, and of economic collapse. The campaign actually affected the Chilean economy adversely and a major financial panic ensued.[30]

In private, Chilean military officers were warned that American military aid would come to a halt if Allende were seated.[31]

During this interim period, according to the CIA, over 700 articles, broadcasts, editorials and similar items were generated in the Latin American and European media as a direct result of Agency activity. This is apart from the "real" media stories inspired by the planted ones. Moreover, journalists in the pay of the CIA arrived in Chile from at least ten different countries to enhance their material with on-the-spot credibility.[32]

The following portion of a CIA cable of 25 September 1970 offers some indication of the scope of such media operations:

Sao Paulo, Tegucigalpa, Buenos Aires, Lima, Montevideo, Bogota, Mexico City report continued replay of Chile theme materials. Items also carried in *New York Times* and *Washington Post*. Propaganda activities continue to generate good coverage of Chile developments along our theme guidance.[33]

The CIA also gave "inside" briefings to American journalists about the situation in Chile. One such briefing provided to *Time* enlightened the magazine as to Allende's intention to support violence and destroy Chile's free press. This, observed the Senate report, "resulted in a change in the basic thrust" of the *Time* story.[34]

When Allende criticized the leading conservative newspaper *El Mercurio* (heavily funded by the CIA), the Agency "orchestrated cables of support and protest from foreign newspapers, a protest statement from an international press association, and world press coverage of the association's protest."[35]

A cable sent from CIA headquarters to Santiago on 19 October expressed concern that the coup still had

no pretext or justification that it can offer to make it acceptable in Chile or Latin America. It therefore would seem necessary to create one to bolster what will probably be [the military's] claim to a coup to save Chile from communism.

One of headquarters' suggestions was the fabrication of:

Firm intel[ligence] that Cubans planned to reorganize all intelligence services along Soviet/Cuban mold thus creating structure for police state ... With appropriate military contact can determine how to "discover" intel[ligence] report which could even be planted during raids planned by Carabineros [the police].[36]

Meanwhile, the Agency was in active consultation with several Chilean military officers who were receptive to the suggestion of a coup. (The difficulty in finding such officers was described by the CIA as a problem in overcoming "the apolitical, constitutional-oriented inertia of the Chilean military".)[37] They were assured that the United States would give them full support short of direct military involvement. The immediate obstacle faced by the officers was the determined opposition of the Commander-in-Chief of the Army, René Schneider, who insisted that the constitutional process be followed. He would have to be "removed".

In the early morn of 22 October the CIA passed "sterilized" machine guns and ammunition to some of the conspirators. (Earlier they had passed tear gas.) That same day, Schneider was mortally wounded in an attempted kidnap (or "kidnap") on his way to work. The CIA station in Santiago cabled its headquarters that the general had been shot with the same kind of weapons it had delivered to the military plotters, although the Agency later claimed to the Senate that the actual assassins were not the same ones it had passed the weapons to.[38]

The assassination did not avail the conspirators' purpose. It only served to rally the army around the flag of constitutionalism; and time was running out. Two days later, Salvador Allende was confirmed by the Chilean Congress. On 3 November he took office as president.

The stage was set for a clash of two experiments. One was Allende's "socialist" experiment aimed at lifting Chile from the mire of underdevelopment and dependency and the poor from deprivation. The other was, as CIA Director William Colby later put it, a "prototype or laboratory experiment to test the techniques of heavy financial investment in an effort to discredit and bring down a government."[39]

Although there were few individual features of this experiment which were unique for the CIA, in sum total it was perhaps the most multifarious intervention ever undertaken by the United States. In the process it brought a new word into the language: destabilization.

"Not a nut or bolt [will] be allowed to reach Chile under Allende", warned then-American Ambassador Edward Korry before the confirmation.[40] The Chilean economy, so extraordinarily dependent upon the United States, was the country's soft underbelly, easy to pound. Over the next three years, new US government assistance programs for Chile plummeted almost to the vanishing point; similarly with loans from the US Export-Import Bank and the Inter-American Development Bank, in which the United States held what amounted to a veto; and the World Bank made no new loans at all to Chile during 1971-73. US government financial assistance or guarantees to American private investment in Chile were cut back sharply and American businesses were given the word to tighten the economic noose.[41]

What this boycott translated into were things like the many buses and taxis out of commission in Chile due to a lack of replacement parts; and similar difficulties in the copper, steel, electricity and petroleum industries. American suppliers refused to sell needed parts despite Chile's offer to pay cash in advance.[42]

Multinational ITT, which didn't need to be told what to do, stated in a 1970 memorandum: "A more realistic hope among those who want to block Allende is that a swiftly-deteriorating economy will touch off a wave of violence leading to a military coup."[43]

In the midst of the near disappearance of economic aid, and contrary to its warning, the United States increased its military assistance to Chile during 1972 and 1973 as well as training Chilean military personnel in the United States and Panama.[44] The Allende government, caught between the devil and the deep blue sea, was reluctant to refuse this "assistance" for fear of antagonizing its military leaders.

Perhaps nothing produced more discontent in the population than the shortages, the little daily annoyances when one couldn't get a favorite food, or flour or cooking oil, or toilet paper, bed sheets or soap, or the one part needed to make the TV set or the car run; or, worst of all, when a nicotine addict couldn't get a cigarette. Some of the scarcity resulted from Chile being a society in transition: various changeovers to state ownership, experiments in workers' control, etc. But this was minor compared to the effect of the aid squeeze and the practices of the omnipresent American corporations. Equally telling were the extended strikes in Chile, which relied heavily on CIA financial support for their prolongation.[45]

In October 1972, for example, an association of private truck owners instituted a work-stoppage aimed at disrupting the flow of food and other important commodities, including in their embargo even newspapers which supported the government (subtlety was not the order of the day in this ultra-polarized country). On the heels of this came store closures, countless petit-bourgeois doing their bit to turn the screws of public inconvenience— and when they were open, many held back on certain goods, like cigarettes, to sell them on the black market to those who could afford the higher prices. Then most private bus companies stopped running; on top of this, various professional and white-collar workers, largely unsympathetic to the government, walked out, with or without CIA help.

Much of this campaign was aimed at wearing down the patience of the public, convincing them that "socialism can't work in Chile". Yet there had been worse shortages for most of the people before the Allende government—shortages of food, housing, health care, and education, for example. At least half the population had suffered from malnutrition. Allende, who was a medical doctor, explained his free milk program by pointing out that "Today in Chile there are over 600,000 children mentally retarded because they were not adequately nourished during the first eight months of their lives, because they did not receive the necessary proteins."[46]

Financial aid was not the CIA's only input into the strike scene. More than 100 members of Chilean professional associations and employers' guilds were graduates of the school run by the American Institute for Free Labor Development in Front Royal, Virginia—"The Little Anti-Red Schoolhouse". AIFLD, the CIA's principal Latin America labor organization, also assisted in the formation of a new professional association in May 1971: the Confederation of Chilean Professionals. The labor specialists of AIFLD had more than a decade's experience in the art of fomenting economic turmoil (or keeping workers quiescent when the occasion called for it).[47]

CIA propaganda merchants had a field day with the disorder and the shortages, exacerbating both by instigating panic buying. All the techniques, the whole of the media saturation, the handy organizations created for each and every purpose, so efficiently employed in 1964 and 1970, were facilitated by the virtually unlimited license granted the press: headlines and stories which spread rumors about everything from nationalizations to bad meat and undrinkable water ... "Economic Chaos! Chile on Brink of Doom!" in the largest type one could ever expect to see in a newspaper ... raising the specter of civil war, when not actually *calling* for it, literally ... alarmist stories which anywhere else in the world would have been branded seditious ... the worst of London's daily tabloids or the National Enquirer of the United States appear as staid as a journal of dentistry by comparison.[48]

In response, on a few occasions, the government briefly closed down a newspaper or magazine, on the left as well as on the right, for endangering security.[49]

The Agency's routine support of the political opposition was extended to include the extreme rightist organization *Patria y Libertad*, which the CIA reportedly helped to form, and whose members it trained in guerrilla warfare and bombing techniques at schools in Bolivia and Los Fresnos, Texas. *Patria y Libertad* marched in rallies in full riot gear, engaged repeatedly in acts of violence and provocation, and its publications openly called for a military coup.[50]

The CIA was engaged in courting the military for the same end. Providing military equipment meant the normal presence of US advisers and the opportunity for Americans to work closely with the Chileans. Since 1969, the Agency had been establishing "intelligence assets" in all three branches of the Chilean armed services, and included "command-level officers, field- and company-grade officers, retired general staff officers and enlisted men." Employing its usual blend of real and fabricated information, along with forged documents, the CIA endeavored to keep the officers "on the alert". One approach was to convince them that, with Allende's approval, the police investigations unit was acting in concert with Cuban intelligence to gather information prejudicial to the army high command.[51]

Newspapers in Santiago supported by the CIA, particularly *El Mercurio*, often concentrated on influencing the military. They alleged communist plots to disband or destroy the armed services, Soviet plans to establish a submarine base in Chile, North Korea setting up a training base, and so forth. The papers stirred up hatred against the government in the ranks, and in some cases entire columns were published which were calculated to change the opinion of a single officer, in one case an officer's wife.[52]

The Agency also subsidized a number of books and other kinds of publications in

Chile. One was a short-lived anti-government newsletter directed at the military.[53] Later the CIA made use of a weekly humor and political magazine, *SEPA*, aimed at the same audience. The cover of the 20 March 1973 issue featured the headline: "Robert Moss. An English Recipe for Chile—Military Control." Moss was identified by the magazine as a British sociologist. A more relevant description would have been that he was a "news" specialist associated with known CIA media fronts. One of these, Forum World Features of London (see Western Europe chapter), published Moss's book, *Chile's Marxist Experiment*, in 1973, which was widely circulated by the junta to justify its coup.[54]

Moss was associated with a CIA-funded think-tank in Santiago which went by the supremely innocuous name of the Institute of General Studies. The IGS, amongst other activities, conducted seminars for Chilean military officers in which it was explained, in technical, apolitical terms, why Allende was a disaster for the economy and why a laissez-faire system offered a solution to Chile's ills. There is no way of measuring to what extent such lectures influenced future actions of the military, although after the coup the junta did appoint several IGS people to top government posts.[55]

The CIA's Santiago station was meanwhile collecting the operational intelligence necessary in the event of a coup: "arrest lists, key civilian installations and personnel that needed protection, key government installations which need to be taken over, and government contingency plans which would be used in case of a military uprising."[56] The CIA later asserted that this information was never passed to the Chilean military, a claim that does not give one the feeling of having been united with the probable. It should be noted in this context that in the days immediately following the coup the Chilean military went directly to the residences of many Americans and other foreigners living in Santiago who had been sympathetic to the Allende government.[57]

The government contingency plans were presumably obtained by the Agency through its infiltration of the various parties which made up Allende's *Unidad Popular* (UP) coalition. CIA agents in the upper echelons of Allende's own Socialist Party were "paid to make mistakes in their jobs".[58] In Washington, burglary was the Agency's tactic of choice for obtaining documents. Papers were taken from the homes of several employees of the Chilean Embassy; and the embassy itself, which had been bugged for some time, was burgled in May 1972 by some of the same men who the next month staged the Watergate break-in.[59]

In March 1973, the UP won about 44 percent of the vote in congressional elections, compared to some 36 percent in 1970. It was said to be the largest increase an incumbent party had ever received in Chile after being in power more than two years. The opposition parties had publicly expressed their optimism about capturing two-thirds of the congressional seats and thus being able to impeach Allende. Now they faced three more years under him, with the prospect of being unable, despite their best and most underhanded efforts, to prevent his popularity from increasing even further.

During the spring and summer the destabilization process escalated. There was a whole series of demonstrations and strikes, with an even longer one by the truckers. *Time* magazine reported: "While most of the country survived on short rations, the truckers seemed unusually well equipped for a lengthy holdout." A reporter asked a group of truckers who were camping and dining on "a lavish communal meal of steak, vegetables, wine and empanadas" where the money for it came from. "From the CIA," they answered laughingly.[60]

There was as well daily sabotage and violence, including assassination. In June, an abortive attack upon the Presidential Palace was carried out by the military and *Patria y Libertad*.

In September the military prevailed. "It is clear," said the Senate investigating committee, "the CIA received intelligence reports on the coup planning of the group which carried out the successful September 11 coup throughout the months of July, August, and September 1973."[61]

The American role on that fateful day was one of substance and shadow. The coup began in the Pacific coast port of Valparaiso with the dispatch of Chilean naval troops to Santiago, while US Navy ships were present offshore, ostensibly to participate in joint maneuvers with the Chilean Navy. The American ships stayed outside of Chilean waters, but remained on the alert. A US WB-575 plane—an airborne communications control system—piloted by US Air Force officers, cruised in the Chilean sky. At the same time, 32 American observation and fighter planes were landing at the US air base in Mendoza, Argentina, not far from the Chilean border.[62]

In Valparaiso, while US military officers were meeting with their Chilean counterparts, a young American, Charles Horman, who lived in Santiago and was stranded near Valparaiso by the coup, happened to engage in conversation with several Americans, civilian and military. A retired naval engineer told him: "We came down to do a job and it's done." One or two American military men also gave away clues they shouldn't have. A few days later, Horman was arrested in his Santiago residence. They knew where to find him. He was never seen again.[63]

Thus it was that they closed the country to the outside world for a week, while the tanks rolled and the soldiers broke down doors; the stadiums rang with the sounds of execution and the bodies piled up along the streets and floated in the river; the torture centers opened for business; the subversive books were thrown to the bonfires; soldiers slit the trouser legs of women, shouting that "In Chile women wear dresses!"; the poor returned to their natural state; and the men of the world in Washington and in the halls of international finance opened up their check-books.

One year later, President Gerald Ford was moved to declare that what the United States had done in Chile was "in the best interest of the people in Chile and certainly in our own best interest."[64] The remark could have been punctuated with a pinch of snuff.

What the United States had done in Chile, thought Gerald Ford, or so he said, "was to help and assist the preservation of opposition newspapers and electronic media and to preserve opposition political parties."[65] The reporters present were kind, or obsequious, enough not to ask Ford what he thought of the junta's Chile where all opposition, of any kind, in any form, in any medium, was forbidden.

It was of course *de rigueur* for some other officials and congressmen to assert that what the United States had really done in Chile was repel the Soviet threat to the Western hemisphere. But Soviet behavior toward the Allende government simply did not tally with any such hypothesis; the language of US intelligence reports confirms that: "Soviet overtures to Allende ... characterized by caution and restraint"; "Soviet desire to avoid" another Cuba-type commitment; Russians "advising Allende to put his relations with the United States in order ... to ease the strain between the two countries."[66]

Much has been made of the multinational-corporation angle, particularly the nationalization of the US copper-mining companies without compensation (the *Unidad Popular* calculated that due to "excess profits" over many years the companies actually owed Chile money). But that decision was not announced until September 1971, a full year after the White House had decided to overthrow and/or assassinate Allende. Some indication of Washington's actual interest in the issue may be derived from a comment made in November 1973 by Orlando Saenz, one of the junta's main economic advisers, who declared: "Now the Government of the US considers this is a problem for the American mining companies."[67] And before the coup, the CIA and other US government agencies were "counseling the White House to rebuff Allende's attempts to work out a settlement on the compensations to be paid for nationalized American property."[68]

Moreover, a Washington official who followed Henry Kissinger throughout the Chile policy put it thusly: Kissinger, he said, "never gave a shit about the business community. What really underlay it was ideology."[69]

A CIA study of 7 September 1970, three days after Allende's electoral victory, concluded in part:

The U.S. has no vital national interests within Chile.
The world military balance of power would not be significantly altered by an Allende government.
An Allende victory would represent a definite psychological set-back to the U.S and a definite psychological advantage for the Marxist idea.[70]

Washington knows no heresy in the Third World but independence. In the case of Salvador Allende independence came clothed in an especially provocative costume—a Marxist constitutionally elected who continued to honor the constitution. This would not do. It shook the very foundation stones upon which the anti-communist tower is built: the doctrine, painstakingly cultivated for decades, that "communists" can take power only through force and deception, that they can retain that power only through terrorizing and brainwashing the population. There could be only one thing worse than a Marxist in power—an *elected* Marxist in power.

35. Greece 1964-1974

"Fuck your Parliament and your Constitution," said the President of the United States

"It's the best damn Government since Pericles," the American two-star General declared.[1] (The news report did not mention whether he was chewing on a big fat cigar.)

The government, about which the good General was so ebullient, was that of the Colonels' junta which came to power in a military coup in April 1967, followed immediately by the traditional martial law, censorship, arrests, beatings, torture, and killings, the victims totaling some 8,000 in the first month. This was accompanied by the equally traditional declaration that this was all being done to save the nation from a "communist takeover". Corrupting and subversive influences in Greek life were to be removed. Among these were miniskirts, long hair, and foreign newspapers; church attendance for the young would be compulsory.[2]

So brutal and so swift was the repression, that by September, Denmark, Norway, Sweden and the Netherlands were before the European Commission of Human Rights to accuse Greece of violating most of the Commission's conventions. Before the year was over,

Amnesty International had sent representatives to Greece to investigate the situation. From this came a report which asserted that "Torture as a deliberate practice is carried out by the Security Police and the Military Police."[3]

The coup had taken place two days before the campaign for national elections was to begin, elections which appeared certain to bring the veteran liberal leader George Papandreou back as prime minister. Papandreou had been elected in February 1964 with the only outright majority in the history of modern Greek elections. The successful machinations to unseat him had begun immediately, a joint effort of the Royal Court, the Greek military, and the American military and CIA stationed in Greece.

Philip Deane (the pen name of Gerassimos Gigantes) is a Greek, a former UN official, who worked during this period both for King Constantine and as an envoy to Washington for the Papandreou government. He has written an intimate account of the subtleties and the grossness of this conspiracy to undermine the government and enhance the position of the military plotters, and of the raw power exercised by the CIA in his country.[4] We saw earlier how Greece was looked upon much as a piece of property to be developed according to Washington's needs. A story related by Deane illustrates how this attitude was little changed, and thus the precariousness of Papandreou's position: During one of the perennial disputes between Greece and Turkey over Cyprus, which was now spilling over onto NATO, President Johnson summoned the Greek ambassador to tell him of Washington's "solution". The ambassador protested that it would be unacceptable to the Greek parliament and contrary to the Greek constitution. "Then listen to me, Mr. Ambassador," said the President of the United States, "fuck your Parliament and your Constitution. America is an elephant. Cyprus is a flea. If these two fleas continue itching the elephant, they may just get whacked by the elephant's trunk, whacked good. ... We pay a lot of good American dollars to the Greeks, Mr. Ambassador. If your Prime Minister gives me talk about Democracy, Parliament and Constitutions, he, his Parliament and his Constitution may not last very long."[5]

In July 1965, George Papandreou was finally maneuvered out of office by royal prerogative. The king had a coalition of breakaway Center Union Deputies (Papandreou's party) and rightists waiting in the wings to form a new government. It was later revealed by a State Department official that the CIA Chief-of-Station in Athens, John Maury, had "worked in behalf of the palace in 1965. He helped King Constantine buy Center Union Deputies so that the George Papandreou Government was toppled."[6]

For nearly two years thereafter, various short-lived cabinets ruled until it was no longer possible to avoid holding the elections prescribed by the constitution.

What concerned the opponents of George Papandreou most about him was his son. Andreas Papandreou, who had been head of the economics department at the University of California at Berkeley and a minister in his father's cabinet, was destined for a leading role in the new government. But he was by no means the wide-eyed radical. In the United States, Andreas had been an active supporter of such quintessential moderate liberals as Adlai Stevenson and Hubert Humphrey.[7] His economic views, wrote Washington Post columnist Marquis Childs, were "those of the American New Deal".[8]

But Andreas Papandreou did not disguise his wish to take Greece out of the cold war. He publicly questioned the wisdom of the country remaining in NATO, or at least remaining in it as a satellite of the United States. He leaned toward opening relations with the Soviet Union and other Communist countries on Greece's border. He argued that the swollen American military and intelligence teams in Greece compromised the nation's freedom of action. And he viewed the Greek Army as a threat to democracy, wishing to purge it of its most dictatorial- and royalist-minded senior officers.[9]

Andreas Papandreou's bark was worse than his bite, as his later presidency was to amply demonstrate. (He did not, for example, pull Greece out of NATO or US bases out of Greece.) But in Lyndon Johnson's Washington, if you were not totally and unquestioningly with us, you were agin' us. Johnson felt that Andreas, who had become a naturalized US citizen, had "betrayed America". Said LBJ:

> We gave the son of a bitch American citizenship, didn't we? He was an American, with all the rights and privileges. And he had sworn allegiance to the flag. And then he gave up his American citizenship. He went back to just being a Greek. You can't trust a man who breaks his oath of allegiance to the flag of these United States.[10]

What, then, are we to make of the fact that Andreas Papandreou was later reported to have worked with the CIA in the early 1960s? (He criticized publication of the report, but did not deny the charge.)[11] If true, it would not have been incompatible with being a liberal, particularly at that time. It was incompatible, as he subsequently learned, only with his commitment to a Greece independent from US foreign policy.

As for the elder Papandreou, his anti-communist credentials were impeccable, dating back to his role as a British-installed prime minister during the civil war against the left in 1944-45. But he, too, showed stirrings of independence from the Western superpower. He refused to buckle under Johnson's pressure to compromise with Turkey over Cyprus. He accepted an invitation to visit Moscow, and when his government said that it would accept Soviet aid in preparation for a possible war with Turkey, the US Embassy *demanded* an explanation. Moreover, in an attempt to heal the old wounds of the civil war, Papandreou began to reintroduce certain civil liberties and to readmit into Greece some of those who had fought against the government in the civil war period.[12]

When Andreas Papandreou assumed his ministerial duties in 1964 he was shocked to discover what was becoming a fact of life for every techno-industrial state in the world: an intelligence service gone wild, a shadow government with powers beyond the control of the nation's nominal leaders. This, thought Papandreou, accounted for many of the obstacles the government was encountering in trying to carry out its policies.[13]

The Greek intelligence service, KYP, as we have seen, was created by the OSS/CIA in the course of the civil war, with hundreds of its officers receiving training in the United States. One of these men, George Papadopoulos, was the leader of the junta that seized power in 1967. Andreas Papandreou found that the KYP routinely bugged ministerial conversations and turned the data over to the CIA. (Many Western intelligence agencies have long provided the CIA with information about their own government and citizens, and the CIA has reciprocated on occasion. The nature of much of this information has been such that if a private citizen were to pass it to a foreign power he could be charged with treason.)

As a result of his discovery, the younger Papandreou dismissed the two top KYP men and replaced them with reliable officers. The new director was ordered to protect the cabinet from surveillance. "He came back apologetically," recalls Papandreou, "to say he couldn't do it. All the equipment was American, controlled by the CIA or Greeks under CIA supervision. There was no kind of distinction between the two services. They duplicated functions in a counterpart relationship. In effect, they were a single agency."[14]

Andreas Papandreou's order to abolish the bugging of the cabinet inspired the Deputy Chief of Mission of the US Embassy, Norbert Anshutz (or Anschuetz), to visit him.

Anshutz, who has been linked to the CIA, demanded that Papandreou rescind the order. Andreas demanded that the American leave his office, which he did, but not before warning that "there would be consequences".[15]

Papandreou then requested that a thorough search be made of his home and office for electronic devices by the new KYP deputy director. "It wasn't until much later," says Andreas, "that we discovered he'd simply planted a lot of new bugs. Lo and behold, we'd brought in another American-paid operative as our No. 2."[16]

An endeavor by Andreas to end the practice of KYP's funds coming directly from the CIA without passing through any Greek ministry also met with failure, but he did succeed in transferring the man who had been liaison between the two agencies for several years. This was George Papadopoulos. The change in his position, however, appears to have amounted to little more than a formality, for the organization still took orders from him; even afterwards, Greek "opposition politicians who sought the ear (or the purse) of James Potts, CIA [deputy] chief in Athens before the coup, were often told: 'See George—he's my boy'."[17]

In mid-February 1967, a meeting took place in the White House, reported Marquis Childs, to discuss CIA reports which "left no doubt that a military coup was in the making ... It could hardly have been a secret. Since 1947 the Greek army and the American military aid group in Athens, numbering several hundred, have worked as part of the same team ... The solemn question was whether by some subtle political intervention the coup could be prevented" and thus preserve parliamentary government. It was decided that

> no course of action was feasible. As one of the senior civilians present recalls it, Walt Rostow, the President's adviser on national security affairs, closed the meeting with these words: I hope you understand, gentlemen, that what we have concluded here, or rather have failed to conclude, makes the future course of events in Greece inevitable.[18]

A CIA report dated 23 January 1967 had specifically named the Papadopoulos group as one plotting a coup, and was apparently one of the reports discussed at the February meeting.[19]

Of the cabal of five officers which took power in April, four, reportedly, were intimately connected to the American military or to the CIA in Greece. The fifth man had been brought in because of the armored units he commanded.[20] George Papadopoulos emerged as the *de facto* leader, taking the title of prime minister later in the year.

The catchword amongst old hands at the US military mission in Greece was that Papadopoulos was "the first CIA agent to become Premier of a European country". "Many Greeks consider this to be the simple truth," reported Charles Foley in *The Observer* of London.[21]

At the time of the coup, Papadopoulos had been on the CIA payroll for some 15 years.[22] One reason for the success of their marriage may have been Colonel Papadopoulos's World War II record. When the Germans invaded Greece, Papadopoulos served as a captain in the Nazis' Security Battalions whose main task was to track down Greek resistance fighters.[23] He was, it is said, a great believer in Hitler's "new order", and his later record in power did little to cast doubt upon that claim. Foley writes that when he mentioned the junta leader's pro-German background to an American military adviser he met at a party in Athens, the American hinted that it was related to Papadopoulos's subservience to US wishes: "George gives good value," he smiled, "because there are documents in Washington he wouldn't like let out."[24]

Foley relates that under Papadopoulos:

intense official propaganda portrayed Communism as the only enemy Greece had ever had and minimized the German occupation until even Nazi atrocities were seen as provoked by the Communists. This rewriting of history clearly reflects the dictator's concern at the danger that the gap in his official biography may some day be filled in.[25]

As part of the rewriting, members of the Security Battalions became "heroes of the resistance".[26]

It was torture, however, which most indelibly marked the seven-year Greek nightmare. James Becket, an American attorney sent to Greece by Amnesty International, wrote in December 1969 that "a conservative estimate would place at not less than two thousand" the number of people tortured.[27] It was an odious task for Becket to talk to some of the victims:

> People had been mercilessly tortured simply for being in possession of a leaflet criticizing the regime. Brutality and cruelty on one side, frustration and helplessness on the other. They were being tortured and there was nothing to be done. It was like listening to a friend who has cancer. What comfort, what wise reflection can someone who is comfortable give? Torture might last a short time, but the person will never be the same.[28]

Becket reported that some torturers had told prisoners that some of their equipment had come as US military aid: a special "thick white double cable" whip was one item; another was the headscrew, known as an "iron wreath", which was progressively tightened around the head or ears.[29]

The Amnesty delegation described a number of the other torture methods commonly employed. Among these were:

a) Beating the soles of the feet with a stick or pipe. After four months of this, the soles of one prisoner were covered with thick scar tissue. Another was crippled by broken bones.

b) Numerous incidents of sexually-oriented torture: shoving fingers or an object into the vagina and twisting and tearing brutally; also done with the anus; or a tube is inserted into the anus and water driven in under very high pressure.

c) Techniques of gagging: the throat is grasped in such a way that the windpipe is cut off, or a filthy rag, often soaked in urine, and sometimes excrement, is shoved down the throat.

d) Tearing out the hair from the head and the pubic region.

e) Jumping on the stomach.

f) Pulling out toe nails and finger nails.[30]

These were not the worst. The worst is what one reads in the many individual testimonies. But these are simply too lengthy to be repeated here.[31]

The junta's response to the first Amnesty report was to declare that it was comprised of charges emanating from "International Communism" and to hire public relations firms in New York and London to improve its image.[32]

In 1969, the European Commission of Human Rights found Greece guilty of torture, murder and other violations. For these reasons and particularly for the junta's abolition of parliamentary democracy, The Council of Europe—a consultative body of, at that time, 18 European states, under which the Commission falls—was preparing to expel Greece. The Council rejected categorically Greece's claim that it had been in danger of a communist takeover. Amnesty International later reported that the United States, though not a member of the Council, actively applied diplomatic pressure on member states not to vote for the expulsion. (Nonetheless, while the Council was deliberating, the *New York Times* reported that "The State Department said today that the United States had deliberately avoided taking any position on the question of continued Greek membership in the Council of Europe.") The European members, said Amnesty, believed that only the United States had the power to bring about changes in Greece, yet it chose only to defend the junta.[33]

On the specific issue of torture, Amnesty's report concluded that:

> American policy on the torture question as expressed in official statements and official testimony has been to deny it where possible and minimize it where denial was not possible. This policy flowed naturally from general support for the military regime.[34]

As matters transpired, Greece walked out before the Council could formalize the expulsion.

In a world grown increasingly hostile, the support of the world's most powerful nation was *sine qua non* for the Greek junta. The two governments thrived upon each other. Said the American ambassador to Greece, Henry Tasca, "This is the most anti-communist group you'll find anywhere. There is just no place like Greece to offer these facilities with the back up of the kind of Government you have got here." ("You", not "we", noted the reporter, was the only pretense.)[35]

The facilities the ambassador was referring to were dozens of US military installations, from nuclear missile bases to major communication sites, housing tens of thousands of American servicemen. The United States, in turn, provided the junta with ample military hardware despite an official congressional embargo, as well as the police equipment required by the Greek authorities to maintain their rigid control.

In an attempt to formally end the embargo, the Nixon administration asked Papadopoulos to make some gesture towards constitutional government which the White House could then point to. The Greek prime minister was to be assured, said a secret White House document, that the administration would take "at face value and accept without reservation" any such gesture.[36]

US Vice-president Spiro Agnew, on a visit to the land of his ancestors, was moved to exalt the "achievements" of the Greek government and its "constant co-operation with US needs and wishes".[37] One of the satisfied needs Agnew may have had in mind was the contribution of $549,000 made by the junta to the 1968 Nixon-Agnew election campaign. Apart from any other consideration, it was suspected that this was money given to the junta by the CIA finding its way back to Washington. A Senate investigation of this question was abruptly canceled at the direct request of Henry Kissinger.[38]

Perhaps nothing better captures the mystique of the bond felt by the Greeks to their American guardians than the story related about Chief Inspector Basil Lambrou, one of Athens' well-known torturers:

> Hundreds of prisoners have listened to the little speech given by Inspector Basil Lambrou, who sits behind his desk which displays the red, white, and blue clasped-hand symbol of American aid. He tries to show the prisoner the absolute futility of resistance: "You make yourself ridiculous by thinking you can do anything. The world is divided in two. There are the communists on that side and on this side the free world. The Russians and the Americans, no one else. What are we? Americans. Behind me there is the government, behind the government is NATO, behind NATO is the U.S. You can't fight us, we are Americans."[39]

Amnesty International adds that some torturers would tell their victims things like: "The Human Rights Commission can't help you now ... The Red Cross can do nothing for you ... Tell them all, it will do no good, you are helpless." "The torturers from the start," said

Amnesty, "had said that the United States supported them and that was what counted."[40]

In November 1973, a falling-out within the Greek inner circle culminated in the ousting of Papadopoulos and his replacement by Col. Demetrios Ioannidis, Commander of the Military Police, torturer, graduate of American training in anti-subversive techniques, confidant of the CIA.[41] Ioannidis named as prime minister a Greek-American, A. Androutsopoulos, who came to Greece after the Second World War as an official employee of the CIA, a fact of which Mr. Androutsopoulos had often boasted.[42]

Eight months later, the Ioannidis regime overthrew the government of Cyprus. It was a fatal miscalculation. Turkey invaded Cyprus and the reverberations in Athens resulted in the military giving way to a civilian government. The Greek nightmare had come to an end.

Much of the story of American complicity in the 1967 coup and its aftermath may never be known. At the trials held in 1975 of junta members and torturers, many witnesses made reference to the American role. This may have been the reason a separate investigation of this aspect was scheduled to be undertaken by the Greek Court of Appeals.[43] But it appears that no information resulting from this inquiry, if it actually took place, was ever announced. Philip Deane, upon returning to Greece several months after the civilian government took over, was told by leading politicians that "for the sake of preserving good relations with the US, the evidence of US complicity will not be made fully public".[44]

Andreas Papandreou had been arrested at the time of the coup and held in prison for eight months. Shortly after his release, he and his wife Margaret visited the American ambassador, Phillips Talbot, in Athens. Papandreou related the following:

> I asked Talbot whether America could have intervened the night of the coup, to prevent the death of democracy in Greece. He denied that they could have done anything about it. Then Margaret asked a critical question: What if the coup had been a Communist or a Leftist coup? Talbot answered without hesitation. Then, of course, they would have intervened, and they would have crushed the coup.[45]

36. Bolivia 1964-1975
Tracking down Che Guevara in the land of *coup d'état*

Victor Paz Estenssoro was given a choice when he was overthrown by yet another Bolivian military coup. He could be taken—one of the officers told him—"either to the cemetery, or to the airport". The president opted to fly to Lima and exile.[1]

The man who led the coup in November 1964 and replaced Paz was none other than his vice-president, General René Barrientos Ortuño. It marked something like the 185th change of government (no one seems certain of the precise number) in Bolivia's 139 years of independence from Spanish rule, very few by elections.

Paz was unseated despite support from the American ambassador, Douglas Henderson, for it happened that both the CIA and the Pentagon wanted the president out. Barrientos, the former commander of the air force, had formed a close relationship with both institutions, primarily through the person of Col. Edward Fox, his "flying instructor and drinking companion", dating back to the Bolivian's military-training days in the United States. The year 1964 found Fox in the Bolivian capital of La Paz working with the CIA, though listed officially as a military attaché.[2]

Not surprisingly, Cuba was one of the sore points between the American colonel and the Bolivian president. Paz had directly opposed American policy by voting against Cuba's expulsion from the Organization of American States in 1962, by declining to join in on the OAS sanctions against the Castro government two years later, and by refusing to break diplomatic relations with Havana. It was not until August 1964, when Bolivian-American relations were "just short of an open quarrel",[3] that Paz finally broke with the United States' bête noire. "It was a case of conforming or of facing a severe cut in United States aid", observed a New York Times editorial.[4]

The Bolivian government's attempts to attract economic aid and investment from countries other than the United States, such as the Soviet Union, Czechoslovakia and Yugoslavia, were a further source of friction between the two countries. Here, too, the Bolivians eventually yielded.[5]

Although Fox and Ambassador Henderson were divided—deeply it was said—on the question of Paz remaining in office,[6] both were uneasy about the political and economic power wielded by the tin miners and their leader Juan Lechín, the former vice-president who was an open candidate for Paz's job. The miners controlled their own area of the country; they had their own radio station and their own armed militia; they were intensely opposed to the military; and they were seen as a force potentially more radical than the president. A volatile four-month strike in the mines in mid-1963 which reached crisis proportion could only have served to ring the alarm bells louder in the American Embassy. The Minister of Mines under Paz, René Zavaleta Mercado, later wrote that "For over a year and a half, the American Embassy, in the form of Mr. Henderson, urged with almost weekly regularity that the army be sent to the mining zones, and threatened that otherwise [an American financial program for the mines] would be suspended."[7]

Paz recognized the challenge to his own rule posed by the miners and Lechín, but the likely political damage ensuing from an armed intervention was more than he was willing to risk.

The very existence of an army to send in owed more than a little to American efforts to rebuild the shattered Bolivian armed forces. In 1952 that rarity had occurred—an armed popular revolt had defeated the military, displaced the oligarchy, nationalized the tin mines, instituted land reform, and set up a new government under the Movimiento Nacionalista Revolucionario. The MNR reduced the military to a small, impotent and discredited force, at the same time fostering "people's militias". Decades of coups and other abuses had cut a wide swathe of anti-military sentiment across the Bolivian population. Despite the entreaties of certain segments of the left, however, the traditional armed forces were not completely dismantled. It proved to be a fatal error for the MNR and the country's fledgling democratic institutions.

Primarily to serve as a counterweight to the strength of the militias, and because of American pressure, both Paz and his predecessor had permitted, however reluctantly, the slow but certain rejuvenation of the military. Under US guidance, the Bolivian army became the first in Latin America to launch a "civic action" program, building roads, schools, etc., designed to improve its image amongst the population.

"No country in the Western hemisphere is more dependent on Washington's aid," wrote the New York Times shortly after the coup, "and nowhere has the United States

Embassy played a more obtrusive role in establishing that fact."[8] Washington employed its potent economic leverage to spur a distinctly more favorable government policy towards the military, one which allowed the US to "professionalize" the armed forces. More money followed, more recruits, new equipment ... selected officers were sent to the United States for training ... political indoctrination courses for officers given by MNR adherents and academics were allowed to lapse, and were replaced by indoctrination at the US School of the Americas in the Panama Canal Zone ... by 1964, some 1,200 Bolivian officers and men had received training either in the United States or Panama, including 20 of the 23 senior Army officers ... the military had come a long way towards recouping its former size and efficiency, its prestige and its independence.[9]

The School of the Americas, observed the *Washington Post* in 1968, "counts so many important Latin officers as alumni ... that it is known throughout Latin America as the 'escuela de golpes' or coup school".[10]

Whether the American motivation for reviving the military derived from a desire for an eventual military takeover is impossible to say. At a minimum, it evidenced a basic distrust of the Bolivian revolution with its potential for genuine independence from the United States; and, given the country's history, the culmination of the military process would appear to have been plainly inevitable. The Pentagon has long seen the military of Latin America as its natural partners, the proper "nation builders". This conviction was spelled out by Col. Truman F. Cook of the American military assistance mission in Bolivia in the foreword to a pamphlet on the use of the army in civic action programs. In the pamphlet, published in Bolivia in 1964 and authored by Bolivian Lt. Col. Julio Sanjinés, a confidant of Pentagon and CIA officers, Cook wrote:

> the military organization is perhaps the only institution endowed with the organization, order, discipline, and self-sacrificing attitude towards objectives for the common good ... Should political and economic institutions fail ... then there is a real possibility that the military would move in against graft and corruption in government ... [It is] naive to assume that they might not move to power in a classic sense.[11]

Another unknown is at what point General Barrientos and his co-conspirators actually decided to oust Paz. What is certain is: (1) the general's ascendancy to the office of vice-president was a crucial part of the process; (2) the role played by the CIA and the Pentagon in obtaining that office for Barrientos was *sine qua non*.

At the MNR's convention in January 1964, Paz sidestepped Barrientos, who had made his candidacy known, and chose a civilian, Frederico Fortún, to be his running mate. Barrientos proved to be a bad loser. He declared publicly that the nomination was a mistake and continued politicking, finally compelling the president to ask for his resignation as air force chief. The general was given one week in which to submit it.[12] A few days later, however, a scenario began to unfold which grabbed Barrientos from the edge of the abyss.

On the evening of 25 February, there supposedly took place a shooting attempt on Barrientos's life. Some accounts have the general near death, others "only wounded". In either event, it does appear rather incongruous that he was moved by military vehicle to the airport and then flown in a US Air Force plane to an American hospital in the Panama Canal Zone—2,000 miles away. No Bolivian doctor ever examined Barrientos.[13]

In the days following, while Barrientos was still in the hospital following a "lengthy operation", he was extolled as a national hero by the press in Bolivia. This was particularly the case with *El Diario*, an influential, conservatives and strongly anti-Paz newspaper. According to the later testimony of a member of Barrientos's new cabinet, some of the newspaper's staff worked with the CIA. Moreover, one of *El Diario*'s board members was the aforementioned Lt. Col. Sanjinés. Sanjinés, a graduate of West Point, was an employee of the US Embassy, working on Alliance for Progress programs. After the coup he was appointed minister of economics, later ambassador to Washington.[14]

The press coverage included the story that Barrientos's life was spared only because the bullet had struck the US Air Force silver wings which he wore on his uniform. This became the "silver bullet" affair and great sympathy was generated for the courageous general. On top of this, notes one historian of Bolivia, the commander of the army and the political opposition

> hinted publicly that Paz's police had been responsible for the alleged attack. Strong pressures from other high officers as well were exerted upon Paz to vindicate both himself and Barrientos by belatedly including the general on the ticket, and Paz felt he could not refuse.[15]

Ten days after the mysterious incident, the president dumped Fortún, replaced him with Barrientos, and went on to re-election.

Barrientos himself later conceded that without the "silver bullet" (or "magic bullet", as others dubbed it), he would never have become vice-president.[16] His eight months as candidate and as vice-president in office served, in turn, to tie up all the loose ends required for the military to return from 12 years in the political wilderness and stage their coup with a minimum of opposition; indeed, with a measure of support.

Barrientos's ascendancy furnished a distinct legitimacy to the military, and the general regularly used his platform to champion the armed forces and defend it against the deep-seated anti-militarism. He denounced the militias, called for their dissolution, and took the anomalous step of undermining the government of which he was the vice-president (or to be) by publicly reproaching the president and the MNR—particularly when they were critical of the military—and by throwing his support to anti-government groups. These tactics served to show up the president's weakness and succeeded in rallying to Barrientos's side many of the military officers who had been dubious about the wisdom or safety of re-entering the political arena and unsure of their own political muscle.[17]

It appears that little if anything further was heard of Barrientos's "injury", although during this period he "miraculously" escaped several other reported assassination attempts, including a bomb which blew up his car when no one was in it and another bomb which somehow found its way to under his bed. He used the latter occasion to declare that he "had more enemies within the MNR than in the ranks of the opposition".[18]

Paz Estenssoro had been "re-elected" because the opposition—claiming, amongst other things, unfair electoral procedure—had decided to abstain. Without pausing for breath, the masochistic, tangled mess that is Bolivian politics continued at his throat. Widespread discontent, arising from long-standing grievances and fueled by a conflux of personal ambitions, erupted in a series of strikes, demonstrations and violent confrontations, with Barrientos lending his weight to the dissident elements, attacking the beleaguered president, and taking upon himself the role of the defender of order. In October, the vice-president withdrew to his home town and declared himself a rebel.

This period of public chaos and government crisis may have hastened the timing of the coup, at the same time convincing some still-reluctant officers who were disgusted by the constant civilian warfare. When the military finally made its move against Paz at the beginning of November it was not unwelcomed by various segments of the population.

Three years later, the *Washington Post*'s veteran Latin America correspondent, John

Goshko, reported that Paz "still insists that Fox was behind his ouster. Among Bolivians with an awareness of politics, it is hard to find anyone who disagrees."[19]

René Barrientos pressed an unrelenting hard line against the tin miners. He inflicted upon them an extraordinary 50 percent cut in salary. Miners' boss Juan Lechín and other union and MNR leaders were ordered into exile and a principal labor confederation was banned. All Bolivian unions were directed to reorganize under guidelines designed to produce an apolitical labor movement.

Then the army moved in. Repeated invasions and occupations of the mining camps over a period of time were needed to pacify the ultra-militant miners. The fighting was bloody, 70 miners losing their lives in one raid alone—*La Noche de San Juan* as it came to be known.[20] The Revolution of 1952 had come to an end.

The United States was not a disinterested observer. In February 1966, Secretary of Defense Robert McNamara, presenting his department's regular "Assessment of the International Situation", told a congressional committee: "Violence in the mining areas and in the cities of Bolivia has continued to occur intermittently, and we are assisting this country to improve the training and equipping of its military forces."[21]

This was all that the Defense Secretary had to report about Bolivia—a routine report, routinely written by some faceless Pentagon researcher, routinely delivered by the quintessential technocrat, as if the American action was the most natural and innocuous thing in the world.

As natural as American financial contributions to Barrientos. Antonio Arguedas, Minister of the Interior under Barrientos, later disclosed that the CIA contributed $600,000 to the Bolivian leader in 1966 when he decided to hold an election. Several right-wing parties received lesser sums. Arguedas, an admitted agent of the CIA who, in 1968, gave the world Che Guevara's diary, claiming that the Agency had pushed him too hard, also revealed that Gulf Oil Corp. donated $200,000 to Barrientos's campaign as well as a helicopter for his tours around the provinces. Gulf subsequently admitted that it had paid Bolivian officials, mainly Barrientos, a total of $460,000 in "political contributions" during the period 1966-69 at the CIA's recommendation, although the company may have needed but little prodding, for the Bolivian president had opened up the economy to multinationals to a greater degree than his predecessors, bestowing upon Gulf especially generous concessions.[22]

In the two years following the disappearance of Che Guevara from public view in early 1965, rumours had placed him at different times in the Dominican Republic, Brazil, Venezuela, Colombia, Peru, Chile, Guatemala, the Congo (which was true), China, Vietnam, and even New York, "always plotting revolution with some menacing and inscrutable bunch of desperados".[23] Word also had it that he had gone mad and was confined to an asylum somewhere, or that he had been imprisoned or executed by his erstwhile comrade-in-arms Fidel Castro for challenging Castro's authority. These latter stories or others like them may well have been CIA handiwork. The Agency, ever inventive, had begun generating unfavorable press speculation about Guevara's disappearance as early as autumn 1965 in the hope that he would reappear in order to put an end to the tales.[24]

When evidence began to drift back to CIA headquarters in early 1967 that Che was leading a band of guerrillas in the southern mountains of Bolivia, there was understandable skepticism amongst some Agency officials. Nevertheless, obsessed as the CIA was with tracking down the legendary guerrilla, a multi-phased operation was put into motion. In

April, American military supplies suitable for combatting guerrilla forces began to arrive in Bolivia: light arms, communication equipment, helicopters, etc. At the end of the month, a unit of 16 Green Berets was dispatched from Fort Gulick in the Panama Canal Zone to Bolivia to provide on-the-spot training in counter-insurgency tactics to a hand-picked battalion of Bolivian Rangers who had little or no experience in the real thing. The Green Berets had at their disposal a team of experts in communications, intelligence and reconnaissance work, and, before long, aerial photographs taken of approximately 23,500 square miles of southern Bolivia. This undertaking made use of an infra-red detection system, sensitive to thermal radiation rather than visible light, and as such could be employed at night and on cloudy days. The infra-red cameras were able to discriminate targets having less than one degree temperature difference with their background, thus picking up campfires, vehicles, even people. Or so the technocrats would have one believe. In any event, the guerrillas rarely built fires or used vehicles.[25]

In La Paz, the CIA station informed Interior Minister Arguedas that it was sending him several "advisors" whose presence was required, it was stated, because of the ineffectiveness of Bolivia's intelligence services. A few days later, according to Arguedas, four Cuban exiles arrived and assumed their "advisory" positions in his ministry. One of them proceeded to set up two houses of interrogation where Bolivians suspected of aiding the guerrillas were brought for questioning. When Arguedas learned of this, and that in some cases the Cubans were resorting to torture, he was furious and demanded that the CIA put a stop to the operation.[26]

Other Cuban CIA agents were attached to the military high command and sent to the area of guerrilla fighting to collect detailed information from prisoners and peasants. This kind of investigation probably contributed more to locating the elusive Guevara than did the CIA's assortment of technological marvels, although the ultimate value of the Agency's role cannot be stated with any precision. What is clear, however, is that it was a case of overkill. Che's guerrilla movement never amounted to much of a threat. Barely more than 50 men and one woman at its peak, reduced to less than half that number at the end, the rebels could show to their credit only a scattering of skirmishes with the army. They had been largely ignored by the left in Bolivia and hardly "swam like fish in the peasants' sea".

"The inhabitants of this region," wrote Che in his diary, "are as impenetrable as rocks. You speak to them, but in the deepness of their eyes you can see that they do not believe you." As in the Congo, this man who made social revolution his life had failed to win over the peasantry. "You can waken men," said Alexander Hertzen a century ago in Russia, "only by dreaming their dreams more clearly than they can dream them themselves."

On 8 October 1967, Che Guevara was captured. The next day the Bolivian government ordered his execution in cold blood to prevent him from becoming the object of a worldwide clemency campaign, and despite the vociferous objections of CIA men in the country who clung to the hope that Guevara would eventually talk openly about his sundry guerrilla adventures.

Following the death of René Barrientos in April 1969 (crashing in Gulf's helicopter), Bolivia's statesmen soon reverted to their normal Byzantine convolutions. For a start, the vice-president who succeeded Barrientos lasted but five months before being ousted by General Alfredo Ovando Candia.

Ovando's long-held nationalist sentiments came to the fore. In his first month, he nationalized the Gulf Oil Corporation. The prevailing attitude toward the multinational, said Bolivian leaders, was that Gulf "constituted itself as a shadow government of vast powers over a poor land".[27]

The nationalization left Bolivia open, as the *New York Times* expressed it in December, to "the wrath of the United States".

> Since the seizure, the United States, which has been the mainstay of Bolivia's economy for years, has indicated that further aid will not be forthcoming ... Washington has not been impressed by Bolivia's offer to compensate Gulf for the property, which is valued at $140 million, about 50 per cent more than Bolivia's annual budget ... Two Bolivian cabinet ministers interviewed this week said privately that the United States and Argentina were aware, as were most educated people in this capital, that well financed groups were plotting to overthrow the new Bolivian regime.[28]

This was followed by a dispatch from La Paz of Interpress Service (a major Latin American news agency) reporting that the United States was planning to bring down the Ovando government through economic strangulation.[29] Then, two days later, the government alerted the public about a conspiracy "that was being organized by the CIA in close collaboration with Gulf Oil and some Bolivian rightists."[30]

What fire all this smoke pointed to is not known. Ovando, who had walked the corridors of the Bolivian power structure for many years (it was he who had presented Paz with the choice of cemetery or airport), was no stranger to CIA intrigue in his country, and he may have seen the bright spotlight of publicity as the only means of forestalling his overthrow. This would also explain why, in January 1970, the government made it a point to announce the ordinary: that it had uncovered a CIA office in La Paz with radio transmission and bugging equipment.[31] The same month, Ovando also advocated a rapprochement with Cuba, and it looked like he and the CIA were on a collision course.

But then ... it seems ... someone got to Ovando with an offer he couldn't refuse. Slowly but surely, the president drifted to the right; amongst other indications: several anti-US student demonstrations were firmly put down by the police, nothing more was heard about Cuba, and Ovando removed General Juan José Torres as commander of the armed forces, a man highly regarded by most of the Bolivian left.[32] By September, matters had progressed to the point that State Department officials were publicly expressing concern that a deepening split between the Ovando government and its former leftist allies was on the brink of open showdown and might result in a "communist" government.[33]

By whatever label, there was indeed fresh political conflict in Bolivia. Two weeks later, the power struggle erupted into a military revolt.

General Ovando was out. General Torres was in. Ovando had lasted one year.

Juan José Torres's ten months in office produced the archetypical Latin American political drama. In the opening act, Torres did all the things which make Washington officials see Red: He made overtures of friendship to Allende's Chile and Castro's Cuba; increased commercial ties with the Soviet Union; nationalized tin mines owned by American interests (leading the US to threaten to release large amounts of its tin stockpile onto the world market to deflate the international price); expelled the Peace Corps; and closed down the Inter-American Regional Labor Organization (ORIT, an important vehicle for CIA labor operations in Latin America); on top of all this, Torres indulged at times in Marxist rhetoric, talking of workers' and peasants' power and the like.[34]

Act Two brought on stage one Hugo Banzer, a Bolivian colonel with long and close ties to the American military establishment. He too had attended the *escuela de golpes* in Panama. Later there was further military training at Fort Hood in Texas; eventually, a posting to Washington as Bolivian military attaché. Along the way he picked up the Order of Military Merit from the United States government. Banzer was also reported to be one of the beneficiaries of Gulf Oil's largesse when he served in Barrientos's cabinet.

In January 1971, Col. Banzer led a coup attempt which came to nothing except his own exile to Argentina. The CIA in La Paz had known of Banzer's plan at least two weeks earlier, and had advised Washington of it.[35] Over the next six months, as Banzer and his military cohorts diligently plotted their next attempt to oust Torres, Banzer regularly crossed over the Argentine border into Bolivia where he was in close contact with US Major Robert Lundin, an adviser to the Bolivian Air Force School in Santa Cruz.[36]

Act Three, or the coup that succeeded, took place in August, a few days after Torres had announced an agreement with the Soviet Union for a major development of the Bolivian iron industry,[37]a few days before he was to meet with Salvador Allende to re-establish diplomatic relations with Chile.

When the plotters were in military control of Santa Cruz, a breakdown in their radio communications network caused a delay in rallying other Bolivian military units to their side. At this moment, Major Lundin stepped in to fill the breach by placing the US Air Force radio system at the rebels' disposal.[38]

How important this aid was to the success of the coup, which turned out to be very bloody, or what Lundin's role was otherwise, has not been determined.

One week later, the *San Francisco Chronicle* reported: "Although it has been officially denied, CIA money, training and advice was liberally given to the rebel strategists who masterminded [the] overthrow of Bolivia's leftist President Juan José Torres."[39]

In the finale, we find that the military-political coalition that took power was so far to the right that one of its member parties called itself by the customary fascist designation "Falange", and that Banzer immediately announced that: his government would maintain very close relations with the United States, efforts to restore ties with Cuba and Chile would be abandoned, the trend toward nationalizations would halt, some already-completed nationalizations would be rescinded, the government would welcome private foreign investment, and all schools would be closed for at least four months because they were hotbeds of "political subversive agitation provoked by anarchists opposed to the new institutional order".[40] Before long, the government ordered the entire Soviet Embassy to leave the country, and Banzer eventually raised a foreign loan to pay Gulf Oil greatly increased compensation.

At the same time, the time-honored scene known popularly as "reign of terror" was performed: Within the first two years of the new regime, more than 2,000 persons were arrested for political reasons without being brought to trial, "all the fundamental laws protecting human rights were regularly violated", torture was "commonly used on prisoners during interrogation ... beaten, raped and forced to undergo simulated executions ... hung for hours with their hands tied behind their backs".[41]

By 1975, Catholic religious groups and clergy had taken upon themselves the dangerous burden of speaking out in defense of human rights in Bolivia. The Banzer government responded with a calculated and methodical campaign to divide the church, to isolate its progressive members, harass and censor them, and smear them as communists. Foreign priests and nuns, who made up the bulk of the country's clergy, were especially vulnerable to arrest and deportation. One of them, an American missionary from Iowa, Father Raymond Herman, was found murdered.

The CIA, it has been reported, assisted the Bolivian government in this endeavor by "providing full information on certain priests—personal data, studies, friends, addresses, writings, contacts abroad, etc." The Agency, with its international data network, was particularly valuable concerning the foreign clergy.[42]

"I will observe the constitution," said Banzer, "whenever it does not contradict military decrees."[43]

"Since the formulation of the current Bolivian Government in August 1971," stated a report of the US Comptroller General's Office in 1975, "the objective of U.S. military assistance has been to provide stability and security. To assist in the objective, the United States provides materiel and training to develop adequate counter-insurgent forces."[44]

In 1978, Hugo Banzer was overthrown in yet another Bolivian coup. The new Bolivian strongman, former Air Force General Juan Pereda Asbun, announced, as Banzer had announced, that he was saving the nation from "international communism".[45]

37. Guatemala 1962 to 1980s
A less publicized "final solution"

Indians tell harrowing stories of village raids in which their homes have been burned, men tortured hideously and killed, women raped, and scarce crops destroyed. It is Guatemala's final solution to insurgency: only mass slaughter of the Indians will prevent them joining a mass uprising.[1]

This newspaper item appeared in 1983. Very similar stories have appeared many times in the world press since 1966, for Guatemala's "final solution" has been going on rather longer than the more publicized one of the Nazis.

It would be difficult to exaggerate the misery of the mainly-Indian peasants and urban poor of Guatemala who make up three-quarters of the population of this beautiful land so favored by American tourists. The particulars of their existence derived from the literature of this period sketch a caricature of human life. In a climate where everything grows, very few escape the daily ache of hunger or the progressive malnutrition ... almost half the children die before the age of five ... the leading cause of death in the country is gastro-enteritis. Highly toxic pesticides sprayed indiscriminately by airplanes, at times directly onto the heads of peasants, leave a trail of poisoning and death ... public health services in rural areas are virtually non-existent ... the same for public education ... near-total illiteracy. A few hundred families possess almost all the arable land ... thousands of families without land, without work, jammed together in communities of cardboard and tin houses, with no running water or electricity, a sea of mud during the rainy season, sharing their bathing and toilet with the animal kingdom. Men on coffee plantations earning 20 cents or 50 cents a day, living in circumstances closely resembling concentration camps ... looked upon by other Guatemalans more as beasts of burden than humans. A large plantation to sell, reads the advertisement, "with 200 hectares and 300 Indians" ... this, then was what remained of the ancient Mayas, whom the American archeologist Sylvanus Morely had called the most splendid indigenous people on the planet.[2]

The worst was yet to come.

We have seen how, in 1954, Guatemala's last reform government, the legally-elected regime of Jacobo Arbenz, was overthrown by the United States. And how, in 1960, nationalist elements of the Guatemalan military who were committed to slightly opening the door to change were summarily crushed by the CIA. Before long, the ever-accumulating discontent again issued forth in a desperate lunge for alleviation—this time in the form of a guerrilla movement—only to be thrown back by a Guatemalan-American operation reminiscent of the Spanish *conquistadores* in its barbarity.

In the early years of the 1960s, the guerilla movement, with several military officers of the abortive 1960 uprising prominent amongst the leadership, was slowly finding its way: organizing peasant support in the countryside, attacking an army outpost to gather arms, staging a kidnapping or bank robbery to raise money, trying to avoid direct armed clashes with the Guatemalan military.

Recruitment amongst the peasants was painfully slow and difficult; people so drained by the daily struggle to remain alive have little left from which to draw courage; people so downtrodden scarcely believe they have the right to resist, much less can they entertain thoughts of success; as fervent Catholics, they tend to believe that their misery is a punishment from God for sinning.

Some of the guerrilla leaders flirted with Communist Party and Trotskyist ideas and groups, falling prey to the usual factional splits and arguments. Eventually, no ideology or sentiment dominated the movement more than a commitment to the desperately needed program of land reform aborted by the 1954 coup, a simple desire for a more equitable society, and nationalist pride vis-à-vis the United States. *New York Times*, correspondent Alan Howard, after interviewing guerrilla leader Luis Turcios, wrote:

> Though he has suddenly found himself in a position of political leadership, Turcios is essentially a soldier fighting for a new code of honor. If he has an alter ego, it would not be Lenin or Mao or even Castro, whose works he has read and admires, but Augusto Sandino, the Nicaraguan general who fought the U.S. Marines sent to Nicaragua during the Coolidge and Hoover Administrations.[3]

In March 1962, thousands of demonstrators took to the streets in protest against the economic policies, the deep-rooted corruption, and the electoral fraud of the government of General Miguel Ydigoras Fuentes. Initiated by students, the demonstrations soon picked up support from worker and peasant groups. Police and military forces eventually broke the back of the protests, but not before a series of violent confrontations and a general strike had taken place.

The American military mission in Guatemala, permanently stationed there, saw and heard in this, as in the burgeoning guerrilla movement, only the omnipresent "communist threat". As US military equipment flowed in, American advisers began to prod a less-alarmed and less-than-aggressive Guatemalan army to take appropriate measures. In May the United States established a base designed specifically for counter-insurgency training. (The Pentagon prefers the term "counter-insurgency" to "counter-revolutionary" because of the latter's awkward implications.) Set up in the northeast province of Izabal, which, together with adjacent Zacapa province, constituted the area of heaviest guerrilla support, the installation was directed by a team of US Special Forces (Green Berets) of Puerto Rican and Mexican descent to make the North American presence less conspicuous. The staff of the base was augmented by 15 Guatemalan officers trained in counter-insurgency at the US School of the Americas at Fort Gulick in the Panama Canal Zone.[4]

American counter-insurgency strategy is typically based on a carrot-and-stick philosophy. Accordingly, while the Guatemalan military were being taught techniques of ambush, booby-traps, jungle survival and search-and-destroy warfare, and provided with aircraft and pilot training, a program of "civil action" was begun in the northeast area: some wells were built, medicines distributed, school lunches provided etc., as well as promises of other benefits made, all aimed at stealing a bit of the guerrillas' thunder and reducing the peasants' motivation for furnishing support to them; and with the added bonus of allowing American personnel to reconnoitre guerrilla territory under a non-military cover. Land reform, overwhelmingly the most pressing need in rural Guatemala, was not on the agenda.

As matters were to materialize, the attempt at "winning the hearts and minds" of the peasants proved to be as futile in Guatemala as it was in southeast Asia. When all the academic papers on "social systems engineering" were in, and all the counter-insurgency studies of the RAND Corporation and the other think-tanks were said and done, the recourse was to terror: unadulterated, dependable terror. Guerrillas, peasants, students, labor leaders, and professional people were jailed or killed by the hundreds to put a halt, albeit temporarily, to the demands for reform.[5]

The worst was yet to come.

In March 1963, General Ydigoras, who had been elected in 1958 for a six-year term, was overthrown in a coup by Col. Enrique Peralta Azurdia. Veteran Latin American correspondent Georgie Anne Geyer later reported that "Top sources within the Kennedy administration have revealed the U.S. instigated and supported the 1963 coup." Already in disfavor with Washington due to several incidents, Ydigoras apparently sealed his fate by allowing the return to Guatemala of Juan José Arévalo who had led a reform government before Arbenz and still had a strong following. Ydigoras was planning to step down in 1964, thus leaving the door open to an election and, like the Guatemalan army, Washington, including President Kennedy personally, believed that a free election would reinstate Arévalo to power in a government bent upon the same kind of reforms and independent foreign policy that had led the United States to overthrow Arbenz.[6] Arévalo was the author of a book called *The Shark and the Sardines* in which he pictured the US as trying to dominate Latin America. But he had also publicly denounced Castro as "a danger to the continent, a menace".[7]

The tone of the Peralta administration was characterized by one of its first acts: the murder of eight political and trade union leaders, accomplished by driving over them with rock-laden trucks.[8] Repressive and brutal as Peralta was, during his three years in power US military advisers felt that the government and the Guatemalan army still did not appreciate sufficiently the threat posed by the guerrillas, still were strangers to the world of unconventional warfare and the systematic methods needed to wipe out the guerrillas once and for all; despite American urging, the army rarely made forays into the hills.

Peralta, moreover, turned out to be somewhat of a nationalist who resented the excessive influence of the United States in Guatemala, particularly in his own sphere, the military. He refused insistent American offers of Green Beret troops trained in guerrilla warfare to fight the rebels, preferring to rely on his own men, and he restricted the number of Guatemalan officers permitted to participate in American training programs abroad.

Thus it was that the United States gave its clear and firm backing to a civilian, one Julio Cesar Mendez Montenegro, in the election held in March 1966. Mendez won what passes for an election in Guatemala and granted the Americans the free hand they had been chafing at the bit for. He served another important function for the United States: as a civilian, and one with genuine liberal credentials, Mendez could be pointed to by the Johnson administration as a response to human rights critics at home,

However, whatever social conscience Julio Cesar Mendez may have harbored deep within, he was largely a captive of the Guatemalan army, and his administration far exceeded Peralta's in its cruelty. Yet the army did not trust this former law school professor—in the rarefied

231

atmosphere of Guatemala, some military men regarded him as a communist—and on at least two occasions, the United States had to intervene to stifle a coup attempt against him.

Within days after Mendez took office in July, US Col. John D. Webber, Jr. arrived in Guatemala to take command of the American military mission. *Time* magazine later described his role:

> Webber immediately expanded counterinsurgency training within Guatemala's 5,000-man army, brought in U.S. Jeeps, trucks, communications equipment and helicopters to give the army more firepower and mobility, and breathed new life into the army's civic-action program. Towards the end of 1966 the army was able to launch a major drive against the guerrilla strongholds ... To aid in the drive, the army also hired and armed local bands of "civilian collaborators" licensed to kill peasants whom they considered guerrillas or "potential" guerrillas. There were those who doubted the wisdom of encouraging such measures in violence-prone Guatemala, but Webber was not among them. "That's the way this country is," he said. "The communists are using everything they have including terror. And it must be met."[9]

The last was for home consumption. There was never any comparison between the two sides as to the quantity and cruelty of their terror, as well as in the choice of targets; with rare exceptions, the left attacked only legitimate political and military enemies, clear and culpable symbols of their foe; and they did not torture, nor take vengeance against the families of their enemies.

Two of the left's victims were John Webber himself and the US naval attaché, assassinated in January 1968. A bulletin later issued by a guerrilla group stated that the assassinations had "brought to justice the Yanqui officers who were teaching tactics to the Guatemalan army for its war against the people".[10]

In the period October 1966 to March 1968, Amnesty International estimated, somewhere between 3,000 and 8,000 Guatemalans were killed by the police, the military, right-wing "death squads" (often the police or military in civilian clothes, carrying out atrocities too bloody for the government to claim credit for), and assorted groups of civilian anti-communist vigilantes. By 1972, the number of their victims was estimated at 13,000. Four years later the count exceeded 20,000, murdered or disappeared without a trace.

Anyone attempting to organize a union or other undertaking to improve the lot of the peasants, or simply suspected of being in support of the guerrillas, was subject ... unknown armed men broke into their homes and dragged them away to unknown places ... their tortured or mutilated or burned bodies found buried in a mass grave, or floating in plastic bags in a lake or river, or lying beside the road, hands tied behind the back ... bodies dropped into the Pacific from airplanes. In the Gualán area, it was said, no one fished any more; too many corpses were caught in the nets ... decapitated corpses, or castrated, or pins stuck in the eyes ... a village rounded up, suspected of supplying the guerrillas with men or food or information, all adult males taken away in front of their families, never to be seen again ... or everyone massacred, the village bulldozed over to cover the traces ... seldom were the victims actual members of a guerrilla band.

One method of torture consisted of putting a hood filled with insecticide over the head of the victim; there was also electric shock—to the genital area is the most effective; in those days it was administered by using military field telephones hooked up to small generators; the United States supplied the equipment and the instructions for use to several countries, including South Vietnam where the large-scale counter-insurgency operation was producing new methods and devices for extracting information from uncooperative prisoners; some of these techniques were finding their way to Latin America.[11]

The Green Berets taught their Guatemalan trainees various methods of "interrogation", but they were not solely classroom warriors. Their presence in the countryside was reported frequently, accompanying Guatemalan soldiers into battle areas; the line separating the advisory role from the combat role is often a matter of public relations.

Thomas and Marjorie Melville, American Catholic missionaries in Guatemala from the mid-1950s until the end of 1967, have written that Col. Webber "made no secret of the fact that it was his idea and at his instigation that the technique of counter-terror had been implemented by the Guatemalan Army in the Zacapa and Izabal areas."[12] The Melvilles wrote also of Major Bernard Westfall of Iowa City who:

> perished in September 1967 in the crash of a Guatemalan Air Force jet that he was piloting alone. The official notices stated that the US airman was "testing" the aeroplane. That statement may have been true, but it is also true that it was a common and public topic of conversation at Guatemala's La Aurora air base that the Major often "tested" Guatemalan aircraft in strafing and bombing runs against guerrilla encampments in the Northeastern territory.[13]

F-51(D) fighter planes modified by the United States for use against guerrillas in Guatemala ... after modification, the planes are capable of patrolling for five hours over a limited area ... equipped with six .50-calibre machine guns and wing mountings for bombs, napalm and 5-inch air-to-ground rockets.[14] The napalm falls on villages, on precious crops, on people ... American pilots take off from Panama, deliver loads of napalm on targets suspected of being guerrilla refuges, and return to Panama[15] ... the napalm explodes like fireworks and a mass of brilliant red foam spreads over the land, incinerating all that falls in its way, cedars and pines are burned down to the roots, animals grilled, the earth scorched ... the guerrillas will not have this place for a sanctuary any longer, nor will they or anyone else derive food from it ... halfway around the world in Vietnam, there is an instant replay.

In Vietnam they were called "free-fire zones"; in Guatemala, "*zonas libres*": "Large areas of the country have been declared off limits and then subjected to heavy bombing. Reconnaissance planes using advanced photographic techniques fly over suspected guerrilla country and jet planes, assigned to specific areas, can be called in within minutes to kill anything that moves on the ground."[16]

"The military guys who do this are like serial killers. If Jeffrey Dahmer had been in Guatemala, he would be a general by now." ... In Guatemala City, right-wing terrorists machine-gunned people and houses in full light of day ... journalists, lawyers, students, teachers, trade unionists, members of opposition parties, anyone who helped or expressed sympathy for the rebel cause, anyone with a vaguely leftist political association or a moderate criticism of government policy ... relatives of the victims, guilty of kinship ... common criminals, eliminated to purify the society, taken from jails and shot. "See a Communist, kill a Communist", the slogan of the New Anticommunist Organization ... an informer with hooded face accompanies the police along a city street or into the countryside, pointing people out: who shall live and who shall die ... "this one's a son of a bitch" ... "that one ... " Men found dead with their eyes gouged out, their testicles in their mouth, without hands or tongues, women with breasts cut off ... there is rarely a witness to a killing, even when people are dragged from their homes at high noon and executed in the street ... a relative will choose exile rather than take the matter to the authorities ... the government joins the family in mourning the victim ... [17]

One of the death squads, *Mano Blanca* (White Hand), sent a death warning to a student leader. Former American Maryknoll priest Blase Bonpane has written:

I went alone to visit the head of the Mano Blanca and asked him why he was going to kill this lad. At first he denied sending the letter, but after a bit of discussion with him and his first assistant, the assistant said, "Well, I know he's a Communist and so we're going to kill him."

"How do you know?" I asked.

He said, "I know he's a Communist because I heard him say he would give his life for the poor."[18]

Mano Blanca distributed leaflets in residential areas suggesting that doors of left-wingers be marked with a black cross.[19]

In November 1967, when the American ambassador, John Gordon Mein, presented the Guatemalan armed forces with new armored vehicles, grenade launchers, training and radio equipment, and several HU-1B jet powered helicopters, he publicly stated:

> These articles, especially the helicopters, are not easy to obtain at this time since they are being utilized by our forces in defense of the cause of liberty in other parts of the world [i.e., southeast Asia]. But liberty must be defended wherever it is threatened and that liberty is now being threatened in Guatemala.[20]

In August 1968, a young French woman, Michele Kirk, shot herself in Guatemala City as the police came to her room to make "inquiries". In her notebook Michele had written:

> It is hard to find the words to express the state of putrefaction that exists in Guatemala, and the permanent terror in which the inhabitants live. Every day bodies are pulled out of the Motagua River, riddled with bullets and partially eaten by fish. Every day men are kidnapped right in the street by unidentified people in cars, armed to the teeth, with no intervention by the police patrols.[21]

The US Agency for International Development (AID), its Office of Public Safety (OPS), and the Alliance for Progress were all there to lend a helping hand. These organizations with their reassuring names all contributed to a program to greatly expand the size of Guatemala's national police force and develop it into a professionalized body skilled at counteracting urban disorder. Senior police officers and technicians were sent for training at the Inter-American Police Academy in Panama, replaced in 1964 by the International Police Academy in Washington, at a Federal School in Los Fresnos, Texas (where they were taught how to construct and use a variety of explosive devices—see Uruguay chapter), and other educational establishments, their instructors often being CIA officers operating under OPS cover. This was also the case with OPS officers stationed in Guatemala to advise local police commands and provide in-country training for rank-and-file policemen. At times, these American officers participated directly in interrogating political prisoners, took part in polygraph operations, and accompanied the police on anti-drug patrols.

Additionally, the Guatemala City police force was completely supplied with radio patrol cars and a radio communications network, and funds were provided to build a national police academy and pay for salaries, uniforms, weapons, and riot-control equipment.

The glue which held this package together was the standard OPS classroom tutelage, similar to that given the military, which imparted the insight that "communists", primarily of the Cuban variety, were behind all the unrest in Guatemala; the students were further advised to "stay out of politics", that is, support whatever pro-US regime happens to be in power.

Also standard was the advice to use "minimum force" and to cultivate good community relations. But the behavior of the police and military students in practice was so far removed from this that continued American involvement with these forces over a period of decades makes this advice appear to be little more than a self-serving statement for the record, the familiar bureaucratic maxim: Cover your ass.[22]

According to AID, by 1970, over 30,000 Guatemalan police personnel had received OPS training in Guatemala alone, one of the largest OPS programs in Latin America.[23]

"At one time, many AID field offices were infiltrated from top to bottom with CIA people," disclosed John Gilligan, Director of AID during the Carter administration. "The idea was to plant operatives in every kind of activity we had overseas, government, volunteer, religious, every kind."[24]

By the end of 1968, the counter-insurgency campaign had all but wiped out the guerrilla movement by thwarting the rebels' ability to operate openly and casually in rural areas as they had been accustomed to, and, through sheer terrorization of villagers, isolating the guerrillas from their bases of support in the countryside.

It had been an unequal match. By Pentagon standards it had been a "limited" war, due to the absence of a large and overt US combat force. At the same time, this had provided the American media and public with the illusion of their country's non-involvement. However, as one observer has noted: "In the lexicon of counterrevolutionaries, these wars are 'limited' only in their consequences for the intervening power. For the people and country under assault, they are total."[25]

Not until 1976 did another serious guerrilla movement arise, the Guatemalan Army of the Poor (EGP) by name. Meanwhile, others vented their frustration through urban warfare in the face of government violence, which reached a new high during 1970 and 1971 under a "state of siege" imposed by the president, Col. Carlos Arana Osorio. Arana, who had been close to the US military since serving as Guatemalan military attaché in Washington, and then as commander of the counter-insurgency operation in Zacapa (where his commitment to his work earned him the title of "the butcher of Zacapa"), decreed to himself virtually unlimited power to curb opposition of any stripe.[26]

Amnesty International later stated that Guatemalan sources, including the Committee of the Relatives of Disappeared Persons, claimed that over 7,000 persons disappeared or were found dead in these two years. "Foreign diplomats in Guatemala City," reported *Le Monde* in 1971, "believe that for every political assassination by left-wing revolutionaries fifteen murders are committed by right-wing fanatics."[27]

During a curfew so draconian that even ambulances, doctors and fire engines reportedly were forbidden outside ... as American police cars and paddy wagons patrolled the streets day and night ... and American helicopters buzzed overhead ... the United States saw fit to provide further technical assistance and equipment to initiate a reorganization of Arana's police forces to make them yet more efficient.[28]

"In response to a question [from a congressional investigator in 1971] as to what he conceived his job to be, a member of the US Military Group (MILGP) in Guatemala replied instantly that it was to make the Guatemalan Armed Forces as efficient as possible. The next question as to why this was in the interest of the United States was followed by a long silence while he reflected on a point which had apparently never occurred to him."[29]

As for the wretched of Guatemala's earth ... in 1976 a major earthquake shook the land, taking over 20,000 lives, largely of the poor whose houses were the first to crumble ... the story was reported of the American church relief worker who arrived to help the victims; he was shocked at their appearance and their living conditions; then he was informed that he was not in the earthquake area, that what he was seeing was normal.[30]

"The level of pesticide spraying is the highest in the world," reported the *New York Times* in 1977, "and little concern is shown for the people who live near the cotton fields" ... 30 or 40 people a day are treated for pesticide poisoning in season, death can come within hours, or a longer lasting liver malfunction ... the amounts of DDT in mothers' milk in Guatemala are the highest in the Western world. "It's very simple," explained a cotton planter, "more insecticide means more cotton, fewer insects mean higher profits." In an attack, guerrillas destroyed 22 crop-duster planes; the planes were quickly replaced thanks to the genius of American industry[31] ... and all the pesticide you could ever want, from Monsanto Chemical Company of St. Louis and Guatemala City.

During the Carter presidency, in response to human-rights abuses in Guatemala and other countries, several pieces of congressional legislation were passed which attempted to curtail military and economic aid to those nations. In the years preceding, similar prohibitions regarding aid to Guatemala had been enacted into law. The efficacy of these laws can be measured by their number. In any event, the embargoes were never meant to be more than partial, and Guatemala also received weapons and military equipment from Israel, at least part of which was covertly underwritten by Washington.[32]

As further camouflage, some of the training of Guatemala's security forces was reportedly maintained by transferring it to clandestine sites in Chile and Argentina.[33]

Testimony of an Indian woman:

My name is Rigoberta Menchú Tum. I am a representative of the "Vincente Menchú" [her father] Revolutionary Christians ... On 9 December 1979, my 16-year-old brother Patrocino was captured and tortured for several days and then taken with twenty other young men to the square in Chajul ... An officer of [President] Lucas Garcia's army of murderers ordered the prisoners to be paraded in a line. Then he started to insult and threaten the inhabitants of the village, who were forced to come out of their houses to witness the event. I was with my mother, and we saw Patrocino; he had had his tongue cut out and his toes cut off. The officer jackal made a speech. Every time he paused the soldiers beat the Indian prisoners.

When he finished his ranting, the bodies of my brother and the other prisoners were swollen, bloody, unrecognizable. It was monstrous, but they were still alive.

They were thrown on the ground and drenched with gasoline. The soldiers set fire to the wretched bodies with torches and the captain laughed like a hyena and forced the inhabitants of Chajul to watch. This was his objective—that they should be terrified and witness the punishment given to the "guerrillas".[34]

In 1992, Rigoberta Menchú Tum was awarded the Nobel Peace Prize.

Testimony of Fred Sherwood (CIA pilot during the overthrow of the Arbenz government in 1954 who settled in Guatemala and became president of the American Chamber of Commerce), speaking in Guatemala, September 1980:

Why should we be worried about the death squads? They're bumping off the commies, our enemies. I'd give them more power. Hell, I'd get some cartridges if I could, and everyone else would too ... Why should we criticize them? The death squad—I'm for it ... Shit! There's no question, we can't wait 'til Reagan gets in. We hope Carter falls in the ocean real quick ... We all feel that he [Reagan] is our saviour.[35]

The Movement for National Liberation (MLN) was a prominent political party. It was the principal party in the Arana regime. An excerpt from a radio broadcast in 1980 by the head of the party, Mario Sandoval Alarcon ...

> I admit that the MLN is the party of organized violence. Organized violence is vigor, just as organized color is scenery and organized sound is harmony. There is nothing wrong with organized violence; it is vigor, and the MLN is a vigorous movement.[36]

Mario Sandoval Alarcon and former president Arana ("the butcher of Zacapa") "spent inaugural week mingling with the stars of the Reagan inner circle", reported syndicated columnist Jack Anderson. Sandoval, who had worked closely with the CIA in the overthrow of Arbenz, announced that he had met with Reagan defense and foreign-policy advisers even before the election. Right-wing Guatemalan leaders were elated by Reagan's victory. They looked forward to a resumption of the hand-in-glove relationship between American and Guatemalan security teams and businessmen which had existed before Carter took office.[37]

Before that could take place, however, the Reagan administration first had to soften the attitude of Congress about this thing called human rights. In March 1981, two months after Reagan's inaugural, Secretary of State Alexander Haig told a congressional committee that there was a Soviet "hit list ... for the ultimate takeover of Central America". It was a "four phased operation" of which the first part had been the "seizure of Nicaragua". "Next," warned Haig, "is El Salvador, to be followed by Honduras and Guatemala."[38]

This was the kind of intelligence information which one would expect to derive from a captured secret document or KGB defector. But neither one of these was produced or mentioned, nor did any of the assembled congressmen presume to raise the matter.

Two months later, General Vernon Walters, former Deputy Director of the CIA, on a visit to Guatemala as Haig's special emissary, was moved to proclaim that the United States hoped to help the Guatemalan government defend "peace and liberty".[39]

During this period, Guatemalan security forces, official and unofficial, massacred at least 2,000 peasants (accompanied by the usual syndrome of torture, mutilation and decapitation), destroyed several villages, assassinated 76 officials of the opposition Christian Democratic Party, scores of trade unionists, and at least six catholic priests.[40]

19 August 1981 ... unidentified gunmen occupy the town of San Miguel Acatan, force the Mayor to give them a list of all those who had contributed funds for the building of a school, pick out 15 from the list (including three of the Mayor's children), make them dig their own graves and shoot them.[41]

In December, Ronald Reagan finally spoke out against government repression. He denounced Poland for crushing by "brute force, the stirrings of liberty ... Our Government and those of our allies, have expressed moral revulsion at the police-state tactics of Poland's oppressors."[42]

Using the loopholes in the congressional legislation, both real and loosely interpreted, the Reagan administration, in its first two years, chipped away at the spirit of the embargo: $3.1 million of jeeps and trucks, $4 million of helicopter spare parts, $6.3 million of other military supplies.[43] These were amongst the publicly announced aid shipments; what was transpiring covertly can only be guessed at in light of certain disclosures: Jack Anderson revealed in August 1981 that the United States was using Cuban exiles to train security forces in Guatemala; in this operation, Anderson wrote, the CIA had arranged "for secret training in the finer points of assassination".[44] The following year, it was reported that the Green Berets had been instructing Guatemalan Army officers for over two years in the finer points of warfare.[45] And in 1983, we learned that in the previous two years Guatemala's Air Force helicopter fleet had somehow increased from eight to 27, all of them American made, and that Guatemalan officers were once again being trained at the US School of the Americas in Panama.[46]

In March 1982, a coup put General Efraín Ríos Montt, a "born-again Christian" in power. A month later, the Reagan administration announced that it perceived signs of an improvement in the state of human rights in the country and took the occasion to justify a shipment of military aid.[47] On the first of July, Ríos Montt announced a state of siege. It was to last more than eight months. In his first six months in power, 2,600 Indians and peasants were massacred, while during his 17-month reign, more than 400 villages were brutally wiped off the map.[48] In December 1982, Ronald Reagan, also a Christian, went to see for himself. After meeting with Ríos Montt, Reagan, referring to the allegations of extensive human-rights abuses, declared that the Guatemalan leader was receiving "a bad deal."[49]

Statement by the Guatemalan Army of the Poor, made in 1981 (by which time the toll of people murdered by the government since 1954 had reached at least the 60,000 mark, and the sons of one-time death-squad members were now killing the sons of the Indians killed by their fathers):

The Guatemalan revolution is entering its third decade. Ever since the government of Jacobo Arbenz was overthrown in 1954, the majority of the Guatemalan people have been seeking a way to move the country towards solving the same problems which were present then and have only worsened over time.

The counterrevolution, put in motion by the U.S. Government and those domestic sectors committed to retaining every single one of their privileges, dispersed and disorganized the popular and democratic forces. However, it did not resolve any of the problems which had first given rise to demands for economic, social and political change. These demands have been raised again and again in the last quarter century, by any means that seemed appropriate at the time, and have received each time the same repressive response as in 1954.[50]

Statement by Father Thomas Melville, 1968:

Having come to the conclusion that the actual state of violence, composed of the malnutrition, ignorance, sickness and hunger of the vast majority of the Guatemalan population, is the direct result of a capitalist system that makes the defenseless Indian compete against the powerful and well-armed landowner, my brother [Father Arthur Melville] and I decided not to be silent accomplices of the mass murder that this system generates.

We began teaching the Indians that no one will defend their rights, if they do not defend themselves. If the government and oligarchy are using arms to maintain them in their position of misery, then they have the obligation to take up arms and defend their God-given right to be men.

We were accused of being communists along with the people who listened to us, and were asked to leave the country by our religious superiors and the U.S. ambassador [John Gordon Mein]. We did so.

But I say here that I am a communist only if Christ was a communist. I did what I did and will continue to do so because of the teachings of Christ and not because of Marx or Lenin. And I say here too, that we are many more than the hierarchy and the U.S. government think.

When the fight breaks out more in the open, let the world know that we do it not for Russia, not for China, nor any other country, but for Guatemala. Our response to the present situation is not because we have read either Marx or Lenin, but because we have read the New Testament.[51]

Postscript, a small sample:

1988: Guatemala continues to suffer the worst record of human-rights abuses in Latin America, stated the Council on Hemispheric Affairs in its annual report on human rights in the Western Hemisphere.[52]

1990: Guatemalan soldiers at the army base in Santiago Atitlán opened fire on unarmed townspeople carrying white flags, killing 14 and wounding 24. The people had come with their mayor to speak to the military commander about repeated harassment from the soldiers.[53]

1990: "The United States, said to be disillusioned because of persistent corruption in the government of President Vinicio Cerezo Arevalo, is reportedly turning to Guatemala's military to promote economic and political stability ... even though the military is blamed for human rights abuses and is believed to be involved in drug trafficking."[54]

This was reported in May. In June, a prominent American businessman living in Guatemala, Michael DeVine, was kidnapped and nearly beheaded by the Guatemalan military after he apparently stumbled upon the military's drug trafficking and/or other contraband activities. The Bush administration, in a show of public anger of the killing, cut off military aid to Guatemala, but, we later learned, secretly allowed the CIA to provide millions of dollars to the military government to make up for the loss. The annual payments of $5 to $7 million apparently continued into the Clinton administration.

1992: In March, Guatemalan guerilla leader, Efrain Bamaca Velasquez, was captured and disappeared. For the next three years, his American wife, attorney Jennifer Harbury, waged an impassioned international campaign—including public fasts in Guatemala City (nearly to death) and in Washington—to pressure the Guatemalan and American governments for information about her husband's fate. Both governments insisted that they knew nothing. Finally, in March 1995, Rep. Robert Torricelli of the House Intelligence Committee revealed that Bamaca had been tortured and executed the same year of his capture, and that he, as well as DeVine, had been murdered on the orders of Col. Julio Roberto Alpírez, who had been on the CIA payroll for several years. (Alpírez thus becoming another illustrious graduate of Fort Benning's School of the Americas). The facts surrounding these cases were known early on by the CIA, and by officials at the State Department and National Security Council at least a few months before the disclosure. Torricelli's announcement prompted several other Americans to come forward with tales of murder, rape or torture of themselves or a relation at the hands of the Guatemalan military. Sister Dianna Ortiz, a nun, related how, in 1989, she was kidnapped, burned with cigarettes, raped repeatedly, and lowered into a pit full of corpses and rats. A fair-skinned man who spoke with an American accent seemed to be in charge, she said.[55]

38. Costa Rica 1970-1971
Trying to topple an ally, part II

Jose Figueres, who headed the Costa Rican government three times, was always a rather improbable target of destabilization by the United States. He was a bona fide (North) Americaphile, fluent in English, educated at MIT, lecturer at Harvard and other American universities, well-connected in US intellectual circles, particularly among Kennedyites, accorded an honorary membership in the Americans for Democratic Action. Figueres was typically referred to as an "outstanding friend" of the United States, and had long been associated with the CIA in a variety of activities and fronts in Latin America. And if that weren't enough, both of Figueres's wives had been American.

Yet, the CIA tried to overthrow him during his term in office in the 1950s and twice tried to assassinate the man (see Costa Rica, mid-1950s chapter) and perhaps tried again to overthrow him in the 1970s.

To liberal American political figures, Figueres was the quintessential "liberal democrat", the kind of statesman they liked to think, and liked the world to think, was the natural partner of US foreign policy rather than the military dictators who, somehow, keep popping up as allies.

To American conservatives, Figueres was of questionable ilk, the type that, if not actually a communist himself, doesn't sufficiently appreciate the nature and degree of The International Communist Conspiracy and consequently allows communists too much room to maneuver.

It was the latter conviction that was stirred up by Figueres soon after becoming president again in May 1970. He began "building bridges" to the Communist bloc, with Costa Rica becoming the first Central American country to establish diplomatic relations with the Soviet Union and Eastern Europe.

"This diplomatic recognition in no way shakes our loyalty to the United States or to the democratic cause," Figueres cautioned. "People everywhere are tired of the cold war. Russia controls half of Europe, and we want to make the Russians drink coffee [Costa Rica's principal export] instead of tea."[1]

In the previous two years the Soviet Union had purchased $10 million worth of coffee from Costa Rica, an "economic offensive" which reportedly "disturbed United States officials".[2]

Earl (Ted) Williamson, officially listed as First Secretary of the US Embassy in San José, but actually CIA Chief of Station, was heard to declare at a party that the Figueres government would not last much longer. He spoke openly against the president's bridge-building endeavors.

Williamson's comments got back to Costa Rican officials, as did reports of his close ties with Figueres's conservative political opponents, and indiscreet remarks made by his Cuban wife regarding the country's alleged march toward communism. Williamson, who had served in Cuba before the revolution and married the niece of a wealthy sugar baron, was also blamed for the seizure and burning of some Marxist literature coming in through the Costa Rican airport. The blame arose through his involvement in a CIA "technical assistance program on security".

By autumn, the Costa Rican government felt compelled to make an informal suggestion through the State Department's Costa Rican desk in Washington that Williamson be removed. The request was ignored.

Then, on 17 December, a fisherman reported sighting a mysterious ship which had unloaded "long wooden boxes" on a remote Costa Rican beach. The ship was identified as the *Waltham* and the Costa Rican government later received information that the vessel was registered to the "commercial section of the State Department". This was never verified. However, the US Commerce Department at that time did own a 455-foot vessel named the *Waltham Victory*.

It was first reported that the boxes contained weapons. Subsequently, a story was circulated that it was contraband whisky that had been put ashore.

The *Miami Herald*, which had first broken this story, commented that: "The contraband story presumably was put out to dispel rumors of a coup against the government." Americaphile that he was, Figueres was probably anxious to downplay the entire controversy which must have been acutely embarrassing to him. Three congressmen of his party, however, unencumbered by such loyalties, released a statement that accused the CIA of being involved in the ship movements and the alleged arms drop.

By early January 1971, the Costa Rican government seriously feared an uprising. It again asked the Nixon administration to recall Williamson. Not long before, Williamson had publicly forecast that the Figueres government would not survive another two weeks.

The *Guardia Civil*, Costa Rica's only armed force, was alerted and plans were made to remove Figueres from the capital to a hiding place in the mountains. At Figueres's request, the Panama government covertly delivered over 100 semi-automatic rifles to Costa Rica.

During this entire period, the American Embassy in San José was reported to be deeply divided between liberals and conservatives. Perhaps the most conservative, along with Williamson, was Ambassador Walter Ploeser, a Nixon political appointee with a long history of ultra-anti-communist activity. Ploeser vehemently defended Williamson and was said to have made no effort to curb the CIA official's public outbursts against Figueres. At the same time, Ploeser fired the director of the US AID program in Costa Rica, Lawrence Harrison, who took a pro-Figueres stand. The two men reportedly clashed over priorities, with Ploeser wanting an increase in military assistance, although Costa Rica, ostensibly, had little use for such, and a reduction in American economic aid to the country.

Official cables reaching Washington from Ploeser's embassy described the situation in Costa Rica as "dangerous". Figueres was accused of abandoning the West and facing East, of having accepted financial assistance from the communists for his campaign, and of permitting communists to infiltrate his government.[3]

In February, Williamson was finally recalled by Washington. Costa Rican officials hoped and expected that Ploeser would be replaced as well, as soon as it could be done with the customary diplomatic face-saving. As it was, Ploeser lingered on at his post for a full year before resigning for "personal reasons".

The announcement of Williamson's departure was perhaps hastened by the fact that a few days earlier the House Subcommittee on Inter-American Affairs had held a briefing to look into the matter. But the congressmen were not about to become the authors of an exposé. After hearing the testimony of two State Department officials, the committee announced that it had all been a big misunderstanding due to "personality conflicts" within the embassy which had "repercussions" outside its walls, and "overzealous actions" by some US officials who would remain nameless, as would everything else heard at the closed-door briefing.[4]

The same day, the *Miami Herald* stated in an editorial: "What is abundantly clear ... is the power and influence of the United States Embassy in a small country such as Costa Rica. An embassy that even quietly passes the word that it opposes the government can stimulate opposition and perhaps inspire efforts to overthrow it. Open antipathy almost asks for it."[5]

39. Iraq 1972-1975

Covert action should not be confused with missionary work

Into the land of ancient Mesopotamia reached the long arm of the CIA, and the Kurdish people of the Zagros and Taurus mountains, but a few decades removed from the life of nomads, joined the Agency's list of clients.

In May of 1972, President Richard Nixon and his National Security Affairs adviser, Henry Kissinger, went to the Soviet Union to meet their Russian counterparts. Afterward, Kissinger told a press conference in Moscow that the two nations had agreed to defuse the tensions in the Middle East and "to contribute what they can to bringing about a general settlement ... such a settlement would also contribute to a relaxation of the armaments race in that area. ... Speaking for our side," he added, "I can say we will attempt to implement these principles in the spirit in which they were promulgated."[1]

Kissinger and Nixon were moved by the spirit for perhaps 24 hours. On their way home, they stopped in Teheran to visit their friend, the Shah of Iran. It seems that Iran and Iraq were embroiled once again in their perennial feud—a border dispute and the like—and the Shah asked his pal Richard for a little favor. Could he help arm the Kurds in Iraq who were fighting for autonomy? Just generally heat things up so as to sap the Iraqi resources and distract them from Iran?[2]

Anything for a friend and loyal ally, said Richard Milhous, two weeks before the Watergate burglary and still on top of the world.

The Shah was quite capable of arming the Kurds himself, and in fact was doing so to some extent, but the Kurds didn't trust him. They trusted the United States and wanted to be armed by them. Several years later, the congressional committee known as the Pike Committee, which investigated various CIA operations, put it thusly: "The U.S. acted in effect as a guarantor that the Kurds would not be summarily dropped by the Shah."[3]

Before long, the CIA was reaching into its warehouses and a range of Soviet and Chinese small arms and rifles and millions of rounds of ammunition were on their way to the Kurdish rebels, the Communist origin of the weapons being a standard means of ensuring the standard "plausible denial". Ultimately, the military aid was to total some $16 million.

The Kurds are a distinct ethnic group, Muslim but, unlike most other Iraqis, not Arab. Their people are to be found primarily in Turkey, Iran, Iraq, and Syria. For decades, the Iraqi Kurds had been engaged in intermittent warfare against the government in pursuance of a goal of "autonomy", a concept not terribly well-defined by them, it being clear only that it fell short of being an independent state, perhaps.

The political history of the Iraqi Kurds in their recent past was a baffling piece of patchwork. Ten years earlier, they had been in close alliance with the Iraqi Communist Party, such that when the ruling Ba'ath party began to persecute the Communists, they took refuge amongst the Kurds. The Kurdish leader, Mustafa al-Barzani, a man in his seventies, had spent a dozen years in the Soviet Union and spoke Russian. Now, in 1972, the Communists were allies of the Ba'aths in an attempt to suppress the "imperialist agent Barzani", and Kurdish propaganda emphasized Soviet military support of the Iraqi government, including claims that Russians were flying bombing missions against the Kurds. At the same time the Kurds painted themselves as "social democrats" of the European variety, going so far as to apply for membership in the Socialist International.[4] Nonetheless, Barzani stated frequently that "he trusted no other major power" than the United States and asserted that if his cause were successful, the Kurds were "ready to become the 51st state".[5] All this on top of desiring to establish a Muslim society.

In October 1973, when the Yom Kippur surprise attack on Israel took place, and Iraq was preoccupied as an ally of Egypt and Syria, the Kurds were willing to launch a major attack, at Israel's suggestion, that might have been very beneficial to their own cause as well as taking some pressure off Israel by tying down the Iraqi army. But Kissinger refused to let the Kurds move. On 16 October he had the CIA send them a cable which read: "We do not repeat not consider it advisable for you to undertake the offensive military actions that Israel has suggested to you." The Kurds obeyed.[6]

The Pike Report regarded this incident as an example of the apparent "no win" policy of the United States and Iran. The committee stated:

The progressively deteriorating position of the Kurds reflected the fact that none of the nations who were aiding them seriously desired that they realize their objective of an autonomous state. A CIA memo of March 22, 1974 states Iran's and the United States' position clearly: "We would think that Iran would not look with favor on the establishment of a formalized autonomous government. Iran, like ourselves, has seen benefit in a stalemate situation ... in which Iraq is intrinsically weakened by the Kurds' refusal to relinquish [their] semi-autonomy. Neither Iran nor ourselves wish to see the matter resolved one way or the other."[7]

"This policy," said the report, "was not imparted to our clients, who were encouraged to continue fighting. Even in the context of covert action, ours was a cynical enterprise."[8]

The day after the CIA memo referred to above, 23 March 1974, Soviet Defense Minister Andrei Grechko, who had befriended Barzani when the latter lived in the Soviet Union, arrived in Iraq to help the government reach a settlement with the Kurds. On the advice of Iran and the United States, however, Barzani refused to come to any terms.[9] Earlier that month, the Iraqi government had actually passed a law offering a limited amount of autonomy to the Kurds, but they had rejected that as well, whether or not at the request of their "allies" is not known.

The congressional committee discovered that "The CIA had early information which suggested that the Shah would abandon the Kurds the minute he came to an agreement with Iraq over border disputes." Agency documents characterized the Shah's view of the Kurds as "a card to play" in this dispute with Iraq. And a CIA memo characterized the Kurds as "a uniquely useful tool for weakening Iraq's potential for international adventurism".[10]

The last may have been a reference to Iraq signing a pact of Friendship and Cooperation with the Soviet Union in April 1972, under which it received military aid and granted the Soviet Navy certain port privileges. Then, in June, super oil-rich Iraq had nationalized the Western-owned consortium, the Iraq Petroleum Company (23.75 percent US), a move warmly applauded by the Soviets, after which the two countries proceeded to conclude a trade and economic accord.[11]

As it was, it was oil that brought Iran and Iraq together. In 1973, the Shah wanted to strengthen Iran's position with the Organization of Petroleum Exporting Countries (OPEC), and a crucial part of the inducement to Iraq and other Arab neighbors was Iran's willingness to double-cross the troublesome Kurds.[12] None of these countries wanted their own minorities to be getting any ideas from a Kurdish success.

It was not until March 1975 that the Shah was ready to make his move. Events moved swiftly then. The Shah met with the vice-president of Iraq and, by agreement, the Shah cut off all supplies to the Kurds, including the American part. The next day the Iraqis unleashed their biggest offensive ever. Several days later the stunned Kurds sent a desperate message to the CIA: "There is confusion and dismay among our people and forces. Our people's fate in unprecedented danger. Complete destruction hanging over our head. No explanation for all this. We appeal you and USG [United States government] intervene according to your promises ..."[13]

The same day, the Kurds appealed to Kissinger as well:

Your Excellency, having always believed in the peaceful solution of disputes including those between Iran and Iraq, we are pleased to see that their two countries have come to some agreement ... However, our hearts bleed to see that an immediate byproduct of their agreement is the destruction of our defenseless people ... Our movement and people are being destroyed in an unbelievable way with silence from everyone. We feel your Excellency that the United States has a moral and political responsibility towards our people who have committed themselves to your country's policy.[14]

The hapless Kurds received no response to their pleas, from either the CIA or Henry Kissinger. By the end of the month their forces had been decimated. Several hundred Kurdish leaders were executed.

In conclusion, the Pike report noted:

Over 200,000 refugees managed to escape into Iran. Once there, however, neither the United States nor Iran extended adequate humanitarian assistance. In fact, Iran was later to forcibly return over 40,000 of the refugees and the United States government refused to admit even one refugee into the United States by way of political asylum even though they qualified for such admittance.[15]

When Henry Kissinger was interviewed by the staff of the Pike Committee about the United States' role in this melodrama, he responded with his now-famous remark: "Covert action should not be confused with missionary work."[16]

40. Australia 1973-1975
Another free election bites the dust

When the leader of a Communist country was removed from office by the Politburo, this was confirmation to the Western mind of the totalitarian, or, at best, the arbitrary, nature of the Communist system.

What then are we to make of the fact that in 1975 Edward Gough Whitlam, the legally elected prime minister of Australia, was summarily dismissed by a single non-elected individual, one functioning under the title of "Governor-General"?

Whitlam took office in December 1972 as the head of the first Labor Party government in Australia in 23 years. In short order he set about proving to the opposition parties the correctness of their historical prediction that Labor in power would be "irresponsible and dangerous"[1]—to *whom*, of course, had always been the question.

The war in Vietnam was an immediate example. Australian military personnel serving there under the command of the United States were called home, conscription was halted, and young men jailed for refusing military service were released.[2] Moreover, the Whitlam government recognized North Vietnam, several of his ministers publicly denounced American bombing of Hanoi and called for rallies to oppose it, and protesting dock workers felt inspired to impose a temporary boycott on American shipping, although the last was opposed by Whitlam.[3]

Condemnation of President Nixon and his administration volunteered by Labor ministers was most undiplomatic: "corrupt" ... "maniacs" ... "mass murderers" ... were some of the epithets hurled at Washington. American officials were reported to be "shocked and angered".[4]

The overseas side of Australian intelligence (ASIS by acronym), it turned out, was working with the CIA in Chile against the Allende government. Whitlam ordered an immediate halt to the operation in early 1973, although at the time of Allende's downfall in September, ASIS was reportedly still working with the Agency.[5]

The Labor government showed itself less than committed to the games security people play at home as well. Whitlam let it be known immediately that he did not wish to have his staff members undergo the usual security checks because he knew and trusted them. The Australian Security and Intelligence Organization (ASIO) was taken aback by such unorthodoxy and informed its CIA colleagues in Australia; cables went to Washington; before long, a political officer at the American Embassy was informing Richard Hall, one of Whitlam's advisers, "Your Prime Minister has just cut off one of his options." Hall took the remark to be a threat to cut off intelligence information.[6] Whether bowing to American/ASIO pressure or not, Whitlam soon afterward agreed to the security checks.

The new administration also put an end to the discrimination against immigrants who were being denied naturalization for having opposed the military juntas in places like Greece and Chile.[7] Most exceptional and alarming to the security professionals was the behavior of the Attorney General who showed up unannounced at ASIO headquarters one day in March 1973 with the police and carted away certain files because he suspected that the intelligence agency was withholding information from him. In all likelihood, ASIO *was* deliberately keeping certain information from its own government, as does every other intelligence agency in the world. The difference here, once again, was that the Labor government simply refused to accept such a state of affairs as normal.

A few years later, after Whitlam's ouster, James Angleton, who had been a high CIA officer in 1973 and directly concerned with intelligence relations with Australia, complained to an Australian television interviewer about the "Attorney General moving in, barging in, we were deeply concerned as to the sanctity of this information which could compromise sources and methods and compromise human life." The CIA, he said, seriously considered breaking intelligence relations with Australia.[8]

As a consequence of Whitlam's unconventional way of running a government, the CIA became rather concerned about the security and continued functioning of its many military and intelligence facilities in Australia. By the Agency's standards, it was a highly important setup, employing thousands of persons—a vital part of the early warning system; a key tracking station in the United States' global spy satellite system of extremely sophisticated photography and monitoring of activities within the Soviet Union; a US naval communications station which dealt with nuclear submarines; a huge electronics control center set up by the US National Security Agency (NSA) to intercept messages, of voice, telex, etc., coming in and out of Australia and its Pacific region—that is, eavesdropping on everybody and everything.[9]

Most of this had been built in the latter part of the 1960s and was run in such secrecy that not even senior members of the Australian Foreign Ministry had been briefed on exactly what went on in those buildings in Australia's wide open spaces, and the CIA connection was never officially acknowledged.

After the Labor Party took power, some of its members voiced strong criticism of the secret facilities. They increasingly demanded an official explanation for their presence and at times even voted for their removal. This was not carried out because the leaders of the Whitlam administration, for all their radical posturing, were not about to leap into political no-man's-land by cutting off ties to the West. They spoke of neutralism and non-alignment on occasion, but they were willing to settle for independence; which is all the Papandreous wanted before they were ousted in Greece, another site of an American electronics state-within-a-state in which the host intelligence and defense establishments typically demonstrate more loyalty to their American counterparts than to their own "government of the day".

In 1976, an investigation by the Australian Royal Commission on Intelligence and Security concluded that for many years members of ASIO had been providing the CIA with potentially damaging information about prominent Australian politicians and governmental officials. The information reportedly ranged from accusations of subversive tendencies to details about personal peccadillos.[10]

Moreover, it was later learned that in addition to Chile, Australian intelligence had aided US operations in Vietnam, Cambodia and Indonesia.[11]

The Whitlam government displayed its independence where it could. In 1973, Whitlam disclosed the existence of an Australian Defence Signals Directorate unit in Singapore—another cold-war toy of the CIA and ASIO which monitored military and civilian radio traffic in Asia. (The DSD is comparable to the American NSA and the British GCHQ.) Later, the Australian prime minister closed the unit down, although he re-established part of it in Australia. His administration also expressed its disapproval of US plans to build up the Indian Ocean island of Diego Garcia as another military-intelligence-nuclear outpost.[12] And in February 1975, the Labor Party conference voted to allow the Provisional Revolutionary Government of Vietnam (the Vietcong) to set up an office in Australia. This was before the fall of Saigon.

"By the end of 1974," writes Joan Coxsedge, a Labor Party member of Parliament in the state of Victoria,

> almost every move by the Whitlam Government or by individual Labor parliamentarians, whether it was a departmental decision, a staff appointment, an international cable, a telex, a phone call, or a confidential letter, quickly became the property of the news media. There was an unparalleled campaign of personal vituperation, hinting at incompetence, dissension, corruption and private scandal within the ranks of the government.[13]

Matters reached the spark point in autumn 1975. Whitlam dismissed the heads of both ASIO and ASIS in separate incidents, the latter because his agency had been secretly assisting the CIA in covert activities in nearby East Timor.[14] Then, at the beginning of November, it was revealed in the press that a former CIA officer, Richard Lee Stallings, had been channeling funds to J. Douglas Anthony, leader of the National Country Party, one of the two main opposition parties. It was reported that Stallings was a close friend and former tenant of Anthony's, that the secret facilities in the hinterland were indeed CIA creations, and that Stallings had been the first head of much of the operation.[15]

A year earlier, an Australian political journalist, Ray Aitchison, had published a book called *Looking at the Liberals* (the Liberal Party, the other important opposition party, was actually rather conservative), in which he claimed that the CIA had offered the opposition unlimited funds in their unsuccessful attempt to defeat the Labor Party in the May 1974 parliamentary elections.[16] Subsequently, a Sydney newspaper reported that the Liberals had been on the receiving end since the late 1960s, and quoted the remarks of former CIA officer Victor Marchetti, who confirmed that the CIA had funded both of the major opposition parties.[17]

Whitlam publicly repeated the charges about Stallings and insisted upon an investigation of the facilities, to identify once and for all their true nature and purpose. (Whether any of it was part of a weapons system was one question which seriously concerned the administration.) At the same time he demanded a list of all CIA operatives in Australia.

The Australian military-intelligence complex appears to have been spurred into a flurry of activity. On 6 November, the head of the Defence Department reportedly met with the Governor-General, Sir John Kerr, and afterward declared publicly: "This is the greatest risk to the nation's security there has ever been."[18]

On the eighth, another senior defence official held a meeting with Kerr in which he briefed the Governor-General about allegations from the CIA that Whitlam was jeopardizing the security of the American bases in Australia.[19] The same day, the CIA in Washington informed the ASIO station there that all intelligence links with Australia would be cut off unless a satisfactory explanation was given of Mr. Whitlam's behavior.[20] The Agency had already expressed reservations about releasing intelligence information to certain government ministers.[21]

If this had been a Third World country, the CIA would likely have already sent the government packing.

On 9 November, Kerr was received at the Defence Signals Directorate for yet another briefing.[22] The following day, the ASIO station in Washington, at the request of the CIA, sent a telex to its headquarters in Australia in which it stated that "CIA can not see how this dialogue with continued reference to CIA can do other than blow the lid off these installations".[23] In addition to Stallings, the names of his successors (senior CIA officers) and the CIA station chief in Canberra had appeared in the press.

Kerr, who was taken with the world of spookery and regularly saw classified material, in all likelihood was aware of the ASIO telex and the CIA ultimatum.[24] On the 11th, he dismissed Whitlam as Prime Minister, dissolved both houses of Parliament, and appointed Malcolm Fraser, the leader of the Liberal Party, to head an interim government until new elections could be held on 13 December. In the hours between the appointment of Fraser and the dissolution of Parliament, the Labor majority in the House of Representatives pushed through a no-confidence motion against Fraser, an act which obliged the Governor-General to dismiss the Liberal leader in turn. Kerr chose to ignore this maneuver, which was a legalistic one, although his dismissal of Whitlam was no less a legalistic act.

On 15 October, the opposition-controlled Senate had refused to vote on a new budget appropriation bill (called "Supply" in Australia) in order to force the government to dissolve Parliament and hold new elections, hoping thus to regain power. Though the constitution gave the Senate the technical right to withhold approval of the budget, it was seldom interpreted literally, as it is in the United States. Precedent was of greater importance, and the fact was that in Australia's 75-year history as a Federation the Senate had never exercised this right against the federal government. Only days earlier, eight leading law professors had publicly declared such action to be constitutionally improper. The opposition tactic was thus at least debatable.

When Whitlam refused to dissolve Parliament and tried to govern without the budget, a constitutional and financial crisis steadily built up over the course of several weeks. Then Kerr invoked a power as archaic and as questionable as that employed by the Senate. It was the first time a Governor-General had ever dismissed a federal prime minister; it had occurred but once before on a state level.[25]

The Melbourne newspaper, *The Age* (which, said the *New York Times*, was "generally held to be one of the nation's most responsible papers"),[26] wrote that Kerr's action was "a triumph of narrow legalism over common sense and popular feeling". It added:

> By bringing down the Government because the Senate refused it Supply, Sir John Kerr acted at least against the spirit of the Australian Constitution. Since 1901, it has been a firmly held convention that the Senate should not reject budgets ... Sir John has created an awesome precedent—that a hostile Senate can bring down a government whenever it denies it Supply. [Kerr] breathed life into a constitutional relic—the right of kings and queens to unilaterally appoint governments.[27]

The office of Governor-General had traditionally been only that of a figurehead representative of the Queen of England. Kerr's decision, however, appears as a calculated political act. He gave Whitlam no warning or ultimatum before dismissing him, no opportunity to request the dissolution of parliament, which would have permitted him to remain in office. One must read Kerr's own account of his confrontation with Whitlam to appreciate how he maneuvered the Prime Minister into stalking out of the Governor-General's office without requesting the dissolution. Kerr claims he refrained from issuing Whitlam an ultimatum because he feared that the prime minister would leave and then ask the Queen for his removal as Governor-General.[28] But he fails to explain why he didn't give Whitlam an ultimatum that had to be responded to on the spot.

Kerr had been appointed, at least in theory, by the Queen. Ironically, she had done so at Whitlam's recommendation, which he had made against the wishes of his party's left-wing. Kerr's action added to Whitlam's reputation as a bad judge of character, a man easily taken in.

Certainly the warning signs were there, for John Kerr had been intimately involved with CIA fronts for a number of years. In the 1950s he joined the Australian Association for Cultural Freedom, an organization spawned by the CIA's Congress for Cultural Freedom (see Western Europe chapter). Kerr became a member of the organization's executive board in 1957 and also wrote for its magazine *Quadrant*. One article, in 1960, was entitled "The struggle against communism in the trade unions", a program and tactic, as we have seen, the CIA has consistently accorded a high priority to throughout the world.

In 1966 Kerr helped to found Lawasia (or Law Asia), an organization of lawyers in the Far East funded by the Asia Foundation. The Foundation was one of the most prominent CIA fronts for over a decade, with offices and representatives in all the major capitals of Asia; one of its prime missions, Victor Marchetti has written, was "to disseminate throughout Asia a negative vision of mainland China, North Vietnam, and North Korea".[29] Kerr became Lawasia's first president, a position he held until 1970. He describes the organization as "a non-communist group of Asian lawyers" which the Asia Foundation supported because "the rule of law is a good thing, a strong legal profession is a good thing, and talk between lawyers is a good thing."[30]

"There was a bit of a celebration" in the CIA when Whitlam was dismissed by Kerr, reported Christopher Boyce. Boyce is an American who was working at the time for TRW Systems, Inc., Los Angeles, in a cryptographic communications center which linked CIA headquarters in Virginia with the Agency's satellite surveillance system in Australia. In his position, Boyce was privy to telex communications between the two stations. The CIA, he said, referred to Kerr as "our man".[31]

Boyce also revealed that the CIA had infiltrated Australian labor unions, had been "manipulating the leadership", and had "suppressed their strikes", particularly those involving railroads and airports. The last was reportedly because the strikes were holding up deliveries of equipment to the Agency's installations. Some unions as well had been in the forefront of opposition to the installations.[32]

As matters turned out, Whitlam lost the new election.

One other CIA operation in Australia deserves mention. This is the Nugan Hand Merchant Bank of Sydney, truly a CIA bank. Founded in 1973 by Frank Nugan, an Australian, and Michael Hand, an American formerly with the Green Berets in Vietnam and with the CIA airline Air America, the bank exhibited phenomenal growth over the next few years. It opened branch offices in Saudi Arabia, Hamburg, Malaysia, Thailand, Hong Kong, Singapore, the Philippines, Argentina, Chile, Hawaii, Washington and Annapolis, Maryland, run by men with backgrounds in the CIA, OSS, Green Berets, and similar specialty areas of banking. Former CIA Director William Colby was one of the bank's attorneys.

The Nugan Hand Bank succeeded in expanding the scope of normal banking services. Among the activities it was reportedly involved in were: drug trafficking, international arms dealing, links to organized crime, laundering money for President Suharto of Indonesia, unspecified services for President and Mrs. Marcos of the Philippines, assisting the Shah of Iran's family to shift money out of Iran, channeling CIA money into pro-American political parties and operations in Europe, transferring $2.4 million to the Australian Liberal Party through one of the bank's many associated companies, attempting to blackmail an Australian state minister who was investigating organized crime (the CIA opened a Swiss bank account in his name and threatened to leak the information), and a host of other socially useful projects.

In addition, several mysterious deaths have been connected to the bank, including that of a ranking CIA officer in Maryland. And on 27 January 1980, Frank Nugan was himself found shot dead in his car. In June, Michael Hand disappeared without a trace. The Nugan Hand Merchant Bank collapsed, $50 million or so in debt.[33]

41. Angola 1975 to 1980s
The Great Powers Poker Game

It is spring 1975. Saigon has just fallen. The last of the Americans are fleeing for their lives. Fallout from Watergate hangs heavy in the air in the United States. The morning papers bring fresh revelations about CIA and FBI misdeeds. The Pike Committee of the House of Representatives is investigating CIA foreign covert activities. On the Senate side, the Church Committee is doing the same. And the Rockefeller Commission has set about investigating the Agency's domestic activities.

The CIA and its influential supporters warn that the crescendo of disclosures will inhibit the Agency from carrying out the functions necessary for national security.

At CIA headquarters in Langley, Virginia, they are busy preparing for their next secret adventure: Angola.

To undertake a military operation at such a moment, the reasons, one would imagine, must have been both compelling and urgent. Yet, in the long history of American interventions it would be difficult to find one more pointless or with less to gain for the United States or the foreign people involved.

The origin of our story dates back to the beginning of the 1960s when two political movements in Angola began to oppose by force the Portuguese colonial government: the MPLA, led by Agostinho Neto, and the FNLA, led by Holden Roberto. (The latter group was known by other names in its early years, but for simplicity will be referred to here only as FNLA.)

The United States, not normally in the business of supporting "liberation" movements, decided that inasmuch as Portugal would probably be unable to hold on to its colony forever, establishing contact with a possible successor regime might prove beneficial. For reasons lost in the mists of history, the United States, or at least someone in the CIA, decided that Roberto was their man and around 1961 or '62 onto the Agency payroll he went.[1]

At the same time, and during the ensuing years, Washington provided their NATO ally, the Salazar dictatorship in Lisbon, with the military aid and counter-insurgency training needed to suppress the rebellion. John Marcum, an American scholar who walked 800 miles through Angola into the FNLA guerrilla camps in the early 1960s, has written:

> By January 1962 outside observers could watch Portuguese planes bomb and strafe African villages, visit the charred remains of towns like Mbanza M'Pangu and M'Pangala, and copy the data from 750-point napalm bomb casings from which the Portuguese had not removed the labels marked "Property U.S. Air Force".[2]

The Soviet Union, which had also given some support to Roberto, embraced Neto instead in 1964, arguing that Roberto had helped the discredited Moise Tshombe in the Congo and curtailed his own guerrilla operations in Angola under pressure from Washington.[3] Before long, another movement, UNITA by name, entered the picture and China dealt itself into The Great Powers Poker Game, lending support to UNITA and FNLA.

Although MPLA may have been somewhat more genuine in its leftist convictions than FNLA or UNITA, there was little to distinguish any of the three groups from each other ideologically. When the press made any distinction amongst them it was usually to refer to MPLA as "Marxist", but this was ill-defined, if defined at all, and simply took on a media life of its own. Each of the groups spoke of socialism and employed Marxist rhetoric when the occasion called for it, and genuflected to other gods when it did not. In the 1960s, each of them was perfectly willing to accept support from any country willing to give it without excessive strings attached. Neto, for example, went to Washington in December 1962 to put his case before the American government and press and to emphasize the fallacy of categorizing the MPLA as communist. During the following two years, Roberto appealed for aid to the Soviet Union, Cuba, China, Algeria, and Nasser's Egypt. Later, Jonas Savimbi, the leader of UNITA, approached the same countries (with the exception perhaps of the Soviet Union) as well as North Vietnam, and accepted military training for his men from North Korea.

Each group was composed predominantly of members of a particular tribe; each tried to discourage aid or recognition being given to the others; they each suffered from serious internal splits and spent as much time fighting each other as they did the Portuguese army. The Vietcong they were not.[4]

Author Jonathan Kwitny has observed that the three tribal nations had a long history of fighting each other ...

It was not until the latter part of the twentieth century, however, that Dr. Henry Kissinger and other political scientists discovered that the real reason the Mbundu, the Ovimbundu, and the Kongo had been fighting off and on for the past 500 years was that the Mbundu were "Marxist" and the Ovimbundu and Kongo were "pro-Western".[5]

That the CIA's choosing of its ally was largely an arbitrary process is further underlined by a State Department cable to its African Embassies in 1963 which stated: "U.S. policy is not, repeat not, to discourage [an] MPLA ... move toward West and not to choose between these two movements."[6]

Even in 1975, when the head of the CIA, William Colby, was asked by a congressional committee what the differences were between the three contesting factions, he responded:

They are all independents. They are all for black Africa. They are all for some fuzzy kind of social system, you know, without really much articulation, but some sort of let's not be exploited by the capitalist nations.

And when asked why the Chinese were backing the FNLA or UNITA, he stated: "Because the Soviets are backing the MPLA is the simplest answer."

"It sounds," said Congressman Aspin, "like that is why we are doing it."

"It is," replied Colby.[7]

Nonetheless, the committee, in its later report, asserted that in view of Colby's statement, "The U.S.'s expressed opposition to the MPLA is puzzling".[8]

Finally, it is instructive to note that all three groups were denounced by the Portuguese as communists and terrorists.

Before April 1974, when a coup in Portugal ousted the dictatorship, the aid given to the Angolan resistance movements by their various foreign patrons was sporadic and insignificant, essentially a matter of the patrons keeping their hands in the game. The coup, however, raised the stakes, for the new Portuguese government soon declared its willingness to grant independence to its African colonies.

In an agreement announced on 15 January 1975, the three movements formed a transitional government with elections to be held in October and formal independence to take place the following month.

Since 1969, Roberto had been on a $10,000-a-year retainer from the CIA.[9] On 22 January, the Forty Committee of the National Security Council in Washington authorized the CIA to pass $300,000 to Roberto and the FNLA for "various political action activities, restricted to non-military objectives."[10] Such funds of course can always free up other funds for military uses.

In March, the FNLA, historically the most warlike of the groups, attacked MPLA headquarters and later gunned down 51 unarmed, young MPLA recruits.[11] These incidents served to spark what was to be a full-scale civil war, with UNITA aligning itself with FNLA against MPLA. The scheduled elections would never take place.

Also in March, the first large shipment of arms reportedly arrived from the Soviet Union for the MPLA.[12] The House investigating committee subsequently stated that "Later events have suggested that this infusion of US aid [the $300,000], unprecedented and massive in the underdeveloped colony, may have panicked the Soviets into arming their MPLA clients".[13]

The Soviets may have been as much influenced by the fact that China had sent a huge arms package to the FNLA the previous September and had dispatched over one hundred military advisers to neighboring Zaire to train Roberto's soldiers only a month after the coup in Portugal.[14]

The CIA made its first major weapons shipment to the FNLA in July 1975. Thus, like the Russians and the Chinese, the United States was giving aid to one side of the Angolan civil war on a level far greater than it had ever provided during the struggle against Portuguese colonialism.

The United States was directly involved in the civil war to a marked degree. In addition to training Angolan combat units, US personnel did considerable flying between Zaire and Angola carrying out reconnaissance and supply missions,[15] and the CIA spent over a million dollars on an ambitious mercenary program.[16] Several reports appeared in the US press stating that many American mercenaries were fighting in Angola against the MPLA—from "scores" to "300"—and that many others were being recruited and trained in the United States to join them. But John Stockwell, the head of the CIA's Angola task force, puts the number of American mercenaries who actually made it to Angola at only 24.[17] However, Holden Roberto was using CIA money, with the Agency's tacit approval, to recruit many other mercenaries—over 100 British plus a scattering of French and Portuguese.[18] The CIA was also directly financing the arming of British mercenaries.[19] (The mercenaries included amongst their number the well-known Englishman and psychopath George Cullen who lined up 14 of his fellow soldiers-of-fortune and shot them all dead because they had mistakenly attacked the wrong side.)[20]

Subsequently, Secretary of State Henry Kissinger informed the Senate that "the CIA is not involved" in the recruitment of mercenaries for Angola.[21]

There were also well over a hundred CIA officers and American military advisers scurrying about Angola, Zaire, Zambia and South Africa helping to direct the military operations and practicing their propaganda skills.[22] Through recruited journalists representing major news services, the Agency was able to generate international coverage for false reports of Soviet advisers in Angola. One CIA story, announced to the press by UNITA, was that 20 Russians and 35 Cubans had been captured. Another fabrication concerned alleged rapes committed by Cuban soldiers in Angola; this was elaborated to include their capture, trial, and execution, complete with photos of the young women killing the Cubans who had raped them.[23]

Both stories were reported widely in the American and British press and elsewhere. Some of the major newspapers, such as the *New York Times*, *Washington Post*, and *The Guardian* of London, were careful to point out that the only source of the information was UNITA and their articles did not attempt to ascribe any special credence to the reports.[24] But this could not of course prevent the placing of seeds of belief in the minds of readers already conditioned to believe the worst about communists.

The disinformation campaign took place within the United States as well. FNLA delegates came to New York in September to lobby for support at the UN and with the New York press, distributing as they went copies of a "white paper" on the Angolan conflict prepared at CIA headquarters but made to look like it was produced in Zaire, French and all.[25] John Stockwell described the paper as sometimes "false to the point of being ludicrous" and other times "simply inaccurate".[26]

Afterward, representatives of UNITA went to Washington and presented to members of Congress, the State Department, the White House and the media, verbal reports about the situation in Angola which were the product of briefings given them by their CIA case officers.[27]

In January 1976, William Colby sat before the Senate investigating committee and solemnly assured the Senators:

We have taken particular caution to ensure that our operations are focused abroad and not at the United States to influence the opinion of the American people about things from the CIA point of view.[28]

There was virtually no important aspect of the Angolan intervention which Colby, Kissinger, and other high officials did not misrepresent to Congress and the media.

The odds never favored a military victory for the US-backed forces in Angola, particularly in the absence of a relatively large-scale American commitment which, given the political atmosphere, was not in the cards. The MPLA was the most organized and best led of the three factions and early on controlled the capital city of Luanda, which housed almost the entire governmental machinery. Yet, for no reason, apparently, other than anti-Soviet spite, the United States was unwilling to allow a negotiated settlement. When Savimbi of UNITA sent out feelers to the MPLA in September 1975 to discuss a peaceful solution he was admonished by the CIA. Similarly, the following month when an MPLA delegation went to Washington to once again express their potential friendliness to the United States, they received a cool reception, being seen only by a low-level State Department official.[29]

In November MPLA representatives came to Washington to plead for the release of two Boeing jet airliners which their government had paid for but which the State Department would not allow to be exported. John Stockwell relates the unusual development that the MPLA men were accompanied by Bob Temmons, who until shortly before had been the head of the CIA station in Luanda, as well as by the president of Boeing. While the two Angolans and the man from Boeing petitioned the State Department, the CIA man made known to Agency headquarters that he had come to share the view of the US Consul General in Luanda "that the MPLA was best qualified to run the country, that it was not demonstrably hostile to the United States, and that the United States should make peace with it as quickly as possible."

The State Department's response to the MPLA representatives was simple: the price for any American co-operation with the Angolan government was Soviet influence out, US influence in.[30]

At one time or another almost two dozen countries, East and West, felt the urge to intervene in the conflict. Principal amongst these were the United States, China, South Africa and Zaire on the side of FNLA/UNITA, and the Soviet Union, Cuba, the Congo Republic and Katangese troops (Zairian rebels) supporting MPLA. The presence of South African forces on their side cost the United States and its Angolan allies dearly in support from other countries, particularly in Africa. Yet, South Africa's participation in the war had been directly solicited by the United States.[31] In sharp contrast to stated American policy, the CIA and the National Security Agency had been collaborating with Pretoria's intelligence service since the 1960s and continued to do so in regard to Angola. One of the principal focuses of the intelligence provided by the US to South Africa was the African National Congress, the leading anti-apartheid organization which had been banned and exiled.[32] In 1962, the South African police arrested ANC leader Nelson Mandela based on information as to his whereabouts and disguise provided them by CIA officer Donald Rickard. Mandela spent almost 28 years in prison.[33]

In 1977, the Carter administration banned the sharing of intelligence with South Africa, but this was largely ignored by the American intelligence agencies. Two years earlier, the CIA had set up a covert mechanism whereby arms were delivered to the South Africans; this practice, in violation of US law, continued until at least 1978, and a portion of the arms were more than likely put to use in Angola.[34] South Africa in turn helped to ferry American military aid from Zaire into Angola.[35]

In fairness to the CIA, it must be pointed out that its people were not entirely oblivious or insensitive to what South Africa represented. The Agency was very careful about letting its black officers into the Angola program.[36]

A congressional cutoff of aid to the FNLA/UNITA, enacted in January 1976, hammered a decisive nail into their coffin. Congressmen did not yet know the full truth about the American operation, but enough of the public dumbshow had been exposed to make them incensed at how Kissinger, Colby, et al. had lied to their faces. The consequence was one of the infrequent occasions in modern times that the US Congress has exercised a direct and pivotal influence upon American foreign policy. In the process, it avoided the slippery slope to another Vietnam, on top of which stood Henry Kissinger and the CIA with shoes waxed.[37]

By February, the MPLA, with indispensable help from Cuban troops and Soviet military equipment, had all but routed their opponents. The Cuban presence in Angola was primarily a direct response to South African attacks against the MPLA. Wayne Smith, director of the State Department's Office of Cuban Affairs from 1977 to 1979, has written that "in August and October [1975] South African troops invaded Angola with full U.S. knowledge. No Cuban troops were in Angola prior to this intervention."[38]

Savimbi at this time again considered reaching an understanding with the MPLA. The response from Washington was: Keep fighting. Kissinger personally promised UNITA continued support if they maintained their resistance, knowing full well that there was no more support to give. During the two weeks that Savimbi waited for his answer, he lost 600 men in a single battlefield.[39] Yet, incredibly, less than two months before, the Secretary of State had stated: "We are not opposed to the MPLA as such ... We can live with any of the factions in Angola."[40] The man was wholly obsessed with countering Soviet moves anywhere on the planet—significant or trivial, real or imagined, *fait accompli* or anticipated. He was perhaps particularly driven in this case, for as he later wrote: "Angola represents the first time that the Soviets have moved militarily at long distance to impose a regime of their choice."[41]

If this seems far removed from how the academics tell us American foreign policy is made, it's still more plausible than the other explanation commonly advanced for the policy in Angola, viz: it was done to please Sese Seko Mobutu, the head of Zaire, characterized as America's most important ally/client in Africa, if not in the Third World.[42] (Zaire was home to the CIA's largest station in Africa.) Mobutu desired an Angolan government he could sway, primarily to prevent Angola being used as a sanctuary by his arch foes, the rebels from Katanga province in Zaire. Accordingly, the Zairian leader committed his US-equipped armed forces into combat in Angola, on the side of the FNLA, for Holden Roberto happened to be a relation of his, although Roberto and the FNLA had little else going for them. As Professor Gerald Bender, a leading American authority on Angola, testified before Congress in 1978:

> Although the United States has supported the FNLA in Angola for 17 years, it is virtually impossible to find an American official, scholar or journalist, who is familiar with that party, who will

testify positively about its organization or leadership. After a debate with a senior State Department official at the end of the Angolan civil war, I asked him why the United States ever bet on the FNLA. He replied, "I'll be damned if I know; I have never seen a single report or memo which suggests that the FNLA has any organization, solid leaders, or an ideology which we could count on." Even foreign leaders who have supported Holden Roberto, such as General Mobutu, agree with that assessment. When asked by a visiting U.S. Senator if he thought Roberto would make a good leader for Angola, Mobutu replied, "Hell no!"[43]

Kissinger himself told the House investigating committee that promoting the stability of Mobutu was one of the prime reasons for the American policy in Angola.[44] Yet, even if this were one of Kissinger's rare truthful remarks about the Angola situation, and even if this could be a valid justification for serious intervention in a civil war in a third country, his statement challenges, if it does not defeat, comprehension; for in June 1975, a month before the United States shipped its first major arms package to the FNLA, Mobutu had accused the US of plotting his overthrow and assassination, whereupon he expelled the American ambassador (see Zaire chapter).

The Secretary of State, never at a loss for the glib line custom-made for his immediate audience, also told Israeli officials that failure to stop the Russians in Angola "could encourage Arab countries such as Syria to run risks that could lead to a new attack on Israel, backed up by the Russians."[45]

The American ambassador to the United Nations, Daniel Moynihan, did not greatly enhance the level of discussion when he declared that if the United States did not step in "the Communists would take over Angola and will thereby considerably control the oil shipping lanes from the Persian Gulf to Europe. They will be next to Brazil. They will have a large chunk of Africa, and the world will be different in the aftermath if they succeed."[46] A truly baroque train of thought, and another example of what cold-war conditioning could do to an otherwise intelligent and educated person.

With only a change in place names, similar geo-political-domino theories have been put forth to give a veneer of rationality to so many American interventions. In this case, as in the others where the "communists" won, nothing of the sort ensued.

"In all respect to Kissinger," Jonathan Kwitny has written, "one really has to question the sanity of someone who looks at an ancient tribal dispute over control of distant coffee fields and sees in it a Soviet threat to the security of the United States."[47]

The MPLA in power was restricted by the same domestic and international economic realities which the FNLA or UNITA would have faced. Accordingly, it discouraged union militancy, dealt sternly with strikes, exhorted the workers to produce more, entered into commercial contracts with several multinationals, and did not raise the hammer and sickle over the president's palace.[48] The MPLA urged Gulf Oil Co. to continue its exclusive operation in Cabinda province and guaranteed the safety of the American corporation's employees while the fighting was still heavy. Gulf was completely amenable to this offer, but the CIA and the State Department put pressure on the company to discontinue its royalty payments to the MPLA, thus jeopardizing the entire oil venture in a way that the "Marxist" government never did. One aspect of this pressure was a threat by Kissinger to open an investigation of international bribery by the company. Gulf compromised by putting its payments into an escrow bank account until the civil war came to an end of sorts a few months later, at which time payments to the MPLA were resumed.[49]

Contrary to accepted Western belief, Cuba did not enter the Angolan war as a

Soviet surrogate. John Stockwell has noted that after the war the CIA "learned that Cuba had not been ordered into action by the Soviet Union" but that "the Cuban leaders felt compelled to intervene for their own ideological reasons."[50] In 1977, the New York magazine *Africa Report* stated that "The Cubans have supported [MPLA leader Neto's] pragmatic approach toward Western investment and his attempts to maintain a foreign policy of non-alignment." The magazine also reported that on 27 May the Angolan government had announced that, aided by Cuban troops, it had crushed a rebellion by a faction of the MPLA whose leader claimed to have Soviet support.[51]

The civil war in Angola did not actually come to an end in 1976 as it appeared to, for the fighting lingered on intermittently, sometimes moderately, sometimes ferociously.

In 1984 a confidential memorandum smuggled out of Zaire revealed that the United States and South Africa had met in November 1983 to discuss destabilization of the Angola government. Plans were drawn up to supply more military aid to UNITA (the FNLA was now defunct) and discussions were held on ways to implement a wide range of tactics: unify the anti-government movements, stir up popular feeling against the government, sabotage factories and transport systems, seize strategic points, disrupt joint Angola-Soviet projects, undermine relations between the government and the Soviet Union and Cuba, bring pressure to bear on Cuba to withdraw its troops, sow divisions in the ranks of the MPLA leadership, infiltrate agents into the Angolan army, and apply pressure to stem the flow of foreign investments into Angola.

The United States branded the document a forgery, but UNITA's representative in Washington would neither confirm nor deny that the meeting took place. He stated, however, that UNITA had "contacts with US officials at all levels on a regular basis".

The aim of the operation, according to the memorandum, was to force part of the Angolan leadership to negotiate with UNITA, precisely what Washington had successfully discouraged years earlier.[52]

A month after the reported US-South Africa meeting, the UN Security Council censured South Africa for its military operations in Angola, and endorsed Luanda's right to reparations. Only the United States, abstaining, did not support the resolution.[53]

In August 1985, after a three-year battle with Congress, the Reagan administration won a repeal of the 1976 prohibition against US military aid to rebel forces in Angola. Military assistance began to flow to UNITA overtly as well as covertly. In January 1987, Washington announced that it was providing the rebels with Stinger missiles and other anti-aircraft weaponry. Three months earlier, Jonas Savimbi had spoken before the European Parliament in Strasbourg, France in an appeal for support. Following his talk, however, a plenary session of the Parliament criticized American support for the guerrilla leader and passed a resolution which described UNITA as a "terrorist organization which supports South Africa."[54]

Finally, in September 1992, elections were held, but when it became apparent that the MPLA would be the winner in a run-off—in polling which the UN certified to be free and fair—Savimbi refused to accept the result. He ended a year-old cease-fire and launched one of UNITA's largest, most sustained offensives of the war, still being supplied by South Africa, and, in recent years, by American "private" airlines and "relief" organizations with interesting histories such as previous contacts to the Nicaraguan contras.[55]

In May 1993, Washington finally recognized the Angolan government. In January, just before the Clinton administration took over, a senior State Department official had declared: "Unita is exactly like the Khmer Rouge: elections and negotiations are just one more method of fighting a war; power is all."[56]

The war—which had taken more than 300,000 lives—was still raging in 1994, continuing to produce widespread hunger and what is said to be the highest amputee rate in the world, caused by the innumerable land mines.

42. Zaire 1975-1978

Mobutu and the CIA,
a marriage made in heaven

By 1975, President Mobutu Sese Seko (née Joseph Mobutu), the Zairian (née Congo) strongman regarded by the CIA as one of its "successes" in Africa, had ruled over his hapless, impoverished subjects for 10 long years. In the process, with a flair for conspicuous corruption that ranks amongst the best this century has to offer, Mobutu amassed a personal fortune estimated to run into the billions of dollars sitting in the usual Swiss, Paris, and New York banks, while most of the population suffered from severe malnutrition.[1]

It can reasonably be said that his corruption was matched only by his cruelty. Mobutu, one observer of Zaire has written,

> rules by decree with a grotesque impulsiveness that seems to shock even his former [CIA] case officers. One recalled that in June 1971 Mobutu had forcibly enlisted in the armed forces the entire student body of Lovanium University. "He was put out by some student demonstrations," remembered the official. Mobutu finally relented, but ten of the students were sentenced to life imprisonment for crimes of "public insult" to the Chief of State.... One intelligence source recalls a fervent Mobutu approach, eventually deflected, that either Zaire with CIA help or the Agency alone undertake an invasion against "those bastards across the river" in the Congo Republic (Brazzaville). He's a "real wild man," said one former official, "and we've had trouble keeping him under rein."[2]

This may not have been for lack of trying. In June 1975 Mobutu announced that he had uncovered and suppressed a coup attempt aimed at his "physical elimination". He blamed an unnamed "large foreign power" and Zairian citizens "thirsty for money" (sic). The charges appeared in a government-controlled newspaper in the form of a letter from Mobutu, with an accompanying editorial indicating plainly that the large foreign power was the United States. A few days later, Zairian newspapers asserted that the CIA had organized tribal dissidents and black Americans for a coup against Mobutu planned for 30 September. It is not clear what relation this allegation had to the earlier one.

Mobutu declared that the "imperialists" were displeased with his breaking off relations with Israel, his nationalization of many foreign-owned businesses, and the "sincere and reciprocal" friendships which were developing between Zaire and China and North Korea. Several high-ranking Zairian military officers as well as other military men and civilians were arrested, their number reportedly including most of the CIA's indigenous agents in Zaire. The government announced that one of the arrested officers had returned four months ago from a US military school, another had been the Zairian military attaché in Washington until two weeks before, and a third had recently returned from studies at Fort Bragg, North Carolina where, as a class assignment, he had prepared a report on "How to plan and carry out a coup d'état against the government of Zaire." This last is not as ridiculous as it may sound. Such "hypothetical" exercises have been reported before by former students at CIA schools, although without the name of a real country being used and under the cover of learning how to *suppress* a coup attempt (as torture methods were taught in Vietnam under the cover of "countermeasures to hostile interrogation"; similarly, as we have seen, for the teaching of bombing techniques and chemical/biological warfare).

Eventually, seven of those arrested were condemned to death for the alleged plot (including some of the CIA's agents), seven men were acquitted, and 27 others given prison sentences. No Americans were named as conspirators, but the US ambassador, Deane R. Hinton, was ordered to leave the country and Zaire recalled its ambassador from Washington.

The State Department denied the allegations and called upon the Zairian government to provide evidence, which the latter failed to do. Secretary of State Henry Kissinger announced that the charges were based on "totally wrong information that fell into the hands of Zaire" and "was probably the result of forgery". It is difficult to evaluate Kissinger's assertion inasmuch as the Zairian government had made no public mention of any documents.[3]

Mobutu may indeed have been taken in by forged documents or, scoundrel that he was, he may have built a mountain out of a molehill of truth. It was suggested that his action was a pretext to get rid of certain Zairian military officers or that he was looking for a scapegoat for domestic problems.

On the other hand, it would not have been the first time that the CIA was involved in a plot to eliminate an ostensible ally of the United States—Trujillo, Figueres and Diem are cases in point. Mobutu, at this time, for his own reasons was deeply involved in the civil war in Angola on the side of the CIA-supported forces. Zaire was serving as an indispensable rear base and training and supply point, and Zairian troops were engaged in the fighting. The Agency may have felt very uneasy that the head of this vital ally in war was a man as erratic, unpredictable and uncontrollable as Mobutu Sese Seko. "Mobutu is screwing up Zaire pretty good, you know," commented a senior CIA officer upon returning to Washington from a meeting with the Zairian leader, shortly after his accusation against the United States. "He simply has no idea of how to run a country."[4]

Moreover, although Chinese and North Korean military advisers in Zaire were training forces fighting on the same side as the United States in the Angolan free-for-all, the simple tenet of cold-war life was that an American ally does not do things like invite Chinese and North Korean military advisers to their country. And the Zairian "wild man" had twice broken relations with the Soviet Union and twice re-established them. There was no telling what whimsy he might pursue next.

There is also the matter of the expelled American Ambassador. Deane Roesch Hinton was no ordinary Foreign Service career diplomat. He had worked closely with the CIA since the 1950s and was no stranger to extra-diplomatic operations. From 1967 to 1969 in Guatemala and the following two years in Chile (against Allende), Hinton, under the cover of the Agency for International Development (AID), had played a role in the CIA operations. He then served on a subcommittee of the National Security Council until taking up his post in Zaire in 1974.[5]

After the brouhaha about the alleged coup, both the CIA and Mobutu acted as if nothing out of the ordinary had happened, although the Agency did make an appeal to the Zairian president for the freedom of their agents sitting on death row[6] (outcome unknown), and did seem to be remarkably submissive to Mobutu's usual obnoxious and impulsive behavior. In October, Mobutu asked the CIA to help him annex Cabinda, a province of

Angola that was separated from the rest of Angola by a narrow strip of Zairian territory. Mobutu had coveted the province since coming to power in 1965. His greed for it was heightened a few years later when oil was discovered off the Cabindan coastline. The CIA, although busily involved in the Angolan civil war at this time, promptly flew in a one-thousand-man arms package for use by Zairian troops who marched into Cabinda. Agency officials helped to co-ordinate this almost casual invasion of a sovereign nation, but the operation proved to be singularly unsuccessful.[7]

Six months later, in April 1976, the CIA gave Mobutu close to $1.4 million to distribute to US-backed Angolan forces, thousands of whom were refugees in Zaire, desperate and hungry. Mobutu simply pocketed the money. The Agency had been aware of this possibility when they delivered the money to him but, in the words of CIA Africa specialist John Stockwell, "They rationalized that it would mollify him, bribe him not to retaliate against the CIA." Stockwell added this observation:

> It is an interesting paradox that the Securities and Exchange Commission has since 1971 investigated, and the Justice Department has prosecuted, several large U.S. corporations for using bribery to facilitate their overseas operations. At the same time, the U.S. government, through the CIA, disburses tens of millions of dollars each year in cash bribes. Bribery is a standard operating technique of the U.S. government, via the CIA, but it is a criminal offense for U.S. business.[8]

The same can be said of murder. A few months earlier, in January 1976, the Justice Department had concluded that no grounds existed for federal prosecution of CIA officials involved in plots to assassinate several heads of state, including Patrice Lumumba of the Congo.[9]

In early March 1977, during a pause in the Angola war, members of the Lunda (or Balunda) tribal group of Zaire who had been in exile in Angola and fighting along with their Angolan tribal kin on the side of the MPLA, crossed the border and invaded Zaire in a resumption of their own civil war. The invaders, numbering at least 2,000, were composed largely of former residents of Katanga (now Shaba) province who had fled the Congo during the early 1960s following the failure of their secessionist movement (see Congo chapter).

Mobutu urgently requested help from Zaire's traditional arms suppliers, Belgium, France and the United States, to put down this threat to his control of the mineral-rich Shaba province which accounted for about 70 percent of Zaire's foreign exchange. The United States responded immediately with some $2 million of military supplies, reaching $15 million worth within a month, while Belgium and France provided large amounts of arms and ammunition as well as 14 Mirage jet bombers from the latter.

Jimmy Carter had been in office less than two months when the Zairian conflict broke out, and he was reluctant to involve his administration deeply in a foreign adventure whose ultimate commitment could not be foreseen. The Angolan involvement had only recently wound down under severe congressional criticism. Compared to this and other American interventions, Carter's action in Zaire constituted a fairly mild response, mild enough to enable Washington to pass off its policy as one of "non-intervention" and effectively obscure the fact that it was actively taking sides in a civil war.

The administration pointed out that its aid was all of a "non-lethal" type (that is, a military transport plane, spare parts, fuel, communication equipment, parachutes, etc.); that the aid represented a drawing of credits already authorized by Congress for Zaire—as if the United States government therefore had no other choice in the matter; and that it had refused a Zairian request for further assistance. President Carter asserted on more than one occasion that the Zaire crisis was an African problem, best solved by Africans, yet he apparently saw no contradiction to this thesis in his own policy, nor did he offer any criticism of France or Belgium, or of China, which sent Mobutu a substantial amount of military equipment.

Carter denied the suggestion that US aid to Zaire was part of a coordinated venture with France, Belgium, Morocco, Egypt and the Sudan; and, at the same time, the State Department characterized American policy as "a neither help-nor-hinder position" towards Zaire. Yet, only a few days earlier, the United States had given its tacit approval to Morocco's decision to send 1,500 of its American-armed troops to aid Mobutu's cause, while confirming that "both by law and bilateral agreement, Morocco would have to obtain Washington's permission in advance if its army used American weapons outside Morocco".[10] Whether the Zairian rebels felt put out by the American non-lethal, non-help-nor-hinder, non-intervention policy was not reported.[11]

In mid-April, *Newsday* broke a story that the CIA was secretly supporting efforts to recruit several hundred mercenaries in the United States and Great Britain to serve alongside Zaire's notoriously ineffective army. David Bufkin, a 38-year-old Californian who reportedly was an experienced mercenary himself and had recruited other Americans for Angola, said that American "soldiers of fortune" would leave within a week for Zaire to fight against the rebels. Bufkin had advertised for former military men with combat experience for this particular mission.

The New York newspaper stated that the CIA had "strong links" to Bufkin and had told the Justice Department that it would not cooperate in any investigation of the Californian. (It is a criminal offense in the United States to recruit an American citizen for service with foreign armed forces or to enlist for such service.)

"Diplomats in Washington," the *New York Times* reported, "said they understood that President Mobutu Sese Seko had indicated several weeks ago that Zaire might have to recruit mercenaries to repel the invasion." They added that the aid from France, Belgium, Morocco, the United States and others may have led Mobutu to abandon the idea.

Bufkin denied that he was being financed by the CIA. He claimed that his financial aid "is coming from Africa and that's all I can tell you".[12] (This, of course, would not rule out the CIA channeling money to Bufkin via Zaire.) Several months later, the soldier of fortune revealed that he had worked with the CIA, without specifying when or where, as well as with the Korean CIA, going into some detail about his operations with the latter.[13] What role, if any, was actually played by mercenaries in Zaire has not come to light.

The more experienced rebels had the upper hand during the first month of the 80-day war, and the continuance of Mobutu's rule was reported to be uncertain. But the repeated pumping of men and supplies into Zaire by at least eight Western and African nations proved too much for the Lunda tribesmen. By the end of May, their offensive had been crushed and they were forced to retreat into Angola once again.

Although the Lunda were engaged in a struggle for tribal autonomy, of the kind which has erupted in one African country after another following independence, Mobutu knew that it was the cold-war, anti-communist card he had to play if he was to provoke greater military support, particularly from the United States. Accordingly, Zaire began to issue regular accusations against Cuba, which had a large military contingent still stationed in Angola.

Cuba had trained and armed the rebels, it was charged. This was true to some extent, but it had not been done necessarily to invade Zaire. Some quarters of the international left cloaked the Lunda in a revolutionary mantle, but the inspiration for this had more to do with the rebels being opposed by the likes of Mobutu, the United States and France than with any demonstrated revolutionary virtues. On the contrary, they were originally trained by white mercenaries and supported by Belgium and other Western interests in their secession attempt in Katanga. After fleeing to Angola, in return for sanctuary they served with the colonial Portuguese army in its campaign to put down the black nationalist guerrillas of the MPLA. Then, during the ensuing civil war in Angola, they switched over to fighting on the side of the MPLA and the Cubans.[14]

Cuba was leading the rebels ... Cuban, Russian and Portuguese troops were fighting with them, insisted the Zairian government.

The invasion "could not have taken place—and it could not continue—without the material support or acquiescence of the Soviet Union—whether or not Cuban troops are present", announced (now former) Secretary of State Henry Kissinger, in a choice example of knee-reflex anti-communism/wishful thinking, without any evidence whatsoever.[15]

And so it went. To the credit of the Carter administration, it resisted the temptation to embrace all the unfounded and sometimes silly charges, stating on several occasions that there was no evidence of Cuban involvement, and that the United States did not view the conflict as a confrontation between the Soviet Union and the West. An increasingly petulant Mobutu was finally moved to declare that if the United States had indeed "capitulated" in the face of communist danger, it should announce this clearly.[16]

Why then, did the United States intervene at all?

The day after the first American shipment of military aid, Washington expressed its concern about the possible "loss" to American mining interests in Zaire. However, there was not necessarily a logical connection between a Lunda capture of Shaba province, or even toppling Mobutu, and a threat to foreign investment and loans, and the Carter administration offered no elaboration of its statement. No matter who controlled the mines, they would be looking to sell the copper, the cobalt, and the other minerals. In 1960, the secession movement of these same Lunda forces in then-called Katanga province had been supported by both Washington and Belgium. (Why Belgium now opposed them was not made clear by events, except that the rebels' sabotage combined with power failure had halted the mines' water pumps, leading to widespread flooding.) And in neighboring Angola, as we have seen, when the "Marxist" MPLA took over control of oil-rich Cabinda province, it cooperated fully in business-as-usual with Gulf Oil Company. The Zaire government, on the other hand, in 1974, took over most small businesses and plantations without compensating the owners, and divided the spoils among political leaders loyal to Mobutu, which went well beyond anything the MPLA did.[17]

The expressed concern about US investments may have been no more than one type of "throwaway" remark that has often been put forth by Washington officials to make a particular foreign involvement sound more reasonable to the American public (most ironic in this case in light of traditional Marxist analysis), while giving the administration time to decide what it is they're actually trying to achieve. No further reference to American investments was made.

The American intervention in this case seems to have been little more than a highly-developed cold-war reflex action triggered by an invasion originating in a country classified as a member of the Soviet camp, and against a country ostensibly in the American or Western camp. Subsequent developments, or lack of them, may have inspired second thoughts in the administration, producing a dilemma which was succinctly summed up by a New York Times editorial observation a month into the war: "The instinct for intervention seems great but the case for it is not at all clear."[18]

Earlier, the Washington Post had expressed similar doubts. In an editorial entitled

"Why Zaire?", the newspaper stated that it was "a highly dubious proposition for the United States to deepen its involvement in the murk of Zaire in the way that it has." President Carter, it added, "has not explained the contingencies or stakes which require such an abrupt American response, nor the risks of delay".[19]

By his second year in the White House, Jimmy Carter had managed to acquire the unfortunate image of an "indecisive" man, a president who was yet to demonstrate the proverbial sterling qualities of leadership. His moderate response to the events in Zaire the previous year had contributed to this reputation, particularly amongst the hardline anti-communists in the United States and amongst some of the European and African nations which had come to Mobutu's aid.

Thus it was, in the middle of May 1978, when the Lunda again left Angola and invaded their home province in Zaire, that the Carter administration was once again drawn into the conflict, for reasons no more compelling than in the year before ... "determination this time, particularly with a meeting in 11 days in Washington of heads of NATO Governments, to act decisively", was the way the *New York Times* paraphrased "high administration officials".[20]

Within days the United States had sent several million dollars more of "non-lethal" military aid to Mobutu (condemned for human-rights violations only three months earlier by the State Department, under a president who championed human rights) while a fleet of 18 American military transport planes began ferrying Belgian and French troops into Zaire in a rescue mission of (white) foreigners trapped by the war. In the process of evacuating the foreigners, the French troops took a markedly active part in the war against the rebels, inflicting a serious military setback upon them.

Subsequently, the American airlift was extended to delivering Moroccan armed forces into Shaba province, then army units from Senegal and Gabon, and transporting French troops out of the region as they were replaced by African forces.[21]

The fighting in Shaba this time was over in less than a month. At its conclusion, the *New York Times* reported that "Discussions with officials in recent days, have produced no single cohesive explanation" for American policy in Zaire.[22]

The *Times* apparently was not placing too much weight upon the explanations already put forth by the administration. There were several of these in addition to the rescue mission and the need to act decisively. The president, for example, had discovered something which, it seems, he had not realized the year before; namely, that aiding Zaire was "in the national security interests of the United States".[23] As is customary with such crucial declarations, it was not felt necessary to explain what this actually meant in real-life terms.

Administration officials also professed "concern for the territorial integrity of all countries in Africa and elsewhere".[24] This marvelous platitude not only managed to do away with the previous 80 years of American foreign policy, including the very recent intervention into Angola, but was irrelevant in the context of a civil war ... more throwaways.

Several African governments which came to the aid of Mobutu during these two years likewise expressed regard for the territorial integrity of African states, but what these states found disquieting was that a victory for the Shaba rebels might encourage tribal dissidents within their own vulnerable borders.[25]

Another reason offered by the administration was the belief that Cuba and the Soviet Union, and even Angola, were, after all, somehow responsible. (Mobutu added Algeria and Libya.) But no more evidence to support these charges was forthcoming from any quarter than had been the case the year before, and Carter was obliged to fall back on an accusation of guilt by omission. On 25 May 1978 he declared that Cuba "obviously did nothing" to hold back the invasion. It then came to light that Castro had informed the US government a week earlier that he had learned of the rebel plans to invade Shaba and had tried unsuccessfully to stop it. Administration officials, clearly embarrassed, had no choice but to reply that they had not believed him.

"It is not a half-lie," commented Fidel Castro to charges of Cuban involvement. "It is an absolute, total, complete lie."

Two days later, the president rejoined: "Castro could have done much more had he genuinely wanted to stop the invasion. He could have interceded with the Katangese themselves; he could certainly have imposed Cuban troops near the border."[26]

In the final scene of this light comedy, Mobutu announced that he was holding Cuban prisoners captured in the fighting—the long-awaited proof of Cuban involvement. But when the American embassy in Zaire checked into the matter it found nothing to substantiate the claim. "Let's call it charitably a mistake," said one official."[27]

It remains a mystery why Mobutu Sese Seko commanded such support from the Western powers. In 1978 a "key European diplomat" told the *Washington Post:* "There's no alternative to the [Mobutu] regime. So we have to support him in hopes of reforming him." No further explanation, from the diplomat or the newspaper, was recorded.[28]

43. Jamaica 1976-1980
Kissinger's ultimatum

"I can give you my personal word," said Henry Kissinger to Jamaican Prime Minister Michael Manley, "that there is no attempt now underway involving covert action against the Jamaican government."[1]

Manley has written that at this moment "similar assurances given concerning Chile flashed a little ominously across my mind."[2] (Kissinger had given his personal word about American non-intervention to the Chilean Ambassador in Washington in 1971 at a time when the US government, and Kissinger in particular, were actively plotting the downfall of the Chilean government. When the ambassador mentioned press references to covert American actions against his country, Kissinger responded: "Absolutely absurd and without foundation.")[3]

Michael Manley also knew first-hand that American non-intervention in the affairs of Jamaica was not something to be taken for granted. During the 1972 election campaign, the American Ambassador in Jamaica, Vincent de Roulet, had promised Manley that the United States would not interfere in the campaign if Manley did not make nationalization of the foreign-owned bauxite industry an election issue. De Roulet feared that if Manley did so, he would oblige the opposition Jamaica Labour Party to vie with Manley's party for popular support on the question. According to de Roulet, Manley agreed and both sides kept their promise.[4]

Secretary of State Kissinger had arrived in Jamaica in December 1975 to suggest to Manley that he change his policies or else US-Jamaican relations "would be reviewed".[5] Kissinger raised the subject of Jamaica's request for a $100 million trade credit. "He said they were looking at it," wrote Manley later, "and let the comment hang in the room for a moment. I had the feeling he was sending me a message."[6]

The Jamaican prime minister—a graduate of the London School of Economics and the son of Norman Manley who had led Jamaica to independence from the British in 1962—had incurred Washington's displeasure since taking office in 1972 by behavior such as the following:

- Expressing support for the MPLA regime in Angola which the United States was attempting to topple at the very moment of the Kissinger-Manley meeting, an issue that was one of the Secretary of State's obsessions and one which he raised during the talk.

- Establishing diplomatic relations with Cuba and the Soviet Union and maintaining close ties with the Castro government, although "no closer," said Manley, "than ... with Mexico and Venezuela".[7]

- Advocating a form of democratic socialism, though maintaining a decidedly mixed economy which featured nothing more radical than could be found in many countries of Western Europe in the areas of health, education, minimum wage, and social services. Manley's party, the People's National Party—whose slogan was "Socialism is Love"—belonged to the Socialist International, as have ruling parties in modern times in Austria, Great Britain, West Germany and Sweden.

- Prevailing against the transnational aluminum companies, principally American, which operated on the island because it is rich in bauxite, the raw material of aluminum. The Jamaican government had imposed a production levy to obtain a significant—and what was regarded as long-overdue—increase in the payments made to it by the companies, and had then persuaded other bauxite-producing countries in the Third World to do the same. The government also intended to buy out 51 percent of the foreign bauxite mining operations, and planned, along with Venezuela and Mexico, to build an international aluminum processing complex outside the multinational system.[8]

Manley was pressured by both Washington and the Jamaican left. "Everyone wants me to be either a capitalist or a communist," he said at one point. "Why can't they just let me be? ... I've always been a democratic socialist and that's what I want in Jamaica."[9] He viewed the multinational corporations in a similar vein, declaring that they "have grown used to two types. One is the mendicant of the neo-colonial syndrome. The other is the revolutionary who simply sends in the army to take over the operation. Here they were dealing with neither. This was part of our search for the third path."[10]

The Jamaican prime minister did not toe the line Kissinger had drawn. Five days after the Secretary of State had departed, Manley informed him that "Jamaica had decided to support the Cuban army presence in Angola because we were satisfied that they were there because of the South African invasion ... I never heard another word about the hundred million dollar trade credit."[11]

At the time of Kissinger's visit, certain destabilization operations had already gotten off the ground, particularly in the area of propaganda, but it was primarily afterward, beginning in the election year of 1976, that covert actions started to escalate. In January, a few weeks after Kissinger had left, the US Embassy in Kingston was increased by seven. Manley has noted: "Yet all aid to Jamaica suddenly slowed to a virtual halt. The pipelines suddenly became clogged. Economic co-operation contracted as the embassy expanded."[12]

Investigative reporters Ernest Volkman and John Cummings, writing in *Penthouse* magazine in 1977 and citing "several senior American intelligence sources", stated that the destabilization program drawn up by the CIA station chief in Jamaica (Norman Descoteaux) contained the following elements:

a) "Covert shipments of arms and other equipment to opposition forces": Politics in Jamaica had long been spiced with strong-arm tactics, but this now intensified in both frequency and deadliness, and in the use of arson, bombing and assassination. "The CIA quickly sought to organize and expand the violence: shipments of guns and sophisticated communications equipment began to be smuggled into the island. In one shipment alone, which was grabbed by Manley's security forces, there were 500 submachine guns."[13]

Some of the CIA's traveling army of Cuban exiles arrived on the scene. One was Luis Posada Carriles, a former officer in Cuban dictator Batista's secret police, now a CIA-trained explosives expert who was implicated in the mid-air bombing of a Cubana Airlines plane in 1976 which killed 73 people. Posada was reportedly spotted at the scene of more than one bombing in Jamaica.[14]

The well-publicized violence was a body-blow to Jamaica's vital tourist business. The foreign tourists stayed away in droves, forcing many hotels to close their doors and consigning thousands of workers to the ranks of the unemployed.

b) "Extensive labor unrest": A wave of strikes by transport, electrical and telephone workers hit the island, reportedly provoked in part by graduates of the American Institute for Free Labor Development, the CIA's principal labor organization in Latin America.[15]

c) "Economic destabilization": In addition to the US credit squeeze and curtailment of aid, and the damage to tourism, the fragile Jamaican economy suffered from the actions of the aluminum companies. As an act of retaliation for the bauxite production levy—which had become law in May 1974—and with the tacit encouragement of Washington, the companies systematically reduced production, which hurt Jamaica in several ways.[16] In August 1975, the American firm, Revere Copper and Brass Company, closed its aluminum refinery after only four years of operation, saying that it was uneconomical.[17] In January 1976, the company announced that it was suing the Jamaican government over the levy.[18] Whether there was any underlying destabilization motive connected to these actions is not known.

A cargo of flour, brought to Jamaica on a German ship, the *Heidelberg*, was discovered to have been contaminated with the poison parathion, an insecticide which had been banned from Jamaica for many years. Much of the flour had already been sold and about 17 people died from it in December 1975 and January 1976. Later in the year, in October, a large shipment of rice from Costa Rica, on board the ship *City of Bochum*, arrived to relieve a rice shortage Jamaicans had been suffering through for months. This too was found to be contaminated by parathion and had to be destroyed.[19] The two incidents are reminiscent of the contaminations of sugar carried out by the CIA against Cuba (q.v.).

d) "Covert financial support for the opposition": This was principally the conservative Jamaica Labour Party (JLP). In June 1976, Jamaican security forces announced the uncovering of a plot to overthrow the government involving leading members of the JLP; another arrested party member was found to be making Molotov cocktails in a mineral-bottling plant he owned.[20] No evidence of CIA involvement in the conspiracy has been revealed.

e) "Mobilization of the middle class into CIA-created anti-government organizations to carry out well-publicized demonstrations": Groups with names such as "Silent Majority" and "Christian Women Agitators for Truth" were formed, the latter attacking those who criticized the United States and the CIA. In one instance, the group brought up the example of the famed and revered American doctor, Tom Dooley, who had founded seven hospitals for the poor in southeast Asia. The Christian Women could not have known then that Dr. Dooley had been a witting, active CIA operative in Indochina.[21] There was also an attempt by a newly formed "National Council of Women" to replay the pots-and-pans scenario which had worked so well in Chile, but this fizzled out.[22] (This featured women, mostly of the upper classes with their maids, banging on pots and pans in a street march to demonstrate the government's inability to provide enough food for their families.)

f) "Infiltration of security services and armed forces to turn them against the government": "With liberal bribes, the CIA turned many security personnel into paid informants for the agency." Several soldiers were part of a plot to assassinate Manley in July, one of at least three such attempts which "the CIA was directly involved in"; another, in September, employed Cuban exiles; the third turned to Jamaican gunmen to do the job. This last was in December, a final act of desperation on election night; all three attempts failed, not even a shot was fired, and Manley easily won re-election.[23]

During the campaign, CIA officer James Holt was accused of contriving a plot to turn the military against Manley's People's National Party. According to the accusation, a tape of a PNP youth rally was spliced with a message, purporting to be from Fidel Castro, urging young people to rise up in armed struggle against the police and the army. The tape was supposed to fall into the hands of the military and cause dissension.[24]

Press attacks against the government were carried out at a level of integrity only slightly above that of Holt's alleged tape. This was particularly the case with the *Daily Gleaner* whose campaign was very similar to that of *El Mercurio* in Chile before the fall of Allende, and it is eminently reasonable to assume that it was similarly financed by the CIA. Both newspapers had close links to the Inter-American Press Association (IAPA) of Miami, the *Gleaner's* Managing Director, Oliver Clarke, being elected to the association's executive in 1976. The IAPA, though not a formal CIA front, had received funding from the Agency and had been a reliable and valuable press asset for it since the 1950s.[25]

The *Gleaner* emphasized the omnipresent Cuban menace and how Manley was a prisoner of Castro and the KGB. One recurrent theme, echoed in the American press, was the presence of Cuban troops in Jamaica, a bald lie and something that would be impossible to conceal on the small island.

Propagandists arrived from the United States as well. Evangelists and faith healers came down to set up their tents and preach against communism and the government to the highly religious population,[26] à la the Christian Anti-Communist Crusade in British Guiana during the CIA's campaign against the government of Cheddi Jagan (q.v.).

With Henry Kissinger removed from formal power, and with the less interventionist Carter administration taking office in January 1977, American policy toward Jamaica was tempered: the economic pipelines were unclogged to some extent and the CIA, without the urgency of an upcoming election, diminished its activities.

It cannot be said, however, that Washington officialdom had learned to respect Manley's wish to "just let me be". Pulitzer prize-winner Les Payne reported in *Newsday* in February 1980 that "the Carter Administration remains determined to drive the country's Socialist prime minister from office unless he moderates his pro-Cuban policies." In an earlier article, Payne quoted a State Department source: "If within a 6-month testing period, Manley shows some signs of moderating his position, then we will take a softer line. If not, then we will continue to pursue a hard line."[27]

There was no let-up in the *Gleaner's* diatribes against Manley and his government. The newspaper reprinted numerous articles from all over the world which bore the standard CIA themes and syntax and undocumented assertions that the Agency's press assets are paid for. The *Gleaner* openly encouraged disaffection and mutiny in the security forces, and overthrow of the government. The following, from a column by John Hearne in June 1980, was not very unusual:

In many other countries, somebody with a disciplined force of men behind him would have long ago taken the Government away from them ... In most Third World countries, our Ministers, Ministers of State, Party commanders, heads of statutory boards, among others, would now be in forced exile or buried in common graves.[28]

Throughout, the *Gleaner* and other anti-Manley newspapers in Jamaica bemoaned the threat to freedom of the press posed by the government—on the premise, apparently, that this is only what one can expect from a "communist" government—and continued to print freely what in other countries would lead to arrest for sedition.

Manley was defeated for re-election in October 1980, due primarily to a continuing deterioration in the standard of living of the masses of people. While recognizing the importance of this factor, the former prime minister attributed his defeat also to "propaganda and finely calculated violence", the latter having persisted throughout his second term, being particularly heavy during the election year when 800 people lost their lives in political violence. Manley wrote that "Unless there is overwhelming and widely accepted evidence laying the blame for violence at the door of one party, it tends to damage the government in power, since it is the government that people look to for their personal security."[29] He added:

The Jamaican establishment had mastered the ways of destabilization. It knew how to use fact and create fiction for maximum effect. We do not know what was the part played by the CIA in the last year. By then it may not have mattered because the *Gleaner* and the JLP had clearly reached postgraduate level.[30]

44. Seychelles 1979-1981

Yet another area of great strategic importance

Mr. Michael Hoare, in 1981, was an elderly accountant leading a relatively sedate life in Durban, South Africa. There was, however, another side to the man that was somewhat different. In this other role he was "Mad Mike" Hoare, veteran mercenary. He had fought for the CIA in various "trouble spots" of the world, including the Congo in the 1960s, and had done the same for the government of South Africa. In 1981, at the age of 62, he led a mercenary invasion of the Seychelles on behalf of both his old employers.

The Seychelles is a country made up of a number of small islands in the Indian Ocean, about 800 miles off the coast of Kenya, with a population of some 62,000. The former British Crown Colony is also the site of a US Air Force installation, officially described as a satellite tracking station, and part of an area that the United States regards as being of great strategic importance. (This should be seen in light of the fact that it would be an arduous task to locate an area of the globe that Washington policy makers, at one time or another, have not regarded as being of great strategic importance.)

After France-Albert René, a socialist, took power in a 1977 coup, he withdrew South African landing rights, and the United States had to use all its formidable powers of economic and political persuasion to retain its base in the country. Moreover, the lease on the installation was to expire in 1990, and Washington, which worries about long-term "national security" needs as well as current trouble spots, was apprehensive that it might not be renewed. The United States was also worried about what it saw as the growing friendship between the Seychelles and the Soviet Union, a concern seemingly as common in

Washington as areas of great strategic importance.

René pursued a policy of non-alignment, a concept which did not preclude friendship with either superpower as long as the terms were not unduly exploitative. He was also a strong advocate of turning the Indian Ocean into a nuclear-free zone, without foreign military bases, including, ideally, the one in his own country. The Seychelles president was particularly critical of American efforts to develop the British-owned Indian Ocean island of Diego Garcia into a major air and naval base.[1]

In 1979, a plot to invade the Seychelles and overthrow René was aborted when it was discovered by his government before the mercenaries were able to leave Durban. An official investigation into the matter by the Seychelles government concluded that the United States and France had been directly involved with the plotters, that the American ambassador in Kenya had been in contact with supporters of James Mancham, the man deposed by René, and that the US Charge d'Affaires in the Seychelles was the link man in the conspiracy.[2] Several of the 120 Americans employed at the US base were expelled from the country.[3]

Two years later, in November 1981, an invasion force of more than 40 men, pretending to be members of a rugby club, traveled from South Africa to Swaziland whence they flew to the Seychelles aboard a regular commercial flight of the Royal Swazi Airlines. It appears that the attack was not planned for the arrival but for some time later, after the soldiers of fortune had settled in. But some of the arms hidden in their luggage were discovered upon arrival, and a battle broke out at the airport. The would-be invaders were forced to hijack an Air India plane back to Durban, although seven of their number were not so lucky, being caught and detained in the Seychelles.[4] But Mad Mike Hoare had survived another close call.

A few days after this debacle, the *Sunday Tribune*, published in Durban, where the invasion plot was reportedly hatched, cited "reliable local and foreign sources" for the assertion that the CIA had financed the raising and equipping of the invasion force. "Despite a terse, one-sentence denial by the U.S government yesterday," the conservative newspaper declared, "separate mercenary sources in South Africa are emphatic that funding for the operation originated with the CIA." At the same time, the *Tribune* made clear the complicity of its own government, an act for which several South African editors were duly prosecuted by the authorities.[5]

In 1982, Hoare and 44 other men went on trial in South Africa for airplane hijacking. Five weeks earlier, all but five of them had been released by the government with a "good-ol'-boys" wave of the hand, but diplomatic protests from Western nations, including the United States, which pointed out that South Africa had formally associated itself with a 1978 anti-hijacking declaration, led to a reversal of the earlier decision.

Twenty-three of the men were South Africans and most of these, it turned out, were reservists in elite units of the South African Defense Force. The head of the security police said that the men had not been charged at first because they had been misled into thinking they were on an official mission. Who had misled them, or why, was not reported. The picture which emerged from the trial was that the government, at a minimum, was well aware of the plot and ready to be helpful. Hoare produced an invoice, purportedly from the military, certifying the delivery to his home of weapons and ammunition before the flight to the Seychelles. This apparently was not contested by the prosecution. The government also requested that evidence from some defendants about their involvement in army activities in 1981 should not be heard because it could prejudice state security.

Hoare testified further that he had met someone from the CIA in Pretoria and informed him of the coup plans. The United States was interested, the soldier of fortune said, but he described the CIA man's attitude as "extremely timid" and Hoare didn't suggest that the United States had played an active role. Under cross-examination, however, he acknowledged telling his troops that the CIA had approved the plan.[6]

Motivation seems not to have been an issue raised at the trial. For the mercenaries, the coup attempt was undertaken presumably for money. Of the two governments involved in the matter, the United States had a much greater interest than South Africa in toppling the René government, and had, apparently, tried it before. But it would need the help of South Africa in that part of the world. As we have seen, the US intelligence establishment had been collaborating with Pretoria's intelligence service since the 1960s and continued to do so in the mid-1970s in regard to Angola. Circumstances indicate that this relationship continued, or was renewed, under the Reagan administration, which took office in 1981.

It appears that Mad Mike Hoare was made a scapegoat, for he was imprisoned—an action he called a "double-cross", and which he attributed to the government wanting to appear as an innocent party which defended international justice—and was not released until 1985. Almost all his co-conspirators were released in November 1982, after serving but four months in prison.[7]

On 15 December 1981, the UN Security Council decided to send a commission to the Seychelles to investigate the invasion. Although the United States voted for the motion, the American ambassador, Jeane Kirkpatrick, suggested that to send the commission was to assume that the "Seychelles affair was not purely internal", and was "prejudging the situation".[8] Even by the standards of Kirkpatrick's renowned cold-war-impaired logic, this was a remarkable statement, when it is considered that South Africans made up about half the invasion force, with the others emanating from Great Britain, Rhodesia, the US, Germany, Austria, and elsewhere. The number of Seychellois dissidents amongst their number came to zero.

It seems that someone was still determined that the René government should not remain in power. In December 1983, South Africa announced that it had arrested five men for attempting to recruit mercenaries in yet another plot to invade the Seychelles.[9]

45. Grenada 1979-1984

Lying—one of the few growth industries in Washington

What can be said about an invasion launched by a nation of 240 million people against one of 110 thousand? And when the invader is, militarily and economically, the most powerful in the world, and the target of its attack is an underdeveloped island of small villages 1,500 miles away, 133 square miles in size, whose main exports are cocoa, nutmeg and bananas ... ?

The United States government had a lot to say about it. The relation which its pronouncements bore to the truth can be accurately gauged by the fact that three days after the invasion the deputy White House press secretary for foreign affairs resigned, citing "damage to his personal credibility".[1]

One of the fundamental falsehoods concerning the invasion of Tuesday, 25 October 1983 was that the United States had been requested to intervene by an urgent plea on the 21st from the Organization of Eastern Caribbean States (OECS), comprising six countries, and joined in this instance by Barbados and Jamaica. These countries purportedly feared some form of aggressive act from the new ultra-leftist regime in Grenada which had deposed socialist leader Maurice Bishop. Bishop had been expelled from the ruling party on 12 October, placed under house arrest the next day, and murdered on the 19th.

Even if the fears were valid, it would constitute a principle heretofore unknown under international law, namely that state A could ask state B to invade state C in the absence of any aggressive act toward state A by state C. In Washington, State Department lawyers worked overtime, finally settling on sections of an OECS mutual assistance pact, the Charter of the OAS, and the United Nations Charter as legal justifications for the American action. These documents, however, even with the most generous interpretation, provide for nothing of the sort. Moreover, Article Six of the OECS pact requires *all* members to approve decisions of the organization's Authority (the heads of government). Grenada, a member, certainly did not approve. It was not even at the meeting, although US officials were present to steer the direction of the discussions.[2]

As matters later transpired, Tom Adams, the Prime Minister of Barbados, stated that the United States had approached him on 15 October concerning a military intervention. (The State Department declined to comment when asked about Adams' statement.)[3] Then, "sources close to Jamaican Prime Minister Edward Seaga" asserted that the plea by the Caribbean nations "was triggered by an offer from the United States"—"Issue an appeal and we'll respond" was the message conveyed by Washington.[4] Furthermore, on 26 October, the US ambassador to France, Evan Galbraith, stated over French television that the Reagan administration had been planning the invasion for the previous two weeks;[5] that is, not only well before the putative request from the Caribbean countries, but, if Galbraith is to be taken literally, even before Bishop was overthrown or before this outcome could have been known with any certainty, unless the CIA had been mixed up in the intra-party feud.

Eventually it was disclosed that at some point before the invasion the government of Eugenia Charles, the Prime Minister of Dominica, who headed the OECS, had been the recipient of covert CIA money "for a secret support operation".[6]

At the same time, the United States, as if to cover its bets, endorsed (if not in fact devised) the claim by the OECS that the governor-general of Grenada, Paul Scoon, had also sent an urgent appeal for military intervention to the organization. Apart from the highly debatable question of whether Scoon—appointed by the British Queen to his largely cere-monial, figurehead position, a vestige of the days of the Empire—had the constitutional right to make such a momentous decision on behalf of an independent Grenada, there was the mystery of how and when he had sent his request, or, indeed, whether he had sent it at all.

On 31 October, the London press reported that British Foreign Secretary Sir Geoffrey Howe "was emphatic that there had been no request for intervention from Sir Paul Scoon". Prime Minister Thatcher unequivocally confirmed this. Scoon, said Sir Geoffrey, "had been seen by a British diplomat last Monday—the day before the invasion—and had not men-tioned any such desire."[7] The same day (another report places it on Sunday) Scoon spoke by phone to the Commonwealth Secretariat in London and to Buckingham Palace, but, again, made no mention of intervention.[8]

Interviewed later by the BBC, Scoon himself said that an invasion was the "last thing" he wanted.[9]

In the end, after the invasion was underway, Scoon signed a piece of paper aboard the USS *Guam* that made the whole operation nice and legal.[10]

Another justification advanced by the United States for its action, what President Reagan termed "of overriding importance", was the need to evacuate many hundreds of Americans from the island, mainly students at St George's Medical College who were supposedly in a dangerous position because of the new regime and the chaos surrounding its accession to power.

To refute this contention one does not have to dig for evidence; there is a surfeit lying on the surface, viz. ...

Two members of the US Embassy in Barbados, Ken Kurze and Linda Flohr, reported over the weekend before the invasion that "US students in Grenada were, for the most part, unwilling to leave or be evacuated. They were too intent on their studies."[11] Another report, in the London press, that three US diplomats visited Grenada at the same time and appeared to have agreed on orderly departures for any Americans wishing to leave, may or may not refer to the same thing.[12]

The White House acknowledged that two days before the invasion, Grenada had offered the United States "an opportunity to evacuate American citizens. But officials said the Reagan administration came to distrust the offer." This was, they said, because the Grenadian government had promised that the airport would be open on Monday for evacuation flights, but it was instead closed.[13] Only later did the White House admit that four charter flights had indeed left the airport on Monday.[14]

Some of those who left on Monday were American medical students. The Chancellor of the medical school, Dr. Charles Modica, who was visiting New York, declared on the day of the invasion that he was in touch with amateur radio operators at the college. "I think the President's information is very wrong," he said, "because some of the Americans started to go out yesterday."[15]

The Grenadian government issued instructions that the American students should be treated with utmost consideration by the army; vehicles and escorts were provided for them to shuttle between their two campuses.[16]

The Cuban government released documents which showed that it had notified the United States on 22 October that no American or other foreign citizen was in danger and said it was ready "to cooperate in the solution of problems without violence or intervention". It received no reply until after the invasion had begun.[17] On the 23rd the Cubans sent a message to the Grenadian leaders suggesting that the area around the medical school be demilitarized to avoid providing the United States with an excuse for invasion: "the pretext of evacuating its citizens".[18]

Asked by journalists if there was any concrete information about threats to Americans in Grenada, the White House spokesman responded: "Nothing that I know of."[19]

After subduing the minor resistance of Grenadian soldiers and Cuban construction workers, the US forces discovered several other things to justify their coming: they found, said Ronald Reagan, "a complete base of weapons and communication equipment which makes it clear a Cuban occupation of the island had been planned". One warehouse "contained weapons and ammunition stacked almost to the ceiling, enough to supply thousands of terrorists". Grenada, the president declared, was "a Soviet-Cuban colony being readied as a major military bastion to export terror and undermine democracy, but we got there just in time."[20]

Documents discovered by the American military allegedly showed that "the Cubans were planning to put their own government in Grenada" (later, CIA Director William Casey was to admit that the documents "were not a real find") and there was found what "appeared to have been a terrorist training center".[21] Moreover, missile silos were being built in Grenada ... there were 1,100 Cubans on the island, it was announced, almost all professional soldiers; soon the number was 1,600 ...[22]

The US/Grenada/Cuba scenario staged in Washington was comparable at the time to the Soviet Union invading Great Britain and then announcing that it had prevented an American takeover, and Marx-knows what else, because it had discovered 30,000 US servicemen there, over 100 American military bases, a huge arsenal of nuclear weapons, and "enough arms to supply millions of terrorists". The Soviet president could then have declared that "We got there just in time."

Comparable, except that the Soviet discoveries would have been real. The American claims turned out to be as phantom as the other components of the media package, or, at best, highly questionable—a correspondent for *The Guardian* of London reported that in the warehouse "that contained most of the weapons, there were only five mortars to be seen, one recoilless rifle, one Soviet-made quadri-barrelled anti-aircraft gun, and two Korean-vintage British Bren guns on display".[23] The *New York Times* reported, without further detail, "significant stockpiles of Soviet arms but also a number of antiquated guns, including rifles manufactured in the 1870s".[24] Years later it was revealed that a US intelligence report of 30 October had concluded that "the caches of arms and weapons on Grenada were for the army and the militia and were not sufficient or intended to be used in overthrowing the governments in the neighboring islands."[25]

More to the point, however, is the fact that the Grenadian government had been threatened with destabilization for over four years by the United States. The leaders of the country knew that they had to develop the country's defenses. They were people who had read some recent history.

The Cuban government announced that there were 784 of their people in Grenada and specified all their jobs: 636 were construction workers, mostly in their forties and fifties (an observation made by several American and British journalists); the remainder, which included 44 women, were doctors, dentists, nurses, public health workers, teachers, etc., and 43 military personnel; thereafter, the United States went by the Cuban figures.[26]

The world was asked to believe that there was a major Cuban military presence with imminent control of the country. Yet the Cubans in Grenada were unable even to save Maurice Bishop and his government which Castro had strongly and warmly supported. The Cuban government had expressed in no uncertain terms its distaste for the Military Revolutionary Council (MRC) which had overthrown Bishop. Before the US invasion, Castro had blamed Bishop's death on "grave errors" by extremists,[27] and later referred to them as the "Pol Pot Group".[28] He had turned down a request from the MRC for more troops when the American action seemed imminent. The MRC was told that its request was "impossible and unthinkable" after what had happened.[29]

The Russians, on the other hand, had indicated their support for the MRC and its coup, although the Soviet interest in Grenada was generally minimal. Cuba was enough of a Caribbean burden and potential spark-point for Moscow. The Soviet Union condemned the American invasion, comparing it to "a daring cavalry attack of armed-to-the-teeth white settlers on a village of Redskins".[30] But this was *de rigueur* cold-war fare. The lack of real concern on the part of Soviet leaders about the invasion, and the fate of Grenada, was made evident six months later when they announced that the USSR would not take part in the Olympics in Los Angeles. Grenada was not even mentioned amongst their reasons although the circumstances truly cried out for it—four years earlier, the United States had cited the Soviet invasion of Afghanistan as its sole reason for boycotting the Moscow Olympics.

Finally, there was the question of why Cuba or the Soviet Union would have needed Grenada as a springboard for their dastardly deeds in Latin America when there was already Cuba itself, militarily and politically more secure and stable than Grenada.

After the invasion, after the overthrow of the Grenadian government, after the US forces had killed or wounded hundreds of people ... officials of the Reagan administration, reported the *New York Times*, "acknowledge that in their effort to rally public support for the invasion of Grenada, they may have damaged the Government's credibility by making sweeping charges about Soviet and Cuban influence on the island without so far providing detailed evidence." The officials simply asked that the public "reserve judgement until all the information is in".[31]

The New Jewel Movement (NJM) under Maurice Bishop had taken power in March 1979 by ousting, to popular acclaim, Eric Gairy, an erratic personality given increasingly to thuggery to maintain his rule. That accomplished, Bishop, a London-educated lawyer, had to deal with the exceedingly more formidable task which faces a socialist revolutionary in power: spurring an underdeveloped country to lift itself up by its own bootstraps when it doesn't have any boots.

They had to start with the basics: jobs, new schools, teacher training, adult literacy, social services, clean water ... the NJM left private business undisturbed, but instituted free health care, free milk for young children, agricultural co-operatives, and the like.

Nicholas Brathwaite, the Chairman of the US-approved Interim Government following the invasion, and his colleagues, reported *The Guardian*, "readily praise the [NJM] for giving Grenadians new awareness, self-confidence and national pride and admit it is a hard act to follow."[32]

The World Bank gave the Grenadian government good grades also. In 1980 the Bank praised the NJM's sound fiscal management and two years later wrote that "Government objectives are centered on the critical development issues and touch on the country's most promising development areas."[33]

The New Jewel Movement did not hold elections. Bishop explained this decision on one occasion in the following way:

> There are those (some of them our friends) who believe that you cannot have a democracy unless there is a situation where every five years, and for five seconds in those five years, a people are allowed to put an "X" next to some candidate's name, and for those five seconds in those five years they become democrats, and for the remainder of the time, four years and 364 days, they return to being non-people without the right to say anything to their government, without any right to be involved in running the country.[34]

In lieu of the traditional system, the NJM claimed, democracy in Grenada was manifested through numerous mass organizations and decentralized structures which received and seriously considered input from large numbers of citizens. However well this form of democracy may have worked, or would have if not interrupted, it inevitably produced resentment as well. People were expected to attend meeting after meeting and were subject to various forms of pressure to conform to the exigencies of the revolution.

Before long, the leaders of nearby Caribbean states, particularly Tom Adams of Barbados and Eugenia Charles of Dominica, who were prime supporters of the invasion, evidenced hostility towards the Grenadian government. Bishop believed that this derived from fear of their own people's enthusiasm for Grenada's example, an enthusiasm, he said, which was demonstrated at every public appearance by the Grenadian leaders in the region.[35] Charles was regarded by Reagan administration people as passionately pro-American, a "Caribbean Jeane Kirkpatrick," who "made British Prime Minister Margaret Thatcher seem like a kitten".[36]

The United States adopted its adversarial position almost immediately. Washington recognized instinctively that the new Grenadian leaders would not fall easily into line in regard to the American obsession with quarantining Cuba. Indeed, Grenada itself might turn out to be that long-dreaded beast—"another Cuba". Less than a month after Bishop assumed power, the American ambassador delivered a note to him which read in part:

> Although my government recognizes your concern over allegations of a possible counter-coup, it also believes that it would not be in Grenada's best interests to seek assistance from a country such as Cuba to forestall such an attack. We would view with displeasure any tendency on the part of Grenada to develop closer ties with Cuba.[37]

The counter-coup the ambassador was referring to was Bishop's fear that Eric Gairy, in exile in the United States, would put together a mercenary army to invade the island. The NJM feared a CIA destabilization operation even more but, in either case, who but "a country such as Cuba" could they turn to for help?

Before the year 1979 was out, Grenada had discovered hidden transmitters in its UN Mission,[38] and representatives of the US government were visiting travel agents in the United States, spreading travel-scare rumours to discourage tourism to the island's sunny beaches, a most important source of foreign exchange.[39]

Over the next four years, Washington tried to harass Grenada in some of the other ways in which it was practiced, more so under Ronald Reagan beginning in 1981 than under President Carter. The United States aggressively lobbied the International Monetary Fund and several other international lending organizations in an attempt to block loans to Grenada although, surprisingly, not with marked success. The IMF, for example, approved a loan to Grenada "despite vigorous opposition from the Reagan Administration", opposition based ostensibly on "economic grounds".[40]

In the summer of 1981, the CIA developed plans "to cause economic difficulties for Grenada in hopes of undermining the political control of Prime Minister Maurice Bishop." The operation reportedly was scrapped because of objections by the Senate Intelligence Committee. One committee member, however, remarked that "If they were going to do something ... I'm not sure they would tell us. I think they would wait until it was all over."[41]

The main thrust of the American campaign against Grenada was in the form of propaganda, the theme of which was that Grenada was a fully paid-up member of the Soviet-Cuban-Nicaraguan Terrorist Network which held a dagger at America's throat. Associating Grenada thusly could serve to further discourage tourism as well as justify an invasion.

The propagation of this general theme was punctuated by specific accusations which were simply fraudulent. One early hoax was that a Soviet submarine base was being constructed on the south coast of the island. This report was given wide currency until 1983 when a correspondent for the *Washington Post* visited the supposed site and pointed out that no submarine base could possibly be built in an area where the sea was so shallow.[42]

In February 1983, an official of the US Defense Department announced, apparently with a straight face, that the Soviet Union had shipped to Grenada assault helicopters, hydrofoil torpedo boats, and supersonic MIG fighters which gave Grenada an air force of 200 (sic) modern planes.[43] The whereabouts of this mighty armada have remained a mystery ever since.

The charge which received the greatest media play was the canard that the new airport being built in Grenada was intended as a military facility for the Russians and Cubans. Grenada insisted that it was only to encourage tourism, its one growth industry. In March 1983, President Reagan told an American television audience that the airfield would have a 10,000-foot runway, but that

> Grenada doesn't even have an air force [see previous paragraph]. Who is it intended for? ... The rapid build-up of Grenada's military potential is unrelated to any conceivable threat ... The Soviet-Cuban militarization of Grenada ... can only be seen as a power projection into the region.[44]

The president displayed aerial photos of the construction site—there were regular American spy flights over the island—as if to imply something hidden and furtive in the operation when, in fact, the site was very much open to the public.

There is a plethora of evidence that puts Reagan's analysis into question: At least five other Caribbean islands, including Barbados, had similar-sized or larger airfields yet did not possess air forces.[45] The building of the airfield was encouraged by the World Bank, which also discussed with Grenada the erection of new tourist hotels.[46] The excavation work was being done by the Layne Dredging Co. of Florida and the communications system installed by Plessey, a British multinational, the Cubans donating labor and machinery.[47] Plessey rejected the US claim: "The airport ... was being built to purely civilian specifications," it said, and listed a number of technical characteristics of a military airport/base which the new airport would not have.[48]

Further, the European Common Market had contributed money toward the construction—"In our view the airport is for tourism," said a spokesman. "We stand by our commitment."[49] The airport was being funded by about a dozen nations as well, including Canada, Mexico and Venezuela. The United States had turned down a request for assistance, and instead had exerted pressure to deter international financing.[50]

After the invasion, the airport was completed, by the United States. "The decision has been taken to complete it by the military, for the military," said one of the sub-contractors. "Equipment for that purpose is already being moved on to the site."[51] (As far as is known, the United States has not yet used the airport for military purposes.)

There were also several instances of the Grenadian opposition press featuring entirely unfounded stories of the type mentioned above, as well as fostering harmful local economic rumors. In one case in 1979 a Grenadian newspaper reprinted a story from, of all places, the West German magazine *Bunte*, which reported that large military and missile bases were being built in Grenada, something which would be impossible to hide on the tiny island, but it was a lie made of whole cloth.[52] The reprinting-from-abroad tactic, as we have seen, is one often employed by the CIA, and to the NJM leaders it was a clear signal that the Agency had arrived in town. It led eventually to the government closing down independent newspapers. The country, they felt, was simply too vulnerable, even more so than Chile and Jamaica, where the same CIA tactic had been employed.

It was the same with political prisoners, most of them former members of Gairy's secret police.[53] The government was afraid to release some of them lest they wind up in a Gairy and/or CIA mercenary force or engage in actions like the June 1980 bombing at an outdoor rally which was apparently designed to remove the entire NJM leadership with one blow, but instead took the lives of three young women.

As to the invasion itself ... code-named "Urgent Fury" ... 2,000 American marines and paratroopers the first day, by week's end 7,000 on the island, even more waiting offshore ... planes fitted with murderous multi-barreled Gatling guns spraying positions of the People's Revolutionary Army ... "The People's Revolutionary Army—are they on our side or theirs?" asks the young Marine[54]... the home of the Cuban ambassador damaged and looted by American soldiers; on one wall is written "AA", symbol of the 82nd Airborne Division; beside it the message: "Eat shit, commie faggot"[55] ... captured Cubans used as hostages, ordered to march in front of American jeeps as they advanced on Cuban positions, a violation of the Geneva Convention[56] ... promises of all kinds were made to Cuban prisoners, said Castro, to get them to go to the United States; none accepted[57] ... "I want to fuck communism out of this little island," says a marine, "and fuck it right back to Moscow."[58] ... "Britain announced that it was sending a destroyer to assist in the rescue," said the American radio station to the Grenadian people the first morning; not a half-truth, but a complete lie ... Grenadians who heard the broadcasts said they were a powerful encouragement to accept the occupation[59] ... the fighting was over in a week, 135 Americans killed or wounded, 84 Cubans, 400 Grenadians, more or less ...

The land conquered, there remained the people's hearts and minds. At the outset, the invasion radio station engaged in fiery attacks against Bishop—he had brought Grenada into captivity said the announcer.[60] But then the Americans evidently learned that this was a tactical error, that Bishop was still enormously popular, because for some time afterward, criticism of his regime was usually made more indirectly and without naming him.

Before long the Psychological Operations Battalion of the US Army was cruising over the island in a helicopter offering the Grenadians, via a loudspeaker, a large serving of anti-Cuban fare: the Cubans had supported those who had killed Bishop, Grenada had been a pawn of Cuba, Castro/communism were still a threat, and so forth. Posters were put up showing alleged captured Cuban weapons with the slogan, "Are these the tools that build airports?" Other posters linked the MRC leaders to Moscow.[61]

In March 1984, a visiting London journalist could report:

> The island remains visibly under American occupation. Jeeps patrol constantly. Helicopters fly over the beaches. Armed military police watch the villagers and frequent the cafes. CIA men supervise the security at the courthouse. The island's only newspaper pours out weekly vitriol about the years of the revolutionary government, "this gruesome period in our history". The pressures, in a small community, are heavy.[62]

And in June we learned that schools called after "heroes of the revolution" had been given back their old names, though not without pupil protests. And the US Information Service was showing school children a film entitled "Grenada: Return to Freedom".[63]

The invasion was almost universally condemned in Latin America, only the military dictatorships of Chile, Guatemala and Uruguay expressing support. The United Nations voted its disapproval overwhelmingly. To this President Reagan responded: "One hundred nations in the UN have not agreed with us on just about everything that's come before them where we're involved, and it didn't upset my breakfast at all."[64]

One of the evils of Communist states, we were always told, is that they were oblivious to world opinion.

There was, however, the supreme irony that most of the people of Grenada welcomed the invasion. In addition to the conservative minority who knew that the "socialist" experiment would now be decisively put to rest, there were the greater number who were overjoyed to see the murderers of their beloved Maurice Bishop receive the punishment due them. Despite all the hostility and lies directed at Bishop by Washington for over four years, it did not seem to occur to the islanders that the invasion had nothing to do with avenging his death and that the United States had merely used the event as a convenient pretext for an action it had desired to carry out for a long time.

If the average Grenadian seems thus rather ingenuous, with a short political memory, we must consider also that the average American lustily cheered the invasion, believed everything which crossed the lips of Ronald Reagan (as if this were the first US intervention in history), and to this day would be hard pressed to recite a single falsehood associated with the entire affair. The president himself later appeared to have completely repressed the incident. In March 1986, when asked about the possibility of an American invasion of Nicaragua, he replied:

> You're looking at an individual that is the last one in the world that would ever want to put American troops into Latin America, because the memory of the great Colossus in the north is so widespread in Latin America. We'd lose all our friends if we did anything of that kind.[65]

On the fourth day of the invasion Reagan made a speech which succeeded in giving jingoism a bad name. The president managed to link the invasion of Grenada with the shooting down of a Korean airliner by the Soviet Union, the killing of US soldiers in Lebanon, and the taking of American hostages in Iran. Clearly, the invasion symbolized an end to this string of humiliations for the United States. Even Vietnam was being avenged. To commemorate the American Renaissance, some 7,000 US servicemen were designated heroes of the republic and decorated with medals. (Many had done no more than sit on ships near the island.) America had regained its manhood, by stepping on a flea.

Postscript:

At the end of 1984, former Premier Herbert Blaize was elected prime minister, his party capturing 14 of the 15 parliamentary seats. Blaize, who in the wake of the invasion had proclaimed to the United States: "We say thank you from the bottom of our hearts,"[66] had been favored by the Reagan administration.[67] The candidate who won the sole opposition seat announced that he would not occupy it because of what he called "vote rigging and interference in the election by outside forces."[68]

One year later, the Washington-based Council on Hemispheric Affairs reported on Grenada as part of its annual survey of human rights abuses:

> Reliable accounts are circulating of prisoners being beaten, denied medical attention and confined for long periods without being able to see lawyers. The country's new US-trained police force has acquired a reputation for brutality, arbitrary arrest and abuse of authority.

The report added that an offending all-music radio station had been closed and that US-trained counter-insurgency forces were eroding civil rights.[69]

By the late 1980s, the government began confiscating many books arriving from abroad, including Graham Greene's *Our Man in Havana* and *Nelson Mandela Speaks*. In April 1989, it issued a list of more than 80 books which were prohibited from being imported.[70]

Four months later, Prime Minister Blaize suspended Parliament to forestall a threatened no-confidence vote resulting from what his critics called "an increasingly authoritarian style".[71]

46. Morocco 1983
A video nasty

The government of Morocco, in January 1983, had the sad duty to announce the "grievous death" in a car accident of General Ahmed Dlimi, a confidant of King Hassan for more than 20 years and commander of the Moroccan Army's southern forces.

When the *Le Monde* correspondent had the temerity to suggest that Dlimi's death was perhaps not an accident, he was summarily expelled from the country.[1]

Then, in March, Ahmed Rami, a Moroccan political scientist living in exile in Sweden, stated unequivocally that Dlimi had been murdered by Hassan and his security men and that the CIA was deeply implicated.[2]

Ahmed Rami had been a lieutenant in the Moroccan Army and a leader of *Le Mouvement des Officiers Libres*, the underground movement of army officers dedicated to overthrowing the king and the monarchy as well as the king's personal corruption and his "crimes against human rights". Rami was living abroad under sentence of death in Morocco for his part in a failed attempt to shoot down a plane carrying Hassan in 1972.

The dissident officers supported the establishment of a "democratic Islamic Arab Republic of Morocco" and a negotiated settlement in the country's ruinous war with the Polisario guerrillas in the Western Sahara, a war in which US military aid and personnel had reportedly enabled Morocco to maintain a deadlock.[3]

Ahmed Dlimi, while serving as the king's right-hand man, had been secretly associated with *Officiers Libres*. When he went abroad he would meet with Rami and during 1982 the two men were discussing plans for a coup attempt in July of the following year.

"Unknown to us, however," said Rami, "the CIA was investigating him [Dlimi]. When the CIA handed over a dossier to King Hassan in January [1983] it contained videofilm of General Dlimi and I meeting in Stockholm last December. That was enough for Dlimi to be eliminated."[4]

Morocco, said the *New York Times*, had become the United States' "closest and most useful ally in the Arab world."[5] Hassan had clearly tied his fortunes to the Reagan administration. In 1981 alone, he was visited by Secretary of Defense Caspar Weinberger and Secretary of State Alexander Haig, as well as the Deputy Director of the CIA, the chairman of the Senate Foreign Relations Committee, and a host of other high-level Washington officials. The Assistant Secretary of Defense for International Security arrived with a team of 23 military advisers and experts; more than 100 Americans were reported to be working with the Moroccan armed forces.[6]

In the years previous, Hassan had co-operated extensively with US policies in Africa. In both 1977 and 1978 he sent Moroccan troops to Zaire in support of the American actions there, and since the mid-1970s he had been aiding the UNITA forces in Angola along with the United States and South Africa in their continuing effort to overthrow the MPLA government. At the same time, King Hassan had allowed the CIA to build up its station in Morocco to where it was probably one of the Agency's key posts in Africa.[7]

In these and other important ways, Hassan had earned the gratitude and protection of the United States. Thus it was that the CIA exposed General Dlimi's double life to the king. Dlimi, moreover, had reportedly advocated that Morocco receive aid from France, the former colonial power, rather than from the United States. The CIA saw this as a threat to the American position in the country and insisted that Hassan get rid of his confidants who favored closer relations with France.[8]

At eleven o'clock on the night of 23 January 1983, says Ahmed Rami, Dlimi was called to the palace in Marrakesh. There, ten security men escorted him to an underground interrogation room. At one a.m., "two American officers" arrived with the king and went into the interrogation room for several hours. Dlimi was tortured, and, at five a.m., he was shot. His body was later placed in his car which was exploded in a suburb of the city. No one, not even his family, was allowed to see the body.[9]

47. Suriname 1982-1984
Once again, the Cuban bogeyman

It was unusual, to be sure, that the Director of the CIA would inform Congress in advance of an Agency plan to overthrow a foreign government. President Reagan, said William Casey to the House and Senate intelligence committees in December 1982, had authorized the CIA to try to topple Suriname ruler Col. Desi Bouterse. The Agency's plan reportedly called for the formation of an exile paramilitary force to invade Suriname because Bouterse, who had taken power in a 1980 military coup, was leading the small South American country into the proverbial and dreaded "Cuban orbit".[1]

The congressional committee members, "while not opposed in principle to the idea of attempting to overthrow a foreign government"[2] did object to the proposal on the grounds that there was no evidence that Cuba was "manipulating the government in Suriname, or gaining a military foothold in the country".[3]

Inasmuch as rational argument of this sort had never made too deep an impression upon the mind of Ronald Reagan or excessively inhibited the CIA, there was no reason to believe that this was the end of the story.

Or even the beginning. Two months earlier, in October, the Bouterse regime had threatened to expel two US diplomats it accused of encouraging the country's conservative trade unions and of playing a key role in organizing anti-government demonstrations and strikes aimed at bringing the government down.[4] Then, on 8 December, Suriname announced that a coup attempt had been made against the government. A number of alleged plotters were arrested, some of them winding up "shot while trying to escape", evidently a euphemism for their execution. Bouterse claimed that the arrested men had been conspiring with the CIA.[5] One of those who lost his life was conservative union leader Cyril Daal, who had helped organize anti-government demonstrations earlier in the year and who was said to have connections with the CIA through his Moederbond Union's association with the CIA's ubiquitous American Institute for Free Labor Development (AIFLD).[6]

The following month, the two US diplomats were actually asked to leave because of their "destabilizing activities".[7]

In July 1983 the plot thickened. The *New York Times* reported that an invasion of Suriname scheduled for the first of the month by Florida-based mercenaries was called off after the plans for it were discovered by the internal security agency of the Netherlands, the former colonial power in Suriname when it was known as Dutch Guiana. The invasion force reportedly would have been composed of some 300 men—half of them US and South American nationals, the others Surinamese—who were to be flown from Florida to the Suriname capital of Paramaribo on the northern tip of South America. The invaders were then to be augmented by Surinamese exiles from the Netherlands. It was this latter group which the Dutch had infiltrated to learn of the plans.[8]

As had become customary concerning American targets in Latin America, stories about the presence of large numbers of Cuban soldiers in Suriname found their way into international circulation. Like their counterparts in Jamaica and Grenada, these warriors remained mythical figures.

In spring 1983, Suriname entered into agreements with the neighboring right-wing government of Brazil which provided for economic and military aid and military training. By the reasoning of the Reagan administration, Suriname should then have been in "the Brazilian orbit". The simple truth was that Suriname, like other developing nations, was willing to accept help from wherever it could get it. And in fact, Brazil, which openly admitted that its purpose was "saving Suriname from Cuba", had made the move at Washington's prodding.[9]

As matters turned out, in October Bouterse expelled almost all Cuban advisers and embassy personnel, including the ambassador, and suspended all agreements with Havana. The expulsion was announced on the day the United States invaded Grenada and was influenced by Bouterse's belief that Cuba had played a part in the overthrow of Maurice Bishop and that he might suffer a similar fate, if not a similar invasion.[10] This belief about Cuba, as we have seen, bore no relation to the truth, and may have been encouraged by the United States. *Newsweek* magazine later reported that "U.S. diplomats in the capital of Paramaribo made sure to keep Bouterse current on evidence that Cuba had aided the Grenadian coup, and the rest was left to his well-prepped paranoia."[11]

Desi Bouterse, by all accounts, left much to be desired as a leader and as a person. Long before the events of October, Cuba and Grenada were reported to be privately "irritated, even angry, at the harm done to the Left's image in the region by what they see as immature revolutionaries leading a premature revolution."[12] Although Bouterse had learned to parrot socialist and anti-imperialist clichés, his principles appeared to lie elsewhere. In the words of one diplomat in Suriname, "Bouterse is a chameleon. The first thing for him is his own personal survival. The second thing is his survival as the man-in-charge."[13] Bouterse was accused at times of claiming plots against him as a pretext to get rid of some of those opposed to his rule. (Several other coup attempts were alleged in addition to the one of December 1982 mentioned above.)

During the period December 1983 to January 1984, Suriname was shaken by thousands of striking workers protesting against tax increases and steep price rises, and calling for the dismissal of Prime Minister Errol Alibux; serious acts of sabotage to power and water supplies were carried out as well. Bouterse gave in, removing Alibux and canceling the price rises, but he did not accede to the demand that the military hand power back to civilians.[14] Although the scenario was reminiscent of CIA activities in British Guiana, Jamaica, and elsewhere, as well as what the Suriname government had accused the United States of in October 1982, there is no report of the Agency's hand in the disturbances of this period. However, in 1985 it was revealed that the National Endowment for Democracy, which is financed by Congress to support foreign organizations sympathetic to US foreign policy objectives, had been funding organizations in Suriname during the 1983-85 period.[15]

48. Libya 1981-1989
Ronald Reagan meets his match

The great masses of the people in the very bottom of their hearts tend to be corrupted rather than consciously and purposely evil ... therefore, in view of the primitive simplicity of their minds, they more easily fall a victim to a big lie than to a little one, since they themselves lie in little things, but would be ashamed of lies that were too big.

Adolf Hitler[1]

"Our evidence is direct, it is precise, it is irrefutable," announced the President of the United States. He was explaining that the American bombing attack upon Libya of 14 April 1986 was in retaliation for the Libyan bombing nine days earlier of a West Berlin nightclub frequented by American servicemen which had killed two soldiers and one civilian and injured many others.[2]

In actuality, the evidence of Libyan culpability in the bombing was never directly or precisely presented to the world, but little notice was taken of that. For over a decade the American public had been told that Libyan leader Muammar el-Qaddafi was behind one terrorist act after another in every part of the world. A few days before the American attack, President Reagan had referred to him as the "mad dog of the Middle East". This was just one more example. It all fit.

The bombs dropped on Libya took the lives of a reported 40 to 100 people, all civilians but one, and wounded another hundred or so. The French Embassy, located in a residential district, was destroyed. The dead included Qaddafi's young adopted daughter and a teenage girl visiting from London; all of Qaddafi's other seven children as well as his wife were hospitalized, suffering from shock and various injuries.[3]

It was not claimed by the United States that any of the people killed or wounded had any connection to the Berlin bombing. Like the mideast terrorists who threw hand grenades at an El Al ticket counter to kill Israelis simply because they were Israelis, and those who planted a bomb on PanAm flight 103 in order to kill Americans simply because they were Americans, the bombing of Libya was an attempt to kill Libyans simply because they were Libyans. After the air attack, White House spokesman Larry Speakes announced that "It is our hope this action will preempt and discourage Libyan attacks against innocent civilians in the future."[4]

The Libyan the United States most wanted to kill of course was Qaddafi. The bombing had been an assassination attempt. Said a "well-informed Air Force intelligence officer" cited by the *New York Times*, "There's no question they were looking for Qaddafi. It was briefed that way. They were going to kill him."[5] Which is what you have to do with a mad dog.

Subsequently, two of Qaddafi's children filed suit in the United States to stop President Reagan from launching more "assassination attempts" on their family. The suit, which was rejected in court, alleged that Reagan and other top officials, in ordering the raids, had violated an executive order that bars attempted assassinations of foreign government leaders.[6] Another suit filed in Washington was in behalf of 65 people killed or injured by the bombing.[7] Meanwhile, the US Navy was awarding 158 medals to the pilots who dropped 500-pound and 2,000-pound bombs in the dark of night upon sleeping people.[8]

The notion of targeting Qaddafi's family originated with the CIA, which claimed that in Bedouin culture Qaddafi would be diminished as a leader if he could not protect his home: "If you really get at Qaddafi's house—and by extension his family—you've destroyed an important connection for the people in terms of loyalty."[9]

To make sure the Libyan people got the message, the Voice of America repeatedly told them, following the bombing, things like "Colonel Qaddafi is your tragic burden" and that as long you obey his orders you must "accept the consequences".[10]

The president's claim of irrefutable evidence was based on alleged interceptions of communications between the Libyan capital of Tripoli and the Libyan Embassy in East Berlin. Reagan declared that on 25 March, Libya had sent orders to the embassy "to conduct a terrorist attack against Americans, to cause maximum and indiscriminate casualties"; then the embassy alerted Tripoli on 4 April that the attack would be carried out the next day, that "Tripoli will be happy when you see the headlines tomorrow", and that after the bombing the embassy reported that the action had been successful and could not be traced to it.[11]

These are, at best, interpretations and paraphrases. The complete, unedited, unexpurgated, literal texts of the relevant communications were not made public. They were intercepted by the National Security Agency and decoded with the help of the German BND (Federal Intelligence Service) which had broken the Libyan code years before. After the decoding was completed, reported *Der Spiegel*, Germany's leading newsmagazine, it was still not clear what the wires actually said, there being different versions. Moreover, the NSA and BND came to different conclusions about the meaning of the messages, "but these disagreements were quickly pushed aside for political reasons". German security officials, who insisted that Libya should not be the only focus of investigation and who cautioned against a "premature accusation", also looked into rival groups of disco competitors and drug dealers. In January 1987, a senior official in Bonn told investigative reporter Seymour Hersh that the German government continued to be "very critical and skeptical" of the American position linking Libya to the bombing; and at the end of the following year, Germany announced that the investigation was being ended.[12]

"Some White House officials had immediate doubts that the case against Libya was clear-cut," Hersh reported. "What is more, the discotheque was known as a hangout for black soldiers, and the Libyans had never been known to target blacks or other minorities."[13]

As in many other instances that we have seen, however, official Washington's official position, repeated often enough, became official truth. Three years after the incident, *Time* magazine could state matter-of-factly that "Libyan-backed terrorists bombed a disco in West Berlin", thereby provoking the American "retaliatory" bombing.[14]

Much of Washington's secret planning for the Libyan operation took place at the same time as the secret talks and arms dealing with Iran. Thus, the Reagan administration was pursuing the elimination of one Middle East source of terrorism while it was arming another. Moreover, the two missions involved some of the same national security people, notably John Poindexter and Oliver North.

Although the Carter administration did not carry out any overt military attacks upon Libya, it was possibly involved in a very serious covert action. On 27 June 1980, an Italian passenger plane was destroyed by a missile over the Mediterranean, taking 81 lives. At the same time, a Libyan plane which may have been carrying Qaddafi was flying in the vicinity. Italian air controllers listed it as a "VIP 56" flight, denoting that top officials were aboard. In 1988, Italian state television reported that the plane had been mistakenly shot down by a missile belonging to a NATO country, possibly Italy. A year later, an Italian defense ministry report revealed that it was probably a Sidewinder air-to-air missile that was used, a weapon employed by NATO. The Italian press began speculating that a plan to assassinate the Libyan leader had gone awry, and instead the Italian plane had been shot down by a NATO power. (At the time of the disaster, Qaddafi had hinted that the United States was responsible.) The US and France—Libya's chief foes—issued denials, as well as NATO itself, but the Italian military was taking great pains to conceal information about the case. Nevertheless, an air force officer admitted to destroying the radar tape for that evening, and a civilian investigation suggested that many air force personnel were persuaded to lie or "forget" about the incident.[15]

Ronald Reagan and his ultra-ideological comrades took office in January 1981 committed to a massive transfer of wealth from the poor to the rich. One of the pivotal ways in which they so artfully reached this end was through huge increases in the military budget; i.e., welfare for the rich, for defense industry friends and business associates, past, present, and future. But in order for the military-industrial-intelligence complex to sell this to the American public and Congress, there had to be a fresh supply of wars, armed conflict, insurgencies, counter-insurgencies ... or rumors and "threats" of same ... and enemies, ideally of the monster type, to be defended against.

Qaddafi was a designer-monster: a quirky, unpredictable, super-uppity Third World leader, sitting on the world's ninth largest oil reserve; a man with deep-seated pan-Islamic, pan-Arabic, anti-imperialist, and anti-Zionist convictions; an artless braggart mouthing revolutionary rhetoric so juvenile he could serve equally well as bogeyman or buffoon; a man carrying out or supporting enough real terrorist acts so that any exaggeration would be believed.

There were elements of a bitter personal feud between the two men. Ronald Reagan—a man who played with air strikes as if he were directing movie scenes—had chosen to take on a man who, like himself, was a prisoner of ideology and had left his mark on the world media with a trail of dogmatic observations and actions, as well as plain stupid remarks. (All of the great prophets of modern times, Qaddafi said, have come from the desert and were uneducated: "Mohammed, Jesus and myself.")[16] The Libyan leader, however, did have a social conscience, not a quality known to be part of Ronald Reagan's DNA. ("You don't see poverty or hunger here. Basic needs are met to a greater degree than in any other Arab country," reported *Newsweek* in 1981 about Libya.[17])

Qaddafi's principal crime in Reagan's eyes was not that he supported terrorist groups, but that he supported the *wrong* terrorist groups; i.e., Qaddafi was not supporting the same terrorists that Washington was, such as the Nicaraguan Contras, UNITA in Angola, Cuban exiles in Miami, the governments of El Salvador and Guatemala, and the US military in Grenada. The one band of terrorists the two men supported in common was the Moujahedeen in Afghanistan.

Some of the belligerent American operations against Qaddafi, actual and threatened, and charges of Libyan terrorism, actual and fabricated, were timed to stir up American jingoist juices when Congress was debating the military budget or aid to Reagan's favorite terrorists, whom he called freedom fighters. The 14 April 1986 bombing of Libya, for example, came one day before the House opened a new round of debate on aid to the Contras. Then, speaking on the 15th, Reagan said: "I would remind the House voting this week that this archterrorist Qaddafi has sent $400 million [sic] and an arsenal of weapons and advisers into Nicaragua."[18]

Very shortly after taking office, Reagan announced the appointment of a special group to study "the Libyan problem". The State Department appeared to have two schools of thought: diplomatic pressure on Qaddafi or a more confrontational view. "Nobody," one official pointed out, "advocates being nice to him."[19]

Soon a master plan had been drawn up by the CIA, which *Newsweek* exposed in August, 1981: "a large-scale, multiphase and costly scheme to overthrow the Libyan regime" and obtain what the CIA called Qaddafi's "ultimate" removal from power. The plan called for a "disinformation" program designed to embarrass Qaddafi and his government; the creation of a "counter government" to challenge his claim to national leadership; and an escalating paramilitary campaign of small-scale guerrilla operations.[20]

The escalation was immediate. On 19 August, American planes crossed Qaddafi's "line of death", the 120-mile limit claimed by Libya in the Gulf of Sidra, and shot down two Libyan jets. The United States, which considered it international waters, as did most of the rest of the world—although this concept is more debatable when applied to aircraft than when applied to ships[21]—purposely chose the area to conduct military exercises. As expected, Libya rose to the bait, at least according to Washington, which claimed that the Libyan planes had fired first.

An enraged Qaddafi accused the US of "international terrorism" and, in a phone call to the leader of Ethiopia, reportedly threatened to assassinate Reagan.[22] An official who served in a national security position under Reagan responded that there was no question that the "only thing to do with Qaddafi was kill him. He belonged dead."[23]

Soon the US media were reporting a barrage of Qaddafi death threats against the life of Reagan or other senior officials. In October, a story appeared that the American ambassador to Italy was hastily flown out of the country after Italian authorities discovered a Libyan plot to assassinate him, "that was aborted when Italian police deported ten suspected Libyan hit men". But some American officials in Washington and Rome disputed the story, while another government source confirmed it.[24]

A month later, there was a report of an attempt upon the life of an American diplomat in Paris—seven shots were fired at Christian Chapman, but he escaped unharmed. That same day Secretary of State Alexander Haig—who referred to Qaddafi as "the patron saint of terror"—suggested that Libya was behind the attempt, although he admitted that he had "no other information" directly implicating Libya. But Chapman had recently received some threats, said the French government, some of which had been traced to Tripoli.[25] A *New York Times* analysis of the incident, however, concluded that "something less than an organized assassination attempt might have been involved."[26]

In late November, the administration announced that a number of terrorists trained in Libya had entered the United States with plans to assassinate President Reagan or other officials. This prompted a huge nationwide search for "the Libyan hit squad" and for Americans to whom they might turn for assistance, including the Weather Underground. Then the infamous international terrorist "Carlos" was brought into the picture, and the administration said that it had received first-hand descriptions from informers of the training and plans of the terrorists. Each day new and ominous details arose in the media, which had already forgotten the exposure in August of the initiation of a government disinformation campaign against Libya.[27] "We have the evidence," Reagan told newsmen, "and he [Qaddafi] knows it." Reporters pressed the White House to make the evidence public, but were refused. Some officials, however, including some senior FBI officials, were said to be skeptical about the reports.[28]

Syndicated columnist Jack Anderson then described what a shadowy, unreliable group the suppliers of the hit-squad information were, adding that several of them were known to have connections with Israeli intelligence, "which would have its own reasons to encourage a U.S.-Libyan rift," there being a deep and mutual animosity between Israel and Qaddafi.[29]

In mid-1981 a task force under William Clark, Deputy Secretary of State, had been set up to look into the whole Qaddafi issue. Years later, Seymour Hersh was to report:

> According to key sources, there was little doubt inside Clark's task force about who was responsible for the spate of anti-Qaddafi leaks—the CIA, with the support of the President, Haig and Clark. "This item [the Libyan hit squad] stuck in my craw," one involved official recalls. "We came out with this big terrorist threat to the U.S. Government. The whole thing was a complete fabrication." ... One task force official eventually concluded that [CIA Director William] Casey was in effect running an operation inside the American Government: "He was feeding the disin-

formation into the (intelligence) system so it would be seen as separate, independent reports" and taken seriously by other Government agencies.[30]

As matters turned out, most of the presumed assassins were Lebanese who had helped Reagan negotiate the release of US hostages in Beirut and who hated Qaddafi.[31] When the story's purpose had been served, it faded away.

However much some of Qaddafi's reported threats were disinformation, there were real plans by the West to kill him. A February 1981 French plot, with US cooperation under discussion, had to be canceled when French President Giscard was unexpectedly defeated at the polls.[32] In 1984 it went further, with the CIA sharing highly sensitive intelligence, including satellite photographs and communications intercepts, with the French secret service to aid them in at least two major, but unsuccessful, operations to assassinate or overthrow Qaddafi, who was perceived by the French as a threat to what they thought of as their interests in Africa. One of the operations resulted in a pitched battle in Libya between exiles and Qaddafi loyalists.[33]

And in 1985, the State Department had to go to great lengths to head off a White House-sponsored plan for a joint US-Egyptian land and air invasion of Libya. Secretary of State George Schultz called the plan "crazy," while his department colleagues referred to the free-wheeling staff of the National Security Council as "those madmen in the White House".[34]

At Christmas of that year, after bomb attacks at the Rome and Vienna airports killed about 20 people, including five Americans, all the usual suspects were quickly accused, with Iran and the Palestinian splinter group of the nefarious Abu Nidal heading the list.[35] The Reagan administration soon added Qaddafi, announcing that the CIA had found a strong Libyan connection, when all they had was that the Tunisian passports of three of the terrorists had purportedly been traced to Libya. Within days, Reagan declared that there was "irrefutable" evidence of Qaddafi's role in the airport bombings, although he knew that this was not true. At the same time, new economic sanctions against Libya were announced, "to get economic sanctions out of the way so the next time [we] could do more".[36] The next time was in March 1986. US Navy jets again crossed Qaddafi's "line of death", daring retaliation. When there wasn't any, they returned the next day and the day after, twice attacking a Libyan anti-aircraft site and destroying three or four ships. Washington asserted that on the second day, Libya had first fired several missiles at the American planes.

Shortly afterward, one of a group of British electronics engineers working in Libya at the time was interviewed by the *Sunday Times* of London. The engineer said that he had been watching the radar screens during the two days of fighting and saw American warplanes cross not only into the 12 miles of Libyan territorial waters, but over Libyan land as well.

"I watched the planes fly approximately eight miles into Libyan air space," said the engineer. "I don't think the Libyans had any choice but to hit back. In my opinion they were reluctant to do so."[37]

Following the first American attack in March on Libya, Qaddafi spoke on the phone with King Fahd of Saudi Arabia, who subsequently told US officials that the Libyan leader appeared deeply affected by the violence unleashed against him. The king described Qaddafi as "incomprehensible and disoriented", a description similar to other reports which appeared during the 1980s which spoke of a very depressed Qaddafi who didn't seem to understand what the United States had against him. Before and after the events of March, he made half a dozen attempts through third parties to open a dialogue with Washington, but Reagan administration officials rebuffed them all. The would-be European and Arab mediators, including King Fahd, were firmly told that the United States was not interested either in "a direct or indirect dialogue" with Qaddafi.[38]

That at least was the official policy, the face turned to the public. There were, however, reports that the White House was secretly dealing with the Libyan leader; to what extent is not known. The only certain contact was a November 1985 visit with Qaddafi in Libya by the US ambassador to the Vatican, William Wilson. The meeting was disavowed by official Washington as being unauthorized and Wilson lost his post after it was disclosed.[39]

Meanwhile, and throughout the term of the Reagan administration, the United States was increasing military assistance to Libya's immediate neighbors and conducting military exercises with Egypt designed to provoke Qaddafi; instituting diverse forms of economic sanctions against Libya with varying degrees of ineffectiveness; trying to unify Libyan exile opposition groups and giving them financial support and encouragement; the same to the governments of Egypt and France for various anti-Qaddafi actions, not excluding assassination. It should be noted that France—the United States' chief "anti-terrorism" partner—in 1985 deliberately sank the Greenpeace ship *Rainbow Warrior*, killing a Greenpeace photographer. This, with the express approval of French President Francois Mitterand.[40]

Disinformation was a regular part of the process: using the foreign and American press to publicize fictitious new Libyan terrorist plans, and to announce—with each new terrorist act that occurred in the Western world—that Libya "may" be responsible; to make Qaddafi believe that key trusted aides were disloyal, that the Libyan military was plotting against him, that his Russian military advisers were plotting against him, that his troops were deserting en masse, or that a new US military attack was on the horizon; a process they hoped would push the man into "irrational" acts. His imminent downfall was predicted as regularly as that of Castro.[41] One operation involved Navy Seal commandos landing on Libyan beaches and leaving tell-tale signs of the incursions—such as matchboxes and Israeli cigarette butts—to make the Libyans nervous, ever more paranoid.[42]

An August 1986 memo from John Poindexter, the president's national security adviser, which spelled out some of the disinformation program, mentions itself that at the time Qaddafi was "quiescent" on the terrorist front.[43] Shortly afterward, a key Reagan administration official admitted to American reporters that if pressed for "hard evidence" of the charges against Libya they wouldn't have any. "It will look like we're crying wolf once again."[44] In response to the Poindexter memo—the exposure of which had caused a mini-scandal—the senior spokesman for the State Department, Bernard Kalb, resigned in protest, because he was "worried about faith in America ... American credibility" and "anything which hurts America".[45]

The issue spilled over to the British, whose officials described US intelligence analyses about Libya's intentions as "wildly inaccurate", which they said were passed to the British in "a deliberate effort to deceive".[46]

In this same period, in light of new US news reports (engendered by the Poindexter memo), of possible further strikes against Libya in retaliation for terrorist actions allegedly being planned by Qaddafi's regime, Libya's effective prime minister called upon the United States to furnish details on the alleged actions so that Libya could "cooperate fully to avert and abort such attacks and apprehend the individuals and put them on trial." He said that his request, sent to Washington through diplomatic channels, had gone unanswered.[47] The next day, Qaddafi, in a speech in Libya, challenged the United States to produce bank statements showing that Libya financed terrorism.[48]

"Half the lies they tell about the Irish aren't true," a son of Erin once observed. The regular employment of disinformation about Qaddafi and Libya by the United States so clouded the historical picture that it is extremely difficult in most cases to separate fact from fiction, to distinguish Libyan moral or token backing or simply promises to a revolutionary movement from major, vital support. The fact that the Reagan administration felt the need to undertake disinformation campaigns against Libya indicates a paucity of smoking guns.

On 1 September 1969, Captain Muammar el-Qaddafi had led a group of fellow officers in a bloodless overthrow of the monarchy and established the Libyan Arab Republic. Despite his "troublemaking" abroad, he initially kept in the good graces of the West—the US thwarting three serious plots against his rule during his first two years[49]—because of his fierce anti-communism, which stemmed basically from his taking Marxism's implicit atheism at face value and viewing it as irreconcilably at odds with his Islamic faith. But this did not keep him from trying to institute revolutionary social and economic changes in Libyan society which others called Marxist. This, plus entering into oil development and arms agreements with the Soviet Union, may have spelled the beginning of the end for the West's tolerance of his foreign adventures.[50]

During the 1970s and '80s, Qaddafi was accused of using his large oil revenues to support—with funds, arms, training, offices, havens, diplomacy and/or general subversion—a wide array of radical/insurgent/terrorist organizations, particularly certain Palestinian factions and Muslim dissident and minority movements in various parts of the Middle East, Africa, and Asia; as well as the IRA and Basque and Corsican separatists in Europe; several groups engaged in struggle against the apartheid regime in South Africa; Noriega in Panama, opposition groups and politicians in Costa Rica, St. Lucia, Jamaica, Dominica, and France's Caribbean colonies of Guadeloupe, French Guiana, and Martinique; the Japanese Red Army, the Italian Red Brigades, Germany's Baader-Meinhof gang ... the list is without end.

It was claimed as well that Libya was behind, or at least somehow linked to, the attempt on Pope John Paul's life, the assassination of Egyptian President Anwar Sadat, mining the Suez Canal, attempting to blow up the US Embassy in Cairo, various plane hijackings, a bomb explosion on an American airliner over Greece, blowing up a synagogue in Istanbul, and seeking to destabilize the governments of Chad, Liberia, the Sudan, and other African countries ... and ... Qaddafi took drugs, was an extreme womanizer, was bisexual, dressed in women's clothing, wore makeup, carried a teddy bear, had epileptic fits ...[51]

More established is the fact that for several years Qaddafi made use of former CIA staffers, notably Edwin Wilson and Frank Terpil, to supply him with aircraft and pilots, mechanics and Green Beret instructors, all manner of sophisticated weaponry, equipment and explosives, and to help set up paramilitary training camps in Libya.[52]

And Amnesty International, in 1987, concluded that Libya had carried out attacks on at least 37 anti-Qaddafi dissidents abroad since 1980, with 25 being killed.[53]

In January 1989, the State Department added to Qaddafi's credits by asserting that Libya was funding and training "radical individuals and groups whose activities exacerbate local problems" in Thailand, the Philippines, Indonesia, Japan and New Caledonia. A few months earlier, the CIA had accused Libya of building the largest poison gas plant in the world.[54] In March 1990, a fire broke out at the plant in question and burned it to the ground. President Bush immediately and personally assured the world that the United States "absolutely" had nothing to do with the fire. A week earlier, the White House spokesman had been asked if the US might take military action to destroy the plant. "We don't rule out anything," was the reply.[55]

And in Chicago, members of a street gang ...

were convicted in late 1987 of planning terrorist activities. U.S. prosecutors charged that the gang expected to receive $2.5 million from Libya for assassination attempts on American politicians and for attacks on U.S. aircraft and government facilities.[56]

That, in its entirety, is how the *Los Angeles Times* reported it, and it sounded like the bizarre Libyan strongman was at it again. In actuality, "assassination", planned or concrete, was not one of the charges, and no evidence at all was presented at the trial that Libya had anything to do with originating or encouraging these acts, or had paid or promised any money. The El Rukn gang members, a Moslem sect, and naive in the extreme, had met with Libyan representatives in New York, Panama and Libya, and pathetically tried to impress them with their prowess and loyalty to Qaddafi. They had been inspired by Nation of Islam leader Louis Farrakhan purportedly receiving a Libyan promise of $5 million. If El Rukn received a promise of $2.5 million—and we have only their word for it—it would appear that both promises were no more than Qaddafi's revolutionary self-indulgence. (The IRA also claimed that they had not received any money from Libya, contrary to Qaddafi's claim.[57]) It is perhaps a measure of the hostility toward Libya that had been inculcated in the American people for more than a decade, that the gang members—through government use of a questionable informer and through entrapment—were found guilty by a jury of federal conspiracy charges and sentenced to extraordinarily long sentences. It was reportedly the first time ever that US citizens had been convicted on terrorism charges.[58]

It is like a grade B horror movie. A dozen times it rises from the dead and lurches towards the audience; a dozen times it is cut to ribbons, staggering back, collapsing in a heap; and a dozen times it rises again and clomps slowly forward. But it is not the mummy's ghost, and it is not haunting the upper Nile. It is the notion that the Libyan leader, Col. Muammar Qaddafi, is responsible for every act of terrorism in the entire world, and it haunts the pages of the western press and the screens of western television sets.[59]

PanAm flight 103

On 21 December 1988, PanAm flight 103 exploded over Lockerbie, Scotland, killing 270 people, more than half of them Americans. Five months later, the State Department announced that the CIA was "confident" that the villains who planted the bomb were members of the Popular Front for the Liberation of Palestine-General Command (PFLP-GC), led by Ahmed Jibril, based in Syria, and hired by Iran to avenge the American shooting down of an Iranian airliner.[60] Though little could be done to apprehend Jibril and his cohorts, this remained the US government's official, certain, and oft-repeated judgment, even though Syria and Iran were viewed as the keys to the release of Western hostages held in Lebanon. Then, in 1990, something strange happened. The United States was preparing to go to war against Iraq, when who should pop up as one of its allies, sending troops to Saudi Arabia in the *jihad* against Saddam Hussein? None other than the terrorist-haven land of Syria. And whose cooperation in the war was Washington angling for? The wicked Iran. This would not do. In early October, American officials declared that newly uncovered evidence indicated that Libyan intelligence agents may have assembled and planted the bomb. But this, they were quick to point out, did not clear Iran, Syria or the PFLP-GC of complicity.[61]

After the war, little by little, a putative case against Libya was leaked, until 14 November 1991 when two Libyan intelligence operatives were indicted in absentia as the perpetrators. The head of the Justice Department's criminal division asserted the same day that there was no evidence to link either Syria or Iran to the bombing "and he brushed aside suggestions that the conclusion had been influenced by the United States' desire for improved relations with Syria".[62] Within the next 20 days, the remaining four American hostages held in Lebanon were released along with the most prominent hostage, Britisher Terry Waite.

And the evidence against the two Libyans? Two pieces of metal the size of fingernails, allegedly from electronic timing devices. One has to read the detailed account of what the case against Libya rests upon to appreciate its full shakiness.[63] Moreover, in December 1993, a BBC program, "Silence Over Lockerbie", presented new findings which cast significant doubt about the case against Libya and indicated that Britain and the United States may have fingered Libya to divert suspicion from Syria and Iran. The key new information was that the Swiss manufacturer of the electronic timers changed his previous story which had named Libya as the only purchaser of such devices. He now remembered that he had sold some of the timers to East Germany as well. There were close links between the East German secret police and the PFLP-GC and other Arab terrorist groups. Even more significant, an engineer with the Swiss company declared that he had told the Lockerbie investigators about the East German connection in late 1990, which means that the international investigators knew that their accusation against Libya had a large, if not fatal, hole in it either before the accusation was made public in October, or shortly thereafter.[64] "No German judge could, with the present evidence, put the two suspects into jail," declared Volker Rath, German government prosecutor and specialist in Lockerbie, in 1994.[65]

The new Qaddafi?

It may be that the oft-depressed Muammar el-Qaddafi finally began to understand—finding his way past the verbiage and the disinformation—what the United States and other governments had against him. In the latter half of 1988 he seemed to grow up, instituting a host of progressive changes into Libyan society—freeing up civil liberties, releasing hundreds of political prisoners, removing restrictions on travel abroad, loosening up the economy ("All Libyans are called upon to become bourgeois."); at the same time, making peace or improving relations with a number of African neighbors.[66]

But as the year 1989 opened and Washington prepared to shift from Ronald Reagan to George Bush, the United States marked the occasion by conducting some more "military exercises" in Libya's back yard and shooting down two more Libyan planes. The State Department then saw fit at this particular time to issue its most detailed account to date of Libyan involvement in international terrorism—"an attempt to maintain international pressure" on Libya, wrote the *Los Angeles Times*.[67]

Nonetheless, Qaddafi continued to display his new persona. He announced that he had decided to cut off or trim the flow of funds to various foreign groups and he told several Palestinian groups that they would no longer receive direct funding from his government and would have to close their offices in Libya. He also admitted that Libya had bankrolled terrorist groups, but said that it no longer did so—"when we discovered that these groups were causing more harm than benefit to the Arab cause, we halted our aid to them completely and withdrew our support"—adding that he did not wish for any confrontation with Washington.[68]

Equally surprising, the Libyan leader went out of his way to resume friendly relations with Egypt after years of enmity characterized by repeated attempts to destabilize each other.[69] By 1991, Egyptian officials were trying, without success, to nudge the US into a more open policy toward Libya, saying that Qaddafi was showing signs of restraining his military behavior.[70]

Washington may have felt that it had nothing to gain by relaxing its crusade against Qaddafi, but it did have an enemy to lose.

49. Nicaragua 1981-1990
Destabilization in slow motion

I have the most conclusive evidence that arms and munitions in large quantities have been on several occasions ... shipped to the revolutionists in Nicaragua ... I am sure it is not the desire of the United States to intervene in the internal affairs of Nicaragua or of any other Central American republic. Nevertheless, it must be said, that we have a very definite and special interest in the maintenance of order and good Government in Nicaragua at the present time ... The United States cannot, therefore, fail to view with deep concern any serious threat to stability and constitutional government in Nicaragua tending toward anarchy and jeopardizing American interests, especially if such state of affairs is contributed to or brought about by outside influence or by any foreign power.[1]

In this manner did President Calvin Coolidge address the Congress of the United States in 1927. The revolutionaries he was voicing alarm about were those supporters of the Liberal Party (one of whom was Augusto Cesar Sandino) who had taken up arms against the Conservative Party government which they claimed was illegally in office. The foreign power accused of arming the Liberals was the Mexican government, which the Coolidge administration viewed as being "impregnated with Bolshevist ideas". The American interests thought to be in jeopardy were the usual business investments, flaunted more openly in those days than later. Thus it came to pass that the Marines landed in Nicaragua for the twelfth time in less than three-quarters of a century. (See Appendix II.)

In the 1980s, it was the revolutionary Nicaraguan government of the Sandinistas which alarmed the administration of Ronald Reagan (who described Coolidge as his political patron saint); the foreign power castigated for arming the Sandinistas was the Soviet Union, impregnated with Bolshevist ideas to be sure; the counter-revolutionaries known as the "contras" were Washington's Marines; as to American "interests"—to the "rationality" of economic imperialism had been affixed a desire for political hegemony bordering on the pathological.

When the American military forces left Nicaragua for the last time, in 1933, they left behind a souvenir by which the Nicaraguan people could remember them: the National Guard, placed under the direction of one Anastasio Somoza (just as in 1924 the United States had left Trujillo behind for the people of the Dominican Republic). Three years later, Somoza took over the presidency and with the indispensable help of the National Guard established a family dynasty which would rule over Nicaragua, much like a private estate, for the next 43 years. While the Guardsmen, consistently maintained by the United States, passed their time on martial law, rape, torture, murder of the opposition, and massacres of peasants, as well as less violent pursuits such as robbery, extortion, contraband, running brothels and other government functions, the Somoza clan laid claim to the lion's share of Nicaragua's land and businesses. When Anastasio Somoza II was overthrown by the Sandinistas in July 1979, he fled into exile leaving behind a country in which two-thirds of the population earned less than $300 a year. Upon his arrival in Miami, Somoza admitted to being worth $100 million. A US intelligence report, however, placed it at $900 million.[2]

It was fortunate for the new Nicaraguan leaders that they came to power while Jimmy Carter sat in the White House. It gave them a year and a half of relative breathing space to take the first steps in their planned reconstruction of an impoverished society before the relentless hostility of the Reagan administration descended upon them; which is not to say that Carter welcomed the Sandinista victory.

In 1978, with Somoza nearing collapse, Carter authorized covert CIA support for the press and labor unions in Nicaragua in an attempt to create a "moderate" alternative to the Sandinistas.[3] Towards the same end, American diplomats were conferring with non-leftist Nicaraguan opponents of Somoza. Washington's idea of "moderate", according to a group of prominent Nicaraguans who walked out on the discussions, was the inclusion of Somoza's political party in the future government and "leaving practically intact the corrupt structure of the *somocista* apparatus", including the National Guard, albeit in some reorganized form.[4] Indeed, at this same time, the head of the US Southern Command (Latin America), Lt. General Dennis McAuliffe, was telling Somoza that, although he had to abdicate, the United States had "no intention of permitting a settlement which would lead to the destruction of the National Guard".[5] This was a notion remarkably insensitive to the deep loathing for the Guard felt by the great majority of the Nicaraguan people.

The United States, moreover, tried, unsuccessfully, to convince the Organization of American States to send in a "peace-keeping force",[6] a body which could only have stood in the way of the insurgents' military progress; and in neighboring Costa Rica the American ambassador saw fit to complain to the government that Cuba had set up a center to oversee its military support of the Sandinistas, resulting in the Cubans being forced to move their headquarters to their consulate.[7]

After the Sandinistas took power, Carter authorized the CIA to provide financial and other support to their opponents.[8] At the same time, Washington pressured the Sandinistas to include certain men in the new government.[9] Although these tactics failed, the Carter administration did not refuse to give aid to Nicaragua. Ronald Reagan was later to point to this and ask: "Can anybody doubt the generosity and good faith of the American people?" What the president failed to explain was:

a) Almost all of the aid had gone to non-governmental agencies and to the private sector, including the American Institute for Free Labor Development, the long-time CIA front. (In 1981, the US Solicitor General, while arguing before the Supreme Court, inadvertently touched upon the link between the AIFLD and the CIA. When this was picked up by the press, he lamely said that he had been speaking hypothetically.)[10]

b) The primary and expressed motivation for the aid was to strengthen the hands of the so-called moderate opposition and undercut the influence of socialist countries in Nicaragua.

c) All military aid was withheld despite repeated pleas from the Nicaraguan government about its need and right to such help[11]—the defeated National Guardsmen and other supporters of Somoza had not, after all, disappeared; they had regrouped as the "contras" and maintained primacy in the leadership of this force from then on.

In January 1981, Ronald Reagan took office under a Republican platform which asserted that it "deplores the Marxist Sandinista takeover of Nicaragua". The president moved quickly to cut off virtually all forms of assistance to the Sandinistas, the opening salvos of his war against their revolution. The American whale, yet again, felt threatened by a minnow in the Caribbean.

Among the many measures undertaken: Nicaragua was excluded from US government programs which promote American investment and trade; sugar imports from Nicaragua were slashed by 90 percent; and, without excessive subtlety but with notable success, Washington pressured the International Monetary Fund (IMF), the Inter-American Development Bank (IDB), the World Bank, and the European Common Market to withhold loans to Nicaragua.[12] The director of the IDB, Mr. Kevin O'Sullivan, later revealed that in

1983 the US had opposed a loan to aid Nicaraguan fishermen on the grounds that the country did not have adequate fuel for their boats. A week later, O'Sullivan pointed out, "saboteurs blew up a major Nicaraguan fuel depot in the port of Corinto",[13] an action described by an American intelligence source as "totally a CIA operation".[14]

Washington did, however, offer $5.1 million in aid to private organizations and to the Roman Catholic Church in Nicaragua. This offer was rejected by the government because, it said, "United States congressional hearings revealed that the [aid] agreements have political motivations, designed to promote resistance and destabilize the Revolutionary Government."[15] Nicaragua had already arrested members of several of the previous recipient organizations such as the Moravian Church and the Superior Council of Private Enterprise (COSEP) for involvement in armed plots against the government.[16]

The Reagan administration was not deterred. Cardinal Miguel Obando and the Catholic Church in Nicaragua received hundreds of thousands of dollars in covert aid, from the CIA until 1985, and then—after official US government aid was stopped by congressional oversight committees—from Oliver North's off-the-books operation in the White House basement. One end to which Obando reportedly put the money was "religious instruction" to "thwart the Marxist-Leninist policies of the Sandinistas".[17]

As part of a concerted effort to deprive the Nicaraguan economy of oil, several attacks on fuel depots were carried out. Contra/CIA operations emanating in Honduras also blew up oil pipelines, mined the waters of oil-unloading ports, and threatened to blow up any approaching oil tankers; at least seven foreign ships were damaged by the mines, including a Soviet tanker with five crewmen reported to be badly injured. Nicaragua's ports were under siege: mortar shelling from high-speed motor launches, aerial bombing and rocket and machine-gun attacks were designed to blockade Nicaragua's exports as well as to starve the country of imports by frightening away foreign shipping.[18] In October 1983, Esso announced that its tankers would no longer carry crude oil to Nicaragua from Mexico, the country's leading supplier; at this point Nicaragua had a 10-day supply of oil.[19]

Agriculture was another prime target. Raids by contras caused extensive damage to crops and demolished tobacco-drying barns, grain silos, irrigation projects, farm houses and machinery; roads, bridges and trucks were destroyed to prevent produce from being moved; numerous state farms and cooperatives were incapacitated and harvesting was prevented; other farms still intact were abandoned because of the danger.[20]

And in October 1982, the Standard Fruit Company announced that it was suspending all its banana operations in Nicaragua and the marketing of the fruit in the United States. The American multinational, after a century of enriching itself in the country, and in violation of a contract with the government which extended to 1985, left behind the uncertainty of employment for some 4,000 workers and approximately six million cases of bananas to harvest with neither transport nor market.[21]

Nicaragua's fishing industry suffered not only from lack of fuel for its boats. The fishing fleet was decimated by mines and attacks, its trawlers idled for want of spare parts due to the US credit blockade. The country lost millions of dollars from reduced shrimp exports.[22]

It was an American war against Nicaragua. The contras had their own various motivations for wanting to topple the Sandinista government. They did not need to be instigated by the United States. But before the US military arrived in Honduras in the thousands and set up Fortress America, the contras were engaged almost exclusively in hit-and-run forays across the border, small-scale raids on Nicaraguan border patrols and farmers, attacks on patrol boats, and the like; killing a few people here, burning a building down there,[23] there was no future for the contras in a war such as this against a much larger force. Then the

American big guns began to arrive in 1982, along with the air power, the landing strips, the docks, the radar stations, the communications centers, built under the cover of repeated joint US-Honduran military exercises,[24] while thousands of contras were training in Florida and California.[25]

US and "Honduran" reconnaissance planes, usually piloted by Americans, began regular overflights into Nicaragua to photograph bombing and sabotage targets, track Sandinista military maneuvers and equipment, spot the planting of mines, eavesdrop on military communications and map the terrain. Electronic surveillance ships off the coast of Nicaragua partook in the bugging of a nation.[26] Said a former CIA analyst: "Our intelligence from Nicaragua is so good ... we can hear the toilets flush in Managua."[27]

Meanwhile, American pilots were flying diverse kinds of combat missions against Nicaraguan troops and carrying supplies to contras inside Nicaraguan territory. Several were shot down and killed.[28] Some flew in civilian clothes, after having been told that they would be disavowed by the Pentagon if captured.[29] Some contras told American congressmen that they were ordered to claim responsibility for a bombing raid organized by the CIA and flown by Agency mercenaries.[30] Honduran troops as well were trained by the US for bloody hit-and-run operations into Nicaragua[31] ... and so it went ... as in El Salvador, the full extent of American involvement in the fighting will never be known.

The contras' brutality earned them a wide notoriety. They regularly destroyed health centers, schools, agricultural cooperatives, and community centers—symbols of the Sandinistas' social programs in rural areas. People caught in these assaults were often tortured and killed in the most gruesome ways. One example, reported by *The Guardian* of London, suffices. In the words of a survivor of a raid in Jinotega province, which borders on Honduras:

> Rosa had her breasts cut off. Then they cut into her chest and took out her heart. The men had their arms broken, their testicles cut off, and their eyes poked out. They were killed by slitting their throats and pulling the tongue out through the slit.[32]

Americas Watch, the human-rights organization, concluded that "the contras systematically engage in violent abuses ... so prevalent that these may be said to be their principal means of waging war."

In November 1984, the Nicaraguan government announced that since 1981 the contras had assassinated 910 state officials and killed 8,000 civilians.[33]

The analogy is inescapable: if Nicaragua had been Israel, and the contras the PLO, the Sandinistas would have long before made a lightning bombing raid on the bases in Honduras and wiped them out completely. The United States would have tacitly approved the action, the Soviet Union would have condemned it but done nothing, the rest of the world would have raised their eyebrows, and that would have been the end of it.

After many contra atrocity stories had been reported in the world press, it was disclosed in October 1984 that the CIA had prepared a manual of instruction for its clients which, amongst other things, encouraged the use of violence against civilians. In the wake of the furor in Congress caused by the exposé, the State Department was obliged to publicly condemn the contras' terrorist activities. Congressional intelligence committees were informed by the CIA, by present and former contra leaders, and by other witnesses that the contras indeed "raped, tortured and killed unarmed civilians, including children" and that "groups of civilians, including women and children, were burned, dismembered, blinded and beheaded".[34] These were the same rebels whom Ronald Reagan, with his strange mirror language, called "freedom fighters" and the "moral equal of our founding fathers". (The rebels in El Salvador, in the president's studied opinion, were "murderers and terrorists".)[35]

The CIA manual, entitled *Psychological Operations in Guerrilla Warfare*, gave advice on such niceties as political assassination, blackmailing ordinary citizens, mob violence, kidnapping, and blowing up public buildings. Upon entering a town, it said, "establish a public tribunal" where the guerrillas can "shame, ridicule and humiliate" Sandinistas and their sympathizers by "shouting slogans and jeers". "If ... it should be necessary ... to fire on a citizen who was trying to leave the town," guerrillas should explain that "he was an enemy of the people" who would have alerted the Sandinistas who would then "carry out acts of reprisals such as rapes, pillage, destruction, captures, etc."

The contras were advised to explain to the people that "our struggle is not against the nationals but rather against Russian imperialists". This "will foster the sympathy of the peasants, and they will immediately become one of us." (Mao himself couldn't have put it better.) Workers were to be told that "the state is putting an end to factories", and doctors informed that "they are being replaced by Cuban paramedics".

When the population sees the light and begins to rise against the government, "professional criminals should be hired to carry out selective jobs" such as "taking the demonstrators to a confrontation with the authorities to bring about uprisings and shootings that will cause the death of one or more people to create a martyr for the cause." Other people will be "armed with clubs, iron rods and placards and, if possible, small firearms, which they will carry hidden." Still other "shock troops", equipped "with knives, razors, chains, clubs and bludgeons", will "march slightly behind the innocent and gullible participants" as the uprising progresses.

Finally, a section called "Selective Use of Violence for Propagandistic Effects" informed the contra student that "It is possible to neutralize carefully selected and planned targets, such as court judges, police and state security officials," and others.[36]

Throughout, the manual reads like what the Western world has always been taught is the way communists scheme and indoctrinate. It proved intensely embarrassing to the Reagan administration, not least because it unequivocally punctured the official balloon which had been floating about bearing the message that the United States was not pursuing the overthrow of the Sandinista government; although at that late date, anyone who still believed that was far enough removed from reality to continue believing it.

White House officials and President Reagan twisted their tongues into knots trying to explain away the manual: the manual made public was only a first draft which was not the one distributed, they said falsely ... the word "neutralize" didn't mean to assassinate, only to remove from office ... the author of the manual was some low-level, irresponsible "freelancer" ... [37]

Not long afterward, the manual, with minor changes, could be found in distribution again in Honduras, put out ostensibly by a private American organization, *Soldier of Fortune* magazine.[38]

The CIA may have tried to provide its students with some object lessons in neutralization, of the Mafia kind. In June 1983, the Nicaraguan government expelled three US Embassy officials—one of whom was reported to be the CIA's Chief of Station in Managua—charging them with being part of an Agency destabilization network which, amongst other things, was attempting to assassinate Foreign Minister Miguel d'Escoto. The intended murder weapon was to be a bottle of Benedictine liqueur containing thalium, a poison almost undetectable in the human body. At a press conference, the government presented evidence which included photos and videotapes of American diplomats meeting with the Nicaraguan officials who had pretended to go along with the plot, as well as copies of intercepted CIA messages.[39]

Two months later, another Agency plot to kill d'Escoto (who is also a Roman Catholic priest) as well as two other Sandinista officials was alleged by the Nicaraguan government. A CIA agent named Mike Tock was charged with being behind this particular conspiracy.[40]

The following June, according to one of the participants, the CIA sent a contra hit team from Honduras to Managua to do away with all nine *comandantes* of the Sandinista National Directorate in one fell swoop by blowing up the building they were meeting in. The team made it to Managua, but the explosives failed to arrive and the plot was aborted.[41]

The Lord and the fight for freedom have something in common: they both move in mysterious ways. If the CIA's guerrilla manual was not an odd enough tool of liberty, the Agency's comic book surely was. Entitled *Freedom Fighters' Manual*, the 16-page booklet was supplied to contra forces presumably to distribute amongst the Nicaraguan population. Its 40 illustrations showed the reader how s/he could "liberate Nicaragua from oppression and misery" by "a series of useful sabotage techniques". Amongst these were: stop up toilets with sponges ... pull down power cables ... put dirt into gas tanks ... put nails on roads and highways ... cut and perforate the upholstery of vehicles ... cut down trees over highways ... telephone to make false hotel reservations and false alarms of fires and crimes ... hoard and steal food from the government ... leave lights and water taps on ... steal mail from mailboxes ... go to work late ... call in sick ... short circuit electricity ... break light bulbs ... rip up books ... spread rumors ... threaten supervisors and officials over the phone ...[42]

Until at least the mid-1980s, the primary official explanation for American belligerence towards the Sandinista government, at least the explanation most frequently advanced, was that a significant quantity of military supplies was being sent to the Salvadorean rebels from Nicaragua. (The fact that the United States was at the same time heavily arming the Salvadorean government and that the Salvadorean government was assisting the contras did not enter into Washington's equation.) We shall see in the chapter on El Salvador how lacking in evidence Washington was in support of this charge. Whatever organized supply operation of any significance that had existed appears to have ended in early 1981. In January of that year a Salvadorean cabinet minister announced that Nicaragua was no longer allowing its territory to be used for arms shipments.[43] A few weeks later, the Sandinista government, alarmed by the suspension of US economic aid, pressed the Salvadorean guerrillas to seek a political settlement.[44] (Similar requests were made by the Sandinistas during the following years.)[45] And in March, in a meeting at CIA headquarters of Director William Casey and others, the cessation of the supply operation was confirmed.[46]

David MacMichael, who served with the CIA from 1981 to 1983 as an analyst of military and political developments in Central America, attended an inter-agency meeting held to discuss CIA plans to support the contras. Of this meeting he noted that "Although the stated objective was to interdict arms going into El Salvador, there was hardly any discussion of the arms traffic ... I couldn't understand this failure until months later when I realized, like everyone else, that arms interdiction had never been a serious objective."

The former CIA man said that he had had access to the most sensitive intelligence on Nicaragua, including arms shipments to El Salvador, based on which he concluded that "the Administration and the CIA have systematically misrepresented Nicaraguan involvement in the supply of arms to Salvadorean guerrillas to justify [their] efforts to overthrow the Nicaraguan Government."[47] For a man who spent ten years as an officer in the US

Marine Corps and four years as a counter-insurgency expert in southeast Asia, in addition to his tour of service at the CIA, David MacMichael's political thinking about US foreign policy in Latin America landed in strange territory.

> We have control and we don't want to lose it. The ideology of anti-communism then provides the rationalization, although this determination to hold on is actually pathology. Then you have an entire generation of people raised in the foreign policy establishment and specializing in this region who for 25 years have gotten up in the morning and said: "We'll get that bastard Castro today."[48]

The failure of the United States to show large Nicaraguan tracks on the Salvadorean landscape apparently led the ubiquitous Oliver North to try and place some artificial footprints in the ground. In 1988, José Blandón, a former close adviser to Panama's defense chief and de facto ruler, General Manuel Noriega, stated that North had set up a secret operation in 1986 that called for Panama to arrange a large shipment of Soviet-bloc arms and vehicles that could be captured in El Salvador and falsely linked to the Sandinistas. The effort collapsed in June when the ship carrying the military goods was seized by Panamanian officials, two days after the New York Times had published an article concerning illegal activities of Noriega.[49]

Washington's explanation Number Two put forth for its policy appeared to be that Nicaragua was a military threat to other Central American countries—not simply to the bases in Honduras, which were a daily, calculated provocation—but to Honduras itself and the other nearby states. This was a weak reed to lean on, for Nicaragua had virtually no air force (and it would have been suicidal to attack anyone without proper air cover), even less of a navy, and its tanks were demonstrably unsuitable for the terrain of Honduras.[50] Still less did the Sandinistas have a sane reason for invasion. It is questionable whether the men of the State Department believed this story themselves, any more than did the supposed neighboring targets. At a conference for journalists in Costa Rica in 1985, the Costa Rican Minister of Information, Armando Vargas, said cheerfully: "No one here really expects Nicaragua to invade us." ... "And nobody in Honduras does either," said Manuel Gamero, the editor-in-chief of Tiempo, one of that country's leading newspapers.[51]

On other days we were told other reasons why the Sandinistas had to be restrained. It may have been to protect the Panama Canal (sic) or "the free use of the sea lanes in the Caribbean basin and the Gulf of Mexico". (The danger-to-the-sea-lanes bit has been trotted out by Washington for every corner of the globe in the past 40 years; not once has it materialized.) Or it may have been the threat of "another Cuba" or its corollary, "a Soviet beachhead" in the region. These warnings came complete with pictures—an exhibition of aerial photos of Nicaragua showing "Cuban-style military barracks", a "Soviet-style physical training area with chin-bars and other types of equipment to exercise the forces, and a running track", and, most damning of all, a Sandinista garrison "having a standard rectangular configuration like we have seen in Cuba".[52] Leave it to those cunning Castroites to devise a rectangular building.

"The strategic issue is a simple one," asserted Patrick Buchanan, Reagan's Director of Communications. "Who wants Central America more—the West or the Warsaw Pact?"[53]

Fidel Castro was not in any doubt. On at least two occasions he expressed in no uncertain terms his frustration and annoyance with the Soviet Union for not sufficiently aiding Nicaragua and for what he saw as the Russians' weak and indecisive response to American pressure against the Sandinista government, even in the face of a Russian ship being damaged by CIA mines. The Cuban leader failed to attend the funeral of Soviet leader Chernenko in March 1985 and did not sign the book of condolences at the Soviet Embassy in Havana, apparently to register his displeasure with Soviet policy. Responded a Soviet diplomat: "We obviously place a priority on improving relations with our adversary. We have to seek a balance with the US, so naturally we will say [to the Cubans] calm down, we are not interested in sharpening the situation in Angola and Nicaragua."[54]

"In the ... think-tanks and the academic institutes in Moscow where Soviet policy towards Central America is discussed and debated ...", reported *The Guardian* of London, "the emphasis is on dialogue and negotiation, and if the Soviet Union agrees on one thing with the United States, it is that there should be 'no more Cubas'," a reference to the heavy economic and political burden Cuba had placed upon Moscow over the years.[55]

Oliver North was not in any doubt either as to who wanted Central America more. Said the lieutenant colonel to one of the private American contributors to the contras: "Russia would never go up against us to save Nicaragua."[56]

Neither was Poland in doubt. The Warsaw Pact member sold arms to the contras, as did the Communist Chinese.[57]

In 1987, Soviet leader Michael Gorbachev offered to end Soviet military aid to Nicaragua if the United States ended its military support of the contras. Reagan confirmed that Gorbachev had raised this matter with him, but there is no indication that the president followed up in any way.[58]

In January 1983, the so-called Contadora group, composed of Mexico, Panama, Colombia and Venezuela, began to meet periodically in an attempt to still the troubled waters of Central America. Rejecting at the outset the idea that the conflicts of the region could or should be seen as part of an East-West confrontation, they conferred with all the nations involved, including the United States. The complex and lengthy discussions eventually gave birth to a 21-point treaty which dealt with the most contentious issues: civil war, foreign intervention, elections, and human rights. Washington, which was not itself to be a signatory to the treaty, though obviously indispensable to its implementation, pressed Managua to sign, partly for domestic consumption—congressional support of the administration's Nicaragua policy and the 1984 presidential elections—and partly to be able to take jabs at Nicaragua, saying that it would make the country a democracy and halt their "export of revolution".

Then, much to Washington's surprise, on 7 September 1984 Nicaragua announced its intention to sign the treaty. Until this moment, the United States had not publicly criticized the treaty's provisions, but immediately Washington began to find things wrong with it and called for changes. The State Department declared that the Contadora group "didn't intend that this [treaty document] be the end of the process", but a high-ranking diplomat from one of the Contadora countries insisted that "Everyone had treated it as a final document from the beginning", as had the US representatives.[59]

What alarmed Washington about the treaty was its provisions for the removal from each country of all foreign military bases; restrictions on foreign military personnel, armaments, and military exercises; and a prohibition on aid to insurgent forces seeking to overthrow a government. It was enough to put an interventionist power out of business.

The United States refused to give its blessings to the agreement. Commented Rep. Michael Barnes, chairman of the House Foreign Affairs Subcommittee on the Western Hemisphere: "The Administration's objections to the treaty reinforce my belief that it's never had any real interest in a negotiated settlement."[60]

After the Managua announcement, State Department officials admitted that they were concerned that it "might undermine the Administration's efforts to portray the Sandinistas as the primary source of tension in Central America". Some officials argued that a trip scheduled by Sandinista leader Daniel Ortega to Los Angeles "should not be approved, in part, to punish Mr. Ortega and the Sandinistas for accepting the Contadora peace proposal."[61] Nicaragua's willingness to sign the treaty was labeled "a propaganda ploy".[62]

One month later, an internal National Security Council paper was able to note that the United States, through intensive lobbying efforts, had "effectively blocked" adoption of the treaty as it was written.[63]

During the following three years, the Reagan administration successfully sought to thwart the peace talks among the Contadora group because the talks complicated administration attempts to win funds for the contras in Congress, as well as working against their primary goal of toppling the Nicaraguan government.[64]

National Security adviser John Poindexter let Panama strongman General Manuel Noriega understand that the United States did not appreciate Panama's role in the Contadora process and suggested that Noriega step down from power. When Noriega refused, the US cut off $40 million in economic assistance. Then, in June 1986, Washington officials briefed American journalists about Noriega's involvement in drug trafficking and money laundering. Thus was a CIA client in good standing suddenly transformed into Public Enemy Number One in the United States. (Similarly, in 1985, when Honduran President Roberto Suazo impeded contra aid shipments, the US blocked an aid package to Honduras and leaked some dirt about Suazo.)

In February 1986, the US threatened Mexico—which was, along with Panama, the most active member of the Contadora group—that if it lobbied Congress on behalf of the Contadora process, the administration would throw its support behind the opposition National Action Party (PAN) in upcoming Mexican elections. Convicted Contragate player Carl Channell later told representatives of PAN that Reagan would help them if they helped the contras. In an extremely unusual move, administration officials went before Congress in May to denounce the Mexican government for corruption, drug trafficking and economic mismanagement.[65]

In August 1987, a "Central American Peace Accord", generated by President Oscar Arias of Costa Rica as a successor to the unsuccessful Contadora process, was signed by Salvador, Honduras, Guatemala, Nicaragua, and Costa Rica. Its key provisions concerning foreign military intervention were similar to those in the various Contadora versions.

The Reagan administration, however, still had its heart set on a military victory. According to former officials, some in the administration wanted to see the failure of peace talks convened under the Arias plan.[66] The war in Nicaragua continued.

The argument most often advanced by the Reagan administration to explain its reluctance to accept a Contadora agreement during 1983 and 1984 was that Nicaragua was not prepared to hold a truly free election as called for by the treaty. Washington labeled the election held in November 1984, which the Sandinistas won by a two-to-one margin, a "sham".

On the face of it, by the (flawed) standards of Western elections, the Nicaraguan election cannot be much faulted; by the standards of Latin America, it was a veritable paragon of democracy; the fact that there were no deaths reported in connection with the election, by itself, made it rather unique in Latin America; the appearance of minor parties on the ballot in every department (state) of the nation distinguished it from the typical presidential election in the United States.

The election was open to all parties and candidates, no fraud in the polling was reported, or even seriously charged; it was observed by a reported 400 foreigners from 40 different countries, and on election day the *Washington Post* could report:

> even U.S. diplomats here acknowledge that the Sandinistas have allowed expression of a wide range of political views, including some that were harshly critical of the government. The Sandinistas eased censorship of the sole opposition newspaper, *La Prensa*, at the start of the campaign, and the state television and radio channels have given air time—although limited—for the small but vocal opposition parties to make their case.[67]

Washington's criticism of the election centered on the boycott of it by the Democratic Coordinating Alliance (DCA), a significant coalition of opposition groups headed by Arturo José Cruz. On several occasions, Cruz and his followers were physically harassed by crowds when they appeared in public and on at least one occasion it was reported that many of the protestors had been brought to town in government vehicles. Whether the Sandinistas deliberately intended to harass Cruz or discourage him from running is not clear; what is clear is that the government had much more to lose than to gain by keeping the DCA off the ballot. In any event, harassment of a serious nature appears to have been short-lived and did not remain as a stumbling block to Cruz running. The DCA's most persistent stated objection was that not enough time had been allowed for campaigning.

The chronology of events is as follows: the 4 November election date was announced on 21 February; in May, registration of parties and candidates was set for 25 July, at which time seven parties registered: the Sandinistas, three parties which could be considered to their left, and three to their right.[68] The DCA declined to register and Cruz announced that he would not run unless the government opened a dialogue with the contras, as if the contras had been fervently demanding this for some time, only to be rebuffed by the government. The DCA dropped this request three weeks later, stating that the contras had told them they would abide by any accord reached between the party and the government.[69] The failure to register, it should be noted, occurred before any special harassment had taken place.

Cruz also contended at this time that for five years the population had been too indoctrinated by the government for the opposition to stand a chance,[70] a charge which could be made with considerable validity by any opposition party in any nation of the world.

The day of registration, several of Cruz's aides met with the government and asked that the deadline for registration be extended,[71] a move indicating perhaps a split in the DCA ranks. The Sandinistas at first refused, but on 22 September announced that registration was being extended to 1 October. The DCA again failed to register, stating that the election date had to be moved from November to January.[72] The Sandinistas suspected, and said so openly, that the DCA knew it would lose anyway and was abstaining from the election at the behest of the United States in order to throw a question mark over the whole process. In August, some of Cruz's backers had in fact stated that they hoped to "discredit the election and force the Sandinistas to grant political concessions". "What we really need," they declared, "is Arturo in jail."[73]

One unmistakable sign of the CIA's hand in the election was the full-page advertisements which appeared in August in newspapers in Venezuela, Costa Rica and Panama. Signed by a fictitious organization called "Friends of Tomas Borge", the ads attempted to split the Sandinista leadership by promoting Borge's candidacy over that of Daniel Ortega who had already been chosen as the Sandinista candidate. "Neither Ortega nor Cruz!" proclaimed the ads.[74]

Throughout this period, the DCA made one demand after another concerning electoral procedures as its price for taking part in the election. By any reasonable standard of power relationships, the government showed itself to be flexible. On 21 September, the *New York Times* reported that the opposition had stated that the Sandinistas had made substantial concessions and that the only major proposal left was postponing the election until January. This was important, said the DCA, because the campaign could not have properly begun before certain things had been agreed upon. The government's position was that it would grant the postponement—a major concession and inconvenience—only if the DCA would arrange a ceasefire with the contras. The party replied that it didn't have the power to do so, and negotiations continued through all of October with many confusing and contradictory reports coming out of the talks until, finally, time ran out.

The United States could certainly have arranged a ceasefire if it was interested in testing the Sandinistas' commitment to what Washington would call a free election. That the US had such an interest is questionable in light of what the *New York Times* revealed two weeks before the election:

> The Reagan Administration, while publicly criticizing the Nov. 4 elections in Nicaragua as "a sham," has privately argued against the participation of the leading opposition candidate for fear his involvement would legitimize the electoral process, according to some senior Administration officials.
>
> Since May, when American policy toward the election was formed, the Administration has wanted the opposition candidate, Arturo José Cruz, either not to enter the race or, if he did, to withdraw before the election, claiming the conditions were unfair, the officials said.
>
> "The Administration never contemplated letting Cruz stay in the race," one official said, "because then the Sandinistas could justifiably claim that the elections were legitimate, making it much harder for the United States to oppose the Nicaraguan Government."
>
> Several Administration officials who are familiar with the Administration's activities in Nicaragua said the Central Intelligence Agency had worked with some of Mr. Cruz's supporters to insure that they would object to any potential agreement for his participation in the election.[75]

A few days before election day, some rightist parties on the ballot claimed that US diplomats had been pressing them to drop out of the race.[76] One of these, the Independent Liberal Party, had already announced that it was no longer in the running.

Having exposed the administration's plan to sabotage the election's credibility, a plan centering around Arturo Cruz, and having reported the above about parties being pressured to drop out, the *New York Times*, after the election, inexplicably published an editorial which said in part:

> Only the naive believe that Sunday's election in Nicaragua was democratic or legitimizing proof of the Sandinista's popularity. ... The Sandinistas made it easy to dismiss their election as a sham. Their decisive act was to break off negotiations with Arturo Cruz, an opposition democrat whose candidacy could have produced a more credible contest. ... The opposition ... was finally shrunk to four small left-wing groups and factions of two traditional parties. Even so, and after five years of unchallenged power, the Sandinistas appear to have won less than two-thirds of the vote.[77]

The American ambassador to Costa Rica likened Nicaragua under the Sandinistas to an "infected piece of meat" that attracts "insects".[78] President Reagan called the country a "totalitarian dungeon",[79] and insisted that the people of Nicaragua were more oppressed than blacks in South Africa.[80]

Members of the Kissinger Commission on Central America indicated that Nicaragua under the Sandinistas was as bad or worse than Nicaragua under Somoza. Henry Kissinger believed it to be as bad as or worse than Nazi Germany.[81] Reagan was in accord—he compared the plight of the contras to Britain's stand against Germany in World War II.[82]

"Central America," noted Wayne Smith, former head of the US Interests Section in Havana, "now exercises the same influence on American foreign policy as the full moon does on werewolves."[83]

So all-consuming, so unrelenting, was the hatred, that Kissinger demanded that the American ambassador to Nicaragua be removed simply because he reported that the Sandinista government was "performing fairly well in such areas as education".[84] And in the wake of the terrible devastation in Nicaragua wrought by Hurricane Joan in October 1988, the Reagan administration refused to send any aid nor to help private American organizations do so.

So eager was the State Department to turn the Sandinistas into international pariahs, that it told the world, without any evidence, that Nicaragua was exporting drugs, that it was anti-Semitic, that it was training Brazilian guerrillas.[85] When the CIA was pressed about the alleged Sandinista drug connection, it backed down from the administration's claim.[86]

Secretary of State Alexander Haig referred to a photograph of blazing corpses and declared it an example of the "atrocious genocidal actions that are being taken by the Nicaraguan Government" against the Miskito Indians. We then learned that the photo was from 1978, Somoza's time.[87]

Loathing of this magnitude had to be institutionalized. Thus it was that an Office of Public Diplomacy was set up in 1983, nominally in the State Department, but operating as an arm of the National Security Council. The OPD was characterized by a US official as "a huge psychological operation of the kind the military conducts to influence a population in denied or enemy territory".[88] Only in this case the target population was the American people. OPD Deputy Director Col. Daniel Jacobowitz, a military "psy-ops" specialist, described the media campaign in a March 1985 "confidential-sensitive" strategy paper: "Overall theme: the Nicaraguan Freedom Fighters (NFF) are fighters for freedom in the American Tradition, FSLN [Sandinistas] are evil."[89]

Rolling off the OPD disinformation assembly line, with the imagination of Oliver North ever active, were stories about Nicaragua acquiring chemical weapons, an "Iran-Nicaragua" link (not to be confused with the real US/Oliver North-Iran link we later learned of), a "Soviet MIGs in Nicaragua" hoax, the Sandinista massacre of 50 political prisoners ... as well as a number of other claims, misleading at best.[90]

Opinion pieces and "news" stories prepared by OPD staffers or contractors were planted in major media outlets under the signatures of contra leaders or ostensibly independent scholars, pretending to offer independent confirmation of White House claims, while other materials were distributed to thousands of university libraries, faculties, editorial writers, and religious organizations. Private sector public relations experts, lobbying groups, and think tanks were also enlisted for the cause and paid large chunks of taxpayer money to promote the OPD agenda. By OPD's own assessment, its work significantly changed public and congressional opinion, including winning approval in the House of $100 million in contra aid in June 1986.[91]

Within a rational framework, it would be proper to inquire what the Sandinistas had done that made it impossible for the United States to share the same planet with them. David MacMichael observed that there was no *casus belli* between the two countries:

> There are no examples of US citizens being killed there. No US property has been expropriated without due process or compensation. These people are so backward that they haven't even bothered to kill any American priests or nuns.
>
> Now any half-respectable country in the world can do that, but the Sandinistas don't seem to get round to it.[92]

What the United States did to the Nicaraguan revolution is clearer.

To transform Nicaraguan society, even if left in peace, would have been uphill all the way. The Sandinistas inherited a country of crushing poverty, backward in most respects (there were, reportedly, but two elevators in Nicaragua), and with a foreign debt of $1.6 billion which they decided to honor (with the exception of money owed to Israel and Argentina for arms shipments to Somoza).[93]

Then came the American body-blows to foreign trade and credit, to industry and agriculture, and a war which forced the government to devote an increasing portion of its national budget and an inordinate amount of its labor power to warfare and security. In 1980, half the national budget had been allocated to health and education, and military spending accounted for about 18 percent. By 1987, the military effort consumed more than half the budget, health and education less than 20 percent.

On top of this: the historically familiar post-revolutionary flight abroad of capital and middle-class professionals; the equally familiar sabotage by those who remain[94]—facile in a society where most of the businesses and farms were still in private hands—and the Nicaraguan economy went onto a life-support machine: a trail of inefficiencies and shortages of all kinds; taxis and buses and machines grinding to a halt for want of an American spare part; a failure to meet the great expectations of the population, mitigated only partly by the progress in agrarian reform, health care, literacy, and other social programs ... many who had been sympathetic to the revolution drifted away, some into protest and opposition.

Individuals are turned away from, or attracted to, social revolutions for a multitude of reasons, ideological and/or personal. All must be approached with caution. The most prominent defector from the Sandinistas, Edén Pastora, in between (semi-coherent) political statements, declared that "They [the Sandinistas] attack me for my success with women, out of jealousy because they are all queer and I can make love to their women."[95]

"Few US officials now believe the contras can drive out the Sandinistas soon," reported the *Boston Globe* in February 1986. "Administration officials said they are content to see the contras debilitate the Sandinistas by forcing them to divert scarce resources toward the war and away from social programs."[96]

Forty years of anti-communist indoctrination under Somoza and American cultural influence had also left their marks. A government militant put it this way:

> Tell a Nicaraguan factory worker ... that we are building a system in which workers will control the means of production, in which income will be redistributed to benefit the proletariat, and he will say "yes—that's what we want." Call it Socialism and he will tell you he doesn't want any part of it. Tell a peasant—in whom the problem of political education is even more acute—that the revolution is all about destroying the power of the big *latifundistas*, that the agrarian reform and the literacy campaign will incorporate the peasantry into political decisions ... and he will be enthusiastic, he will recognize that this is right and just. Mention the word Communism and he will run a mile.[97]

In the face of dissension, the Sandinistas often showed themselves unable to distinguish sincere and valid criticism from intentions to destabilize. Some opponents were harassed and jailed, civil liberties were curtailed, although never in a draconian manner. And credentials of loyalty to the revolution increasingly became a priority in filling positions high and low. This, interestingly enough, was precisely what was taking place in Washington at the same time, as the ultra-ideological Reagan administration was stuffing the bureaucracy with confirmed conservative loyalists.

Subsequent disclosures, however, established that the Sandinistas were not simply paranoid. In September 1988, the Speaker of the US House of Representatives, Jim Wright, citing "clear testimony from CIA people", revealed that the Agency had employed people in Nicaragua to organize and promote anti-government rallies and protests in hopes of provoking a crackdown or some other overreaction by the government, which, besides making the Sandinistas look bad, "was calculated to be disruptive to the peace talks" that the Reagan administration was publicly supporting.[98]

The shutting down of the prominent opposition newspaper *La Prensa* on several occasions was also judged harshly by civil libertarians. But this policy raised an important historical question: During World War II, did the US government allow the publication of pro-German or pro-Japanese newspapers in the United States? Has any government at war, particularly a war for its very survival, fought on its own soil, permitted the enemy to freely publish or broadcast at home, or allowed unrestricted dissent? During the American Civil War, Lincoln suspended the writ of habeas corpus and put enemy sympathizers in army jails without trial.

La Prensa indeed represented the enemy. At various times in the 1980s, one of the paper's chief editors was Pedro Joaquin Chamorro, Jr. During part of the same time, he was a member of the directorate of a contra umbrella group, The Nicaraguan Resistance of Washington, D.C.[99] And Chamorro would go off on speaking tours in the United States to enlist support for the contras.

The newspaper was financed by the enemy as well, covertly by the CIA since 1979, and by millions of dollars from the National Endowment for Democracy (NED) in Washington and various "private" American groups beginning in 1984.[100] NED receives its money from Congress and was set up in 1983 in the wake of all the negative revelations about the CIA in the 1970s. Its *raison d'être* is to do somewhat overtly what the CIA had been doing covertly for decades—manipulate the political process in a target country by financing political parties, labor unions, book publishers, newspapers, etc.—and thus, hopefully, eliminate the stigma associated with CIA covert activities.[101] Allen Weinstein, who helped draft the legislation establishing NED, and also founded the Center for Democracy, one of NED's funding middlemen, was candid about this when he said in 1991: "A lot of what we do today was done covertly 25 years ago by the CIA."[102] NED, like the CIA before it, calls what it does supporting democracy. The governments against whom the financing is targeted call it destabilization.

In any event, covert funding did not pass away. Both the CIA and Oliver North's multifarious operation channeled large sums of money to anti-Sandinista politicians and other elements of the internal opposition, including, as we have seen, the Catholic Church.[103]

During a period in which military aid to the contras was prohibited by Congress, North's network purchased large quantities of arms for the rebels from Manzer al-Kassar, a man whose US criminal record labels him "TERRORIST!" at the top of the page. Kassar was a known associate of those reputed to be responsible for the 1985 Christmas massacres in the Rome and Vienna airports, the hijacking of the liner Achille Lauro, and other notorious attacks.[104]

Another apostle of decency enlisted for the cause was the government of South Africa, which sent 200,000 pounds of military equipment to contra leader Edén Pastora.[105]

By the time the war in Nicaragua began to slowly atrophy to a tentative conclusion during 1988-89, the Reagan administration's obsession with the Sandinistas had inspired both the official and unofficial squads to embrace tactics such as the following in order to maintain a steady flow of financing, weaponry and other aid to the contras: dealings with other middle-eastern and Latin American terrorists, frequent drug smuggling in a variety of imaginative ways, money laundering, embezzlement of US government funds, perjury, obstruction of justice, burglary of the offices of American dissidents, covert propaganda to defeat domestic political foes, violation of the neutrality act, illegal shredding of government documents, plans to suspend the Constitution in the event of widespread internal dissent against government policy ... and much more, as revealed in the phenomenon known as Iran/Contra ... all of it to support the band of rapists, torturers and killers known as the contras.[106]

This, then, was the level of charm reached by anti-communism after 70 years of refinement. The imperial sensibility of America's leaders could be compared favorably with that of Britain circa 1925.

But it worked.

On 25 February 1990, the Sandinistas were defeated in national elections by a coalition of political parties running under the name National Opposition Union (UNO). President George Bush called it "a victory for democracy"... Senator Robert Dole declared that "The final outcome is a vindication of the Reagan policies."[107] ... Elliott Abrams, former State Department official and Iran/Contra leading light, said "When history is written, the contras will be folk heroes."[108]

The opposing analysis of the election was that ten years of all-encompassing war had worn the Nicaraguan people down. They were afraid that as long as the Sandinistas remained in power, the contras and the United States would never relent in their campaign to overthrow them. The people voted for peace. (As the people of the Dominican Republic had voted in 1966 for the US-supported candidate to forestall further American military intervention.)

"We can't take any more war. All we have had is war, war, war, war," said Samuel Reina, a driver for Jimmy Carter's election monitoring team in Juigalpa. In some families "one son has been drafted by the Sandinistas and another has joined the contras. The war has torn families apart."[109]

The US invasion and bombing of Panama just two months earlier, with all its death and destruction, could only have intensified the commitment of hardcore Sandinistas to resist *yanqui imperialismo*, but it could not have failed to serve as a caution to the large bloc of undecided voters.

The Nicaraguans were also voting, they hoped, for some relief from the grinding poverty that five years of a full American economic embargo, as well as the war, had heaped upon their heads. Commented Paul Reichler, a US lawyer who represented the Nicaraguan government in Washington at the time: "Whatever revolutionary fervor the people once might have had was beaten out of them by the war and the impossibility of putting food in their children's stomachs."[110]

Aqui no se rinde nadie. For ten years the people of Nicaragua had shouted that slogan—Here, no one gives up. But in February 1990, they did exactly that. (Just as the people of Chile had chanted "The people united will never be defeated", before succumbing to American power.)

The United States had more than war and embargo at its disposal to determine the winner of the election. The National Endowment for Democracy spent more than $11 million dollars, directly and indirectly, on the election campaign in Nicaragua.[111] This is comparable to a foreign government pouring more than $700 million dollars into an American election, and is in addition to several million dollars more allocated by Congress to "supporting the electoral infrastructure" and the unknown number of millions the CIA passed around covertly.

As a result of a controversy in 1984—when NED funds were used to aid a Panamanian presidential candidate backed by Noriega and the CIA—Congress enacted a law prohibiting the use of NED funds "to finance the campaigns of candidates for public office." The ways to circumvent the letter and/or spirit of such a prohibition were not difficult to conceive. NED first allocated millions to help organize UNO, building up the parties and organizations that formed and supported the coalition. Then a variety of other organizations—civic, labor, media, women's, etc.—run by UNO activists received grants for all kinds of "nonpartisan" and "pro-democracy" programs, for voter education, voter registration, job skills, and so on. Large grants made to UNO itself were specified for items such as office equipment and vehicles. (Rep. Silvio Conte of Massachusetts pointed out that the $1.3 million requested for vehicles would pay for renting 2,241 cars for a month at $20 per day.) UNO was the only political party to receive US aid, even though eight other opposition parties fielded candidates. Money received by UNO for any purpose of course freed up their own money for use in the campaign and helped all of their candidates. Moreover, the US continued to fund the contras, some of whom campaigned for UNO in rural areas.[112]

Afterwards, critics of the American policy in Nicaragua called it "a blueprint" for successful US intervention in the Third World. A Pentagon analyst agreed: "It's going right into the textbooks."[113]

50. Panama 1969-1991

Double-crossing our drug supplier

El Chorrillo, that's what they called the tenement barrio in Panama City ... 20,000 people had been packed into it; the invasion—nine or ten hours of heavy assault—left 15,000 of them homeless. ... Marcia McFarland was asleep with her daughters when the assault on the nearby military building began; she was leading them out of her house when a shard of shrapnel took a pound of her thigh and all but tore off her two-year old daughter's foot. ... Artillery shells and rockets; tanks, machine guns, and flame throwers; and then the ground troops, "the *Yanqui* soldiers, with their faces painted, they were all screaming, they looked like Indians"; people burning to death in the incinerated dwellings, leaping from windows, running in panic through the streets, cut down in cross fire, crushed by tanks, human body fragments everywhere. ... Heriberto Pitti worked for Eastern Airlines; when US troops attacked the airport, Pitti, Pablo Diaz and another colleague jumped into an Eastern pickup and raced out of the hanger; the truck took seven rounds through the windshield, killing all three men; Pitti left a widow and two daughters; Diaz left a widow and 12 children.[1]

Five hundred-something Panamanian dead is the official body count, what the US and Panamanian governments admit to; other sources, with no less evidence, insist that thousands died, their numbers obscured in mass graves; 3,000-something wounded; 23 American dead, 324 wounded.

Question from reporter: "Was it really worth it to send people to their death for this? To get Noriega?"

George Bush: "... every human life is precious, and yet I have to answer, yes, it has been worth it."[2]

"Born to Inform" would be a suitable inscription on a T-shirt worn by Manuel Antonio Noriega. In his younger days, in the 1950s and early '60s, he was already passing on information to one or another US intelligence agency, about colleagues in a socialist party he belonged to, about leftist students at his Peruvian military academy.[3]

Noriega followed a military career, falling under the right mentor, National Guard General Omar Torrijos. On two occasions the general had to intervene to save the ruthless Noriega from rape charges. In October 1968, Torrijos took power in Panama in a coup. He was, by Latin American standards, a not-very-brutal dictator; he was as well a liberal reformer, who was wary of the excesses of North American power in Central America.

In December 1969, conservative military officers tried, unsuccessfully, to overthrow Torrijos, claiming the government was heading toward a pro-communist dictatorship. Only hours before the coup attempt began, one of the principal plotters had met with a US official. After the coup, the same plotter and others escaped from a high-security jail in a sophisticated commando operation and turned up in the US-run Panama Canal Zone before going into exile in Miami.[4]

Noriega, who had proven his loyalty to Torrijos during the coup attempt, was soon elevated to head the intelligence unit of the National Guard. He was now in the right place to carry out all forms of mischief and enhance his reputation as a thug.

As early as 1971, the Bureau of Narcotics and Dangerous Drugs (forerunner of the Drug Enforcement Administration), had "hard evidence" about Noriega's heavy involvement in drug trafficking, "sufficient for indictment". But the legal and diplomatic obstacles involved were considerable, and Noriega was already too valuable to the CIA. President Nixon, however, wanted him "removed". Among the options discussed to achieve this end was assassination. It went as far as sending a member of the infamous "plumbers" unit to Mexico to await further orders to go to Panama and carry out the execution. But the would-be assassin got no further.[5]

During the Watergate hearings in 1973, former White House counsel John Dean testified that the White House had contracted E. Howard Hunt, "former" CIA officer and Watergate burglar, to assassinate Omar Torrijos because of his uncooperative stance on the Panama Canal treaty negotiations and his government's role in drug trafficking. (Inasmuch as Hunt may have been the "plumber" referred to above, and since Dean stated that Hunt had his team in Mexico before the mission was aborted, there is possibly some confusion here; however, the two testimonies appear to be quite clear as to the intended target.)[6]

Meanwhile, US government cash (primarily that of the CIA and the Pentagon) was making its way into Manuel Noriega's bank accounts. With the exception of President Carter's term, 1977-81,[7] the payments to Noriega continued until 1986; this included the period that George Bush was the Director of the CIA (1976), at which time the Panamanian intelligence chief was reportedly receiving in excess of $100,000 per year.[8]

And a lot of looking the other way. During the Panama Canal negotiations in October 1976, three bombs went off under cars parked in the Canal Zone. American officials believed that the bombings were an expression of nationalism carried out by Noriega's National Guard.[9] Yet, in December, Bush met with the Panamanian in Washington and gave him a VIP tour of the CIA. Noriega spent his time in Washington as the house guest of Bush's Deputy Director, the infamous Vernon Walters.[10]

When Omar Torrijos died in an air crash in 1981, Noriega became part of a ruling military junta. (In 1987, Colonel Robert Díaz Herrera, who was a cousin of Torrijos and had been one of the members of the junta, declared that Torrijos had died because of a bomb placed aboard his plane. Díaz named Noriega, the CIA, US General Wallace Nutting, head of the U.S. Southern Command in Panama at the time of the air crash, and others as being part of the conspiracy.)[11]

By August 1983, Noriega had maneuvered himself into the position of commander of the National Guard (whose name he soon changed to Panama Defense Forces). He was the effective chief of state, and his value to his American paymasters increased accordingly.

Six months earlier, the Senate Permanent Subcommittee on Investigations had reported that "Witnesses in Panama consider it common knowledge that the [National] Guard has links—and receives payments—from various traffickers in drugs, arms and other kinds of contraband."[12]

In November, however, Noriega received the red-carpet treatment in Washington, marked by luxury and meetings with officials of the White House, State Department and Pentagon, and enjoyed a four-hour lunch with CIA Director William Casey. Casey, probably Noriega's biggest supporter in Washington, met with the Panama strongman at least six times in Washington and Panama during the 1980s.[13]

Noriega earned Washington's money and tolerance over the years by providing numerous services, such as information about a host of regional matters, including his meetings with Fidel Castro and Daniel Ortega; giving haven to the Shah of Iran in December 1979; allowing the United States to set up listening posts in Panama, with which they monitored sensitive communications in all of Central America and beyond; and aiding the American warfare against the rebels in El Salvador and the government of Nicaragua; in the latter conflict, Noriega facilitated the flow of money and arms to the contras, allowed the US to base spy planes in Panama in clear violation of the canal treaties, gave the US permission to train contras in Panama (it is not certain that this actually took place), and provided information and direct action for the American campaign of sabotage inside of Nicaragua.[14]

But what information, American officials wondered, was the same Manuel Antonio Noriega giving Fidel Castro and Daniel Ortega about the United States? Washington already knew that he was helping Cuba circumvent the American economic embargo and that at various times in his career he'd helped to get weapons for the Sandinistas and for the guerrillas in El Salvador and Colombia, as well as transferring high technology to Eastern Europe.

On 12 June 1986, the *New York Times* carried a front-page story recounting many of Noriega's questionable activities, including his drug-trafficking and money-laundering operations, and the murder of a political opponent. It was the most detailed and damning report on Noriega to appear in the US media.

Noriega assumed, probably incorrectly, that the article had the blessings of the White House. And though the Reagan administration reassured him that he need not be overly concerned about the story, the Panamanian felt threatened.[15]

In August, through a go-between, he proposed to Oliver North that in exchange for a promise from Washington to help clean up his image and a commitment to lift the US government ban on military sales to the Panamanian Defense Forces (imposed because of the *Times* article), Noriega would assassinate the Sandinista leadership. North evidently declined the offer, noting in a written memo that an executive order barred American participation in assassinations.[16] However, as we have seen, the CIA in Nicaragua, not long before, had been engaged in precisely the same undertaking.

The following month North and Noriega met in London to discuss the latter's contribution to the Nicaraguan sabotage campaign. In return, North arranged for an American public relations firm to work on improving Panama's and Noriega's image.[17]

Noriega's principal periods of drug trafficking and money laundering appear to have been the early 1970s and the early 1980s, the latter period involving the Medellin, Colombia cartel. At other times, for reasons best known to his opportunistic self, he generally enforced the law against such activities. On his orders, Panamanian-flagged ships were searched in international waters, fugitive drug traffickers were sent to the United States for trial, and Panamanian banking laws were breached—all at the behest of American authorities.[18]

Noriega's American patrons were pleased. At various times, he received warm letters of praise from the State Department, the U.S. Southern Command in Panama, US Attorney General William French Smith, CIA Director William Webster, and more than one DEA official. In 1987, more than a year after the *New York Times* had revealed his drug involvements in a front-page story, the head of the DEA, John Lawn, praised Noriega's "personal commitment" in helping to solve a major money-laundering case.[19] The same year found high US law enforcement officials, including Lawn, working alongside Noriega at a meeting of Interpol, even advising him on how to achieve a better public image.[20]

Eventually, his luck ran out. A few enthusiastic DEA agents and US Attorneys, keeping a low profile, set the ball rolling in 1985 that eventually led to an indictment of Noriega in Florida on Federal drug charges in February 1988. In the interim, the Iran-Contra scandal broke out, followed by congressional hearings, making it much more awkward for Noriega's prominent administration defenders, such as Oliver North and William Casey, to pull the strings of the law. Then, in November 1986, North was relieved of his duties. The following May, Casey died. In June, the Senate passed a resolution calling for Noriega's immediate removal. It passed over the objections of the administration.

Ironically, it appears that Noriega had really gone straight. With one exception—a drugs-for-arms deal in March 1986—all the crimes he was indicted for in 1988 occurred in June 1984 or earlier. The DEA was deeply divided between those who investigated him as a criminal and those who swore by the authenticity of his cooperation with their agency.[21]

"The Yankees," Noriega said shortly before they invaded, "seem to adore the product [drugs] and then become upset with Latin Americans, as if we somehow were seducing them."[22]

Thus it was that the Reagan administration found itself with an indictment on its hands. The situation called for disassociation. George Bush, campaigning for the presidency in 1988, said repeatedly that he knew of no clear evidence that the Panamanian leader was involved in drugs until he was indicted.[23] (He also initially denied, but later acknowledged, that he had met with Noriega when he was CIA Director in 1976.)[24] It should be noted that Bush was head of the Reagan administration's Task Force on Drugs.

It would clearly be better for all concerned if Noriega would step down. Consequently, the Reagan administration offered to drop the indictment if he resigned and went into exile; they isolated him diplomatically; and undertook a campaign of severe and multifaceted economic sanctions against Panama; but Noriega held fast, although the sanctions eventually led to what the *New York Times* described as "a festering economic depression and the collapse of thousands of businesses."[25]

In the summer of 1988, the United States drew up a covert plan for a group of dissident Panamanian officers to oust Noriega without violence. If this failed, the proposal called for the support of military action of a rebel force composed of a Panamanian military officer and his followers, who were in exile in Miami and on the CIA payroll.

The Senate Intelligence Committee turned down the plan on the ground that it might result in the illegal assassination of Noriega.[26]

A presidential election was scheduled in Panama for May 1989, and the United States expected that it would be stolen for Noriega's candidate, as had been the case in the previous election of 1984. Accordingly, the CIA provided more than $10 million in aid to the opposition, as well as clandestine radio and television broadcasts.[27] Noriega didn't disappoint his critics. When the ballot counting indicated his man losing heavily, he simply put an end to the whole process and allowed his goons to beat up opposition candidates and their supporters.

Washington expressed its moral indignation about the fraudulent election, but this should be viewed in light of what had transpired five years earlier. In that election, Noriega's man, Nicolás Barletta, was declared the winner, the final count being announced ten days after the election. The opposition cried "fraud" and demonstrated for weeks, but the result stood. The CIA, it turned out, along with the Medellin cocaine cartel, had helped finance Barletta's campaign.[28] And after his victory, Barletta was welcomed by President Reagan to the Oval Office, Secretary of State George Schultz attended the inauguration, and heaven was in its place. Meanwhile, a political officer at the American Embassy in Panama was meticulously examining huge stacks of voting documents and reports he had managed to collect. His conclusion was inescapable: there had been egregious fraud. Barletta had been defeated by at least four thousand votes.

The US ambassador's main concern was that the report not reach the press. No American official pressured Panama for a recount. The political officer's report lies somewhere in a file in the bowels of Foggy Bottom.[29]

On 3 October 1989, elements of the Panamanian Defense Forces (PDF) attempted a very short-lived military overthrow of Noriega. When they apprised US officials in Panama of their plan beforehand, they were not discouraged from undertaking it. But during the execution they received virtually no help at all, even though they had Noriega in custody for at least two hours and were willing to turn him over to the US military.

The reasons which were later advanced by the Bush administration at different times to explain the lack of American support included: we didn't know what was going on; we didn't think the rebels had Noriega in custody; they may have had him in custody but they didn't want to release him to us; the US military commander in Panama was not authorized to seize Noriega (later we learned that he was); the rebels were not to our liking politically; our hands were tied by congressional intelligence committees; and, we suspected the whole thing was a ruse to provoke and embarrass the US government.[30]

The US military in Panama failed to block the road loyalist forces used to rescue Noriega. The administration said later that by the time it was certain of the troop movements it was too late. However, a convoy of loyalist trucks rumbled by the American Embassy itself; moreover, the United States had a number of helicopters in the air (reportedly as many as a dozen) observing developments.[31]

Some reports have it that the rebels were willing to turn Noriega over to the US military only if the Americans would come and grab him to make it appear that he was being seized against the will of his Panamanian captors. But the administration has denied this as well.[32]

At one point, the American Embassy reported to the State Department and the CIA in Washington that the rebels wanted to turn Noriega over, and the CIA went to brief members of the congressional intelligence committees. Administration officials later said that the embassy had misunderstood what the US military had told it because telephone communications in Panama were poor at the time.[33]

Did the Bush administration decline Noriega as a gift during the October coup attempt because it was determined to have its invasion? One circumstance may indicate a negative response to this question: On 12 October, US officials met at the State Department with Noriega's attorney to negotiate, once again, the Panamanian peacefully stepping down from power. Nothing came of this meeting.[34]

After the US invasion began at one a.m. on 20 December, another incident occurred which further raises the question of whether the apprehension of Noriega was the White House's sole, or even primary, concern.

A European diplomat in Panama City (representing a major US ally) claimed that less than three hours after the invasion began he telephoned the US military to inform them that Noriega was two houses away in the flat of his mistress's grandmother, but the military disregarded the information. The diplomat said later that he was "100 percent certain" of Noriega's location. "But when I called, SouthCom [the U.S. Southern Command] said it had other priorities." The diplomat had met several times with Noriega and his mistress, who had recently moved into the diplomat's own apartment building. Other residents of the two apartment buildings confirmed the diplomat's assertion about Noriega's presence. Neither Southern Command officials nor the American Embassy would respond to inquiries about the matter.[35]

Did the US decline to capture Noriega in the first few hours of the invasion because it was determined to first cripple his base of power, the PDF, and score a grand military triumph that would enable George Bush to shred the wimp image that plagued him? Did military muscle have to be flexed to illustrate the need for a big combat-ready force even in the absence of a "Soviet threat"? Or to send a clear message to the people of Nicaragua who had an election scheduled in three months?

When George Bush and Secretary of Defense Dick Cheney were asked why they had made 180-degree turns on previous explicit rejections of a war against Panama, they each referred to the same incident of the night of 16-17 December.[36]

According to the Defense Department, four American servicemen, unarmed and in civilian clothes, got lost and inadvertently drove up to a PDF roadblock, where they were manhandled. As they drove away, they were shot at, killing one and wounding another. At the same time, an American Navy officer and his wife who witnessed this scene were roughed up considerably by the PDF.[37]

One year later, the *Los Angeles Times* reported that the incident was not the unprovoked act of aggression by the PDF portrayed by Washington. Instead, it was a step in a pattern of aggressive behavior by a small group of US troops who frequently tested the patience and reaction of Panamanian forces, particularly at roadblocks, which they would "dare" by driving up and then refusing to stop or suddenly pulling away. The Americans in this case were not lost; and they were armed. They drove up to a very sensitive roadblock and when told to leave the car by the PDF, the Americans all gave them the finger, shouted an obscenity, and drove off. The Panamanians then opened fire.[38]

Lending credence to this report is, oddly enough, a recorded phone conversation of a young Marine guard at the American Embassy speaking to his mother in the United States the next morning. The four Americans, he said, "were out of bounds, owing to the fact that they had no reason to be there. The whole world knows that they shouldn't have gone there. They messed up. If the United States set up a barricade anywhere and someone acted in the same way we would also start firing."[39]

There had been other provocation as well. For months prior to the incident, the United States had been engaging in military posturing in Panama. US troops, bristling with assault weapons, would travel in fast-moving convoys, escorted by armored vehicles, looking for all the world as if they planned to attack someone. US Marines descended from helicopters by rope to practice emergency evacuation of the embassy. Panamanian military camps were surrounded and their gates rattled amid insults by US servicemen. In one episode, more than 1,000 US military personnel conducted an exercise that appeared to be a rehearsal of a kidnap raid, as helicopters and jet aircraft flew low over Noriega's house and American raiders splashed ashore nearby.[40]

In late September, Gen. Max Thurman had been appointed the new Commander-in-Chief of the Southern Command. He was briefed by Adm. William Crowe, Chairman of the Joint Chiefs of Staff, who apprised him that there was a very high probability that Bush would call for large-scale military action in Panama in the near future. "We're going to go [but] I can't tell you when."[41]

After the invasion, the mother of one of the American soldiers killed said that her son had called her on 14 December to say he was going on a dangerous mission. "He called to say goodbye ... and that (he) might not be home again." This was before the roadblock incident. Another serviceman, speaking to reporters after the invasion, said that the soldiers had found out about it "maybe four or five days before you did". When a reporter asked when that was, an Army officer prevented the soldier from answering.[42]

It would appear from this evidence that the war had been planned before the American serviceman was shot. All that was needed was a pretext, an incident.

Two days after the incident, an off-duty American lieutenant was leaving a laundry when he was approached by a Panamanian police (or army) officer. The American shot and wounded the Panamanian twice. "The U.S. serviceman felt threatened," the Bush administration claimed, admitting that its earlier story that the Panamanian had pulled a gun was false.[43] It was not reported that Panama invaded the United States as a result of this incident.

Thus it came to be that a superpower crushed one of the smallest armies in the hemisphere. (It was the seventh time the United States had invaded Panama since it had kidnapped the province from Colombia in 1903 to build the canal—see Appendix II.) The new Chairman of the Joint Chiefs of Staff, Gen. Colin Powell, declared at the time of the invasion: "We have to put a shingle outside our door saying, 'Superpower lives here'."[44]

But the Superpower still had to show *a decent respect to the opinions of mankind.* Accordingly, the leading legal minds of the Justice Department, the State Department, and the Defense Department put their heads together and came to the unanimous conclusion that the invasion of the sovereign nation of Panama, the abduction of its leader, and his criminal trial in the United States were all legal and proper.

The invasion was called "Operation Just Cause", perhaps for acts like the following carried out by the American military:

- searched out and arrested hundreds of civilian supporters of Noriega even though they did not face American or Panamanian criminal charges; houses were broken into to apprehend some of the individuals;
- forced ambulances—with emergency lights flashing and sirens sounding as they rushed patients to hospitals—to halt, to be searched for Noriega loyalists disguised as patients;
- fired into the air without warning while walking through busy streets;
- imposed and enforced curfews;
- organized tours of Noriega's home and office for reporters to gawk at and pry into all of the man's personal belongings, from his photos to his underwear; publicized and ridiculed everything from his sexual practices to his religious beliefs;

- invaded prisons and released prisoners; the commander of the new Panamanian Public Force, appointed by the US, blamed the extraordinary wave of crime and violence that hit Panama after the invasion on what he said were hundreds of dangerous criminals freed by the US; he declared that the rate of assaults, murders, and other crimes was "much worse" than under the Noriega regime;

- wearing painted faces and firing machine guns into the air, raided the Nicaraguan ambassador's home; the ambassador was wrestled to the ground; he and seven other people were held at gunpoint while US soldiers ransacked the house and confiscated weapons, $3,000 in cash, and personal items; the money was never returned, the ambassador said;

- surrounded the Vatican Embassy, where Noriega had taken sanctuary, and for several days blasted the ears of the entire neighborhood with ear-splitting rock and roll music over loudspeakers. US soldiers near the Vatican Embassy sang a parody of Woody Guthrie's old song: "This land is my land, that land is my land, there's no land here that isn't my land."[45]

"Many Panamanians initially welcomed the U.S. intervention," reported the *Los Angeles Times*. "But as fighting continued through a fourth day on Saturday, some reports from Panama suggested that resentment of the U.S. presence was also widespread. ... The Panamanian people feel more threatened since the Americans arrived than they did when Noriega still held power, an [American] administration official said."[46]

On the first anniversary of the invasion, Panamanians couldn't agree whether to mark the day as a holiday or a day of mourning. So President Endara proclaimed a National Day of Reflection.[47]

"From Mexico to Argentina, Latin American governments today roundly condemned the use of force by the United States against Gen. Manuel Antonio Noriega of Panama."

News report, 20 December 1989[48]

"I appreciate the support that we've received, strong support from the United States Congress, and from our Latin American neighbors."

George Bush, 21 December 1989[49]

The Organization of American States approved a resolution "to deeply regret the military intervention in Panama" by a vote of 20 to 1 (the one being the United States).

"We are outraged," said State Department spokesman Richard Boucher. The OAS, he declared, "missed an historic opportunity to get beyond its traditional narrow concern with non-intervention."[50]

Afterword

During 1990, the United States was instrumental in setting up a highly secretive intelligence office, with the all-encompassing name of the Council of Public Security and National Defense. The new agency was headed by a man who twice served as a senior minister in Noriega's puppet governments. A government official said that the CIA was assisting in personnel training for the new agency and that further assistance was being received from a US Justice Department police training mission in Panama.

Reportedly, one of the agency's missions was to gather information on "troublemakers", including opposition figures organizing mass demonstrations. Another target was the newly organized National Police, formed from remnants of Noriega's old army. "We'll watch the police," said an official. "We can't let the monster arise again." This left open the question of who would watch the new agency.[51] At the same time, the US Army's 4th Psychological Operations Group established a hotline for the public to denounce Noriega backers, criminals, subversives and anti-US fighters, who were then picked up by American troops and consigned to detention camps.[52]

In December 1990, when President Guillermo Endara was faced with a military rebellion he was unable to put down, he called upon US troops to intervene and quell the uprising.[53] Endara had been sworn in as president on a US military base in Panama during the invasion a year earlier. The official Pentagon study of the Panama occupation notes that the original post-invasion plans called for outright US military government, with the head of the Southern Command as Panama's de facto ruler. At the last minute a decision was made to install Endara as president, but his government was, as the study put it, "merely a facade".[54]

The United States confiscated thousands of boxes of Noriega government documents and refused to hand over any of them to Panamanian investigators. "The United States is protecting robbers and thieves and obstructing justice," complained the government's chief prosecutor. "We are the owners of the documents. If I am to complete my work, I have to see the documents."[55]

Panamanian businessmen reported that they'd lost as much as $700 million because of the looting and rioting that followed the invasion, very little of it covered by insurance. One year after the invasion, unemployment was running at more than 25 percent, and invasion damage, looting, and the US sanctions of 1988-89 had shrunk Panama's economy by 30 percent.[56]

The new president, one of the two vice-presidents, and the attorney general, it turned out, all had links to drug trafficking and money laundering.[57]

By the spring of 1991 it could be reported that Colombian drug cartels and associates of Noriega had once again turned Panama into a narcotics trans-shipment center; there were as well far more cocaine production facilities than ever existed under Noriega, and drug use in Panama was reportedly at a far higher level. The new drug trafficking and money laundering activity centered on associates of cabinet officials, particularly in the president's and the attorney general's offices. When American officials told the Panamanians that Foreign Ministry legal adviser Julio Berrios was under US investigation for money laundering, the Panamanians did nothing. Berrios was subsequently appointed to Panama's delegation for negotiations with the United States on the treaty to end money laundering.[58]

Washington insisted that Panama change its prized banking secrecy laws to facilitate US efforts to pursue suspected lawbreakers, principally launderers of drug money. Panama's Controller General pointed out that the United States wanted Panama to pursue acts which were crimes in the US but not in Panama. "We can't change the whole legal system because of one thing [drugs]," he argued.

Eventually, after many American threats to cut off aid, Panama signed a treaty in April 1991 giving US authorities partial access to Panamanian banking records and the right to prosecute individuals depositing illegal drug profits. However, foreign banks, particularly Colombian ones, found ways to circumvent the new requirements and were soon back in the money-laundering business.[59]

* *

An American helicopter gunship was strafing what it perceived to be enemies in the street. Ernesto Cubilla was in his kitchen. A stray round went through his roof. His son rushed in to find him spread out in the corner. He lost a lung and a kidney and suffered liver damage.[60]

"Women and children naturally went to the window and looked out when they heard the fighting," said Roberto Troncoso, president of the Panamanian Committee for Human Rights, "and the nervous [American] soldiers shot them."[61]

A few hours before the invasion, while all the details were being finalized, George Bush, wearing a bright red and green Christmas tie, holding his granddaughter, sang Christmas carols at a White House Christmas party.[62] Two days later he declared that his "heart goes out to the families of those who have died in Panama."[63]

One of Bush's advisers said that the president felt that Noriega "was thumbing his nose at him".[64]

51. Bulgaria 1990
Teaching communists what democracy is all about

For American anti-communist cold-warriors, for Bulgarian anti-communist cold-warriors, it couldn't have looked more promising.

The cold war was over. The forces of Western Civilization, Capitalism and Goodness had won. The Soviet Union was on the verge of falling apart. The Communist Party of Bulgaria was in disgrace. Its dictatorial leader of 35 years was being prosecuted for abuses of power. The party had changed its name, but that wouldn't fool anybody. And the country was holding its first multiparty election in 45 years.

Then, the communists proceeded to win the election.

For the anti-communists the pain was unbearable. Surely some monstrous cosmic mistake had been made, a mistake which should not be allowed to stand. It should not, and it would not.

Washington had expressed its interest early. In February, Secretary of State James Baker became the most senior American official to visit Bulgaria since World War II. His official schedule said he was in Bulgaria to "meet with opposition leaders as well as Government officials". Usually, the *New York Times* noted, "it is listed the other way around". Baker became deeply involved in his talks with the opposition about political strategies and how to organize for an election. He also addressed a street rally organized by opposition groups, praising and encouraging the crowd. On the State Department profile of Bulgaria handed to reporters traveling with Baker, under the heading "Type of Government", was written "In transition".[1]

In May, three weeks before election day, a row broke out over assertions by the leader of the main opposition group. Petar Beron, secretary of the Union of Democratic Forces, a coalition of 16 parties and movements, said that during UDF's visits to Europe and the United States, many politicians pledged that they would not provide financial assistance to a socialist Bulgaria. This would apply even if the Bulgarian Socialist Party—the renamed Communist Party—won the elections fairly. Beron stated that:

Western leaders want lasting contacts with governments which are building Western-style democracy and economies. The British Foreign Secretary, Douglas Hurd, was particularly categorical. He said he was drawing up a declaration to go before the European Community to refuse help for the remaining socialist governments in Eastern Europe.[2]

Meanwhile, the National Endowment for Democracy, Washington's specially created stand-in for the CIA (see Nicaragua chapter), with funding in this case primarily from the Agency for International Development, was pouring some $2 million into Bulgaria to influence the outcome of the election, a process the NED calls promoting democracy. This was equivalent to a foreign power injecting more than $50 million into an American electoral campaign. One major recipient of this largesse was the newspaper of the opposition Union of Democratic Forces, *Demokratzia*, which received $233,000 worth of newsprint, "to allow it to increase its size and circulation for the period leading up to the national elections". The UDF itself received another $615,000 of American taxpayer money for "infrastructure support and party training" ... "material and technical support" ... and "post-electoral assistance for the UDF's party building program".[3]

The United States made little attempt to mask its partisanship. On June 9, the day before election day, the US ambassador to Bulgaria, Sol Polansky, appeared on the platform of a UDF rally.[4] Polansky, whose early government career involved intelligence research, was a man who had had more than a passing acquaintance with the CIA. Moreover, several days earlier, the State Department had taken the unusual step of publicly criticizing the Bulgarian government for what it called the inequitable distribution of resources for news outlets, especially newsprint for opposition newspapers, as if this was not a fact of life for genuine opposition forces in the United States and every other country in the world. The Bulgarian government responded that the opposition had received newsprint and access to the broadcast outlets in accordance with an agreement between the parties, adding that many of the Socialist Party's advantages, especially its financial reserves, resulted from the party's membership of one million, about a ninth of Bulgaria's population. The government had further provided the printing plant to publish the UDF newspaper and had given the opposition coalition the building from which to run its operations.[5]

The Socialists' lead in the polls in the face of a crumbling economy perplexed the UDF, but the Bulgarian Socialist Party drew most of its support from among pensioners, farmworkers and the industrial workforce, together representing well over half the voting population.[6] These sectors tended to associate the BSP with stability, and the party capitalized on this, pointing to the disastrous results—particularly the unemployment and inflation—of "shock therapy" free enterprise in Russia.[7] Although the three main parties all proposed moving toward a market economy, the Socialists insisted that the changes had to be carefully controlled. How this would be manifested in practice if the BSP were in charge and had to live in an extremely capitalist world, could not be predicted. What was certain, however, was that there was no way a party named "Socialist", née "Communist", recently married to the Soviet Union, could win the trust and support of the West.

As it turned out after the second round of voting, the Socialists had won about 47 percent of the vote and 211 seats in the 400-seat parliament (the Grand National Assembly), to the UDF's 36 percent and 144 seats. Immediately following the first round, the opposition took to the streets with accusations of fraud, chanting "Socialist Mafia!" and "We won't work for the Reds!" However, the European election observers had contrary views. "The results ... will reflect the will of the people," said the leader of a British observer delegation. "If I wanted to fix an election, it would be easier to do it in England than in Bulgaria."

"If the opposition denounces the results as manipulated, it doesn't fit in with what we've seen," a Council of Europe delegate declared.

Another West European observer rejected the opposition claims as "sour grapes".[8]

"Utter rot" was the term chosen by a conservative English MP to describe allegations of serious fraud. He asserted that "The conduct of the poll was scrupulously fair. There were just minor incidents that were exaggerated."

"The opposition appear to be rather bad losers," concluded one Western diplomat.[9]

These opinions were shared by the many hundreds of observers, diplomats and parliamentarians from Western Europe. Nonetheless, most of the American observers were not very happy, saying that fear and intimidation arising from "the legacy of 45 years of totalitarian rule" had produced "psychological" pressures on Bulgarian voters. "Off the record, I have real problems with this," said one of the Americans. Asked if his team's report would have been as critical had the opposition won, he replied: "That's a good question."[10]

Members of the British parliamentary observer group dismissed reports that voting was marred by intimidation and other malpractices. Most complaints were either "trivial" or impossible to substantiate, they said. "When we asked where intimidation had taken place, it was always in the next village," said Lord Tordoff.[11]

Before the election, Socialist Prime Minister Lukanov had called for a coalition with opposition parties if his Bulgarian Socialist Party won the election. "The new government," he said, "needs the broadest possible measure of public support if we are to carry through the necessary changes."[12] Now victorious, he repeated the call for a coalition. But the UDF rejected the offer.[13] There were, however, elements within the BSP which were equally opposed to a coalition.

The opposition refused to accept the outcome of the voting. They were at war with the government. Street demonstrations became a daily occurrence as UDF supporters, backed by large numbers of students, built barricades and blocked traffic, and students launched a wave of strikes and sit-ins. Many of the students were acting as part of the Federation of Independent Student Societies (or Associations), which had been formed before the election. The chairman of the student group, Aptanas Kirchev, asserted that the organization had documentation on electoral abuses which would shortly be made public. But this does not appear to have taken place.[14]

The student movements were amongst the recipients of National Endowment for Democracy grants, to the tune of $100,000 "to provide infrastructure support to the Federation of Independent Student Associations of Bulgaria to improve its outreach capacity in preparation for the national elections". The students received "faxes, video and copying equipment, loudspeakers, printing equipment and low-cost printing techniques", as well as the help of various Polish advisers, American legal advisers, and other experts—the best that NED money could buy.[15]

The first victory for the protest movement came on 6 July, less than a month after the election, when President Mladenov was forced to resign after a week of protests—including a hunger strike outside of Parliament—over his actions during an anti-governmental demonstration the previous December. His resignation came after the UDF released a videotape showing Mladenov talking to his colleagues and appearing to say: "Shouldn't we bring in the tanks?" Said a UDF official of the resignation, "We are rather happy about all this. It has thrown the Socialists into chaos."[16]

The demonstrations, the protests, the agitation continued on a daily basis during July. A "City of Freedom" consisting of more than 60 tents was set up in the center of Sofia, occupied by people who said they would stay there until all senior Bulgarian politicians who served under the old communist regime were removed. When they were denied what they considered adequate access to the media, the protesters added to their demands the resignation of the head of Bulgarian television.[17] At one point, a huge ceremonial pyre was built in the street in which text books from the communist era were burnt, as well as party cards and flags.[18]

The next head to fall was that of the interior minister, Atanas Smerdjiev, who resigned in a dispute over the extent to which the questioning of former dictator Todor Zhivkov should be public or behind closed doors. The Bulgarian people indeed had a lot to protest about; primarily a rapidly declining standard of living and a government without a president which seemed paralyzed and unable to enact desperately-needed reforms. But the question posed by some MPs—as thousands of hostile demonstrators surrounded the Parliament building during the Smerdjiev affair—was "Are we going to be dictated to by the street?" "The problem," said Prime Minister Lukanov, "is whether Parliament is a sovereign body or whether we are going to be forced to make decisions under pressure." His car was attacked as he left the building.[19] Finally, on 1 August the head of the UDF, Zhelyu Zhelev, was elected unopposed by Parliament as the new president.

A few weeks later, another demand of the protesters was met. The government began to remove communist symbols, such as red stars and hammer-and-sickles, from buildings in Sofia. Yet, two days later, the headquarters of the Socialist Party was set afire as 10,000 people swarmed around it. Many of them broke into the building and ransacked it before it wound up a gutted and charred shell.[20]

The protest movement in Bulgaria was beginning to feel and smell like the general strike in British Guiana to topple Cheddi Jagan in 1962, and the campaign to undermine Salvador Allende in Chile in the early '70s—both operations of the CIA—where as soon as one demand was met, newer ones were raised, putting the government virtually under siege, hoping it would over-react, and making normal governing impossible. In Bulgaria, women demonstrated by banging pots and pans to signify the lack of food in the shops,[21] just as women had dramatically done in Chile, and in Jamaica and Nicaragua as well, where the CIA had also financed anti-government demonstrations. In British Guiana, the Christian Anti-Communist Crusade had come down from the US to spread the gospel and money, and similar groups had set up shop in Jamaica. In Bulgaria in August, representatives of the Free Congress Foundation, an American right-wing organization with lots of money and lots of anti-communist and religious ideology, met with about one-third of the opposition members in Parliament and President Zhelev's chief political adviser. Zhelev himself visited the FCF's Washington office the following month. The FCF—which has received money from the National Endowment for Democracy at times—had visited the Soviet Union and most of the Eastern European countries in 1989 and 1990, imparting good ol' American know-how in electoral and political techniques and for shaping public policy, as well as holding seminars on the multiple charms of free enterprise. It is not known whether any of the students were aware of the fact that one of the FCF's chief Eastern European program directors, Laszlo Pasztor, was a man with genuine Nazi credentials.[22] By October, a group of American financial experts and economists, under the auspices of the US Chamber of Commerce, had drawn up a detailed plan for transforming Bulgaria into a supply-side free-market economy, complete with timetables for implementing the plan. President Zhelev said he was confident the Bulgarian government would accept virtually all the recommendations, even though the BSP held a majority in Parliament. "They will be eager to proceed," he said, "because otherwise the government will fall."[23]

Witnesses and police claimed that Konstantin Trenchev, a fierce anti-communist who was a senior figure in the UDF and the leader of the Podkrepa independent trade union, had called on a group of hardcore demonstrators to storm the BSP building during the fire. He had also called for the dissolution of Parliament and presidential rule, "tantamount to a coup d'etat" declared the Socialist Party. Trenchev went into hiding.[24]

Trenchev's Podkrepa union was also being financed by the NED—$327 thousand had been allocated "to provide material and technical support to Bulgaria's independent trade union movement Podkrepa" and "to help Podkrepa organize a voter education campaign for the local elections". There were computers and fax machines, and there were advisers to help the union "get organized and gain strength", according to Podkrepa's vice president. The assistance had reached Podkrepa via the Free Trade Union Institute,[25] set up by the AFL-CIO in 1977 as the successor to the Free Trade Union Committee, which had been formed in the 1940s to combat left-wing trade unionism in Europe. Both the FTUC and the FTUI had long had an intimate relationship with the CIA.[26]

In the first week of November, several hundred students occupied Sofia University once again, demanding now the prosecution, not merely the removal, of leading figures in the former communist regime, as well as the nationalization of the Socialist Party's assets. The prime minister's rule was shaky. Lukanov had threatened to step down unless he gained opposition support in Parliament for his program of economic reform. The UDF, on the other hand, was now demanding that it be allowed to dominate a new coalition government, taking the premiership and most key portfolios. Although open to a coalition, the BSP would not agree to surrender the prime minister's position; the other cabinet posts, however, were open to negotiation.[27]

The movement to topple Lukanov was accelerating. Thousands marched and called for his resignation. University students held rallies, sit-ins, strikes and protest fasts, now demanding the publication of the names of all former secret police informers in the university. They proclaimed their complete distrust in the ability of the government to cope with Bulgaria's political and economic crisis, and called for "an end to one-party rule", a strange request in light of the desire of Lukanov to form a coalition government.[28] In June *The Guardian* of London had described Lukanov as "Bulgaria's impressive Prime minister ... a skilled politician who impresses business executives, bankers and conservative Western politicians, while maintaining popular support at home, even among the opposition."[29]

On the 23rd of November, Lukanov (barely) survived a no-confidence motion, leading the UDF to storm out of Parliament, announcing that they would not return for "an indefinite period". Three days later, the Podkrepa labor organization instituted a "general strike", albeit not with a majority of the nation's workers.[30]

Meanwhile, the student protests continued, although some of their demands had already been partly met. The Socialist Party had agreed to restore to the state 57 percent of its assets, corresponding to subsidies received from the state budget under the previous regime. And the former party leader, Todor Zhivkov, was already facing trial.

Some opposition leaders were not happy with the seemingly boundless student protest movement. UDF leader Petar Beron urged that since Bulgaria had embarked on the road to parliamentary democracy, the students should give democracy a chance and not resort to sit-ins. And a UDF MP added that "The socialists should leave the political arena in a legal manner. They should not be forced into doing it through revolution." Student leaders dismissed these remarks out of hand.[31]

The end for Andrei Lukanov came on 29 November, as the strike spread to members of the media, and thousands of doctors, nurses and teachers staged demonstrations. He announced that since his proposed economic program had not received the broad support he had asked for, he had decided that it was "useless to continue in office". A caretaker coalition would be set up that would lead to new general elections.[32]

Throughout the period of protest and turmoil, the United States continued to give financial assistance to various opposition forces and "whispered advice on how to apply pressure to the elected leaders". The vice president of the Podkrepa union, referring to American diplomats, said: "They wanted to help us and have helped with advice and strategy." This solidarity gave rise to hopes of future American aid. Konstantin Trenchev, the head of Podkrepa, apparently out of hiding now, confirmed that opposition activists had been assured of more US assistance if they managed to wrest power from the former communists.[33]

These hopes may have had as much to do with naiveté as with American support for the UDF. The Bulgarians, like other Eastern Europeans and Soviet citizens, had led very sheltered political and intellectual lives. In 1990, their ideological sophistication was scarcely above the equation: if the communist government was bad, it must have been all bad; if it was all bad, its principal enemy must have been all good. They believed such things as: American government leaders could not stay in office if they lied to the people, and that reports of homelessness and the absence of national health insurance in the United States were just "communist propaganda".

However, the new American ambassador, H. Kenneth Hill, said that Washington officials had made it clear to Bulgarian politicians that future aid depended on democratic reform and development of an economic recovery plan acceptable to Western lenders, the same terms laid down all over Eastern Europe.

The Bulgarian Socialists, while not doubting Washington's commitment to exporting capitalism, did complain that the United States had at times violated democratic principles in working against the leadership chosen by the Bulgarian people. One reform-minded Socialist government official contended that Americans had reacted to his party's victory as if it represented a failure of US policy. "The U.S. government people have not been the most clean, moral defenders of democracy here," he said. "What cannot be done at home can be gotten away with in this dark, backward Balkan state."[34]

In the years since, the Bulgarian people, particularly the students, may have learned something, as the country has gone through the now-familiar pattern of freely-rising prices, the scrapping of subsidies on basic goods and uilities, shortages of all kinds, and IMF and World Bank demands to tighten the belts even further. Politically, there's been chaos. The UDF came to power in the next elections (with the BSP a very close second) but, due to the failing economy, lost a confidence vote in Parliament, saw its entire cabinet resign, then the vice president, who warned that the nation was heading for dictatorship. Finally, in July 1993, protesters prevented the president from entering his office for a month and demanded his resignation.

By 1994, we could read in the *Los Angeles Times,* by their most anti-communist foreign correspondent:

> Living conditions are so much worse in the reform era that Bulgarians look back fondly on communism's "good old days," when the hand of the state crushed personal freedom but ensured that people were housed, employed and had enough to eat. [35]

But for Washington policy makers, the important thing, the ideological bottom line, was that the Bulgarian Socialist Party could not, and would not, be given the chance to prove that a democratic, socialist-oriented mixed economy could succeed in Eastern Europe while the capitalist model was failing all around it.

Nor, apparently, would it be allowed in nearby Albania. On 31 March 1991, a Communist government won overwhelming endorsement in elections there. This was followed immediately by two months of widespread unrest, including street demonstrations and a general strike lasting three weeks, which finally led to the collapse of the new regime by June. [36] The National Endowment for Democracy had been there also, providing $80,000 to the labor movement and $23,000 "to support training and civic education programs".[37]

52. Iraq 1990-1991
Desert holocaust

"This is the one part I didn't want to see," said a 20-year-old private. "All the homeless, all the hurting. When we came through the refugee camp, man, that's something I didn't need."

"It's really sad," said the sergeant. "We've got little kids come up and see my gun, and they start crying. That really tears me up."

"At night, you kill and you roll on by," said another GI. "You don't stop. You don't have to see anything. It wasn't until the next morning the rear told us the devastation was total. We'd killed the entire division."[1]

While many nations have a terrible record in modern times of dealing out great suffering face-to-face with their victims, Americans have made it a point to keep at a distance while inflicting some of the greatest horrors of the age: atomic bombs on the people of Japan; carpet-bombing Korea back to the stone age; engulfing the Vietnamese in napalm and pesticides; providing three decades of Latin Americans with the tools and methods of torture, then turning their eyes away, closing their ears to the screams, and denying everything ... and now, dropping 177 million pounds of bombs on the people of Iraq in the most concentrated aerial onslaught in the history of the world.

What possessed the United States to carry out this relentless devastation for more than 40 days and nights against one of the most advanced and enlightened nations in the Middle East and its ancient and modern capital city?

It's the first half of 1990. The dismantling of the Berlin wall is being carried out on a daily basis. Euphoria about the end of the cold war and optimism about the beginning of a new era of peace and prosperity are hard to contain. The Bush administration is under pressure to cut the monster military budget and institute a "peace dividend". But George Bush, Commander-in-Chief of the Armed Forces, former Texas oil man, and former Director of the CIA, is not about to turn his back on his many cronies in the military-industrial-intelligence complex. He rails against those who would "naively cut the muscle out of our defense posture", and insists that we must take a cautious attitude towards reform in the USSR.[2] In February, it's reported that "the administration and Congress are expecting the most acrimonious hard-fought defense budget battle in recent history"; and in June that "tensions have escalated" between Congress and the Pentagon "as Congress prepares to draft one of the most pivotal defense budgets in the past two decades."[3] A month later, a Senate Armed Services subcommittee votes to cut military manpower by nearly three times more than recommended by the Bush administration ... "The size and direction of the cuts indicate that

President Bush is losing his battle on how to manage reductions in military spending."[4]

During this same period Bush's popularity was plummeting: from an approval rating of 80 percent in January—as he rode the wave of public support for his invasion of Panama the previous month—to 73 in February, down to the mid-60s in May and June, 63 on 11 July, 60 two weeks later.[5]

George Herbert Walker Bush needed something dramatic to capture the headlines and the public, and to convince Congress that a powerful military was needed as much as ever because it was still a scary and dangerous world out there.

Although the official Washington version of events presented Iraq's occupation of neighboring Kuwait as an arbitrary and unwarranted aggression, Kuwait had actually been a district of Iraq, under Ottoman rule, up to the First World War. After the war, to exert leverage against the abundantly oil-rich Iraq, the British Colonial Office established tiny Kuwait as a separate territorial entity, in the process cutting off most of Iraq's access to the Persian Gulf. In 1961, Kuwait became "independent," again because Britain declared it to be so, and Iraq massed troops at the border, backing down when the British dispatched their own forces. Subsequent Iraqi regimes never accepted the legitimacy of this state of affairs, making similar threats in the 1970s, even crossing a half-mile into Kuwait in 1976, but Baghdad was also open to a compromise with Kuwait under which Iraq would gain access to its former islands in the Gulf.[6]

The current conflict had its origins in the brutal 1980-88 war between Iraq and Iran. Iraq charged that while it was locked in battle, Kuwait was engaged in stealing $2.4 billion of oil from the Rumaila oil field that ran beneath the vaguely defined Iraq-Kuwait border and was claimed in its entirety by Iraq; that Kuwait had built military and other structures on Iraqi territory; and worst of all, that immediately after the war ended, Kuwait and the United Arab Emirates began to exceed the production quotas established by the Organization of Petroleum Exporting Countries (OPEC), flooding the oil market, and driving prices down. Iraq was heavily strapped and deeply in debt because of the long war, and Iraqi President Saddam Hussein declared this policy was an increasing threat to his country—"economic war", he called it, pointing out that Iraq lost a billion dollars a year for each drop of one dollar in the oil price.[7] Besides compensation for these losses, Hussein insisted on possession of the two Gulf islands which blocked Iraq's access to the Gulf as well as undisputed ownership of the Rumaila oilfield.

In the latter part of July 1990, after Kuwait had continued to scorn Iraq's financial and territorial demands, and to ignore OPEC's request to stick to its assigned quota, Iraq began to mass large numbers of troops along the Kuwaiti border.

The reaction to all this by the world's only remaining superpower and self-appointed global policeman became the subject of intense analysis and controversy after Iraq actually invaded. Had Washington given Iraq a green light to invade? Was there, at a minimum, the absence of a flashing *red* light? The controversy was fueled by incidents such as the following:

19 July: Secretary of Defense Dick Cheney stated that the American commitment made during the Iran-Iraq war to come to Kuwait's defense if it were attacked was still valid. The same point was made by Paul Wolfowitz, Undersecretary of Defense for Policy, at a private luncheon with Arab ambassadors. (Ironically, Kuwait had been allied with Iraq and feared an attack from Iran.) Later, Cheney's remark was downplayed by his own spokesman, Pete Williams, who explained that the secretary had spoken with "some degree of liberty". Cheney was then told by the White House: "You're committing us to war we might not

want to fight," and advised pointedly that from then on, statements on Iraq would be made by the White House and State Department.[8]

24 July: State Department spokeswoman Margaret Tutweiler, in response to a question, responded: "We do not have any defense treaties with Kuwait, and there are no special defense or security commitments to Kuwait." Asked whether the United States would help Kuwait if it were attacked, she said: "We also remain strongly committed to supporting the individual and collective self-defense of our friends in the gulf with whom we have deep and longstanding ties"—a statement that some Kuwaiti officials said privately was too weak.[9]

24 July: The US staged an unscheduled and rare military exercise with the United Arab Emirates, and the same Pete Williams then announced: "We remain strongly committed to supporting the individual and collective self-defense of our friends in the gulf with whom we have deep and longstanding ties." And the White House declared: "We're concerned about the troop buildup by the Iraqis. We ask that all parties strive to avoid violence."[10]

25 July: Saddam Hussein was personally told by the US ambassador to Iraq, April Glaspie, in a now-famous remark, that "We have no opinion on the Arab-Arab conflicts, like your border disagreement with Kuwait." But she then went on to tell the Iraqi leader that she was concerned about his massive troop deployment on the Kuwaiti border in the context of his government's having branded Kuwait's actions as "parallel to military aggression".[11]

25 July: John Kelly, Assistant Secretary of State for Near Eastern and South Asian Affairs, killed a planned Voice of America broadcast that would have warned Iraq with the identical party-line words used by Tutweiler and Williams.[12] Hussein may not have known of this incident, although in April he had been personally assured by visiting Senate Minority Leader Robert Dole, speaking in behalf of the president, that the Bush administration dissociated itself from a Voice of America broadcast critical of Iraq's human-rights abuses and also opposed a congressional move for economic sanctions against Iraq.[13]

27 July: The House and Senate each voted to impose economic sanctions against Iraq because of its human-rights violations. However, the Bush administration immediately reiterated its opposition to the measure.[14]

28 July: Bush sent a personal message to Hussein (apparently after receiving Glaspie's report of her meeting with the Iraqi leader) cautioning him against the use of force, without referring directly to Kuwait.[15]

31 July: Kelly told Congress: "We have no defense treaty relationship with any Gulf country. That is clear. ... We have historically avoided taking a position on border disputes or on internal OPEC deliberations."

Rep. Lee Hamilton asked if it would be correct to say that if Iraq "charged across the border into Kuwait" the United States did "not have a treaty commitment which would obligate us to engage U.S. forces" there.

"That is correct," Kelly responded.[16]

The next day (Washington time), Iraqi troops led by tanks charged across the Kuwaiti border, and the United States instantly threw itself into unmitigated opposition.

Official statements notwithstanding, it appears that the United States did indeed have an official position on the Iraq-Kuwait border dispute. After the invasion, one of the documents the Iraqis found in a Kuwaiti intelligence file was a memorandum concerning a November 1989 meeting between the head of Kuwaiti state security and CIA Director William Webster, which included the following:

We agreed with the American side that it was important to take advantage of the deteriorating economic situation in Iraq in order to put pressure on that country's government to delineate our common border. The Central Intelligence Agency gave us its view of appropriate means of pressure, saying that broad cooperation should be initiated between us on condition that such activities be coordinated at a high level.

The CIA called the document a "total fabrication". However, as the *Los Angeles Times* pointed out, "The memo is not an obvious forgery, particularly since if Iraqi officials had written it themselves, they almost certainly would have made it far more damaging to U.S. and Kuwaiti credibility."[17] It was apparently real enough and damaging enough to the Kuwaiti foreign minister—he fainted when confronted with the document by his Iraqi counterpart at an Arab summit meeting in mid-August.[18]

When the Iraqi ambassador in Washington was asked why the document seemed to contradict US Ambassador Glaspie's avowal of neutrality on the issue, he replied that her remark was "part and parcel of the setup".[19]

Was Iraq set up by the United States and Kuwait? Was Saddam provoked into his invasion—with the conspirators' expectation perhaps that it would not extend beyond the border area—so he could be cut down to the size both countries wanted?

In February 1990, Hussein made a speech before an Arab summit which could certainly have incited, or added impetus to, such a plot. In it he condemned the continuous American military presence in the Persian Gulf waters and warned that "If the Gulf people and the rest of the Arabs along with them fail to take heed, the Arab Gulf region will be ruled by American will." Further, that the US would dictate the production, distribution and price of oil, "all on the basis of a special outlook which has to do solely with U.S. interests and in which no consideration is given to the interests of others."[20]

In examining whether there was a conspiracy against Iraq and Saddam Hussein, we must consider, in addition to the indications mentioned above, the following:

Palestine Liberation Organization Chairman Yasser Arafat has asserted that Washington thwarted the chance for a peaceful resolution of the differences between Kuwait and Iraq at an Arab summit in May, after Saddam had offered to negotiate a mutually acceptable border with Kuwait. "The US was encouraging Kuwait not to offer any compromise," said Arafat, "which meant there could be no negotiated solution to avoid the Gulf crisis." Kuwait, he said, was led to believe it could rely on the force of US arms instead.[21]

Similarly, King Hussein of Jordan revealed that just before the Iraqi invasion the Kuwaiti foreign minister stated: "We are not going to respond to [Iraq] ... if they don't like it, let them occupy our territory ... we are going to bring in the Americans." And that the Kuwaiti emir told his military officers that in the event of an invasion, their duty was to hold off the Iraqis for 24 hours; by then "American and foreign forces would land in Kuwait and expel them." King Hussein expressed the opinion that Arab understanding was that Saddam had been goaded into invading, thereby stepping into a noose prepared for him.[22]

The emir refused to accede to Iraq's financial demands, instead offering an insulting half-million dollars to Baghdad. A note from him to his prime minister before the invasion speaks of support of this policy from Egypt, Washington and London. "Be unwavering in your discussions," the emir writes. "We are stronger than they [the Iraqis] think."[23]

After the war, the Kuwaiti Minister of Oil and Finance acknowledged:

> But we knew that the United States would not let us be overrun. I spent too much time in Washington to make that mistake, and received a constant stream of visitors here. The American policy was clear. Only Saddam didn't understand it.[24]

But we have seen perhaps ample reason why Saddam would fail to understand.

Iraqi Foreign Minister Tariq Aziz declared that a sharp drop in the price of oil was something the Kuwaitis, with their vast investment holdings in the West, could easily afford, but which undercut the oil revenues essential to a cash-hungry Baghdad. "It was inconceivable," said Aziz, that Kuwait "could risk engaging in a conspiracy of such magnitude against a large, strong country such as Iraq, if it were not being supported and protected by a great power; and that power was the United States of America."[25] There is, in fact, no public indication that the United States, despite its very close financial ties, tried to persuade Kuwait to cease any of its provocative actions against Iraq.

And neither Washington nor Kuwait seemed terribly concerned about heading off an invasion. In the week prior to the Iraqi attack, intelligence experts were telling the Bush administration with increasing urgency that an invasion of at least a part of Kuwait was likely. These forecasts "appear to have evoked little response from Government agencies."[26] During this period Bush was personally briefed and told the same by CIA Director William Webster, who showed the president satellite photos of the Iraqi troops massed near the Kuwaiti border. Bush, reportedly, showed little interest.[27] On 1 August, the CIA's National Intelligence Officer for Warning (sic) walked into the offices of the National Security Council's Middle East Staff and announced: "This is your final warning." Iraq, he said, would invade Kuwait by day's end, which they did. This, too, did not produce a rush to action.[28] Lastly, a Kuwaiti diplomat stationed in Iraq before the invasion sent many reports back to his own government warning of an Iraqi invasion; these were ignored as well. His last warning had specified the exact date (Kuwaiti time) of 2 August. After the war, when the diplomat held a press conference in Kuwait to discuss the government's ignoring of his warnings, it was broken up by a government minister and several army officers.[29]

In July, while all these warnings were ostensibly being ignored, the Pentagon was busy running its computerized command post exercise (CPX), initiated in late 1989 specifically to explore possible responses to "the Iraqi threat"—which, in the new war plan 1002-90, had replaced "the Soviet threat"—the exercise dealing with an Iraqi invasion of Kuwait or Saudi Arabia or both.[30] At a war-games exercise at the Naval War College in Newport, R.I., participants were also being asked to determine the most effective American response to a hypothetical invasion of Kuwait by Iraq.[31] While at Shaw Air Force Base in South Carolina, another war "game" involved identifying bombing targets in Iraq.[32]

And during May and June, the Pentagon, Congress and defense contractors had been extensively briefed by the Center for Strategic and International Studies of Georgetown University on a study of the future of conventional warfare, which concluded that the most likely war to erupt requiring an American military response was between Iraq and Kuwait or Saudi Arabia.[33]

Another person who seems to have known something in advance was George Shultz, who was Reagan's Secretary of State and then returned to the Bechtel Corp., the multinational construction giant. In the spring of 1990, Schultz convinced the company to withdraw from a petrochemicals project in Iraq. "I said something is going to go very wrong in Iraq and blow up and if Bechtel were there it would get blown up too. So I told them to get out."[34]

Finally, there was this disclosure in the *Washington Post*:

> Since the invasion, highly classified U.S. intelligence assessments have determined that Saddam took U.S. statements of neutrality ... as a green light from the Bush administration for an invasion. One senior Iraqi military official ... has told the agency [CIA] that Saddam seemed to be sincerely surprised by the subsequent bellicose reaction.[35]

On the other hand we have the statement from Iraqi Foreign Minister Aziz, who was present at the Glaspie-Hussein meeting.

> She didn't give a green light, and she didn't mention a red light because the question of our presence in Kuwait was not raised. ... And we didn't take it as a green light ... that if we intervened militarily in Kuwait, the Americans would not react. That was not true. We were expecting an American attack on the morning of the second of August.[36]

But one must be skeptical about so casual an attitude toward an American attack. And these remarks, in effect denying that Iraq was played for a sucker, must be considered in light of the Iraqi government's stubborn refusal for some time to admit the harm done to the country by US bombing, and to downplay the number of their casualties.

The Bush administration's position was that Iraq's Arab neighbors, particularly Egypt, Saudi Arabia, and Jordan, had urged the United States all along not to say or do anything that might provoke Saddam. Moreover, as Ambassador Glaspie emphasized, no one expected Hussein to take "all" of Kuwait, at most the parts he already claimed: the islands and the oilfield.

But, of course, Iraq had claimed "all" of Kuwait for a century.

The Invasion

When Iraq invaded, the time for mixed signals was over. Whatever devious plan, if any, George Bush may have been operating under, he now took full advantage of this window of opportunity. Within hours, if not minutes, of the border crossing, the United States began mobilizing, the White House condemned Iraq's action as a "blatant use of military aggression", demanded "the immediate and unconditional withdrawal of all Iraqi forces", and announced that it was "considering all options"; while George Bush was declaring that the invasion "underscores the need to go slowly in restructuring U.S. defense forces".[37]

Before 24 hours had passed, an American naval task force loaded with fighter planes and bombers was on its way to the Persian Gulf, Bush was seeking to enlist world leaders for collective action against Iraq, all trade with Iraq had been embargoed, all Iraqi and Kuwaiti assets in the United States had been frozen; and the Senate had "decisively defeated efforts to end or freeze production of the B-2 Stealth bomber after proponents seized on Iraq's invasion of Kuwait to bolster their case for the radar-eluding weapon"; the attack, they said, "demonstrates the continuing risk of war and the need for advanced weapons" ... Said Senator Dole: "If we needed Saddam Hussein to give us a wake-up call at least we can thank him for that."[38]

"One day after using Iraq's invasion of Kuwait to help save the high-tech B-2 bomber, senators invoked the crisis again Friday to stave off the mothballing of two World War II-vintage battleships."[39]

Within days, thousands of American troops and an armored brigade were stationed in Saudi Arabia. It was given the grand name of Operation Desert Shield, and a heightened appreciation for America's military needs was the prevailing order of the day ...

> Less than a year after political changes in Eastern Europe and the Soviet Union sent the defense industry reeling under the threat of dramatic cutbacks, executives and analysts say the crisis in the Persian gulf has provided military companies with a tiny glimmer of hope.

"If Iraq does not withdraw and things get messy, it will be good for the industry. You will hear less rhetoric from Washington about the peace dividend," said Michael Lauer, an analyst with Kidder, Peabody & Co. in New York.

"The possible beneficiaries" of the crisis, added the *Washington Post*, "cover the spectrum of companies in the defense industry."[40]

By September, James Webb, former Assistant Secretary of Defense and Secretary of the Navy in the Reagan administration, felt moved to speak out:

The President should be aware that, while most Americans are laboring very hard to support him, a mood of cynicism is just beneath their veneer of respect. Many are claiming that the buildup is little more than a "Pentagon budget drill," designed to preclude cutbacks of an Army searching for a mission as bases in NATO begin to disappear.[41]

Remarkably, yet another cynical former Assistant Secretary of Defense was heard from. Lawrence Korb wrote that the deployment of troops to Saudi Arabia "seems driven more by upcoming budget battles on Capitol Hill than a potential battle against Saddam Hussein."[42]

But can anything be too cynical for a congressman stalking re-election? By the beginning of October we could read:

The political backdrop of the U.S. military deployment in Saudi Arabia played a significant role in limiting defense cuts in Sunday's budget agreement, halting the military spending "free fall" that some analysts had predicted two months ago, budget aides said. Capitol Hill strategists said that Operation Desert Shield forged a major change in the political climate of the negotiations, forcing lawmakers who had been advocating deep cuts on the defensive.

The defense budget compromise ... would leave not only funding for Operation Desert Shield intact but would spare much of the funding that has been spent each year to prepare for a major Soviet onslaught on Western Europe.[43]

Meanwhile, George Bush's approval rating had recovered. The first poll taken in August after the US engagement in the Gulf showed a jump to 74 percent, up from 60 percent in late July. However, it seems that the American public needs the rush of a regular patriotic-fix to maintain enthusiasm for the man occupying the White House, for by mid-October, due to Bush's extreme obfuscation of why the US was in the Persian Gulf, the rating they granted him was down to 56—since Bush's first month in office, it had never been lower; and it stayed close to that level until the citizenry's next patriotic-invasion-fix in January, as we shall see.[44]

Prelude to War

As Iraq went about plundering Kuwait and turning it into Iraqi Province 19, the United States was building up its military presence in Saudi Arabia and the surrounding waters, and—employing a little coercion and history's most spectacular bribes—creating a "coalition" to support US-fostered United Nations resolutions and the coming war effort in a multitude of ways: a figleaf of "multinational" respectability, as Washington had created in Korea, Grenada and Afghanistan, for what was essentially an American mission, an American war. Egypt was forgiven many billions of dollars in debt, while Syria, China, Turkey, the Soviet Union, and other countries received military or economic aid and World

Bank and IMF loans, had sanctions lifted, or were given other perks, not only from the US but, under Washington's pressure, from Germany, Japan and Saudi Arabia. As an added touch, the Bush administration stopped criticizing the human rights record of any coalition member.[45]

But Washington and the media were unhappy with Germany for not enthusiastically jumping on the war bandwagon. The Germans who only yesterday were condemned as jackbooted fascists marching through Poland, were now called "cowards" for marching for peace in large demonstrations.

Washington pushed a dozen resolutions through the Security Council condemning Iraq, imposing severe economic sanctions, and getting "authorization" to wage war. Only Cuba and Yemen voted against any of them. When Yemen's delegate received some applause for his negative vote on the key use-of-force resolution of 29 November, US Secretary of State Baker, who was presiding, said to his delegation: " I hope he enjoyed that applause, because this will turn out to be the most expensive vote he ever cast." The message was relayed to the Yemenis, and within days, the tiny Middle-East nation suffered a sharp reduction in US aid.[46]

UN Secretary General Javier Perez de Cuellar acknowledged that "It was not a United Nations War. General Schwarzkopf [commander of the coalition forces] was not wearing a blue helmet."[47] The American control of the United Nations prompted British political commentator Edward Pearce to write that the UN "functions like an English medieval parliament: consulted, shown ceremonial courtesy, but mindful of divine prerogative, it mutters and gives assent."[48]

The paramount issue in the United States soon became: how long should we wait for the sanctions to work before resorting to direct military force? The administration and its supporters insisted that they were giving Hussein every chance to find a peaceful, face-saving way out of the hole he had dug himself into. But the fact remained that each time President Bush made the Iraqi leader any kind of offer, it was laced with a deep insult, and never offered the slightest recognition that there might be any validity to Iraq's stated grievances.[49] Indeed, Bush had characterized the Iraqi invasion as being "without provocation".[50] The president's rhetoric became increasingly caustic and exaggerated; he was putting it on a personal level, demonizing Saddam, as he had done with Noriega, as Reagan had done with Qaddafi, as if these foreigners did not have pride or reason like Americans have. Here's how the *Los Angeles Times* viewed it:

> Shortly after Iraq's invasion ... Bush carefully compared Iraq's aggression with the German aggression against Poland that launched World War II. But he stopped short of a personal comparison of Iraqi President Saddam Hussein with Adolf Hitler. That caution went out the window last month, when Bush not only compared Hussein to Hitler but also threatened Nuremberg-style war crime trials. Then, last week, Bush went further, briefly maintaining that the Iraqi leader is worse than Hitler because the Germans never held U.S. citizens as "human shields" at military sites.

After this trivializing of the Holocaust, Bush went on to warn that any acceptance of uncontrolled aggression "could be world war tomorrow". Said one of his own officials: "Got to get his rhetoric under control."[51]

Saddam Hussein could not help but soon realize that by seizing all of Kuwait—not to mention sacking and pillaging it—he had bitten off substantially more than he could chew. In early August and again in October, he signaled his willingness to pull Iraqi forces out of the country in return for sole control of the Rumaila oil field, guaranteed access to the Persian Gulf, the lifting of sanctions, and resolution of the oil price/production problem.[52]

He also began to release some of the many foreigners who had had the misfortune of being in Iraq or Kuwait at the wrong time. In mid-December the last of them was freed. Earlier that month, Iraq began laying out a new Iraqi-Kuwait border, which might have meant a renunciation of its claim of Kuwait being a part of Iraq, though its meaning was not clear.[53] And in early January, as we shall see, his strongest peace signal was reported.

The Bush administration chose to not respond in a positive manner to any of these moves. After Saddam's August offer, the State Department "categorically" denied it had even been made; then the White House confirmed it.[54] A later congressional summary of the matter stated:

> The Iraqis apparently believed that having invaded Kuwait, they would get everyone's attention, negotiate improvements to their economic situation, and pull out. ... a diplomatic solution satisfactory to the interests of the United States may well have been possible since the earliest days of the invasion.

The Bush administration, said the congressional paper, wanted to avoid seeming in any way to reward the invasion. But a retired Army officer, who was acting as a middle man in the August discussions, concluded afterward that the peace offer "was already moving against policy".[55]

After a certain point in the American military buildup, could the United States have given peace a chance even if it wanted to? Former Assistant Defense Secretary Lawrence Korb observed in late November that all the components of the defense establishment were pushing to get in on the action, to prove their worth, to prove that there was still a need for them, to assure their continued funding ...

> By mid-January ... the United States will have over 400,000 troops in the Gulf [it turned out to be over 500,000] from all five armed services (yes, even the Coast Guard is there). This is about 100,000 more troops than we had in Europe at any time during the Cold War. The Army will eventually have eight divisions on the ground in Saudi Arabia, twice as many as it had in Europe. ... two-thirds of the entire Marine Corps' combat power [will be there] ... The Navy will deploy six of its 14 aircraft carrier battle groups, two of its four battleships and one of its two amphibious groups ... The Air Force already has fighters from nine of its 24 active tactical wings ... as well as bombers ... Even the combat reserves are scheduled to be sent ... The reserve lobby recognized that their future funding may be jeopardized if their units do not get involved. ... Just as every service wants to be involved in the deployment, will not each want a piece of the real action?

And would the military high-command be able to resist the pressures from each service, Korb wondered. The Navy, which had moved some its carriers into the narrow and dangerous waters of the Gulf just to be closer to the action? The Marines, who might want to demonstrate the continuing viability of amphibious warfare by staging an assault on the coast? And could the Army lay back while air power carried the day?[56] [They couldn't, and it prolonged the war.]

The US military and President Bush would have their massive show of power, their super-hi-tech real war games, and no signals from Iraq or any peacenik would be allowed to spoil it. *Fortune* magazine, in an ingenuous paean to Bush's fortitude, later summed up the period before the war began thusly:

> The President and his men worked overtime to quash freelance peacemakers in the Arab world, France, and the Soviet Union who threatened to give Saddam a face-saving way out of the box Bush was building. Over and over, Bush repeated the mantra: no negotiations, no deals, no face-saving, no rewards, and specifically, no linkage to a Palestinian peace conference [a point raised

by Iraq on several occasions].[57]

On 29 November, the UN Security Council authorized the use of "all necessary means" to compel Iraq to vacate Kuwait if it didn't do so by 15 January. Over Christmas, we have learned, George Bush pored over every one of the 82 pages of Amnesty International's agonizing report of Iraqi arrests, rape, and torture in Kuwait. After the holiday, he told his staff that his conscience was clear: "It's black and white, good vs. evil. The man has to be stopped."[58]

It's not reported whether Bush ever read any of Amnesty's many reports of the period on the equally repulsive violations of human rights and the human spirit perpetrated by Washington's allies in Guatemala, El Salvador, Afghanistan, Angola and Nicaragua. If he did, the literature apparently had little effect, for he continued to support these forces. Amnesty had also been reporting about Iraq's extreme brutality for more than a decade, and only a few months before the August invasion had testified about these abuses before the Senate, but none of this had filled George Bush with righteous indignation.

As the 15 January deadline neared, the world held its breath. Was it possible that in five and a half months no way could have been found to avoid inflicting another ghastly war upon this sad planet? On the 11th, Arab diplomats at the UN said that they had received reports from Algeria, Jordan and Yemen, all on close terms with Iraq, that Saddam planned an initiative soon after the 15th that would express his willingness "in principle" to pull out of Kuwait in return for international guarantees that Iraq would not be attacked, an international conference to address Palestinian grievances, and negotiations on disputes between Iraq and Kuwait. The Iraqi leader, the diplomats said, wanted to wait a day or two after the deadline had passed to demonstrate that he had not been intimidated.

For the United States, with half-a-million troops poised for battle in Saudi Arabia, this was unacceptable. Saddam Hussein will "pass the brink at midnight, January 15", said Secretary of State Baker, and could not expect to save himself by offering to pull out of Kuwait after that time.[59]

The multiple explanations of George Bush

Our jobs, our way of life, our own freedom, and the freedom of friendly countries around the world will suffer if control of the world's great oil reserves fell in the hands of that one man, Saddam Hussein.[60]

Thus spaketh George Herbert Walker Bush to the people of America. As Theodore Draper observed:

These reasons were both mundane and implausible. That "jobs" should have been mentioned first suggested that Bush, as in a domestic political campaign, sought primarily to appeal to the voters' pocketbook. It was, however, a peculiarly crass reason to go to war, if it came to that, halfway around the world.[61]

During the entire lengthy buildup to the war, during the war, after the war, no one was sure they understood why Bush had intervened in the Persian Gulf, and then taken the United States into war. Congressmen, journalists, editors, plain citizens kept asking, almost pleading at times, for the president to clearly and unambiguously explain his motivations, and without contradicting what he had said the previous week. (Economists and think-tank intellectuals found it professionally awkward to admit their uncertainty, and thus wound up writing lots of authoritative-sounding mumbo-jumbo.)

The prevailing bewilderment prompted the *Wall Street Journal* to assemble a group of "voters" to discuss the issues. "They are confused about what's happening and are crying out for more information," reported the newspaper about the participants. "And they are unsettled by the perception that Mr. Bush seems to be switching his reasoning day to day." Said one participant: "So far it's been like David Letterman's Top 10 Reasons for Being There. There's a different story every week or so."[62]

Taking place in the Persian Gulf, as it all did, of course lent itself to the belief that the liquid gold had a lot, if not everything, to do with the conflict. This, however, is a thesis which cannot be supported by the immediate circumstances. Supply was not a problem—the Energy Department acknowledged that there was not an oil shortage, and Saudi Arabia and other countries increased their production to more than make up for the oil lost from Iraq and Kuwait, which, in any event, together accounted for only about five percent of American consumption. There was a whole world ready to supply more oil, from Mexico to Russia, as well as large untapped American sources. This indicates the difficulties faced by any single producer—Hussein or anyone else—who might try to control or dominate the market; which in turn raises the question: what would such a country do with all the oil, drink it? By December it was reported that "OPEC is pumping oil at the highest levels since early summer, and unless a war in the Middle East disrupts supplies, there's a prospect again of an oil glut and sharply lower prices."[63]

As to the price of oil: did oilmen George Bush and James Baker and the depressed American oil states want it to go up or down? A case could be made for either hypothesis. (In January 1990 the US had secretly urged Saddam to try to raise the OPEC oil price to $25 a barrel.)[64] And how easily could Washington control it either way in a chaotic situation? As it is, oil prices fluctuate on a regular basis, often sharply—between 1984 and 1986, for example, the price of a barrel of oil fell from around $30 to less than $10, despite the ongoing Iraq-Iran war which cut into the production of both countries.

However, this analysis of the immediate circumstances does not take into consideration the formidable and continual influence of the "mystique of oil" upon the thinking of American policy makers. If Bush was looking for a "crisis" to impress upon the congressional mind the enduring danger of the world we live in, then getting involved in a conflict between two major oil producing countries would certainly generate the desired effect much more readily than if he had seized upon Bolivia attacking Paraguay, or Ghana occupying Ivory Coast.

The president's remark about the American way of life and everyone's freedom reflects the life-and-death seriousness that he and other policy makers publicly ascribe to oil. (What these men really believe and feel in each instance is something we are not privy to.) Earlier in the year, CIA Director William Webster had told Congress that oil "will continue to have a major impact on U.S. interests" because "Western dependence on Persian Gulf oil will rise dramatically" in the next decade; while General Schwarzkopf, who had lifelong ties to the Middle East, testified:

> Mideast oil is the West's lifeblood. It fuels us today, and being 77 percent of the Free World's proven oil reserves, is going to fuel us when the rest of the world has run dry. ... It is estimated that within 20 to 40 years the U.S. will have virtually depleted its economically available oil reserves, while the Persian Gulf region will still have at least 100 years of proven oil reserves.[65]

It was actually 69 percent at the time, and since the Soviet Union has joined the "Free World", it's even less.[66] It should also be noted that the good general's prediction for the

US is rather speculative, and that the term "economically available" is a reference to the fact that US domestic oil reserves are more costly to exploit than those in the Gulf. But this only makes it a profit problem, not an oil-supply problem. Moreover, the vast potential residing in alternative energy sources must be included in the equation.

At this time, the United States—seemingly in a panic about danger to the Gulf oil supply—was receiving about 11 percent of its oil from the region, while Japan, which got 62 percent of its oil, and Europe which got 27 percent from there, were hardly stirred up at all, except for Margaret Thatcher who foamed at the mouth when it came to Saddam and former colony Iraq.[67] Germany's figure was about 35 percent, yet both Bonn and Tokyo had to have their arms twisted by Washington to support the war effort. The two countries may, in fact, have been leery about helping the United States acquire greater influence and control over the region's oil.

Official Washington's embrace of the oil mystique has given rise to a long-standing policy, expressed as follows by political analyst Noam Chomsky:

> It's been a leading, driving doctrine of U.S. foreign policy since the 1940s that the vast and unparalleled energy resources of the Gulf region will be effectively dominated by the United States and its clients, and, crucially, that no independent, indigenous force will be permitted to have a substantial influence on the administration of oil production and price.[68]

This has not always meant the use of force. In 1973, when OPEC, led by Saudi Arabia, used substantial price increases and an oil boycott in an attempt to force Washington to influence Israel into withdrawing from its recently occupied territories, the United States did not launch, or even threaten, an invasion. The matter was resolved through extensive diplomacy without a shot being fired. What saved the OPEC states from a violent fate may have been the combination of the Vietnam war still hanging heavy in the air in Washington, and the Nixon administration on the verge of being swallowed up by Watergate.

In addition to issuing several dire warnings early on about the invasion's severe economic consequences for the United States, which never came to pass, Bush warned of an even worse fate if Iraq took over Saudi Arabia. The danger-to-Saudi Arabia explanation was a non-starter. Iraq never had any designs on Saudi Arabia, as a simple look at a map makes clear. The Iraqis have a long border with that country; they didn't have to go through Kuwait to invade the Saudis; and even if they did, they could have moved into Saudi Arabia virtually unopposed during the three weeks following their takeover of Kuwait, as General Colin Powell later conceded.[69] Bush administration officials in fact admitted that neither the CIA nor the Defense Intelligence Agency thought it probable that Iraq would invade Saudi Arabia.[70] The Saudis didn't think so either, until Defense Secretary Cheney flew to Riyadh on 5 August and personally told King Fahd that his country stood in great potential danger and desperately needed a very large infusion of American military forces to defend it.[71]

Bush backed away from the oil rationale when critics charged that he was only trying to protect the interests of the oil industry. In October, he was interrupted while making a speech by some people calling out: "Mr. President, bring our troops home from Saudi Arabia! No blood for oil!" To which George Bush replied—as the hecklers were hustled out —"You know, some people never get the word. The fight isn't about oil. The fight is about naked aggression that [we] will not stand." A month later, if not sooner, the president again began to play the oil card, tying America's economic security to that of Saudi Arabia. Shortly afterward, he returned to "the devastating damage being done every day" to the US and international economies by the disruption of oil markets.[72]

As to Iraq's naked aggression—a remark requiring selective-memory skills of a high order coming from a government that held all modern records for international aggression, naked or otherwise, and from a man who, less than a year before, had nakedly invaded Panama—both Syria and Israel had invaded Lebanon and still occupied large portions of that country, Israel bombarding Beirut mercilessly in the process, without a threat of war emanating from Washington. Saddam Hussein, perhaps wondering when they had changed the rules, said to the United States: "You are talking about an aggressive Iraq ... if Iraq was aggressive during the Iran war, why then did you speak with [us] then?"[73]

During Iraq's epic struggle against the Ayatollah Khomeini, the United States of course had more than spoken to Baghdad. Washington—choosing Iraq as the lesser evil against Shiite extremism—was responsible for huge amounts of weaponry, military training, sophisticated technology, satellite-photo intelligence, and billions of dollars reaching a needy Hussein, who was also lavishly supported by Kuwait and Saudi Arabia, they being concerned that Iran's anti-monarchist sentiments might spread to their own realms. Indeed, there is evidence that Washington encouraged Iraq to attack Iran and ignite the war in the first place.[74] And during this period of American support of Hussein, he was certainly the same odious, repressive, beastly thug as when he later came under American moralistic rhetorical fire. Similarly, absent Washington's prodding, the UN did not condemn Iraq's invasion, nor did it impose any sanctions or lay down any demands.

Even as it officially banned arms sales to either combatant, the US secretly provided weapons to both. The other *bête noire* of the region, the Ayatollah, received American arms and military intelligence on Iraq during the war, so as to enhance the ability of the two countries to inflict maximum devastation upon each other and stunt their growth as strong Middle-East nations.

In contrast to Iraq-the-enemy now were the two "allies" most involved, Saudi Arabia and Kuwait. Although Washington did not make a big thing about the "virtue" of either country, official policy was always that the United States had a principled commitment to defending the former and liberating the latter. And they were not a pretty pair. Saudi Arabia regularly featured extreme religious intolerance, extrajudicial arrest, torture, and flogging.[75] It also practiced gender apartheid and systematic repression of women, virtual slavery for its foreign workers, stoning of adulterers, and amputation of the hands of thieves. US chaplains stationed in the country were asked to remove crosses and Stars of David from their uniforms and call themselves "morale officers".[76]

Kuwait, oddly enough, was virulently anti-American in its foreign policy.[77] Though more socially enlightened than Saudi Arabia (but less than Iraq), it was nonetheless run by one family as an elitist oligarchy, which closed down the parliament in 1986, had no political parties, and forbade criticism of the ruling emir; no more than 20 percent of the population possessed any political rights at all. After the country had been returned to its rightful dictators, it behaved very brutally toward its large foreign-worker population, holding them without charge or trial for several months; death squads executed scores of people. "Torture of political detainees was routine and widespread," said Amnesty International, and at least 80 "disappeared" in custody. The targets of the campaign, which took place in the presence of thousands of US troops, were primarily those who were accused of collaboration with the Iraqis, although this was something most of them had no choice in, and those who were involved in a nascent pro-democracy movement. Additionally, some 400 Iraqis were forced to return to Iraq despite fears that they would be harmed or executed there.[78]

The elite of the region did not display much gratitude for all that George Bush said America was doing for them. Said one Gulf official: "You think I want to send my teenaged son to die for Kuwait?" He chuckled and added, "We have our white slaves from America to do that." A Saudi teacher saw it this way: "The American soldiers are a new kind of foreign worker here. We have Pakistanis driving taxis and now we have Americans defending us." Explaining the absence of expressed gratitude on the part of Gulf leaders, a Yemeni diplomat said: "A lot of the Gulf rulers simply do not feel that they have to thank the people they've hired to do their fighting for them."[79] Apart from anything else, people in the Arab world were very sensitive about the killing of Muslims and Arabs by foreigners, as well as foreign military presence on Arab soil, a reminder of a century of Western, white colonialism.

Bush also warned that Iraq posed a nuclear threat. True enough. But so did the United States, France, Israel, and every other country that already had nuclear weapons. Iraq, on the other hand, according to American, British and Israeli experts, was five to ten years away from being able to build and use nuclear weapons.[80] It's unlikely that the president himself believed there was any such danger. His warning came only after a poll showed that a plurality of Americans felt that preventing Iraq from acquiring nuclear weapons was the most persuasive argument for going to war.[81]

One factor not mentioned by Bush as a reason for the intervention, but which, in fact, probably played an important role, was the Pentagon's desire to make or strengthen agreements with Gulf-region countries for an ongoing US military presence; and considerable progress along these lines appears to have been made.[82] General Schwarzkopf had earlier told Congress that "U.S. presence" in the Gulf is one of the three pillars of overall military strategy, along with security assistance and combined exercises, all of which lead to all-important "access", which one can take as a euphemism for influence and control.[83] After the war, the existence of a network of military-communication-systems "superbases" in Saudi Arabia was revealed. Ten years in the building by the United States, in maximum secrecy, its cost of almost $200 billion paid for by the Saudis, its use during the Gulf War indispensable, it may explain why Bush moved so quickly to defend Saudi Arabia, albeit against a non-existent threat.[84]

"Stop me before I kill again!"

Josef Stalin studied for the priesthood ... Adolf Hitler was a vegetarian and anti-smoking ... Herman Goering, while his Luftwaffe rained death upon Europe, kept a sign in his office that read: "He who tortures animals wounds the feelings of the German people." ... this fact Elie Wiesel called the greatest discovery of the war: that Adolf Eichmann was cultured, read deeply, played the violin ... Charles Manson was a staunch anti-vivisectionist ...

About Panama, as we have seen, after he ordered the bombing, George Bush said that his "heart goes out to the families who have died in Panama." And when he was asked, "Was it really worth it to send people to their death for this? To get Noriega?", he replied, "... every human life is precious, and yet I have to answer, yes, it has been worth it."

About Iraq, Bush said: "People say to me: 'How many lives? How many lives can you expend?' Each one is precious."[85]

Just before ordering the start of the war against Iraq in January, Bush prayed, as tears ran down his cheeks. "I think," he later said, "that, like a lot of others who had positions of responsibility in sending someone else's kids to war, we realize that in prayer what mattered is how it might have seemed to God."[86]

God, one surmises, might have asked George Bush about the kids of Iraq. And the adults. And, in a testy, rather un-godlike manner, might have cracked: "So stop wasting all the precious lives already!"

Tanks pulling plows moved alongside trenches, firing into the Iraqi soldiers inside the trenches as the plows covered them with great mounds of sand. Thousands were buried, dead, wounded, or alive.[87]

US forces fired on Iraqi soldiers after the Iraqis had raised white flags of surrender. The navy commander who gave the order to fire was not punished.[88]

The bombing destroyed two operational nuclear reactors in Iraq. It was the first time ever that live reactors had been bombed, and may well have set a dangerous precedent. Hardly more than a month had passed since the United Nations, under whose mandate the United States was supposedly operating, had passed a resolution reaffirming its "prohibition of military attacks on nuclear facilities" in the Middle East.[89] Sundry chemical, including chemical-warfare, facilities and alleged biological-warfare plants, were also targets of American bombs. General Schwarzkopf then announced that they had been very careful in selecting the means of destruction of these as well as the nuclear facilities, and only "after a lot of advice from a lot of very, very prominent scientists," and were "99.9 percent" certain that there was "no contamination".[90] However, European scientists and environmentalists detected traces of chemical-weapons agents that the bombings had released; as well as chemical fallout and toxic vapors, also released by the air attacks, that were killing scores of civilians.[91]

The American government and media had a lot of fun with an obvious piece of Iraqi propaganda—the claim that a bombed biological warfare facility had actually been a baby food factory. But it turned out that the government of New Zealand and various business people from there had had intimate contact with the factory and categorically confirmed that it had indeed been a baby food factory.[92]

The United States also made wide use of advanced depleted uranium (DU) shells, rockets and missiles, leaving tons of radioactive and toxic rubble in Kuwait and Iraq. The United Kingdom Atomic Energy Authority, in an April 1991 secret report, warned that "if DU gets in the food chain or water this will create potential health problems." The uranium-238 used to make the weapons can cause cancer and genetic defects if inhaled. Uranium is also chemically toxic, like lead. Inhalation causes heavy metal poisoning or kidney or lung damage. Iraqi soldiers, pinned down in their bunkers during assaults, were almost certainly poisoned by radioactive dust clouds.[93]

The civilian population suffered in the extreme from the relentless bombing. Middle East Watch, the human-rights organization, has documented numerous instances of the bombing of apartment houses, crowded markets, bridges filled with pedestrians and civilian vehicles, and a busy central bus station, usually in broad daylight, without a government building or military target of any kind in sight, not even an anti-aircraft gun.[94]

On 12 February, the Pentagon announced that "Virtually everything militarily ... is either destroyed or combat ineffective."[95] Yet the next day there was a deliberate bombardment of a civilian air raid shelter that took the lives of as many as 1,500 civilians, a great number of them women and children; this was followed by significant bombardment of various parts of Iraq on a daily basis for the remaining two weeks of the war, including what was reported for the 18th in The Guardian of London as "one of [the coalition's] most ferocious attacks on the centre of Baghdad."[96] What was the purpose of the bombing campaign after the 12th?

The United States said it thought that the shelter was for VIPs, which it had been at one time, and claimed that it was also being used as a military communications center, but neighborhood residents insisted that the constant aerial surveillance overhead had to observe the daily flow of women and children into the shelter.[97] Western reporters said they could find no signs of military use.[98]

An American journalist in Jordan who viewed unedited videotape footage of the disaster, which the American public never saw, wrote:

> They showed scenes of incredible carnage. Nearly all the bodies were charred into blackness; in some cases the heat had been so great that entire limbs were burned off. ... Rescue workers collapsed in grief, dropping corpses; some rescuers vomited from the stench of the still-smoldering bodies.[99]

Said White House spokesman Marlin Fitzwater after the bombing of the shelter: It was "a military target ... We don't know why civilians were at this location, but we do know that Saddam Hussein does not share our value in the sanctity of life."[100] Said George Bush, when criticized for the bombing campaign: "I am concerned about the suffering of innocents."[101]

The crippling of the electrical system multiplied geometrically the daily living horror of the people of Iraq. As a modern country, Iraq was reliant on electrical power for essential services such as water purification and distribution, sewage treatment, the operation of hospitals and medical laboratories, and agricultural production. Bomb damage, exacerbated by shortages attributable to the UN/US embargo, dropped electricity to three or four percent of its pre-war level; the water supply fell to five percent, oil production was negligible, the food distribution system was devastated, the sewage system collapsed, flooding houses with raw sewage, and gastroenteritis and extreme malnutrition were prevalent.[102]

Two months after the war ended, a public health team from Harvard University visited health facilities in several Iraqi cities. Based on their research, the group projected, conservatively, that "at least 170,000 children under five years of age will die in the coming year from the delayed effects" of the destruction of electrical power, fuel and transportation; "a large increase in deaths among the rest of the population is also likely. The immediate cause of death in most cases will be water-borne infectious disease in combination with severe malnutrition."[103] One member of both the Harvard group and a later research group which visited Iraq testified before Congress that "Children play in the raw sewage which is backed up in the streets ... Two world renowned child psychologists stated that the children in Iraq were 'the most traumatized children of war ever described'."[104]

Despite repeated statements by American authorities about taking the greatest of care to hit only military targets, using "smart bombs" and laser-guided bombs, and "surgical strikes", we now know that this was little more than an exercise in propaganda, just as referring to this suffering as "collateral damage" was. After the war, the Pentagon admitted that non-military facilities had been extensively targeted for political reasons.[105] Comprehensive post-World War II government studies had concluded that "the dread of disease and the hardships imposed by the lack of sanitary facilities were bound to have a demoralizing effect upon the civilian population", and that there was a "reliable and striking" correlation between the disruption of public utilities and the willingness of the German population to accept unconditional surrender.[106]

In the Iraqi case there was a further motivation: to encourage desperate citizens to rise up and overthrow Saddam Hussein. Said a US Air Force planner:

Big picture, we wanted to let people know, "Get rid of this guy and we'll be more than happy to assist in rebuilding. We're not going to tolerate Saddam Hussein or his regime. Fix that, and we'll fix your electricity."[107]

Those who tried to escape the bombing horror in Iraq by fleeing to Jordan were subjected to air attacks on the highway between Baghdad and the Jordanian border—buses, taxis, and private cars were repeatedly assaulted, literally without mercy, by rockets, cluster bombs and machine guns; usually in broad daylight, the targets clearly civilian, with luggage piled on top, with no military vehicles or structures anywhere to be seen, surrounded by open desert, the attacking planes flying extremely close to the ground ... busloads of passengers incinerated, and when people left the vehicles and fled for their lives, planes often swooped down upon them firing away. ... "You're killing us!" cried a Jordanian taxi driver to an American reporter. "You're shooting us everywhere we move! Whenever they see a car or truck, the planes dive out of the sky and chase us. They don't care who we are or what we are. They just shoot." His cry was repeated by hundreds of others. ... The US military, it appears, felt that any vehicle, including those filled with families, might be a cover for carrying military fuel or other war materiel, some perhaps related to Scud missiles; and even carrying civilian fuel was a violation of the embargo.[108]

At the very end, when the hungry, wounded, sick, exhausted, disoriented, demoralized, ragged, sometimes barefoot Iraqi army, which had scarcely shown any desire to fight, left Kuwait and headed toward Basra in southern Iraq, Saddam tried to salvage a pathetic scrap of dignity by announcing that his army was withdrawing because of "special circumstances". But even this was too much for George Bush to grant. "Saddam's most recent speech is an outrage," declared the president, forcefully. "He is not withdrawing. His defeated forces are retreating. He is trying to claim victory in the midst of a rout."

This could not be permitted. Thus it was that American air power in all its majesty swept down upon the road to Basra, bombing, rocketing, strafing everything that moved in the long column of Iraqi military and civilian vehicles, troops and refugees. The nice, god-fearing, wholesome American GIs, soon to be welcomed as heroes at home, had a ball ... "we toasted him" ... "we hit the jackpot" ... "a turkey shoot" ... "This morning was bumper-to-bumper. It was the road to Daytona Beach at spring break ... and spring break's over."

Again and again, as loudspeakers on the carrier Ranger blared Rossini's "William Tell Overture", the rousing theme song of the Lone Ranger, one strike force after another took off with their load of missiles and anti-tank and anti-personnel Rockeye cluster bombs, which explode into a deadly rain of armor-piercing bomblets; land-based B-52s joined in with 1000-pound bombs. ... "It's not going to take too many more days until there's nothing left of them." ... "shooting fish in a barrel" ... "basically just sitting ducks" ... "There's just nothing like it. It's the biggest Fourth of July show you've ever seen, and to see those tanks just 'boom,' and more stuff just keeps spewing out of them ... they just become white hot. It's wonderful."

The British daily, The Independent, although it supported the war, denounced the glee with which the Americans carried out the barrage, saying it "turned the stomachs" and was "sickening to witness a routed army being shot in the back".[109]

A BBC Radio reporter summed up the attack by asking: "What threat could these pathetic remnants of Saddam Hussein's beaten army have posed? Wasn't it obvious that the people of the convoy would have given themselves up willingly without the application of such ferocious weaponry?"[110]

And all this against a foe that had for five days been calling for a cease-fire.

But heaven forbid that the Americans should offend any of the people of the Gulf. Thus it was that GIs were taught things like never to use their left hand when offering food or drink, for that hand is traditionally reserved for sanitary functions; and the proper way to beckon an Arab with one's hand and fingers, so as not to confuse it with beckoning a dog.[111]

We also have the story of the American pilot who, during an earlier bombing operation, stuffed into his identification packet a $20 bill and a note written in Arabic, Farsi, Turkish and English. It said: "I am an American and do not speak your language. I bear no malice toward your people." Then he was off, roaring through the skies toward Iraq with his payload of bombs.[112]

Did the GIs bear any malice toward their female soldiers-in-arms? One post-war study found that more than half the women who served in the Gulf War felt that they had been sexually harassed verbally, while eight percent (almost 3,000) had been the objects of attempted or completed sexual assaults.[113]

And immediately after George Bush ordered the bombing to begin, his rating with the American people jumped for joy: an 82 percent approval rating, the highest ever in his two years in office, higher even than after his invasion of Panama.[114] One journalist later noted:

> One minute of nightly truth on this "popular" war would have changed American public opinion. ... if for just 60 seconds the 6 o'clock Monday news had shown 5,000 Iraqi soldiers with hideous phosphorous burns that alter human anatomy followed by 60 seconds Tuesday night of the slaughter at the Baghdad bomb shelter ... What if on Wednesday Americans had seen 10,000 Iraqi soldiers incinerated by American high-tech weapons?[115]

Ever since the Iraqi invasion in August, and despite the many confusing soundbites and heavy rhetoric emanating from the White House, one thing seemed clear enough: if Iraq agreed to withdraw from Kuwait, military attacks against it would not take place, or would cease, whatever other punishment or sanctions might continue. Thus, it seemed like a ray of hope, however late, when the Soviet Union succeeded on 21-22 February 1991 in getting Iraq to agree to withdraw completely the day after a cease-fire of all military operations went into effect. The agreement came with specified timetables and monitoring.[116]

George Bush refused to offer a cease-fire, per se. He could not even bring himself to mention the word in his replies. All he would say was that the retreating Iraqi forces would not be attacked (which turned out to be untrue), and that the coalition "will exercise restraint." Saddam could have chosen to take this as the cease-fire, but he was as proud and stubborn as George.

The point Bush emphasized the most during these two crucial days, as well as earlier, was that Iraq must comply with all 12 UN resolutions. In evaluating Bush's legalistic demands, it should be kept in mind that the policy and practice of the American war had repeatedly violated the letter and the spirit of the United Nations Charter, the Hague Conventions, the Geneva Conventions, the Nuremberg Tribunal, the protocols of the International Committee of the Red Cross, and the US Constitution, amongst other cherished documents.[117]

In the end, Bush gave Saddam 24 hours to begin withdrawing from Kuwait, period. When the time came and went, the United States launched the long-expected ground war, while the aerial attacks—including the carnage on the road to Basra—continued until the end of the month.

Said Vitaly Ignatenko, a spokesman for Soviet President Mikhail Gorbachev: "It seems that President Gorbachev cares more about saving the lives of American soldiers than George Bush does."[118]

In a postwar survey, a United Nations inspection team declared that the allied bombardment had had a "near apocalyptic impact" on Iraq and had transformed the country into a "pre-industrial age nation" which "had been until January a rather highly urbanized and mechanized society."[119]

It will never be known how many hundreds of thousands of Iraqis died from the direct and indirect effects of the war; the count is added to every day. With the United States refusing to end the embargo against Iraq, everything has continued: malnutrition, starvation, lack of medicines and vaccines, contaminated drinking water, human excrement piling up, typhoid, a near-epidemic of measles, several other diseases ... Iraq's food supply had been 70 percent dependent on imports, now billions of dollars were frozen in overseas accounts, and with prohibitive restrictions on selling its oil ... an inability to rebuild because vital parts could not be imported, industry closing its doors, mass unemployment, transportation and communications broken down[120] ... By September 1994, with the US government still refusing to release its death grip on the embargo, still hoping that the suffering would reach critical mass and the Iraqi people would overthrow Saddam, the Iraqi government announced that since the sanctions had begun in August 1990 about 400,000 children had died of malnutrition and disease.[121]

After the war, when the Iraqi government was repressing a Kurdish revolt—which the US had encouraged, then failed to support—Bush said: "I feel frustrated any time innocent civilians are being slaughtered."[122]

This was the second time the United States had led the Kurdish lambs to slaughter with a broken commitment. (See Iraq 1972-75 chapter.)

The United States had also encouraged the Shiite muslims in Iraq to rebel, then did not back them, presumably because Washington only wanted to drive Saddam up the wall some more, make him irrational enough to incite a coup against him; but Washington was not looking to foster a pro-Iranian regime and inspire muslim fundamentalists elsewhere in the Middle East.

American mental hospitals and prisons are home to many people who claim to have heard a voice telling them to kill certain people, people they'd never met before, people who'd never done them any harm, or threatened any harm.

American soldiers went to the Persian Gulf to kill the same kind of people after hearing a voice command them: the voice of George Herbert Walker Bush.

53. Afghanistan 1979-1992
America's *Jihad*

His followers first gained attention by throwing acid in the faces of women who refused to wear the veil. CIA and State Department officials I have spoken with call him "scary," "vicious," "a fascist," "definite dictatorship material".[1]

This did not prevent the United States government from showering the man with large amounts of aid to fight against the Soviet-supported government of Afghanistan. His name was Gulbuddin Hekmatyar. He was the head of the Islamic Party and he hated the United

States almost as much as he hated the Russians. His followers screamed "Death to America" along with "Death to the Soviet Union", only the Russians were not showering him with large amounts of aid.[2]

The United States began supporting Afghan Islamic fundamentalists in 1979 despite the fact that in February of that year some of them had kidnapped the American ambassador in the capital city of Kabul, leading to his death in the rescue attempt. The support continued even after their brother Islamic fundamentalists in next-door Iran seized the US Embassy in Teheran in November and held 55 Americans hostage for over a year. Hekmatyar and his colleagues were, after all, in battle against the Soviet Evil Empire; he was thus an important member of those forces Ronald Reagan called "freedom fighters".

On 27 April 1978, a coup staged by the People's Democratic Party (PDP) overthrew the government of Mohammad Daoud. Daoud, five years earlier, had overthrown the monarchy and established a republic, although he himself was a member of the royal family. He had been supported by the left in this endeavor, but it turned out that Daoud's royal blood was thicker than his progressive water. When the Daoud regime had a PDP leader killed, arrested the rest of the leadership, and purged hundreds of suspected party sympathizers from government posts, the PDP, aided by its supporters in the army, revolted and took power.

Afghanistan was a backward nation: a life expectancy of about 40, infant mortality of at least 25 percent, absolutely primitive sanitation, widespread malnutrition, illiteracy of more than 90 percent, very few highways, not one mile of railway, most people living in nomadic tribes or as impoverished farmers in mud villages, identifying more with ethnic groups than with a larger political concept, a life scarcely different from many centuries earlier.

Reform with a socialist bent was the new government's ambition: land reform (while still retaining private property), controls on prices and profits, and strengthening of the public sector, as well as separation of church and state, eradication of illiteracy, legalization of trade unions, and the emancipation of women in a land almost entirely Muslim.

Afghanistan's thousand-mile border with the Soviet Union had always produced a special relationship. Even while it was a monarchy, the country had been under the strong influence of its powerful northern neighbor which had long been its largest trading partner, aid donor, and military supplier. But the country had never been gobbled up by the Soviets, a fact that perhaps lends credence to the oft-repeated Soviet claim that their hegemony over Eastern Europe was only to create a buffer between themselves and the frequently-invading West.

Nevertheless, for decades Washington and the Shah of Iran tried to pressure and bribe Afghanistan in order to roll back Russian influence in the country. During the Daoud regime, Iran, encouraged by the United States, sought to replace the Soviet Union as Kabul's biggest donor with a $2 billion economic aid agreement, and urged Afghanistan to join the Regional Cooperation for Development, which consisted of Iran, Pakistan and Turkey. (This organization was attacked by the Soviet Union and its friends in Afghanistan as being a "branch of CENTO" the 1950s regional security pact that was part of the US policy of "containment" of the Soviet Union.) At the same time, Iran's infamous secret police, SAVAK, was busy fingering suspected Communist sympathizers in the Afghan government and military. In September 1975, prodded by Iran which was conditioning its aid on such policies, Daoud dismissed 40 Soviet-trained military officers and moved to reduce future Afghan dependence on officer training in the USSR by initiating training arrangements with India and Egypt. Most important, in Soviet eyes, Daoud gradually broke off his alliance with the PDP, announcing that he would start his own party and ban all other political activity under a projected new constitution.[3]

Selig Harrison, the *Washington Post's* South Asia specialist, wrote an article in 1979 entitled "The Shah, Not the Kremlin, Touched off Afghan Coup", concluding:

> The Communist takeover in Kabul [April 1978] came about when it did, and in the way that it did, because the Shah disturbed the tenuous equilibrium that had existed in Afghanistan between the Soviet Union and the West for nearly three decades. In Iranian and American eyes, Teheran's offensive was merely designed to make Kabul more truly nonaligned, but it went far beyond that. Given the unusually long frontier with Afghanistan, the Soviet Union would clearly go to great lengths to prevent Kabul from moving once again toward a pro-western stance.[4]

When the Shah was overthrown in January 1979, the United States lost its chief ally and outpost in the Soviet-border region, as well as its military installations and electronic monitoring stations aimed at the Soviet Union. Washington's cold warriors could only eye Afghanistan even more covetously than before.

After the April revolution, the new government under President Noor Mohammed Taraki declared a commitment to Islam within a secular state, and to non-alignment in foreign affairs. It maintained that the coup had not been foreign inspired, that it was not a "Communist takeover", and that they were not "Communists" but rather nationalists and revolutionaries. (No official or traditional Communist Party had ever existed in Afghanistan.)[5] But because of its radical reform program, its class-struggle and anti-imperialist-type rhetoric, its support of all the usual suspects (Cuba, North Korea, etc.), its signing of a friendship treaty and other cooperative agreements with the Soviet Union, and an increased presence in the country of Soviet civilian and military advisers (though probably less than the US had in Iran at the time), it was labeled "communist" by the world's media and by its domestic opponents.

Whether or not the new government in Afghanistan should properly have been called communist, whether or not it made any difference what it was called, the lines were now drawn for political, military, and propaganda battle: a *jihad* (holy war) between fundamentalist Muslims and "godless atheistic communists"; Afghan nationalism vs. a "Soviet-run" government; large landowners, tribal chiefs, businessmen, the extended royal family, and others vs. the government's economic reforms. Said the new prime minister about this elite, who were needed to keep the country running, "every effort will be made to attract them. But we want to re-educate them in such a manner that they should think about the people, and not, as previously, just about themselves—to have a good house and a nice car while other people die of hunger."[6]

The Afghan government was trying to drag the country into the 20th century. In May 1979, British political scientist Fred Halliday observed that "probably more has changed in the countryside over the last year than in the two centuries since the state was established." Peasant debts to landlords had been canceled, the system of usury (by which peasants, who were forced to borrow money against future crops, were left in perpetual debt to moneylenders) was abolished, and hundreds of schools and medical clinics were being built in the countryside. Halliday also reported that a substantial land-redistribution program was underway, with many of the 200,000 rural families scheduled to receive land under this reform already having done so. But this last claim must be approached with caution. Revolutionary land reform is always an extremely complex and precarious undertaking even under the best of conditions, and ultra-backward, tradition-bound Afghanistan in the midst of nascent civil war hardly offered the best of conditions for social experiments.

The reforms also encroached into the sensitive area of Islamic subjugation of women by outlawing child marriage and the giving of a woman in marriage in exchange for money or commodities, and teaching women to read, at a time when certain Islamic sectors were openly calling for the reinforcement of *purdah*, the seclusion of women from public observation.

Halliday noted that the People's Democratic Party saw the Soviet Union as the only realistic source of support for the long-overdue modernization.[7] The illiterate Afghan peasant's ethnic cousins across the border in the Soviet Union were, after all, often university graduates and professionals.

The argument of the Moujahedeen ("holy warriors") rebels that the "communist" government would curtail their religious freedom was never borne out in practice. A year and a half after the change in government, the conservative British magazine *The Economist* reported that "no restrictions had been imposed on religious practice".[8] Earlier, the *New York Times* stated that the religious issue "is being used by some Afghans who actually object more to President Taraki's plans for land reforms and other changes in this feudal society."[9] Many of the Muslim clergy were in fact rich landowners.[10] The rebels, concluded a BBC reporter who spent four months with them, are "fighting to retain their feudal system and stop the Kabul government's left-wing reforms which [are] considered anti-Islamic".[11]

The two other nations which shared a long border with Afghanistan, and were closely allied to the United States, expressed their fears of the new government. To the west, Iran, still under the Shah, worried about "threats to oil-passage routes in the Persian Gulf". Pakistan, to the south, spoke of "threats from a hostile and expansionist Afghanistan".[12] A former US ambassador to Afghanistan saw it as part of a "gradually closing pincer movement aimed at Iran and the oil regions of the Middle East."[13] None of these alleged fears turned out to have any substance or evidence to back them up, but to the anti-communist mind this might prove only that the Russians and their Afghan puppets had been stopped in time.

Two months after the April 1978 coup, an alliance formed by a number of conservative Islamic factions was waging guerrilla war against the government.[14] By spring 1979, fighting was taking place on many fronts, and the State Department was cautioning the Soviet Union that its advisers in Afghanistan should not interfere militarily in the civil strife. One such warning in the summer by State Department spokesman Hodding Carter was another of those Washington monuments to *chutzpah*: "We expect the principle of nonintervention to be respected by all parties in the area, including the Soviet Union."[15] This while the Soviets were charging the CIA with arming Afghan exiles in Pakistan; and the Afghanistan government was accusing Pakistan and Iran of also aiding the guerrillas and even of crossing the border to take part in the fighting. Pakistan had recently taken its own sharp turn toward strict Muslim orthodoxy, which the Afghan government deplored as "fanatic";[16] while in January, Iran had established a Muslim state after overthrowing the Shah. (As opposed to the Afghan fundamentalist freedom fighters, the Iranian Islamic fundamentalists were regularly described in the West as terrorists, ultra-conservatives, and anti-democratic.)

A "favorite tactic" of the Afghan freedom fighters was "to torture victims [often Russians] by first cutting off their noses, ears, and genitals, then removing one slice of skin after another", producing "a slow, very painful death".[17] The Moujahedeen also killed a Canadian tourist and six West Germans, including two children, and a U.S. military attaché was dragged from his car and beaten; all due to the rebels' apparent inability to distinguish Russians from other Europeans.[18]

In March 1979, Taraki went to Moscow to press the Soviets to send ground troops to help the Afghan army put down the Moujahedeen. He was promised military assistance, but ground troops could not be committed. Soviet Prime Minister Kosygin told the Afghan leader:

> The entry of our troops into Afghanistan would outrage the international community, triggering a string of extremely negative consequences in many different areas. Our common enemies are just waiting for the moment when Soviet troops appear in Afghanistan. This will give them the excuse they need to send armed bands into the country.[19]

In September, the question became completely academic for Noor Mohammed Taraki, for he was ousted (and his death soon announced) in an intra-party struggle and replaced by his own deputy prime minister, Hafizullah Amin. Although Taraki had sometimes been heavy-handed in implementing the reform program, and had created opposition even amongst the intended beneficiaries, he turned out to be a moderate compared to Amin who tried to institute social change by riding roughshod over tradition and tribal and ethnic autonomy.

The Kremlin was unhappy with Amin. The fact that he had been involved in the overthrow and death of the much-favored Taraki was bad enough. But the Soviets also regarded him as thoroughly unsuitable for the task that was Moscow's *sine qua non*: preventing an anti-communist Islamic state from arising in Afghanistan. Amin gave reform an exceedingly bad name. The KGB station in Kabul, in pressing for Amin's removal, stated that his usurpation of power would lead to "harsh repressions and, as a reaction, the activation and consolidation of the opposition".[20] Moreover, as we shall see, the Soviets were highly suspicious about Amin's ideological convictions.

Thus it was, that what in March had been unthinkable, in December became a reality. Soviet troops began to arrive in Afghanistan around the 8th of the month—to what extent at Amin's request or with his approval, and, consequently, whether to call the action an "invasion" or not, has been the subject of much discussion and controversy.

On the 23rd the *Washington Post* commented "There was no charge [by the State Department] that the Soviets have invaded Afghanistan, since the troops apparently were invited."[21]

However, at a meeting with Soviet-bloc ambassadors in October, Amin's foreign minister had openly criticized the Soviet Union for interfering in Afghan affairs. Amin himself insisted that Moscow replace its ambassador.[22] Yet, on 26 December, while the main body of Soviet troops was arriving in Afghanistan, Amin gave "a relaxed interview" to an Arab journalist. "The Soviets," he said, "supply my country with economic and military aid, but at the same time they respect our independence and our sovereignty. They do not interfere in our domestic affairs." He also spoke approvingly of the USSR's willingness to accept his veto on military bases.[23]

The very next day, a Soviet military force stormed the presidential palace and shot Amin dead.[24]

He was replaced by Babrak Karmal, who had been vice president and deputy prime minister in the 1978 revolutionary government.

Moscow denied any part in Amin's death, though they didn't pretend to be sorry about it, as Brezhnev made clear:

> The actions of the aggressors against Afghanistan were facilitated by Amin who, on seizing power, started cruelly repressing broad sections of Afghan society, party and military cadres, members of the intelligentsia and of the Moslem clergy, that is, the very sections on which the April revolution relied. And the people under the leadership of the People's Democratic Party, headed by Babrak Karmal, rose against Amin's tyranny and put an end to it. Now in Washington and some other capitals they are mourning Amin. This exposes their hypocrisy with

particular clarity. Where were these mourners when Amin was conducting mass repressions, when he forcibly removed and unlawfully killed Taraki, the founder of the new Afghan state?[25]

After Amin's ouster and execution, the public thronged the streets in "a holiday spirit". "If Karmal could have overthrown Amin without the Russians," observed a Western diplomat, "he would have been seen as a hero of the people."[26]

The Soviet government and press repeatedly referred to Amin as a "CIA agent", a charge which was greeted with great skepticism in the United States and elsewhere.[27] However, enough circumstantial evidence supporting the charge exists so that it perhaps should not be dismissed entirely out of hand.

During the late 1950s and early '60s, Amin had attended Columbia University Teachers College and the University of Wisconsin.[28] This was a heyday period for the CIA—using impressive bribes and threats—to regularly try to recruit foreign students in the United States to act as agents for them when they returned home. During this period, at least one president of the Afghanistan Students Association (ASA), Zia H. Noorzay, was working with the CIA in the United States and later became president of the Afghanistan state treasury. One of the Afghan students whom Noorzay and the CIA tried in vain to recruit, Abdul Latif Hotaki, declared in 1967 that a good number of the key officials in the Afghanistan government who studied in the United States "are either CIA trained or indoctrinated. Some are cabinet level people."[29] It has been reported that in 1963 Amin became head of the ASA, but this has not been corroborated.[30] However, it is known that the ASA received part of its funding from the Asia Foundation, the CIA's principal front in Asia for many years, and that at one time Amin was associated with this organization.[31]

In September 1979, the month that Amin took power, the American *chargé d'affaires* in Kabul, Bruce Amstutz, began to hold friendly meetings with him to reassure him that he need not worry about his unhappy Soviet allies as long as the US maintained a strong presence in Afghanistan. The strategy may have worked, for later in the month, Amin made a special appeal to Amstutz for improved relations with the United States. Two days later in New York, the Afghan Foreign Minister quietly expressed the same sentiments to State Department officials. And at the end of October, the US Embassy in Kabul reported that Amin was "painfully aware of the exiled leadership the Soviets [were] keeping on the shelf" (a reference to Karmal who was living in Czechoslovakia).[32] Under normal circumstances, the Amin-US meetings might be regarded as routine and innocent diplomatic contact, but these were hardly normal circumstances—the Afghan government was engaged in a civil war, and the United States was supporting the other side.

Moreover, it can be said that Amin, by his ruthlessness, was doing just what an American agent would be expected to do: discrediting the People's Democratic Party, the party's reforms, the idea of socialism or communism, and the Soviet Union, all associated in one package. Amin also conducted purges in the army officer corps which seriously undermined the army's combat capabilities.

But why would Amin, if he were actually plotting with the Americans, request Soviet military forces on several occasions? The main reason appears to be that he was being pressed to do so by high levels of the PDP and he had to comply for the sake of appearances. Babrak Karmal has suggested other, more Machiavellian, scenarios.[33]

The Carter administration jumped on the issue of the Soviet "invasion" and soon launched a campaign of righteous indignation, imposing what President Carter called "penalties"—from halting the delivery of grain to the Soviet Union to keeping the US team out of the 1980 Olympics in Moscow.

The Russians countered that the US was enraged by the intervention because Washington had been plotting to turn the country into an American base to replace the loss of Iran.[34]

Unsurprisingly, on this seemingly clear-cut anti-communist issue, the American public and media easily fell in line with the president. The *Wall Street Journal* called for a "military" reaction, the establishment of US bases in the Middle East, "reinstatement of draft registration", development of a new missile, and giving the CIA more leeway, adding: "Clearly we ought to keep open the chance of covert aid to Afghan rebels."[35] The last, whether the newspaper knew it or not, had actually been going on for some time. In February 1980, the *Washington Post* disclosed that while the United States was now supplying weapons to the guerrillas,

> U.S. covert aid prior to the December invasion, according to sources, was limited to funneling small amounts of medical supplies and communications equipment to scattered rebel tribes, plus what is described as "technical advice" to the rebels about where they could acquire arms on their own.[36]

US foreign service officers had been meeting with rebel leaders to determine their needs at least as early as April 1979,[37] and the CIA had been training guerrillas in Pakistan and beaming radio propaganda into Afghanistan since the year before.[38]

Intervention in the Afghan civil war by the United States, Iran, Pakistan, China and others gave the Russians grave concern about who was going to wield power next door. They consistently cited these "aggressive imperialist forces" to rationalize their own intervention into Afghanistan, which was the first time Soviet ground troops had engaged in military action anywhere in the world outside its post-World War II Eastern European borders. The potential establishment of an anti-communist Islamic state on the borders of the Soviet Union's own republics in Soviet Central Asia that were home to some 40 million Muslims could not be regarded with equanimity by the Kremlin any more than Washington could be unruffled about a communist takeover in Mexico.

As we have seen repeatedly, the United States did not limit its defense perimeter to its immediate neighbors, or even to Western Europe, but to the entire globe. President Carter declared that the Persian Gulf area was "now threatened by Soviet troops in Afghanistan", that this area was synonymous with US interests, and that the United States would "defend" it against any threat by all means necessary. He called the Soviet action "the greatest threat to peace since the Second World War", a statement that required overlooking a great deal of post-war history. But 1980 was an election year.

Brezhnev, on the other hand, declared that "the national interests or security of the United States of America and other states are in no way affected by the events in Afghanistan. All attempts to portray matters otherwise are sheer nonsense."[39]

The Carter administration was equally dismissive of Soviet concerns. National Security Adviser Zbigniew Brzezinski later stated that "the issue was not what might have been Brezhnev's subjective motives in going into Afghanistan but the objective consequences of a Soviet military presence so much closer to the Persian Gulf."[40]

The stage was now set for 12 long years of the most horrific kind of warfare, a daily atrocity for the vast majority of the Afghan people who never asked for or wanted this war. But the Soviet Union was determined that its borders must be unthreatening. The Afghan government was committed to its goal of a secular, reformed Afghanistan. The United States was determined that, at a minimum, this should be the Soviets' Vietnam, that they should slowly bleed as the Americans had; at a maximum ... that was perhaps not as well thought out, but American policymakers could not fail to understand—though they dared not say it publicly and explicitly—that support of the Moujahedeen (many of whom carried pictures of the Ayatollah Khomeini with them) could lead to a fundamentalist Islamic state being established in Afghanistan every bit as repressive as in next-door Iran, which in the 1980s was Public Enemy Number One in America. Neither could the word "terrorist" cross the lips of Washington officials in speaking of their new allies/clients, though these same people shot down civilian airliners and planted bombs at the airport. In 1986, British Prime Minister Margaret Thatcher, whose emotional invectives against "terrorists" were second to none, welcomed Abdul Haq, an Afghan rebel leader who admitted that he had ordered the planting of a bomb at Kabul airport in 1984 which killed at least 28 people.[41] Such, then, were the scruples of cold-war anti-communists in late 20th century. As Anastasio Somoza had been "our son of a bitch", the Moujahedeen were now "our fanatic terrorists".

At the beginning there had been some thought given to the morality of the policy. "The question here," a senior official in the Carter administration said, "was whether it was morally acceptable that, in order to keep the Soviets off balance, which was the reason for the operation, it was permissible to use other lives for our geopolitical interests."[42]

But such sentiments could not survive. Afghanistan was a cold-warrior's dream: The CIA and the Pentagon, finally, had one of their proxy armies in direct confrontation with the forces of the Evil Empire. There was no price too high to pay for this Super Nintendo game, neither the hundreds of thousands of Afghan lives, nor the destruction of Afghan society, nor three billion (sic) dollars of American taxpayer money poured into a bottomless hole, much of it going only to make a few Afghans and Pakistanis rich. Congress was equally enthused—without even the moral uncertainty that made them cautious about arming the Nicaraguan contras—and became a veritable bipartisan horn of plenty as it allocated more and more money for the effort each year. Rep. Charles Wilson of Texas expressed a not-atypical sentiment of official Washington when he declared:

There were 58,000 dead in Vietnam and we owe the Russians one ... I have a slight obsession with it, because of Vietnam. I thought the Soviets ought to get a dose of it ... I've been of the opinion that this money was better spent to hurt our adversaries than other money in the Defense Department budget.[43]

The CIA became the grand coordinator: purchasing or arranging the manufacture of Soviet-style weapons from Egypt, China, Poland, Israel and elsewhere, or supplying their own; arranging for military training by Americans, Egyptians, Chinese and Iranians; hitting up Middle-Eastern countries for donations, notably Saudi Arabia which gave many hundreds of millions of dollars in aid each year, totaling probably more than a billion; pressuring and bribing Pakistan—with whom recent American relations had been very poor—to rent out its country as a military staging area and sanctuary; putting the Pakistani Director of Military Operations, Brigadier Mian Mohammad Afzal, onto the CIA payroll to ensure Pakistani cooperation.[44] Military and economic aid which had been cut off would be restored, Pakistan was told by the United States, if they would join the great crusade. Only a month before the Soviet intervention, anti-American mobs had burned and ransacked the US embassy in Islamabad and American cultural centers in two other Pakistani cities.[45]

The American ambassador in Libya reported that Muammar Qaddafi was sending the rebels $250,000 as well, but this, presumably, was not at the request of the CIA.[46]

Washington left it to the Pakistanis to decide which of the various Afghan guerrilla groups should be the beneficiaries of much of this largesse. As one observer put it: "According to conventional wisdom at the time, the United States would not repeat the mistake of Vietnam—micro-managing a war in a culture it did not understand."[47]

Not everyone in Pakistan was bought out. The independent Islamabad daily newspaper, the *Muslim*, more than once accused the United States of being ready to "fight to the last Afghan" ... "We are not flattered to be termed a 'frontline state' by Washington." ... "Washington does not seem to be in any mood to seek an early settlement of a war whose benefits it is reaping at no cost of American manpower."[48]

It's not actually clear whether there was any loss of American lives in the war. On several occasions in the late '80s, the Kabul government announced that Americans had been killed in the fighting,[49] and in 1985 a London newspaper reported that some two dozen American Black Muslims were in Afghanistan, fighting alongside the Moujahedeen in a *jihad* that a fundamentalist interpretation of the Koran says all believers in Islam must do at least once in their lives.[50] Several of the Black Muslims returned to the United States after being wounded.

Soviet aggression ... Soviet invasion ... Soviet swallowing up another innocent state as part of their plan to conquer the world, or at least the Middle East ... this was the predominant and lasting lesson taught by Washington official pronouncements and the mainstream US media about the war, and the sum total of knowledge for the average American, although Afghanistan had retained its independence during 60 years of living in peace next door to the Soviet Union. Zbigniew Brzezinski, albeit unrelentingly anti-Soviet, repeatedly speaks of the fact of Afghanistan's "neutrality" in his memoirs.[51] The country had been neutral even during the Second World War.

One would have to look long and hard at the information and rhetoric offered to the American public following the Soviet intervention to derive even a hint that the civil war was essentially a struggle over deep-seated social reform; while an actual discussion of the issue was virtually non-existent. Prior to the intervention, one could get a taste of this, such as the following from the *New York Times*:

> Land reform attempts undermined their village chiefs. Portraits of Lenin threatened their religious leaders. But it was the Kabul revolutionary Government's granting of new rights to women that pushed orthodox Moslem men in the Pashtoon villages of eastern Afghanistan into picking up their guns. ... "The government said our women had to attend meetings and our children had to go to schools. This threatens our religion. We had to fight." ... "The government imposed various ordinances allowing women freedom to marry anyone they chose without their parents' consent."[52]

Throughout the 1980s, the Karmal, and then the Najibullah regimes, despite the exigencies of the war, pursued a program of modernization and broadening of their base: bringing electricity to villages, along with health clinics, a measure of land reform, and literacy; releasing numerous prisoners unlawfully incarcerated by Amin; bringing mullahs and other non-party people into the government; trying to carry it all out with moderation and sensitivity instead of confronting the traditional structures head-on; reiterating its commitment to Islam, rebuilding and constructing mosques, exempting land owned by religious dignitaries and their institutions from land reform; trying, in short, to avoid the gross mistakes of the Amin government with its rush to force changes down people's throats.[53]

Selig Harrison, writing in 1988, stated:

> The Afghan Communists see themselves as nationalists and modernizers ... They rationalize their col-

laboration with the Russians as the only way available to consolidate their revolution in the face of foreign "interference". ... The commitment of the Communists to rapid modernization enables them to win a grudging tolerance from many members of the modern-minded middle class, who feel trapped between two fires: the Russians and fanatic Muslims opposed to social reforms.[54]

The program of the Kabul government eventually encouraged many volunteers to take up arms in its name. But it was a decidedly uphill fight, for it was relatively easy for the native anti-reformists and their foreign backers to convince large numbers of ordinary peasants that the government had ill intentions by blurring the distinction between the present government and its detested and dogmatic predecessor, particularly since the government was fond of stressing the continuity of the April 1978 revolution.[55] One thing the peasants, as well as the anti-reformists, were undoubtedly not told of was the US connection to the selfsame detested predecessor, Hafizullah Amin.

Another problem faced by the Kabul government in winning the hearts and minds of the people was of course the continuing Soviet armed presence, although it must be remembered that Islamic opposition to the leftist government began well before the Soviet forces arrived; indeed, the most militant of the Moujahedeen leaders, Hekmatyar, had led a serious uprising against the previous (non-leftist) government as well, in 1975, declaring that a "godless, communist-dominated regime" ruled in Kabul.[56]

As long as Soviet troops remained, the conflict in Afghanistan could be presented to the American mind as little more than a battle between Russian invaders and Afghanistan resistance/freedom fighters; as if the Afghanistan army and government didn't exist, or certainly not with a large following of people who favored reforms and didn't want to live under a fundamentalist Islamic government, probably a majority of the population.

"Maybe the people really don't like us, either," said Mohammed Hakim, Mayor of Kabul, a general in the Afghan army who was trained in the 1970s at military bases in the United States, and who thought that America was "the best country", "but they like us better than the extremists. This is what the Western countries do not understand. We only hope that Mr. Bush and the people of the United States take a good look at us. They think we are very fanatic Communists, that we are not human beings. We are not fanatics. We are not even Communists."[57]

They were in the American media. Any official of the Afghan government, or the government as a whole, was typically referred to, a priori, as "Communist", or "Marxist", or "pro-Communist", or "pro-Marxist", etc., without explanation or definition. Najibullah, who took over when Karmal stepped down in 1986, was confirmed in his position in 1987 under a new Islamized constitution that was stripped of all socialist rhetoric and brimming with references to Islam and the holy Koran. "This is not a socialist revolutionary country," he said in his acceptance speech. "We do not want to build a Communist society."[58]

Could the United States see beyond cold war ideology and consider the needs of the Afghan people? In August 1979, three months before the Soviet intervention, a classified State Department Report stated:

> the United States's larger interests ... would be served by the demise of the Taraki-Amin regime, despite whatever setbacks this might mean for future social and economic reforms in Afghanistan. ... the overthrow of the D.R.A. [Democratic Republic of Afghanistan] would show the rest of the world, particularly the Third World, that the Soviets' view of the socialist course of history as being inevitable is not accurate.[59]

Repeatedly, in the 1980s, as earlier, the Soviet Union contended that no solution to the conflict could be found until the United States and other nations ceased their support of the

Moujahedeen. The United States, in turn, insisted that the Soviets must first withdraw their troops from Afghanistan.

Finally, after several years of UN-supported negotiations, an accord was signed in Geneva on 14 April 1988, under which the Kremlin committed itself to begin pulling out its estimated 115,000 troops on 15 May, and to complete the process by 15 February of the next year. Afghanistan, said Soviet President Mikhail Gorbachev, had become "a bleeding wound".

In February, after the last Soviet forces had left Afghanistan, Gorbachev urged the United States to support an embargo on arms shipments into Afghanistan and a cease-fire between the two warring sides. Both proposals were turned down by the new Bush adminis-tration, which claimed that the Afghan government had been left with a massive stockpile of military equipment. It is unclear why Washington felt that the rebels who had fought the government to a standstill despite the powerful presence of the Soviet armed forces with all their equipment, would now be at a dangerous disadvantage with the Russians gone. The key to the American response may lie in the State Department statement of the prior week that the United States believed that the Kabul government on its own would not last more than six months.[60]

By raising the question of an arms gap (whether it was for real or not), Washington was assuring the continuation of the arms race in Afghanistan—a microcosm of the cold war. At the same time, the Bush administration called upon the Soviets to support "an inde-pendent, nonaligned Afghanistan", although this was precisely what the United States had worked for decades to thwart.

Two days later, President Najibullah criticized the American rejection of Gorbachev's proposal, offering to return the Soviet weapons if the rebels agreed to lay down their weapons and negotiate. There was no reported response to this offer from the US, or from the rebels, who in the past had refused such offers.

It would appear that Washington was thinking longer term than cease-fires and negoti-ations. On the same day as Najibullah's offer, the United States announced that it had deliv-ered 500,000 made-in-America textbooks to Afghanistan which were being used to teach Grades one through four. The books, which "critics say bordered on propaganda", told of the rebels' fight against the Soviet Union and contained drawings of guerrillas killing Russian soldiers.[61] Since the beginning of the war, the Moujahedeen had reserved its worst treatment for Russians. Washington possessed confirmed reports that the rebels had drugged and tortured 50 to 200 Soviet prisoners and imprisoned them like animals in cages, "living lives of indescribable horror".[62] Another account, by a reporter from the conserva-tive *Far Eastern Economic Review*, relates that :

> One [Soviet] group was killed, skinned and hung up in a butcher's shop. One captive found him-self the centre of attraction in a game of buzkashi, that rough and tumble form of Afghan polo in which a headless goat is usually the ball. The captive was used instead. Alive. He was literally torn to pieces.[63]

Meanwhile, much to the surprise of the United States and everyone else, the Kabul gov-ernment showed no sign of collapsing. The good news for Washington was that since the Soviet troops were gone (though some military advisers remained), the "cost-benefit ratio" had improved,[64] the cost being measured entirely in non-American deaths and suffering, as the rebels regularly exploded car bombs and sent rockets smashing into residential areas of Kabul, and destroyed government-built schools and clinics and murdered literacy teachers (just as the US-backed Nicaraguan contras had been doing on the other side of the world, and for the same reason: these were symbols of governmental benevolence).

The death and destruction caused by the Soviets and their Afghan allies was also extensive, such as the many bombings of villages. But individual atrocity stories must be approached with caution, for, as we have seen repeatedly, the propensity and the ability of the CIA to disseminate anti-communist disinformation—often of the most far-fetched variety—was virtually unlimited. With the Soviet Union the direct adversary, the creativity lamp must have burning all night at Langley.

Amnesty International, with its usual careful collection methods, reported in the mid-'80s on the frequent use of torture and arbitrary detention by the authorities in Kabul.[65] But what are we to make, for example, of the report, without attribution, by syndicated columnist Jack Anderson—who had ties to the American Afghan lobby—that Soviet troops *often* marched into unfriendly villages in Afghanistan and "massacred every man, woman and child"?[66] Or the *New York Times* recounting a story told them by an Afghan citizen of how Afghan soldiers had intentionally blinded five children with pieces of metal and then strangled them, as a government supporter he was with just laughed. To the newspaper's credit, it added that "There is no way of confirming this story. It is possible that the man who told it was acting and trying to discredit the regime here. His eyes, however, looked like they had seen horror."[67] Or a US congressman's charge in 1985 that the Soviets had used booby-trapped toys to maim Afghan children,[68] the identical story told before about leftists elsewhere in the world during the cold war, and repeated again in 1987 by CBS News, with pictures. The *New York Post* later reported the claim of a BBC producer that the bomb-toy had been created for the CBS cameraman.[69]

Then there was the Afghan Mercy Fund, ostensibly a relief agency, but primarily in the propaganda business, which reported that the Soviets had burned a baby alive, that they were disguising mines as candy bars and leaving other mines disguised as butterflies to also attract children. The butterfly mines, it turned out, were copies of a US-designed mine used in the Vietnam war.[70]

There was also the shooting down of a Pakistan fighter plane over Afghanistan in May 1987 that was reported by Pakistan and Washington—knowing with certainty that their claim was untrue—to be the result of a Soviet-made missile. It turned out that the plane had been shot down by a companion Pakistani plane in error.[71]

Throughout the early and mid-'80s, the Reagan administration declared that the Russians were spraying toxic chemicals over Laos, Cambodia and Afghanistan—the so-called "yellow rain"—and had caused more than ten thousand deaths by 1982 alone, (including, in Afghanistan, 3,042 deaths attributed to 47 separate incidents between the summer of 1979 and the summer of 1981, so precise was the information). Secretary of State Alexander Haig was a prime dispenser of such stories, and President Reagan himself denounced the Soviet Union thusly more than 15 times in documents and speeches.[72] The "yellow rain", it turned out, was pollen-laden feces dropped by huge swarms of honeybees flying far overhead. Then, in 1987, it was disclosed that the Reagan administration had made its accusations even though government scientists at the time had been unable to confirm any of them, and considered the evidence to be flimsy and misleading.[73] Even more suspicious: the major scientific studies that later examined Washington's claims spoke only of Laos, Cambodia and Thailand; no mention at all was made of Afghanistan. It was as if the administration—perhaps honestly mistaken at first about Indochina—had added Afghanistan to the list with full knowledge of the falsity of its allegation.

Such disinformation campaigns are often designed to serve a domestic political need. Consider Senator Robert Dole's contribution to the discussion when he spoke in 1980 on the floor of Congress of "convincing evidence" he had been provided "that the Soviets had developed a chemical capability that extends far beyond our greatest fears ... [a gas that] is unaffected by ... our gas masks and leaves our military defenseless." He then added: "To even suggest a leveling off of defense spending for our nation by the Carter administration at such a critical time in our history is unfathomable."[74] And in March 1982, when the Reagan administration made its claim about the 3,042 Afghan deaths, the New York Times noted that: "President Reagan has just decided that the United States will resume production of chemical weapons and has asked for a substantial increase in the military budget for such weapons."[75]

The money needed to extend American propaganda campaigns internationally flowed from the congressional horn of plenty as smoothly as for military desires—$500,000 in one moment's flow to train Afghan journalists to use television, radio, and newspapers to advance their cause.[76]

It should be noted that in June 1980, before any of the "yellow rain" charges had been made against the Soviet Union, the Kabul government had accused the rebels and their foreign backers of employing poison gas, citing an incident in which 500 pupils and teachers at several secondary schools had been poisoned with noxious gases; none were reported to have died.[77]

One reason victory continued to elude the Moujahedeen was that they were terribly split by centuries-old ethnic and tribal divisions, as well as the relatively recent rise of Islamic fundamentalism in conflict with more traditional, but still orthodox, Islam. The differences often led to violence. In one incident, in 1989, seven top Moujahedeen commanders and more than 20 other rebels were murdered by a rival guerrilla group. This was neither the first nor the last of such occurrences.[78] By April 1990, 14 months after the Soviet withdrawal, the Los Angeles Times described the state of the rebels thusly:

> they have in recent weeks killed more of their own than the enemy. ... Rival resistance commanders have been gunned down gangland-style here in the border town of Peshawar [Pakistan], the staging area for the war. There are persistent reports of large-scale political killings in the refugee camps ... A recent execution ... had as much to do with drugs as with politics. ... Other commanders, in Afghanistan and in the border camps, are simply refusing to fight. They say privately that they prefer [Afghan President] Najibullah to the hard-line Moujahedeen fundamentalists led by Gulbuddin Hekmatyar.[79]

The rebel cause was also corrupted by the huge amounts of arms flooding in. Investigative reporter Tim Weiner reported the following:

> The CIA's pipeline leaked. It leaked badly. It spilled huge quantities of weapons all over one of the world's most anarchic areas. First the Pakistani armed forces took what they wanted from the weapons shipments. Then corrupt Afghan guerrilla leaders stole and sold hundreds of millions of dollars' worth of anti-aircraft guns, missiles, rocket-propelled grenades, AK-47 automatic rifles, ammunition and mines from the CIA's arsenal. Some of the weapons fell into the hands of criminal gangs, heroin kingpins and the most radical faction of the Iranian military. ... While their troops eked out hard lives in Afghanistan's mountains and deserts, the guerrillas' political leaders maintained fine villas in Peshawar and fleets of vehicles at their command. The CIA kept silent as the Afghan politicos converted the Agency's weapons into cash.[80]

Amongst the weapons the Moujahedeen sold to the Iranians were highly sophisticated Stinger heat-seeking anti-aircraft missiles, with which the rebels had shot down many hundreds of Soviet military aircraft, as well as at least eight passenger planes. On 8 October

1987, Revolutionary Guards on an Iranian gunboat fired one of the Stingers at American helicopters patrolling the Persian Gulf, but missed their target.[81]

Earlier the same year, the CIA told Congress that at least 20 percent of its military aid to the Moujahedeen had been skimmed off by the rebels and Pakistani officials. Columnist Jack Anderson stated at the same time that his conservative estimate was that the diversion was around 60 percent, while one rebel leader told Anderson's assistant on his visit to the border that he doubted that even 25 percent of the arms got through. By other accounts, as little as 20 percent was making it the intended recipients. If indeed there was a deficiency of arms available to the Moujahedeen compared to the government forces, as George Bush implied, this was clearly a major reason for it. Yet the CIA and other administration officials simply looked upon it as part of doing business in that part of the world.[82]

Like many other CIA clients, the rebels were financed as well through drug trafficking, and the Agency was apparently as little concerned about it as ever as long as it kept their boys happy. Moujahedeen commanders inside Afghanistan personally controlled huge fields of opium poppies, the raw material from which heroin is refined. CIA-supplied trucks and mules, which had carried arms into Afghanistan, were used to transport some of the opium to the numerous laboratories along the Afghan-Pakistan border, whence many tons of heroin were processed with the cooperation of the Pakistani military. The output provided an estimated one-third to one-half of the heroin used annually in the United States and three-quarters of that used in Western Europe. US officials admitted in 1990 that they had failed to investigate or take action against the drug operation because of a desire not to offend their Pakistani and Afghan allies.[83] In 1993, an official of the US Drug Enforcement Administration called Afghanistan the new Colombia of the drug world.[84]

The war, with all its torment, continued until the spring of 1992, three years after the last Soviet troops had gone. An agreement on ending the arms supply, which had been reached between the United States and the Soviet Union, was now in effect. The two super-powers had abandoned the war. The Soviet Union no longer existed. And the Afghan people could count more than a million dead, three million disabled, and five million made refugees, in total about half the population.

At the same time, a UN-brokered truce was to transfer power to a transitional coalition government pending elections. But this was not to be. The Kabul government, amidst food riots and army revolts, virtually disintegrated, and the guerrillas stormed into the capital and established the first Islamic regime in Afghanistan since it had become a separate and independent country in the mid-18th century.

A key event in the downfall of the government was the eleventh-hour defection to the guerrillas of General Abdul Rashid Dostum. Dostum, who previously had been referred to in the US media as a "Communist general", now metamorphosed into an "ex-Communist general".

The Moujahedeen had won. Now they turned against each other with all their fury. Rockets and artillery shells wiped out entire neighborhoods in Kabul. By August at least 1,500 people had been killed or wounded, mostly civilians. (By 1994, the body count in this second civil war would reach 10,000.) Of all the rebel leaders, none was less compromising or more insistent upon a military solution than Gulbuddin Hekmatyar.

Robert Neumann, a former US ambassador to Afghanistan, observed at this time:

Hekmatyar is a nut, an extremist and a very violent man. He was built up by the Pakistanis. Unfortunately, our government went along with the Pakistanis. We were supplying the money and the weapons but they [Pakistani officials] were making the policy.

Washington was now very concerned that Hekmatyar would take power. Ironically, they were afraid that if he did, his brand of extremism would spread to and destabilize the former Soviet republics of large Moslem populations, the same fear which had been one of the motivations behind the Soviets intervening in the civil war in the first place.[85]

It was to the forces of Hekmatyar that the "Communist general" Dostum eventually aligned himself.

Suleiman Layeq, a leftist and a poet, and the fallen regime's "ideologue", watched from his window as the Moujahedeen swarmed through the city, claiming building after building. "Without exception," he said of them, "they follow the way of the fundamentalist aims and goals of Islam. And it is not Islam. It is a kind of theory against civilization—against modern civilization."[86]

Even before taking power, the Moujahedeen had banned all non-Muslim groups. Now more of the new law was laid down: All alcohol was banned in the Islamic republic; women could not venture out in the streets without veils, and violations would be punished by floggings, amputations and public executions. And this from the more "moderate" Islamics, not Hekmatyar. By September, the first public hangings were carried out. Before a cheering crowd of 10,000 people, three men were hung. They had been tried behind closed doors, and no one would say what crimes they had committed.[87]

In February 1993, a group of Middle Easterners blew up the World Trade Center in New York City. Most of them were veterans of the Moujahedeen. Other veterans were carrying out assassinations in Cairo, bombings in Bombay, and bloody uprisings in the mountains of Kashmir.

This, then, was the power and the glory of President Reagan's "freedom fighters", who had become yet more anti-American in recent years, many of them backing Iraqi leader Saddam Hussein in the Persian Gulf conflict of 1990-91. Surely even Ronald Reagan and George Bush would have preferred the company of "communist" reformers like President Noor Mohammed Taraki, Mayor Mohammed Hakim or poet Suleiman Layeq.

But the Soviet Union had bled. They had bled profusely. For the United States it had also been a holy war.

54. El Salvador 1980-1994
Human rights, Washington style

The United States was supporting the government of El Salvador, said President Ronald Reagan, because it was trying "to halt the infiltration into the Americas, by terrorists and by outside interference, and those who aren't just aiming at El Salvador but, I think, are aiming at the whole of Central and possibly later South America and, I'm sure, eventually North America."[1]

Psychiatrists have a term for such perceptions of reality. They call it paranoid schizophrenia.

If the insurgents in El Salvador, the smallest country by far in all of Central and South

America, were engaged in what Ronald Reagan perceived as a plot to capture the Western Hemisphere, others saw it as the quintessential revolution.

Viewed in the latter context, it cannot be asserted that the Salvadorean people rushed precipitously into revolution at the first painful sting of repression, or turned to the gun because of a proclivity towards violent solutions, or a refusal to "work within the system", or because of "outside agitators", or any of the other explanations of why people revolt so dear to the hearts of Washington opinion makers. For as long as anyone could remember, the reins of El Salvador's government had resided in the hands of one military dictatorship or another, while the economy had been controlled by the celebrated 14 coffee and industrial families, with only the occasional, short-lived bursting of accumulated discontent to disturb the neat arrangement.

In December 1980, *New York Times*, reporter Raymond Bonner asked José Napoleón Duarte "why the guerrillas were in the hills". Duarte, who had just become president of the ruling junta, responded with an answer that surprised Bonner: "Fifty years of lies, fifty years of injustice, fifty years of frustration. This is a history of people starving to death, living in misery. For fifty years the same people had all the power, all the money, all the jobs, all the education, all the opportunities."[2]

In the decades following the famed peasant rebellion in 1932, which was crushed by an unholy massacre, a reform government had occupied the political stage only twice: for nine months in 1944, then again in 1960. The latter instance was precipitated by several thousand students of the National University who staged a protest against the curtailment of civil liberties. The government responded by sending in the police, who systematically smashed offices, classrooms, and laboratories, beat up the school's president, killed a librarian, bayoneted students, and raped dozens of young women. Finally, when the students amassed anew, troops opened fire upon them point-blank.

The bloody incident was one of the turning points for a group of junior military officers. They staged a coup in October aimed at major social and political reforms, but the new government lasted only three months before being overthrown in a counter-coup which the United States was reportedly involved in.[3] Dr. Fabio Castillo, a former president of the National University and a member of the ousted government, testified years later before the US Congress that in the process of overthrowing the reform government, the American Embassy immediately began to "intervene directly", and "members of the U.S. Military Mission openly intensified their invitation to conspiracy and rebellion".[4]

Throughout the 1960s, multifarious American experts occupied themselves in El Salvador by enlarging and refining the state's security and counter-insurgency apparatus: the police, the National Guard, the military, the communications and intelligence networks, the co-ordination with their counterparts in other Central American countries ... as matters turned out, these were the forces and resources which were brought into action to impose widespread repression and wage war. Years later, the *New York Times* noted:

In El Salvador, American aid was used for police training in the 1950's and 1960's and many officers in the three branches of the police later became leaders of the right-wing death squads that killed tens of thousands of people in the late 1970's and early 1980's.[5]

If during the 1960s, the apparatus could not be charged with the level of murder or torture or disappearance of political opponents reached in Guatemala and elsewhere in Latin America, it had more to do with the modest degree of outspoken dissent and violent unrest it faced than with greater respect for human rights; those opposition groups which were not outlawed were those regarded as unthreatening; the bloated stomachs of malnourished peasant children were not regarded as threatening at all.

For apparently no better reason than the fact that even militarists cherish a veneer of legitimacy, during the 1960s certain political organizations of generally urban middle-class membership were allowed to run candidates for municipal and legislative office. They did well, though the government-calculated returns consistently left the opposition as a minority in the legislature; i.e., without real power. In 1967, the government went through the motions of the first contested election for the presidency since 1931. After declaring its party, PCN, the winner, the government promptly banned one of the major contending parties, PAR, on the grounds that it supported principles "contrary to the Constitution". According to a PAR spokesperson, the "principle" involved was support for agrarian reform. Another source reports that the party was declared illegal "allegedly for dispensing Communist ideologies", which, within the government's frame of reference, may well have been one and the same.[6]

Undeterred, a center-left coalition, UNO by acronym, was formed and put forth Christian Democrat José Napoleón Duarte as its presidential candidate in 1972. Though UNO was confronted by violence against its candidates and campaigners, including the murder of an aide of Duarte, and the sabotaging of the coalition's radio broadcasts, it arrived at election day with high expectations. Two days after the polling, the Central Election Board, after first announcing a victory for PCN, shocked everyone by declaring that a recount had shown UNO to be the winner instead. The government quickly imposed a news blackout and for the next two days nothing was heard concerning the election results. On the third day, the Election Board announced that PCN was indeed the winner after all.

In the 1974 and 1976 legislative elections, and again in the 1977 presidential election, the government employed similar creative counting along with gross physical intimidation of candidates, voters, and poll watchers, to assure its continuance in office.[7]

A mass demonstration following the 1977 polling, protesting against electoral fraud, was surrounded by government security forces who opened fire. The result was nothing less than a bloodbath, the death toll measurable in the hundreds. In the immediate aftermath, top leaders of UNO were exiled and the party's followers became liable to arrest, torture and murder.[8] The country's president, Col. Arturo Molina, blamed the protests on "foreign Communists". His response to charges of electoral fraud was: "Only God is perfect."[9]

Government political violence of this sort had been sporadic in the 1960s, but became commonplace in the 1970s as more and more Salvadoreans, frustrated by the futility of achieving social change through elections, resorted to other means. While some limited themselves to more militant demonstrations, strikes, and occupations of sites, an increasing number turned to acts of urban guerrilla warfare such as assassination of individuals seen as part of the repressive machinery, bombings, and kidnappings for ransom. The government and its paramilitary right-wing vigilante groups—"death squads" is the self-named modern genre—countered with a campaign centered upon leaders of labor unions, peasant organizations and political parties, as well as priests and lay religious workers. "Be Patriotic—Kill a Priest" was the slogan of one death squad. Church people were accused of teaching subversion to the peasants, what the church people themselves would call the word of God, in this the only country in the world named after Christ. The CIA and the US military played an essential role in the conception and organization of the security agencies from which the death squads emanated. CIA surveillance programs routinely supplied these agencies with information on, and the whereabouts of, various individuals who wound up as death squad victims.[10]

In October 1979, a cabal of younger military officers, repelled by the frequent government massacres of groups of protesters and strikers, and wishing to restore the military's "good name", ousted General Carlos Romero from the presidency and took power in a bloodless coup. A number of prominent civilian political figures were given positions in the new administration, which proclaimed an impressive program of reforms. But it was not to be. The young and politically inexperienced officers were easily co-opted by older, conservative officers, and by pressure exerted by the United States, to install certain military men into key positions.[11] The civilian members of the government found themselves unable to exercise any control over the armed forces and were left to function only as reformist camouflage.

Washington had supported the removal of the brutal Romero because only three months earlier the Sandinistas had overthrown the Somoza dictatorship in Nicaragua, and the Carter administration did not wish to risk the loss of a second client state in Central America in so short a space of time, but brakes had to be applied to keep the process within manageable bounds.

Meanwhile, the security forces did not miss a beat as they continued to fire into crowds: the body count in the first month of the "reformist" government was greater than in the first nine months of the year. By January 1980, almost all the civilian members had resigned in disgust over government-as-usual.[12] The experience was the straw which broke the backs of many moderates and liberals, as well as members of the Salvadorean Communist Party, who still clung to hopes of peaceful reforms. The Communist Party had supported the new government, even contributed the Minister of Labor, "because we believe it is going to comply with its promises and open the possibility of democratizing the country." The party was the last group on the left to join the guerrilla forces.[13]

One of the civilians, Minister of Education Salvador Samayoa, in front of the TV cameras, simultaneously announced his resignation and his enlistment with a guerrilla group.[14] For those who continued to harbor illusions, a steady drumbeat of terrorism soon brought them into the fold. A demonstration march by a coalition of popular organizations on 22 January was first sprayed with DDT by crop-duster planes along the route of the march; then, when the demonstrators reached San Salvador's central plaza, snipers fired at them from surrounding government buildings; at least 21 dead and 120 seriously wounded was the toll, some of which reportedly resulted from the demonstrators' undisciplined return of fire.

On 17 March, a general strike was met by retaliatory violence—54 people killed in the capital alone.

A week later, the Archbishop of San Salvador, Oscar Romero, an outspoken critic of the government's human-rights violations, who had called upon President Carter, "Christian to Christian", to cease providing military aid, was assassinated. In his last sermon, he had addressed the security forces with these words: "I beseech you, I beg you, I order you, in the name of God: *stop the repression.*" The next day he became the eleventh priest murdered in El Salvador in three years.

At the funeral of the martyred Archbishop—who had been a nominee for the Nobel Peace Prize the year before, 23 members of the US House of Representatives being among his nominators—a bomb was thrown amongst the mourners in the plaza, followed by rifle and automatic fire, all emanating from the National Palace and some of the office buildings flanking the plaza, just as in January. At least 40 people were reported killed and hundreds injured.[15]

Junta president Duarte tried to put the blame for the funeral carnage on the left. His case rested apparently on bald statement and nothing else, for all eyewitness reports stated that the bomb and gunfire came from the National Palace and the other government buildings. A statement issued by eight bishops and 16 other foreign church visitors who had been present denied the government's version.[16]

Seven years were to pass before Duarte, elected to the presidency in 1984, accused former army Major Roberto d'Aubuisson, the prominent leader of the country's right wing, with having ordered Romero's murder. Though this was a belief already widely held, the public accusation created a stir in El Salvador and the United States. The CIA, it turned out, knew the facts no later than one year after the assassination. (D'Aubuisson, it should be noted, was a man who once told three European reporters: "You Germans are very intelligent. You realized that the Jews were responsible for the spread of communism, and you began to kill them.") The American-trained former intelligence officer was never arrested because of immunity arising from his being a deputy in the National Assembly. He died in 1992.[17]

During the early months of 1980, the government, with direct American influence and input, enacted a program of agrarian reform, the *sine qua non* of social change in El Salvador. Its key provision—tenant farmers gaining title to the plots they worked—was similar to programs the US had advocated in a number of other Third World hot spots since the 1950s, and for the same reasons: as a counter-insurgency tactic—stealing the guerrillas' thunder; and to make the government receiving US military aid appear more deserving, in the eyes of Congress and the world. A memorandum from the Agency for International Development (AID) in mid-1980, commenting on reaction in El Salvador to the program of "Land to the Tiller", says in part:

> Many believe it is a "symbolic" and "cosmetic" measure which was proposed because it would look good to certain American politicians and not necessarily because it would be beneficial or significant in the Salvadorean context.[18]

The reaction of the Salvadorean agrarian elite could have been predicted. They expelled many thousands of peasants from their meager plots to preclude land being turned over to them. This was not the worst ...

The testimony of a technician of the *Instituto Salvadoreño de Transformación Agraria*, established to oversee the program:

> The troops came and told the workers the land was theirs now. They could elect their own leaders and run it themselves. The peasants couldn't believe their ears, but they held elections that very night. The next morning the troops came back and I watched as they shot every one of the elected leaders.[19]

This was not an isolated case. The Assistant Minister of Agriculture, Jorge Alberto Villacorta, in his resignation letter in March 1980, stated that "During the first days of the reform—to cite one case—5 directors and 2 presidents of new campesino organizations were assassinated and I am informed that this repressive practice continues to increase."[20]

"Force," wrote Karl Marx, "is the midwife of every old society pregnant with a new one." Revolution was now the only item of importance on the political agenda of the opposition, united as never before—united more by a common enemy than by a common ideology, but many saw this pluralism as strength rather than weakness. Leftists would now be fighting alongside (former) Christian Democrats whom, only shortly before, they had accused of serving US imperialism.

If Jimmy Carter's trumpeted devotion to human rights was to be taken seriously, his administration clearly had no alternative but to side with the Salvadorean opposition, or at least keep its hands strictly out of the fighting. The Carter administration, however, with only an occasional backward glance at its professed principles, continued its military support of the government. Within days before his term ended in January 1981, Carter ordered a total of $10 million in military aid along with additional American advisers to be sent to El Salvador, an action characterized by one observer as "President Carter's foreign policy establishment's last convulsive effort to evade responsibility for having been 'too soft' in dealing with the Salvadorean rebels." (Two years later, private citizen Carter stated: "I think the government in El Salvador is one of the bloodthirstiest in [the] hemisphere now.")[21]

The Reagan administration, to whom "human rights" was a suspect term invented by leftists, had little fear of the too-soft label. Its approach to the conflict was threefold: (a) a sharp escalation, both quantitatively and qualitatively, in the American military involvement in El Salvador; (b) a public relations campaign to put a human face on the military junta; (c) a concurrent exercise in news management to convince the American public and the world that the Salvadorean opposition had no legitimate cause for revolution; which was to say that what the Salvadoreans had experienced during the previous two decades, indeed for half a century, had little or nothing to do with their uprising—this, it turned out, was the inspiration of (unprovoked, mindless) "left-wing terrorists" abetted by the Soviet Union, by Nicaragua, by Cuba. The Red Devils were at it again.

Military Escalation

El Salvador did not turn into another Vietnam quicksand for the United States as many critics of the left and center warned. But for the Salvadorean people the war and its horror dragged on as interminably as it did for the Vietnamese, and for the same reason: American support of a regime—one even more loathsome than in Vietnam—which would have crumbled dismally if left to its own resources. Despite overwhelmingly superior military might, the government could hold the insurgents to no more than a stalemate.

The amount of American military aid to El Salvador from 1980 to the early 1990s, for the hardware alone, ran into the billions of dollars. Six billion is the figure commonly used in the press, but the true figure will never be known. The Arms Control and Foreign Policy Caucus, a bipartisan congressional group, accused the Reagan administration in the mid-1980s of supplying "insufficient, misleading and in some cases false information" concerning aid to El Salvador. The administration, concluded the Caucus study, categorized most military aid as "development" aid, and undervalued the real cost of the hardware even when it was properly categorized as military aid.[22]

To this must be added the cost of training Salvadorean military personnel by the thousands in the United States, and the Panama Canal Zone, as well as in El Salvador; the further training which was provided in the earlier years by Argentina, Chile and Uruguay at US behest; and the substantial military aid routed through Israel, a maneuver employed by the United States elsewhere in Central America as well.[23]

One telling result of this massive provision of weapons and training, as well as the money to pay higher salaries, was the sizeable expansion of the Salvadorean armed forces and other security services. From an estimated seven to twelve thousand men in 1979, the army alone jumped to more than 22,000 by 1983, with an additional 11,000 civilian security forces; three years later, the total of these two forces had spiraled to 53,000.[24] The equipment available to them flowed endlessly; when, for example, in January 1982, the rebels destroyed 16 to 18 aircraft in a raid upon an airport, the United States replaced them in a matter of weeks with 28 new aircraft.[25] Part of the air power available to the government were US reconnaissance planes fitted with sophisticated surveillance equipment which could provide almost instant intelligence on guerrilla movements before and after combat operations, and designate bombing targets.[26] The guerrillas had neither air power nor a practical anti-aircraft capability until November 1990 when they used a Soviet-made surface-to-air missile for the first time.

Predictably, the bombing, as well as the strafing and napalming, took the lives of many more civilians than guerrillas who had better learned how to avoid the attacks; countless dwellings were leveled in the process, villages destroyed, a nation of refugees created. Civilian deaths, whether from air or ground raids, were not necessarily accidental, as the many massacre stories make evident. It is a basic tenet of counter-insurgency: kill the sympathizers and you win the war.

Officially, the US military presence in El Salvador was limited to an advisory capacity. In actuality, military and CIA personnel played a more active role on a continuous basis from as early as 1980. About 20 Americans were killed or wounded in helicopter and plane crashes while flying reconnaissance or other missions over combat areas.[27] Moreover, the American program for training Salvadorean pilots, bombardiers and gunners could easily serve to conceal the advisers' direct participation in these operations while accompanying their trainees.

Considerable evidence surfaced of a US role in the ground fighting as well. There were numerous reports of armed Americans spotted in combat areas,[28] a report by CBS News of US advisers "fighting side by side" with government troops,[29] and reports of other Americans, some ostensibly mercenaries, killed in action.[30] The extent of American mercenary involvement in El Salvador is not known, but Lawrence Bailey, a former US Marine, has stated that he was part of a team of 40 American soldiers of fortune paid by wealthy Salvadorean families living in Miami to protect their plantations from takeover by the rebels.[31]

During the Iran-Contra hearings in 1987, it was disclosed that at least until 1985, CIA paramilitary personnel had been organizing and leading special Salvadorean army units into combat areas to track down guerrillas and call in air strikes.[32]

These bit-by-bit disclosures pointed to a frequent, if not routine, American involvement in the ongoing combat. In September 1988 another news item related that US military advisers were caught in a gun battle between Salvadorean army forces and guerrillas and that, in "self-defense", they opened fire on the rebels.[33]

The degree of overall control of the military operation by the United States is perhaps best captured by an excerpt from an interview given to *Playboy* magazine in 1984 by President Duarte, one of the few Christian Democrat leaders of the earlier days still working within the government.

Playboy: Do the American military advisers also tell you how to run the war?

   Duarte: This is the problem, no? The root of this problem is that the aid is given under such conditions that its use is really decided by the Americans and not by us. Decisions like how many planes or helicopters we buy, how we spend our money, how many trucks we need, how many bullets and of what caliber, how many pairs of boots and where our priorities should be—all of that ... And all the money is spent over there. We never even see a penny of it, because everything arrives here already paid for.[34]

In Duarte's previous incarnation as a government opponent, his view of the Yanquis was even harsher. US policy in Latin America, he said in 1969, was designed to "maintain the Iberoamerican countries in a condition of direct dependence upon the international political decisions most beneficial to the United States, both at the hemisphere and world levels. Thus [the North Americans] preach to us of democracy while everywhere they support dictatorships."[35]

Duarte's ideology, however, appears to have been a flexible and marketable commodity. At some point in the 1970s, if not earlier, he began to covertly supply the CIA with intelligence.[36]

A Human Face

On 28 January 1982, President Reagan certified to Congress that the El Salvador government was "making a concerted and significant effort to comply with internationally recognized human rights" and that it was "achieving substantial control over all elements of its own armed forces, so as to bring to an end the indiscriminate torture and murder of Salvadorean citizens by these forces." The language was that imposed by Congress upon the administration if the flow of arms and American military personnel was to continue.

Two days earlier, the American and foreign press had carried the story of how government troops had engaged in a massacre of the people of the village of El Mozote in December. From 700 to 1,000 persons were reported killed, mostly the elderly, women and children. When a very long, detailed account of this incident appeared eventually, in 1993, it became more apparent than ever that this was one of the most repulsive and cruelest massacres of the 20th century carried out by ground troops face-to-face with their victims— people hacked to death by machetes, many beheaded, a child thrown in the air and caught on a bayonet, an orgy of rapes of very young girls before they were killed ... "If we don't kill them [the children] now, they'll just grow up to be guerrillas," barked an army officer to a reluctant soldier ... anti-communism at its zenith.

Both immediately and thereafter, the massacre was attended by denials and a coverup by the State Department, with abundant media complicity.[37] The State Department's defense of its position before a congressional committee left the committee members conspicuously underwhelmed, even though the congressmen did not yet know the full story.[38]

Two days after the president's certification, the world could read how Salvadorean soldiers had pulled about 20 people out of their beds in the middle of the night, tortured them, and then killed them, meanwhile finding the time to rape several teenage girls.[39]

Earlier the same month, the *New York Times* had published an interview with a deserter from the Salvadorean Army who described a class where severe methods of torture were demonstrated on teenage prisoners. He stated that eight US military advisers, apparently Green Berets, were present. Watching "will make you feel more like a man," a Salvadorean officer apprised the recruits, adding that they should "not feel pity of anyone" but only "hate for those who are enemies of our country."[40]

Another Salvadorean, a former member of the National Guard, later testified: "I belonged to a squad of twelve. We devoted ourselves to torture, and to finding people whom we were told were guerrillas. I was trained in Panama for nine months by the [unintelligible] of the United States for anti-guerrilla warfare. Part of the time we were instructed about torture."[41]

Officers of the National Guard were also trained in the United States. In August 1986, CBS Television reported that three senior Guard officers who had been linked to rightwing death squads received training at a police academy in Phoenix.[42]

In 1984, Amnesty International reported that it had received:

> regular, often daily, reports identifying El Salvador's regular security and military units as responsible for the torture, "disappearance" and killing of non-combatant civilians from all sectors of Salvadorean society ... A number of patients have allegedly been removed from their beds or operating theaters and tortured and murdered ... Types of torture reported ... by those who have survived arrest and interrogation included beatings, sexual abuse, use of chemicals to disorient, mock executions, and the burning of flesh with sulphuric acid.[43]

In light of the above, and many other reports of a similar nature,[44] it can be appreciated that the Reagan administration had to exercise some creativity in getting around congressional hesitation about continued military aid to the government of El Salvador. Thus it was that in March 1984 the administration tacked on a request for additional military aid to legislation to send US food supplies to starving Africans.[45] (A few days later, it tacked on a request for support of the Nicaraguan contras to a bill to provide emergency fuel spending for the poor in parts of the United States which were suffering a severe winter.)[46]

Death squad executions ... military massacres ... the legion of the disappeared ... the numbers reached well into the tens of thousands. And the death squads may have reached their arm into the United States. A number of Americans and Salvadoreans living in Los Angeles and working with refugees or actively opposing US military aid to El Salvador received death threats in 1987. Rev. Luis Olivares, a Catholic priest whose church is part of the "sanctuary" movement, was sent an anonymous letter bearing the letters "EM", which were often found on the doors or buildings of people who were targeted in El Salvador. The letters stand for *Escuadrón Muerto* [death squad].[47]

In July 1987, a Salvadorean woman named Yanira Corea who had received threatening phone calls and letters was kidnapped outside the Los Angeles office of the Committee in Solidarity with the People of El Salvador (CISPES). Two men, speaking with what she described as Salvadorean accents, forced her at knifepoint into a van, interrogated her about her political activities and colleagues, cut her hands with a knife, burnt her fingers with cigarettes, sexually assaulted her with a stick, then raped her. A month earlier, she had narrowly escaped being abducted, along with her three-year-old son. Other activists had their cars smashed or vandalized.[48]

For several years under the Reagan administration, the FBI conducted a nationwide investigation of CISPES. During this period, some of the organization's offices were broken into with nothing of value taken except files. "It is imperative at this time to formulate some plan of attack against CISPES ... ", reads one FBI teletype later made public.[49]

On some days during the 1980s, Washington officials issued warnings to the Salvadorean government to improve its human rights record, or told Congress that the record was improving, or told the world how much worse that record would be if not for American influence. On most other days, the United States continued to build up each and every component of the military and paramilitary forces engaged in the atrocities. In 1984, in an interview with the *New York Times*, Col. Roberto Eulalio Santibáñez, a former Salvadorean military official who had served at the highest level of the security police, confirmed—for those who may still have entertained doubts—that the network of death squads had been shaped by leading Salvadorean officials and was still directed by them. He also revealed that one of these officials, Col. Nicolas Carranza, the head of the Treasury Police, which "have long been considered the least disciplined and most brutal of the Salvadorean security forces", had been receiving more than $90,000 a year during the previous five or six years from the CIA. Although some members of the Treasury Police were linked by the Reagan administration itself to death-squad activities, the United States continued to train and equip them.[50]

In a visit to San Salvador in February 1989, Vice President Dan Quayle told army leaders that death squad killings and other human rights violations attributed to the military had to be ended. Ten days later, the US-trained Atlacatl Battalion—which was believed to have a US trainer assigned to it at all times—attacked a guerrilla field hospital, killing at least ten people, including five patients, a doctor and a nurse, and raping at least two of the female victims before shooting them. Sources close to the El Salvador military said afterward that Quayle's warning was not taken seriously, but as rhetoric aimed at the US Congress and the American public.[51]

In October 1989, former Salvadorean Army commando Cesar Vielman Joya Martinez, in an interview on the CBS Evening News, related that he and others in his unit—the intelligence section of the army's First Brigade—had acted as a clandestine death squad, that the two US military advisers attached to the unit were aware of the assassinations, although they refused to hear the details, and that the advisers supplied money to his unit that helped maintain two civilian vehicles used for death-squad operations and a safehouse that served as a secret base of operations and storage of weapons. In subsequent interviews with the American press, Joya Martinez stated that the advisers had used the names Mauricio Torres and Raul Antonio Lazo, that his unit had carried out 74 assassinations of Salvadorean dissidents between April and July of 1989, and that he himself had been personally involved in eight torture murders. Apropos of deadly bombings in El Salvador in November of dissident organizations (a union hall and an organization of mothers of the disappeared), he added that his unit had received explosives training from US advisers. The Salvadorean Embassy in Washington, while denying any government involvement in death-squad activities, did confirm that "Joya Martinez was a member of the intelligence unit of the First Brigade".[52]

In July 1990, an aide to Rep. Joseph Moakley (D-Mass.), chairman of the Speaker's Task Force on El Salvador, declared: "The fact that Joya Martinez has been in the U.S. since last August, given all kinds of interviews, been arrested, and no one from the government has bothered to question him, seems pretty strange, unless people don't want to find the answers."[53]

On the twelfth of that month Joya Martinez had been arrested for having illegally entered the United States after being deported six years earlier. After a lengthy legal battle, he was ordered deported back to El Salvador in October 1992. His supporters in the United States expressed their concern about his safety in El Salvador, to which a State Department official responded, presumably with a straight face, that Joya Martinez "has admitted to killings and torture and it would be callous to the victims to prevent him from standing trial."[54]

A few weeks after Joya Martinez went public in the United States, one of the most shocking atrocities in this war of shocking atrocities occurred. Six Jesuit priests at the University of Central America in San Salvador were shot to death in cold blood at their campus residence, along with their housekeeper and her young daughter. A witness, whom the killers failed to observe, Lucia Barrera de Cerna, said she saw five armed men in uniform carry out the murders. The Salvadorean military—whom the Roman Catholic order had often criticized for human rights violations—were the immediate and logical suspects. Because of an extraordinary outcry against the crime, in the United States and internationally, including the creation of the special congressional task force referred to above, two months later nine officers and enlisted men were arrested—a platoon from the Atlacatl

Battalion, seven of whom, it turned out, had only two days before the murders participated in combat training exercises supervised by the U.S. Special Forces (Green Berets) in El Salvador.

Almost two years passed before any of those arrested were convicted of the crime—two relatively low-level officers; their higher-ups who gave the order were not touched. Yet, this was an achievement in a country where thousands of people had been killed by military death squads, and no officer had ever before been tried, let alone convicted, for murder or other human-rights abuse. The Salvadorean military tolerated the trial of the officers because Congress had made prosecution of the killers a condition for continuing military aid.

During the two-year period, as well as after the convictions, officials of the Bush administration appeared to be trying to thwart the investigation and aid in a coverup, by such tactics as the following:

a) grossly intimidating Cerna and labeling her a liar;

b) refusing on grounds of national security to provide a Salvadorean court with classified documents that dealt with the case; withholding, on the same grounds, substantive material from journalists making Freedom of Information Act requests;

c) refusing for a long time to allow questioning, by the investigating judge, of US Army Major Eric Buckland, stationed in El Salvador, who had learned of the Salvadorean military's culpability shortly after the murders from Salvadorean Col. Carlos Aviles; then imposing a series of conditions on Buckland's questioning that served to conceal much of his story;

d) putting Buckland through such horrendous interrogation that he underwent an apparent nervous breakdown;

e) immediately informing the Salvadorean high command about what Aviles had revealed to Buckland (which caused Aviles much grief).

Father Charles Beirne, vice rector of the Jesuit university, declared in 1991 that "the Americans were helping to protect the [Salvadorean army] high command all along. They were afraid the whole house of cards would fall if the investigation went any further." A year later, United Nations investigators were still complaining that the United States was slow in turning over vital information about the case.[55]

The cruelty level of the guerrillas' military and political campaign generally stood in sharp contrast to that of the government. *Newsweek* reported in 1983 that when the rebels "capture a town, they treat the civilians well, paying for food and holding destruction to a minimum. And they have begun to free most of the government troops they capture, which helps to persuade other soldiers to surrender rather than fight to the death."[56] Eventually, however, the guerrillas began to treat civilians more harshly, in particular those suspected of informing or of other collaboration with the government, or those refusing to collaborate with rebel forces; some peasants reportedly were forced to leave their villages and farms as punishment; several village mayors were killed; young men were forcibly recruited to join the rebels.

However, given the numerous instances of disinformation disseminated by the Salvadorean government about the rebels, reports of guerrilla ruthlessness must be approached with caution. The following case is instructive (see the notes for reference to other examples):

In February 1988, the *New York Times*, reported that:

Villagers say guerrillas publicly executed two peasants ... because they had applied for and received new voter registration cards. According to the villagers, the guerrillas placed the voting cards of [the two men] in their mouths after executing them as a warning to others not to take part in the elections.[57]

The story was included in a State Department booklet to highlight the guerrillas' "campaign of intimidation and terrorism". The booklet was mailed to Congress, newspaper editors, and other opinion makers. But the story, it turned out, was the invention of a Salvadorean Army propaganda specialist who had placed it in the San Salvador newspaper *El Mundo*. From there it was picked up by the *New York Times* reporter who gave the impression that he had interviewed villagers with firsthand knowledge of the incident, instead of attributing the story to the military as had *El Mundo*. The *Times* later recanted the story.[58]

Outside Agitators

"Sometimes I feel like Sisyphus," said a senior Reagan administration official involved in developing US Latin America policy in March 1982. "Every time we head up the hill to explain or justify our policy, the stone comes crashing down on top of us."[59]

Two weeks earlier, Secretary of State Alexander Haig had asserted that the United States had "overwhelming and irrefutable" evidence that the insurgents were controlled from outside by non-Salvadoreans. Haig, however, declined to provide any details of the evidence, saying it would jeopardize intelligence sources. Challenged to prove his charges two days later, the good general insisted that the United States had "unchallengeable" evidence of Nicaraguan and Cuban involvement in the command and control of the operation in El Salvador and, oddly enough, only the day before a Nicaraguan military man had been captured there. As it turned out, according to the Mexican Embassy in San Salvador, the man was a student on his way back to school in Mexico from Nicaragua, traveling overland because he couldn't afford to fly.[60]

The following week, a Nicaraguan was captured fighting with the guerrillas. He told US Embassy and Salvadorean Army officials that he had been trained in Cuba and Ethiopia, then sent to El Salvador by the Nicaraguan government. The State Department was understandably excited. It presented the young man at a press conference in Washington, at which time he declared that he had never been to Cuba or Ethiopia, had joined the guerrillas on his own, and had made his previous statements under torture by his Salvadorean captors. He added that he had never seen another Nicaraguan or Cuban in El Salvador and denied that Nicaragua had provided aid to the guerrillas.[61]

"Then there were two Nicaraguan air force defectors," reported *Time* magazine during the same period, "who were scheduled to bear witness to their country's involvement in El Salvador but by week's end were judged 'not ready' to face the press." *Time* entitled its story: "A Lot of Show, but No Tell: The U.S. bungles its evidence of foreign subversion in El Salvador."[62]

In January 1981, US diplomats disclosed that five boats had landed in El Salvador containing 100 "well-armed, well-trained guerrillas", allegedly from Nicaragua. They knew the boats had come from Nicaragua because "they were made from wood of trees not native to El Salvador."[63] No sign, dead or alive, of any of the hundred invaders was ever found, however.

One hundred seemed to be the number of choice for the Reagan administration. That was the count of Cuban combat troops, said a senior State Department policy maker, who were sent to El Salvador in the fall of 1981 by way of Nicaragua. "They were brought in clandestinely and given operational responsibilities in El Salvador," he asserted.[64] The later whereabouts and actions of the Cubans likewise remained a mystery.

The world was also informed that Soviet and Chinese weapons had been seized from rebels and this was cited as further proof of outside Communist aid.[65] The weapons capture may have been real—although the CIA has long had warehouses full of Communist weapons of all kinds, suitable for all occasions—but then what were we to make of the US, Israeli, Belgian and German weapons which, by Washington's admission a month later, were also to be found amongst the rebels?[66] The world arms traffic is indeed wide open and fluid. (In neighboring Honduras, the US-supported contras were using Soviet-made missiles to shoot down Soviet-made helicopters of Nicaragua.)[67] Moreover, the Salvadorean rebels captured weapons from government forces and they claimed that they also purchased arms from corrupt Salvadorean Army officers, a practice common to other Latin American guerrilla wars. A source cited by the *New York Times* corroborated the rebels' claim.[68]

The centerpiece of the Reagan administration's campaign to prove the international-conspiracy nature of the revolution in El Salvador was its White Paper issued a month after taking office and based largely on purported "captured guerrilla documents", some of which were included in the report. Amongst the various analyses of the White Paper which cast grave doubts upon its claims was the one in the *Wall Street Journal* by Jonathan Kwitny. This included an interview with a State Department official, Jon D. Glassman, who was given the major credit for the White Paper. Admitted Mr Glassman: parts of the paper were possibly "misleading" and "over-embellished" ... it contained "mistakes" and "guessing". Said the *Wall Street Journal*: "A close examination ... indicates that, if anything, Mr. Glassman may be understating the case in his concession that the White Paper contains mistakes and guessing."

Amongst the many specific shortcomings of the paper pointed out in the article was that:

> Statistics of armament shipments into El Salvador, supposedly drawn directly from the documents, were extrapolated, Mr. Glassman concedes. And in questionable ways, it seems. Much information in the White Paper can't be found in the documents at all.[69]

It was not merely the accuracy of the White Paper that was questioned, but the authenticity of the documents themselves. Apropos of this, former US Ambassador to El Salvador, Robert White (sacked by Reagan because of excessive commitment to human rights and reforms), commented: "The only thing that even makes me think that these documents were genuine was that they proved so little."[70]

When pressed to state what proof his government had of Nicaraguan intervention, President Duarte declined to answer on the grounds that the world would not believe him anyway.[71] But President Reagan had some evidence to offer. He saw the hand of foreign masters pulling strings in the fact that demonstrators in Canada carried "the same signs" as demonstrators in the United States: "U. S. Out of El Salvador."[72]

But all of this was essentially besides the point. Revolutions are not exported like so many cartons of soap. We have seen what the circumstances were in El Salvador for decades which finally provoked people to take up the gun. Ambassador White, no champion of the rebels' cause, observed that "The revolution situation came about in El Salvador because you had what was one of the most selfish oligarchies the world has ever seen, combined with a corrupt security force ... Whether Cuba existed or not, you would still have a revolutionary situation in El Salvador."[73]

Education-minister-turned-guerrilla, Salvador Samayoa, speaking in 1981, asserted that US charges that the Soviet bloc was directing the guerrilla movement "reveals Washington's deep ignorance of our movement". He pointed out that three of the five guerrilla groups that made up the Farabundo Marti National Liberation Front (FMLN) were "strongly anti-Soviet". Samayoa added: "To say we are run by Cuba because we have a relationship with Cuba is like saying we're a Christian movement because we have received enormous help from the church. ... Instead of seeing us as Communist subversives, the U.S. should see us as a people struggling to survive."[74]

Despite American patrol boats in the Gulf of Fonseca (which separates El Salvador from Nicaragua), AWAC surveillance planes in the skies over the Caribbean, and an abundance of aerial photographs, despite a large US radar installation in Honduras manned by 50 American military technicians, the finest electronic monitoring equipment modern technology had to offer, and all the informers that CIA money could buy[75]... despite it all, the Reagan administration singularly failed to support its case that the fires of the Salvadorean revolution were stoked by Nicaraguan and Cuban coals; nor by the Soviet Union, Vietnam, the PLO, Ethiopia, or any of the other countries indicted at one time or another as important suppliers of military aid.

In any case, whatever military support the Salvadorean insurgents actually received from abroad—necessarily limited to what could be carried by the occasional clandestine small truck or boat—plainly did not belong in the same league, nor on the same planet, as the huge transport-planefuls and shipfuls of American aid, in all its forms, to the Salvadorean government. The United States had waged ruthless war against the Salvadorean revolution, and threatened worse—in April 1991, Chairman of the Joint Chiefs of Staff, General Colin Powell, announced that "if necessary, [the civil war in El Salvador] can be resolved the way it was in the Persian Gulf."[76]

In early 1992, the war came to an official end when a United Nations commission, after a year-and-a-half effort, finally got the warring sides to agree to a cease fire and a peace agreement. A major offensive launched by the guerrillas in late 1989—in which they "brought the war home" to wealthy neighborhoods and Americans in the capital—had made clear to Washington and its Salvadorean allies, once again, finally, that the war was unwinnable. In February 1990, Gen. Maxwell Thurman, the head of the US Southern Command, told Congress that the El Salvador government was not able to defeat the rebels and that the only way to end the fighting was through negotiation.[77] Moreover, the ostensible end of the cold war had undermined the United States' professed rationale for—and may have relaxed its obsession with—defeating "communism" in El Salvador. At the same time, Congress was balking more and more about continuing military aid to the Salvadorean government, an attitude that had been growing ever since the November 1989 murder of the Jesuit priests.

One of the many provisions of the complex peace agreement was the establishment of a UN Commission of the Truth "to investigate the worst acts of violence since 1980". In March of 1993 the Commission presented its report. Among its findings and conclusions were the following:

The military forces, supported by the government and the civilian establishment, were plainly the main perpetrators of massacres, executions, torture and kidnappings during the civil war. These acts could not be blamed on the excesses of war but on premeditated and ideologically inspired decisions to kill.

The commission called for the dismissal of more than 40 high-ranking military personnel—including Defense Minister Gen. Rene Emilio Ponce, a long-time favorite of US officials—whom it found had given the orders that led to the murders of the priests, and stipulated that none should ever be allowed to return to military or security duty and should be banned from other public and political life for 10 years.

Dismissal and a 10-year ban was also specified for government officials and bureaucrats who abused human rights or took part in a cover-up of the abuses, including the President of the Supreme Court. (Right-wing parties in the Salvadorean National Assembly quickly pushed through an amnesty law barring prosecution for any crimes committed during the war.)

Several leaders of the left were singled out for the assassinations of 11 mayors during the war.

A special investigation of death squads was called for. These squads, said the report, were "often operated by the military and supported by powerful businessmen, landowners and some leading politicians." (The peace accords did not put an end to this: dozens of leaders and members of the FMLN were assassinated during 1992 and 1993, as well as a few from the right.)

Cited as the most notorious of the death squad leaders by the report was Roberto d'Aubuisson, the principal founder of the Nationalist Republican Alliance (Arena) party, the party of the country's current president, Alfredo Cristiani. D'Aubuisson, the report confirmed, hired the sharpshooter who killed Archbishop Romero.

Other sins laid at the doorstep of the government were the rapes and killings of three American nuns and a female religious worker in 1980, the murder of two American labor advisers in 1981, and the assassination, in 1982, of four Dutch journalists, whose reports were evidently considered favorable to the guerrillas.

The Commission did not focus on any American role in the abuses and cover-up. "The role of the United States in El Salvador is a role more effectively studied by the U.S. Congress," said Commission member Thomas Buergenthal, an American jurist, at a news conference. However, the Commission did chastise the United States for failing to rein in Salvadorean exiles in Miami who "helped administer death squad activities between 1980 and 1983, with apparently little attention from the U.S. government. Such use of American territory for acts of terrorism abroad should be investigated and never allowed to be repeated."[78] (Cuban exiles, of course, have been using Miami as a base for terrorism abroad, as well as in the US, for 30 years.)

Members of Congress, outraged by the findings of the Commission of the Truth, called for the declassification of State Department, Defense Department, and CIA files on El Salvador to help determine whether the Reagan and Bush administrations had concealed evidence from Congress about widespread human rights abuses by their Salvadorean allies. "It [the Commission's report] simply verifies what a number of us knew all through the '80s," said Rep. David Obey, "that our own government was lying like hell to us." The report proves that the Reagan administration was willing to "lie ... and ... certify to anything ... to get the money it wanted."[79]

Various of the more than 12,000 once-secret documents released by the Clinton administration unequivocally confirmed Obey's charge. Other papers revealed that ...

The current Vice President, Francisco Merino, had organized death squads.

The CIA referred to Roberto d'Aubuisson as "egocentric, reckless and perhaps mentally unstable"; he trafficked in drugs and smuggled arms; his paramilitary unit was responsible for thousands of murders; and in 1983 he and his advisers were invited by American Ambassador Deane Hinton to have lunch with the visiting US representative to the United Nations, Jeane Kirkpatrick. Six years later, shortly before the CIA reported that d'Aubuisson's inner circle had plotted to assassinate President Cristiani, Ambassador William G. Walker invited him to the embassy's Fourth of July party.[80]

American military advisers trained a militia of some 50 wealthy Salvadoreans, ostensibly for them to be able to defend their own lavish homes against a rebel attack, but the group was actually linked to d'Aubuisson and their militia was a "cover for the recruitment, training and possible dispatch of paramilitary civilian death squads". Ambassador Walker halted the training as soon as he learned of it, despite protests from the chief of the US military advisory mission. (Another memo, written by a Defense Department official, argued that the wealthy Salvadoreans might fund death squads, but would not get blood on their own hands.)[81]

On 20 March 1994, the ruling party Arena and its main ally scored a victory in elections held to choose a new president, National Assembly, and hundreds of municipal governments. With the exception of a few reforms touching upon civil liberties, whose significance remains to be seen, the outcome left the society at essentially the same place it was in 1980 when the war had just begun and José Napoleón Duarte had said: "For fifty years the same people had all the power, all the money, all the jobs, all the education ..." One could now say: "For more than sixty years ..."

Why had more than half the people of El Salvador, most of them very poor, voted for parties intimately connected with not only the wealthy, but with death squads? The new president, Armando Calderon Sol, had long and close ties to death-squad godfather Roberto d'Aubuisson, a large portrait of whom hung in his office. The declassified documents referred to above raised questions about Calderon Sol himself—connections to a kidnapping and to a group of young Arena militants who bombed the Ministry of Agriculture and wreaked other havoc in the early 1980s in an attempt to destabilize the government whose new agrarian reform was supposed to take land from the wealthy.

Arena's sophisticated multimillion-dollar campaign relied heavily on nurturing two kinds of fears: the traditional fear of "communism", inculcated by decades of authoritarian rule; and the supposed economic incompetence of the left, as typified by the Sandinista rule in Nicaragua. Further, ignoring their own violent history, Arena portrayed the left as terrorists who were exclusively responsible for the war's death and destruction.

How honest and fair had the actual voting been? Was the right willing to end a half-century of political exclusion of the left? Besides having a great deal more money at its disposal than its opponents, the Arena party in power had controlled the press in El Salvador for many years—the one daily paper, *Diario Latino*, which had dared to show a brief independence, was destroyed by bombs.[82] Moreover, the makeup of the Supreme Electoral Tribunal (TSE), which supervised the election, was based on the election of 1991 which the FMLN had boycotted; it was thus dominated by Arena, with no one from the FMLN.

Many points of contention were raised about the voting, such as the following:

A large number of people who registered to vote were unable to do so because they didn't receive their voting card. According to United Nations monitors, as of 1 February these cases came to more than half a million, equal to 20 percent of the electorate. After the election, the FMLN estimated the number of such non-voters at 340,000.

74,000 other applicants were rejected because they couldn't produce a birth certificate; often this was because the local office of records had been destroyed in the war.

Another large block of people held valid voting cards but couldn't vote because they had no transportation to a distant polling station. This was exacerbated, reportedly, by a slowdown in bus service by bus companies owned by Arena supporters and the Arena-controlled bus drivers' union.

Many made it to the polling stations with their voting cards only to be kept from voting because their names did not appear on the voter-registration lists, or were spelled incorrectly (at least 25,000 such cases according to the UN; several times that, said the FMLN).

Other potential voters left the stations without casting their ballots because very long lines and an extremely cumbersome and snail-paced processing system left them still waiting when the polls closed.

These problems of course affected the poor, the rural, the less educated, and the first-time voters the most, the base of the FMLN's support.

The TSE refused international advice, declined to spend money to transport voters to the polls, and made voting unnecessarily complicated, UN observers said. "There was frightening mismanagement of the election beyond our worst expectations," said a senior UN official. "There was widespread lack of trust by the electorate before the voting, [and] now it's much worse. The [TSE] is completely discredited and has therefore tarnished the election."

The FMLN claimed the irregularities cheated the party out of several municipal and legislative seats, a contention lent credence by the UN observers who stated that thousands of people were denied voting cards in 30 towns where the FMLN was strong. The party challenged the results in 37 cities and towns, but the TSE rejected all the claims—a decision that Rafael Lopez Pintor, who headed the UN electoral division, called "shocking".

A team of observers representing the US government also said it was "troubled" that "many of the procedures cited as administrative defects" in previous elections continued to be practiced.

In the days immediately following the vote, election authorities delayed the release of official results. Then on the third day, they abruptly cut off access to party monitors to computerized tabulations. The FMLN said that initial tabulations showed that many ballot boxes contained more votes than the legal maximum of 400, some of them two to three times as many. They also claimed that in San Miguel, one of the country's largest cities, a group of Arena militants had absconded with 15 ballot boxes.

As it turned out, in the announced result for the presidency, Arena got 641,000 votes, 49 percent of the total, while the Democratic Coalition, which included the FMLN, was credited with 326,000 votes, or 25 percent. Failure of any party to win a majority necessitated a run-off election a month later, at which time Arena won 68 percent of the vote to the Coalition's 32 percent. Because the winner of the run-off was a completely foregone conclusion, there were undoubtedly many poor people who didn't vote because they were unwilling to go through the great inconvenience and uncertainty a second time.

There was also the matter of intimidation. According to observers from the Committee in Solidarity with the People of El Salvador (CISPES):

> Meanwhile, army helicopters buzzed cities where the opposition was strong. Soldiers set up checkpoints and machine-gun nests in towns traumatized by army massacres during the war. The government did its best to instill fear in the electorate, and must have scared many voters into staying home.

Before the election, some workers were warned that if the FMLN won, heads would roll, or they would be fired. Inasmuch as a polling official tore off the corner of each ballot, containing the same number as on the ballot, a voter could see that someone could save his number and check how he voted later.

The *Los Angeles Times* reported the story of the master of ceremonies at a rally staged by Arena, attended by a number of peasants, farmers and market vendors.

"All those who support Arena, raise your hats!" the emcee implored the crowd.

A few people lifted their hats.

"All those who support Arena, raise your hats!" he tried again. "And those who don't raise their hats are terengos!" he added, invoking a slang word for "terrorists" used by the army throughout this country's brutal civil war.

A lot of people took their hats off.[83]

For the benefit of which Salvadoreans did Arena remain in power? For which of them had 75,000 civilians been killed? For whom was the US Treasury reduced by $6 billion? Two reports from the *New York Times* ...

Over canapes served by hovering waiters at a party, a guest said she was convinced that God had created two distinct classes of people: the rich and people to serve them. She described herself as charitable for allowing the poor to work as her servants. "It's the best you can do," she said.

The woman's outspokenness was unusual, but her attitude is shared by a large segment of the Salvadoran upper class.

The separation between classes is so rigid that even small expressions of kindness across the divide are viewed with suspicion. When an American, visiting an ice cream store, remarked that he was shopping for a birthday party for his maid's child, other store patrons immediately stopped talking and began staring at the American. Finally, an astonished woman in the checkout line spoke out. "You must be kidding," she said.

One of their class, who had had enough and was leaving, commented to the *Times*: "I can't accept the fact that if you're born a peasant here, you die a peasant and your children are going to be peasants. There's no vision that kids of farmhands should be going to Harvard and running this country one day. There's no vision of a modern society."[84]

After taking part in Washington's decade-long effort to train and reform the Salvadoran Army, many American military advisers have left here angry over the Salvadorans' resistance to change ... [they] say they feel manipulated and betrayed by the Salvadoran officers. ... the advisers described Salvadoran officers as being mainly interested in amassing wealth and power, as willing to deprive troops of equipment to further the officers' own ends and as allowing the regular killing or mistreatment of prisoners. ... None went so far as to say the effort to help the Salvadoran armed forces in their war against a leftist insurgency had been futile. They thought human rights abuses would have been worse or that the guerrillas might have won the war without their presence.[85]

The *Times* apparently did not ask the advisers whether they believed that the United States government had in some way been *forced* to take sides in the civil war. And if not, what had their government's ultimate motive been? And if so, why had they not taken the side of the insurgents? And how bad would the human rights abuses have been if the armed forces had not been provided by Washington with a never-ending supply of every weapon and implement and training known to man to bring destruction, pain and suffering to the greatest number of people?

55. Haiti 1986-1994
Who will rid me of this man?

When I give food to the poor,
they call me a saint.
When I ask why the poor have no food,
they call me a communist.

Dom Helder Câmara

What does the government of the United States do when faced with a choice between supporting: (a) a group of totalitarian military thugs guilty of murdering thousands, systematic torture, widespread rape, and leaving severely mutilated corpses in the streets ... or (b) a non-violent priest, legally elected to the presidency by a landslide, whom the thugs have overthrown in a coup? ...

But what if the priest is a "leftist"?

During the Duvalier family dictatorship—Francois "Papa Doc", 1957-71, followed by Jean-Claude "Baby Doc", 1971-86, both anointed President for Life by papa—the United States trained and armed Haiti's counter-insurgency forces, although most American military aid to the country was covertly channeled through Israel, thus sparing Washington embarrassing questions about supporting brutal governments. After Jean-Claude was forced into exile in February 1986, fleeing to France aboard a US Air Force jet, Washington resumed open assistance. And while Haiti's wretched rabble were celebrating the end of three decades of Duvalierism, the United States was occupied in preserving it under new names.

Within three weeks of Jean-Claude's departure, the US announced that it was providing Haiti with $26.6 million in economic and military aid, and in April it was reported that "Another $4 million is being sought to provide the Haitian Army with trucks, training and communications gear to allow it to move around the country and maintain order."[1] Maintaining order in Haiti translates to domestic repression and control; and in the 21 months between Duvalier's abdication and the scheduled elections of November 1987, the successor Haitian governments were responsible for more civilian deaths than Baby Doc had managed in 15 years.[2]

The CIA was meanwhile arranging for the release from prison, and safe exile abroad, of two of its Duvalier-era contacts, both notorious police chiefs, thus saving them from possible death sentences for murder and torture, and acting contrary to the public's passionate wish for retribution against its former tormenters.[3] In September, Haiti's main trade union leader, Yves Richard, declared that Washington was working to undermine the left before the coming elections. US aid organizations, he said, were encouraging people in the countryside to identify and reject the entire left as "communist",[4] though the country clearly had a fundamental need for reformers and sweeping changes. Haiti was, and is, the Western Hemisphere's best known economic, medical, political, judicial, educational, and ecological basket case.

At this time Jean-Bertrand Aristide was a charismatic priest with a broad following in the poorest slums of Haiti, the only church figure to speak out against repression during the

Duvalier years. He now denounced the military-dominated elections and called upon Haitians to reject the entire process. His activities figured prominently enough in the electoral campaign to evoke a strong antipathy from US officials. Ronald Reagan, Aristide later wrote, considered him to be a communist.[5] And Assistant Secretary of State for Inter-American Affairs, Elliott Abrams, saw fit to attack Aristide while praising the Haitian government in a letter to *Time* magazine during the election campaign.[6]

The Catholic priest first came to prominence in Haiti as a proponent of liberation theology, which seeks to blend the teachings of Christ with inspiring the poor to organize and resist their oppression. When asked why the CIA might have sought to oppose Aristide, a senior official with the Senate Intelligence Committee stated that "Liberation theology proponents are not too popular at the agency. Maybe second only to the Vatican for not liking liberation theology are the people at Langley [CIA headquarters]."

Aristide urged a boycott of the elections, saying "The army is our first enemy." The CIA, on the other hand, funded some of the candidates. The Agency later insisted that the purpose of the funding program had not been to oppose Aristide but to provide a "free and open election", by which was meant helping some candidates who didn't have enough money and diminishing Aristide's attempt to have a low turnout, which would have "reduced the election's validity". It is not known which candidates the CIA funded or why the Agency or the State Department, which reportedly chose the candidates to support, were concerned about such goals in Haiti, when the same electoral situation exists permanently in the United States.

The CIA was "involved in a range of support for a range of candidates", said an intelligence official directly active in the operation. Countering Aristide's impressive political strength appears to be the only logical explanation for the CIA's involvement, which was authorized by President Reagan and the National Security Council.

When the Senate Intelligence Committee demanded to know exactly what the CIA was doing in Haiti and which candidates it was supporting, the Agency balked. Eventually, the committee ordered the covert electoral action to cease. A high-ranking source working for the committee said the reason the program was killed was that "there are some of us who believe in the neutrality of elections."[7] Nevertheless, it cannot be stated with any certainty that the program was actually halted.

The elections scheduled for 29 November 1987 were postponed because of violence. In the rescheduled elections held in January, the candidate favored by the military government was declared the winner in balloting widely perceived as rigged, and in the course of which the CIA was involved in an aborted attempt of unknown nature to influence the elections.[8]

There followed more than two years of regular political violence, coup attempts, and repression, casting off the vestiges of the Duvalier dictatorship and establishing a new one, until, in March 1990, the current military dictator, General Prosper Avril, was forced by widespread protests to abdicate and was replaced by a civilian government of sorts, but with the military still calling important shots.

The United States is not happy with "chaos" in its client states. It's bad for control, it's bad for business, it's unpredictable who will come out on top, perhaps another Fidel Castro. It was the danger of "massive internal uprisings" that induced the United States to inform Jean-Claude Duvalier that it was time for him to venture a life of struggle on the French Riviera,[9] and a similar chaotic situation that led the US Ambassador to suggest to Avril that it was an apt moment to retire; transportation into exile for the good general was once again courtesy of Uncle Sam.[10]

Thus it was that the American Embassy in Port-au-Prince pressured the Haitian officer corps to allow a new election. Neither the embassy nor Aristide himself at this time had reason to expect that he would be a candidate in the election scheduled for December, although he had already been expelled from his religious order, with the blessings of the Vatican, because, amongst other things, of "incitement to hatred and violence, and a glorifying of class struggle". Aristide's many followers and friends had often tried in vain to persuade him to run for office. Now they finally succeeded, and in October he became the candidate of a loose coalition of reformist parties and organizations.[11]

On the eve of the election, former US Ambassador to the UN, Andrew Young, visited Aristide and asked him to sign a letter accepting Marc Bazin, the US-backed and funded candidate, as president should Bazin win. Young reportedly said there was fear that if Aristide lost, his followers would take to the streets and reject the results.[12] Young was said to be acting on behalf of his mentor, former president Jimmy Carter, but presumably the White House also had their finger in the pie, evidencing their concern about Aristide's charisma and potential as a leader outside their control.

Despite a campaign marred by terror and intimidation, nearly a thousand UN and Organization of American States (OAS) observers and an unusually scrupulous Haitian general insured that a relatively honest balloting took place, in which Aristide was victorious with 67.5 percent of the vote. "People chose him over 10 comparatively bourgeois candidates," wrote an American Haiti scholar who was an international election observer, "because of his outspoken and uncompromising opposition to the old ways."[13] Aristide's support actually included a progressive bourgeois element as well as his larger popular base.

The president-priest took office in February 1991 after a coup attempt against him in January failed. By June, one could read in the *Washington Post*:

> Proclaiming a "political revolution," Aristide, 37, has injected a spirit of hope and honesty into the affairs of government, a radical departure after decades of official venality under the Duvalier family dictatorship and a series of military strongmen. Declaring that his $10,000 monthly salary is "not just a scandal, but a crime", Aristide announced on television that he would donate his paychecks to charity.[14]

The Catholic priest had long been an incisive critic of US foreign policy because of Washington's support of the Duvalier dynasty and the Haitian military, and he was suspicious of foreign "aid", commenting that it all wound up in the pockets of the wealthy. "Since 1980, this amounted to two hundred million dollars a year, and these were the same ten years during which the per capita wealth of the country was reduced by 40 percent!"[15]

Aristide did not spell out a specific economic program, but was clear about the necessity of a redistribution of wealth, and spoke more of economic justice than of the virtues of the market system. He later wrote:

> I have often been criticized for lacking a program, or at least for imprecision in that regard. Was it for lack of time?—a poor excuse. ... In fact, the people had their own program. ... dignity, transparent simplicity, participation. These three ideas could be equally well applied in the political and economic sphere and in the moral realm. ... The bourgeoisie should have been able to understand that its own interest demanded some concessions. We had recreated 1789. Did they want, by their passive resistance, to push the hungry to demand more radical measures?[16]

Seriously hampered by the absence in Haiti of a strong traditional left, and confronted by a gridlocked parliament that constitutionally had more power than the president, Aristide didn't succeed in getting any legislation enacted. He did, however, initiate programs in literacy, public health and agrarian reform, and pressed for an increase in the daily wage, which was often less than three dollars, a freeze on prices of basic necessities, and a public-works program to create jobs. He also increased the feeling of security amongst the population by arresting a number of key paramilitary thugs, and setting in motion a process to eliminate the institution of rural section chiefs (sheriffs), the military's primary instrument of unfettered authority over the lives of the peasants.

In office, though not the uncompromising revolutionary firebrand many anticipated, Aristide frequently angered his opponents in the wealthy business class, the parliament, and the army by criticizing their corruptness. The military was particularly vexed by his policies against smuggling and drug trafficking, as well as his attempt to de-politicize them. As for the wealthy civilians—or as they are fondly known, the morally repugnant elite—they did not much care for Aristide's agenda whereby they would pay taxes and share their bounty by creating jobs and reinvesting profits locally rather than abroad. They were, as they remain, positively apoplectic about this little saintly-talking priest and his love for the (ugh) poor.

However, Aristide's administration was not, in practice, actually anti-business, and he made it a point to warm up to American officials, foreign capitalists and some elements of the Haitian military. He also discharged some 2,000 government workers, which pleased the International Monetary Fund and other foreign donors, but Aristide himself regarded these positions as largely useless and corrupt bureaucratic padding.[17]

Jean-Bertrand Aristide served less than eight months as Haiti's president before being deposed, on 29 September 1991, by a military coup in which many hundreds of his supporters were massacred, and thousands more fled to the Dominican Republic or by sea. The slightly-built Haitian president who, in the previous few years, had survived several serious assassination attempts and the burning down of his church while he was inside preaching, was saved now largely through the intervention of the French ambassador.

Only the Vatican recognized the new military government, although the coup of course was backed by the rich elite. They "helped us a lot," said the country's new police chief and key coup plotter, Joseph Michel Francois, "because we saved them."[18]

No evidence of direct US complicity in the coup has arisen, though, as we shall see, the CIA was financing and training all the important elements of the new military regime, and a Haitian official who supported the coup has reported that US intelligence officers were present at military headquarters as the coup was taking place; this was "normal", he added, for the CIA and DIA (Defense Intelligence Agency) were always there.[19]

We have seen in Nicaragua how the National Endowment for Democracy—which was set up to do overtly, and thus more "respectably", some of what the CIA used to do covertly—interfered in the 1990 election process. At the same time, the NED, in conjunction with the Agency for International Development (AID), was busy in Haiti. It gave $189,000 to several civic groups that included the Haitian Center for the Defense of Rights and Freedom, headed by Jean-Jacques Honorat. Shortly after Aristide's ouster, Honorat became the prime minister in the coup government. In a 1993 interview with the Canadian Broadcasting Corporation, he declared, "The coup was justified by the human rights record of Aristide." Asked what he himself had done as prime minister to halt the massive human rights violations that followed the overthrow, Honorat responded: "I don't have my files here."

In the years prior to the coup, the NED also gave more than $500,000 to the Haitian Institute for Research and Development (IHRED). This organization played a very partisan role in the 1990 elections when it was allied with US-favorite Marc Bazin, former World Bank executive, and helped him create his coalition (just as NED was instrumental in creating the coalition in Nicaragua which defeated the Sandinistas earlier in the year). IHRED was led by Leopold Berlanger who, in 1993, supported the junta's sham election aimed at ratifying the prime ministership of Bazin, Honorat's successor and a political associate of Berlanger.

Another recipient of NED largesse was Radio Soleil, run by the Catholic Church in a manner calculated to not displease the dictatorship of the day. During the 1991 coup—according to the Rev. Hugo Triest, a former station director—the station refused to air a message from Aristide.

The NED has further reduced the US Treasury by grants to the union association *Federation des Ouvriers Syndiques*, founded in 1984 with Duvalier's approval, so that Haiti, which previously had crushed union-organizing efforts, would qualify for the US Caribbean Basin Initiative economic package.[20]

But despite its name and unceasing rhetoric, the National Endowment for Democracy did not give a dollar to any of the grassroots organizations that eventually merged to form Aristide's coalition.

Within a week of Aristide's overthrow, the Bush administration began to distance itself from the man, reported the *New York Times*, "by refusing to say that his return to power was a necessary pre-condition for Washington to feel that democracy has been restored in Haiti." The public rationale given for this attitude was that Aristide's human rights record was questionable, since some business executives, legislators and other opponents of his had accused him of using mobs to intimidate them and tacitly condoning their violence.[21] Some of Haiti's destitute did carry out acts of violence and arson against the rich, but it's a stretch to blame Aristide, whatever his attitude, given that these were enraged people seeking revenge for a lifetime of extreme oppression against their perceived oppressors, revenge they had long been waiting for.

A year later, the *Boston Globe* could editorialize that the Bush administration's "contempt for Haitian democracy has been scandalous ... By refusing to acknowledge the carnage taking place in Haiti, the administration has all but bestowed its blessing on the putschists."[22]

Two months earlier, in testimony before Congress, the CIA's leading analyst of Latin American affairs, Brian Latell, had described coup leader Lieut. Gen. Raoul Cédras as one of "the most promising group of Haitian leaders to emerge since the Duvalier family dictatorship was overthrown in 1986". He also reported that he "saw no evidence of oppressive rule" in Haiti.[23]

Yet the State Department annual human-rights report for the same year stated:

Haitians suffered frequent human rights abuses throughout 1992, including extra-judicial killings by security forces, disappearances, beatings and other mistreatment of detainees and prisoners, arbitrary arrests and detention and executive interference with the judicial process.[24]

The *New York Times'* one-year-post-coup status report was remarkably blunt:

Since shortly after the overthrow—when Secretary of State James Baker echoed President Bush's famous "this aggression will not stand" statement about Iraq—little consideration has been given to backing up American principles in Haiti with American muscle. ... Recently, an adviser of the [coup government] repeated Father Aristide's longtime complaint when he said that "all it would take is one phone call" from Washington to send the army's leadership packing. ... supporters and opponents of Father Aristide agree, nothing more threatening than a leaky and ineffective embargo, quickly imposed ... has ever been seriously contemplated, which reflects Washington's deep-seated ambivalence about a leftward-tilting nationalist [who] often depicted the United States as a citadel of evil and the root of many of his country's problems. ... Despite much blood on the army's hands, United States diplomats consider it a vital counterweight to Father Aristide, whose class-struggle rhetoric ... threatened or antagonized traditional power centers at home and abroad.[25]

During this period, numerous nocturnal arrivals of US Air Force planes in Port-au-Prince were reported in Haitian clandestine newspapers. Whether this had any connection to the leaking embargo may never be known. When asked, a US embassy official said the flights were "routine".[26]

The CIA's Clients

I. From the mid-1980s until at least the 1991 coup, key members of Haiti's military and political leadership were on the Agency's payroll. These payments were defended by Washington officials and a congressman on the House Intelligence Committee as being a normal and necessary part of gathering intelligence in a foreign country.[27] This argument, which has often been used to defend CIA bribery, ignores the simple reality (illustrated repeatedly in this book) that payments bring more than information, they bring influence and control; and when one looks at the anti-democratic and cruelty levels of the Haitian military during its period of being bribees, one has to wonder what the CIA's influence was. Moreover, one has to wonder what the defenders of the payments would have thought upon learning during the cold war that congressmen and high officials in the White House were on the KGB payroll. Even after the supposed end of the cold war, we must consider the shocked reaction to the case of CIA officer Aldrich Ames. He was, after all, only accepting money from the KGB for information. In any event, money paid by the CIA to these men, as well as to the groups mentioned below, was obviously available to finance their murderous purposes. When Qaddafi of Libya did this, it was called "supporting terrorism".

Did the information provided the CIA by the Haitian leaders include advance notice of the coup? No evidence of this has emerged, but four decades of known CIA behavior would make it eminently likely. And if so, did the Agency do anything to stop it? What did the CIA do with its knowledge of the drug trafficking which the Haitian powers-that-be, including Baby Doc, were long involved in?[28]

II. In 1986 the CIA created a new organization, the National Intelligence Service (SIN). The unit was staffed solely by officers of the Haitian army, widely perceived as an unprofessional force with a marked tendency toward corruption. SIN was purportedly created to fight the cocaine trade, though SIN officers themselves engaged in the trafficking, and the trade was aided and abetted by some of the Haitian officials also on the Agency payroll.

SIN functioned as an instrument of political terror, persecuting and torturing Father Aristide's supporters and other "subversives", and using its CIA training and devices to spy on them; in short, much like the intelligence services created by the CIA elsewhere in the world during the previous several decades, including Greece, South Korea, Iran, and Uruguay; and created in Haiti presumably for the same reason: to give the Agency a properly trained and equipped, and loyal, instrument of control. At the same time that SIN was receiving between half and one million dollars a year in equipment, training and financial support, Congress was withholding about $1.5 million in aid for the Haitian military because of its abuses of human rights.

Aristide had tried, without success, to shut SIN down. The CIA told his people that the United States would see to it that the organization was reformed, but that its continued operation was beyond question. Then came the coup. Afterwards, American officials say, the CIA cut its ties to SIN, but in 1992 a US Drug Enforcement Administration document described SIN in the present tense as "a covert counternarcotics intelligence unit which often works in unison with the C.I.A." In September of the same year, work by the DEA in Haiti led to the arrest of a SIN officer on cocaine charges by the Haitian authorities.[29]

III. Amongst the worst violators of human rights in Haiti was the Front for the Advancement and Progress of Haiti (FRAPH), actually a front for the army. The paramilitary group spread deep fear amongst the Haitian people with its regular murders, public beatings, arson raids on poor neighborhoods, and mutilation by machete. FRAPH's leader, Emannuel Constant, went onto the CIA payroll in early 1992 and, according to the Agency, this relation ended in mid-1994. Whatever truth lies in that claim, the fact is that by October the American Embassy in Haiti was openly acknowledging that Constant—now a born-again democrat—was on *its* payroll.

The FRAPH leader says that soon after Aristide's ouster an officer of the US Defense Intelligence Agency, Col. Patrick Collins, pushed him to organize a front that could balance the Aristide movement and do intelligence work against it. This resulted in Constant forming what later evolved into FRAPH in August 1993. Members of FRAPH were working, and perhaps still are, for two social service agencies funded by the Agency for International Development, one of which maintains sensitive files on the movements of the Haitian poor.

Constant—who has told in detail of having attended, on invitation, the Clinton inauguration balls—was the organizer of the dockside mob that, on 11 October 1993, chased off a ship carrying US military personnel arriving to retrain the Haitian military under the UN agreement (see below). This was while Constant was on the CIA payroll. But that incident may have been something out of the Agency's false-bottom world. Did Washington really want to challenge the military government? Or only *appear* to do so? Constant actually informed the United States beforehand of what was going to happen, then went on the radio to urge all "patriotic Haitians" to join the massive demonstrations at the dock. The United States did nothing before or after but allow its ship to turn tail and run.[30]

In the summer of 1993, United Nations-mediated talks on Governors Island in New York between Aristide, living in exile in Washington, and the Haitian military government, resulted in an accord whereby the leader of the junta, Gen. Cédras, would step down on 15 October and allow Aristide to return to Haiti as president on 30 October. But the dates came and went without the military fulfilling their promise, meanwhile not pausing in their assaults upon Aristide supporters, including the September murder of a prominent Aristide confidant who was dragged out of church and shot in full view of UN officials, and the assassination a month later of Aristide's justice minister, Guy Malary.

Pleased with its "foreign-policy-success" in securing the agreement in New York, the Clinton administration seemingly was willing to tolerate any and all outrages.

But an adviser to Cédras declared afterward that when the military had agreed to negotiate, "the whole thing was a smokescreen. We wanted to get the sanctions lifted. ... But we never had any intention of really agreeing to Governors Island, as I'm sure everyone can now figure out for themselves. We were playing for time."

Aristide himself never liked the UN plan, which granted amnesty to those who mounted the coup against him. He declared that the United States had pressured him to sign.[31]

Speaking to congressmen in early October, CIA official Brian Latell—who had previously praised Cédras and his rule—now characterized Aristide as mentally unbalanced. Was this perhaps amongst the information provided the CIA by their agents in the Haitian military? (During the election campaign, Aristide's detractors in Haiti had in fact spread the rumor that he was mentally ill.)[32] Latell also testified that Aristide "paid little mind to democratic principles", and had urged supporters to murder their opponents with a technique called "necklacing", in which gasoline-soaked tires are placed around victims' necks and set afire. Neither Latell nor anyone else has provided any evidence of Aristide engaging in an explicit provocation, although this is not to say that necklacing was not carried out as an act of revenge by Haiti's masses, as it was in 1986 following the ouster of Duvalier.

At the same time, congressman were exposed to a document purporting to describe Aristide's medical history, claiming that he had been treated in a mental hospital in Canada in 1980, diagnosed as manic depressive and prescribed large quantities of drugs. This claim was described in the media as emanating from the CIA, but the Agency denied this, saying it had seen the document before and had judged it to be a partial or complete fake, but adding that it still stood by its 1992 psychological profile of Aristide which concluded that the deposed president was possibly unstable.

The claims were denied by Aristide and his spokesman and independent checks with the hospital in Canada showed no record of his being a patient there. Nonetheless, congressional opponents of Aristide now had a rationale for trying to limit the extent of US support to him, and some of them argued that the United States should not embroil itself in Haiti on behalf of such a leader.[33]

"He [Latell] made it the most simplistic, one-dimensional message he could—murderer, psychopath," said an administration official familiar with Latell's briefing.[34] (In 1960, the Eisenhower administration had regarded another black foreign leader who didn't buy into Pax Americana, Patrice Lumumba, as "unstable", "irrational, almost psychotic".[35] Nelson Mandela was often described in a similar fashion by his opponents. Some of those who make such charges may indeed believe that conspicuously rejecting the established order is a sign of insanity.)

The junta, which was concerned that President Clinton might order military action against Haiti, was pleased. A spokesman observed that "after the information about Aristide got out from our friends in the CIA, and Congress started talking about how bad he is, we figured the chances of an invasion were gone."[36]

Though the Clinton administration publicly repudiated the claims about Aristide's mental health in no uncertain terms, it nonetheless continued to negotiate with Haiti's military leaders, a policy which stunned supporters of the Catholic priest. "Apparently," marveled Robert White, a former US ambassador to El Salvador and an unpaid adviser to Aristide, "nothing will shake the touching faith the Clinton administration has in the Haitian military's bona fides."

Aristide supporters asserted that such faith reflected long and continuing relations between American military officers and Haiti's top commanders, Cédras and Francois, the police chief, both of whom had received military training in the United States. *Time* magazine suggested that "the U.S. attitude toward some of Haiti's henchmen is not as hostile as American rhetoric would indicate."[37]

This attitude was commented upon by the Lawyers Committee for Human Rights:

> Faced with [Aristide's] talk of radical reform, an old and deep-rooted American instinct has taken hold. Repeated in countless countries, both during and after the Cold War, it is this: When in doubt, look to the military as the only institutional guarantee of stability and order.[38]

It had indeed been to the military that the Reagan and Bush administrations had looked to provide these qualities, praising the sincerity of the Haitian army's commitment to democracy on several occasions.[39]

The Clinton administration was as hypocritical on the Haiti question as were its predecessors, exemplified by its choice for Secretary of Commerce—Ron Brown had been a well-paid and highly-active lobbyist for Baby-Doc Duvalier.[40] Cédras's spit-in-the-face deceit on the Governors Island accord appeared to bother Washington officials much less than the fact that Aristide would not agree to form a government with the military.[41] By February 1994, it was an open secret that Washington would as soon be rid of the Haitian priest as it would the Haitian strongmen. The *Los Angeles Times* reported: "Officially it [the US] supports the restoration of Aristide. In private, however, many officials say that Aristide ... is so politically radical that the military and the island's affluent elite will never allow him to return to power."[42]

Ideologically, if not emotionally, the antipathy of the administration's senior officials to Aristide's politics was hardly less than that of his country's ruling class. Moreover, the predominant reason the strongmen were in disfavor in Washington's eyes had little to do with their dreadful human-rights record per se, but rather that the repression in Haiti was provoking people to flee by the tens of thousands, causing the United States an enormous logistical headache and image problem in the Caribbean and Florida, as well as costing hundreds of millions of dollars.

The gulf between the administration and Aristide widened yet further when Secretary of State Warren Christopher announced that a group of Haitian parliamentarians, whom he characterized as "centrists", had put forth a plan which would pardon the army officers who engineered the coup, and which called for Aristide to name a prime minister, who in turn would create a cabinet acceptable to Aristide's domestic foes. These steps, the plan anticipated, would establish a coalition government and clear the way for Aristide's eventual return to office.

Aristide, who had not been consulted at all, flatly rejected the proposal that would have allowed some awful villains to escape punishment, made no mention of a date or timetable for his restoration, contained no guarantee that he would ever be able to return to power at all, and would require him to share power with a politically incompatible prime minister and some cabinet members of similar ilk.

Christopher added that any strengthening of the embargo against Haiti would depend on Aristide's acceptance of the plan. The United States, he said, was wary of tougher sanctions because they would increase the suffering in Haiti.[43] At the same time, the State Department's chief Haiti expert, Michael Kozak, blamed "extremists on both sides" for scuttling the plan. This, said a Haitian supporter of Aristide, "created a moral equivalency between Aristide and the military. That put Aristide on the same level as the killers."[44]

The Bush administration, employing the UN and the OAS as well, had pressed similar proposals and ultimatums upon the beleaguered Aristide on several occasions. His failure to embrace them had stamped him as "intransigent" amongst some officials and media.[45]

Aristide's rejection of the plan can perhaps be better understood if one considers whether Washington would ever insist to the Cuban exiles in Miami that if they wanted US support for their return to Cuba, they would have to agree to a coalition government with Castroites, or that Iraqian exiles would have to learn to live with Saddam Hussein. The repeated insistence that Aristide accept a "broad-based" government, or a government of "national consensus" is ironic coming from the Bush and Clinton administrations, in which one cannot find an open left-liberal, much less a leftist or socialist, scarcely even a plain genuine liberal, in any middle- or high-level position. Nor has the severe suffering of the Cuban people from the American embargo had any noticeable effect upon the policy of either administration.

It soon developed that the plan, which had been labeled "a bipartisan Haitian legislative initiative" had actually originated with a State Department memo; worse, the Haitian input had come from supporters of Aristide's overthrow, including Police Chief Francois himself.[46]

A further symptom of the administration's estrangement from Aristide was a report from the US Embassy in Haiti to the State Department in April. While conceding widespread and grave violations of human rights by the military regime, the report claimed that Aristide "and his followers consistently manipulate and even fabricate human-rights abuses as a propaganda tool." The Aristide camp was described as "hardline ideological".[47]

Congressional liberals, particularly the Congressional Black Caucus, were becoming disturbed. In the midst of their growing criticism and pressure, State Department Special Envoy to Haiti Lawrence Pezzullo, by this time openly described as the author of the "legislative" plan, resigned. A week later several congressmen, attended by wide media coverage, were arrested in a protest outside the White House.

By early May, given the congressional pressure, the Grand Haitian Plan discredited and abandoned, the sanctions an international joke, the refugees still washing up on Florida shores, while many thousands of others were filling up Guantànamo base in Cuba, the Clinton administration was forced to the conclusion that—though they still didn't like this man Jean-Bertrand Aristide with his non-centrist thoughts—they were unable to create anything that smelled even faintly like a rose without restoring him to the presidency. Bill Clinton had painted himself into a corner. During the campaign in 1992, he had denounced Bush's policy of returning refugees to Haiti as "cruel". "My Administration," he declared, "will stand up for democracy".[48] Since that time the word "Haiti" could not cross his lips without being accompanied by at least three platitudes about "democracy".

Something had to be done or another "foreign-policy failure" would be added to the list the Republicans were drooling over in this election year ... but what? Over the next four months, the world was treated to a continuous flip-flop—numerous permutations concerning sanctions, handling of the refugees, how much time the junta had to pack up and leave (as much as six months), what kind of punishment or amnesty for the murderous military and police, whether the US would invade ... this time we mean it ... now we *really* mean it ... "our patience has run out", for the third time ... "we will not rule out military force", for the fifth time ... the junta was not terribly intimidated.

Meanwhile, an OAS human-rights team was accusing the Haiti regime of "murder, rape, kidnaping, detention and torture in a systematic campaign to terrorize Haitians who want the return of democracy and President Jean-Bertrand Aristide", and Amnesty International was reporting the same.[49]

Time was passing, and each day meant less time for Aristide to govern Haiti. He had already lost almost three of the five years of his term, plus the eight months he had served.

By the summer, what Bill Clinton wanted desperately was to get the junta out of power without having to deal with the thorny question of congressional approval, without a US invasion, without any American casualties, without going to war on behalf of a socialist priest. If Washington's heart had really been set on the return to power of Father Jean-Bertrand Aristide, the CIA could have been directed to destabilize the Haitian government any time during the previous three years, using its tried and trusted bribery, blackmail, and forged documents, its disinformation, rumors, and paranoia, its weapons, mercenaries, and assassinations, its multinational economic strangleholds, its instant little armies, its selective little air assaults imbuing the right amount of terror in the right people at the right time ... the Agency had done so with much stronger and more stable governments; governments with much more public support, from Iran and Guatemala, to Ecuador and Brazil, to Ghana and Chile.

Much of what was needed in Haiti was already in place, beginning with the CIA's own creation, the National Intelligence Service, as well as a large network of informants and paid assets within other security forces such as FRAPH, and knowledge of who the reliable military officers were.[50] US intelligence even had a complete inventory of Haitian weaponry.[51]

The failure of Clinton to make use of this option is particularly curious in light of the fact that many members of Congress and some of the administration's own foreign policy specialists were urging him to do so for months.[52] Finally, in September 1994, officials revealed that the CIA had "launched a major covert operation this month to try to topple Haiti's military regime ... but so far the attempt has failed". One official said the effort "was too late to make a difference". The administration, we were told, had spent months debating what kind of actions to undertake, and whether they would be legal or not.[53]

Or they could have made the famous "one phone call". Like they meant it.

Betrayal

"The most violent regime in our hemisphere" ... "campaign of rape, torture and mutilation, people starved" ... "executing children, raping women, killing priests" ... "slaying of Haitian orphans" suspected of "harboring sympathy toward President Aristide, for no other reason than he ran an orphanage in his days as a parish priest" ... "soldiers and policemen raping the wives and daughters of suspected political dissidents—young girls, 13, 16 years old—people slain and mutilated with body parts left as warnings to terrify others; children forced to watch as their mothers' faces are slashed with machetes" ...[54]

Thus spaketh William Jefferson Clinton to the American people to explain why he was seeking to "restore democratic government in Haiti".

The next thing we knew, the Haitian leaders were told that they could take four weeks to resign, they would not be charged with any crimes, they could remain in the country if they wished, they could run for the presidency if they wished, they could retain all their assets no matter how acquired. Those who chose exile were paid large amounts of money by the United States to lease their properties, any improvements made to remain free of charge; two jets were chartered to fly them with all their furniture to the country of their choice, transportation free, housing and living expenses paid for the next year for all family members and dozens of relatives and friends, totaling millions of dollars.[55]

The reason Bill Clinton the president (as opposed, perhaps, to Bill Clinton the human being) could behave like this is that he—as would be the case with any other man sitting in the White House, like Jimmy Carter who told Cédras that he was a man of honor and that he had great respect for him—was not actually repulsed by Cédras and company, for they posed no ideological barrier to the United States continuing the economic and strategic control of Haiti it's maintained for most of the century. Unlike Jean-Bertrand Aristide, a man who only a year earlier had declared: "I still think capitalism is a mortal sin."[56] Or Fidel Castro in Cuba. Lest there be doubt here, it should be noted that shortly before Clinton made the remarks cited above, Vice President Gore declared on television that Castro has a worse record on human rights than the military leaders of Haiti.[57]

The atrocities of the Haitian government were simply trotted out by President Clinton to build support for military intervention, just as he cited the junta's drug trafficking; after all these years, this was now discovered, as Noriega's long-time dealings were finally condemned when it was time for a military intervention into Panama.

But the worst of the betrayal was yet to come.

Per the above agreement with Raoul Cédras, US armed forces began arriving in Haiti 19 September to clear the way for Aristide's arrival in mid-October. The Americans were welcomed with elation by the Haitian people, and the GIs soon disarmed, arrested, or shot dead some of the worst dangers to life and limb and instigators of chaos in Haitian society. But first they set up tanks and vehicles mounted with machine guns to block off the streets leading to the residential neighborhoods of the morally repugnant elite, the rich being Washington's natural allies.[58]

Jean-Bertrand Aristide's reception was a joyous celebration filled with optimism. However, unbeknownst to his adoring followers, while they were regaining Aristide, they may have lost Aristidism. The *Los Angeles Times* reported:

> In a series of private meetings, Administration officials admonished Aristide to put aside the rhetoric of class warfare ... and seek instead to reconcile Haiti's rich and poor. The Administration also urged Aristide to stick closely to free-market economics and to abide by the Caribbean nation's constitution—which gives substantial political power to the Parliament while imposing tight limits on the presidency. ... Administration officials have urged Aristide to reach out to some of his political opponents in setting up his new government ... to set up a broad-based coalition regime. ... the Administration has made it clear to Aristide that if he fails to reach a consensus with Parliament, the United States will not try to prop up his regime.[59]
>
> Almost every aspect of Aristide's plans for resuming power—from taxing the rich to disarming the military—has been examined by the U.S. officials with whom the Haitian president meets daily and by officials from the World Bank, the International Monetary Fund and other aid organizations. The finished package clearly reflects their priorities. ... Aristide obviously has toned down the liberation theology and class-struggle rhetoric that was his signature before he was exiled to Washington.[60]

Tutored by leading Clinton administration officials, "Aristide has embraced the principles of democracy [sic], national reconciliation and market economics with a zeal that Washington would like to see in all leaders of developing nations."[61]

Aristide returned to Haiti 15 October 1994, three years and two weeks after being deposed. The United States might well have engineered his return under the same terms—or much better of course—two to three years earlier, but Washington officials kept believing that the policy of returning refugees to Haiti, and when that was unfeasible, lodging them at Guantánamo, would make the problems go away—the refugee problem, and the Jean-Bertrand Aristide problem. Faced ultimately with an Aristide returning to power, Clinton demanded and received—and then made sure to publicly announce—the Haitian president's guarantee that he would not try to remain in office to make up for the time lost in exile.

Clinton of course called this "democracy", although it represents a partial legitimization of the coup.[62] As can be deduced from the above compilation of news reports, this was by no means the only option Aristide effectively surrendered.

His preference for the all-important position of prime minister—who appoints the cabinet—was Claudette Werleigh, a woman very much in harmony with his thinking, but he was forced to rule her out because of strong opposition to her "leftist bent" from political opponents who argued that she would seriously hurt efforts to obtain foreign aid and investment. Instead, Aristide wound up appointing Smarck Michel, one of Washington's leading choices.[63] At the same time, the Clinton administration and the international financial institutions (IFIs) were carefully watching the Haitian president's appointments for finance minister, planning minister, and head of the Central Bank.[64]

Two of the men favored by Washington to fill these positions had met in Paris on 22 August with the IFIs to arrange the terms of an agreement under which Haiti would receive about $700 million of investment and credit. Typical of such agreements for the Third World, it calls for a drastic reduction of state involvement in the economy and an enlarged role for the private sector through privatization of public services. Haiti's international function will be to serve the transnational corporations by opening itself up further to foreign investment and commerce, with a bare minimum of tariffs or other import restrictions, and offering itself, primarily in the assembly industries, as a source of cheap export labor— extremely cheap labor, little if any increase in the current 10 to 25 cents per hour wages, distressingly inadequate for keeping body and soul together and hunger at bay; a way of life promoted for years to investors by the US Agency for International Development and other US government agencies.[65] (The assembly industries are regarded by Washington as important enough to American firms that in the midst of the sanctions against Haiti, the US announced that it was "fine-tuning" the embargo to permit these firms to import and export so they could resume work.)[66]

The agreement further emphasizes that the power of the Parliament is to be strengthened. The office of the president is not even mentioned. Neither is the word "justice".[67]

As of this writing (late October 1994), Aristide's dreams of a living wage and civilized working conditions for the Haitian masses, a social security pension system, decent education, housing, health care, public transportation, etc. appear to be little more than that— dreams. What appears to be certain is that the rich will grow richer, and the poor will remain at the very bottom of Latin America's heap. Under Aristide's successor—whomever the United States is already grooming—it can only get worse.

Aristide the radical reformer knew all this, and at certain points during September and October he may have had the option to get a much better deal, for Clinton needed him almost as much as he needed Clinton. If Aristide had threatened to go public, and noisily so, about the betrayal in process, spelling out all the sleazy details so that the whole world could get beyond the headlined platitudes and understand what a sham Bill Clinton's expressed concerns about "democracy" and the welfare of the Haitian people were, the American president would have been faced with an embarrassment of scandalous proportion.

But Aristide the priest sees the world in a different light:

> Let us compare political power with theological power. On the one hand, we see those in control using the traditional tools of politics: weapons, money, dictatorship, coups d'état, repression. On the other hand, we see tools that were used 2,000 years ago: solidarity, resistance, courage, determination, and the fight for dignity and might, respect and power. We see transcendence. We see faith in God, who is justice. The question we now ask is this: which is stronger, political power or theological power? I am confident that the latter is stronger. I am also confident that

the two forces can converge, and that their convergence will make the critical difference.[68]

Noam Chomsky has noted that the end of the cold war has enabled the US government to achieve its ultimate goal—"to set the terms of discussion" for virtually any international issue, and thus become the ultimate empire.

Notes

Introduction to the New Edition

1. David Evans, "Catch F-22", *In These Times* (Chicago biweekly newsmagazine), 11-24 July 1994, pp. 14-18.
2. 11/2 wars: *San Francisco Chronicle*, 27 January 1978; 2 wars: *New York Times*, 10 December 1993, p. 1.
3. *New York Times*, 8 March 1992, p. 14.
4. Cited by Michael Klare in *The Nation*, 15 October 1990.
5. St. George: *The Guardian* (London), 6 March 1984; Bikini: ibid., 29 November 1983; CIA/Army: see China chapter herein; 1947: letter from Col. O. G. Haywood, AEC, to Dr. Fidler, AEC, Oak Ridge, Tenn., 17 April 1947 (cited in *Covert Action Quarterly* [Washington, DC] Summer 1994, No. 49, p. 28); Ike: *San Francisco Chronicle*, 20 April 1979.
6. Mark F. Brzezinski (son of former national security adviser Zbigniew Brzezinski), *Los Angeles Times*, 2 September 1994, op-ed column.
7. Robert Scheer, *Los Angeles Times Book Review*, 27 September 1992, review of Georgi Arbatov, *The System: An Insider's Life in Soviet Politics* (Times Books, New York, 1992)
8. *International Herald Tribune*, 29 October 1992, p. 4.
9. *The New Yorker*, 2 November 1992, p. 6.
10. *Los Angeles Times*, 2 December 1988: emigration of Soviet Jews peaked at 51,330 in 1979 and fell to about 1,000 a year in the mid-1980s during the Reagan administration (1981-89); in 1988 it was at 16,572.
11. a) Frank Kofsky, *Harry S. Truman and the War Scare of 1948: A Successful Campaign to Deceive the Nation* (St. Martin's Press, New York 1993), passim, particularly Appendix A; the book is replete with portions of such documents written by diplomatic, intelligence and military analysts in the 1940s; the war scare was undertaken to push through the administration's foreign policy program, inaugurate a huge military buildup, and bail out the near-bankrupt aircraft industry.
   b) *Declassified Documents Reference System*: indexes, abstracts, and documents on microfiche, annual series, arranged by particular government agencies and year of declassification.
   c) *Foreign Relations of the United States* (Department of State), annual series, internal documents published about 25 to 35 years after the fact.
12. *Los Angeles Times*, 29 December 1991, p. M1.
13. *The Guardian* (London), 10 October 1983, p. 9.
14. Ruth Leger Sivard, *World Military and Social Expenditures 1986* (Ann Arbor, Mich. 1986)
15. a) Anne H. Cahn, "How We Got Oversold on Overkill", *Los Angeles Times*, 23 July 1993, based on testimony before Congress, 10 June 1993, of Eleanor Chelimsky, Assistant Comptroller-General of the General Accounting Office, about a GAO study.
   b) *Los Angeles Times*, 15 September 1991, p. 1; 26 October 1991.
   c) *The Guardian* (London), 4 March 1983; 20 January 1984; 3 April 1986.
   d) Arthur Macy Cox, "Why the U.S., Since 1977, Has Been Misperceiving Soviet Military Strength", *New York Times*, 20 October 1980, p. 19; Cox was formerly an official with the State Department and the CIA.
16. For further discussion of these points, see:
   a) Walden Bello, *Dark Victory: The United States, Structural Adjustment and Global Poverty* (Institute for Food and Development Policy, Oakland, CA, 1994), passim.
   b) *Multinational Monitor* (Washington), July/August 1994, special issue on The World Bank.
   c) Doug Henwood, "The U.S. Economy: The Enemy Within", *Covert Action Quarterly* (Washington, DC), Summer 1992, No. 41, pp. 45-9.
   d) Joel Bleifuss, "The Death of Nations", *In These Times* (Chicago) 27 June - 10 July 1994, p. 12 (UN Code).
17. *Los Angeles Times*, 26 June 1988, p. 8.
18. Newsbroadcast on American radio, 3 November 1989.
19. During the spring and summer of 1945, the Japanese made it very clear through third parties and through internal messages that they were ready to surrender. But the United States, which had broken the Japanese code and thus was fully aware of these communications, did not respond. The only condition specified by the Japanese was the retention of the emperor system, and, as matters eventually turned out, the emperor system was maintained anyway. See:Stewart Udall, *The Myths of August* (Pantheon Books, NY, 1994), chapters 4 and 5; Hearings Before the Committee on Armed Services and the Committee on Foreign Relations, US Senate, 25 June 1951, pp. 3113-4, re the Japanese offer in July via the Soviet Union; *New York Times*, 11 August 1993, p.9.

Introduction to the Original Edition

1. *Washington Post*, 24 October 1965, article by Stanley Karnow.
2. Winston Churchill, *The Second World War, Vol. IV, The Hinge of Fate* (London, 1951), p. 428.
3. Winston Churchill, *The World Crisis: The Aftermath* (London, 1929), p. 235.
4. D.F. Fleming, "The Western Intervention in the Soviet Union, 1918-1920", *New World Review* (New York), Fall 1967; see also Fleming, *The Cold War and its Origins, 1917-1960* (New York, 1961), pp. 16-35.
5. *Los Angeles Times*, 2 September 1991, p. 1.
6. Frederick L. Schuman, *American Policy Toward Russia Since 1917* (New York, 1928), p. 125.
7. Ibid., p. 154.

Notes

8. *San Francisco Chronicle*, 4 October 1978, p. 4.
9. *New Republic*, 4 August 1920, a 42-page analysis by Walter Lippmann and Charles Merz.
10. *Life*, 29 March 1943, p. 29.
11. *New York Times*, 24 June 1941; for an interesting account of how US officials laid the groundwork for the cold war during and immediately after World War 2, see the first two chapters of Blanche Wiesen Cook, *The Declassified Eisenhower* (New York, 1981), a study of previously classified papers at the Eisenhower Library.
12. This has been well documented and would be "common knowledge" if not for its shameful implications. See, e.g., the British Cabinet papers for 1939, summarized in the *Washington Post*, 2 January 1970 (reprinted from the *Manchester Guardian*); also Fleming, *The Cold War*, pp. 48-97.
13. *Los Angeles Times*, 15 December 1987; the figure of 28% disagreeing was obtained by the author from the *Times* reporter.
    For a highly insightful and readable description of the anti-communist mentality in the United States, see Michael Parenti, *The Anti-Communist Impulse* (Random House, New York, 1969).
14. Related by former French Foreign Minister Christian Pineau in a recorded interview for the Dulles Oral History Project, Princeton University Library; cited in Roger Morgan, *The United States and West Germany, 1945-1973: A Study in Alliance Politics* (Oxford University Press, London, 1974), p. 54, my translation from the French.
15. Parenti, p. 35.
16. John Stockwell, *In Search of Enemies* (New York, 1978), p. 101. The expressions "CIA officer" or "case officer" are used throughout the present book to denote regular, full-time, career employees of the Agency, as opposed to "agent", someone working for the CIA on an ad hoc basis. Other sources which are quoted, it will be seen, tend to use the word "agent" to cover both categories.
17. Ibid., p. 238.
18. Kwame Nkrumah, *Dark Days in Ghana* (London, 1968), pp. 71-2.
19. The full quotation is from the *New York Times*, 11 January 1969, p. 1; the inside quotation is that of the National Commission.
20. *Mother Jones* magazine (San Francisco), April 1981, p. 5.
21. *San Francisco Chronicle*, 14 January 1982, p. 2.
22. Richard F. Grimmett, *Reported Foreign and Domestic Covert Activities of the United States Central Intelligence Agency: 1950-1974*, (Library of Congress) 18 February 1975.
23. *The Pentagon Papers* (N.Y. Times edition, 1971), p. xiii.
24. *Newsweek*, 22 November 1971, p. 37.
25. Speech before the World Affairs Council at the University of Pennsylvania, 13 January 1950, cited in the Republican Congressional Committee Newsletter, 20 September 1965.
26. The last sentence is borrowed from Michael Parenti, op. cit., p. 7.

1. CHINA 1945 to 1960s

1. David Barrett, *Dixie Mission: The United States Army Observer Group in Yenan, 1944* (Center for Chinese Studies, University of California, Berkeley, 1970), passim; R. Harris Smith, *OSS: The Secret History of America's First CIA* (University of California Press, Berkeley, 1972), pp. 262-3; *New York Times*, 9 December 1945, p. 24.
2. Chiang's policies during and after war: Smith, pp. 259-82; *New York Times*, 19 December 1945, p. 2.
3. Harry S. Truman, *Memoirs, Vol. Two: Years of Trial and Hope, 1946-1953* (Great Britain, 1956), p. 66.
4. Smith, p. 282.
5. D.F. Fleming, *The Cold War and its Origins, 1917-1960* (New York, 1961), p. 570.
6. *New York Times*, September-December 1945, passim; Barbara W.Tuchman, *Stilwell and the American Experience in China 1911-45* (New York, 1972), pp. 666-77.
7. *Congressional Record*, Appendix, Vol. 92, part 9, 24 January 1946, p. A225, letter to Congressman Hugh de Lacy of State of Washington.
8. *New York Times*, 6 November 1945, p. 1; 19 December 1945, p. 2
9. Ibid., 9 December 1945, p. 24; 26 December 1945, p. 5.
10. Ibid., 26 December 1945, p. 5.
11. Fleming, p. 587.
12. Christopher Robbins, *Air America* (U.S., 1979), pp. 46-57; Victor Marchetti and John Marks, *The CIA and the Cult of Intelligence* (New York, 1975), p. 149.
13. Hearings held in executive session before the US Senate Foreign Relations Committee during 1949-50: *Economic Assistance to China and Korea 1949-50*, testimony of Dean Acheson, p. 23; made public January 1974 as part of the Historical Series.
14. Tuchman, p. 676.
15. For some detail of the oppression and atrocities carried out by the Chiang regime against the Taiwanese, see Scott Anderson and Jon Lee Anderson, *Inside the League* (New York, 1986), pp. 47-9, citing prominent American Generals and a State Department official who was in Taiwan at the time. Also see Fleming, p. 578-9. In 1992, the Taiwan government admitted that its army had killed an estimated 18,000 to 28,000 native-born Taiwanese in the 1947 massacre. (*Los Angeles Times*, 24 February 1992).
16. Felix Greene, *A Curtain of Ignorance* (New York, 1964)

17. Tuchman, p. 676; Fleming, pp. 572-4, 577, 584-5; Milovan Djilas, *Conversations with Stalin* (London, 1962), p. 164; *New York Times*, 7 November 1945, p. 12; 14 November, p. 1; 21 November, p.2; 28 November, p. 1; 30 November, p. 3; 2 December, p. 34.
18. *New York Times*, 12 January 1947, p. 44.
19. William Manchester, *American Caesar: Douglas MacArthur 1880-1964* (London, 1979), p. 535.
20. *Foreign Relations of the United States, 1949, Vol. VIII, The Far East: China* (U.S. Government Printing Office, Washington, 1978), passim between pp. 357 and 399; 768, 779-80; publication of this volume in the State Department's series was held up precisely because it contained the reports about Chou En-Lai's request (*San Francisco Chronicle*, 27 September 1978, p. F-1).
21. See Indonesia 1957-1958 chapter and *The Guardian* (London), 24 August 1985.
22. *New York Times*, 25 April 1966, p. 20.
23. Burma: David Wise and Thomas Ross, *The Invisible Government* (New York, 1965, paperback edition), pp. 138-44; Joseph Burkholder Smith, *Portrait of a Cold Warrior* (New York, 1976), pp. 77-8; *New York Times*, 28 July 1951; 28 December 1951; 22 February 1952; 8 April 1952; 30 December 1952; opium: Robbins, pp. 84-7.
24. *Washington Post*, 20 August 1958, Joseph Alsop, a columnist who had been a staff officer under General Chennault and was well connected with Taiwan. Over the years he performed a variety of undercover tasks for the CIA, as did his brother Stewart Alsop. (see Carl Bernstein, "The CIA and the Media", *Rolling Stone* magazine, 20 October 1977.)
25. Quemoy and Matsu: Stewart Alsop (formerly with the OSS; also see note 24), 'The Story Behind Quemoy: How We Drifted Close to War', *Saturday Evening Post*, 13 December 1958, p. 26; Andrew Tulley, *CIA: The Inside Story* (New York, 1962), pp. 162-5; Fleming, pp. 930-1; Wise and Ross, p. 116; *New York Times*, 27 April 1966, p. 28.
26. Wise and Ross, p. 114.
27. Air drops: Wise and Ross, pp. 112-5; Thomas Powers, *The Man Who Kept the Secrets* (New York, 1979), pp. 43-4; *Newsweek*, 26 March 1973.
28. Overflights: Marchetti and Marks, pp. 150, 287; *Washington Post*, 27 May 1966; *New York Times*, 28 March 1969, p. 40.
29. *Foreign Relations of the United States, 1943, China* (U.S. Government Printing Office, Washington, 1957), p. 630.
30. Tibet: David Wise, *The Politics of Lying* (New York, 1973, paperback edition), pp. 239-54; Robbins, pp. 94-101; Marchetti and Marks, pp. 128-31 and p. 97 of the 1983 edition.
31. *People's China*, English-language magazine, Foreign Languages Press, Peking, 17 September 1952, p. 28.
32. Callum A. MacDonald, *Korea: The War Before Vietnam* (New York, 1986), pp. 161-2, cites several sources for this well known occurrence.
33. Germ Warfare: *People's China*, 1952, passim, beginning 16 March.
34. *New York Times*, 9 August 1970, IV, p. 3.
35. *Washington Post*, 17 December 1979, p. A18, "whooping cough cases recorded in Florida jumped from 339 and one death in 1954 to 1,080 and 12 deaths in 1955." The CIA received the bacteria from the Army's biological research center at Fort Detrick, Md.
36. *San Francisco Chronicle*, 4 December 1979, p. 12. For a detailed account of US Government experiments with biological agents within the United States, see: Leonard A. Cole, *Clouds of Secrecy: The Army's Germ Warfare Tests over Populated Areas* (Maryland, 1990), passim.
37. *Department of State Bulletin*, 2 May 1966.

2. ITALY 1947-1948

1. Addressing the Cathedral Club of Brooklyn, 15 January 1948; cited in David Caute, *The Great Fear: The Anti-Communist Purge Under Truman and Eisenhower* (Simon and Schuster, New York, 1979), p. 15.
2. Robert T. Holt and Robert W. van de Velde, *Strategic Psychological Operations and American Foreign Policy* (University of Chicago Press, 1960) p. 169.
3. Dissolving the cabinet: *New York Times*, 21 January 1947, p. 5; 26 January, p. 31; 3 February, p. 1; 5 May, p. 13; 13 May; 14 May; 29 May, p.3; 2 June, p. 24.
4. *New York Times*, 5 May 1947, p. 1; 11 May, IV, p. 5; 14 May, pp. 14 and 24; 17 May, p. 8; 18 May, IV, p. 4; 20 May, p. 2; Howard K. Smith, *The State of Europe* (London, 1950), p. 151 (includes Ramadier quote; similar quote in *New York Times*, 20 May).
5. *Time*, 22 March 1948, p. 35.
6. William Colby, *Honorable Men: My Life in the CIA* (New York, 1978), p. 109.
7. Except where otherwise indicated, the items in the succeeding list are derived from the following:
   a) *New York Times*, 16 March to 18 April 1948, passim;
   b) Howard K. Smith, pp. 198-219;
   c) William E. Daugherty and Morris Janowitz, *A Psychological Warfare Casebook* (Johns Hopkins Press, Baltimore, 1958), pp. 319-26;
   d) Holt and van de Velde, pp. 159-205;
   e) E. Edda Martinez and Edward A. Suchman, "Letters from America and the 1948 Elections in Italy", *The Public Opinion Quarterly* (Princeton University), Spring 1950, pp. 111-25.

8. Cited in Smith, p. 202, no date of issue given.
9. Tom Braden, "I'm Glad the CIA is 'Immoral'", *Saturday Evening Post*, 20 May 1967; Braden had been a high-ranking CIA officer.
10. Miles Copeland, *Without Cloak and Dagger* (New York, 1974), pp. 235-6; also published as *The Real Spy World*.
11. CIA memorandum to the Forty Committee (National Security Council), presented to the Select Committee on Intelligence, US House of Representatives (The Pike Committee) during closed hearings held in 1975. The bulk of the committee's report which contained this memorandum was leaked to the press in February 1976 and first appeared in book form as *CIA — The Pike Report* (Nottingham, England, 1977). The memorandum appears on pp. 204-5 of this book. (See also: Notes: Iraq.)
12. Stephen Goode, *The CIA* (Franklin Watts, Inc., New York, 1982), p. 45; William R. Corson, *The Armies of Ignorance: The Rise of the American Intelligence Empire* (The Dial Press, New York, 1977) pp. 298-9. Corson had an extensive career in military intelligence and was Staff Secretary of the President's Special Group Joint DOD-CIA Committee on Counterinsurgency R & D.
13. *Public Papers of the Presidents of the United States: Harry S. Truman, 1947* (U.S. Government Printing Office, Washington, 1963) pp. 178-9.
14. *New York Times*, 8 April 1948.
15. Ibid., 12 April 1948.
16. Smith, p. 200.
17. Ibid., p. 202.
18. *New York Times*, 15 April 1948.

3. GREECE 1947 to early 1950s

1. Jorge Semprun, *What a Beautiful Sunday!* (English translation, London, 1983), pp. 26-7; Semprun wrote the screenplays for 'Z' and 'La Guerre est finie'.
2. For a summary of some of the literature about ELAS and EAM, see Todd Gitlin, "Counter-Insurgency: Myth and Reality in Greece" in David Horowitz, ed., *Containment and Revolution* (Boston, 1967) pp. 142-7. See also D.F. Fleming, *The Cold War and its Origins, 1917-1960* (New York, 1961) pp. 183-5; Howard K. Smith, *The State of Europe* (London, 1950) pp. 225-30; William Hardy McNeill, *The Greek Dilemma: War and Aftermath* (US, 1947) passim.
3. For accounts of the thoroughly unprincipled British policy in Greece and its dealings with collaborators during 1944-46, see Fleming, pp. 174-87; Smith, pp. 227-31, 234; Lawrence S. Wittner, *American Intervention in Greece, 1943-1949* (Columbia University Press, NY, 1982) passim.
4. Churchill quote: Kati Marton, *The Polk Conspiracy: Murder and Cover-Up in the Case of CBS News Correspondent George Polk* (New York, 1990), p. 23. EAM sign: Hearst Metrotone News, N.Y., film shot 3 November 1944, copy in author's possession.
5. *Parliamentary Debates, House of Commons*, 16 October 1946, column 887 (reference is made here to Bevin's statement of 10 August). See also Christopher Simpson, *Blowback: America's Recruitment of Nazis and its Effects on the Cold War* (New York, 1988), p. 81.
6. Gitlin, p. 157; Wittner, p. 25.
7. Winston Churchill, *The Second World War, Vol. VI, Triumph and Tragedy* (London, 1954), pp. 198, 255. For further evidence of Soviet non-intervention, see Wittner, pp. 26-7.
8. Fleming, p. 182; see also Smith, p. 228.
9. See sources listed in notes 2 and 3 above; see also James Becket, *Barbarism in Greece* (New York, 1970) p. 6; Richard Barnet, *Intervention and Revolution* (London, 1970) pp. 99-101; Edgar O'Ballance, *The Greek Civil War, 1944-1949* (London, 1966) pp. 155, 167.
10. Smith, p. 232. To capture the full flavor of how dreadful the Greek government of that time was, see Marton, op. cit., passim. This book recounts the story of how the Greek authorities, with US approval, fabricated a case to prove that CBS news correspondent George Polk had been murdered by communists, and not by the government, because he was about to reveal serious corruption by the prime minister.
11. Stephen G. Xydis, *Greece and the Great Powers, 1944-1947* (Institute for Balkan Studies, Thessaloniki, Greece, 1963) p. 479, information from the archives of the Greek Embassy in Washington.
12. *Foreign Relations of the United States, 1947, Vol. V* (U.S. Government Printing Office, Washington, 1971) p. 222.
13. *New York Times Magazine*, 12 October 1947, p. 10.
14. *Foreign Relations*, op. cit., pp. 222-3.
15. Cited in Fleming, p. 444.
16. Barnet, p. 109.
17. *Public Papers of the Presidents of the United States: Harry S. Truman, 1947* (U.S. Government Printing Office, Washington, 1963) p. 177.
18. Milovan Djilas, *Conversations with Stalin* (London, 1962) p. 164. Djilas was imprisoned in 1962 for divulging state secrets in this book.
19. For details of the American military effort:
    a) O'Ballance, passim

b) Wittner, p. 242

c) CIA Report to the President, March 1948, appendices D and F, *Declassified Documents Reference System* (Arlington, Va.) 1977, document 168A

d) Department of the Army internal memorandum, 15 June 1954, *DDRS* 1980, document 253C

e) Simpson, pp. 81-2 (Secret Army Reserve)

20. O'Ballance, p. 156.

21. Ibid., p. 173

22. Christopher M. Woodhouse, *The Struggle for Greece, 1941-1949* (London, 1976) pp. 260-1.

23. *New York Times*, 28 August 1947, p. 1; 5 September 1947, p. 1.

24. *Foreign Relations*, op. cit., p. 327.

25. John O. Iatrides, "American Attitudes Toward the Political System of Postwar Greece" in Theodore A. Couloumbis and John O. Iatrides, eds., *Greek-American Relations: A Critical Review* (New York, 1980) pp. 64-65; Lawrence Stern, *The Wrong Horse: The Politics of Intervention and the Failure of American Diplomacy* (N.Y. Times Books, 1977) pp. 16-17.

26. Philip Deane, *I Should Have Died* (Atheneum, New York, 1977) pp. 102, 103; Andreas Papandreou, *Democracy at Gunpoint* (Doubleday, New York, 1970) pp. 84-5.

27. Papandreou, p. 80.

28. *New York Times*, 13 July 1947, p. 11.

29. Ibid., 11 September 1947, p. 19; 17 October 1947, p. 11.

30. Papandreou, p. 5.

31. Sent by Horace Smith of AMAG; U.S. National Archives, Record Group 59, cited in Michael M. Amen, *American Foreign Policy in Greece 1944/1949: Economic, Military and Institutional Aspects* (Peter Lang Ltd., Frankfurt, W. Germany, 1978), pp. 114-5.

4. THE PHILIPPINES 1940s and 1950s

1. Charles S. Olcott, *The Life of William McKinley* (Boston, 1916) vol. 2, pp. 110-11; from a talk given to a visiting group from the Methodist Episcopal Church.

2. US actions against Huks during Second World War:

a) D.M. Condit, Bert H. Cooper, Jr., et al., *Challenge and Response in Internal Conflict, Volume 1, The Experience in Asia* (Center for Research in Social Systems, The American University, Washington, D.C., 1968), p. 481, research performed for the Department of the Army.

b) Luis Taruc, *Born of the People* (New York, 1953, although completed in June 1949) pp. 147-62, 186-211, the autobiography of the Huks' commander-in-chief who surrendered to the government in 1954.

c) William J. Pomeroy, *An American Made Tragedy* (New York, 1974) pp. 74-7; Pomeroy is an American who served in the Philippines during the war where he encountered the Huks. After the war, he returned to fight with them he until he was captured in 1952.

d) George E. Taylor, *The Philippines and the United States: Problems of Partnership* (New York, 1964) p. 122 (see note 13 below).

e) Eduardo Lachica, *Huk: Philippine Agrarian Society in Revolt* (Manila, 1971) pp. 112-3, 116-7.

f) *Philippines: A Country Study* (Foreign Area Studies, The American University, Washington, D.C., 1983-84) p. 43, prepared for the Department of the Army.

3. Taruc, chapter 22; Pomeroy, pp. 77-8; Taylor, pp. 116-20.

4. *New York Times*, 19 December 1952, p. 13

5. *Philippines: A Country Study*, p. 44

6. *New York Times*, 5 January 1946, p. 26

7. Hearings before the House Committee on Foreign Affairs in executive session, 7 June 1946, released in 1977, p. 31. Arnold was the Deputy Assistant Chief of Staff, Operations Division, War Department General Staff.

8. American servicemen's protests: *New York Times*, 8 January 1946, p. 3; 11 January, p. 4; for more information see Mary-Alice Waters, *G.I.'s and the Fight Against War* (New York, 1967), pamphlet published by *Young Socialist* magazine.

9. *New York Times*, 20 May 1946, p. 8; 2 June, p. 26; 4 June, p. 22 (letter from Tomas Confessor, prominent Filipino political figure, detailing the illegality of not seating the men); 18 September, p. 4; 19 September, p. 18; Pomeroy, p. 20; Taruc, pp. 214-27; Lachica, pp. 120-1.

10. *New York Times*, 12 March 1947, p. 15; the words are those of the *Times*; Lachica, p. 121.

11. Pomeroy, p. 28, explains how this came about.

12. Taruc, chapters 23 and 24; Pomeroy, p. 78; the Philippine Army reported that 600 deaths had occurred from their incursions into Huk areas in the month following the election (*New York Times*, 20 May 1946, p. 8) but no breakdown between military and non-military casualties was given in the press account; see also Lachica, p. 121.

13. Taylor, pp. 114, 115. The book was published by Frederick A. Praeger, Inc. for the Council on Foreign Relations, the ultra high-level think-tank whose officers and directors at the time included Allen Dulles, David Rockefeller, and John J. McCloy. Praeger, it was later disclosed, published a number of books in the 1960s under CIA sponsorship. This book, though generally reasonable on most matters, descends to the puerile and semi-hysterical when discussing the Huks or 'communism'.

14. Department of State, *Treaties and Other International Agreements of the United States of America, 1776-1949*

(Washington, 1974) pp. 84-9; Pomeroy, pp. 21-3; Taylor, p. 129.

15. *New York Times*, 1 July 1946, $50 million furnished; 11 February 1950, p. 6, $163.5 million furnished under the 1947 agreement.

16. Edward G. Lansdale, *In the Midst of Wars* (New York, 1972) passim; Stephen Shalom, "Counter-Insurgency in the Philippines" in Daniel Schirmer and Stephen Shalom, eds., *The Philippine Reader* (Boston, 1987) pp. 112-3.

17. William Worden, 'Robin Hood of the Islands', *Saturday Evening Post*, 12 January 1952, p. 76.

18. Lansdale, pp. 24-30, 47.

19. Joseph Burkholder Smith, *Portrait of a Cold Warrior* (New York, 1976) p. 95 (see note 30 for Smith's background).

20. Lansdale, pp. 72-3.

21. Ibid., pp. 47-59.

22. Ibid., pp. 70-1, 81-3, 92-3; Smith, p. 106; Taruc, pp. 68-9; for further description of this propaganda campaign, see Shalom, pp. 115-6.

23. Col. L. Fletcher Prouty, US Air Force, Ret., *The Secret Team: The CIA and its Allies in Control of the World* (Ballantine Books, New York, 1974, paperback) pp. 38-9.

24. Ibid., pp. 102-3.

25. Smith, p. 95, quoting CIA officer Paul Lineberger.

26. *New York Times*, 17 September 1953.

27. Interviews by author Thomas Buell of Ralph Lovett, CIA Chief of Station in the Philippines in the early 1950s, and of Lansdale; cited in Raymond Bonner, *Waltzing With a Dicatator: The Marcoses and the Making of American Policy* (New York, 1987) pp. 39-40.

28. Bonner, p. 41

29. Sherman Adams, *Firsthand Report* (New York, 1961) p. 123.

30. For an overall detailed description of CIA manipulation of Philippine political life, and of Magsaysay in particular, see Smith, chapters 7, 15, 16, 17. Smith was a CIA officer who, in the early 1950s, worked in the Far East Division, which includes the Philippines, concerned with political and psychological-warfare matters.

31. Smith, p. 280

32. Buell interview of Lovett (see note 27), cited in Bonner, p. 42.

33. *Reader's Digest*, April 1963, article entitled "Democracy Triumphs in the Philippines".

34. Smith, p. 290

35. House Bill No. 6584, Republic Act No. 1700, approved 20 June 1957.

36. Huks' condition: *New York Times*, 3 April 1949, p. 20; 30 June 1950, p. 4.

37. Lachica, p. 131

38. Taylor, p. 192

5. KOREA 1945-1953

1. *New York Times*, 1 October 1950, p. 3.

2. *The U.S. Imperialists Started the Korean War* is the subtle title of the book published in Pyongyang, North Korea, 1977, pp. 109-10.

3. Radio address of 13 April 1950, reprinted in *The Department of State Bulletin*, 24 April 1950, p. 627.

4. For a discussion of the war's immediate origin, see:

a) Karunakar Gupta, "How Did the Korean War Begin?", *The China Quarterly* (London) October/December 1972, No. 52, pp. 699-716.

b) "Comment: The Korean War", *The China Quarterly*, April/June 1973, No. 54, pp. 354-68. This consists of responses to Gupta's article in issue No. 52 and Gupta's counter-response.

c) *New York Times*, 26 June 1950. Page 1 — South Korea's announcement about Haeju. Page 3 — North Korea's announcement about Haeju.

d) Glenn D. Paige, *The Korean Decision (June 24-30, 1950)* (New York, 1968) passim, particularly p. 130.

e) I.F. Stone, *The Hidden History of the Korean War* (New York, 1952) chapter 7 and elsewhere.

5. John Gunther, *The Riddle of MacArthur* (London, 1951), pp. 151-2.

6. *New York Times*, 25 July 1950, p. 4; 30 July, p. 2.

7. *Khrushchev Remembers* (London, 1971) chapter 11. Study of transcription vs. book: John Merrill, Book Reviews, *Journal of Korean Studies* (University of Washington, Seattle) Vol. 3, 1981, pp. 181-91.

8. Joseph C. Goulden, *Korea: The Untold Story of the War* (New York, 1982), p. 64.

9. *New York Times*, 26 June 1950.

10. Ibid., 1 October 1950, p. 4.

11. Goulden, pp. 87-8; Stone, pp. 75, 77.

12. For further discussion of the UN's bias at this time see Jon Halliday, "The United Nations and Korea", in Frank Baldwin, ed., *Without Parallel: The American-Korean Relationship Since 1945* (New York, 1974), pp. 109-42.

13. Trygve Lie, *In the Cause of Peace* (New York, 1954) chapters 18 and 19.

14. Shirley Hazzard, *Countenance of Truth: The United Nations and the Waldheim Case* (New York, 1990), pp. 13-22. In his book, p. 389, Lie states that it was he who initiated this practice.

15. CIA memorandum, 28 June 1950, *Declassified Documents Reference System* (Arlington, Virginia) Retrospective Volume, Document 33C.

16. Stone, pp. 77-8.
17. The full text of the Security Council Resolution of 7 July 1950 can be found in the *New York Times*, 8 July 1950, p. 4.
18. Dwight Eisenhower, *The White House Years: Mandate for Change, 1953-1956* (New York, 1963) p. 340.
19. For a discussion of post-war politics in South Korea see:
a) Bruce Cumings, *The Origins of the Korean War: Liberation and the Emergence of Separate Regimes, 1945-1947* (Princeton University Press, New Jersey, 1981) passim.
b) E. Grant Meade, *American Military Government in Korea* (King's Crown Press, Columbia University, New York, 1951) chapters 3-5.
c) George M. McCune, *Korea Today* (Institute of Pacific Relations, New York, 1950) passim, pp. 46-50 (KPR). Professor McCune worked with the US Government on Korean problems during World War II.
d) D. F. Fleming, *The Cold War and its Origins, 1917-1960* (Doubleday & Co., New York, 1961) pp. 589-97.
e) Alfred Crofts, "The Case of Korea: Our Falling Ramparts", *The Nation* (New York) 25 June 1960, pp. 544-8. Crofts was a member of the US Military Government in Korea beginning in 1945.
20. Crofts, p. 545.
21. Gunther, p. 165.
22. Crofts, p. 545.
23. Ibid.
24. Ibid., p. 546.
25. Collaborators: Cumings, pp. 152-6; Meade, p. 61; McCune, p. 51; plus elsewhere in these sources, as well as in Fleming and Crofts. Japanese and collaborators retaining positions to thwart the KPR: Cumings, pp. 138-9.
26. McCune, pp. 83-4, 129-39, 201-9.
27. 1946 election: Mark Gayn, *Japan Diary* (New York 1948) p. 398; 1948 election: Crofts, p. 546; Halliday, pp. 117-22; 1950 election and US warning: Fleming, p. 594. For a discussion of Rhee's thwarting of honest elections in 1952 and later, and his consistently tyrannical rule, see William J. Lederer, *A Nation of Sheep* (W.W. Norton & Co., New York, 1961), chapter 4.
28. Gunther, pp. 166-7.
29. Gayn, p. 388.
30. Ibid., p. 352.
31. John Kie-Chiang Oh, *Korea: Democracy on Trial* (Cornell University Press, Ithaca, NY, 1968) p. 35.
32. *The Nation* (New York), 13 August 1949, p. 152.
33. Gunther, p. 171.
34. Oh, p. 206; see also *New York Times*, 11 April 1951, p. 4 for an account of a massacre of some 500 to 1,000 people in March in the same place, which appears to refer to the same incident.
35. Jon Halliday, "The Political Background", in Gavan McCormack and Mark Selden, eds., *Korea, North and South: The Deepening Crisis* (New York, 1978) p. 56.
36. *New York Times*, 11 April 1951, p.4.
37. René Cutforth, "On the Korean War", *The Listener* (BBC publication, London) 11 September 1969, p. 343.
38. Gregory Henderson, *Korea: The Politics of the Vortex* (Harvard University Press, Cambridge, Mass., 1968) p. 167.
39. *New York Times*, 9 February 1951, George Barrett.
40. Goulden, pp. 471-2. This information derives from Goulden's interview of Tofte.
41. *New York Times*, 27 November 1951, p. 4.
42. Eugene Kinkead, *Why They Collaborated* (London, 1960) p. 17; published in the US in 1959 in slightly different form as *In Every War But One*. The Army study was not contained in any one volume, but was spread out over a number of separate reports. Kinkead's book, written with the full co-operation of the Army, is composed of a summary of some of these reports, and interviews with many government and military officials who were directly involved in or knowledgeable about the study or the subject. For the sake of simplicity, I have referred to the book as if it were the actual study.
It is to the Army's credit that much of the results of the study were not kept secret; the study, nonetheless, contains some anti-communist statements of the most bizarre sort: lying is often punished in China by death ... communists live like animals all their lives ... [pp. 190, 193]
43. *Keesings Contemporary Archives*, 5-12 January 1952, p. 11931, an announcement on 31 December 1951 from General Ridgeway's headquarters.
44. Kinkead, p. 34.
45. Robert J. Lifton, *Thought Reform and the Psychology of Totalism: A Study of 'Brainwashing' in China* (London, 1961), p. 4
46. John Marks, *The Search for the Manchurian Candidate: The CIA and Mind Control* (New York, paperback edition, 1988), p. 25, based on CIA documents.
47. *Sunday Times* (London), 6 July 1975, p. 1. Narut at the time was working at a US naval hospital in Naples, Italy, and made his remarks at a NATO-sponsored conference held in Oslo, Norway the week before.
48. Kinkead, p. 31.
49. Ibid., pp. 17, 34.
50. Ibid., pp. 105-6.

Notes

51. Ibid., p. 197.
52. For a concise description of the "terror bombing" of 1952-53, see John Gittings, "Talks, Bombs and Germs: Another Look at the Korean War", *Journal of Contemporary Asia* (London) Vol. 5, No. 2, 1975, pp. 212-6.
53. Air Force Communiqué, 2 February 1951, cited by Stone, p. 259
54. *Military Situation in the Far East*, Hearings Before the Senate Committees on Armed Services and Foreign Relations, 25 June 1951, p. 3075.
55. Louis Heren, "The Korean Scene", in Rear-Admiral H.G. Thursfield, ed., *Brassey's Annual: The Armed Forces Year-Book 1951* (London, 1951) p. 110.
56. *San Francisco Chronicle*, 15 December 1977, p. 11, based on documents released under the Freedom of Information Act.
57. *New York Times*, 12 November 1951, p. 3.
58. Ibid., 14 November 1951, p. 1.

6. ALBANIA 1949-1953

1. Douglas Sutherland, *The Fourth Man* (London, 1980) p. 88.
2. Thomas Powers, *The Man Who Kept the Secrets: Richard Helms and the CIA* (New York, 1979), p. 54.
3. Nicholas Bethell, *The Great Betrayal: The Untold Story of Kim Philby's Biggest Coup* (London, 1984) passim, for the most detailed discussion of the recruitment, training and fate of the émigrés (published in New York, 1984 as *Betrayed*). See also Bruce Page, David Leitch, and Philip Knightly, *The Philby Conspiracy* (New York, 1968) pp. 196-203.
4. Philby, p. 117.
5. E. Howard Hunt, *Undercover: Memoirs of an American Secret Agent* (London, 1975) p. 93.
6. See note 3 above.
7. Political background of the émigrés: *New York Times*, 20 June 1982, p. 22; Bethell, passim; Christopher Simpson, *Blowback: America's Recruitment of Nazis and Its Effects on the Cold War* (New York, 1988), p. 123 (Xhafer Deva).
8. Radio station, unrest: *New York Times*, 31 March 1951, p. 5; 9 April 1951, p. 1; 26 September 1951.
9. Philby, p. 118.
10. *New York Times*, 27 March 1950; 9 April 1951, p. 1.
11. Bethell, p. 183.
12. *New York Times*, 9 April 1951, p. 1.
13. Bethell, p. 200.

7. EASTERN EUROPE 1948-1956

1. *New York Times*, 29 September 1954.
2. The story of Operation Splinter Factor comes from the book of the same name by Stewart Steven published in London in 1974. Steven, a veteran British journalist and Editor of *The Mail on Sunday* (London), provides much greater detail than the short summary appearing here. He presents a strong case, and one has to read the entire book to appreciate this. Nonetheless, his central thesis remains undocumented. Steven states that this thesis — Allen Dulles instigating Jozef Swiatlo to use Noel Field in the manner described — comes from personal interviews with former members of the CIA, the SIS (the British Secret Intelligence Service) and other people involved in the conspiracy who insisted on remaining anonymous.
   Flora Lewis, the *Washington Post* correspondent who wrote *Red Pawn: The Story of Noel Field* (New York, 1965; published in London the same year as *The Man Who Disappeared: The Strange History of Noel Field*), stated in that book that she ran into an "official barrier of silence" when she requested information from American, Swiss, French, British and German intelligence centers on even "plain questions of dates and places". And she was not inquiring about Operation Splinter Factor *per se*, which she knew nothing about, only about Noel Field a decade after he had been released. Similarly, the US government, without explanation, flatly refused her access to Jozef Swiatlo.
   Richard Harris Smith, *OSS: The Secret History of America's First Central Intelligence Agency* (University of California Press, paperback edition, 1972), p. 238 note, writes that "It was later suggested that Field's arrest was actually part of a British plot to split the East European Communists, as outlined in John Le Carré's *The Spy Who Came in From the Cold*."
   Thomas Powers, *The Man Who Kept the Secrets: Richard Helms and the CIA* (Pocket Books, New York, 1979, paperback) pp. 405-6, suggests that Stewart Steven's "central premise apparently came from someone in the British SIS who did not like Dulles."
3. *New York Times*, 25 October 1954, p. 1.
4. Ibid., 19 February 1955, p. 1.
5. Ibid., 17 November 1954, p. 1.
6. Blanche W. Cook, *The Declassified Eisenhower* (New York, 1981) p. 129.
7. Ibid.
8. Cord Meyer, *Facing Reality: From World Federalism to the CIA* (New York, 1980) p. 120; Steven, pp. 208-9; Lewis, p. 238 (torture).
9. *New York Times*, 23 July 1948, p. 5; Robert Bishop and E. S. Crayfield, *Russia Astride the Balkans* (New York,

1948), pp. 264-71.
10. *New York Times*, 9 April 1951 (column by C. Sulzberger).
11. Cook, pp. 130-1; George Clay, "Balloons for a Captive Audience", *The Reporter* (New York) 18 November 1954; Robert T. Holt and Robert W. van de Velde, *Strategic Psychological Operations and American Foreign Policy* (University of Chicago Press, 1960) ch. VII.
12. *New York Times*, 24 January 1952, p. 4.
13. Ibid., 30 August 1955, p. 1.
14. Ibid., 30 November 1976.
15. Stephen Ambrose, *Ike's Spies* (Doubleday & Co., New York, 1981) pp. 235, 238.

8. GERMANY 1950s
1. Dean Acheson, *Present at the Creation: My Years in the State Department* (New York, 1969) p. 260.
2. Ibid.
3. Failure of deindustrialization: for further discussion, see Richard J. Barnet, *Allies: America, Europe and Japan since the War* (London, 1984) pp. 33-9.
4. Dwight Eisenhower, *The White House Years: Mandate for Change, 1953-1956* (New York, 1963) pp. 79-80.
5. *New York Times*, 6 November 1952, p. 3
6. *Democratic German Report*, 13 February 1953; see description of this publication below.
7. Victor Marchetti and John Marks, *The CIA and the Cult of Intelligence*, (New York, 1975) p. 147.
8. Sabotage and subversion campaign:
a) *Democratic German Report*, various issues from 1952 to 1957 (consult its annual indexes under 'Sabotage', 'Espionage', etc.). This was a small English-language news magazine published fortnightly in East Berlin by Britisher John Peet, former chief correspondent for Reuters News Agency in West Berlin.
b) *Nation's Business* (published by the United States Chamber of Commerce) April 1952, pp. 25-7, 68-9, discusses many of the tactics employed.
c) Sanche de Gramont, *The Secret War* (New York, 1963) pp. 479-80.
d) *The New Yorker*, 8 September 1951, article on the Investigating Committee of Freedom-minded Jurists of the Soviet Zone.
e) *The Nation*, (New York) 24 June 1961, pp. 551-2.
f) Andrew Tully, *CIA: The Inside Story* (Fawcett, New York, 1962) pp, 133-4, CIA activity in June 1953 East German uprising.
g) *Saturday Evening Post*, 6 November 1954, p. 64, refers to CIA-promoted train derailments in East Germany, and blowing up a railway bridge and promoting factory work slowdowns in unspecified East European countries. This was part of a series on the CIA prepared in collaboration with the Agency. [See Jonathan Kwitny, *Endless Enemies: The Making of an Unfriendly World* (New York, 1984) p. 165.]
9. Secret army, hit-list, etc.:
a) *Newsweek*, 20 October 1952, p. 42.
b) *New York Times*, 9 October 1952, p. 8; 10 October, p. 3 (under the remarkable headline: "German Saboteurs Betray U.S. Trust"); 12 October, p. 14.
c) *Der Spiegel* (West German weekly news magazine), 15 October 1952, pp. 6-8.
d) *Democratic German Report*, 15 and 24 October 1952; 21 November 1952.
10. *New York Times*, 14 October 1952, p. 13.

9. IRAN 1953
A general account and overview of the events in this chapter can be obtained from the following:
a) Kermit Roosevelt, *Countercoup: The Struggle for the Control of Iran* (New York, 1979) passim.
b) Bahman Nirumand, *Iran: The New Imperialism in Action* (New York, 1969), chapters 2 to 4, particularly the Iranian case for nationalization, British and American reaction, and post-coup developments.
c) Stephen Ambrose, *Ike's Spies* (Doubleday & Co., New York, 1981) chapters 14 and 15.
d) Barry Rubin, *Paved With Good Intentions: The American Experience and Iran* (New York, 1980) chapter 3.
e) David Wise and Thomas B. Ross, *The Invisible Government* (New York, 1965, paperback edition), pp. 116-21.
f) Andrew Tully, *CIA: The Inside Story* (New York, 1962), pp. 76-84.
g) Fred J. Cook in *The Nation* (New York) 24 June 1961, pp. 547-51, particularly conditions in Iran after the coup.
1. Roosevelt, p. 8.
2. Ibid., pp. 18-19.
3. Anthony Eden, *The Memoirs of the Right Honourable Sir Anthony Eden: Full Circle* (London, 1960) p. 194.
4. Dean Acheson, *Present at the Creation: My Years in the State Department* (New York, 1969) pp. 679-85; Eden, pp. 201-2: Nirumand, pp. 73-4.
5. Roosevelt, p. 107.
6. Ibid., pp. II, 2, 3, 91-2, 126, 134, 164, 119.
7. Acheson, p. 504.
8. Relations between Mossadegh, Tudeh, and the Soviet Union:
a) Manfred Halpern, "Middle East and North Africa", in C.E. Black and T.P. Thornton, eds., *Communism and Revolution* (U.S., 1964) pp. 316-19

b) Donald N. Wilber, *Iran: Past and Present* (Princeton University Press, Third Edition, 1955), p. 115. Wilber is an historian who, by his own admission, was also a CIA operative. He claims, in a later book, to have been the principal planner for the operation to overthrow Mossadegh (known as Operation AJAX), and that Roosevelt's book is full of factual errors. See *Adventures in the Middle East* (1986), pp. 187-8.

c) Nirumand, op. cit.

d) Rubin, op. cit.

9. *The Declassified Documents Reference System* (Arlington, Va.) 1979 volume, document 79E.

10. Ibid.

11. Roosevelt interview by Robert Scheer in the *Los Angeles Times*, 29 March 1979, p. 1.

12. *New York Times*, 10 July 1953, p. 4.

13. Roosevelt, p. 168.

14. Fitzroy Maclean, *Eastern Approaches* (London, 1949) pp. 266, 274; Maclean was a British officer in World War II who kidnapped Zahedi (or Zahidi) to keep him from further aiding the Nazis.

15. The details of the last days of the Mossadegh regime can be found in Roosevelt, chapters 11 and 12; Wilber pp. 124-7 (purposely makes no mention of the CIA — see Note 8); Ambrose, chapter 15, as well as in other books mentioned in this section.

16. Demonstration: Wilber, p. 125; Roosevelt, p. 179; *New York Times*, 19 August 1953.

17. Brian Lapping, *End of Empire* (Great Britain/US 1985) p. 220, based on the Granada Television series of the same name broadcast in Britain in 1985.

18. Halpern, p. 318; Wilber, p. 125.

19. Henderson meeting with Mossadegh: Ambrose, pp. 208-9, interview with Henderson by the author; Roosevelt, pp. 183-5.

20. *New York Times*, 19 August 1953.

21. Roosevelt, p. 191-2.

22. *New York Times*, 20 August 1953, p. 1: *The Times* (London), 20 August 1953.

23. David Leigh, *The Wilson Plot: How the Spycatchers and Their American Allies Tried to Overthrow the British Government* (New York, 1988) pp. 14-15.

24. Hearings in 1954 before the House Foreign Affairs Committee on "The Mutual Security Act of 1954", pp. 503, 569-70. Stewart was the Director of the Office of Military Assistance, Department of Defense.

25. Kennett Love, *The American Role in the Pahlevi Restoration on 19 August 1953* (Pahlevi was the Shah's name), unpublished manuscript residing amongst the Allen Dulles papers, Princeton University; excerpted in Jonathan Kwitny, *Endless Enemies: The Making of an Unfriendly World* (New York, 1984) pp. 164-177.

26. *New York Times*, 18 January 1953, IV, p. 8.

27. Arthur L. Richards, Director, Office of Greek, Turkish and Iranian Affairs, testimony 17 July 1953, before House Committee on Foreign Affairs in executive session, released in 1981, p. 148.

28. *New York Times*, 21 July 1953.

29. Ibid., 23 August 1953, IV, p. 1.

30. Scheer interview.

31. *The Guardian* (London) 2 January 1984, British Government papers of 1953, released 1 January 1984.

32. Testimony at "Hearings on the Situation in the Middle East", Senate Committee on Foreign Relations, 24 February 1956, p. 23.

33. Nirumand, pp. 100-108 explains the contract in detail.

34. Roosevelt's post-CIA career: Scheer interview; Wise and Ross, pp. 116-7; Kwitny, p. 183.

35. Robert Engler, *The Politics of Oil: A Study of Private Power and Democratic Directions* (New York, 1961) p. 310.

36. *San Francisco Chronicle*, 26 December 1979.

37. Roosevelt, p. 145.

38. *New York Times*, 6 August 1954.

39. Allen Dulles, *The Craft of Intelligence* (New York, 1965) p.216.

40. *Fortune* (New York) June 1975, p. 90.

41. Love, op. cit., cited in Kwitny, p. 175.

42. Roosevelt, p. 9.

43. Jesse J. Leaf, Chief CIA analyst on Iran for five years before resigning in 1973, interviewed by Seymour Hersh in the *New York Times*, 7 January 1979.

44. Martin Ennals, Secretary-General of Amnesty International, cited in an article by Reza Baraheni in *Matchbox* (Amnesty publication in New York) Fall, 1976.

45. Tully, p. 76.

46. See, e.g. Michael Klare, *War Without End* (New York, 1972) pp. 375, 379, 382, based on official US Government tables covering the 1950s and 1960s.

47. Cook, p. 550.

48. *San Francisco Chronicle*, 3 March 1980, p. 15.

10. GUATEMALA 1953-1954

The details of the events described in this chapter were derived principally from the following sources:

a) Stephen Schlesinger and Stephen Kinzer, Bitter Fruit: *The Untold Story of the American Coup in Guatemala* (Doubleday & Co., New York, 1982) passim, based partly on documents obtained under the Freedom of Information Act from the State Department, the Defense Department, the CIA, the National Archives, the Navy Department, and the FBI, as well as documents at the Eisenhower Library and amongst the John Foster Dulles and Allen Dulles papers at Princeton University, and interviews with individuals who played a role in the events. This is the primary source where another source is not indicated.

b) Blanche Wiesen Cook, *The Declassified Eisenhower* (Doubleday & Co., New York, 1981) pp. 222-92, based partly on documents at the Eisenhower Library and the Guatemala archives at the Library of Congress. The latter is composed of papers confiscated by the US after the coup.

c) Richard H. Immerman, *The CIA in Guatemala: The Foreign Policy of Intervention* (University of Texas Press, Austin, 1982) pp. 118-22, ch. 6 and 7, based partly on papers at the Truman and Eisenhower Libraries and interviews.

d) David Wise and Thomas Ross, *The Invisible Government* (New York, 1965, paperback edition) chapter 11.

e) Thomas and Marjorie Melville, *The Politics of Land Ownership* (New York, 1971), ch. 4 to 6; published in Great Britain the same year in slightly different form as *Guatemala — Another Vietnam?*

1. Schlesinger and Kinzer, pp. 143-4.
2. *New York Times*, 16 June 1954.
3. Ibid., 20 May 1954, p. 18.
4. *Time* magazine, 11 January 1954.
5. *Congressional Record*, 8 February 1954, p. 1475.
6. *Time*, 19 July 1954, p. 34.
7. Cook, p. 274; Schlesinger and Kinzer, p. 148.
8. Cook, p. 234.
9. Ibid., pp. 240-41.
10. Schlesinger and Kinzer, p. 12.
11. Cook, pp. 242-3, quoting former Guatemalan Foreign Minister Raul Oesegueda.
12. Schlesinger and Kinzer, p. 61.
13. *Washington Post*, 15 November 1953, p. 3B.
14. Schlesinger and Kinzer, pp. 58-9.
15. CIA National Intelligence Estimate, 11 March 1952, pp. 1-3, *Declassified Documents Reference System* (Woodbridge, Connecticut) 1982 Volume, Document no. 6.
16. Immerman, pp. 118-22.
17. Thomas P. McCann, *An American Company: The Tragedy of United Fruit* (New York, 1976) p. 49. McCann had been an official with United Fruit. Almost all sources differ as to the amount offered by the Guatemalan Government, ranging from McCann's figure to almost $1,200,000.
18. Schlesinger and Kinzer, pp. 106-7 and passim; McCann, chapter 4.
19. Schlesinger and Kinzer, p. 52.
20. Ibid., pp. 102-3.
21. Derived primarily from Schlesinger and Kinzer, to a lesser extent from the other sources listed at the beginning of this section, as well as those specified below.
22. Dwight Eisenhower, *The White House Years: Mandate for Change, 1953-1956* (New York, 1963) p. 424.
23. Cook, pp. 270-71.
24. Ibid., pp. 249-52.
25. *Time*, 8 February 1954, p. 36.
26. *New York Times*, 30 January 1954, pp. 1, 6.
27. McCann, p. 60.
28. David Atlee Phillips, *The Night Watch: Twenty-five Years of Peculiar Service* (Atheneum, New York, 1977) pp. 34-5.
29. *Life* magazine, 5 July 1954, p. 8.
30. *Newsweek*, 5 July 1954, p. 46.
31. State Department memo, 23 June 1954, cited in Schlesinger and Kinzer, p. 189.
32. James Hagerty, White House Press Secretary, Diaries 1954 (Eisenhower Library), 24 June 1954, cited in Schlesinger and Kinzer, p. 181.
33. Brian Urquhart, *Hammarskjold* (Knopf, New York, 1972), pp. 91-4.
34. *New York Times*, 24 June 1954; Schlesinger and Kinzer, p. 175.
35. Guillermo Toriello, *La Batalla de Guatemala* (Mexico City, 1955) p. 189; the Guatemalan Foreign Minister related what he was told by Col. Díaz; cited in Schlesinger and Kinzer, p. 207.
36. Cook, p. 285; Wise and Ross, p. 192-3.
37. Paul Kennedy, *The Middle Beat* (Teachers College Press, Columbia University, New York, 1971) p. 142; Schlesinger and Kinzer, pp. 219-20.
38. *Time*, 12 July 1954, p. 31.
39. Wise and Ross, pp. 194-5; John Gerassi, *The Great Fear in Latin America* (New York, 1965, revised edition) p. 183.
40. Melville, p. 93.

Notes

41. Schlesinger and Kinzer, pp. 218-9.
42. Ibid., pp. 60, 221-2; Cook, p. 231; Gerassi, p. 183.
43. Wise and Ross, p. 187.
44. Schlesinger and Kinzer, 222-3.
45. Hilda Gadea, *Ernesto: A Memoir of Che Guevara* (London, 1973, translated from the Spanish) p. 54.
46. *New York Times*, 1 July 1954.
47. CIA memo, 16 August 1954, *Declassified Documents Reference System* (Woodbridge, Connecticut) 1983 Volume, Document No. 32.
48. Statement before the Subcommittee on Latin America, House Select Committee on Communist Aggression, 8 October 1954, as reprinted in *Department of State Bulletin*, 8 November 1954, p. 690.
49. Eisenhower, pp. 421-7.
50. *New York Times*, 28 October 1955.

11. COSTA RICA Mid-1950s
1. *Los Angeles Times*, 10 March 1975.
2. *Miami Herald*, 10 March 1975.
3. *Christian Science Monitor* (Boston), 11 March 1975. Notes one to three all refer to the same television interview of Figueres in Mexico City, 9 March 1975. Figueres may have admitted to his CIA connections at this time because shortly before, Philip Agee's book had come out identifying Figueres as "a long-time Agency collaborator". (*Inside the Company: CIA Diary*, New York, 1975, p. 244; published in Great Britain in 1974.)
4. David Wise and Thomas Ross, *The Invisible Government* (New York, 1965, paperback edition) p. 127.
5. Ibid., pp. 127-8.
6. Charles D. Ameringer, *Democracy in Costa Rica* (Praeger, New York and Hoover Institution Press, Stanford University, California, 1982) pp. 83-5.
7. John Gerassi, *The Great Fear in Latin America* (New York, 1965, revised edition) p. 208.
8. *Miami Herald*, 13 February 1971.
9. Wise and Ross, p. 128.
10. Charles D. Ameringer, *Don Pepe, A Political Biography of José Figueres of Costa Rica* (University of New Mexico Press, 1978) pp. 124-5.
11. *Washington Post*, 9 January 1953; Wise and Ross, p. 127.

12. SYRIA 1956-1957
1. *Department of State Bulletin* (Washington), 18 June 1956, pp. 999-1000.
2. U.S. Mutual Security Act of 1955, Sections 142(a)(4) and 413.
3. *Declassified Documents Reference System*:
1992 volume: document no. 2326, 10 May 1955; no. 2663, 21 September 1955; no. 2973, 9 January 1956; no. 2974, 16 January 1956.
1993 volume: document no. 2953, 14 December 1955; no. 2954, 26 January 1956; no. 2955, 27 January 1956.
With the exception of no. 2663, all the documents bear the heading of the Operations Coordinating Board, a subcommittee of the NSC which coordinated covert activities.
4. Ibid., 1993 volume, no. 2953, 14 December 1955, p. 4.
5. Wilbur Crane Eveland, *Ropes of Sand: America's Failure in the Middle East* (W. W. Norton & Co., New York, 1980) p. 122.
6. Patrick Seale, *The Struggle for Syria: A Study of Post-War Arab Politics, 1945-1958* (London, 1965) pp. 283-306: Eveland, pp. 135, 169-73.
7. Eveland, p. 182.
8. 1956 plot and background: Eveland, chapters 11-20; *New York Times*, 10 April 1956; 17 October 1956.
9. Dwight D. Eisenhower, *The White House Years: Waging Peace, 1956-1961* (New York, 1965) p. 196.
10. *Declassified Documents Reference System*, 1981 volume, document no. 26E, 22 March 1957.
11. Ibid., 1985 volume, document no. 283, March 1957.
12. Ibid., 1981 volume, document no. 471B, 17 June 1957.
13. 1957 plot: Eveland, pp. 253-4; *New York Times*, 14 August 1957, pp. 1, 6; 15 August, pp. 1, 4.
14. *New York Times*, 17 August 1957, p. 3.
15. Ibid., p. 14.
16. Eisenhower, p. 196.
17. CIA internal report, author's name deleted, 18 June 1962, the result of conversations with "Western diplomats" concerning the Kennedy-Macmillan meeting, in *Declassified Documents Reference System*, 1975 volume, document no. 240A.

13. THE MIDDLE EAST 1957-1958
1. Wilbur Crane Eveland, *Ropes of Sand: America's Failure in the Middle East* (W. W. Norton & Co., New York, 1980) p. 240. What Eveland calls "Russia's threat" may not have been all that it appeared to be. Kennett Love (see note re him in chapter) reported later that the CIA had manufactured several reports of Russian military activity which were without any basis in fact, to induce France and Great Britain to call a cease fire — *Suez: The*

395

Twice-Fought War (Great Britain, 1969), p. 615.

2. Events in Jordan: *New York Times*, 5 April 1957, p. 1: 25 April, pp. 13; 26 April, p. 1; the words of the "intervention" quotation are those of the *Times*, 26 April.

3. Richard Barnet, *Intervention and Revolution*, (London, 1972) p. 149.

4. *Washington Post*, 18 February 1977.

5. Kennett Love, op. cit., p. 655.

6. Dwight D. Eisenhower, *The White House Years: Waging Peace, 1956-1961* (New York, 1965) p. 201.

7. *Declassified Documents Reference System*, (Arlington, Va.) 1981 volume, document 471B, 17 June 1957.

8. Eisenhower, p. 198.

9. Emmet John Hughes, *The Ordeal of Power* (London, 1963) pp. 253-4; the remark was made to Hughes "a few months after Herter took office" on 22 February 1957.

10. Barry Blechman and Stephen Kaplan, Force Without War: *U.S. Armed Forces as a Political Instrument* (The Brookings Institution, Washington, 1978) p. 84; although the study was undertaken at the Pentagon's request and with its full co-operation, the book stipulates that the views expressed are the authors' alone.

11. Events concerning Syria: *New York Times*, 6 September 1957, pp. 1, 2; 8 September, p. 3: 10 September, pp. 1, 8, 9; 11 September, p. 10; 12 September, p. 1; 13 September, pp. 1, 3; Barnet, pp. 149-51: Eisenhower, pp. 196-203; Patrick Seale, *The Struggle for Syria: A Study of Post-War Arab Politics, 1945-1958* (London, 1965) p. 303.

12. The norm has been for the CIA to be accused of involvement in a coup which the Agency or its scribes deny. In this case, it appears that the young CIA had a need to blow its own horn and it encouraged the word to be passed that it had been the motivating force behind the Egyptian army coup. But this assertion, found often in the literature, has never been accompanied by any clear description of how this took place, not even an explanation of *why* the CIA preferred Farouk out and the army in. Miles Copeland, one of the Agency's earliest officers and a great admirer of Kermit Roosevelt, goes to some length in his 1969 book, *The Game of Nations*, to propagate the story, but his account is pure crypto-mumbo-jumbo. In the same book, Copeland asserts that the CIA, with himself personally involved, directed a coup in Syria in 1949. This tale, too, is written in a manner that does not inspire credibility. It is probably relevant that CIA colleague Wilbur Crane Eveland (p. 148) has written that "I'd already had evidence that Copeland tended to exaggerate."

13. Saud, Illah, and plot against Nasser: Eveland, pp. 243-4.

14. Ibid., pp. 246-8.

15. Plots:
 a) *New York Times*, 8, 13-15 August 1957; 21 October 1957; 24, 28, December 1957; 14 February 1958; 6-8, 14, 29 March 1958; 8 October 1958.

 b) Eveland, p. 273.

 c) Eisenhower, pp. 263-4.

 d) *The Times* (London), numerous references from July 1957 to October 1958 — see the newspaper's index under "Egypt" and "Syria": "espionage" and "political situation".

16. Eveland, p. 292n.

17. Soviet proposals: *New York Times*, 6 September 1957, p. 2; 11 September, p. 10.

18. Eisenhower, p. 269.

19. David Wise and Thomas Ross, *The Invisible Government* (New York, 1965, paperback edition) p. 337.

20. 1957 election and aftermath: Eveland, pp. 248-53, 256; Eisenhower, p. 265; Barnet, pp. 143-8.

21. Eisenhower quotations: Eisenhower, pp. 266-7.

22. Dulles news conference, 20 May 1958: *Department of State Bulletin*, 9 June 1958, p. 945.

23. Barnet, pp. 147-8.

24. Eisenhower, p. 268.

25. Eveland, p. 276.

26. Robert Murphy, *Diplomat Among Warriors* (US, 1965), p. 450.

27. Eisenhower, p. 273.

28. Murphy, p. 445, 455.

29. Eisenhower, p. 275.

30. Eveland, pp. 294-5; Eisenhower refers to similar situations, p. 277.

31. Eveland, pp. 295-6.

32. Wise and Ross, pp. 337-8; news item from the *St. Louis Post Dispatch*, 23 July 1958, cited on p. 338.

33. Blechman and Kaplan, p. 253.

34. Claudia Wright, *New Statesman* magazine (London), 15 July 1983, p. 20. She doesn't say how the Soviets found out about the plan.

35. *Interim Report: Alleged Assassination Plots Involving Foreign Leaders*, The Select Committee to Study Governmental Operations with Respect to Intelligence Activities (US Senate), 20 November 1975, p. 181, footnote. In the report, Kassem is referred to as "an Iraqi colonel". See also: Thomas Powers, *The Man Who Kept the Secrets: Richard Helms and the CIA* (New York, 1979) pp. 161, 163 for a discussion of how President Eisenhower would have to have given the approval for the action against Kassem.

36. See, e.g., Eisenhower, pp. 274-5.

37. Ibid., pp. 290-1.

Notes

14. INDONESIA 1957-1958

1. Joseph Burkholder Smith, *Portrait of a Cold Warrior* (G.P. Putnam's Sons, New York, 1976) p. 205.
2. *New York Times*, 18 May 1956.
3. *Supplementary Detailed Staff Reports on Foreign and Military Intelligence*, Book 4, Final Report of The Select Committee to Study Governmental Operations with Respect to Intelligence Activities (U.S. Senate), April 1976, p. 133.
4. *New York Times*, 12, 30 April 1955; 3, 4 August 1955; 3 September 1955; 22 November 1967, p. 23.
5. John Discoe Smith, *I Was a CIA Agent in India* (India, 1967) passim; *New York Times*, 25 October 1967, p. 17; 22 November, p. 23; 5 December, p. 12; Harry Rositzke, *The KGB: The Eyes of Russia* (New York, 1981), p. 164.
6. *Interim Report: Alleged Assassination Plots Involving Foreign Leaders*, The Select Committee to Study Governmental Operations with Respect to Intelligence Activities (U.S. Senate), 20 November 1975, p. 4, note.
7. David Wise and Thomas Ross, *The Invisible Government* (New York, 1965, paperback edition) pp. 149-50.
8. Julie Southwood and Patrick Flanagan, *Indonesia: Law, Propaganda and Terror* (London, 1983) pp. 26-7.
9. Wise and Ross, p. 148.
10. J.B. Smith, pp. 210-11.
11. Ibid., pp. 228-9.
12. Ibid., p. 240.
13. Ibid., pp. 229, 246.
14. Ibid., p. 243.
15. Sex-blackmail operations: ibid., pp. 238-40, 248. Smith errs somewhat in his comment about *Round Table*. The article's only (apparent) reference to the Soviet woman is in the comment on p. 133: "Other and more scandalous reasons have been put forward for the President's leaning towards the Communist Party."
16. *New York Times*, 26 January 1976.
17. Truman Smith, "The Infamous Record of Soviet Espionage", *Reader's Digest*, August 1960.
18. J.B. Smith, pp. 220-1.
19. Referred to in a memorandum from Allen Dulles to the White House, 7 April 1961; the memo briefly summarizes the main points of the US intervention: *Declassified Documents Reference System* (Arlington, Va.) released 18 December 1974.
20. The military operation and the Pope affair:
a) Wise and Ross, pp. 145-56.
b) Christopher Robbins, *Air America* (US, 1979), pp. 88-94.
c) Col. L. Fletcher Prouty, US Air Force, Ret., *The Secret Team: The CIA and its Allies in Control of the World* (New York, 1974) pp. 155, 308, 363-6.
d) *New York Times*, 23 March 1958, p. 2; 19 April; 28 May, p. 9.
e) *Sukarno, An Autobiography*, as told to Cindy Adams (Hong Kong, 1966) pp. 267-71; first printed in the US in 1965; although a poor piece of writing, the book is worth reading for Sukarno's views on why it is foolish to call him a Communist; how he, as a Third-Worlder who didn't toe the line, was repeatedly snubbed and humiliated by the Eisenhower administration, apart from the intervention; and how American sex magazines contrived to make him look ridiculous.
f) J. B. Smith, pp. 246-7. There appears to be some confusion about the bombing of the church. Smith states that it was Pope who did it on 18 May before being shot down. Either he or other chroniclers have mixed up the events of April and May.
21. Wise and Ross, p. 145.

15. WESTERN EUROPE 1950s and 1960s

1. Richard Fletcher, "How CIA Money Took the Teeth Out of British Socialism", in Philip Agee and Louis Wolf, eds., *Dirty Work: The CIA in Western Europe* (New Jersey, 1978) p. 200.
2. The CCF, its activities and its publications:
a) For a detailed, and sympathetic, history of the CCF, see Peter Coleman, *The Liberal Conspiracy: The Congress for Cultural Freedom and the Struggle for the Mind of Postwar Europe* (New York, 1989), passim; CCF magazines — chapters 5 and 11; CCF books — Appendix D, plus elsewhere;
b) Russell Warren Howe, "Asset Unwitting: Covering the World for the CIA", *MORE* (New York), May 1978, pp. 20-27, a magazine associated with the Columbia University School of Journalism;
c) *New York Times*, 26 December 1977, p. 37; 27 April 1966, p. 28; 8, 9 May 1967, and other issues in 1967;
d) *Commentary* magazine (New York), September 1967;
e) Fletcher, pp. 188-200.
   Amongst other non-European CCF magazines were: *Thought*, and *Quest* in India, *Aportes*, *Cadernos Brasileiros*, and *Informes de China* in Latin America, *Black Orpheus*, and *Transition* in Africa, *Horison*, *Social Science Review*, *Jiyu* and *Solidarity* in Asia, and *Hiwar* in Beirut.
3. Ray Cline, *Secrets, Spies and Soldiers* (US, 1976), p. 129.
4. *New York Times*, 26 December 1977, p. 37.
5. *Washington Post*, 15 May 1967, p. 1.
6. Forum World Features: Howe, op. cit. Howe is the Forum writer quoted. CIA budget: House Committee report,

cited in Howe, p. 27. For a detailed study of CIA use of American news organizations, see Carl Bernstein, "The CIA and the Media", *Rolling Stone*, 20 October 1977, and *New York Times*, 26 December 1977, pp. 1 and 37.
7. *The Nation* (New York), 19 June 1982, p. 738. The article reports that some CIA officers have maintained that Springer was rather liberal in the early 1950s and he was financed to counter neo-Nazi and rightist elements in Germany. This should be taken with a grain of salt, for the overriding policy of the American occupation administration during this period, regardless of the sentiments of any individual American official, was to suppress the influence of persons and groups to the left of center — Communists, radicals, and social democrats alike; at the same time, the US authorities were employing "former" Nazis in every area of administration and intelligence (see chapter on Germany).
8. Tom Braden, "I'm Glad the CIA is 'Immoral'," *Saturday Evening Post*, 20 May 1967.
9. Ibid.
10. Labour Party/CND: Fletcher, pp. 196-7; *The Times* (London), 5 October 1961.
11. Braden, p. 14.
12. Political parties/CIA:
a) *New York Times*, 7 and 9 January 1976.
b) Jack Anderson in the *San Francisco Chronicle*, 11 and 12 November 1981.
c) Coleman, pp. 183-5.
d) Chapman Pincher, *Inside Story: A Documentary of the Pursuit of Power* (London, 1979) p. 28.
13. Operation Gladio:
a) *The Observer* (London), 7 June 1992.
b) *The Guardian* (New York), 5 December 1990, p. 5, article from Milan citing the Italian news magazine *Panorama*, Agence France Presse, and other European sources.
c) *Washington Post*, 14 November 1990, p. A19.
d) *Die Welt* (Germany), 14 November 1990, p. 7.
e) *Los Angeles Times*, 15 November 1990, p. A6.

16. BRITISH GUIANA 1953-1964

1. Events of 1953: *The Guardian* (London), 28 December 1984, for a detailed description of the raw cynicism behind the British action, based on government documents released in 1984; see also *The Times* (London) 7 and 10 October 1953; Cheddi Jagan, *The West on Trial* (London, 1966) chapters 7 and 8; "The Ordeal of British Guiana", *Monthly Review*, (New York) July-August 1964, pp. 16-19.
2. *Parliamentary Debates, House of Commons*, 22 October 1953, column 2170, speech by Oliver Lyttleton.
3. Ticket incident: Jagan, p. 149. Pan Am: Morton Halperin, et al., *The Lawless State* (Penguin Books, New York, 1976), p. 47; Christopher Robbins, *Air America* (New York, 1979), p. 58; *CounterSpy* magazine (Washington) December 1983-February 1984, p. 21; Trippe was a member of two long-time CIA fronts: The American Institute for Free Labor Development, and The Asia Foundation (formerly called National Committee for a Free Asia)
4. ORIT: Jagan, pp. 296-7; Philip Agee, *Inside the Company: CIA Diary* (New York, 1975) see index; *Survey of the Alliance for Progress: Labor Policies and Programs*, Staff Report of the US Senate Foreign Relations Committee, Subcommittee on American Republics Affairs, 15 July 1968, pp. 8-9; Serafino Romualdi, *Presidents and Peons: Recollections of a Labor Ambassador in Latin America* (New York, 1967), p. 346.
5. Events of 1957-59: *The Sunday Times* (London) 16 and 23 April 1967.
6. *New York Times*, 22 February 1967, pp. 1, 17.
7. *The Sunday Times*, op. cit.
8. Jagan, p. 304.
9. Richard Barnet, *Intervention and Revolution* (London, 1972) p. 244.
10. Arthur Schlesinger, *A Thousand Days* (Boston, 1965) pp. 774-9.
11. *San Francisco Chronicle*, 21 March 1964, p. 27; *New York Times*, 31 October 1964, p. 7; *The Times* (London), 29 June 1963, p. 8.
12. Jagan, p. 255.
13. 1962 strike: *New York Times*, 22 February 1967, p. 17; 30 October 1994, p. 4 (media):Barnet, p. 245; Agee, pp. 293-4; Jagan, pp. 252-69; *The Times* (London) 13 March 1962, p.10.
14. 1963 strike, general description: Jagan, chapters 13 and 14.
15. *Parliamentary Debates, House of Commons*, 4 May 1966, columns 1765-7; see also 29 April 1966, columns 1133-4.
16. *New York Times*, 22 February 1967, p. 17.
17. Thomas J. Spinner Jr., *A Political and Social History of Guyana, 1945-1983* (London, 1984) pp. 115-6; Agee, p. 406; *New York Times*, 4 January 1964, p. 10.
18. *The Sunday Times*, op. cit.
19. Ibid.
20. *New York Times*, 11 August 1963, p. 28.
21. Ibid., 11 September 1963, p. 1.
22. *The Sunday Times* (London) 25 May 1975, p. 4.
23. *San Francisco Chronicle*, 21 March 1964, p. 27.

Notes

24. Jagan, pp. 372-5.
25. *New York Times*, 31 October 1964, p. 7.
26. *The Times* (London) 29 June 1963, p. 8: the words are those of *The Times*.
27. *Parliamentary Debates, House of Commons*, 27 April 1964, column 109.
28. *The Times* (London) 7 December 1964, p. 8.
29. Events of December 1964: *The Times* (London), 4 to 15 December 1964.
30. *The Nation*, June 4, 1990, pp. 763-4
31. *New York Times,* 30 October 1994, p. 4.
32. Ibid., pp. 1 and 4.
33. Ibid., p. 4.

17. SOVIET UNION late 1940s to 1960s

1. Spy Planes:
a) James Bamford, *The Puzzle Palace* (Penguin Books, Great Britain, 1983) pp, 136-9, 180-5.
b) Col. L. Fletcher Prouty, USAF, ret., *The Secret Team: The CIA and its Allies in Control of the World* (New York, 1974) pp. 167-72, 187-9, 369-79, 419-29.
c) Sanche de Gramont, *The Secret War* (New York, 1963) chapter 9.
d) Harry Rositzke, *The CIA's Secret Operations* (New York, 1977) p. 23,
e) *New York Times*, 6 May 1960, p. 7, a list of air incidents to that date.
2. Yeltsin: *Los Angeles Times,* 13 June 1992; Volkogonov: ibid, 12 November 1992. To add to the confusion, the *New York Times* of 12 November reported that Volkogonov said that all 730 airmen, after being interned in Russian prison camps, had been "sent back home". All attempts by the author to locate Volkogonov's exact testimony have been unsuccessful. It appears that his testimony was never published.
3. *New York Times*, 12 May 1960.
4. Emmet John Hughes, *Ordeal of Power* (London, 1963) p. 301.
5. Prouty, pp, 399, 421-4, 427.
6. Francis Gary Powers, *Operation Overflight* (New York, 1970), pp.. 81-5, 113 and elsewhere.
7. Prouty, p. 189.
8. *New York Times*, 8 May 1960, p. 29.
9. Ibid., 10 May 1960. The article referred to the continental United States. Whether any Soviet flights had been made over Alaska, which became a state in 1959, was not mentioned.
10. *Caught in The Act: Facts About U.S. Espionage and Subversion Against the U.S.S.R.* (Foreign Languages Publishing House, Moscow, second revised edition, 1963), p. 95.
11. Thomas Powers, *The Man Who Kept the Secrets: Richard Helms and the CIA* (New York, 1979) pp. 155, 157
12. Emigrés, infiltration into the Soviet Union:
a) De Gramont, pp. 185-9, 480-6.
b) Konstantin Cherezov, *NTS, A Spy Ring Unmasked* (Moscow, 1965) passim; the author worked closely with NTS in Western Europe for several years before returning to the Soviet Union.
c) Rositzke, pp. 18-50.
d) *Caught in the Act*, passim.
e) Wilbur Crane Eveland, *Ropes of Sand: America's Failure in the Middle East* (N.Y. 1980) p. 263.
f) Kim Philby, *My Silent War* (MacGibbon and Kee, London 1968) pp. 199-202.
g) Victor Marchetti and John Marks, *The CIA and the Cult of Intelligence* (New York, 1975) pp. 204-6.
h) Louis Hagen, *The Secret War for Europe* (London, 1968) pp. 163-4.
i) *New York Times*, 30 August 1955, p. 1, training of Eastern Europeans at Fort Bragg, N.C. in guerrilla warfare.
j) *Nation's Business* (published by the United States Chamber of Commerce), April 1952, pp. 25-7, 68-9, discusses many of the sabotage and other tactics employed in the Soviet Union and Eastern Europe.
13. Cherezov, passim; de Gramont, pp. 480-6; Marchetti and Marks, p. 165.
14. *Foreign and Military Intelligence*, Book 1, Final Report of The Select Committee to Study Governmental Operations with Respect to Intelligence Activities (U.S. Senate), April 1976, p. 193.
15. *Book Week* (Washington Post), 5 February 1967.
16. *Foreign and Military Intelligence*, op. cit., p. 194.
17. For further discussion of CIA/USIA books and the source of these and other titles, see the references in notes 14 and 15; also *Washington Post* 28 September 1966; *New York Times*, 22 March 1967 and 22 December 1977; Peter Coleman, *The Liberal Conspiracy: The Congress for Cultural Freedom and the Struggle for the Mind of Postwar Europe* (New York, 1989), Appendix D and elsewhere; Alexander Kendrick, *Prime Time: The Life of Edward R. Murrow* (London, 1970), p. 478; Marchetti and Marks, pp. 180-1; E. Howard Hunt, *Undercover: Memoirs of an American Secret Agent* (London, 1975) pp. 70, 132.
18. Marchetti and Marks, pp. 174-8; de Gramont, pp. 486, 488-92.
19. *Washington Post*, 17 and 20 May 1982; 4 November 1982. For fuller discussions of the use of Nazis and their collaborators by the US Government in the anti-communist crusade, see: Christopher Simpson, *Blowback: America's Recruitment of Nazis and Its Effects on the Cold War* (New York, 1988), passim, and John Loftus, *The Belarus Secret* (New York, 1982), passim.
20. See references for note 12.
21. Hearings before The Select Committee to Study Governmental Operations with Respect to Intelligence Activities

(U.S. Senate), Volume 4, 1975; *Washington Post*, 16 January 1975, p. 18; Rositzke, p. 62.
22. *Washington Post*, 25 April 1979.
23. Rositzke, pp. 21, 33, 37.
24. *San Francisco Chronicle*, 9 October 1978.
25. Rositzke, p. 15.

18. ITALY 1950s to 1970s

1. Unattributed, dated 19 June 1953; copy reproduced in *Declassified Documents Reference System* (Arlington, Va.), 1977, document 137A.
2. Philip Agee and Louis Wolf, eds., *Dirty Work: The CIA in Western Europe* (New Jersey, 1978) pp. 168-9, English translation of interview with Victor Marchetti in *Panorama* (Milan, Italy), 2 May 1974, entitled "Le mani sull'Italia".
3. CIA memorandum to The Forty Committee (National Security Council), presented to the Select Committee on Intelligence, US House of Representatives (The Pike Committee) during closed hearings held in 1975. The bulk of the committee's report which contained this memorandum was leaked to the press in February 1976 and first appeared in book form as *CIA — The Pike Report* (Nottingham, England, 1977). The memorandum appears on pp. 204-5 of this book. (See the Notes section for Iraq for further information about this report.)
4. Victor Marchetti and John D. Marks, *The CIA and the Cult of Intelligence* (New York, 1975) p. 172; William Colby, *Honorable Men: My Life in the CIA* (New York, 1978) p. 119.
5. *CIA — The Pike Report*, p.193.
6. *New York Times*, 7 January 1976, p. 1
7. Bob Woodward, *VEIL: The Secret Wars of the CIA, 1981-1987* (New York, 1987), p. 398.
8. *New York Times*, 7 January 1976, p. 4.
9. Ibid., p. 1.
10. CIA quote: *New York Times*, 26 December 1977, p. 37. *Daily American*: ibid; Carl Bernstein, "The CIA and the Media", *Rolling Stone*, 20 October 1977, p. 59; Thomas Powers, *The Man Who Kept the Secrets: Richard Helms and the CIA* (New York, 1979, paperback edition) p. 414. One of the owners of the newspaper was Robert Cunningham, a CIA employee from 1956 to 1964. (*Washington Post*, 19 September 1985, p. A18)
11. Fred Landis, "Robert Moss, Arnaud de Borchgrave, and Right-Wing Disinformation", *Covert Action Information Bulletin* (Washington), August-September 1980, p. 43.
12. Colby, p. 124. Colby does not mention which year he's referring to, but in 1955, in a shop stewards' election at Fiat, the Communist union's share of the vote fell to 39% from 63% the year before. (*New York Times*, 30 March 1955, p. 9) The *Times* article stated that the dominance of the Communist union had greatly impaired Fiat's value for Western defense and its eligibility for offshore procurement orders from the United States.
13. Agee and Wolf, p. 169.
14. Mark Aarons and John Loftus, *Unholy Trinity: The Vatican, The Nazis and Soviet Intelligence* (New York, 1991), pp. 284-5, 118
15. Agee and Wolf, p. 171.
16. Colby, chapter 4.
17. *The Sunday Times* (London) 21 March 1976, p. 34.

19. VIETNAM 1950-1973

1. *Le Monde*, 13 April 1950, cited in R.E.M. Irving, *The First Indochinese War* (London, 1975) p. 101.
2. Cited in Hans Askenasy, *Are We All Nazis?* (Lyle Stuart, Secaucus, NJ, 1978) p. 64.
3. *New York Times*, 21 March 1954, p. 3;11 April 1954, IV, p. 5. According to Bernard Fall, *The Two Vietnams* (Frederick A. Praeger, Publishers, New York, 1967, second revised edition) p. 472, only $954 million of the $ 1.4 billion had been spent at the time of the ceasefire in 1954.
4. *The Pentagon Papers* (N.Y. Times edition, Bantam Books, 1971), p. xi.
5. Ibid., pp. 4, 5, 8, 26.
6. *Washington Post*, 14 September 1969, p. A25. Lansing was the uncle of John Foster and Allen Dulles. He appointed them both to the American delegation at the Versailles Peace Conference in 1918-19, where it was that Ho Chi Minh presented his appeal.
7. Ho Chi Minh and Vietminh working with OSS, admirers of the US: Archimedes L.A. Patti, *Why Vietnam? Prelude to America's Albatross* (University of California Press, Berkeley, 1980), passim. Patti is the former OSS officer consulted by Ho; Chester Cooper, *The Lost Crusade: The Full Story of US Involvement in Vietnam from Roosevelt to Nixon* (Great Britain, 1971) pp. 22, 25-7, 40. Cooper was a veteran American diplomat in the Far East who served as the Assistant for Asian Affairs in the Johnson White House. He was also a CIA officer, covertly, for all or part of his career.
French collaboration with the Japanese: Fall, pp. 42-9.
Ho Chi Minh not a genuine nationalist: Department of State Bulletin (Washington), 13 February 1950, p. 244, Dean Acheson; 10 April 1950, Ambassador Loy Henderson; 22 May 1950, Dean Acheson.
Ho Chi Minh's desk: Blanche W. Cook, The Declassified Eisenhower (New York, 1981). p. 184.
Declaration of Independence: Full text can be found in Ho Chi Minh, Selected Works, Volume III (Hanoi, 1961), pp. 17-21.
8. Fall, pp. 122, 124.

9. *The Pentagon Papers*, p. 5; Fall, p. 473.
10. Fall, p. 473.
11. Christopher Robbins, *Air America* (G. P. Putnam, New York, 1979) pp. 59-60.
12. *New York Times*, 11 April 1954, IV, p. 5.
13. *The Pentagon Papers*, p. 11.
14. Ibid., p. 36.
15. Ibid., pp. 5, 11; Dwight Eisenhower, *The White House Years: Mandate for Change, 1953-1956* (New York, 1963) pp. 340-41; Cooper, chapter IV; Sherman Adams, *Firsthand Report* (New York, 1961) p. 122; Adams was Eisenhower's White House chief of staff.
16. Adams, p. 124.
17. *The Pentagon Papers*, p. 46.
18. *The Times* (London) 2 June 1954, quoting from an article by Willoughby.
19. Cooper, p. 72.
20. Bernard Fall, *Hell in a Very Small Place: The Siege of Dien Bien Phu* (Great Britain, 1967) p. 307; *Parade* magazine (*Washington Post*) 24 April 1966; Roscoe Drummond and Gaston Coblentz, *Duel at the Brink* (New York, 1960) pp. 121-2.
21. Joseph Burkholder Smith, *Portrait of a Cold Warrior* (New York, 1976) pp. 172-4.
22. Ibid., pp. 173-4.
23. Eisenhower: *Time* magazine, 12 July 1954.
24. US policy toward the Geneva Conference: Cooper, chapter IV; Cooper was a member of the American delegation at the conference.
25. Fall (*Two Vietnams*), pp. 153-4.
26. All other actions: *The Pentagon Papers*, Document No. 15: "Lansdale Team's Report on Covert Saigon Mission in '54 and '55", pp. 53-66.
27. C.L. Sulzberger, *New York Times*, 22 January 1955, p. 10.
28. *New York Times*, 17 July 1955.
29. US Department of Defense, *United States - Vietnam Relations, 1945-67* (the government edition of the Pentagon Papers) book 2, IV, A.5, tab 4, p. 66, cited in Noam Chomsky and Edward Herman, *The Washington Connection and Third World Fascism* (Boston, 1979) p. 370.
30. J.B. Smith, p. 199.
31. Eisenhower, p. 372.
32. *The Pentagon Papers*, p. 22.
33. Ibid., p. 25
34. *Life* magazine, 13 May 1957.
35. *The Pentagon Papers*, p. 23.
36. Emmet John Hughes, *The Ordeal of Power* (London, 1963) p. 208; Hughes was a speech writer for President Eisenhower.
37. Michael Klare, *War Without End* (Random House/Vantage Books, New York, 1972) pp. 261-3; David Wise and Thomas B. Ross, *The Espionage Establishment* (Random House, New York, 1967) p. 152.
38. *Time*, 30 June 1975, p. 32 of European edition.
39. David Wise, "Colby of CIA — CIA of Colby", *New York Times Magazine*, 1 July 1973, p. 9.
40. Donald Duncan, *The New Legions* (London, 1967) pp. 156-9.
41. *Newsweek*, 22 March 1976, pp. 28, 31.
42. *Washington Post*, 20 March 1982, p. A19.
43. In numerous places; see, e.g., *I.F. Stone's Weekly*, (Washington), 4 March 1968; "The 'Phantom Battle' that Led to War", *U.S. News and World Report*, 23 July 1984, pp. 56-67; Joseph C. Goulden, *Truth is the First Casualty: The Gulf of Tonkin Affair — Illusion and Reality* (Rand McNally & Co., U.S., 1969), passim.
44. *Covert Action Information Bulletin* (Washington) No. 10, August-September 1980, p. 43.
45. *Washington Post*, 24 March 1967.
46. *Chicago Daily News*, 20 October 1965; *Washington Post*, 21 October 1965.
47. Copy of Oglesby's speech in author's possession.
48. *Washington Post*, 12 February 1967.
49. Ibid., 18 December 1966.
50. Alexander M. Haig, Jr. *Caveat: Realism, Reagan, and Foreign Policy* (New York, 1984), p. 202.
51. *New York Times*, 28 July 1975, p. 19.
52. *New York Herald Tribune*, 25 April 1965, p. 18.
53. *U.S. Assistance Program in Vietnam*, Hearings before a Subcommittee of the House Committee on Government Operations, 19 July 1971, p. 189.
54. Ibid., p. 183.
55. Victor Marchetti and John Marks, *The CIA and the Cult of Intelligence* (New York, 1975) pp. 236-7.
56. William Colby, *Honorable Men: My Life in the CIA* (New York, 1978) pp. 272, 275-6.
57. Marchetti and Marks, p. 237.
58. Wise, p. 33.
59. *New York Times*, 3 August 1971, p. 10.

60. *Congressional Record*, House, 12 May 1966, pp. 9977-78, reprint of an article by Morley Safer of CBS News.
61. *Washington Post*, 25 November 1966.
62. *U.S. Aid to North Vietnam*, Hearings Before the Subcommittee on Asian and Pacific Affairs, House Committee on International Relations, 19 July 1977, Appendix 2.
63. *Atlanta Journal*, 25 September 1965.
64. *San Francisco Chronicle*, 9 January 1971; also see Telford Taylor, *Nuremberg and Vietnam: An American Tragedy* (New York, 1970).

20. CAMBODIA 1955-1973

1. Prince Norodom Sihanouk, as related to Wilfred Burchett, *My War With The CIA* (London, 1974, revised edition) pp. 75-6. The SEATO treaty of 1954 actually had a protocol attached which unilaterally placed Cambodia, Laos and South Vietnam under its umbrella. Sihanouk later asserted that he had rejected Cambodia's inclusion, although at the time he was reportedly amenable to his country being a member of some sort of Western security system for south-east Asia. In any event, for various reasons, he soon moved away from this position and toward the policy of neutralism he maintained thereafter. For a fuller discussion of these matters, see Michael Leifer, *Cambodia: The Search for Security* (London, 1967) particularly chapter 3.
2. Events of 1956: Sihanouk, pp. 82-6; *New York Times*, 17 March 1956, p. 2; 24 March, p. 3; 20 April, p. 5; 21 April, p. 3.
3. Ibid., p. 94.
4. *Neak Cheat Niyum* ("The Nationalist", Phnom Penh) 29 September 1963, cited in Leifer, p. 144.
5. *Pentagon Papers*, Vol 10, p. 1100, cited by William Shawcross, *Side-Show: Kissinger, Nixon and the Destruction of Cambodia* (New York, 1979, paperback edition) p. 53.
6. Sihanouk, pp. 102-3; *New York Times*, 26 June 1958, p. 1; 25 April 1966, p. 20.
7. Shawcross, p. 54.
8. Ibid.
9. Ibid., p. 122.
10. *Washington Post*, 2 January 1966, p. E4.
11. US involvement with the Khmer Serei and Khmer Krom: Charles Simpson, III, *Inside the Green Berets — The First 30 Years — A History of the US Army Special Forces* (London, 1983) pp. 114-5; Shawcross, passim; Sihanouk, passim.
12. Plot of 1958-59: Sihanouk, pp. 102-109; *Washington Post*, 7 September 1965, p. 1; Shawcross, pp. 54-5; *The Observer* (London) 22 February 1959, p. 8.
13. Sihanouk, p. 125.
14. Ibid., pp. 124-5.
15. William Colby, *Honorable Men: My Life in the CIA* (New York, 1978), pp. 149-50.
16. Sihanouk, pp. 113-115, 118-121.
17. Effects of US aid to Cambodia: Sihanouk, passim, particularly pp. 93-6, 133-8; Shawcross, pp. 58-60; *Washington Post*, 2 January 1966, p. E4.
18. Sihanouk, pp. 139-40.
19. See, e.g., *Washington Post*, 4 August 1966 & 15 October 1966.
20. Francois Ponchaud, *Cambodia Year Zero*, translated from the French (London, 1978) p. 186.
21. *San Francisco Chronicle*, 23 July 1973.
22. Ibid., 16 July 1973; Shawcross, pp. 287-90.
23. Shawcross, pp. 148-9.
24. Ibid., pp. 114-15, based on interviews with Snepp by Shawcross.
25. Ibid., p. 114.
26. Seymour M. Hersh, *Kissinger: The Price of Power* (London, 1983) p. 176. Hersh, in chapter 15, provides further details of the machinations between the US and Lon Nol and others indicating American foreknowledge and encouragement of the coup.
27. Shawcross, p. 122.
28. Ibid., pp. 118-19.
29. Ibid., p. 120.
30. Roger Morris, *Uncertain Greatness: Henry Kissinger and American Foreign Policy* (Great Britain, 1977) p. 173.
31. Shawcross, p. 119; Snepp's remarks based on interview with him by Shawcross.
32. *New York Times*, 21 March 1970, p. 1.
33. Morris, p. 174.
34. *Newsweek*, 22 November 1971, p. 37.
35. Shawcross, p. 400.
36. Testimony before US Senate Foreign Relations Committee, Hearings on Supplemental Assistance to Cambodia, 24 February 1975, p. 64.
37. American support of the Khmer Rouge:
a) Jack Calhoun, "U.S. Supports Khmer Rouge", *Covert Action Information Bulletin*, No. 34, Summer 1990, pp. 37-40.
b) David Munro, "Cambodia: A Secret War Continues", *Covert Action Information Bulletin*, No. 40, Spring 1992,

Notes

pp. 52-57.

c) *Newsweek*, 10 October 1983, p. 41.

d) *Los Angeles Times*, 5 December 1980 (Ray Cline); 27 February 1991 (Bush administration admission of "tactical military cooperation" between US-backed forces and the Khmer Rouge.)

21. LAOS 1957-1973
1. Vientiane (Laos) correspondent, "The Labyrinthine War", *Far Eastern Economic Review* (Hong Kong conservative weekly), 16 April 1970, p. 73.
2. Testimony before the US Senate Armed Services Committee, *Hearings on Fiscal Year 1972 Authorizations*, 22 July 1971, p. 4289.
3. Testimony before the House Subcommittee on Foreign Operations and Monetary Affairs, Committee on Government Operations, *Hearings on US Aid Operations in Laos*, May-June 1959; see also *New York Times*, 20 January 1961, p. 2, and *Washington Post*, 10 April 1966 for statements of Laotian Prime Minister Souvanna Phouma re US opposition to a coalition or neutralist government.
4. *New York Times*, 25 April 1957.
5. Ibid., 18 May 1958, IV, p. 7.
6. Ibid., 23 July 1958, p. 2; 25 July, p. 4.
7. Ibid., 20 January 1961, p. 2; *Washington Post*, 10 April 1966.
8. *New York Times*, 15 January 1959, p. 15.
9. Fred Branfman, *Voices from the Plain of Jars: Life Under an Air War* (Harper & Row, New York, 1972) p. 12; *New York Times*, 18 May 1958, IV, p. 7.
10. *New York Times*, 25 April 1966, p. 20.
11. Arthur Schlesinger, *A Thousand Days* (Boston, 1965), p. 325.
12. 1958: Ibid., pp. 325-6 (this has to do with the events of 1958 referred to earlier - see notes 6 and 7 above); 1959: Ibid., p. 326; Branfman, p. 12; 1960: Chester Bowles, *Promises to Keep: My Years in Public Life, 1941-1969* (New York 1971) p. 334; Bowles was a prominent American diplomat.
13. Roger Hilsman, *To Move a Nation* (New York, 1967) pp, 111-2.
14. *New York Times*, 25 January 1958, p. 6; 25 February, p. 6.
15. Ibid., 9 August 1960.
16. Norman Cousins, "Report from Laos", *Saturday Review*, 18 February 1961, p. 12.
17. Secret Army:
a) *New York Times*, 26 October 1969, p. 1.
b) Fred Branfman, "The President's Secret Army", in Robert Borosage and John Marks, eds., *The CIA File* (New York, 1976) pp. 46-78.
c) Christopher Robbins, *Air America* (New York, 1979) chapters 5 and 8.
d) Col. L. Fletcher Prouty, US Air Force, Ret., *The Secret Team: The CIA and its Allies in Control of the World* (New York, 1974) pp. 190-93, 438.
e) Victor Marchetti and John Marks, *The CIA and the Cult of Intelligence* (New York, 1975) pp. 54, 132.
f) *San Francisco Chronicle*, 25 July 1973 (reporting deaths).
18. *New York Times*, 18 May 1958, IV, p. 7.
19. Robbins, op. cit.
20. Branfman (*CIA File*), p. 65.
21. Robbins, op. cit.
22. For a comprehensive account of CIA involvement in drug trafficking from Latin America to Southeast Asia to Afghanistan, from the 1950s to the 1980s, see:
a) Alfred W. McCoy, *The Politics of Heroin in Southeast Asia* (Harper & Row, New York, 1972) passim; revised and updated edition, *The Politics of Heroin: CIA Complicity in the Global Drug Trade* (Lawrence Hill Books, New York, 1991) passim.
b) Henrik Kruger, *The Great Heroin Coup: Drugs, Intelligence, and International Fascism* (Boston, 1980, originally published in Danish in 1976), passim
c) Christopher Robbins, *Air America* (New York, 1979), pp. 128, 225-243
d) Leslie Cockburn, *Out of Control* (New York, 1987), passim
e) Peter Dale Scott, Jonathan Marshall, *Cocaine Politics: Drugs, Armies, and the CIA in Central America* (University of CA Press, 1991), passim.
f) *Drugs, Law Enforcement and Foreign Policy*, a Report of the Senate Committee on Foreign Relations, Subcommittee on Terrorism, Narcotics and International Operations, 1989
23. Testimony of Daniel Oleksiw, USIA, before US Senate Committee on Foreign Relations, *Hearings on US Security Agreements and Commitments Abroad: Kingdom of Laos*, October 1969, pp. 586-7.
The USIA produced a number of other unattributed publications in Asia during the 1950s and 1960s. A 1954 document lists: *Four Seas* (monthly magazine, southeast Asia), *Free World* (monthly magazine, nine Far Eastern countries), *American Reporter* (bi-weekly newspaper, India), *Panorama* (bi-weekly newspaper, Pakistan), and *News Review* (weekly magazine, Beirut). [White House Memo based on information prepared by USIA, 15 February 1954, *Declassified Documents Reference System*, 1987, document no. 548.]
24. *New York Times*, 25 April 1966, p. 20.

25. Ibid., 20 January 1961, p. 2.
26. Marchetti and Marks, p. 132; Branfman (*Voices*), p. 16.
27. Robbins, p. 116.
28. William Lederer & Eugene Burdick, *A Nation of Sheep* (London, 1961) pp. 12-13; see also Bernard Fall, *Anatomy of a Crisis: The Laotian Crisis of 1960-1961* (New York, 1969), chapter 7.
29. Lederer and Burdick, pp. 15-22.
30. Bernard Fall, *Street Without Joy: Insurgency in Indochina, 1946-63* (London, 1963, Third revised edition) p. 329; *New York Times* 3 January 1961, p. 10.
31. Fall (*Street*), p. 332.
32. Schlesinger, p. 329.
33. Ibid., p. 517; see also Andrew Tully, *The Super Spies* (London, 1970) p. 165.
34. Robbins, p. 115.
35. Prouty, p. 314.
36. *New York Times*, 3 May 1964, p. 1; 7 May, p. 7; 14 May, p. 11.
37. *Congressional Record*, 18 July 1973, pp. 24520-22.
38. Branfman (*Voices*), p. 5; Branfman was in Laos 1967-71, first as an educational adviser to International Voluntary Services ("a Bible Belt version of the Peace Corps" - Robbins), then as a writer and researcher.
39. *Refugee and Civilian War Casualty Problems in Indochina*, Staff Report prepared for the US Senate Subcommittee on Refugees, Committee on the Judiciary, 28 September 1970, pp. 19 and v.
40. Ibid., p. 32.
41. *The Guardian* (London) 14 October 1971, p. 4.
42. Robbins, p. 132.
43. Branfman (*Voices*), p. 15.
44. *New York Times*, 23 February 1973, p. 1.
45. Ibid., 8 April 1954.

22. HAITI 1959-1963

1. Robert I. Rotberg with Christopher K. Clague, Haiti: *The Politics of Squalor* (A Twentieth Century Fund Study, Boston, 1971), p. 244.
2. *New York Times*, 15 and 16 August 1959: Robert Debs Heinl, Jr. and Nancy Gordon Heinl, *The Story of the Haitian People, 1492-1971* (Boston, 1978), p. 600.
3. *Hispanic American Report* (Stanford University, California) October 1959, p. 434.
4. *New York Times*, 17 and 18 August 1959.
5. Heinl, p. 600; *New York Times*, 15 August 1959.
6. Heinl, p. 600; Rotberg, p. 219.
7. *New York Times*, 16 August 1959.
8. Heinl, p. 600.
9. *New York Times*, 16 August 1959.
10. Rotberg, p. 219.
11. Heinl, p. 618.
12. *Interim Report: Alleged Assassination Plots Involving Foreign Leaders*, The Select Committee to Study Governmental Operations with Respect to Intelligence Activities (US Senate), 20 November 1975, p. 4, footnote 1. The Report doesn't specify when this took place, but the *New York Times*, 14 November 1993, p. 12, placed it in 1961.
13. Fritz Longchamp and Worth Cooley-Prost, "Hope for Haiti", *Covert Action Information Bulletin* (Washington), No. 36, Spring 1991, p. 56. Longchamp is Executive Director of the Washington Office on Haiti, an analysis and public education center; Arthur Schlesinger, Jr. *A Thousand Days* (Boston, 1965) pp. 782-3; Heinl, p. 617.

23. GUATEMALA 1960

The principal sources of this chapter are:

a) Richard Gott, *Rural Guerrillas in Latin America* (Great Britain, 1973, revised edition) pp. 68-77; first published in 1970 as *Guerrilla Movements in Latin America*.
b) David Wise and Thomas Ross, *The Invisible Government* (New York, 1965, paperback edition) pp. 22-4, 33.
c) Col. L. Fletcher Prouty, US Air Force, Ret,, *The Secret Team: The CIA and its Allies in Control of the World* (New York, 1974) pp. 45-6.
d) John Gerassi, *The Great Fear in Latin America* (New York, 1965, revised edition) pp. 184-5; Gerassi was a correspondent in Latin America for the *New York Times* and an editor of *Time* magazine.
1. Gott, p. 70.
2. *New York Times*, 18 November 1960.
3. Ibid., 15, 19 November 1960.
4. Gott, p. 71; Wise and Ross, p. 33; Prouty, p. 46.
5. Gerassi, p. 185.
6. *New York Times*, 19 November 1960.
7. Thomas and Marjorie Melville, Guatemala: *The Politics of*

Land Ownership (US, 1971) p. 142; Gott, p. 76.
8. Gott, p. 77.

24. FRANCE/ALGERIA 1960s
1. Andrew Tully, *CIA: The Inside Story* (New York, 1962), p. 44.
2. Allen Dulles, *The Craft of Intelligence* (New York, 1965), p. 175.
3. *New York Times*, 4 May 1961, p. 10.
4. Cited in Tully, p. 45, article by Crosby Noyes, no date of *Washington Star* given.
5. Cited in Sanche de Gramont, *The Secret War* (New York, 1963) pp. 29-30
6. *New York Times*, 24 April 1961.
7. *Washington Post*, 5 May 1961, p. A16.
8. *Time*, 12 May 1961, p. 19.
9. *New York Times*, 29 April 1961, pp. 1, 3
10. Ibid., 1 May 1961, p. 28.
11. Cited in de Gramont, pp. 30-31.
12. *Newsweek*, 15 May 1961, pp. 50-51.
13. *L'Express*/Claude Krief: As reported in Alexander Werth, "The CIA in Algeria", *The Nation* (New York), 20 May 1961, pp. 433-5
14. *Time*, 12 May 1961, p. 19
15. *New York Times*, 29 April 1961, p. 3.
16. Ibid., 2 May 1961, p. 18.
17. Ibid., 24 June 1975, p.11.
18. Christian Plume & Pierre Démaret, *Target: De Gaulle* (translation from the French, London, 1974) passim.
19. *Chicago Tribune*, 15 June 1975, p. 1.
20. David Wise, *The Politics of Lying* (New York, 1973, paperback edition) p. 431.
21. *Military Assistance Training*, Hearings before the House Committee on Foreign Affairs, Subcommittee on National Security Policy and Scientific Developments, October and December 1970, p. 120.
22. Chicago Tribune, 20 June 1975, p. 6.

25. ECUADOR 1960 to 1963
1. Philip Agee, *Inside the Company: CIA Diary* (New York, 1975) pp. 106-316, passim. Agee's book made him Public Enemy No. One of the CIA. In a review of the book, however, former Agency official Miles Copeland — while not concealing his distaste for Agee's "betrayal" — stated that "The book is interesting as an authentic account of how an ordinary American or British `case officer' operates ... As a spy handler in Quito, Montevideo and Mexico City, he has first-hand information ... All of it, just as his publisher claims, is presented `with deadly accuracy'." (*The Spectator*, London, 11 January 1975, p. 40.)
2. *New York Times*, 14 July 1963, p. 20.For an interesting and concise discussion of the political leanings of Velasco and Arosemana, see John Gerassi, *The Great Fear in Latin America* (New York, 1965, revised edition) pp. 141-8.

26. THE CONGO 1960-1964
1. *Interim Report: Alleged Assassination Plots Involving Foreign Leaders*, The Select Committee to Study Governmental Operations with Respect to Intelligence Activities (US Senate), 20 November 1975, pp. 14, 15, 16 respectively; hereafter referred to as Assassination Report.
2. *Washington Post*, 28 August 1960, p. A4.
3. Assassination Report, p. 58.
4. Jonathan Kwitny, *Endless Enemies: The Making of an Unfriendly World* (New York, 1984) p. 57.
5. Alan Merriam, *Congo: Background to Conflict* (Northwestern U. Press, Evanston, 1961) pp. 352-4.
6. David Gibbs, *The Political Economy of Third World Intervention: Mines, Money, and U.S. Policy in the Congo Crisis* (University of Chicago Press, 1991), p. 100, provides the details of these ties; p. 90 re US embassy requesting Belgian intervention.
7. Ibid., pp. 92-3.
8. *New York Times*, 4 September 1960, IV, p. 3; Gibbs, p. 100.
9. Kwitny, pp. 62-3, 65; Stephen R. Weissman, *American Foreign Policy in the Congo, 1960-1964* (Cornell University Press, Ithaca, 1974), pp. 88-95 (Weissman is a former staff member of the Subcommittee on Africa of the House Foreign Affairs Committee); Andrew Tully, *CIA: The Inside Story* (Fawcett, New York, 1962, paperback), pp. 179-80 (CIA men).
10. Assassination Report, p. 16.
11. Victor Marchetti (former executive assistant to the Deputy Director of the CIA) and John D. Marks, *The CIA and the Cult of Intelligence* (Laurel/Dell, 1983), p. 28; this edition contains more of the previously deleted and classified passages.
12. Stephen R. Weissman, "CIA Covert Action in Zaire and Angola: Patterns and Consequences", *Political Science Quarterly* (PSQ), Summer 1979, p. 267 (see information about Weissman above).
13. Assassination Report, pp. 16, 17, 18, 63 respectively. The last three are quotes or paraphrases of the words of

American officials.

14. Ibid., p. 19-30. Gottlieb is referred to as Joseph Scheider in the Assassination Report.
15. Ibid., p. 13.
16. *New York Times*, 22 February 1976, p. 55.
17. Assassination Report, p. 30.
18. Ibid., pp. 18-19.
19. Gibbs, pp. 96-7.
20. Ibid., p. 48.
21. Tully. p. 178; for further discussion of US-Mobutu relationship, see Gibbs, p. 96; Kwitny, pp. 63, 66-7; Weissman (*American Foreign Policy*), pp. 94-9, 108-9; Weissman (PSQ), p. 268.
22. John Stockwell, *In Search of Enemies* (New York, 1978) p. 105; see also 137, 236-7.
23. Cables: 18 January 1961, from US Ambassador in Leopoldville to American Consulate in Elizabethville, and 20 January 1961, from Elizabethville to Washington, *Declassified Documents Reference System* (Arlington, Va.), Retrospective Collection volume, documents 375B, E. Both cables were sent after Lumumba's death, indicating that these State Department officials were not privy to the CIA's actions.
24. Gibbs, chapter 4; Arthur Schlesinger, *A Thousand Days* (Boston, 1965) p. 576.
25. Col. L. Fletcher Prouty, US Air Force, Ret., *The Secret Team: The CIA and its Allies in Control of the World* (Ballantine Books, New York, 1974, paperback) pp. 26, 129-30, 438.
26. Costa Rica in 1955 (cf. this chapter); and Burma in 1970, if not also earlier, when the US military aided the Burmese air force to mount strikes against Burmese rebels, while the CIA was assisting the rebels from its operation in Laos. (*San Francisco Chronicle*, 16 October 1970, p. 22.) Additionally, in Angola during the 1960s and 70s, and in Cuba, 1957-58, the Agency gave funds to insurgents attempting to overthrow governments which were being provided with arms by the United States to suppress the insurgents. (cf. these chapters)
27. Assassination Report, p. 18. Lawrence Devlin is referred to as Victor Hedgman in the Report.
28. Kwitny, p. 67.
29. *Newsweek* 22 November 1971, p. 37.
30. State Department memo, 17 November 1961, from L.D. Battle, Executive Secretary, to McGeorge Bundy, Special Assistant to the President for National Security Affairs; *Declassified Documents Reference System* (Arlington, Va.), Retrospective Collection volume, document 383C.
31. Marchetti and Marks, p. 28.
32. Kwitny, pp. 67-8; Weissman (*American Foreign Policy*) pp. 105, 205; Weissman (PSQ) p. 270; the CIA memorandum was entitled: "Congo: United States Assistance to Adoula Against Gizenga", no date, but apparently written in November 1961, found in the National Security Files, John F. Kennedy Presidential Library, Boston, cited by Weissman (PSQ).
33. "CBS Reports", 26 April 1962, "The Hot and Cold Wars of Allen Dulles", pp. 19-20 of transcript, cited by Stephen R. Weissman in "The CIA and U.S. Policy in Zaire and Angola" in Ellen Ray, et al., eds., *Dirty Work 2: The CIA in Africa* (New Jersey, 1979), p. 200; this is another version of Weissman's article in PSQ referred to above.
34. William Atwood, *The Reds and the Blacks* (London, 1967), p. 194; Atwood was US Ambassador to Kenya, 1964-65; Weissman (PSQ), pp. 271-2; Weissman (*American Foreign Policy*), pp. 226-30.
35. Atwood, p. 192.
36. CIA mercenaries: David Wise and Thomas Ross, *The Espionage Establishment* (New York, 1967) p. 167; Stockwell, pp. 187-8; Marchetti and Marks, p. 104; Roger Morris (former staff member of the National Security Council) and Richard Mauzy, "Zaire (the Congo): An Exercise in Nation Building" in Robert Borosage and John Marks, eds., *The CIA File* (New York, 1976) pp. 35-7.
37. *New York Times*, 26 April 1966, p. 1.
38. Ibid., 17 June 1964, pp. 1, 12; 18 June, p. 1.
39. M. Crawford Young, "Rebellion and the Congo", in Robert Rotberg, ed., *Rebellion in Black Africa* (Oxford University Press, 1971), p. 230.
40. Young, p. 227, and passim; Atwood, p. 192 (witch doctors); Thomas Powers, *The Man Who Kept the Secrets: Richard Helms and the CIA* (New York, 1979) p. 153 (Mulele).
41. Young, p. 209.
42. *New York Times*, 15 November 1964, p. 27.
43. Ibid, 1 November 1964, p. 12: 3 November, p. 14; Atwood, chapter 16.
44. Richard Barnet, *Intervention and Revolution* (London, 1970) p. 250.
45. Atwood, p. 218.
46. *The Times* (London) 25 November 1964.
47. Marchetti and Marks, p. 111.
48. Atwood, p. 194.
49. Dwight Eisenhower, *The White House Years: Waging Peace, 1956-1961* (New York, 1965) p. 270.

27. BRAZIL 1961 to 1964
1. Phyllis R. Parker, *Brazil and the Quiet Intervention, 1964* (University of Texas Press, Austin, 1979) p. 64. This book draws heavily upon declassified documents found at the John F. Kennedy and Lyndon B. Johnson presiden-

tial libraries. The author augmented this information with interviews of key figures in the events discussed here.
2. Ibid., p. 67.
3. Ibid., p. 65.
4. Ibid., p. 20, Washington, April 1962
5. Ibid., pp. 30-31, 34.
6. Ibid., p. 31, meeting in Brazil 17 December 1962.
7. Ibid., pp. 45, 21, Walters' report to the Pentagon, 6 August 1963.
8. Ibid., pp. 41-2.
9. Ibid., p. 44 and passim
10. John Gerassi, *The Great Fear in Latin America* (New York, 1965, revised edition) p. 83.
11. Ibid., p. 82.
12. *New York Times*, 12 July 1961, p. 13.
13. Peter Bell, "Brazilian-American Relations" in Riordan Roett, ed., *Brazil in the Sixties* (Vanderbilt University Press, Nashville, 1972) p. 81; Bell interview of Cabot, Washington, DC, 15 January 1970.
14. Gerassi, p. 84.
15. *New York Times*, 16 March 1962, p. 7.
16. Stephen Schlesinger and Stephen Kinzer, *Bitter Fruit: The Untold Story of the American Coup in Guatemala* (Doubleday & Co., New York, 1982) pp, 103-4, 108.
17. *New York Times*, 16 March 1962, p. 7.
18. Gerassi, pp. 84-8.
19. Thomas E. Skidmore, *Politics in Brazil, 1930-1964: An Experiment in Democracy* (Oxford University Press, New York, 1967) p. 130; Gerassi, pp. 80-81.
20. Jan Knippers Black, *United States Penetration of Brazil* (University of Pennsylvania Press, Philadelphia, 1977), p.40: the words quoted are Black's, based on her interview with Lt. Col. Edward L. King, a member of the Joint Brazil-US Defense Commission in the second half of the 1960s; also see Bell, p. 83 re US doubts about Goulart from the beginning of his presidency.
21. Arthur Schlesinger, *A Thousand Days* (Boston, 1965) pp. 780-2; *New York Times*, 5 December 1961, p. 11.
22. *New York Times*, 5 April 1962, p. 3.
23. *Time*, 3 November 1961, p. 29.
24. Gerassi, pp. 83, 88.
25. Parker, p. 29, interview with Gordon, 19 January 1976.
26. Philip Agee, *Inside the Company: CIA Diary* (New York, 1975),p. 321.
27. Parker, p. 27.
28. A. J. Langguth, *Hidden Terrors* (New York, 1978) p. 92; Langguth was formerly with the *New York Times* and in 1965 served as Saigon Bureau Chief for the newspaper.
29. Parker, p. 26, memo from President Kennedy to AID administrator Fowler Hamilton, 5 February 1962.
30. Ibid., pp. 87-97.
31. Agee, p. 362.
32. Langguth, pp. 77, 89-90, 92, 108.
33. Parker, p. 40.
34. For the most important incident/example of this see the story of the Navy mutiny in Skidmore, pp. 296-7.
35. Philip Siekman, "When Executives Turned Revolutionaries", *Fortune* magazine (New York), September 1964, p. 214.
36. Parker, p. 63, interview of Walters.
37. Langguth, pp. 61-2, 98; *Washington Post*, 5 February 1968, p. 1.
38. Skidmore, p. 330; also see James Kohl and John Litt, *Urban Guerrilla Warfare in Latin America* (The MIT Press, Cambridge, Mass., 1974) p. 39 for further discussion of the strong pro-US, anti-leftist bias of the college's curriculum.
39. Parker, p. 98, cable to State Department, 4 March 1964. In this and the following quotations from cables, missing articles and prepositions have been inserted for the sake of readability. For further discussion of the closeness of US and Brazilian military officers and the presumed influencing of the latter along pro-US, anti-communist lines see: a) Langguth, pp. 94-6, 162-70; b) Black, chapters 9 and 10; c) Michael Klare, *War Without End* (New York, 1972) chapter 10; d) Alfred Stepan, *The Military in Politics: Changing Patterns in Brazil* (Princeton University Press, New Jersey, 1971, a RAND Corp. Study) pp. 123-33.
40. Parker, p. 65.
41. Ibid., p. 68.
42. Ibid., pp. 68-9.
43. Ibid., p. 74.
44. Ibid., p. 75, teletype, Washington to US Embassy, Brazil, 31 March 1964.
45. Ibid., p. 68.
46. Ibid., pp. 74, 77.
47. Ibid., pp. 72, 75-6; also see the statement of former Brazilian Army Col. Pedro Paulo de Baruna, exiled by the junta, about the effect of the naval force upon the thinking of Castelo Branco: Warner Poelchau, ed., *White Paper, Whitewash* (New York, 1981) p. 51.

48. *Survey of the Alliance for Progress: Labor Policies and Programs*, Staff Report of the US Senate Foreign Relations Committee, Subcommittee on American Republics Affairs, 15 July 1968, p. 53; the background of AIFLD can be found in earlier pages of this report; also see Black, chapter 6.
49. US Senate Report cited in the previous note, p. 14, quoting from a radio program in which Doherty took part.
50. Eugene Methvin, "Labor's New Weapon for Democracy", *Reader's Digest*, October, 1966, p. 28.
51. Poelchau, pp. 47-51.
52. Langguth, pp. 110, 113; *Washington Post*, 2 April 1964, p. 23.
53. Langguth, pp. 112-13.
54. Ibid., p. 113; *Washington Post*, 3 April 1964, p. 17.
55. Gordon's cables: Parker, pp. 81-3.
56. Ibid., p. 83.
57. Hearing on the Nomination of Lincoln Gordon to be Assistant Secretary of State for Inter-American Affairs, US Senate Foreign Relations Committee, 7 February 1966, pp. 44-5.
58. *The Department of State Bulletin*, 20 April 1964, news conference of 3 April 1964.
59. Langguth, p. 116, from Langguth's interview of Gordon.
60. Senate Hearing, op. cit.
61. *Foreign Assistance Act of 1965*, Hearings before the House Foreign Affairs Committee, 25 February 1965, p. 346.
62. Langguth, p. 113, citing the *Brazil Herald*, 6 March 1964, p.4.
63. *New York Times*, 11 July 1965, p. 13.
64. Ibid., 25 November 1966, p. 4.
65. Marc Edelman, "The Other Super Power: The Soviet Union and Latin America 1917-1987", *NACLA's Report on the Americas* (North American Congress on Latin America, New York), pp. 32-4; day of mourning: p. 29, citing the CIA's Foreign Broadcast Information Service (FBIS-LAM), 15 November 1982.
66. *Reader's Digest*, November 1964, pp. 135-58.
67. Agee, p. 364.
68. Parker, pp. 85-6.
69. Agee, pp. 364-5.
70. *New York Times*, 6 April 1964, p. 1.
71. *Reader's Digest*, October, 1966, op. cit.
72. Parker, p. 59.
73. The repressiveness of the Branco government and the Washington connection:
a) Penny Lernoux, *Cry of the People: The Struggle for Human Rights in Latin America — The Catholic Church in Conflict with U S. Policy* (Penguin Books, London, 1982) pp. 166-75, 313-32, and elsewhere.
b) Langguth, chapters 4, 5 and 7 and elsewhere.
c) *Torture and Oppression in Brazil*, Hearing before the Subcommittee on International Organizations and Movements of the House Committee on Foreign Affairs, 11 December, 1974; contains testimony by and about torture victims and reprints of articles from the US press.
d) Noam Chomsky and Edward Herman, *The Washington Connection and Third World Fascism* (Boston, 1979) see index.
74. Agency for International Development (AID), *Program and Project Data Presentation to the Congress for Fiscal Year 1971*, p. 26.
75. Langguth, p. 94; Poelchau, p. 65, interview of Langguth.
76. Amnesty International, *Report on Allegations of Torture in Brazil* (London, 1974) p. 40.
77. *Jornal do Brazil*, 25 May 1972, cited in Amnesty International, op. cit., p. 49.
78. Lawrence Weschler, *A Miracle, A Universe: Settling Accounts with Torturers* (Penguin Books, New York, 1991), p. 122.
79. *Special Study Mission to Latin America on Military Assistance Training*, House Committee on Foreign Affairs Report, 1970.
80. *New York Times*, 27 April 1966, p. 28.

28. PERU 1960 to 1965
1. *New York Times*, 22 December 1960, p. 3.
2. Philip Agee, *Inside the Company: CIA Diary* (New York, 1975) pp. 145-6.
3. *Wall Street Journal*, 5 January 1961, p. 1.
4. *New York Times*, 28 December 1960, p. 5.
5. Ibid., 6 and 7 January 1961; Agee, p. 146; Agee does not mention Ramos by name but it appears rather clear that he is referring to the same man.
6. John Gerassi, *The Great Fear in Latin America* (New York, 1965, revised edition) pp. 20, 129; originally published as *The Great Fear* (New York, 1963).
7. For the background, ideology, and fate of the various revolutionary movements in Peru during this period, see Richard Gott, *Rural Guerrillas in Latin America* (Great Britain, 1973, revised edition) pp. 363-463; James Petras and Maurice Zeitlin, eds., *Latin America: Reform or Revolution?* (Fawcett, New York, 1968) pp. 343-50; *New York Times*, 30 August 1966, p. 1.
8. Victor Marchetti and John Marks, *The CIA and the Cult of Intelligence* (New York, 1975) p. 137.

9. Hearings before the Committee on Armed Services and the Subcommittee on Department of Defense of the Committee on Appropriations (US Senate), 23 February 1966, p. 38.
10. Michael Klare, *War Without End* (Random House/Vantage Books, New York, 1972) pp. 297-8.
11. *New York Times*, 12 September 1965, p. 32.
12. Agee, p. 440; see also pp. 267-9, 427.
13. Gott, op. cit; Petras, p. 349; Norman Gall, "The Legacy of Che Guevara", *Commentary* magazine (New York) December 1967, p. 39.
14. Petras, p. 349.

29. DOMINICAN REPUBLIC 1960 to 1966

1. Jerome Slater, "The Dominican Republic, 1961-66" in Barry Blechman and Stephen Kaplan, *Force Without War: U.S. Armed Forces as a Political Instrument* (The Brookings Institution, Washington, 1978) pp. 290-91, a study undertaken at the request of the Pentagon and with its full cooperation, although the book stipulates that the views expressed are the authors' alone.
2. Bernard Diederich, *Trujillo: The Death of the Goat* (London, 1978) p. 43.
3. Ibid., pp. 48-9; *New York Times*, 23 June 1975, p. 17 (this article is more understandable when one knows that Lear Reed was addressed as "Colonel", his World War II rank — Diederich, p. 49).
4. *Interim Report: Alleged Assassination Plots Involving Foreign Leaders*, The Select Committee to Study Governmental Operations with Respect to Intelligence Activities (US Senate), 20 November 1975, p. 192; hereafter referred to as Assassination Report.
5. Ibid.
6. Diederich, p. 44.
7. Assassination Report, 191-215, passim; Diederich, passim, particularly pp. 40-56.
8. Assassination Report, p. 210.
9. Arthur M. Schlesinger, *A Thousand Days* (Boston, 1965) p. 769.
10. Diederich, pp. 170-249, summary on page 265.
11. Schlesinger, p. 661.
12. Events of 1961 following the assassination: Slater, pp. 294-7; Diederich, pp. 220-51.
13. Slater, p. 298; *New York Times*, 20 January 1962, p. 4.
14. John Bartlow Martin, *Overtaken by Events: The Dominican Crisis From the Fall of Trujillo to the Civil War* (New York, 1966) p. 100.
15. Ibid., p. 122.
16. *New York Times*, 9 June 1962, p. 10.
17. US involvement in elections: Martin, pp. 227-9, 347-8.
18. Martin, pp. 455-6; Richard Barnet, *Intervention and Revolution* (London, 1972) p. 168.
19. *Miami News* quote: Cited in *Newsweek*, 7 October 1963, p. 64. Hendrix: Carl Bernstein, "The CIA and the Media", *Rolling Stone*, 20 October 1977, p. 59; Thomas Powers, *The Man Who Kept the Secrets: Richard Helms and the CIA* (Pocket Books, New York, 1979) p. 461.
20. Martin, p. 451.
21. Ibid., pp. 477-8.
22. Sam Halper, "The Dominican Upheaval", *The New Leader* (New York), 10 May 1965, p. 4.
23. Martin, pp. 481-90; *New York Times*, 17 July 1963, p. 10.
24. CONATRAL: *Survey of the Alliance for Progress: Labor Policies and Programs*, Staff Report of the U.S. Senate Foreign Relations Committee, Subcommittee on American Republics Affairs, 15 July 1968, p. 18; Jan Kippers Black, *The Dominican Republic: Politics and Development in an Unsovereign State* (Boston, 1986), pp. 35, 96, 117; Barnet, pp. 170-71.
25. Martin, p. 570.
26. *Newsweek*, 7 October 1963, pp. 64-5.
27. *New York Times*, 14 December 1963, p. 12.
28. *Washington Post*, 27 June 1965, p. E2.
29. *Wall Street Journal*, 25 June 1965, p. 8.
30. Slater, p. 308; Tad Szulc, *Dominican Diary* (New York, 1965) p. 32; Szulc was the *New York Times* correspondent in the Dominican Republic during this period.
31. Slater, p. 307.
32. Martin, pp. 656-7; *New York Times*, 1 May 1965; Slater, p. 309; *Wall Street Journal*, 25 June 1965, p. 8.
33. Martin, p. 658.
34. *Washington Post*, 27 June 1965, p. E5; Slater, pp. 322-3; *New York Times*, 20 May 1965.
35. *New York Times*, 20 May 1965; Slater, p. 325.
36. *New York Times Magazine*, 14 July 1982, p. 20.
37. Ibid.
38. *New York Times*, 25 February 1967.
39. Communists amongst the rebels: *Washington Post*, 27 June 1965, p. E4; CIA cable: *Declassified Documents Reference System* (Arlington, Virginia) 1977 Volume, Document 14G.
40. Philip Agee, *Inside the Company: CIA Diary* (New York, 1975) p. 421.

41. Barnet, pp. 175-6.
42. Ibid.; Szulc, pp. 71-3; *Washington Post*, 27 June 1965, p. E4,
43. Slater, p. 321; *New York Times*, 22 March 1967.
44. David Wise, *The Politics of Lying* (New York, 1973, paperback edition) p. 32.
45. Barnet, pp. 178-9.
46. See, e.g., *Wall Street Journal*, 7 September 1971, "In Dominican Republic, Political Murders Rise, and So Does Poverty"; also, various Amnesty International *Reports on Torture* and *Annual Reports* during the 1970s.

30. CUBA 1959 to 1980s
1   *Khrushchev Remembers* (London, 1971) pp. 494, 496.
2. *Time*, 2 November 1962.
3. Cited by William Appleman Williams, "American Intervention in Russia: 1917-20", in David Horowitz, ed., *Containment and Revolution* (Boston, 1967). Written in a letter to President Wilson by Secretary of State Robert Lansing, uncle of John Foster and Allen Dulles.
4. Facts on File, *Cuba, the U.S. and Russia, 1960-63* (New York, 1964) pp. 56-8.
5. *International Herald Tribune* (Paris), 2 October 1985, p. 1.
6. *New York Times*, 23 October 1959, p. 1.
7. Facts on File, op. cit., pp. 7-8; *New York Times*, 19, 20 February 1960; 22 March 1960.
8. *New York Times*, 5, 6 March 1960.
9. David Wise, "Colby of CIA — CIA of Colby", *New York Times Magazine*, 1 July 1973, p. 9.
10. A report about the post-invasion inquiry ordered by Kennedy disclosed that "It was never intended, the planners testified, that the invasion itself would topple Castro. The hope was that an initial success would spur an uprising by thousands of anti-Castro Cubans. Ships in the invasion fleet carried 15,000 weapons to be distributed to the expected volunteers." *U.S. News & World Report*, 13 August 1979, p. 82. Some CIA officials, including Allen Dulles, later denied that an uprising was expected, but this may be no more than an attempt to mask their ideological embarrassment that people living under a "communist tyranny" did not respond at all to the call of "The Free World".
11. Attacks on Cuba:
a) Taylor Branch and George Crile III, "The Kennedy Vendetta", *Harper's* magazine (New York), August 1975, pp. 49-63
b) Facts on File, op. cit., passim
c) *New York Times*, 26 August 1962, p. 1; 21 March 1963, p. 3; *Washington Post*, 1 June 1966; 30 September 1966; plus many other articles in both newspapers during the 1960s
d) Warren Hinckle and William W. Turner, *The Fish is Red: The Story of the Secret War Against Castro* (Harper & Row, New York, 1981) passim.
12. Branch and Crile, op. cit., pp. 49-63. The article states that there were in excess of 300 Americans involved in the operation, but in "CBS Reports: The CIA's Secret Army", broadcast 10 June 1977, written by Bill Moyers and the same George Crile III, former CIA official Ray Cline states that there were between 600 and 700 American staff officers.
13. *New York Times*, 26 August 1962, p. 1.
14. John Gerassi, *The Great Fear in Latin America* (New York, 1965, revised edition) p. 278.
15. Branch and Crile, op. cit., p. 52.
16. *The Times* (London), 8, 10 January 1964; 12 May, p. 10; 21 July, p. 10; 28, 29 October; *The Guardian* (London), 28, 29 October 1964.
17. *Washington Post*, 14 February 1975, p. C31; Anderson's story stated that there were only 24 buses involved and that they were dried and used in England.
18. Branch and Crile, op. cit., p. 52.
19. *New York Times*, 28 April 1966, p. 1.
20. Branch and Crile, op. cit., p. 52
21. *Washington Post*, 21 March 1977, p. A18.
22. Hinckle and Turner, p. 293, based on their interview with the participant in Ridgecrest, California, 27 September 1975.
23. *San Francisco Chronicle*, 10 January 1977.
24. Bill Schaap, "The 1981 Cuba Dengue Epidemic", *Covert Action Information Bulletin* (Washington), No. 17, Summer 1982, pp. 28-31
25. *San Francisco Chronicle*, 30 October 1980.
26. *Science* (American Association for the Advancement of Science, Washington), 13 January 1967, p. 176.
27. *Covert Action Information Bulletin* (Washington), No. 22, Fall 1984, p. 35; the trial of Eduardo Victor Arocena Perez, Federal District Court for the Southern District of New York, transcript of 10 September 1984, pp. 2187-89.
28. See, e.g., *San Francisco Chronicle*, 27 July 1981.
29. *Washington Post*, 16 September 1977, p. A2.
30. Ibid., 25 October 1969, column by Jack Anderson.
31. Reports of the assassination attempts have been disclosed in many places; see *Interim Report: Alleged*

Notes

Assassination Plots Involving Foreign Leaders, The Select Committee to Study Governmental Operations with Respect to Intelligence Activities (US Senate), 20 November 1975, pp. 71-180, for a detailed, although not complete, account. Stadium bombing attempt: *New York Times*, 22 November 1964, p. 26.

32. *New York Times*, 12 December 1964, p. 1.

33. Ibid., 3 March 1930, p. 1.

34. Terrorist attacks within the United States:

a) Jeff Stein, "Inside Omega 7", *The Village Voice* (New York), 10 March 1980

b) *New York Times*, 13 September 1980, p. 24; 3 March, 1980, p. 1.

c) John Dinges and Saul Landau, *Assassination on Embassy Row* (London, 1981), pp. 251-52, note (also includes attacks on Cuban targets in other countries)

d) *Covert Action Information Bulletin* (Washington), No. 6, October 1979, pp. 8-9.

35. The plane bombing:

a) *Washington Post*, 1 November 1986, pp. A1, A18.

b) Jonathan Kwitny, *The Crimes of Patriots* (New York, 1987), p. 379

c) William Schaap, "New Spate of Terrorism: Key Leaders Unleashed", *Covert Action Information Bulletin* (Washington), No. 11, December 1980, pp.4-8.

d) Dinges and Landau, pp. 245-6.

e) Speech by Fidel Castro, 15 October 1976, reprinted in *Toward Improved U.S.-Cuba Relations*, House Committee on International Relations, Appendix A, 23 May 1977.

The CIA documents: Amongst those declassified by the Agency, sent to the National Archives in 1993, and made available to the public. Reported in *The Nation* (New York), 29 November 1993, p. 657.

36. *Dangerous Dialogue: Attacks on Freedom of Expression in Miami's Cuban Exile Community*, p. 26, published by America's Watch and The Fund for Free Expression, New York and Washington, August 1992.

37. Ibid., passim. Also see: "Terrorism in Miami: Suppressing Free Speech", *CounterSpy* magazine (Washington), Vol. 8, No. 3, March-May 1984, pp. 26-30; *The Village Voice*, op. cit.; *Covert Action Information Bulletin* (Washington), No. 6, October 1979, pp. 8-9.

38. *New York Times*, 4 January 1975, p. 8.

39. *San Francisco Chronicle*, 12 January 1982, p. 14; *Parade* magazine (Washington Post), 15 March 1981, p. 5.

40. *The Village Voice*, op. cit.

41. Jerome Levinson and Juan de Onis, *The Alliance That Lost Its Way: A Critical Report on the Alliance for Progress* (A Twentieth Century Fund Study, Chicago, 1970) p. 56.

42. Ibid., p. 309; the list of Alliance goals can be found on pp. 352-5.

43. Ibid., pp. 226-7.

44. *New York Times*, 26 December 1977, p. 37. See also: Philip Agee, *Inside the Company: CIA Diary* (New York, 1975) p. 380 (Editors Press Service).

45. Tad Szulc, *Fidel, A Critical Portrait* (New York, 1986), pp. 480-1.

46. Richard Nixon, *Six Crises* (New York, 1962, paperback edition) pp. 416-17.

47. Victor Marchetti and John Marks, *The CIA and the Cult of Intelligence* (New York, 1975), p. 289.

48. Marc Edelman, "The Other Super Power: The Soviet Union and Latin America 1917-1987", *NACLA'S Report on the Americas* (North American Congress on Latin America, New York), January-February 1987, p. 16; Szulc, see index.

49. Szulc, pp. 427-8.

50. *Washington Post*, 1 September 1974, p. B7, column by Jack Anderson.

31. INDONESIA 1965

1. *Time*, 17 December 1965.

2. *New York Times Magazine*, 8 May 1966, p. 89.

3. This is the widely-accepted range; see, e.g., various Amnesty International reports on Indonesia published in the 1970s.

4. Rex Mortimer, *Indonesian Communism Under Sukarno: Ideology and Politics, 1959-1965* (Cornell University Press, Ithaca and London, 1974) pp. 413-17; *Indonesia — 1965: The Coup that Backfired* (CIA Research Study, Washington, December 1968) p. 21, hereafter referred to as CIA Study.

5. Mark Selden, ed., *Remaking Asia: Essays on the American Uses of Power* (New York, 1974) pp. 47-8.

6. Noam Chomsky and Edward Herman, *The Washington Connection and Third World Fascism* (Boston, 1979) p. 207.

7. *New York Times*, 12 March 1966, p. 6.

8. *Life*, 11 July 1966.

9. CIA lists: Kathy Kadane, *San Francisco Examiner*, 20 May 1990. See also *Covert Action Information Bulletin*, No. 35, Fall 1990, p. 59, for excerpts from the interviews with the American diplomats conducted by Kadane.

10. Nugroho Notosusanto and Ismail Saleh, *The Coup Attempt of the 'September 30 Movement' in Indonesia* (Jakarta, 1968), cited by Mortimer, p. 419, who notes that "both authors were closely connected with the Indonesian army".

11. CIA Study, p. 199.

12. Notosusanto and Saleh, p. 9, cited by Mortimer, p. 419.

411

13. CIA Study, from the Foreword.
14. Ibid., pp. 3-4; Mortimer, p. 414.
15. Discussion of Sjam's role:
a) CIA Study, pp. 23, 28, 100, 112, 117, and elsewhere
b) Mortimer, pp. 418-40, passim
c) W.F. Wertheim, "Suharto and the Untung Coup —The Missing Link", *Journal of Contemporary Asia* (London) Winter 1970, pp. 53-4
d) Selden, p. 48
e) Julie Southwood and Patrick Flanagan, *Indonesia: Law, Propaganda and Terror* (London, 1983), p. 9
16. CIA Memorandum, 18 June 1962, *Declassified Documents Reference System* (Arlington, Virginia) 1975 volume, Document 240A.
17. Arthur Schlesinger, *A Thousand Days* (Boston, 1965) p. 533.
18. Roger Hilsman, *To Move a Nation* (New York, 1967) p. 377.
19. *Military Assistance Training in East and Southeast Asia,* a Staff Report for the Subcommittee on National Security Policy and Scientific Developments of the House Committee on Foreign Affairs, 16 February 1971, p. 18.
20. Ibid., 2 April 1971, p. 13.
21. *New York Times*, 27 April 1966, p. 28.
22. *Hearings on Foreign Assistance, 1966,* before the Senate Committee on Foreign Relations, 11 May 1966, p. 693.
23. Green has been quoted on this theme in a number of books and periodicals with slight variations here and there, due, apparently, to the fact that he touched upon the same point in several different speeches in Australia. Some sources give only "what we did we had to do"; others provide a fuller quotation. What I have presented here is a combination taken from: a) Denis Freney, *The CIA's Australian Connection* (Australia, 1977), p. 17, citing a talk Green delivered before the Australian Institute for International Affairs in 1973; and b) Peter Britton, "Indonesia's Neo-colonial Armed Forces", *Bulletin Of Concerned Asian Scholars*, July-September 1975.
24. *New York Times*, 19 June 1966, p. 12E.
25. *Journal of Contemporary Asia* (London), Vol. 9, No. 2, 1979, p. 252.
26. Chomsky and Herman, pp. 208-17.
27. *The Guardian* (London), 12 December 1983.
28. *Los Angeles Times*, 15 June 1991, p. 10.
29. Ibid., 13 October 1989, p. A6
30. *New York Times* 13 December 1975, p. 26, editorial.
31. *San Francisco Chronicle*, 9 November 1979, p. 61.
32. For a fuller discussion of these matters, see: Chomsky and Herman, pp. 129-204; Denis Freney, "US-Australian Role in East Timor Genocide", *CounterSpy* magazine (Washington), Vol. 4, No. 2, Spring 1980, pp. 10-21.

32. GHANA 1966
1. Kwame Nkrumah, *Dark Days in Ghana* (London, 1968) p. 96.
2. E.H. Cookridge, 'The Africa Dossier', *The Daily Telegraph Magazine* (London), 21 January 1972, part 2 of a 3-part series on the CIA.
3. John Stockwell, *In Search of Enemies* (New York, 1978) p. 201, note.
4. Ibid.; *New York Times*, 9 May 1978, article by Seymour Hersh.
5. Stockwell, p. 201, note. Another account is that 25 Russians who made up Nkrumah's palace guard were all shot and killed when they tried to surrender: Seymour Friedin and George Bailey, *The Experts* (New York, 1968) p. 210.
6. *New York Times*, op. cit.
7. Ibid.
8. Ibid.
9. *Washington Post*, 17 March 1966.
10. Nkrumah, pp. 97-102 (state-owned industries, price of cocoa).
11. John Barron, *KGB: The Secret Work of Soviet Secret Agents* (Bantam Books, New York, 1981; paperback edition of Reader's Digest Press, 1974), p. 342.

33. URUGUAY 1964 to 1970
1. Manuel Hevia Cosculluela, *Pasaporte 11333: Ocho Años con la CIA* (Havana, 1978), p. 286.
2. A.J. Langguth, *Hidden Terrors* (New York, 1978) pp. 48-9, 51 and passim. Langguth was formerly with the *New York Times* and in 1965 served as Saigon Bureau Chief for the newspaper.
3. *New York Times*, 1 August 1970.
4. Langguth, pp. 285-7; *New York Times*, 15 August 1970.
5. Alain Labrousse, *The Tupamaros: Urban Guerrillas in Uruguay* (Penguin Books, London, 1973, translation from French 1970 edition) p. 103.
6. Langguth, p. 289.
7. Langguth, pp. 232-3, 253-4; Philip Agee, *Inside the Company: CIA Diary* (New York, 1975), see index (Otero's relationship to the CIA).
8. Major Carlos Wilson, *The Tupamaros: The Unmentionables* (Boston, 1974) pp. 106-7; Langguth, p. 236. Agee, p. 478, confirms Cantrell's identity.

Notes

9. Langguth, p. 252.
10. Interview of Langguth in the film "On Company Business" (Directed by Allan Francovich), cited in Warner Poelchau, ed., *White Paper, Whitewash* (New York, 1981) p. 66.
11. Extracts from the report of the Senate Commission of Inquiry into Torture, a document accompanying the film script in *State of Siege* (Ballantine Books, New York, 1973) pp. 194-6; also see "Death of a Policeman: Unanswered Questions About a Tragedy", *Commonweal* (Catholic biweekly magazine, New York), 18 September 1970, p. 457; Langguth, p. 249.
12. Death Squad, TSD: Langguth, pp. 245-6, 253.
13. Michael Klare and Nancy Stein, "Police Terrorism in Latin America", *NACLA's Latin America and Empire Report* (North American Congress on Latin America), January 1974, pp. 19-23, based on State Department documents obtained by Senator James Abourezk in 1973; also see Jack Anderson, *Washington Post*, 8 October 1973, p. C33; Langguth, pp. 242-3.
14. Klare and Stein, p. 19.
15. *New York Times,* 25 September 1968, 1 August 1970; Langguth, p. 241.
16. Hevia, p. 284, translated from the Spanish and slightly paraphrased by author; a similar treatment of this and other passages from Hevia can be found in Langguth, pp. 311-13.
17. *New York Times*, 5 August 1978, p. 3.
18. Mitrione's philosophy: Hevia, pp. 286-7 (see note 16 above).
19. Poelchau, p. 68.
20. Langguth, p. 305.
21. *The Guardian* (London) 19 October 1984.
22. Lawrence Weschler, *A Miracle, A Universe: Settling Accounts With Torturers* (Penguin Books, 1991) p. 121
23. Ibid., p. 147, said to Weschler by Galeano.
24. Nancy Stein and Michael Klare, "Merchants of Repression", *NACLA's Latin America and Empire Report* (North American Congress on Latin America), July-August 1976, p. 31.
25. DEA, arms manufacturers, etc.: Stein and Klare, pp. 31-2; *New York Times*, 23 January 1975, p. 38; 26 January 1975, p 42; Langguth, p. 301.
26. Argentine Commission for Human Rights, Washington, DC: Report entitled "U.S. Narcotics Enforcement Assistance to Latin America", 10 March 1977, reference to a May 1974 press conference in Argentina.
27. *San Francisco Chronicle*, 2 November 1981.
28. Agee, pp. 325-493, passim.
29. From Gott's Introduction to Labrousse, p. 7.

34. CHILE 1964 to 1973

1. *Covert Action in Chile, 1963-1973*, a Staff Report of The Select Committee to Study Governmental Operations with Respect to Intelligence Activities (US Senate) 18 December 1975, p. 16; hereafter referred to as Senate Report.
2. *Washington Post*, 6 April 1973.
3. Senate Report, pp. 14, 18.
4. Ibid., p. 9.
5. *Washington Post*, 6 April 1973.
6. Senate Report, p. 15.
7. Paul E. Sigmund, *The Overthrow of Allende and the Politics of Chile, 1964-1976* (University of Pittsburgh Press, 1977) p. 297.
8. Senate Report, pp. 15-16.
9. Sigmund, p. 34.
10. Propaganda from abroad: Senate Report, p. 16.
11. Sigmund, p. 35; Philip Agee, *Inside the Company: CIA Diary* (New York, 1975) p. 387; Miles Wolpin, *Cuban Foreign Policy and Chilean Politics* (Lexington, Mass., 1972) pp. 88, 176.
12. Senate Report, p. 8.
13. *Washington Post*, 6 April 1973.
14. Senate Report, pp. 9, 16; Wolpin, pp. 175, 372.
15. David Wise, *The Politics of Lying* (New York, 1973, paperback edition) pp. 167-8.
16. *Time* magazine, 11 August 1975, European edition, p. 47.
17. Penny Lernoux, *Cry of the People: The Struggle for Human Rights in Latin America — The Catholic Church in Conflict with U.S. Policy* (Penguin Books, London, 1982) pp. 25-9, 289-92.
18. Senate Report, p. 16.
19. Ibid., p. 5.
20. Ibid., p. 18.
21. Ibid., p. 9.
22. *Survey of the Alliance for Progress: Labor Policies and Programs*, Staff Report of the US Senate Foreign Relations Committee, Subcommittee on American Republics Affairs, 15 July 1968, p. 3.
23. *Newsweek*, 23 September 1974, pp. 51-2, amongst many other places where this now-famous remark can be found.

24. Senate Report, p. 21.
25. Ibid., pp. 21-2.
26. *Interim Report: Alleged Assassination Plots Involving Foreign Leaders*, The Select Committee to Study Governmental Operations with Respect to Intelligence Activities (US Senate) 20 November 1975, p. 227; hereafter referred to as Assassination Report.
27. Senate Report, p. 24.
28. Assassination Report, passim; Senate Report, p. 23.
29. Seymour Hersh, *Kissinger: The Price of Power* (London, 1983) pp. 259, 274, 292.
30. Senate Report, pp. 23, 25; Hersh, p. 273.
31. Senate Report, pp. 26, 37.
32. Ibid., pp. 24, 25.
33. *Foreign and Military Intelligence*, Book 1, Final Report of The Select Committee to Study Governmental Operations with Respect to Intelligence Activities (US Senate), April 1976, p. 200.
34. *Washington Post*, 5 January 1978; Senate Report, p. 25.
35. Senate Report, p. 24.
36. Assassination Report, p. 234.
37. Ibid., p. 240.
38. Ibid., 226, 245, 252, and elsewhere; for another overall description of the 4 September-24 October 1970 period, see Hersh, Chapters 21 and 22.
39. *The Sunday Times* (London), 27 October 1974, p. 15, referring to William Colby's secret testimony before a Congressional committee on 22 April 1974. See the *New York Times*, 8 September 1974, p. 1, for a paraphrase of Colby's statement.
40. Senate Report, p. 33.
41. Almost all books dealing with Chile under Allende go into the economic boycott in some detail; e.g., Edward Boorstein, *Allende's Chile: An Inside View* (New York, 1977) and James Petras and Morris H. Morley, *How Allende Fell* (Great Britain, 1974).
42. Adam Schesch and Patricia Garrett, "The Case of Chile" in Howard Frazier, ed., *Uncloaking the CIA* (The Free Press/Macmillan, New York, 1978) p. 38; Senate Report, pp. 32-3.
43. *The Sunday Times* (London), 27 October 1974, p. 16.
44. Schesch and Garrett, p. 48; Senate Report, pp. 37-8.
45. *Time*, 30 September 1974; Senate Report, p. 31; *New York Times*, 21 September 1974, p. 12.
46. John Dinges and Saul Landau, *Assassination on Embassy Row* (London, 1981) p. 43.
47. AIFLD: Fred Hirsch, *An Analysis of Our AFL-CIO Role in Latin America* (San Jose, California, 1974) passim, Chile, pp. 30-42; *NACLA's Latin America and Empire Report* (North American Congress on Latin America, New York and Berkeley, California) October 1973, p. 11; *The Sunday Times* (London), 27 October 1974, pp. 15, 16; Hortensia Bussi de Allende (Salvador Allende's widow) "The Facts About Chile" in Frazier, op. cit., p. 60.
48. The author's own observations while in Chile from August 1972 to April 1973.
49. One of the publications closed down was *Punto Final*, a magazine put out by the left wing of Allende's own Socialist Party, during a state of emergency declared after an aborted June 1973 military coup.
50. Senate Report, p. 31; Hortensia Bussi de Allende, op. cit., pp. 60, 63; the bombing school in Los Fresnos is described in the chapter on Uruguay.
51. Senate Report, p. 36-8.
52. Ellen Ray and Bill Schaap, "Massive Destabilization in Jamaica", *Covert Action Information Bulletin* (Washington, D.C.) August-September 1980, p. 8; Fred Landis, "Robert Moss, Arnaud de Borchgrave and Right-wing Disinformation" in ibid., p. 42. (Landis was a consultant to the Senate committee which produced the reports cited in this chapter.)
53. Landis, p. 42; Senate Report, p. 39.
54. *The Guardian* (London), 20 December 1976, p. 9; Landis, pp. 37-44.
55. Landis, pp. 38-9; Senate Report, p. 30 (refers to "an opposition research organization"); *Daily Mail* (London) 22 December 1976, p. 6.
56. Senate Report, p. 38.
57. Various published accounts plus the author's personal acquaintance with many Americans and other foreigners who were in Santiago at the time of the coup.
58. *Time* magazine, 30 September 1974.
59. Victor Marchetti and John Marks, *The CIA and the Cult of Intelligence* (New York, 1975), p. 43; Dinges and Landau, p. 50; Hersh, p. 333.
60. *Time*, 24 September 1973, p. 46.
61. Senate Report, p. 39.
62. Hortensia Bussi de Allende, op. cit., p. 64; she adds that the pilots of the WB-575 plane were Majors V. Duenas and T. Schull.
63. Thomas Hauser, *The Execution of Charles Horman* (New York, 1978) Chapters 9 and 10, the book that the film "Missing" is based on.
64. *New York Times*, 17 September 1974, p. 22.

65. Ibid.
66. Senate Report, p. 47; *Washington Post*, 21 October 1973, p. C1.
67. *The Sunday Times* (London), 27 October 1974, p. 16.
68. *Washington Post*, 21 October, 1973, p. C1.
69. Roger Morris, *Uncertain Greatness: Henry Kissinger and American Foreign Policy* (Harper & Row, 1977) p. 241. Morris formerly served under Kissinger on the staff of the National Security Council, although he is not here speaking of himself.
70. Assassination Report, p. 229.

35. GREECE 1964 to 1974

1. *The Observer* (London), 1 July 1973, article by Charles Foley.
2. Junta's actions: James Becket, *Barbarism in Greece* (New York, 1970) p. 1; Bernard Nossiter, "Saving Greece from the Greeks", *New Republic* (Washington), 20 May 1967, p. 10; *The Nation* (New York) 22 May 1967, p. 644.
3. Becket, p. 90 (Amnesty International Report, 27 January 1968).
4. Philip Deane, *I Should Have Died* (Atheneum, New York, 1977) pp. 92-124, composed of conversations with Greek and American individuals in or close to the conspiracy, and references to testimony from the 1975 trials of junta members and torturers.
5. Ibid., pp. 113-14.
6. *New York Times*, 2 August 1974, p. 3; see also *Newsweek*, 12 August 1974, p. 36, concerning CIA buying politicians and votes in Greece before the coup.
7. Stephen Rousseas. "The Deadlock in Greece", *The Nation* (New York), 27 March 1967, p. 392.
8. *Washington Post*, 15 May 1967, p. A18.
9. Andreas Papandreou's political views: Nossiter, p. 9; Deane, p. 116; Lawrence Stern, *The Wrong Horse: The Politics of Intervention and the Failure of American Diplomacy* (N.Y. Times Books, 1977) pp. 20-30.
10. Deane, pp. 116-17.
11. *New York Times*, 2 August 1974, p. 3; 3 August, p. 4.
12. George Papandreou: Rousseas, pp. 390-1; Nossiter, p. 9; Deane, p. 115.
13. *The Observer*, op. cit.
14. Ibid.; see also Deane, p. 96 re bugging ministers.
15. Deane, p. 96, citing Andreas Papandreou as the source. Julius Mader, *Who's Who in CIA* (East Germany, 1968), p. 34, states that Anschuetz served in the Military Intelligence Service of the US Army during World War 2 and joined the CIA in 1950. This book, however, has not always proven to be reliable.
16. *The Observer*, op. cit.
17. Ibid.; Deane, p. 96; Becket, p. 13.
18. *Washington Post*, 15 May 1967, p. A18.
19. Stern, pp. 42-3.
20. *The Observer*, op. cit.
21. Ibid.
22. *New York Times*, 2 August 1974, p. 1; Deane, p. 96.
23. *The Observer*, op. cit.; Deane, p. 126.
24. *The Observer*, op. cit.
25. Ibid.
26. Becket, p. 8.
27. Ibid., p. 10.
28. Ibid., p. xi.
29. Ibid., p. 15.
30. Ibid., p. 91.
31. See, e.g., Becket, pp. 18-85; Deane, pp. 128-33; Amnesty International, *Torture in Greece: The First Torturers' Trial in 1975* (London, 1977) passim.
32. Becket, pp. 4 and 115.
33. Amnesty International, *Report on Torture* (London, 1973), pp. 93-4; also see Deane, p. 119, for evidence of the fraudulent nature of the junta's claims before the coup of a communist threat; State Department statement: *New York Times*, 11 December 1969.
34. *Report on Torture*, op. cit., p. 77; see pages 88, 89, 95, 98 for choice examples of what Amnesty was referring to.
35. *The Observer*, op. cit.
36. Seymour Hersh, *Kissinger: The Price of Power* (Simon & Schuster/Summit Books, New York, 1983) p. 140.
37. *The Observer*, op. cit.
38. Hersh, pp. 137-8, 648; *Los Angeles Times*, 1 August 1990, p. 5.
39. Becket, p. 16; see also p. 127.
40. *Report on Torture*, op. cit., p. 96.
41. Deane, p. 134; *New York Times*, 2 August 1974, p. 1.
42. Deane, p. 134.
43. *New York Times*, 7 September 1975, p. 6.

44. Deane, p. 125.
45. Andreas Papandreou, *Democracy at Gunpoint: The Greek Front* (New York, 1970) p. 294.

36. BOLIVIA 1964 to 1975

The account of the events leading up to the coup of 1964 was derived primarily from the following sources:

a) Cole Blasier, 'The United States and the Revolution' in James M. Malloy and Richard Thorn, eds., *Beyond the Revolution: Bolivia Since 1952* (University of Pittsburgh Press, 1971) pp. 90-105;

b) James Dunkerley, *Rebellion in the Veins: Political Struggle in Bolivia 1952-1982* (London, 1984) pp.112-9;

c) Lawrence Whitehead, *The United States and Bolivia: A Case of Neo-Colonialism* (London, 1969), pp. 11-25;

d) Christopher Mitchell, *The Legacy of Populism in Bolivia: From the MNR to Military Rule* (New York, 1977), Chapter 5;

e) William H. Brill, *Military Intervention in Bolivia: The Overthrow of Paz Estenssoro and the MNR* (Washington, 1967), pp. 18-47.

1. Cornelius H. Zondag, 'Bolivia's 1952 Revolution' in Jerry R. Ladman, ed., *Modern-Day Bolivia* (Arizona State University, 1982) p. 37.

2. *Washington Post*, 5 February 1968. Fox was named as a CIA officer by Antonio Arguedas, Minister of the Interior under Barrientos. This is mentioned in Victor Marchetti and John Marks, *The CIA and the Cult of Intelligence* (New York, 1975), p. 144, but was censored by the CIA in the original manuscript. (Also see note 22 below.)

3. *New York Times*, 9 August 1964, p. 10.

4. Ibid., 24 August 1964, p. 26.

5. Blasier, pp. 89-90; Whitehead, p. 14; Dunkerley, p. 106.

6. Blasier, pp. 97-8; Dunkerley, p. 113; Whitehead, p. 16; *Washington Post*, 5 February 1968.

7. Miners' strength, Zavaleta quote: Whitehead, pp. 24-5. Henderson had actually been ambassador only one year at the time of the coup, so Zavaleta may have been referring to Henderson's predecessor as well.

8. *New York Times*, 22 November 1964, p. 26.

9. US build-up of armed forces: Dunkerley, p. 114; Blasier, pp. 93-5; Whitehead, p. 24; Richard Harris, *Death of a Revolutionary: Che Guevara's Last Mission* (New York, 1970) p. 172.

10. *Washington Post*, 5 February 1968.

11. Blasier, p. 98.

12. Mitchell, p. 94; Dunkerley, pp. 116-17.

13. Shooting incident and aftermath leading to Barrientos replacing Fortún: Dunkerley, p. 117; Mitchell, pp. 94-5.

14. *El Diario* and Sanjinés: Dunkerley, pp. 113-14; Blasier, p. 95; Whitehead, p. 15 (citing cabinet member Antonio Arguedas).

15. Mitchell, p. 95.

16. Brill, p. 28.

17. Ibid., pp. 27-9, 36-8.

18. Ibid., p. 37.

19. *Washington Post*, 5 February 1968.

20. Mitchell, pp. 100-1.

21. Hearings before the Committee on Armed Services and the Subcommittee on Department of Defense of the Committee on Appropriations (US Senate), 23 February 1966, p. 39.

22. *Washington Post*, 17 May 1975; *New York Times*, 17-18 May 1975. Arguedas revealed a number of other things about CIA activities in Bolivia and his own strange connection to the Agency — see Harris, chapter 14; *Intercontinental Press* (New York weekly newsmagazine) 23 September 1968 (transcript of a press conference held by Arguedas).

23. Norman Gall, 'The Legacy of Che Guevara', *Commentary* (New York) December 1967. p. 35.

24. Philip Agee, *Inside the Company: CIA Diary* (New York, 1975) p. 438.

25. Military operation against Guevara: Michael Klare, *War Without End* (Random House, New York, 1972) pp. 173-4, 177-9: Marchetti and Marks, pp. 138-45; Harris, pp. 172-8.

26. Harris, pp. 185-6. See note 22 above.

27. *New York Times*, 14 December 1969, p. 22.

28. Ibid.

29. Interpress Service dispatch of 18 December 1969, cited in Gregorio Selser, *La CIA en Bolivia* (Buenos Aires, 1970) p. 5.

30. Associated Press dispatch from La Paz, appearing in *La Nación* (Buenos Aires' leading newspaper), 21 December 1969, p. 4.

31. *New York Times*, 24 January 1970, p. 9

32. Ibid., 20 July 1970, p. 9.

33. Ibid., 23 September 1970, p. 13.

34. Torres' policies: Latin American Bureau, *Bolivia and Coup d'Etat* (London, 1980) pp. 36-8; Dunkerley, pp. 180, 186.

35. *San Francisco Chronicle*, 30 August 1971.

36. *Washington Post*, 29 August 1971.

37. Dunkerley, p. 197.
38. Dunkerley, p. 200; *Washington Post*, 29 August 1971.
39. *San Francisco Chronicle*, 1 September 1971, reporting from Mexico City and citing "knowledgeable sources here".
40. Banzer's post-coup statements: *Washington Post*, 25 August 1971; *New York Times*, 25 August 1971; *Los Angeles Times*, 24, 25 August 1971.
41. *New York Times*, 30 December 1973.
42. Penny Lernoux, *Cry of the People: The Struggle for Human Rights in Latin America — The Catholic Church in Conflict with U S. Policy* (Penguin Books, London, 1982) pp. 142-5.
43. *The Guardian* (London), 15 July 1985, p. 6.
44. *Bolivia — An Assessment of U S. Policies and Programs: Report to the Congress by the Comptroller General of the United States*, 30 January 1975, p. 29.
45. *New York Times*, 28 July 1978, article by Max Holland.

37. GUATEMALA 1962 to 1980s

The details of the events and issues touched upon in this chapter through 1968 were derived primarily from the following sources:

a) Thomas and Marjorie Melville, *Guatemala — Another Vietnam?* (Great Britain, 1971) Chapters 9 to 16; particularly for the conditions of the poor, and US activities in Guatemala. Published in the United States the same year in a slightly different form as *Guatemala: The Politics of Land Ownership*.
b) Eduardo Galeano, *Guatemala, Occupied Country* (Mexico, 1967; English translation: New York, 1969) passim; for the politics of the guerrillas and the nature of the right-wing terror; Galeano was a Uruguayan journalist who spent some time with the guerrillas.
c) Susanne Jonas and David Tobis, editors, *Guatemala* (Berkeley, California, 1974) passim; particularly "The Vietnamization of Guatemala: U.S. Counter-insurgency Programs" pp. 193-203, by Howard Sharckman; published by the North American Congress on Latin America (NACLA, New York and Berkeley).
d) Amnesty International, *Guatemala* (London, 1976) passim; for statistics about the victims of the terror. Other AI reports issued in the 1970s about Guatemala contain comparable information.
e) Richard Gott, *Rural Guerrillas in Latin America* (Great Britain, 1973, revised edition) Chapters 2 to 8; for the politics of the guerrillas.
1. *The Guardian* (London), 22 December 1983, p. 5.
2. The plight of the poor: a montage compiled from the sources cited herein.
3. *New York Times Magazine*, 26 June 1966, p. 8.
4. US counter-insurgency base: *El Imparcial* (Guatemala City conservative newspaper) 17 May 1962 and 4 January 1963, cited in Melville, pp. 163-4.
5. Stephen Schlesinger and Stephen Kinzer, *Bitter Fruit: The Untold Story of the American Coup in Guatemala* (New York, 1982), p. 242.
6. Georgie Anne Geyer: *Miami Herald*, 24 December 1966. Also see: *New York Herald Tribune*, 7 April 1963, article by Bert Quint, section 2, p. 1; Schlesinger and Kinzer, pp. 236-44.
7. Galeano, p. 55.
8. Ibid., pp. 55-6.
9. *Time*, 26 January 1968, p. 23.
10. Ibid.
11. Atrocities and torture: compiled from the sources cited herein; also see A.J. Langguth, *Hidden Terrors* (New York, 1978) pp. 139, 193 for US involvement with the use of the field telephones for torture in Brazil.
12. Melville, p. 292.
13. Ibid., p. 291.
14. *Washington Post*, 27 January 1968, p. A4, testimony of Rev. Blase Bonpane, an American Maryknoll priest in Guatemala at the time.
15. Panama: revealed in September 1967 by Guatemalan Vice-President Clemente Marroquin Rojas in an interview with the international news agency Interpress Service (IPS), reported in *Latin America*, 15 September 1967, p. 159, a weekly published in London. Eduardo Galeano, p. 70, reports a personal conversation he had with Marroquin Rojas in which the vice-president related the same story. Marroquin Rojas was strongly anti-communist, but he apparently resented the casual way in which the American planes violated Guatemalan sovereignty.
16. Norman Diamond, "Why They Shoot Americans", *The Nation* (New York), 5 February 1968. The title of the article refers to the shooting of John Webber.
17. Opening quotation: Clyde Snow, forensic anthropologist, cited in *Covert Action Quarterly*, spring 1994, No. 48, p. 32. Right-wing terrorism: compiled from the sources cited herein.
18. *Washington Post*, 4 February 1968, p. B1. The historic dialogue in Latin America between Christianity and Marxism, begun in the 1970s, can be traced in large measure to priests and nuns like Bonpane and the Melvilles and their experiences in Guatemala in the 1950s and 60s.
19. Galeano, p. 63.
20. *El Imparcial* (Guatemala City), 10 November 1967, cited in Melville, p. 289.
21. Richard Gott, in the Foreword to the Melvilles' book, p. 8.

22. AID, OPS, Alliance for Progress:
a) "Guatemala and the Dominican Republic", a Staff Memorandum prepared for the US Senate Subcommittee on Western Hemisphere Affairs, Committee on Foreign Relations, 30 December 1971, p. 6;
b) Jonas and Tobis, pp. 199-200;
c) Galeano, pp. 72-3;
d) Michael Klare, *War Without End* (Random House, New York, 1972) pp. 241-69, for discussion of the OPS curriculum and philosophy;
e) Langguth, pp. 242-3 and elsewhere, for discussion of OPS practices, including its involvement with torture; the author confines his study primarily to Brazil and Uruguay, but it applies to Guatemala as well;
f) *CounterSpy* magazine (Washington), November 1980-January 1981, pp. 54-5, lists the names of almost 300 Guatemalan police officers who received training in the United States from 1963 to 1974;
g) Michael Klare and Nancy Stein, "Police Terrorism in Latin America", *NACLA's Latin America and Empire Report* (North American Congress on Latin America, New York), January 1974, pp. 19-23, based on State Department documents obtained by Senator James Abourezk in 1973;
h) Jack Anderson, *Washington Post*, 8 October 1973, p. C33.
23. AID figure cited in Jenny Pearce, *Under the Eagle: U.S. Intervention in Central America and the Caribbean* (Latin American Bureau, London, updated edition 1982) p. 67.
24. George Cotter, "Spies, strings and missionaries", *The Christian Century* (Chicago), 25 March 1981, p. 321.
25. Eqbal Ahmad, "The Theory and Fallacies of Counter-insurgency", *The Nation* (New York), 2 August 1972, p. 73.
26. Relationship of Arana to US military: Joseph Goulden, "A Real Good Relationship", *The Nation* (New York), 1 June 1970, p. 646; Norman Gall, "Guatemalan Slaughter", *N.Y. Review of Books*, 20 May 1971, pp. 13-17.
27. *Le Monde Weekly* (English edition), 17 February 1971, p. 3.
28. *New York Times*, 27 December 1970, p. 2; *New York Times Magazine*, 13 June 1971, p. 72.
29. US Senate Staff Memorandum, op. cit.
30. *New York Times*, 18 February 1976.
31. Ibid., 9 November 1977, p. 2.
32. Jonathan Marshall, Peter Dale Scott, Jane Hunter, *The Iran-Contra Connection: Secret Teams and Covert Operations in the Reagan Era* (South End Press, Boston, 1987), chapter V, passim; *The Guardian* (London), 9 December 1983; *CounterSpy*, op. cit., p. 53, citing Elias Barahona y Barahona, former press secretary at the Guatemalan Ministry of the Interior who had infiltrated the government for the EGP.
33. *CounterSpy*, op. cit. (Barahona) p. 53.
34. Pearce, p. 278; a book was published later which transcribed Menchú's own account of her life, in which she recounts many more atrocities of the Guatemalan military: Elisabeth Burgos-Debray, ed., *I ... Rigoberta Menchú: An Indian Woman in Guatemala* (London, 1984, English translation).
35. Pearce, p. 176; Sherwood's role in 1954: Schlesinger and Kinzer, pp. 116, 122, 128. His statement is partially quoted in Penny Lernoux, *In Banks We Trust* (Doubleday, New York, 1984), p. 238, citing CBS News Special, 20 March 1982: "Update: Central America in Revolt".
36. *Washington Post*, 22 February 1981, p. C7, column by Jack Anderson; Anderson refers only to an "official spokesman" of the MLN; the identity of the speaker as Sandoval comes from other places — see, e.g., *The Guardian* (London), 2 March 1984.
37. *Washington Post*, ibid. For a discussion of the many ties between American conservatives and the Guatemalan power structure, see the report of the Council on Hemispheric Affairs (Washington), by Allan Nairn in 1981.
38. *New York Times*, 19 March 1981, p. 10.
39. *Washington Post*, 14 May 1981, p. A16.
40. Ibid.; *New York Times*, 18 May 1981, p. 18; Report issued by the Washington Office on Latin America (a respected human-rights lobby which has worked in liaison with the State Department's human-rights section), 4 September 1981.
41. Washington Office on Latin America report, op. cit. Presumably it was the traditional right-wing fear of the poor being educated which lay behind this incident.
42. *New York Times*, 28 December 1981.
43. Ibid., 21 June 1981; 25 April 1982; *The Guardian* (London), 10 January 1983.
44. *San Francisco Chronicle*, 27 August 1981, p. 57.
45. *Washington Post*, 21 October 1982, p. A1.
46. *The Guardian* (London), 10 January 1983; 17 May 1983.
47. *New York Times*, 25 April 1982. p. 1.
48. Ibid., 12 October 1982, p. 3 (deaths, citing Amnesty International); *Los Angeles Times*, 20 July 1994, p. 11 (villages, citing "human rights organizations"). For the gruesome details of death squads, disappearances, and torture in Guatemala during the early 1980s, see *Guatemala: A Government Program of Political Murder* (Amnesty International, London, 1981) and *Massive Extrajudicial Executions in Rural Areas Under the Government of General Efraín Ríos Montt* (AI, July 1982).
49. *New York Times*, 6 December 1982, p. 14.
50. *Contemporary Marxism* (San Francisco), No. 3, Summer 1981.
51. *The National Catholic Reporter* (Kansas City, Missouri weekly), 31 January 1968.

52. *Los Angeles Times*, 25 December 1988.
53. Occurred on 2 December 1990; Report, Summer 1991, from Witness for Peace, Washington, a religious-oriented human rights organization concerned with Central America.
54. *Los Angeles Times*, 7 May 1990.
55. DeVine and Bamaca cases: *New York Times*, 23 March 1995, p. 1; 24 March, p. 3; 30 March, p.1; *Los Angeles Times,* 23 March, p. 4; 2 April, p. M2; *Time* magazine, 10 April 1995, p. 43. Alpírez had actually been linked to the Bamaca case two years earlier in testimony to the OAS, information which the State Department of course had access to. (*Los Angeles Times*, 4 April 1995, letter to the editor from Madeline Rios, editor of *Guatemala Review Magazine*, LA).

38. COSTA RICA 1970 to 1971

1. *New York Times*, 11 February 1971.
2. Ibid. The term "economic offensive" was apparently that of the newspaper.
3. The primary sources for the overall story are the *Miami Herald*, 7 February 1971 and the *Los Angeles Times*, 28 February 1971; see also the *Miami Herald*, 9, 10, 11, 13 February 1971.
4. *New York Times*, 11 February 1971; *Miami Herald*, 11 February 1971.
5. *Miami Herald*, 10 February 1971.

39. IRAQ 1972 to 1975

The primary source of information for this chapter is the Staff Report of the Select Committee on Intelligence, US House of Representatives, based on hearings held during 1975. Publication of the report was suppressed by the full House until the White House could censor it. But portions of the uncensored report, which came to be known as The Pike Report after the committee's chairman Rep. Otis G. Pike, were leaked to the press, in particular *The Village Voice* of New York which published much of it in its issues of 16 and 23 February 1976. The first, and probably only, appearance of this material in book form occurred in 1977 in England under the title: *CIA — The Pike Report*, published by Spokesman Books for the Bertrand Russell Peace Foundation, Nottingham. It is this book which is referred to in the present chapter, pp. 56, 195-8, 211-17, hereafter referred to as Pike Report. The report refers to the Kurds as "the ethnic group", Iran or the Shah as "our ally", Iraq as "our ally's enemy", Israel as "another government". Here, the proper names are used.

1. Seymour Hersh, *The Price of Power: Kissinger in the Nixon White House* (Summit Books/Simon & Schuster, New York, 1983) p. 542n.
2. *New York Times*, 5 February 1976, p. 31, column by William Safire.
3. Pike Report, p. 196.
4. Political background of the Kurds: *The Times* (London), 26-28 November 1974.
5. Pike Report, p. 212.
6. Ibid., pp. 197, 214-15.
7. Ibid., p. 214.
8. Ibid., p. 197.
9. *New York Times*, 12 February 1976, p. 31, column by William Safire.
10. Pike Report, p. 214.
11. *New York Times*, 2 June 1972, p. 1; 3 June, p. 1; 8 June, p. 69.
12. Ibid.,5 February 1976, p. 31, column by William Safire.
13. Pike Report, pp. 198, 215.
14. Ibid., 215-216.
15. Ibid., p. 217.
16. *New York Times*, 12 February 1976, p. 31, column by William Safire; Pike Report, p. 198, Kissinger is referred to as "a high U.S. official".

40. AUSTRALIA 1973 to 1975

1. Henry S. Albinski, *Australian External Policy Under Labor* (Australia, 1977) p. 126.
2. Joan Coxsedge, Ken Coldicutt, Gerry Harant, *Rooted in Secrecy: The Clandestine Element in Australian Politics* (Australia, 1982) p. 21.
3. Albinski, p. 125.
4. Ibid.
5. Coxsedge, et al., p. 24; Seymour Hersh, *The Price of Power: Kissinger in the Nixon White House* (Summit Books/Simon & Schuster, New York, 1983) p. 295.
6. Richard Hall, *The Secret State* (Australia, 1978), p. 2.
7. Coxsedge, et al., p. 25-6.
8. Denis Freney, *The CIA's Australian Connection* (Sydney, 1977) pp. 75-80, for the text of the interview. This book deals with many of the events discussed in this chapter.
9. Desmond Ball, *A Suitable Piece of Real Estate: American Installations in Australia* (Sydney, 1980) passim.
10. *The National Times* (Sydney weekly newspaper), 6-12 May 1983, p. 3.
11. Jim Jose, "The Whitlam Years: Illusion and Reality" in Pat Flanagan, ed., *Big Brother or Democracy?* (Great Britain, 1981) p. 50; Albinski, p. 11; Ball, passim.
12. Albinski, pp. 9, 241, 254-6.
13. Coxsedge, et al., p. 26.
14. Jose, p. 50.
15. *The Australian Financial Review* (Sydney daily newspaper), 4 November 1975, p. 1; 5 November, p. 4. In his book on the National Security Agency, *The Puzzle Palace* (New York, 1982), p. 205, James Bamford identifies

Stalling as an official of the NSA, not the CIA.

16. *New York Times*, 24 September 1974, p. 2.

17. Ibid., 5 May 1977, citing the *Sydney Sun*, 4 May 1977.

18. Coxsedge, et al., p. 35.

19. *The Australian Financial Review*, 28 April 1977, p. 1; Jose, p. 51, adds that the official, Dr. Farrands, denied the allegation but did admit to visiting Kerr in October, although he refused to discuss the nature of the meeting.

20. *The Australian Financial Review*, 28 April 1977, p. 1.

21. Albinski, p. 169.

22. Coxsedge, et al., p. 96.

23. Freney, pp. 30-31, for the full text of the telex.

24. Coxsedge, et al., p. 35; Freney, p 33; *The Village Voice* (New York), 1-7 July 1981.

25. Discussion of the political and legal issues surrounding the budget crisis and Kerr's dismissal of Whitlam:

a) Coxsedge, op. cit., Freney, op. cit., Flanagan, op. cit.

b) Sir John Kerr, *Matters for Judgment: An Autobiography* (New York, 1979) chapters 20-22.

c) Russel Ward, *The History of Australia: The Twentieth Century, 1901-1975* (London, 1978) pp. 398-419.

d) *New York Times*, 12, 14 November 1975.

26. *New York Times*, 14 November 1975, p. 7.

27. *The Age*, 12 November 1975, pp. 9 and 3.

28. Kerr, chapters 20-22.

29. Victor Marchetti and John Marks, *The CIA and the Cult of Intelligence* (New York, 1975) p. 178; see pp. 178-9 for a description of the Asia Foundation.

30. Kerr in the Association for Cultural Freedom and Lawasia: Kerr, pp. 172-86, and most of the Australian books mentioned above; the *Quadrant* article was in the Spring, 1960 issue, pp. 27-38.

31. *San Francisco Chronicle*, 24 May 1982. Boyce is the subject of the book and film "The Falcon and the Snowman" by Robert Lindsey.

32. *New York Times*, 28 April 1977, p. 18; *The Guardian* (London), 29 April 1977, p. 7.

33. Nugan Hand Bank:

a) *Sunday Times* (London), 31 August 1980, p. 2;

b) *New York Times*, 13 November 1982, p. 31;

c) *The Village Voice*, 1-7 July 1981;

d) *CounterSpy* magazine (Washington, D.C.), November 1980-January 1981, pp. 30-33;

e) Jonathan Kwitny, *The Crimes of Patriots: A True Tale of Dope, Dirty Money and the CIA* (New York, 1987), passim.

41. ANGOLA 1975 to 1980s

1. *New York Times*, 25 September 1975; 19 December 1975.

2. John A. Marcum, *The Angolan Revolution, Vol. I, 1950-1962* (MIT Press, Cambridge, Mass., 1969) pp. 229-30.

3. *New York Times*, 17 December 1964, p. 14.

4. Comparison of the three groups:

a) Jonathan Kwitny, *Endless Enemies: The Making of an Unfriendly World* (New York, 1984) chapter 9;

b) Marcum, Vol. II, 1962-1976 (1978) pp. 14-15, 132, 172 and elsewhere;

c) Basil Davidson, *In the Eye of the Storm: Angola's People* (London, 1972) passim;

d) Ernest Harsch and Tony Thomas, *Angola: The Hidden History of Washington's War* (New York, 1976) passim.

International appeals for support made by Roberto and Savimbi: see also *New York Times*, 4 January 1964, p. 15; Kwitny, p. 136; *Declassified Documents Reference System*, 1977 volume, document 210D (cable, 17 July 1964, US embassy Congo to State Department).

5. Kwitny, pp. 132-3.

6. State Department Circular 92, 16 July 1963, cited in Marcum II, p. 16.

7. Hearings before the House Select Committee on Intelligence (The Pike Committee) published in *CIA - The Pike Report* (Nottingham, England, 1977) p. 218; hereafter referred to as Pike Report. (See Notes: Iraq for further information.)

8. Ibid., p. 201.

9. *New York Times*, 25 September 1975; 19 December.

10. Pike Report, p. 199, the words in quotes are those of the Pike Committee; the date comes from John Stockwell, *In Search of Enemies* (New York, 1978) p. 67. Stockwell was a CIA officer and head of the Agency's Angola task force.

11. Stockwell, pp. 67-8; Marcum II, pp. 257-8 (he cites several international press accounts).

12. *New York Times*, 25 September 1975

13. Pike Report, p. 199.

14. Stockwell, p. 67.

15. *New York Times*, 12 December 1975; Harsch and Thomas, p. 100, citing CBS-TV News, 17 December 1975, and Senator John Tunney, 6 January 1976.

16. *New York Times*, 16 July 1978, p. 1

17. Interview of Stockwell by author.

18. Stockwell, pp. 223-4; see also Harsch and Thomas, pp. 99-100.

19. Chapman Pincher, *Inside Story: A Documentary of the Pursuit of Power* (London, 1978) p. 20
20. Stockwell, p. 225.
21. *New York Times*, 16 July 1978, referring to Kissinger's statement of 29 January 1976.
22. Stockwell, pp. 162, 177-8
23. Ibid., pp. 194-5, plus interview of Stockwell by author.
24. The capture of Russians and Cubans story appeared in the press 22 November 1975; the rape story, 12 March 1976.
25. Stockwell, p. 196.
26. *San Francisco Chronicle*, 9 May 1978.
27. Stockwell, pp. 196-8.
28. *Foreign and Military Intelligence*, Book 1, Final Report of the Select Committee to Study Governmental Operations with Respect to Intelligence Activities (US Senate), 26 April 1976, p. 129.
29. Stockwell, p. 193.
30. Ibid., pp. 205-6 ("Bob Temmons" is probably a pseudonym); after the war ended, the State Department did release the planes to Angola.
31. *Newsweek* (International Edition), 17 May 1976, p. 23, implicitly admitted to by South African Prime Minister Balthazar Johannes Vorster.
32. *New York Times*, 16 July 1978, p. 1; 23 July 1986, p. 1; Stockwell, pp. 208, 218; Stephen Talbot, "The CIA and BOSS: Thick as Thieves" in Ellen Ray, et al., eds., *Dirty Work 2: The CIA in Africa* (New Jersey, 1979) pp. 266-75 (BOSS is the South African Bureau of State Security); Bob Woodward, *VEIL: The Secret Wars of the CIA 1981-1987* (New York, 1987), p. 269.
33. *The Guardian* (London), 15 August 1986; *The Times* (London) 4 August 1986, p. 10.
34. *New York Times*, 25 March 1982, p. 7, citing a report of the House Foreign Affairs Committee.
35. Stockwell, p. 209.
36. Ibid., p. 75.
37. Stockwell, pp. 216-17 discusses how this came about.
38. Wayne S. Smith, "Dateline Havana: Myopic Diplomacy", *Foreign Policy* (Washington, D.C.) Fall 1982, p. 170.
39. Stockwell, pp. 234-5.
40. *New York Times*, 24 December 1975, p 7.
41. Henry Kissinger, *American Foreign Policy* (New York, 1977, third edition), p. 317.
42. See, for example, *New York Times*, 25 September 1975.
43. Hearings before the Subcommittee on Africa of the House Committee on International Relations, 25 May 1978, p. 7.
44. Pike Report, p. 200.
45. *New York Times*, 9 January 1976, p. 3.
46. *Washington Post*, 18 December 1975, p. A23.
47. Kwitny, p. 148.
48. Harsch and Thomas, pp. 82-91; *New York Times*, 8 February 1981, IV, p. 5.
49. Stockwell, pp. 203-4, 241; plus interview of Stockwell by author.
50. Stockwell, p. 172.
51. Galen Hull, "Internationalizing the Shaba Conflict", *Africa Report* (New York) July-August 1977, p. 9. For further discussion of possible Soviet connection to the rebellion and the Russian attitude toward Angola, see Jonathan Steele, "Soviet Relations with Angola and Mozambique" in Robert Cassen, ed., *Soviet Interests in the Third World* (Published by Sage for the Royal Institute of International Affairs, London, 1985), p. 290.
52. *The Observer* (London), 22 January 1984.
53. *The Guardian* (London), 21 December 1983.
54. *The Times* (London), 23 October 1986, p. 8; the vote in the European Parliament was 152-150.
55. *The Guardian* (London), 25 June 1990, p. 10; Sharon Beaulaurier, "Profiteers Fuel War in Angola", *Covert Action Quarterly* (Washington, DC), No. 45, Summer 1993, pp. 61-65.
56. *New York Times*, 17 January 1993, IV, p. 5.

42. ZAIRE 1975 to 1978

1. Mobutu's fortune: *New York Times*, 3 June 1978, article by Michael Kaufman; *The Nation* (New York) 26 February 1983, p. 230. Malnutrition: World Bank report, 1975, cited in *Africa Today* (Denver, Colorado), October-December 1978, p. 7.
2. Roger Morris (former staff member of the National Security Council) and Richard Mauzy, "Zaire (the Congo): An Exercise in Nation Building" in Robert Borosage and John Marks, eds., *The CIA File* (New York, 1976) pp. 36-7. For a detailed description of Mobutu's corruption and cruelty, see Jonathan Kwitny, *Endless Enemies: The Making of an Unfriendly World* (Penguin Books, New York, 1986), pp. 86-91.
3. Coup accusation and attendant events: *New York Times*, 18-23 June 1975; 2 September 1975, p. 21; John Stockwell, *In Search of Enemies* (New York, 1978) p. 44.
4. Stockwell, p. 96, quoting CIA officer Bill Avery.
5. For a profile of Hinton, see *NACLA's Latin America and Empire Report*, October 1973, pp. 14-15, published by North American Congress on Latin America (NACLA), New York.

6. Stockwell, p. 169.
7. Ibid., p. 164.
8. Ibid., p. 246, and note.
9. *New York Times*, 21 January 1976, p. 1.
10. Ibid., 9 April 1977; the quoted words are those of the newspaper.
11. The overall events of 1977: *New York Times*, 16 March to 3 May 1977, passim; Galen Hull, "Internationalizing the Shaba Conflict", *Africa Report* (New York), July-August 1977, pp. 4-9.
12. Bufkin/mercenaries: *Newsday* (Long Island, NY), 17 April 1977; *New York Times*, 17, 18, 20 April 1977.
13. *New York Times*, 8 August 1977.
14. Background of the Balunda ("Ba" is plural): Gerald Bender, "Zaire: Is There Any Rationale for U.S. Intervention?", *Los Angeles Times*, 27 March 1977, VII, p. 2; Hull, op. cit.; Kwitny, chapter 2; Stockwell, p. 151.
15. *New York Times*, 6 April 1977.
16. Mobutu: Ibid., 13 April 1977.
17. Confiscation of businesses: Bender, op. cit.
18. *New York Times*, 13 April 1977.
19. *Washington Post*, 16 March 1977.
20. *New York Times*, 20 May 1978.
21. 1978 military events: *New York Times*, 15 May to 24 June 1978, passim; *Washington Post*, 21 May 1978, p. 14.
22. *New York Times*, 23 May 1978.
23. Ibid., 19 May 1978.
24. Ibid., 20 May 1978. The words are those of the *Times*, paraphrasing "high administration officials".
25. See, for example, *New York Times*, 10 April 1977.
26. Carter-Castro exchange: Ibid., 11, 13, 15 June 1978.
27. Ibid., 24 June 1978.
28. *Washington Post*, 7 June 1978, p. A21.

43. JAMAICA 1976 to 1980

1. Ernest Volkman and John Cummings, "Murder as Usual", *Penthouse* magazine (New York), December 1977, p. 114, quoting a participant in the meeting of the two men. (Volkman is a former national correspondent for *Newsday*.)
2. Michael Manley, *Jamaica: Struggle in the Periphery* (London, 1982) p. 116.
3. John Dinges and Saul Landau, *Assassination on Embassy Row* (London, 1981) p. 44.
4. Testimony by de Roulet before the US Senate: *Multinational Corporations and United States Foreign Policy*, Hearings before the Subcommittee on Multinational Corporations of the Committee on Foreign Relations, 19 July 1973, pp. 117-18. A State Department official who was testifying at the same time was clearly embarrassed by de Roulet's disclosure and quickly tried to play down the story.
5. Volkman and Cummings, p. 114.
6. Manley, p. 116.
7. Ibid., p. 136.
8. Ibid., pp. 98-103.
9. *New York Times*, 1 October 1979, p. 2.
10. Manley, p.101.
11. Ibid., pp. 116-17.
12. Ibid., p. 117.
13. Volkman and Cummings, p. 182.
14. Ibid., p. 183. Posada and plane bombing: see Cuba chapter and notes.
15. Ellen Ray, "CIA and Local Gunmen Plan Jamaican Coup", *CounterSpy* magazine (Washington), Vol. 3, No. 2, December 1976, p. 39; Volkman and Cummings, p. 182.
16. Volkman and Cummings, p. 182; Manley, p. 103.
17. *New York Times*, 17 July 1976, p. 29.
18. Manley, p. 228.
19. Ray, pp. 38, 40; Manley, pp. 229, 236; *New York Times*, 30 January 1976.
20. Ray, p. 37; Volkman and Cummings, pp. 183, 188.
21. Ray, p. 41; *Washington Post*, 5 July 1979.
22. Volkman and Cummings, p. 182; Ray, p. 41.
23. Assassination attempts: Volkman and Cummings, pp. 112, 183, 188, 190.
24. Ray, p. 40.
25. Fred Landis, "The CIA and the Media: IAPA and the Jamaica Daily Gleaner", *Covert Action Information Bulletin* (Washington) December 1979-January 1980, pp. 10-12; Manley, p. 231; Fred Landis, "CIA Media Operations in Chile, Jamaica and Nicaragua", *CAIB*, March 1982, pp. 32-43; Carl Bernstein, "The CIA and the Media", *Rolling Stone*, 20 October 1977, p. 64.
26. Ray, p. 41.
27. *Newsday* (Long Island, NY), 28 February 1980, cited in Ellen Ray and Bill Schaap, "Massive Destabilization in

Jamaica", *Covert Action Information Bulletin*, August-September 1980, p. 14; the date of the earlier article is not mentioned.
28. *Daily Gleaner* (Kingston, Jamaica), 1 June 1980, p. 10; see also Fred Landis, op. cit. 1982.
29. Manley, pp. 193-4.
30. Ibid., pp. 199-200.

44. SEYCHELLES 1979 to 1981

1. René and US-Seychelles relations: *Sunday Tribune* (Durban, South Africa), 29 November 1981, two separate articles, pp. 1 and 52; Ellen Ray, "Seychelles Beats Back Mercenaries", *CovertAction Information Bulletin* [CAIB] (Washington), No. 16, March 1982, pp. 4-10.
2. *Sunday Tribune*, op. cit., p. 52.
3. CAIB, op. cit., p. 5.
4. *Sunday Tribune*, op. cit., p. 1; CAIB, op. cit., pp. 4-10.
5. Ibid.; *New York Times*, 6 November 1982, p. 4 (prosecution of editors).
6. *New York Times*, 10 May 1982, p. 2; *The Guardian* (London), 19 August 1982, p. 13.
7. The trial and aftermath: *New York Times*, 6 January 1982, p. 9; 11 March, p. 6; 22 April, p. 5; 4 May, p. 10; 10 May, p. 2; 17 June, p. 12; 30 July, p. 6; 28 November, p. 5; *The Guardian* (London), 14 July 1986
8. CAIB, op. cit., p. 10.
9. *The Guardian* (London), 3 December 1983.

45. GRENADA 1979 to 1984

1. *New York Times*, 1 November 1983: Les Janka was the man in whom the FBI security check failed to discover a conscience.
2. US presence: Hugh O'Shaughnessy, *Grenada: Revolution, Invasion and Aftermath* (London, 1984) p. 156 (O'Shaughnessy was the Latin America correspondent for *The Observer* and before that for *The Financial Times*, both London; he won a British Press Award in 1983 for his coverage of the Grenada invasion). For the relevant sections of the OECS treaty: William C. Gilmore, *The Grenada Intervention: Analysis and Documentation* (London, 1984) Part II, "The Grenada Intervention in International Law" and Appendix 2.
3. *The Guardian* (London), 28 October 1983.
4. *The Observer* (London), 30 October 1983 (article by Hugh O'Shaughnessy, see note 2); see also Bob Woodward, *VEIL: The Secret Wars of the CIA 1981-1987* (New York, 1987), p. 290.
5. O'Shaughnessy, p. 153.
6. Woodward, p. 290.
7. *The Guardian*, 31 October 1983.
8. *The Observer*, 30 October 1983.
9. *The Guardian*, 1 November 1983.
10. *The Guardian*, 28, 29 October 1983; *The Observer*, 30 October 1983.
11. O'Shaughnessy, p. 165; this page contains other evidence which refutes Reagan's contention which is not discussed here.
12. *The Guardian*, 26 October 1983.
13. *New York Times*, 27 October 1983.
14. O'Shaughnessy, p. 205.
15. *The Guardian*, 26 October 1983.
16. O'Shaughnessy, p. 160.
17. *The Guardian*, 27 October 1983.
18. Ibid., 28 October 1983.
19. *New York Times*, 27 October 1983.
20. Ibid., 28 October 1983.
21. *The Guardian*, 29 October 1983; Casey: Woodward, p. 294.
22. O'Shaughnessy, p. 204.
23. *The Guardian*, 31 October 1983.
24. *New York Times*, 1 November 1983.
25. Woodward, p. 299, the quote is his paraphrase.
26. O'Shaughnessy, pp. 15, 16, 204.
27. *The Observer*, 23 October 1983.
28. From a speech by Fidel Castro on 14 November 1983 in Havana; reprinted in *The Guardian*, 19 November 1983, p. 8.
29. *The Guardian*, 27 October 1983.
30. Ibid., 1 November 1983.
31. *New York Times*, 1 November 1983.
32. *The Guardian*, 12 June 1984.
33. O'Shaughnessy, pp. 87, 95.
34. Ibid., p. 85.
35. *The Guardian*, 4 November 1983.
36. Woodward, p. 290.

37. Cited by Bishop in his speech of 13 April 1979, in Chris Searle, ed., *In Nobody's Backyard: Maurice Bishop's Speeches 1979-1983* (London, 1984).
38. *New York Times*, 20 August 1979. p. 4.
39. Chris Searle, *Grenada, The Struggle Against Destabilization* (London, 1983), p. 56; this appeared as a news item in the US media as well, and was seen or heard by myself, but I have been unable to locate it again.
40. *New York Times*, 27 August 1983.
41. *Washington Post*, 27 February 1983, p. 1.
42. O'Shaughnessy, p. 192. The correspondent was Ed Cody. Oddly enough, it appears that the *Post* itself did not run the story.
43. *Washington Post*, 27 February 1983, p. 1.
44. *New York Times*, 26 March 1983.
45. *The Nation* (New York), 16 April 1983, p. 467, contains a table which compares the various airports.
46. O'Shaughnessy, p. 90.
47. *The Nation* (New York), 16 April 1983, p. 467; O'Shaughnessy, p. 89.
48. *The Guardian*, 31 October, 2 November 1983.
49. Ibid., 2 May 1983.
50. *Wall Street Journal*, 29 April 1981; *The Guardian*, 2 May 1983.
51. *The Guardian*, 11 November 1983.
52. *New York Times*, 20 August 1979, p. 4.
53. Ibid.
54. The Observer, 30 October 1983, p. 9.
55. *The Guardian*, 25 November 1983.
56. Ibid., 27 October 1983, according to the Cuban ambassador in London.
57. From speech by Fidel Castro on 14 November 1983 in Havana; reprinted in *The Guardian*, 19 November 1983, p. 8.
58. *The Observer*, 30 October 1983, p 9.
59. *The Guardian*, 16 November 1983.
60. The Observer, 30 October 1983.
61. O'Shaughnessy, p. 208; *The Guardian*, 16 November, 19 December 1983.
62. *The Guardian*, 5 March 1984.
63. Ibid., 12 June 1984.
64. *New York Times*, 4 November 1983, p. 16.
65. Ibid., 22 March 1986.
66. *New York Times*, 15 April 1984, p. 10
67. Ibid., 4 December 1984
68. Ibid., 10 December 1984, p. 3
69. *The Guardian* (London), 3 January 1986. Though the Reagan administration described COHA as left-wing, the same annual report strongly criticized Cuba, Nicaragua and the Shining Path guerrillas of Peru for human-rights violations.
70. "Importation of Publications (Prohibition) Order", Statutory Rules and Orders No. 6 of April 11, 1989, government of Grenada.
71. *Los Angeles Times*, 25 August 1989.

46. MOROCCO 1983
1. *The Nation* (New York), 26 March 1983, p. 356.
2. Interview in *Africa Now* (London), March 1983, pp. 14-18.
3. Claudia Wright, "Showdown in the Sahara", *Inquiry* magazine (Washington), 12 April 1982, p. 24; *New York Times*, 1 February 1983, p. 3.
4. *Africa Now*, op. cit., p. 14.
5. *New York Times*, 1 February 1983, p. 3.
6. Wright, p. 24.
7. Ibid., pp. 24-5.
8. *Africa Now*, op. cit., pp. 14-15.
9. Ibid., p. 14.

47. SURINAME 1982 to 1984
1. *Miami Herald*, 1 June 1983.
2. *New York Times*, 1 June 1983, p. 13.
3. *Miami Herald*, 1 June 1983.
4. *The Guardian* (London), 1 November 1982, 7 January 1983; *New York Times*, 7 January 1983, p. 5.
5. *New York Times*, 12 December 1982, p. 4; 30 November 1983.
6. Tom Barry, et al., *The Other Side of Paradise: Foreign Control in the Caribbean* (Grove Press, New York, 1984), p. 361, citing *Soberanía* magazine (Managua, Nicaragua) February/March 1983. See index of the present book for further information on the AIFLD.

7. *New York Times*, 7 January 1983, p. 5.
8. Ibid., 19 July 1983.
9. *Miami Herald*, 2 June 1983; Barry, op. cit., pp. 361-2, citing *Latin America Weekly Report* (London), 9 June 1983.
10. *New York Times*, 27 October 1983, p. 4; 31 October, p. 10; *Miami Herald*, 29 November 1983; *Washington Post*, 5 November 1983.
11. *Newsweek*, 7 November 1983, p. 78.
12. *The Guardian* (London), 22 February 1983, p. 7.
13. *Miami Herald*, 29 November 1983.
14. *The Guardian* (London), 11 and 13 January 1984.
15. Ibid., 28 November 1985. See Nicaragua chapter for further information on the National Endowment for Democracy.

48. LIBYA 1981-1989

1. Adolf Hitler, *Mein Kampf* (Houghton Mifflin Co., Boston, 1971; original version 1925) Vol. 1, chapter 10, p. 231.
2. *New York Times*, 15 April 1986.
3. Seymour Hersh, "Target Qaddafi", *The New York Times Magazine*, 22 February 1987, p. 22.
4. *New York Times*, 15 April 1986, p. 11
5. Hersh, p. 20. A corroborating comment is given by an air force pilot. See also: *The Guardian* (London), 19 April 1986.
6. *San Francisco Chronicle*, 6 October 1987.
7. Ibid., 16 April 1987, p. 15.
8. *The Guardian* (London), 24 February 1987.
9. Hersh, p. 20.
10. *The Guardian* (London), 9 May 1986, p. 11; see also *New York Times*, 15 April 1986, p. 11.
11. *New York Times*, 15 April 1986, transcript of Reagan's address, and Larry Speakes cited in article, p. 11; Bob Woodward, *VEIL: The Secret Wars of the CIA 1981-1987* (New York, 1987), pp. 444-5
12. *Der Spiegel* (Hamburg, West Germany), 21 April 1986, p. 20; *Los Angeles Times*, 11-13 January 1988; *New York Times,* 22 December 1988, p. 14; Hersh, p. 74. In December 1992, German officials charged a Palestinian with the bombing. It is not clear what the outcome of that arrest was.
13. Hersh, p. 74.
14. *Time* magazine, 16 January 1989, p. 20.
15. *The Times* (London), 2 October 1989, p. 10; 28 September 1989, p. 9; *LA Weekly* (Los Angeles), 27 October-2 November 1989, p. 10, column by Alexander Cockburn; *Los Angeles Times*, 2 November 1988.
16. *Los Angeles Times*, 24 November 1988, p. 16.
17. *Newsweek*, 20 July 1981, p. 42, citing a Western ambassador in Tripoli.
18. *New York Times*, 16 April 1986, pp. 1, 20.
19. *Washington Post*, 21 March 1981, p. A3.
20. *Newsweek* 3 August 1981, p. 19.
21. See *Boston Globe*, 25 March 1986, p. 7 for a discussion of this question.
22. *Washington Post*, 13 October 1981, p. D17, Jack Anderson.
23. Hersh, p. 24.
24. *Newsweek*, 19 October 1981, p. 43; *New York Times*, 25 October 1981; 26 October, 1981, p. 4.
25. *Time* magazine, 23 November 1981.
26. *New York Times*, 13 November 1981, p. 3.
27. Ibid., 4 December 1981, p. 1.
28. Ibid., 8 December 1981, p. 7.
29. Jack Anderson, *San Francisco Chronicle*, 7 January 1982.
30. Hersh, pp. 24, 26.
31. Duncan Campbell and Patrick Forbes, "Tale of Anti-Reagan Hit Team Was `Fraud'," *New Statesman* magazine (London), 16 August 1985, p. 6; Jack Anderson, *San Francisco Chronicle*, 13 January 1989, p. E5.
32. *Time* magazine, 23 November 1981, p. 40.
33. Hersh, p. 48.
34. *Washington Post*, 20 February 1987, p. 1.
35. *The Guardian* (London), 30 and 31 December 1985.
36. *San Francisco Chronicle*, 13 July 1987, Jack Anderson column; Hersh, pp. 48, 71.
37. *Sunday Times* (London), 6 April 1986, p. 12.
38. *The Guardian* (London), 3 April 1986.
39. *New York Times*, 19 December 1986, p. 1, and 20 December, p. 6, for a summary of the incident. The Reagan administration acknowledged Wilson's action in March, and he resigned under pressure in May. It would have been earlier if not for the fact that he was a close friend of Reagan.
40. *The Guardian* (London), 30 August 1986, citing the French news magazine *L'Express*.
41. See, e.g., *Wall Street Journal*, 25 August 1986, p. 1, for a story about Qaddafi's plans for new anti-US terrorist

attacks and US plans to attack Libya, and *Washington Post*, 2 October 1986 which reported that the information in the *Journal* article (picked up by much of the US media) had been part of a disinformation program. See also the *Post*, 27 August 1986, p. 1 and 5 October 1986, p. 1.

42. *The Guardian* (London), 18 September 1987, citing *The Montgomery Journal* (presumably the paper in Montgomery, Alabama of that name).

43. *Washington Post*, 2 October 1986, p. 1.

44. *New York Times*, 27 August 1986, p. 7

45. *The Guardian* (London), 9 October 1986.

46. Ibid., 13 October 1986, citing a story in the *Sunday Telegraph* (London) of 12 October.

47. *Washington Post*, 31 August 1986, p. A25.

48. *Wall Street Journal*, 2 September 1986, p. 31.

49. Patrick Seale & Maureen McConville, *The Hilton Assignment* (London, 1973), pp. 176-7 and passim; *New York Times*, 3 October 1971, p. 26.

50. See Jonathan Bearman, *Qadhafi's Libya* (Zed Books, London, 1986) for a detailed discussion of Qaddafi's ideological development and his program of social revolution for Libya.

51. Qaddafi's alleged record of terrorism and idiosyncracies: see, e.g., John K. Cooley, "The Libyan Menace", *Foreign Policy* (Washington), Spring 1981, pp. 75-7; David Blundy and Andrew Lycett, *Qaddafi and the Libyan Revolution* (Little, Brown & Co., Boston, 1987), chapter 6 plus page 21; also, many of the newspaper articles cited herein, such as *Los Angeles Times*, 19 January 1989.

52. Peter Maas, *Manhunt: The Incredible Pursuit of a C.I.A. Agent Turned Terrorist* (Random House, New York, 1986), passim.

53. *San Francisco Chronicle*, 18 July 1987.

54. *Los Angeles Times*, 26 October 1988, 19 January 1989.

55. *New York Times*, 15 March 1990, p. 1.

56. *Los Angeles Times*, 19 January 1989.

57. *New York Times*, 6 July 1972, p. 2. The same article states that the Black Muslims in Chicago (Farrakhan's group) received a loan, not a contribution, of $3 million to build a mosque. (But whether the money was actually given, is not certain.) See Blundy and Lycett, p. 80, re the skepticism of British security forces about the IRA getting much, if any, money from Qaddafi.

58. *Chicago Tribune*, 1987: 3 April, 8 October, 15 October, 28 October, 30 October, 19 November, 25 November.

59. Bill Schaap, *Covert Action Information Bulletin* (Washington, DC). No. 30, Summer 1988, p. 76.

60. *Washington Post*, 11 May 1989, p. 1.

61. *Los Angeles Times*, 10 October 1990, p. 1.

62. Ibid., 15 November 1991, p. 25.

63. Mark Perry, *Eclipse: The Last Days of the CIA* (Wm. Morrow & Co., New York, 1992) pp. 335-48. Despite the title, the author is sympathetic to the CIA and accepts the official version of the guilt of the Libyans, although it's not easy for him or for the reader.

64. *Der Spiegel* (Hamburg, Germany), 18 April 1994, pp. 92-7; *Sunday Times* (London), 19 December 1993, p. 2; *The Times* (London), 20 December 1993, p. 11; *Los Angeles Times*, 20 December 1993.

65. *Der Spiegel*, 18 April 1994, p. 93.

66. *Los Angeles Times*, 24 November 1988, p. 1.

67. Ibid., 19 January 1989.

68. Ibid., 4 September 1989; 26 October 1989, citing an interview in the Egyptian magazine *Al Mussawar*. It can not be determined from the article whether Qaddafi himself referred to any of these groups as "terrorist".

69. Ibid., 30 June 1989, p. 9.

70. *New York Times*, 6 March 1991, p. 16.

49. NICARAGUA 1981-1990

1. *New York Times*, 11 January 1927, p. 2

2. Ibid., 22 July 1979, III, p. 1

3. *Newsweek*, 8 November 1982, p. 44

4. Shirley Christian, *Nicaragua: Revolution in the Family* (Random House, New York, 1985) pp. 73-4; for a description of the discussion process, see chapter 5; also, Bernard Diederich, *Somoza* (London, 1982) chapter 14.

5. Christian, p. 82

6. George Black, *Triumph of the People: The Sandinista Revolution in Nicaragua* (London, 1981) p. 176

7. Christian, p. 81

8. Bob Woodward, *VEIL: The Secret Wars of the CIA 1981-1987* (New York, 1987), p. 113

9. Black, p. 177

10. *New York Times*, 15 January 1981, p. 10

11. Carter administration aid: Christian, pp. 143-4; Jeff McConnell, 'Counterrevolution in Nicaragua: The U.S. Connection', *CounterSpy* magazine (Washington, DC), Vol. 6, No. 3, May-June 1982, pp. 11-23, particularly concerning aid to private organizations.

12. Economic measures: *The Times* (London) 1 October 1984; *The Guardian* (London) 1 July 1983, 30 May 1984, 8 March 1985, 1 May 1985; *New York Times*, 11 October 1984.

13. *The Guardian* (London) 24 May 1985, 14 June 1985
14. *International Herald Tribune*, 18 April 1984; see also *Time*, 31 August 1987, p. 14
15. *San Francisco Chronicle*, 4 August 1982
16. Holly Sklar, *Washington's War on Nicaragua* (Boston, 1988), pp. 46-8, 66; McConnell, pp. 15, 21
17. *Newsweek*, 15 June 1987, pp. 27-8
18. *The Guardian* (London) 8 and 13 October 1983; 9 and 22 March 1984; 9 April 1984
19. Ibid., 17 October 1983
20. Ibid., 18 May 1983, 6 June 1983, 30 May 1984
21. *Barricada International* (English-language weekly newspaper of the Sandinista National Liberation Front, Managua) 8 November 1982, p. 12
22. *The Guardian* (London) 30 May 1984
23. *Bitter Witness: Nicaraguans and the'Covert War', a Chronology and Several Narratives* (Witness for Peace Documentation Project, Santa Cruz, Ca., 1984) pp. 7-16, 18-22 (chronology of events, January 1981-June 1982)
24. *The Guardian* (London) 12 May 1984; *Covert Action Information Bulletin* (Washington, DC) No. 22, Fall 1984, pp. 25-9 — a summary of the military exercises appears on p. 26; *Los Angeles Times*, 17 March 1988
25. Eddie Adams, 'How Latin Guerrillas Train on Our Soil', *Parade Magazine (Washington Post)* 15 March 1981, p. 5 ff; *New York Times,* 17 March 1981; training in the US began in 1980.
26. *San Francisco Chronicle*, 8 June 1982; *The Guardian* (London) 4 and 9 April 1983, 27 April 1984
27. David MacMichael in a television documentary shown on 'Diverse Reports', Channel 4, London, 30 October 1985, p. 2 of transcript.
28. *New York Times*, 29 August 1984, p. 10; 4 September 1984, p. 1; *Washington Post*, 19-22 January 1984 (US helicopter piloted by American shot down in Nicaragua and attempt at cover-up); *International Herald Tribune*, 14 December 1984; *The Guardian* (London), 6 and 7 October 1983, 7 September 1984, 10 October 1986; *Miami Herald*, 26 July 1987; *Time*, 31 August 1987, p. 14
29. *New York Times*, 17 December 1984; *The Guardian* (London) 18 December 1984, both based on a story in the *Detroit Free Press* of 16 December 1984.
30. *The Guardian* (London) 4 May 1984; *San Francisco Chronicle*, 27 July 1987
31. *San Francisco Examiner*, 22 November 1987, article by Seymour Hersh
32. *The Guardian* (London), 15 November 1984. Accounts of contra atrocities are numerous; see, e.g., *Bitter Witness*, op. cit., passim; legal brief filed by the Center for Constitutional Rights and the National Lawyers Guild against the US Government, excerpts in Peter Rosset and John Vandermeer, editors, *The Nicaragua Reader: Documents of a Revolution under Fire* (New York, 1983), pp. 228-36; *New Yorker* magazine, 25 March 1985, "Talk of the Town" section; *New York Times*, 10 March 1985, IV, p. 23, column by Anthony Lewis; Reed Brody, *Contra Terror in Nicaragua* (Boston, 1985), passim.
33. *The Guardian* (London) 15 November 1984
34. *New York Times*, 27 December 1984, p. 1
35. *The Guardian* (London) 3 June 1983
36. *New York Times*, 17 October 1984, pp. 1 and 12
37. Ibid., 20 and 24 October 1984
38. *The Guardian* (London) 25 January 1985
39. Ibid., 7 June 1983; *New York Times*, 7 June 1983
40. *Covert Action Information Bulletin* (Washington, DC) No. 20, Winter 1984, p. 39
41. "World in Action" television program, ITV London, 24 March 1986, documentary on Nicaragua showing an interview with a member of the hit team, part 2, pp. 12-13 of transcript
42. *New York Times*, 19 October 1984, p. 8; *Covert Action Information Bulletin* (Washington, DC) No. 22, Fall 1984, p. 28
43. *New York Times*, 19 January 1981, p. 11.
44. Ibid., 12 February 1981, p. 11
45. *The Guardian* (London) 23 July 1983
46. Bob Woodward, *VEIL: The Secret Wars of the CIA 1981-1987* (New York, 1987), p. 120
47. *New York Times*, 11 June 1984, p. B6
48. *The Guardian* (London) 9 January 1985
49. *New York Times*, 4 February 1988, pp. 1 and 12
50. Statement of Lt. Col. John H. Buchanan, USMC, ret., before the House Subcommittee on Inter-American Affairs, Committee on Foreign Affairs, 21 September 1982, reprinted in Rosset and Vandermeer, pp. 48-57.
51. *The Guardian* (London) 30 March 1985
52. *New York Times*, 10 March 1982, p. 16
53. *The Guardian* (London) 12 March 1986
54. Ibid., 25 March 1985, 24 February 1986 (quotation)
55. Ibid., 28 April 1983; see also *New York Times* 1 October 1987, p. 6 for a similar report of Soviet sentiments.
56. *Washington Post*, 22 May 1987, A18
57. *New York Times*, 2 May 1987
58. *Los Angeles Times*, 16 and 18 December 1987
59. *Washington Post*, 3 October 1984, p. A24, 6 November 1984, p. A1

60. *New York Times*, 3 October 1984, p. 3
61. Ibid., 24 September 1984, p. 12
62. *Washington Post*, 2 October 1984, p. A12
63. Ibid., 6 November 1984, p. A1.
64. See Sklar, chapter 13, for a detailed discussion of the US undermining role in the long Contadora process and the subsequent Central American Peace Accord process.
65. Panama, Honduras, Mexico: *Miami Herald*, 10 May 1987; see also *New York Times*, 18 May 1987
66. *New York Times*, 25 September 1988, p. 15
67. *Washington Post*, 4 November 1984, p. A1; see also *New York Times*, 4 November 1984 for a similar report
68. *New York Times*, 5 November 1984
69. Ibid., 26 July 1984, p. 5; 16 August 1984
70. Ibid., 29 July 1984, IV, p. 2
71. Ibid., 26 July 1984, p.5
72. Ibid., 24 September 1984
73. Ibid., 23 August 1984, p. 10
74. *Covert Action Information Bulletin* (Washington, DC) No. 22, Fall 1984, p. 27 — contains a reproduction of the advertisement
75. *New York Times*, 21 October 1984, p. 12
76. Ibid., 31 October 1984, p. 1
77. Ibid., 7 November 1984, p. 26.
78. Ibid., 5 October 1984, p. 3
79. Ibid., 19 July 1984, p. 6
80. *The Guardian* (London), 13 August 1986
81. *International Herald Tribune*, 22 January 1984; both attributions are from a letter of Eugene Stockwell who testified before the commission following a visit to Nicaragua with the World Council of Churches.
82. *The Guardian* (London) 15 March 1986
83. *Covert Action Information Bulletin* (Washington, DC) No. 20, Winter 1984, p. 25
84. *New York Times*, 31 December 1983, p. 9; the American ambassador, Anthony Quainton, was replaced in May 1984, whether due to Kissinger cannot be determined.
85. *The Guardian* (London) 21 March 1986
86. *San Francisco Chronicle*, 3 June 1987, Jack Anderson column
87. *New York Times*, 3 March 1982, p. 5; the photograph was first printed in the right-wing French newspaper *Le Figaro*, which then admitted its 'mistake' after being exposed by other French publications; it appears that Haig did not make any public retraction.
88. *Miami Herald*, 19 July 1987, p. 18A.
89. Peter Kornbluh, "Propaganda and Public Diplomacy: Selling Reagan's Nicaragua Policy", *Extra!* (Published by Fairness and Accuracy in Reporting, New York), Summer 1989, p. 20.
90. *Miami Herald*, 21 December 1986, p. 30A; Kornbluh, op. cit., pp. 20-22; *Extra!* (FAIR, New York), June 1987, p. 3, October/November 1987, p. 4.
91. Kornbluh, op. cit., pp. 20-22; *Extra!* (FAIR, New York), October/November 1987, p. 4, citing the example of Prof. John Guilmartin's op-ed ("Nicaragua is Armed for Trouble" in the *Wall Street Journal*, 11 March 1985.)
92. *The Guardian* (London) 9 January 1985
93. Black, p. 218
94. Ibid., pp. 215, 332, 356 give a number of examples of the economic sabotage
95. *The Guardian* (London) 13 July 1985, p. 7
96. *Boston Globe*, 9 February 1986, A20
97. Black, p. 306
98. *New York Times*, 21 September 1988, p. 6; 22 September, p. 15; 23 September, p. 5; 25 September, p. 15
99. *In These Times* (Chicago weekly newspaper), 21-27 October 1987, citing a spokeswoman at The Nicaraguan Resistance.
100. William I. Robinson, *A Faustian Bargain: U.S. Intervention in the Nicaraguan Elections and American Foreign Policy in the Post-Cold War Era* (Westview Press, Colorado, 1992) pp. 79-81; *San Francisco Chronicle*, 13 October 1987; Jacqueline Sharkey, "Anatomy of an Election: How U.S. Money Affected the Outcome in Nicaragua," *Common Cause Magazine* (Washington) May/June 1990, p. 24
101. *New York Times*, 1 June 1986; Robinson, passim.
102. *Washington Post*, 22 September 1991, p. C4. The *Post* itself added that NED "did openly what had once been unspeakably covert".
103. *Los Angeles Times*, 23 September 1988, p. 24; *New York Times*, 21 September 1988, p. 6.
104. *San Francisco Chronicle*, 20 April 1987; *Los Angeles Times*, 31 December 1987
105. *New York Times*, 20 August 1987, p. 1, based on an intelligence report dated February 1985
106. Iran/Contra, a sampler:
   a) *Final Report of the Independent Counsel for Iran/Contra Matters,* Washington, D.C., 1993), Volumes I and II, passim
   b) The National Security Archive, *The Chronology* (New York, 1987), passim.

c) Jonathan Marshall, Peter Dale Scott, Jane Hunter, *The Iran-Contra Connection* (Boston, 1987), passim

d) Jonathan Kwitny, *The Crimes of Patriots: A True Tale of Dope, Dirty Money, and the CIA* (New York, 1987), see index

e) Sklar, see index

107. Bush and Dole: Sharkey, pp. 22-3
108. Abrams: *LA Weekly* (Los Angeles) 9-15 March 1990, p. 12.
109. Sharkey, p. 22
110. *LA Weekly* op. cit.
111. National Endowment for Democracy (Washington DC), *Annual Report*, 1989 and 1990.
112. The manipulation of the election by Washington was a wide-ranging and complex operation. For much fuller details than presented here, see Robinson, passim; also Sharkey, passim, and *LA Weekly*, op. cit.
113. Sharkey, p. 23.

50. PANAMA 1969-1991

1. Compiled from: 1) Francisco Goldman, "What Price Panama? A visit to a barrio destroyed by U.S. forces", *Harper's Magazine* (New York), September 1990; 2) *Los Angeles Times*, 1 April 1990, op-ed article by David and John Kiyonaga, lawyers representing more than 100 Panama invasion victims; 3) a speech by Olga Mejia, President of the National Human Rights Commission of Panama, at Town Hall, New York City, 5 April 1990 (excerpted in *Covert Action Information Bulletin* [Washington], No. 34, p. 13).
2. *New York Times*, 22 December 1989, p. 16
3. John Dinges, *Our Man in Panama* (revised edition, New York, 1991) p. 33; *New York Times*, 28 September 1988.
4. Dinges, p. 52. William Jorden, US Ambassador to Panama 1974-78, has written that he's almost certain that US intelligence agents gave the plotters tacit approval for the coup: *Panama Odyssey* (Austin, Texas, 1984), p. 144.
5. "The Noriega Connection", a documentary film aired on "Frontline" (PBS), 30 January 1990, citing former CIA officer John Bacon (on loan to the Bureau of Narcotics and Dangerous Drugs) and other unnamed CIA and federal investigators. See also: article by Joe Conason and John Kelly in *The Village Voice* (New York), 11 October 1988, and Dinges pp. 63-4, for BNDD discussions about assassinating Noriega during the Nixon administration, based on documents of the Attorney General's office and the US Senate.
6. *Newsweek*, 18 June 1973, p. 22.
7. *New York Times*, 2 October 1988, p. 25.
8. Frederick Kempe, "The Noriega Files", *Newsweek*, 15 January 1990, p. 21; "The Noriega Connection", op. cit. At Noriega's trial in Miami in 1991, the prosecution stated that Noriega had been paid a total of only $160,000 over the years by the CIA and a like amount by the US Army. But the prosecution was seeking to counter the claim of Noriega's lawyers that the millions of dollars possessed by their client came not from drug dealing but from US government payments.
9. Dinges, pp. 85-86; *Los Angeles Times,* 16 January 1990, p. 15.
10. Dinges, pp. 88-90.
11. *San Francisco Chronicle*, 11 June 1987.
12. Dinges, p. 158.
13. Dinges, pp. 160, 234, 241; *Newsweek*, 15 January 1990, p. 23; *Los Angeles Times*, 16 January 1990, p. 15 (met at least six times).
14. Re sabotage: *Newsweek*, 15 January 1990, p. 22.
15. For different views of the source of the article, which was by Seymour Hersh, see Dinges, p. 243-4, *Newsweek*, 22 June 1987, p. 37, and Kevin Buckley, *Panama, The Whole Story* (New York, 1991), pp. 53-7.
16. Dinges, p. 253, citing Oliver North's trial stipulations 97-99, 101 and 106; also, see *Los Angeles Times*, 16 January 1990, pp. 14-15.
17. Dinges, pp. 253-4, citing a Foreign Agents Registration Act form signed by an official of the public relations firm and his testimony before the Iran-Contra Committee.
18. Dinges, p. 258.
19. William French Smith: Dinges, p. 27; Lawn: *Los Angeles Times*, 16 January 1990, p. 14. The latter also reports: A March 1984 note from then-DEA Administrator Francis Mullen thanked Noriega for an autographed photograph, saying that he "had it framed, and it is proudly displayed in my office."
20. *Los Angeles Times*, 4 January 1990, p. A12
21. Dinges, 295-6.
22. Saul Landau, "General Middleman", *Mother Jones*, Feb./March 1990, p. 17.
23. *New York Times*, 8 May 1988, p. 1. The same article reports that Edward Everett Briggs, who had been US Ambassador to Panama, had told Bush of Noriega's connection to drugs in 1985.
24. *Los Angeles Times*, 16 January 1990, p. 15; *Newsweek*, 15 January 1990, p. 19. In addition to his meeting with Noriega when he was CIA Director, Bush, as Vice President, met with him in December 1983 in Panama.
25. *New York Times*, 19 February 1989, p. 15.
26. *New York Times*, 24 April 1989, pp. 1, 11. Congressional intelligence committees do not have the formal power to kill covert operations. But they must be notified of them in advance and, very infrequently, their united opposition can dissuade an administration from proceeding. In actual practice, prior to the end of the cold war, the

CIA was normally engaged in continuous, daily covert actions and thus only the most serious actions (and only in recent years) could be brought to the attention of the intelligence committees.

In October 1989, President Bush, perhaps in reaction to this congressional rejection, and in anticipation of the upcoming invasion of Panama, issued a new executive order allowing operations which might result in the death of a foreign political leader as long as it wasn't premeditated murder. (*Los Angeles Times*, 14 October 1989, p. 1)

27. *U.S. News & World Report*, 1 May 1989, p. 40; *Los Angeles Times*, 23 April 1989, p. 1.
28. *Los Angeles Times*, 21 March 1992, p. A2
29. Dinges, pp. 187-9, 195-200, 369-72 (excerpts from the report). Dinges obtained a copy of the embassy report through a Freedom of Information request.
30. Buckley, pp. 197-218; *New York Times*, 8 October 1989, p. 16; *Washington Post*, 5 October 1989, p. 1; 6 October, p. 36; 8 October, p. 1.
31. *New York* Times, 6 October 1989, p. 10; 8 October, p. 16; *Washington Post*, 7 October 1989, pp. 1, 16; 12 October, p. 35; helicopters: *Los Angeles Times*, 4 October 1989.
32. It was reported on the ABC-TV program "Nightline", 4 October 1989, that while the rebels had not offered to turn Noriega over, they had asked that American troops come and get him by helicopter. This was denied by the Pentagon. (As reported in the *New York Times*, 5 October 1989, p. 14.)
33. *New York Times*, 6 October 1989, p. 10; 8 October, p. 16.
34. *Washington Post*, 21 December 1989, p. 37.
35. *Los Angeles Times*, 6 January 1990, p. 18. The *Washington Post*, 23 December 1989, p. 1, reported that in the hours before the invasion, US forces had searched for Noriega at his many known lairs, including his mistress's apartment (which means the same apartment building as the diplomat), but no mention was made of the apartment of the mistress's grandmother.
36. *New York Times*, 21 December 1989 (Cheney), 22 December, p. 16 (Bush).
37. *New York Times*, 18 December 1989, p. 8.
38. *Los Angeles Times*, 22 December 1990, citing three American military and civilian sources who confirmed the facts independently of one another. (It should be noted that as to the claim about the American couple being roughed up, the administration offered no supporting evidence.)
39. Buckley, pp. 228-9. The transcript of the marine's conversation was included in the report of the U.S. Army's Joint Debriefing Center.
40. Buckley, pp. 187, 191; Timothy Harding, "Why Are We In Panama?", *LA Weekly* (Los Angeles), 29 December 1989 - 4 January 1990, p. 16.
41. Buckley, p. 193, citing the *Washington Post National Weekly Edition*, 22-28 January 1990.
42. *New York Times*, 24 December 1989, p. 9. The headline of this story on page one was: "U.S. Invasion: Many Weeks of Rehearsals". An earlier edition of the *Times* that day had headlined the same story: "U.S. Drafted Invasion Plan Weeks Ago".
43. *New York Times*, 19 December, 1989, p. 12.
44. *Washington Post*, 21 December 1989, p. 36.
45. Compiled from: *Los Angeles Times*, 24, 26, 27, 30, 31 December 1989; 2, 4, 8, 25 January 1990; and *Washington Post*, 31 December 1989, p. 1.
46. *Los Angeles Times*, 24 December 1989, pp. 1 and 6.
47. Ibid., 21 December 1990, editorial.
48. Datelined 20 December, but appearing in the *New York Times* 21 December 1989, p. 24.
49. *New York Times*, 22 December 1989, p. 16.
50. *Los Angeles Times*, 23 December 1989.
51. Ibid., 23 December 1990.
52. Alan Nairn, "The Eagle is Landing", *The Nation*, 3 October 1994, p. 347.
53 *New York Times*, 6 December 1990, p. 1; Dinges, p. xxvii.
54. *The Nation*, op. cit., p. 346.
55. *Los Angeles Times*, 23 June 1990.
56. *New York Times*, 22 December 1990, p. 26, editorial; *Los Angeles Times*, 29 December 1989, 1 February 1990.
57. *Extra!* January/February 1990, p. 5 [published by FAIR (Fairness & Accuracy in Reporting), New York].
58. *Los Angeles Times*, 28 April 1991.
59. Ibid., 1 February 1990, p. A8; 27 December 1990, p. A15; 20 April 1991; 28 April 1991, p. A6. An earlier treaty of August 1990 had been repudiated by the Panamanian government.
60. Kiyonaga (*Los Angeles Times*), op. cit.
61. *Los Angeles Times*, 27 October 1990.
62. *New York Times*, 24 December 1989, p. 9.
63. Ibid., 22 December 1989, p. 17.
64. Ibid., 24 December 1989, p. 9.

51. BULGARIA 1990
1. *New York Times*, 11 February 1990, p. 20.
2. *The Guardian* (London), 21 May 1990, p. 6.

Notes

3. National Endowment for Democracy, Washington, D.C., *Annual Report, 1990* (October 1, 1989 - September 30, 1990), pp. 23-4. The NED grants also included $111 thousand for an international election observation team.
4. *Los Angeles Times*, 3 December 1990, p. 13.
5. *New York Times*, 6 June 1990, p. 10; 11 February 1990, p. 20.
6. *The Guardian* (London), 9 June 1990, p. 6.
7. Luan Troxel, "Socialist Persistence in the Bulgarian Elections of 1990-1991", *East European Quarterly* (Boulder, CO), January 1993, pp. 412-14.
8 *Los Angeles Times*, 12 June 1990.
9. *The Guardian* (London), 12 June 1990, p. 7.
10. *Los Angeles Times*, 12 June 1990; *The Times* (London), 12 June 1990, p. 15; *The Guardian* (London), 12 June 1990, p. 7.
11. *The Times* (London), 20 June 1990, p. 10.
12. *The Guardian* (London), 28 May 1990, p. 6.
13. *The Times* (London), 20 June 1990, p. 10.
14. *The Times Higher Educational Supplement* (London), 29 June 1990, p. 11.
15. NED Annual Report, 1990, op. cit., pp. 6-7, 23.
16. *The Times* (London), 7 July 1990, p. 11.
17. *The Times Higher Educational Supplement* (London), 13 July 1990, p. 9.
18. *The Guardian* (London), 12 July 1990, p. 10; *The Times* (London), 20 July 1990, p. 10.
19. *The Times* (London), 28 July 1990, p. 8; 30 July, p. 6.
20. Ibid., 27 August 1990, p. 8.
21. *The Times Higher Education Supplement* (London), 14 December 1990, p. 8.
22. Russ Bellant and Louis Wolf, "The Free Congress Foundation Goes East", *Covert Action Information Bulletin*, Fall 1990, No. 35, pp. 29-32, based substantially on Free Congress Foundation publications.
23. *New York Times*, 9 October 1990, p. D20.
24. *The Guardian* (London), 29, 30 August 1990, both p. 8.
25. NED Annual Report, 1990, op. cit., p. 23; *Los Angeles Times*, 3 December 1990, p. 13.
26. Howard Frazier, editor, *Uncloaking the CIA* (The Free Press/Macmillan Publishing Co., New York, 1978) pp. 241-8.
27. *The Guardian* (London), 7 November 1990, p. 10.
28. *The Times Higher Educational Supplement* (London), 16 November 1990, p. 11.
29. *The Guardian* (London), 9 June 1990, p. 6.
30. *The Times* (London), 24 November 1990, p. 10; 27 November, p. 16.
31. *The Times Higher Educational Supplement* (London), 30 November 1990, p. 8.
32. *The Guardian* (London), 30 November 1990, p. 9; *The Times* (London), 30 November 1990, p. 10.
33. *Los Angeles Times*, 3 December 1990, p. 13.
34. Ibid.
35. Ibid., 6 February 1994, article by Carol J. Williams.
36. Ibid., 13 June 1991, p. 14.
37. National Endowment for Democracy, Washington, D.C., *Annual Report, 1991* (October 1, 1990- September 30, 1991), p. 42.

52. IRAQ 1990-1991

1. *Los Angeles Times*, 17 March 1991, p. 8.
2. *Washington Post*, 13 January 1990, p. 11; 8 February 1990.
3. Ibid., 12 February 1990, 16 June 1990, p. 6.
4. *Los Angeles Times*, 11 July 1990, p. 1.
5. *The Gallup Poll: Public Opinion 1990* (Wilmington, Del. 1991)
6. a) Ramsey Clark, *The Fire This Time: U.S. War Crimes in the Gulf* (Thunder's Mouth Press, NY, 1992), pp. 12-13; this book is based largely on the findings of the Commission of Inquiry for the International War Crimes Tribunal, which gathered testimony from survivors and eyewitnesses.
   b) Ralph Schoenman, *Iraq and Kuwait: A History Suppressed*, pp. 1-11, a 21-page monograph published by Veritas Press, Santa Barbara, CA.
   c) *New York Times*, 15 September 1976, p. 17; the incursion was resolved without war.
7. a) "Note from the Iraqi Minister of Foreign Affairs, Mr. Tariq Aziz, to the Secretary-General of the Arab League, July 15, 1990", Appendix 1 of Pierre Salinger and Eric Laurent, *Secret Dossier: The Hidden Agenda Behind the Gulf War* (Penguin Books, New York 1991), pp. 223-234.
   b) *New York Times*, 3 September 1990, p. 7.
   c) *Los Angeles Times*, 2 December 1990, p. M4 (article by Henry Schuler, director of energy security programs for the Center for Strategic and International Studies, Washington).
   d) John K. Cooley, *Payback: America's Long War in the Middle East* (Brassey's [US], McLean, Va., 1991) pp. 183-6.
8. Murray Waas, "Who Lost Kuwait? How the Bush Administration Bungled its Way to War in the Gulf", *The Village Voice* (New York), 22 January 1991, p. 35; *New York Times*, 23 September 1990.

9. *New York Times*, 23 September 1990.
10. Ibid., 25 July 1990, pp. 1, 8.
11. Ibid., 23 September 1990.
12. Ibid., 17 September 1990, p. 23, column by William Safire.
13. Waas, p. 31.
14. *New York Times*, 28 July 1990, p. 5.
15. *Los Angeles Times*, 21 October 1992, p. 8.
16. "Developments in the Middle East", p. 14, Hearing before the Subcommittee on Europe and the Middle East of the House Committee on Foreign Affairs, 31 July 1990.
17. Kuwaiti document: *Los Angeles Times*, 1 November 1990, p. 14.
18. *Washington Post*, 19 August 1990, p. 29.
19. *Los Angeles Times*, 1 November 1990, p. 14.
20. Schoenman, pp. 11-12; *New York Review of Books*, 16 January 1992, p. 51.
21. *Christian Science Monitor*, 5 February 1991, p. 1.
22. Michael Emery, "How Mr. Bush Got His War" in Greg Ruggiero and Stuart Sahulka, eds., *Open Fire* (The New Press, New York, 1993), pp. 39, 40, 52, based on Emery's interview of King Hussein, 19 February 1991 in Jordan. (Revised version of article in the *Village Voice*, 5 March 1991).
23. Ibid., p. 42; "they" also referred to the Saudis, for reasons not pertinent to this discussion.
24. Milton Viorst, "A Reporter At Large: After the Liberation", *The New Yorker*, 30 September 1991, p. 66.
25. Schoenman, pp. 12-13, from a letter sent by the Iraqi Foreign Minister to the Secretary-General of the UN, 4 September 1990; Emery, pp. 32-3.
26. *New York Times*, 5 August 1990, p. 12.
27. Waas, pp. 30 and 38.
28. *New York Times*, 24 January 1991, p. D22.
29. *Washington Post*, 8 March 1991, p. A26.
30. a) Major James Blackwell, US Army Ret., *Thunder in the Desert: The Strategy and Tactics of the Persian Gulf War* (Bantam Books, New York, 1991), pp. 85-6.
 b) *Triumph Without Victory: The Unreported History of the Persian Gulf War* (U.S. News and World Report/Times Books, 1992) pp. 29-30.
 c) *AIR FORCE Magazine* (Arlington, Va.), March 1991, p. 82.
 d) *Newsweek,* 28 January 1991, p. 61.
31. *Los Angeles Times*, 5 August 1990, p. 1.
32. *Washington Post*, 23 June 1991, p. A16.
33. Blackwell, pp. 86-7.
34. *Financial Times* (London), 21 February 1991, p. 3.
35. Waas, p. 30.
36. *New York Times*, 31 May 1991.
37. Ibid., 2 August 1990, p. 1; *Washington Post*, 3 August 1990, p. 7; the Bush quotation is the *Post* summary of his remarks.
38. *New York Times*, 3 August 1990; *Los Angeles Times*, 3 August 1990, p. 1; *Washington Post*, 3 August 1990, p. 7.
39. *Los Angeles Times*, 4 August 1990, p. 20.
40. *Washington Post*, 10 August 1990, p. F1.
41. *New York Times*, 23 September 1990, IV, p. 21.
42. *Washington Post*, 25 November 1990, p. C4.
43. *Los Angeles Times*, 2 October 1990, p. 18. See *Washington Post*, 10 October 1990, p. 5, and 18 October, p. 1, for some of the actual numbers and programs testifying to how Congress went out of its way not to rock the new war boat.
44. *The Gallup Poll: Public Opinion 1989* (Wilmington, Del. 1990); ditto for 1990, published in 1991.
45. Reported in many places; see, e.g., *Wall Street Journal*, 14 January 1991, p. 14; *Fortune* magazine (New York), 11 February 1991, p. 46; Clark, pp. 153-6; *Washington Post*, 30 January 1991, p. A30 (IMF and World Bank); Daniel Pipes, "Is Damascus Ready for Peace?", *Foreign Affairs* magazine (New York), Fall 1991, pp. 41-2 (Syria); *Los Angeles Times*, 18 June 1992, p. 1 (Turkey); Elaine Sciolino, *The Outlaw State: Saddam Hussein's Quest for Power and the Gulf Crisis* (John Wiley & Sons, New York, 1991), pp. 237-9 (China, Russia).
46. Sciolino, pp. 237-8. Baker's exact words differ slightly in several of the sources reporting this incident; also, whether he said it out loud or not; the amount of aid lost by the Yemenis differs widely as well.
47. *Los Angeles Times*, 4 May 1991, p. 8.
48. *The Guardian* (London), 9 January 1991.
49. For an analysis of the Bush administration's method of negotiating, see John E. Mack and Jeffrey Z. Rubin, "Is This Any Way to Wage Peace?", *Los Angeles Times*, 31 January 1991, op. ed.; also see ibid., 1 October 1990, p. 1, and 2 November 1990, p. 18.
50. *New York Times*, 9 August 1990, p. 15.
51. *Los Angeles Times*, 6 November 1990, p. 4.
52. August: Robert Parry, "The Peace Feeler That Was", *The Nation*, 15 April 1991, pp. 480-2; *Newsweek*, 10

September 1990, p. 17; October: *Los Angeles Times*, 20 October 1990, p. 6.

53. New border: *Wall Street Journal*, 11 December 1990, p. 3.

54. *Newsweek*, 10 September 1990, p. 17

55. Parry, op. cit.

56. *Washington Post*, 25 November 1990, p. C4.

57. *Fortune*, op. cit.

58. Ibid.

59. *The Guardian* (London), 12 January 1991, p. 2.

60. Theodore Draper, "The True History of the Gulf War", *The New York Review of Books*, 30 January 1992, p. 41.

61. Ibid.

62. *Wall Street Journal*, 21 November 1990, p. 16.

63. *New York Times*, 3 August 1990, p. 9; 12 August, p. 1; *Los Angeles Times*, 17 November 1990, p. 14; *Wall Street Journal*, 3 December 1990, p. 3.

64. *The Observer* (London), 21 October 1990.

65. Webster, 23 January 1990, p. 60, and Schwarzkopf, 8 February 1990, pp. 586, 594 of "Threat Assessment; Military Strategy; and Operational Requirements", testimony before Senate Armed Services Committee.

66. *Basic Petroleum Data Book* (American Petroleum Institute, Washington), September 1990, Section II, Table 1a, 1989 figures: Middle East - 572 billion barrels of reserves, "Free World" - 824 billion, USSR - 84 billion.

67. "Threat Assessment; Military Strategy; and Operational Requirements", op. cit., p. 600, for 1989 figures.

68. Speaking on the MacNeil/Lehrer NewsHour, 11 September 1990.

69. Draper, op. cit., p. 41.

70. Judith Miller and Laurie Mylroie, *Saddam Hussein and the Crisis in the Gulf* (Times Books, New York, 1990), p. 192.

71. Bob Woodward, *The Commanders* (Simon & Schuster, New York, 1991), pp. 263-73.

72. *Los Angeles Times*, 17 October 1990 (hecklers); 17 November, p. 14; 1 December, p. 5.

73. *The Guardian* (London), 12 September 1990, p. 7.

74. See, e.g., Christopher Hitchens, *Harper's Magazine*, January 1991, p. 72; Dilip Hiro, *The Longest War: The Iran-Iraq Military Conflict* (London, 1989), p. 71. US policy had to do with the hostages held in the US embassy in Teheran.

75. *Saudi Arabia: Religious intolerance: The arrest, detention and torture of Christian worshippers and Shi'a Muslims* (Amnesty International report, New York, 14 September 1993).

76. Miller and Mylroie, pp. 220, 225; Denis MacShane, "Working in Virtual Slavery", *The Nation*, 18 March 1991.

77. Draper, op. cit., p. 38, provides details.

78. See, as a small sample, *Los Angeles Times*, 7, 13, and 17 March 1991, 12 June 1991, and 10 July 1992 (Amnesty).

79. All three quotations: Arthur Schlesinger, Jr., "White Slaves in the Persian Gulf", *Wall Street Journal*, 7 January 1991, p. 14.

80. *New York Times*, 18 November 1990, p. 1.

81. Sciolino, pp. 139-40.

82. *Los Angeles Times*, 7 May 1991, p. 16; 6 September 1991, p. 17; Clark, p. 92, lists eight countries with whom Washington made such arrangements.

83. "Threat Assessment; Military Strategy; and Operational Requirements", op. cit., pp. 589-90.

84. Scott Armstrong, "Eye of the Storm", *Mother Jones* magazine, November/December 1991, pp. 30-35, 75-6.

85. *Los Angeles Times*, 1 December 1990, p. 1.

86. Ibid., 7 June 1991, pp. 1, 30.

87. *Los Angeles Times*, 12 September 1991, p. 1; *Washington Post*, 13 September 1991, p. 21; this occurred on 24-25 February 1991.

88. *Los Angeles Times*, 12 June 1991, p. 1; 26 September, p. 16; occurred on 18 January 1991.

89. United Nations General Assembly Resolution: "Establishment of a nuclear-weapon-free zone in the region of the Middle East", 4 December 1990, Item No. 45/52.

90. *New York Times*, 24 January 1991, p. 11; 31 January, p. 12; *Los Angeles Times*, 26 January 1991, p. 6.

91. Clark, pp. 97-8; Senate Committee on Veterans' Affairs, "Is Military Research Hazardous to Veterans' Health? Lessons from the Persian Gulf", 6 May 1994, pp. 5-6.

92. *Peacelink* magazine (Hamilton, New Zealand), March 1991, p. 19; *Washington Post*, 8 February 1991, p. 1.

93. Clark, pp. 98-9. The UKAEA report was obtained and published by *The Independent* newspaper of London.

94. *Needless Deaths in the Gulf War: Civilian Casualties During the Air Campaign and Violations of the Laws of War*, a report of Middle East Watch/Human Rights Watch (US and London), November 1991, pp. 95-111, 248-272.

95. *Washington Post*, 13 February 1991, p. 22, citing Rear Admiral Mike McConnell, intelligence director for the Joint Chiefs of Staff.

96. *The Guardian* (London), 20 February 1991, p. 1, entitled: "Bombs rock capital as allies deliver terrible warning".

97. *Needless Deaths ...* op. cit., pp. 128-47; Clark, pp. 70-72, for an explanation of the 1,500 number and for a particularly gruesome description of the carnage and the horror.

98. "The Gulf War and Its Aftermath", *The 1992 Information Please Almanac* (Boston 1992), p. 974.

99. Laurie Garrett (medical writer for *Newsday*), "The Dead", *Columbia Journalism Review* (New York), May/June 1991, p. 32.
100. *Needless Deaths* ... op. cit., p. 135.
101. *Los Angeles Times*, 18 February 1991, p. 11.
102. Effects of the destruction of the electrical system: *Needless Deaths* ... op. cit., pp. 171-93. Also see Clark, pp. 59-72, for a discussion of the destruction of the infrastructure.
103. *Washington Post*, 23 June 1991, p. 16; *Los Angeles Times*, 21 May 1991, p. 1; *Needless Deaths* ... op. cit., pp. 184-5 (The Harvard Study Team Report discusses the methodology used to derive the figure of 170,000.)
104. Julia Devin, Member of the Coordinating Committee for the International Study Team (87 health and environment researchers who visited Iraq in August 1991), testimony before the International Task Force of the House Select Committee on Hunger, 13 November 1991, p. 40.
105. *Washington Post*, 23 June 1991, pp. 1 and 16.
106. *Needless Deaths* ... op. cit., pp. 177-80.
107. *Washington Post*, 23 June 1991, p. 16.
108. *Needless Deaths* ... op. cit., pp. 201-24; Clark, pp. 72-4; *Los Angeles Times*, 31 January 1991, p. 9; 3 February, p. 8; apparently these attacks took place mainly during late January and early February 1991.
109. Road to Basra: *Washington Post*, 27 February 1991, p. 1; *Los Angeles Times*, 27 February 1991, p. 1; Ellen Ray, "The Killing Deserts", *Lies Of Our Times* (New York), April 1991, pp. 3-4 (cites *The Independent*).
110. Stephen Sackur, *On the Basra Road* (London Review of Books, 1991), pp. 25-6, cited in Draper, op. cit., p. 42.
111. *Los Angeles Times*, 24 August 1990.
112. Ibid., 21 January 1991.
113. Ibid., 30 September 1994, p. 26.
114. *The Gallup Poll: Public Opinion 1991* (Wilmington, Del. 1992).
115. Dennis Bernstein, quoted in the *Newsletter of the National Association of Arab Americans* (Greater Los Angeles Chapter), July 1991, p. 2. For an excellent description of the media as government handmaiden during the war, see *Extra!* (Fairness and Accuracy in Reporting, New York), May 1991, Special issue on the Gulf War.
116. Micah L. Sifry & Christopher Cerf, eds., *The Gulf War Reader: History, Documents, Opinions* (Times Books, New York, 1991), p. 345, for the main provisions of the agreement arrived at between the Soviet and Iraqi foreign ministers.
117. Clark, chapters 8 and 9 and appendices, plus elsewhere, explores all this in detail.
118. Interview with Ignatenko on CBS-TV, aired in Los Angeles during the evening of 22 February 1991.
119. "The Gulf War and Its Aftermath", *The 1992 Information Please Almanac* (Boston 1992), p. 974.
120. Clark, pp. 75-84.
121. *Los Angeles Times*, 7 September 1994, p. 6.
122. *International Herald Tribune*, 5 April 1991.

53. AFGHANISTAN 1979-1992
1. Tim Weiner, *Blank Check: The Pentagon's Black Budget* (Warner Books, New York, 1990), p. 149.
2. Ibid., pp. 149-50.
3. a) Selig Harrison, "The Shah, Not the Kremlin, Touched off Afghan Coup", *Washington Post*, 13 May 1979, p. C1; contains other examples of the Shah/US campaign.
b) Hannah Negaran, "Afghanistan: A Marxist Regime in a Muslim Society", *Current History* (Philadelphia), April 1979, p. 173.
c) *New York Times*, 3 February 1975, p. 4.
d) For a brief summary, from the Soviet point of view, of the West's attempts to lure Afghanistan into its fold during the 1950s and 60s, see *The Truth About Afghanistan: Documents, Facts, Eyewitness Reports* (Novosti Press Agency Publishing House, Moscow, 1981, second edition) pp. 60-65.
e) Dwight D. Eisenhower, *The White House Years: Waging Peace, 1956-1961* (New York, 1965) pp. 493, 495, 498 discusses his concern about Soviet influence in Afghanistan.
4. Selig Harrison, op. cit.
5. *New York Times*, 4 May 1978, p. 11; Louis Dupree, "A Communist Label is Unjustified", letter to *New York Times*, 20 May 1978, p. 18. Dupree had been an anthropologist who lived in Afghanistan for many years; he was also at one time a consultant to the U.S. National Security Council, and an activist, both in Pakistan and in the United States, against the leftist Afghan government, which declared him *persona non grata* in 1978.
6. *New York Times Magazine*, 4 June 1978, p. 52 (prime minister's quote).
7. *New York Times*, 18 May 1979, p. 29, article by Fred Halliday, a Fellow at the liberal Transnational Institute, Amsterdam, and author of several books on South Asia.
8. *The Economist* (London), 11 September 1979, p. 44.
9. *New York Times*, 13 April 1979, p. 8.
10. *Newsweek*, 16 April 1979, p. 64.
11. CIA's Foreign Broadcast Information Service, 31 December 1979, p. S-13, cited in *CounterSpy* magazine (Washington, DC), No. 4-2, Spring 1980, p. 36, article by Konrad Ege.
12. *New York Times*, 16 June 1978, p. 11
13. Robert Neumann, in *Washington Review of Strategic and International Studies*, July 1978, p. 117.

Notes

14. *New York Times*, 1 July 1978, p. 4.
15. *San Francisco Chronicle*, 4 August 1979, p. 9.
16. *New York Times*, 24 March 1979, p. 4; 13 April 1979, p. 8.
17. *Washington Post*, 11 May 1979, p. 23. U.S. intelligence officials confirmed that Islamic rebels killed Soviet male and female civilians and mutilated their bodies, *New York Times*, 13 April 1979, p. 8.
18. *New York Times*, 11 September 1979, p. 12.
19. *Washington Post*, 15 November 1992, p. 32, from the official minutes of the conversation, amongst declassified Politburo documents obtained by the newspaper.
20. Ibid., citing an article published in 1992 by the former KGB deputy station chief in Kabul.
21. Ibid., 23 December 1979, p. A8.
22. Selig Harrison, "Did Moscow Fear An Afghan Tito?", *New York Times*, 13 January 1980, p. E23.
23. *The Sunday Times* (London), 6 January 1980, reporting the interview with Amin by the newspaper *Al Sharq Al Awast* ("The Middle East") published in London and Mecca.
24. *Washington Post*, 15 November 1992, p. 32, citing a "recent" account in the Moscow newspaper *Komsomolskaya Pravda*.
25. *The Truth About Afghanistan*, op. cit., p. 15, taken from *Pravda*, 13 January 1980.
26. *The Times* (London), 5 January 1980.
27. *New York Times*, 15 January 1980, p. 6. The newspaper stated that the CIA-accusations appeared to have been dropped by the Soviets at this time, perhaps because they were embarrassed by the incredulous reaction to it from around the world. But it was soon picked up again, conceivably in reaction to the *Times'* story.
28. Phillip Bonosky, *Washington's Secret War Against Afghanistan* (International Publishers, New York, 1985), pp. 33-4. The *Washington Post*, 23 December 1979, p. A8, also mentions Amin being a student at Columbia teachers college.
29. "How the CIA turns foreign students into traitors", *Ramparts* magazine (San Francisco), April 1967, pp. 23-4. This was a month after the magazine printed its famous exposé of the extensive CIA connection to the National Student Association, the leading organization of American students.
30. Bonosky, p. 34. When I spoke to Mr. Bonosky in 1994 about this claim, he said that he couldn't remember its source, but that it may have been something he was informed of in Afghanistan when he was there in 1981.
31. Charles G. Cogan, "Partners in Time: The CIA and Afghanistan since 1979", *World Policy Journal* (New York), Summer 1993, p. 76. Cogan was chief of the Near East and South Asia Division of the CIA's Directorate of Operations (Clandestine Services) from 1979 to 1984. He refers to Amin's connection to the Asia Foundation as "some sort of loose association", and says nothing further about it, but given his past position, Cogan may well know more than he's willing to reveal about a key point of the Afghanistan question, or else the article was censored by the CIA when Cogan submitted it for review, which he would have had to do.
32. Classified State Department cables, 11, 22, 23, 27, 29 September 1979, 28, 30 October 1979, among the documents found in the takeover of the US Embassy in Teheran on 4 November 1979 and gradually published in many volumes over the following years under the title: *Documents from the Den of Espionage*; hereafter referred to as "Embassy Documents". The cables referred to in this note come from vol. 30. These embassy documents and those which follow are cited in *Covert Action Information Bulletin*, No. 30, Summer 1988, article by Steve Galster, pp. 52-4. Except where quotations are used, the language summarizing the documents' content is that of Galster.

    Amin's party knew of these covert activities long before the documents were published. On 16 January 1980, a PDP spokesperson told the Afghan News Agency (Bakhtar): "In September 1979, Amin began preparing the ground for a rapprochement with the United States. He conducted confidential meetings with U.S. officials, sent emissaries to the United States, conveyed his personal oral messages to President Carter." (cited in Bonosky, p. 52)
33. Interview with Karmal in *World Marxist Review* (Toronto), April 1980, p. 36.
34. *New York Times*, 2 January 1980, p. 1.
35. *Wall Street Journal*, 7 January 1980, p. 12.
36. *Washington Post*, 15 February 1980.
37. Amongst the "Embassy Documents", op. cit., vol. 29, p. 99: Classified Department of State cable, 14 May 1979, refers to a previous meeting with a rebel leader in Islamabad on 23 April 1979.
38. Weiner, pp. 145-6.
39. *Truth About Afghanistan*, op. cit., pp. 16-17.
40. Zbigniew Brzezinski, *Power and Principle: Memoirs of the National Security Adviser, 1977-1981* (New York, 1983) p. 430.
41. *The Guardian* (London), 5 March 1986.
42. *Washington Post*, 13 January 1985, p. A30. The unnamed official may have been CIA Director Stansfield Turner who is quoted as saying something very similar in Weiner pp. 146-7.
43. Ibid.
44. Amongst the "Embassy Documents", op. cit.: Classified CIA Field Report, 30 October 1979, vol. 30.
45. *New York Times*, 22 November 1979, p. 1.
46. Weiner, p. 146
47. John Balbach, former staff director of the Congressional Task Force on Afghanistan, article in the *Los Angeles*

Times, 22 August 1993.
48. Cited in *The Guardian* (London), 28 December 1983 and 16 January 1987, p. 19.
49. *Los Angeles Times,* 17 October 1988, 13 March 1989, 16 March 1989.
50. *The Daily Telegraph* (London), 5 August 1985.
51. Brzezinski, p. 356, mentioned three times on this one page alone.
52. *New York Times,* 9 February 1980, p. 3; though written after the Soviet invasion, the article refers to April 1979.
53. For a discussion of some of these and related matters, see Selig Harrison, "Afghanistan: Soviet Intervention, Afghan Resistance, and the American Role" in Michael Klare and Peter Kornbluh, eds., *Low Intensity Warfare: Counterinsurgency, Proinsurgency, and Antiterrorism in the Eighties* (Pantheon Books, New York, 1988) pp. 188-190.
54. Ibid., p. 188; the portion about the middle class was attributed by Harrison to an article by German journalist Andreas Kohlschutter of *Die Zeit.*
55. For a fuller discussion of these matters see the three articles in *The Guardian* of London by their chief foreign correspondent Jonathan Steele, 17-19 March 1986.
56. Lawrence Lifschultz, "The not-so-new rebellion", *Far Eastern Economic Review* (Hong Kong), 30 January 1981, p. 32.
57. *Los Angeles Times,* 22 April 1989, pp. 12-13.
58. Ibid., 1 December 1987, p. 8.
59. Amongst the "Embassy Documents", op. cit., vol. 30 — Department of State Report, 16 August 1979.
60. *Los Angeles Times,* 17 February 1989, p. 8.
61. Najibullah, textbooks: Ibid., 18 February 1989, p. 18.
62. *Washington Post,* 13 January 1985, p. A30. The article speaks of 70 Russian prisoners "living lives of indescribable horror"; it appears, although it's not certain, that they are included in the 50 to 200 figure given earlier in the article.
63. John Fullerton, *The Soviet Occupation of Afghanistan* (London, 1984).
64. *Los Angeles Times,* 28 July 1989.
65. Amnesty International, *Torture in the Eighties* (London, 1984), Afghanistan chapter.
66. Jack Anderson column, *San Francisco Chronicle,* 4 May 1987. For his, and many other persons', ties to the Afghan lobby, see Sayid Khybar, "The Afghani Contra Lobby", *Covert Action Information Bulletin,* No. 30, Summer 1988, p. 65.
67. *New York Times,* 11 September 1979, p. 12.
68. *Washington Post,* 13 January 1985, p. A30.
69. Cited by *Extra!* (published by Fairness & Accuracy in Reporting, New York, October/November 1989), p. 1, referring to a series of articles in the *New York Post* beginning 27 September 1989.
70. Mary Williams Walsh, "Strained Mercy", *The Progressive* magazine (Madison, Wisconsin) May 1990, pp. 23-6. Walsh, as the *Wall Street Journal's* principal correspondent in South and Southeast Asia, had covered Afghanistan. The *Journal* refused to print this article, which led to her resignation.
71. *San Francisco Chronicle,* 20 July 1987.
72. *New York Times,* 9 March 1982, p. 1; 23 March 1982, pp. 1, 14; *The Guardian* (London) 3 November 1983, 29 March 1984; *Washington Post,* 30 May 1986.
73. Julian Robinson, et al, "Yellow Rain: The Story Collapses", *Foreign Policy* magazine, Fall 1987, pp. 100-117; *New York Times,* 31 August 1987, p. 14.
74. *Congressional Record,* 6 June 1980, pp. S13582-3.
75. *New York Times,* 29 March 1982, p. 1.
76. *San Francisco Chronicle,* 16 September 1985, p. 9.
77. *The Truth About Afghanistan,* op. cit., pp. 85, 89, with a photo of the alleged victims lying on the ground and another photo of an American chemical grenade.
78. *Los Angeles Times,* 28 July 1989.
79. Ibid., 30 April 1990, pp. 1 and 9.
80. Weiner, pp. 150, 152.
81. Weiner, p. 151; *Los Angeles Times,* 26 May 1988. Shooting down passenger planes: *New York Times,* 26 September 1984, p. 9; 11 April 1988, p. 6.
82. *San Francisco Chronicle,* Jack Anderson's columns: 29 April and 2 May 1987; 13 July 1987; *Time* magazine, 9 December 1985; *Washington Post,* 13 January 1985, p. A30.
83. Drugs, the Moujahedeen and the CIA:
a) Weiner, pp. 151-2;
b) *New York Times,* 18 June 1986;
c) William Vornberger, "Afghan Rebels and Drugs", *Covert Action Information Bulletin,* No. 28, Summer 1987, pp. 11-12;
d) *Los Angeles Times,* 4 November 1989, p. 14;
e) *Washington Post,* 13 May 1990, p. 1.
84. *Los Angeles Times,* 22 August 1993.
85. Hekmatyar, Neumann: Ibid., 21 April 1992.
86. Ibid., 24 May 1992.

87. Ibid., 4 January, 24 May, 8 September, 1992.

54. EL SALVADOR 1980-1994

1. *New York Times*, 7 March 1981, p. 10.
2. Raymond Bonner, *Weakness and Deceit: U.S. Policy and El Salvador* (Times Books, New York, 1984) p. 24.
3. Events of 1960-1: John Gerassi, *The Great Fear in Latin America* (New York, 1965, revised edition) p. 178; Michael McClintock, *The American Connection: State Terror and Popular Resistance in El Salvador* (Zed Books, London, 1985) pp. 135-7, 149; *New York Herald Tribune*, 7 April 1963, section 2, page 1.
4. *Human Rights in Nicaragua, Guatemala, and El Salvador: Implications for U.S. Policy*, Hearings before the House Subcommittee on International Organizations of the Committee on International Relations, 8 June 1976, pp. 33-4.
5. *New York Times*, 22 October 1987, p. 11. For further discussion of the US role in this process in the 1960s and 70s, see: McClintock, chapter 12; American Civil Liberties Union & Americas Watch Committee, *Report on Human Rights in El Salvador* (Vintage Books, New York, 1982) pp. 179-80, 189-97; James Dunkerley, *The Long War: Dictatorship and Revolution in El Salvador* (London, 1982) pp. 74-5; Jenny Pearce, *Under the Eagle* (London, 1982) pp. 214- 16.
6. McClintock, pp. 158, 226 (note 44).
7. Elections of 1960s and 70s: Robert Armstrong and Janet Shenk, *El Salvador: The Face of Revolution* (London, 1982) pp. 50-87; McClintock, pp. 158-183, passim; Dunkerley, pp. 79-86, 103-6; Gerassi, p. 179; testimony of Fabio Castillo before US Congress, op. cit., pp. 42-4 (see note 4).
8. Armstrong and Shenk, pp. 87-8; McClintock, pp. 183-4; Dunkerley, pp. 106-7.
9. *Facts on File* (New York), 12 March 1977, p. 181.
10. Allan Nairn, "Behind the Death Squads", *The Progressive* magazine (Madison, Wisconsin) May 1984, pp. 1, 20-29 — a detailed account of the CIA's long-standing and close ties to the Death Squads and/or their parent organizations and to the organizations' leaders who were on the CIA payroll. See also *New York Times*, 22 October 1987, p. 11; 6 December 1987, IV, p. 2.
11. Carolyn Forché, "The Road to Reaction in El Salvador", *The Nation* (New York) 14 June 1980, p. 712.
12. October 1979 to January 1980: Dunkerley, pp. 132-44; McClintock, pp. 245-60; Armstrong and Shenk, pp. 115-30.
13. Armstrong and Shenk, p. 122; Dunkerley, pp. 87-8.
14. Dunkerley, p. 144.
15. Events of January to March 1980: *The Guardian* (London) 24 January 1980; 20 March 1980; McClintock, pp. 262-4; Dunkerley, pp. 146, 156-7; Liisa North, *Bitter Grounds: Roots of Revolt in El Salvador* (Toronto, 1981) Appendix I, Chronology of Events — February 1977-June 1981, for further details of government/death squad killings; Armstrong and Shenk, p. 149, quote from Romero's last sermon.
16. James R. Brockman, *Oscar Romero, Bishop and Martyr* (Orbis Books, Maryknoll, New York, 1982) pp. 222, 236 (note 28); Dermit Keogh, *Romero, El Salvador's Martyr* (Dominican Publications, Dublin, 1981) p. 113; *New York Times*, 31 March 1980, p. 1.
17. *Los Angeles Times*, 24 November 1987; *New York Times*, 25 November 1987; CIA knowledge: CIA memo to Reagan's national security adviser Richard Allen, March 1981, *New York Times*, 9 November 1993, p. 9; *Washington Post*, 27 April 1982, p. A3, article by Mary McGrory, quoting d'Aubuisson's remark from the Mexican newspaper *El Día*.
18. McClintock, p. 268; see pages 266-71 for a discussion of agrarian reform in El Salvador in the early 1980s.
19. "El Salvador — A Revolution Brews", *NACLA Report on the Americas* (North American Congress on Latin America, New York), July-August 1980, p. 17, based on an interview with the technician in San Salvador, 2 June 1980.
20. Philip Wheaton, *Agrarian Reform in El Salvador* (Ecumenical Program for Interamerican Communication and Action, Washington, DC, 1980), p. 13.
21. *New York Times*, 18 January 1981, p. 7; 19 January, p. 11; McClintock, p. 286 (the "observer"); *The Guardian* (London) 20 July 1983 (Carter's statement).
22. *New York Times*, 12 February 1985, p. 1; 16 November 1987, p. 5.
23. "Dissent Paper on El Salvador and Central America", 6 November 1980, Section B3, 'International Context' (Argentina Chile, Uruguay) - this document, apparently the work of members of the foreign policy establishment who disagreed with American policy in Central America, was circulated throughout official circles in Washington in 1980, reprinted in Warner Poelchau, ed., *White Paper, Whitewash* (New York, 1981), Appendix B; *New York Times*, 2 December 1981 (Argentina); Clarence Lusane, "Israeli Arms in Central America", *Covert Action Information Bulletin* (Washington, DC) Winter 1984, No. 20, pp. 34-7.
24. McClintock, p. 337; *New York Times*, 12 February 1985; 19 August 1986, p. 3; the "Dissent Paper", op. cit., disclosed that large amounts of US military aid were devoted to expanding the number of Salvadorean troops; *Newsweek*, 14 March 1983, p. 18, reported that of the Salvadorean Army's 22,400 men at that time, about 4,100 had been trained in the US.
25. McClintock, p. 334; *New York Times*, 2 February 1982, p. 10.
26. *New York Times*, 30 March 1984, p. 1.
27. *The Guardian*, (London), 5 February 1983; *New York Times*, 30 March 1984, p. 1; 20 October 1984; 26

February 1991, p. 10; *San Francisco Chronicle*, 17 July 1987.

28. For example, see: *Washington Post*, 14 February 1982, p. 1; *The Guardian* (London) 26 March 1984, 22 October 1984; *New York Times*, 13 February 1982, 21 October 1984, 12 February 1985, 13 February 1986, p. 3, 1 April 1987, p. 1; McClintock, pp. 347-8.

29. *San Francisco Chronicle*, 24 June 1982

30. *Washington Post*, 19 December 1980, p. A26; 1 January 1981, p. A12

31. McClintock, p. 345, citing an article from Bailey's hometown newspaper: "El Salvador: A Mercenary's View", *News-Press* (Fort Myers, Florida daily), 23 Oct 1983.

32. *Los Angeles Times*, 9 July 1987, pp. 1 and 22; see also the *Village Voice* (New York), 11 August 1987, pp. 21-22.

33. *Los Angeles Times*, 27 September 1988, p. 2.

34. *Playboy* magazine (Chicago), November 1984, p. 73, interview by Marc Cooper and Gregory Goldin.

35. Stephen Webre, *Jose Napoleon Duarte and the Christian Democratic Party in Salvadoran Politics, 1960-1972* (Louisiana State University Press, Baton Rouge, La., 1979), p. 57. Duarte's remarks were made in a speech.

36. Bob Woodward, *VEIL: The Secret Wars of the CIA 1981-1987* (New York, 1987), pp. 117. Woodward states that Duarte "had been a good source of intelligence over many years, but he was a man of independence who was in no sense controlled and may not have known he was giving information to the CIA."

37. The detailed account appears in Mark Danner, "The Truth of El Mozote", *The New Yorker*, 6 December 1993, also in expanded form in a book, *The Massacre at El Mozote* (Vintage Books, 1994). Also see, *Los Angeles Times*, 3 January 1993, p. 1; *New York Times*, 27 January 1982, p. 1; *The Guardian* (London) 29 January 1982; McClintock, pp. 308-9.

38. *U.S. Intelligence Performance on Central America: Achievements and Selected Instances of Concern*, Staff Report, House Subcommittee on Oversight and Evaluation, Permanent Select Committee on Intelligence, 22 September 1982, pp. 18-19.

39. *Los Angeles Times*, 1 February 1982, p. 4. Two weeks later an even worse incident: see the *Washington Post*, 14 February 1982, p. C1, for a particularly graphic first-hand account of the indiscriminate barbarity of the Salvadorean armed forces towards the population, another story which Washington officials tried hard to discredit before the Congressional committee, but without success (see *U.S. Intelligence Performance ...* report, op. cit.).

40. *New York Times*, 11 January 1982, p. 2.

41. The National Guardsman, identified only as "Manuel", was interviewed in the television documentary "Torture", produced and directed by Rex Bloomstein for Thames Television Ltd. (Great Britain) in 1986 with the cooperation of Amnesty International. Video copy in author's possession.

42. *The Guardian* (London), 7 August 1986.

43. Amnesty International, *Torture in the Eighties* (London, 1984) pp. 155-6.

44. See, e.g., McClintock, pp. 306-12; *New York Times*, 13 January 1986, p. 3, 1 February 1987, p. 11; Tina Rosenberg, *Children of Cain: Violence and the Violent in Latin America* (William Morrow and Company, New York, 1991) passim.

45. *The Guardian* (London), 9 March 1984.

46. Ibid., 11 March 1984. In a similar humanitarian vein, in 1981 the Reagan administration dissuaded the European Common Market from its plan to distribute cereal and powdered milk to the victims of the fighting in El Salvador because Washington feared that the food would be diverted to the guerrillas. (*New York Times*, 18 February 1981, p. 3.)

47. *San Francisco Chronicle*, 18 July 1987, p. 9.

48. *Los Angeles Times*, 11 July 1987, p. 1.

49. *Los Angeles Reader*, 10 June 1988, special report on FBI spying on domestic dissidents; *Los Angeles Times*, 28 January 1988.

50. *New York Times*, 3 March 1984, p. 1; 22 March 1984, p. 1; 25 February 1986, p. 17; *Newsweek*, 2 April 1984, identified the official as Santibáñez; *The Guardian* (London) 22 March 1985, 29 March 1985.

51. *Los Angeles Times*, 2 February 1989.

52. *Washington Post*, 27 October 1989, p. A1; 19 November 1989, p. F2 (column by Colman McCarthy); *Los Angeles Times*, 27 October 1989; *LA Weekly* (Los Angeles), 19-25 January 1990, 27 July-2 August 1990.

53. *LA Weekly* (Los Angeles), 27 July-2 August 1990, p. 14.

54. *Washington Post*, 22 October 1992, p. A5.

55. *Los Angeles Times*, 1 May 1990, p. 1; 25 August 1990, p. 3; 26 April, 1991 (op-ed essay by Father José María Tojeira); 10 September 1991, p. H6; 15 August 1992, p. 12; *LA Weekly* (Los Angeles), 22-28 December 1989; 2-8 February 1990; *New York Times*, 19 January 1990, p. 3; 30 September 1991. The two officers were sentenced to 30 years in prison on 25 January 1992.

56. *Newsweek*, 14 March 1983, p. 24, international edition.

57. *New York Times*, 29 February 1988, article by James LeMoyne.

58. *Extra!* (Newsletter of FAIR [Fairness & Accuracy in Reporting], New York), July-August 1988, pp. 1, 12, also contains several other examples of Salvadorean government disinformation; September-October 1988, p.2; *New York Times*, 15 September 1988 (recantation); *LA Weekly* (Los Angeles), 27 May - 2 June 1988, column by Marc Cooper.

For further examples of disinformation on the part of Salvadorean officials, see *New York Times*, 29 March

1987, p. 3; 8 January 1988, p. 3; 20 February 1988, p. 3; 18 February 1990, p. 14.
59. *New York Times*, 17 March 1982, p. 1.
60. Ibid., 3, 5 and 6 March 1982, each p. 1.
61. Ibid., 13 March 1982, p. 1.
62. *Time*, 22 March 1982, p. 5, international edition.
63. *New York Times*, 19 January 1981, p. 11.
64. *San Francisco Examiner*, 20 December 1981.
65. *New York Times*, 19 January 1981, p. 11.
66. US State Department, *Communist Interference in El Salvador*, 23 February 1981, Special Report No. 80 (known as the White Paper), Section II, Communist Military Intervention: A Chronology.
67. *The Guardian* (London) 7 December 1985.
68. Dunkerley, p. 182; *New York Times*, 31 July 1983.
69. *Wall Street Journal*, 8 June 1981, pp. 1 and 10; for other analyses of the White Paper (US State Department, *Communist Interference in El Salvador*, 23 February 1981, Special Report No. 80), see: Philip Agee in Warner Poelchau, ed, *White Paper, Whitewash* (New York, 1981), and Ralph McGehee, "The CIA and the White Paper on El Salvador", *The Nation* (New York), 11 April 1981.
70. *Wall Street Journal*, 8 June 1981, p. 10.
71. *Playboy*, op. cit., p. 74.
72. *Covert Action Information Bulletin* (Washington, DC), March 1982, No. 16, p. 27; this was also reported in the daily press.
73. *U.S. News and World Report*, 26 January 1981, p. 37, interview with White.
74. *San Francisco Chronicle*, 24 February 1981.
75. *New York Times*, 30 July 1982 (equipment); 16 April 1983, p. 1 (Awacs); 31 July 1983, p. 1 (radar); *Time*, 22 March 1982 (aerial photos).
76. 9 April 1991 press conference in Honduras.
77. *New York Times*, 9 February 1990, p. 7.
78. Truth Commission, amnesty: *Los Angeles Times*, 16 March 1993, pp. 1 and 6; 21 March; 26 March.
79. Ibid., 19 March 1993
80. *New York Times*, 9 November 1993, p. 9; *Los Angeles Times*, 24 April 1994, p. 10.
81. *Los Angeles Times*, 14 December, 1993; *New York Times*, 14 December 1993, p. 1.
82. *New York Times*, 26 August 1990, p. 24; 10 February 1991, p. 3; 11 February 1991, p. 3.
83. The election:
U.N. and U.S. government observations: *Los Angeles Times*, 24 April 1994, p. 10, 22 March, p. 12, and 21 February, p. 10.
Intimidation story: ibid., 12 March, p. 6.
See also ibid., 23 March, p. 10 and 24 March; *LA Weekly* (Los Angeles), 15-21 April 1994, pp. 12-13;
CISPES observer reports: written papers and talks delivered at meetings in Los Angeles.
84. *New York Times*, 7 October 1990, p. 10.
85. Ibid., 5 August 1991, p. 4.

55. HAITI 1986-1994

1. *New York Times*, 27 February 1986, p. 3; 11 April 1986, p. 4.
2. Fritz Longchamp and Worth Cooley-Prost, "Hope for Haiti", *Covert Action Information Bulletin* (Washington), No. 36, Spring 1991, p. 58. Longchamp is Executive Director of the Washington Office on Haiti, an analysis and public education center; Paul Farmer, *The Uses of Haiti* (Common Courage Press, Monroe, Maine, 1994), pp. 128-9.
3. *The Guardian* (London), 22 September 1986.
4. Ibid.
5. Reagan: *Jean-Bertrand Aristide, An Autobiography* (Orbis Books, Maryknoll, NY, 1993, translation from 1992 French edition), p. 79. Hereafter, Aristide Autobiography.
6. *Time* magazine, 30 November 1987, p. 7.
7. CIA and the 1987-88 election: *Los Angeles Times*, 31 October 1993, p. 1; *New York Times*, 1 November 1993, p. 8.
8. *New York Times*, 1 November 1993, p. 8.
9. Allan Nairn, "The Eagle is Landing", *The Nation*, 3 October 1994, p. 344; citing US Col. Steven Butler, former planning chief for US armed forces in the Caribbean, who was involved in the operation.
10. Farmer, p. 150; *New York Times*, 13 March 1990, p. 1.
11. Aristide Autobiography, pp. 105-6, 118-21.
12. Haitian Information Bureau, "Chronology: Events in Haiti, October 15, 1990 - May 11, 1994", in James Ridgeway, ed., *The Haiti Files: Decoding the Crisis* (Essential Books, Washington, 1994), p. 205.
13. Robert I. Rotberg, *Washington Post*, 20 December 1990, p. A23.
14. *Washington Post*, 6 June, 1991, p. A23. In his autobiography, op. cit., pp. 147-8, Aristide writes that he reduced his salary from ten to four thousand as well as eliminating a number of other expensive perks.

15. Aristide Autobiography, p. 144. He presumably meant the per capita wealth of the poor; the overall per capita wealth wouldn't of course be reduced because of such aid.

16. Ibid., pp. 127-8, 139.

17. Aristide's policies in office:

a. *Washington Post*, 6 June, 1991, p. A23; 7 October 1991, p. 10;

b. Aristide Autobiography, chapter 12;

c. Farmer, pp. 167-180;

d. *Multinational Monitor* (Washington, DC), March 1994, pp. 18-23 (land reform and unions)..

18. *San Francisco Chronicle*, 22 October 1991, p. A16.

19. Alan Nairn, "Our Man in FRAPH: Behind Haiti's Paramilitaries", *The Nation*, 24 October 1994, p. 460, referring to Emannuel Constant, the head of FRAPH.

20. NED, etc.:

a) *The Nation*, 29 November 1993, p. 648, column by David Corn;

b) Haitian Information Bureau, "Subverting Democracy", *Multinational Monitor* (Washington, DC), March 1994, pp. 13-15.

c) National Endowment for Democracy, Washington, D.C., *Annual Report, 1989*, p. 33; *Annual Report, 1990*, p. 41.

d) Aristide Autobiography, p. 111, Radio Soleil's catering to the government.

21. *New York Times*, 8 October 1991, p. 10.

22. *Boston Globe*, 1 October 1992.

23. *New York Times*, 1 November 1993, p. 8; 14 November, p. 12. Latell's report was presented in July 1992.

24. Ibid., 14 November 1993, p. 12.

25. Howard French, *New York Times*, 27 September 1992, p. E5.

26. "Chronology", *The Haiti Files*, op. cit., p. 211.

27. *New York Times*, 1 November 1993, p. 1.

28. Drugs: Ibid., p. 8; *The Nation*, 3 October 1994, p. 344, op. cit.; *Los Angeles Times*, 20 May 1994, p. 11.

29. SIN: *New York Times*, 14 November 1993, p. 1; *The Nation*, 3 October 1994, p. 346, op. cit.

30. a) *The Nation*, 24 October 1994, pp. 458-461, op. cit.; Allan Nairn, "He's Our S.O.B.", 31 October 1994, pp. 481-2.

b) *Washington Post*, 8 October 1994, p. A8;

c) *Los Angeles Times*, 8 October 1994, p. 12;

d) *New York Daily News*, 12 October 1993, article by Juan Gonzales, which lends further credence to the idea that the ship incident was a set-up.

31. *Time* magazine, 8 November 1993, pp. 45-6.

32. Farmer, p. 152.

33. Aristide's mental state:

a) *Los Angeles Times*, 23 October 1993, p. 14; 31 October, p. 16; 2 November, p. 8.

b) *New York Times*, 31 October 1993, p. 12 (re fraudulent document).

c) *Washington Post*, 22 October 1993, p. A26.

d) CBS News, 13 October 1993; 2 December 1993, report by Bob Faw, stated: "This hospital in Montreal told the *Miami Herald* it never treated Aristide for psychiatric disorders."

34. *New York Times*, 23 October 1993, p. 1.

35. Dwight Eisenhower, *The White House Years: Waging Peace, 1956-1961* (New York, 1965) p. 573; Jonathan Kwitny, *Endless Enemies: The Making of an Unfriendly World* (New York, 1984) p. 57.

36. *Time* magazine, 8 November 1993, p. 46.

37. Clinton administration's relation to Haitian leaders: Ibid., p. 45.

38. George Black and Robert O. Weiner, op-ed column in the *Los Angeles Times*, 19 October 1993. Black is editorial director and Weiner coordinator of the Americas program of the Committee.

39. *Washington Post*, 2 December 1987, p. A32; 11 September 1989, p. C22, column by Jack Anderson; *The Guardian* (London), 22 September 1986.

40. Juan Gonzalez, "As Brown Fiddled, Haiti Burned", *New York Daily News*, 9 February 1994.

41. *New York Times*, 18 December 1993, p. 7.

42. *Los Angeles Times*, 16 February 1994, p. 6.

43. Ibid., 24 February 1994, 26 February; *Multinational Monitor*, March 1994, op. cit., p. 15.

44. *Los Angeles Times*, 14 April 1994, p. 4. Kozak's remark was made in February.

45. Kim Ives, "The Unmaking of a President", in *The Haiti Files*, op. cit., pp. 87-103.

46. *Multinational Monitor*, March 1994, op. cit., p. 15; *Los Angeles Times*, 14 April 1994, p. 4.

47. Murray Kempton, syndicated column, *Los Angeles Times*, 12 May 1994.

48. *Los Angeles Times*, 25 September 1994, p. 10.

49. Ibid., 21, 24 May 1994; the words are those of the *Times*; *Amnesty Action* (AI, New York), Fall 1994, p. 4.

50. *The Nation*, 3 October 1994, p. 346, op. cit.

51. *Los Angeles Times*, 23 September 1994, p. 5.

52. Ibid., 24 June 1994, p. 7.

53. Ibid., 16 September 1994.

54. Ibid., 16 September 1994, p. 8.

55. Ibid., 14 October 1994, p. 1.
56. Isabel Hilton, "Aristide's Dream", *The Independent* (London), 30 October 1993, p. 29, cited in Farmer, p. 175; Aristide added, "but the reality's different in the United States."
57. *Los Angeles Times*, 5 September 1994, p. 18, Gore was speaking on "Meet the Press".
58. Ibid., 1 October 1994.
59. Ibid., 17 September 1994, pp. 1 and 10; see also p. 9.
60. Ibid., 1 October 1994, p. 5.
61. Ibid., 8 October 1994, p. 12.
62. *New York Times*, 16 September 1994.
63. *Los Angeles Times*, 24, 25 October 1994.
64. Ibid., 19 October 1994.
65. A slightly condensed version of the Haitian economic plan can be found in *Multinational Monitor* (Washington, DC), July/August 1994, pp. 7-9. For a description of life in Haiti's oppressive assembly sector, see: National Labor Committee, "Sweatshop Development", in *The Haiti Files*, op. cit., pp. 134-54.
66. *New York Times*, 5 February 1992, p. 8.
67. *Multinational Monitor*, July/August 1994, op. cit.
68. Aristide Autobiography, pp. 166-7.

Appendix I

This is How the Money Goes Round

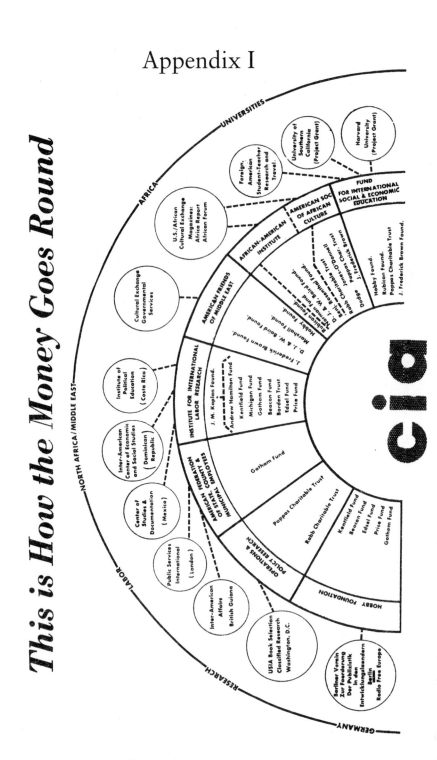

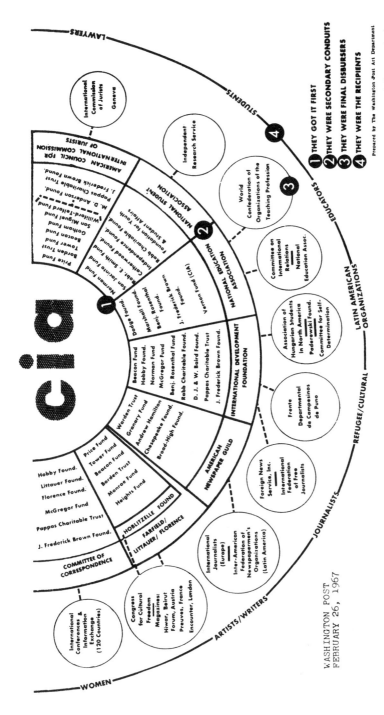

cia

1 THEY GOT IT FIRST
2 THEY WERE SECONDARY CONDUITS
3 THEY WERE FINAL DISBURSERS
4 THEY WERE THE RECIPIENTS

Prepared by The Washington Post Art Department

LAWYERS

International Commission of Jurists Geneva

AMERICAN COUNCIL FOR INTER NATIONAL COMMISSION OF JURISTS

J. Frederick Brown Fund.
M. D. Anderson Found.
Williford-Telford Fund.
San Miguel Fund
Gotham Fund
Beacon Fund
Tower Fund
Borden Trust
Price Fund
Norman Fund
San Jacinto Fund
Gabr. E. Smith Fund
Leatherwood Found.
Kenfield Found.
Rabb Charitable Found.

NATIONAL STUDENT ASSOCIATION

Dodge Found.
Marshall Found.
Benj. Rosenthal Found.
J. Frederick Brown Found.
Vernon Fund (CIA)

Beacon Fund
Hobby Found.
Norman Fund
McGregor Fund
Benj. Rosenthal Fund
Rabb Charitable Found.
D. J. & W. Baird Found.
Pappas Charitable Trust
J. Frederick Brown Found.

INTERNATIONAL DEVELOPMENT FOUNDATION

Warden Trust
Gramercy Fund
Andrew Hamilton
Chesapeake Found.
Broad-High Found.

Price Fund
Tower Fund
Beacon Fund
Borden Fund
Monroe Fund
Heights Fund

Hobby Found.
Littauer Found.
Florence Found.
McGregor Fund
Pappas Charitable Trust
J. Frederick Brown Found.

AMERICAN NEWSPAPER GUILD

HOBLITZELLE FOUND.
FARFIELD/LITTAUER/FLORENCE

COMMITTEE OF CORRESPONDENCE

STUDENTS

EDUCATORS

Independent Research Service

World Confederation of Organizations of the Teaching Profession

Committee on International Relations National Education Assoc.

Association of Hungarian Students In North America Paderewski Found. — Committee for Self-Determination

Frente Departmental de Campesinos de Puno

Foreign News Service, Inc.
International Federation of Free Journalists

International Journalists (Europe)
Inter-American Federation of Newspapermen's Organizations (Latin America)

LATIN AMERICAN ORGANIZATIONS

REFUGEE/CULTURAL

JOURNALISTS

International Conferences & Information Exchange (120 Countries)

Congress for Cultural Freedom
Magazines:
Hiwar, Beirut
Forum, Austria
Preuves, France
Encounter, London

ARTISTS/WRITERS

WOMEN

WASHINGTON POST
FEBRUARY 26, 1967

To provide secret Government funds to private persons and organizations, the CIA gave its money directly to a number of foundations. They are the names in the first band of the chart. Some were largely occupied with other work; some were mainly CIA conduits. These foundations, in turn, gave the money to other private organizations. They are the names in the shaded band. One step away from the source of the money, they could rarely be identified as part of the CIA pipeline. They passed the secret funds along to specific CIA-approved groups, organizations, study projects. Those are named in the last set of circles. Their job was to parcel out the money to individuals.

443

APPENDIX II

Instances of Use of United States Armed Forces Abroad, 1798-1945

(Prepared by Foreign Affairs Division, Congressional Research Service, Library of Congress, US Government Printing Office, Washington, DC, 1975, revision of 1969 version.)

1798-1800 - Undeclared naval war with France: This contest included land actions, such as that in the Dominican Republic, city of Puerto Plata, where marines captured a French privateer under the guns of the forts.

1801-05 - Tripoli: The First Barbary War, including the *George Washington* and *Philadelphia* affairs and the Eaton expedition, during which a few marines landed with United States agent William Eaton to raise a force against Tripoli in an effort to free the crew of the *Philadelphia*. Tripoli declared war but not the United States.

1806 - Mexico (Spanish territory): Capt. Z.M. Pike, with a platoon of troops, invaded Spanish territory at the headwaters of the Rio Grande deliberately and on orders from Gen. James Wilkinson. He was made prisoner without resistance at a fort he constructed in present day Colorado, taken to Mexico, later released after seizure of his papers. There was a political purpose, still a mystery.

1806-10 - Gulf of Mexico: American gunboats operated from New Orleans against Spanish and French privateers, such as *La Fitte*, off the Mississippi Delta, chiefly under Capt. John Shaw and Master Commandant David Porter.

1810 - West Florida (Spanish territory): Gov. Claiborne of Louisiana, on orders of the President, occupied with troops territory in dispute east of Mississippi as far as the Pearl River, later the eastern boundary of Louisiana. He was authorized to seize as far east as the Perdido River. No armed clash.

1812 - Amelia Island and other parts of east Florida, then under Spain: Temporary possession was authorized by President Madison and by Congress, to prevent occupation by any other power; but possession was obtained by Gen. George Matthews in so irregular a manner that his measures were disavowed by the President.

1812-15 - Great Britain: War of 1812. Formally declared.

1813 - West Florida (Spanish territory): On authority given by Congress, General Wilkinson seized Mobile Bay in April with 600 soldiers. A small Spanish garrison gave way. Thus U.S. advanced into disputed territory to the Perdido River, as projected in 1810. No fighting.

1813-14 - Marquesas Islands: Built a fort on island of Nukahiva to protect three prize ships which had been captured from the British.

1814 - Spanish Florida: Gen. Andrew Jackson took Pensacola and drove out the British with whom the United States was at war.

1814-25 - Caribbean: Engagements between pirates and American ships or squadrons took place repeatedly especially ashore and offshore about Cuba, Puerto Rico, Santo Domingo, and Yucatan. Three thousand pirate attacks on merchantmen were reported between 1815 and 1823. In 1822 Commodore James Biddle employed a squadron of two frigates, four sloops of war, two brigs, four schooners, and two gunboats in the West Indies.

1815 - Algiers: The second Barbary War, declared by the opponents but not by the United States. Congress authorized an expedition. A large fleet under Decatur attacked Algiers and obtained indemnities.

1815 - Tripoli: After securing an agreement from Algiers, Decatur demonstrated with his squadron at Tunis and Tripoli, where he secured indemnities for offenses during the War of 1812.

1816 - Spanish Florida: United States forces destroyed Nicholls Fort, called also Negro Fort, which harbored raiders into United States territory.

1816-18 - Spanish Florida - First Seminole War: The Seminole Indians, whose area was a resort for escaped slaves and border ruffians, were attacked by troops under Generals Jackson and Gaines and pursued into northern Florida. Spanish posts were attacked and occupied, British citizens executed.

444

Appendix

There was no declaration or congressional authorization but the Executive was sustained.

1817 - Amelia Island (Spanish territory off Florida): Under orders of President Monroe, United States forces landed and expelled a group of smugglers, adventurers, and freebooters.

1818 - Oregon: The U.S.S. *Ontario*, dispatched from Washington, landed at the Columbia River and in August took possession. Britain had conceded sovereignty but Russia and Spain asserted claims to the area.

1820-23 - Africa: Naval units raided the slave traffic pursuant to the 1819 act of Congress.

1822 - Cuba: United States naval forces suppressing piracy landed on the north-west coast of Cuba and burned a pirate station.

1823 - Cuba: Brief landings in pursuit of pirates occurred April 8 near Escondido; April 16 near Cayo Blanco; July 11 at Siquapa Bay; July 21 at Cape Cruz; and October 23 at Camrioca.

1824 - Cuba: In October the U.S.S. *Porpoise* landed bluejackets near Matanzas in pursuit of pirates. This was during the cruise authorized in 1822.

1824 - Puerto Rico (Spanish territory): Commodore David Porter with a landing party attacked the town of Fajardo which had sheltered pirates and insulted American naval officers. He landed with 200 men in November and forced an apology.

1825 - Cuba: In March cooperating American and British forces landed at Sagua La Grande to capture pirates.

1827 - Greece: In October and November landing parties hunted pirates on the islands of Argenteire, Miconi, and Andross.

1831-32 - Falkland Islands: To investigate the capture of three American sealing vessels and to protect American interests.

1832 - Sumatra - February 6 to 9: To punish natives of the town of Quallah Battoo for depredations on American shipping.

1833 - Argentina - October 31 to November 15: A force was sent ashore at Buenos Aires to protect the interests of the United States and other countries during an insurrection.

1835-36 - Peru - December 10, 1835 to January 24, 1836 and August 31 to December 7, 1836: Marines protected American interests in Callao and Lima during an attempted revolution.

1836 - Mexico: General Gaines occupied Nacogdoches (Tex.), disputed territory from July to December during the Texan war for independence, under orders to cross the "imaginary boundary line" if an Indian outbreak threatened.

1838-39 - Sumatra - December 24, 1838 to January 4, 1839: To punish natives of the towns of Quallah Battoo and Muckie (Mukki) for depredations on American shipping.

1840 - Fiji Islands - July: To punish natives for attacking American exploring and surveying parties.

1841 - Drummond Island, Kingsmill Group: To avenge the murder of a seaman by the natives.

1841 - Samoa - February 24: To avenge the murder of an American seaman on Upolu Island.

1842 - Mexico: Commodore T.A.C. Jones, in command of a squadron long cruising off California, occupied Monterey, Calif., on October 19, believing war had come. He discovered peace, withdrew, and saluted. A similar incident occurred a week later at San Diego.

1843 - China: Sailors and marines from the *St. Louis* were landed after a clash between Americans and Chinese at the trading post of Canton.

1843 - Africa - November 29 to December 16: Four United States vessels demonstrated and landed various parties (one of 200 marines and sailors) to discourage piracy and the slave trade along the Ivory coast, etc., and to punish attacks by the natives on American seamen and shipping.

1844 - Mexico: President Tyler deployed U.S. forces to protect Texas against Mexico, pending Senate approval of a treaty of annexation. (Later rejected.) He defended his action against a Senate resolution of inquiry.

445

1846-48 - Mexico, the Mexican War: President Polk's occupation of disputed territory precipitated it. War formally declared.

1849 - Smyrna: In July a naval force gained release of an American seized by Austrian officials.

1851 - Turkey: After a massacre of foreigners (including Americans) at Jaffa in January, a demonstration by the Mediterranean Squadron was ordered along the Turkish (Levant) coast. Apparently no shots fired.

1851 - Johanna Island (east of Africa), August: To exact redress for the unlawful imprisonment of the captain of an American whaling brig.

1852-53 - Argentina - February 3 to 12, 1852; September 17, 1852 to April 1853: Marines were landed and maintained in Buenos Aires to protect American interests during a revolution.

1853 - Nicaragua - March 11 to 13: To protect American lives and interests during political disturbances.

1853-54 - Japan: The "opening of Japan" and the Perry Expedition.

1853-54 - Ryukyu and Bonin Islands: Commodore Perry on three visits before going to Japan and while waiting for a reply from Japan made a naval demonstration, landing marines twice, and secured a coaling concession from the ruler of Naha on Okinawa. He also demonstrated in the Bonin Islands. All to secure facilities for commerce.

1854 - China - April 4 to June 15 or 17: To protect American interests in and near Shanghai during Chinese civil strife.

1854 - Nicaragua - July 9 to 15; San Juan del Norte (Greytown) was destroyed to avenge an insult to the American Minister to Nicaragua.

1855 - China - May 19 to 21 (?): To protect American interests in Shanghai. August 3 to 5 to fight pirates near Hong Kong.

1855 - Fiji Islands - September 12 to November 4: To seek reparations for depredations on Americans.

1855 - Uruguay - November 25 to 29 or 30: United States and European naval forces landed to protect American interests during an attempted revolution in Montevideo.

1856 - Panama, Republic of New Grenada - September 19 to 22: To protect American interests during an insurrection.

1856 - China - October 22 to December 6: To protect American interests at Canton during hostilities between the British and the Chinese; and to avenge an unprovoked assault upon an unarmed boat displaying the United States flag.

1857 - Nicaragua - April to May, November to December: To oppose William Walker's attempt to get control of the country. In May Commander C.H. Davis of the United States Navy, with some marines, received Walker's surrender and protected his men from the retaliation of native allies who had been fighting Walker. In November and December of the same year United States vessels *Saratoga, Wabash,* and *Fulton* opposed another attempt of William Walker on Nicaragua. Commodore Hiram Paulding's act of landing marines and compelling the removal of Walker to the United States, was tacitly disavowed by Secretary of State Lewis Cass, and Paulding was forced into retirement.

1858 - Uruguay - January 2 to 27: Forces from two United States warships landed to protect American property during a revolution in Montevideo.

1858 - Fiji Islands - October 6 to 16: To chastise the natives for the murder of two American citizens.

1858-59 - Turkey: Display of naval force along the Levant at the request of the Secretary of State after massacre of Americans at Jaffa and mistreatment elsewhere "to remind the authorities (of Turkey) ... of the power of the United States."

1859 - Paraguay: Congress authorized a naval squadron to seek redress for an attack on a naval vessel in the Parana River during 1855. Apologies were made after a large display of force.

1859 - Mexico: Two hundred United States soldiers crossed the Rio Grande in pursuit of the Mexican bandit Cortina.

1859 - China - July 31 to August 2: For the protection of American interests in Shanghai.

1860 - Angola, Portuguese West Africa - March 1: To protect American lives and property at Kissembo when the natives became troublesome.

1860 - Colombia, Bay of Panama - September 27 to October 8: To protect American interests during a revolution.

1863 - Japan - July 16: To redress an insult to the American flag - firing on an American vessel - at Shimonoseki.

1864 - Japan - July 14 to August 3, approximately: To protect the United States Minister to Japan when he visited Yedo to negotiate concerning some American claims against Japan, and to make his negotiations easier by impressing the Japanese with American power.

1864 - Japan - September 4 to 14 - Straits of Shimonoseki: To compel Japan and the Prince of Nagato in particular to permit the Straits to be used by foreign shipping in accordance with treaties already signed.

1865 - Panama - March 9 and 10: To protect the lives and property of American residents during a revolution.

1866 - Mexico: To protect American residents, General Sedgwick and 100 men in November obtained surrender of Matamoras. After 3 days he was ordered by U.S. Government to withdraw. His act was repudiated by the President.

1866 - China - June 20 to July 7: To punish an assault on the American consul at Newchwang; July 14, for consultation with authorities on shore; August 9, at Shanghai, to help extinguish a serious fire in the city.

1867 - Nicaragua: Marines occupied Managua and Leon.

1867 - Island of Formosa - June 13: To punish a horde of savages who were supposed to have murdered the crew of a wrecked American vessel.

1868 - Japan (Osaka, Hiogo, Nagasaki, Yokohama, and Negata) - Mainly, February 4 to 8, April 4 to May 12, June 12 and 13: To protect American interests during the civil war in Japan over the abolition of the Shogunate and the restoration of the Mikado.

1868 - Uruguay - February 7 and 8, 19 to 26: To protect foreign residents and the customhouse during an insurrection at Montevideo.

1868 - Colombia - April 7 - at Aspinwall: To protect passengers and treasure in transit during the absence of local police or troops on the occasion of the death of the President of Colombia.

1870 - Mexico, June 17 and 18: To destroy the pirate ship *Forward*, which had been run aground about 40 miles up the Rio Tecapan.

1870 - Hawaiian Islands - September 21: To place the American flag at half mast upon the death of Queen Kalama, when the American consul at Honolulu would not assume responsibility for so doing.

1871 - Korea - June 10 to 12: To punish natives for depredations on Americans, particularly for murdering the crew of the *General Sherman* and burning the schooner, and for later firing on other American small boats taking soundings up the Salee River.

1873 - Colombia (Bay of Panama) - May 7 to 22, September 23 to October 9: To protect American interests during hostilities over possession of the government of the State of Panama.

1873 - Mexico: United States troops crossed the Mexican border repeatedly in pursuit of cattle and other thieves. There were some reciprocal pursuits by Mexican troops into border territory. The cases were only technically invasions, if that, although Mexico protested constantly. Notable cases were at Remolina in May 1873 and at Las Cuevas in 1875. Washington orders often supported these excursions. Agreements between Mexico and the United States, the first in 1882, finally legitimized such raids. They continued intermittently, with minor disputes, until 1896.

1874 - Hawaiian Islands - February 12 to 20: To preserve order and protect American lives and interests during the coronation of a new king.

1876 - Mexico - May 18: To police the town of Matamoras temporarily while it was without other government.

1882 - Egypt - July 14 to 18: To protect American interests during warfare between British and Egyptians and looting of the city of Alexandria by Arabs.

1885 - Panama (Colon) - January 18 and 19: To guard the valuables in transit over the Panama Railroad, and the safes and vaults of the company during revolutionary activity. In March. April, and May in the cities of Colon and Panama, to re-establish freedom of transit during revolutionary activity.

1888 - Korea - June: To protect American residents in Seoul during unsettled political conditions, when an outbreak of the populace was expected.

1888 - Haiti - December 20: To persuade the Haitian Government to give up an American steamer which had been seized on the charge of breach of blockade.

1888-89 - Samoa - November 14, 1888, to March 20, 1889: To protect American citizens and the consulate during a native civil war.

1889 - Hawaiian Islands - July 30 and 31: To protect American interests at Honolulu during a revolution.

1890 - Argentina: A naval party landed to protect U.S. consulate and legation in Buenos Aires.

1891 - Haiti: To protect American lives and property on Navassa Island.

1891 - Bering Sea - July 2 to October 5: To stop seal poaching.

1891 - Chile - August 28 to 30: To protect the American consulate and the women and children who had taken refuge in it during a revolution in Valparaiso.

1893 - Hawaii - January 16 to April 1: Ostensibly to protect American lives and property; actually to promote a provisional government under Sanford B. Dole. This action was disavowed by the United States.

1894 - Brazil - January: To protect American commerce and shipping at Rio de Janeiro during a Brazilian civil war. No landing was attempted but there was a display of naval force.

1894 - Nicaragua - July 6 to August 7: To protect American interests at Bluefields following a revolution.

1894-95 - China: Marines were stationed at Tientsin and penetrated to Peking for protection purposes during the Sino-Japanese War.

1894-95 - China: Naval vessel beached and used as a fort at Newchwang for protection of American nationals.

1894-96 - Korea - July 24, 1894 to April 3, 1896: To protect American lives and interests at Seoul during and following the Sino-Japanese War. A guard of marines was kept at the American legation most of the time until April 1896.

1895 - Colombia - March 8 to 9: To protect American interests during an attack on the town of Bocas del Toro by a bandit chieftain.

1896 - Nicaragua - May 2 to 4: To protect American interests in Corinto during political unrest.

1898 - Nicaragua - February 7 and 8: To protect American lives and property at San Juan del Sur.

1898 - Spain: The Spanish-American War. Fully declared.

1898-99 - China - November 5, 1898, to March 15, 1899: To provide a guard for the legation at Peking and the consulate at Tientsin during contest between the Dowager Empress and her son.

1899 - Nicaragua: To protect American interests at San Juan del Norte, February 22 to March 5, and at Bluefields a few weeks later in connection with the insurrection of Gen. Juan P. Reyes.

1899 - Samoa - March 13 to May 15: To protect American interests and to take part in a bloody contention over the succession to the throne.

1899-1901 - Philippine Islands: To protect American interests following the war with Spain, and to conquer the islands by defeating the Filipinos in their war for independence.

1900 - China - May 24 to September 28: To protect foreign lives during the Boxer rising, particularly at Peking. For many years after this experience a permanent legation guard was maintained in Peking, and was strengthened at times as trouble threatened. It was still there in 1934.

Appendix

1901 - Colombia (State of Panama) - November 20 to December 4: To protect American property on the Isthmus and to keep transit lines open during serious revolutionary disturbances.

1902 - Colombia - April 16 to 23: To protect American lives and property at Bocas del Toro during a civil war.

1902 - Colombia (State of Panama) - September 17 to November 18: To place armed guards on all trains crossing the Isthmus and to keep the railroad line open.

1903 - Honduras - March 23 to 30 or 31: To protect the American consulate and the steamship wharf at Puerto Cortez during a period of revolutionary activity.

1903 - Dominican Republic - March 30 to April 21: To protect American interests in the city of Santo Domingo during a revolutionary outbreak.

1903 - Syria - September 7 to 12: To protect the American consulate in Beirut when a local Moslem uprising was feared.

1903-04 - Abyssinia: Twenty-five marines were sent to Abyssinia to protect the U.S. Consul General while he negotiated a treaty.

1903-14 - Panama: To protect American interests and lives during and following the revolution for independence from Colombia over the construction of the Isthmian Canal. With brief intermissions, Marines were stationed on the Isthmus from November 4, 1903 to January 21, 1914, to guard American interests.

1904 - Dominican Republic - January 2 to February 11: To protect American interests in Puerto Plata and Sosua and Santo Domingo City during revolutionary fighting.

1904 - Tangier, Morocco: "We want either Perdicaris alive or Raisula dead." Demonstration by a squadron to force release of a kidnapped American Marine guard landed to protect consul general.

1904 - Panama - November 17 to 24: To protect American lives and property at Ancon at the time of a threatened insurrection.

1904-05 - Korea - January 5, 1904 to November 11, 1905: To guard the American Legation in Seoul.

1904-05 - Korea: Marine guard sent to Seoul for protection during Russo-Japanese War.

1906-09 - Cuba - September 1906 to January 23, 1909: Intervention to restore order, protect foreigners, and establish a stable government after serious revolutionary activity.

1907 - Honduras - March 18 to June 8: To protect American interests during a war between Honduras and Nicaragua; troops were stationed for a few days or weeks in Trujillo, Ceiba, Puerto Cortez, San Pedro, Laguna and Choloma.

1910 - Nicaragua - February 22: During a civil war, to get information of conditions at Corinto; May 19 to September 4, to protect American interests at Bluefields.

1911 - Honduras - January 26 and some weeks thereafter: To protect American lives and interests during a civil war in Honduras.

1911 - China: Approaching stages of the nationalist revolution. An ensign and 10 men in October tried to enter Wuchang to rescue missionaries but retired on being warned away.
A small landing force guarded American private property and consulate at Hankow in October.
A marine guard was established in November over the cable stations at Shanghai.
Landing forces were sent for protection in Nanking, Chinkiang, Taku and elsewhere.

1912 - Honduras: Small force landed to prevent seizure by the Government of an American-owned railroad at Puerto Cortez. Forces withdrawn after the United States disapproved of the action.

1912 - Panama: Troops, on request of both political parties, supervised elections outside the Canal Zone.

1912 - Cuba - June 5 to August 5: To protect American interests on the Province of Oriente, and in Habana.

1912 - China - August 24 to 26, on Kentucky Island, and August 26 to 30 at Camp Nicholson: To protect Americans and American interests during revolution activity.

1912 - Turkey - November 18 to December 3: To guard the American legation at Constantinople during a Balkan War.

1912-25 - Nicaragua - August to November 1912: To protect American interests during an attempted revolution. A small force serving as a legation guard and as a promoter of peace and governmental stability, remained until August 5, 1925.

1912-41 - China: The disorders which began with the Kuomintang rebellion in 1912, which were redirected by the invasion of China by Japan and finally ended by war between Japan and the United States in 1941, led to demonstrations and landing parties for the protection of U.S. interests in China continuously and at many points from 1912 to 1941. The guard at Peking and along the route to the sea was maintained until 1941. In 1927, the United States had 5,670 troops ashore in China and 44 naval vessels in its waters. In 1933 U.S. had 3,027 armed men ashore. All this protective action was in general terms based on treaties with China ranging from 1858 to 1901.

1913 - Mexico - September 5 to 7: A few marines landed at Ciaris Estero to aid in evacuating American citizens and others from the Yaqui Valley, made dangerous for foreigners by civil strife.

1914 - Haiti - January 29 to February 9, February 20 to 21, October 19: To protect American nationals in a time of dangerous unrest.

1914- Dominican Republic - June and July: During a revolutionary movement, United States naval forces by gunfire stopped the bombardment of Puerto Plata, and by threat of force maintained Santo Domingo City as a neutral zone.

1914-17 - Mexico: The undeclared Mexican-American hostilities following the *Dolphin* affair and Villa's raids included capture of Vera Cruz and later Pershing's expedition into northern Mexico.

1915-34 - Haiti - July 28, 1915 to August 15, 1934: To maintain order during a period of chronic and threatened insurrection.

1916 - China: American forces landed to quell a riot taking place on American property in Nanking.

1916-24 - Dominican Republic - May 1916 to September 1924: To maintain order during a period of chronic and threatened insurrection.

1917 - China: American troops were landed at Chungking to protect American lives during a political crisis.

1917-18: World War I. Fully declared.

1917-22 - Cuba: To protect American interests during an insurrection and subsequent unsettled conditions. Most of the United States armed forces left Cuba by August 1919, but two companies remained at Camaguey until February 1922.

1918-19 - Mexico: After withdrawal of the Pershing expedition, our troops entered Mexico in pursuit of bandits at least three times in 1918 and six in 1919. In August 1918 American and Mexican troops fought at Nogales.

1918-20 - Panama: For police duty according to treaty stipulations, at Chiriqui, during election disturbances and subsequent unrest.

1918-20 - Soviet Russia: Marines were landed at and near Vladivostok in June and July to protect the American consulate and other points in the fighting between the Bolsheviki troops and the Czech Army which had traversed Siberia from the western front. A joint proclamation of emergency government and neutrality was issued by the American, Japanese, British, French, and Czech commanders in July and our party remained until late August.

In August the project expanded. Then 7,000 men were landed in Vladivostok and remained until January 1920, as part of an allied occupation force.

In September 1918, 5,000 American troops joined the allied intervention force at Archangel, suffered 500 casualties and remained until June 1919.

A handful of marines took part earlier in a British landing on the Murman coast (near Norway) but only incidentally.

All these operations were to offset effects of the Bolsheviki revolution in Russia and were partly supported by Czarist or Kerensky elements. No war was declared. Bolsheviki elements participated at times with us but Soviet Russia still claims damages.

1919 - Dalmatia: U.S. Forces were landed at Trau at the request of Italian authorities to police order

450

between the Italians and Serbs.

1919 - Turkey: Marines from the U.S.S. *Arizona* were landed to guard the U.S. Consulate during the Greek occupation of Constantinople.

1919 - Honduras - September 8 to 12: A landing force was sent ashore to maintain order in a neutral zone during an attempted revolution.

1920 - China - March 14: A landing force was sent ashore for a few hours to protect lives during a disturbance at Kiukiang.

1920 - Guatemala - April 9 to 27: To protect the American Legation and other American interests, such as the cable station, during a period of fighting between Unionists and the Government of Guatemala.

1920-22 - Russia (Siberia) - February 16, 1920 to November 19, 1922: A marine guard to protect the United States radio station and property on Russian Island, Bay of Vladivostok.

1921 - Panama-Costa Rica: American naval squadrons demonstrated in April on both sides of the Isthmus to prevent war between the two countries over a boundary dispute.

1922 - Turkey - September and October: A landing force was sent ashore with consent of both Greek and Turkish authorities, to protect American lives and property when the Turkish Nationalists entered Smyrna.

1922-23 - China: Between April 1922 and November 1923, Marines were landed five times to protect Americans during periods of unrest.

1924 - Honduras - February 28 to March 31, September 10 to 15: To protect American lives and interests during election hostilities.

1924 - China - September: Marines were landed to protect Americans and other foreigners in Shanghai during Chinese factional hostilities.

1925 - China - January 15 to August 29: Fighting of Chinese factions accompanied by riots and demonstrations in Shanghai necessitated landing American forces to protect lives and property in the International Settlement.

1925 - Honduras - April 19 to 21: To protect foreigners at La Ceiba during a political upheaval.

1925 - Panama - October 12 to 23: Strikes and rent riots led to the landing of about 600 American troops to keep order and protect American interests.

1926 - China - August and September: The Nationalist attack on Hankow necessitated the landing of American naval forces to protect American citizens. A small guard was maintained at the consulate general even after September 16, when the rest of the forces were withdrawn. Likewise, when Nationalist forces captured Kiukiang, naval forces were landed for the protection of foreigners November 4 to 6.

1926-33 - Nicaragua - May 7 to June 5, 1926; August 27, 1926 to January 3, 1933: The coup d'état of General Chamorro aroused revolutionary activities leading to the landing of American marines to protect the interests of the United States. United States forces came and went, but seem not to have left the country entirely until January 3, 1933. Their work included activity against the outlaw leader Sandino in 1928.

1927 - China - February: Fighting at Shanghai caused American naval forces and marines to be increased there. In March a naval guard was stationed at the American consulate at Nanking after Nationalist forces captured the city. American and British destroyers later used shell fire to protect Americans and other foreigners. "Following this incident additional forces of marines and naval vessels were ordered to China and stationed in the vicinity of Shanghai and Tientsin."

1932 - China: American forces were landed to protect American interests during the Japanese occupation of Shanghai.

1933 - Cuba: During a revolution against President Gerardo Machado naval forces demonstrated but no landing was made.

1934 - China: Marines landed at Foochow to protect the American Consulate.

1940 - Newfoundland, Bermuda, St. Lucia, Bahamas, Jamaica, Antigua, Trinidad, and British Guiana: Troops were sent to guard air and naval bases obtained by negotiation with Great Britain. These were sometimes called lend-lease bases.

1941 - Greenland: Taken under protection of the United States in April.

1941 - Netherlands (Dutch Guiana): In November the President ordered American troops to occupy Dutch Guiana but by agreement with the Netherlands government in exile, Brazil cooperated to protect aluminum ore supply from the bauxite mines in Suriname.

1941 - Iceland: Taken under the protection of the United States, with consent of its Government, for strategic reasons.

1941 - Germany: Sometime in the spring the President ordered the Navy to patrol ship lanes to Europe. By July U.S. warships were convoying and by September were attacking German submarines. There was no authorization of Congress or declaration of war. In November, the Neutrality Act was partly repealed to protect military aid to Britain, Russia, etc.

1941-45 - Germany, Italy, Japan, etc: World War II. Fully declared.

* * * * *

APPENDIX III

U.S. Government Assassination Plots

The U.S. bombing of Iraq, June 26, 1993, in retaliation for an alleged Iraqi plot to assassinate former president George Bush, "was essential," said President Clinton, "to send a message to those who engage in state-sponsored terrorism ... and to affirm the expectation of civilized behavior among nations."

Following is a list of prominent foreign individuals whose assassination (or planning for same) the United States has been involved in since the end of the Second World War. The list does not include several assassinations in various parts of the world carried out by anti-Castro Cubans employed by the CIA and headquartered in the United States.

1949 - Kim Koo, Korean opposition leader

1950s - CIA/Neo-Nazi hit list of numerous political figures in West Germany

1955 - José Antonio Remon, President of Panama

1950s - Chou En-lai, Prime minister of China, several attempts on his life

1950s - Sukarno, President of Indonesia

1951 - Kim Il Sung, Premier of North Korea

1950s (mid) - Claro M. Recto, Philippines opposition leader

1955 - Jawaharlal Nehru, Prime Minister of India

1957 - Gamal Abdul Nasser, President of Egypt

1959 and 1963 - Norodom Sihanouk, leader of Cambodia

1960 - Brig. Gen. Abdul Karim Kassem, leader of Iraq

1950s-70s - José Figueres, President of Costa Rica, two attempts on his life

1961 - Francois "Papa Doc" Duvalier, leader of Haiti

1961 - Patrice Lumumba, Prime Minister of the Congo (Zaire)

1961 - Gen. Rafael Trujillo, leader of Dominican Republic

1963 - Ngo Dinh Diem, President of South Vietnam

1960s - Fidel Castro, President of Cuba, many attempts on his life

1960s - Raúl Castro, high official in government of Cuba

1965 - Francisco Caamaño, Dominican Republic opposition leader

1965 - Pierre Ngendandumwe, Prime Minister of Burundi

1965-6 - Charles de Gaulle, President of France

1967 - Che Guevara, Cuban leader

1970 - Salvador Allende, President of Chile

1970 - Gen. Rene Schneider, Commander-in-Chief of Army, Chile

1970s, 1981 - General Omar Torrijos, leader of Panama

1972 - General Manuel Noriega, Chief of Panama Intelligence

1975 - Mobutu Sese Seko, President of Zaire

1976 - Michael Manley, Prime Minister of Jamaica

1980-1986 - Muammar Qaddafi, leader of Libya, several plots and attempts upon his life.

1982 - Ayatollah Khomeini, leader of Iran

1983 - Gen. Ahmed Dlimi, Moroccan Army commander

1983 - Miguel d'Escoto, Foreign Minister of Nicaragua

1984 - The nine *comandantes* of the Sandinista National Directorate

1985 - Sheikh Mohammed Hussein Fadlallah, Lebanese Shiite leader (80 people killed in the attempt)

1991 - Saddam Hussein, leader of Iraq

Index

454

Index

457

ABOUT THE AUTHOR

William Blum left the State Department in 1967, abandoning his aspiration of becoming a Foreign Service Officer, because of his opposition to what the United States was doing in Vietnam.

He then became one of the founders and editors of the *Washington Free Press,* the first "alternative" newspaper in the capital.

In 1969, he wrote and published an exposé of the CIA in which was revealed the names and addresses of more than 200 employees of the Agency.

Mr. Blum has been a freelance journalist in the United States, Europe and South America. His stay in Chile in 1972-3, writing about the Allende government's "socialist experiment" and its tragic overthrow in a CIA-designed coup, instilled in him a personal involvement and an even more heightened interest in what his government was doing in various parts of the world.

In the mid-1970's, he worked in London with former CIA officer Philip Agee and his associates on their project of exposing CIA personnel and their misdeeds.

Currently, he is living in Los Angeles and until recently was pursuing a career as a screenwriter. Unfortunately, his screenplays all had two (if not three) strikes against them because they dealt with that thing which makes grown men run screaming in Hollywood: ideas and issues.

email: bblum6@aol.com